T0183430

Lecture Notes in Computer Science 12505

More information about this series at http://www.springer.com/series/7410

Khoa Nguyen · Wenling Wu ·
Kwok Yan Lam · Huaxiong Wang (Eds.)

Provable and Practical Security

14th International Conference, ProvSec 2020 Singapore, November 29 – December 1, 2020 Proceedings

Editors
Khoa Nguyen
Nanyang Technological University
Singapore, Singapore

Kwok Yan Lam
Nanyang Technological University
Singapore, Singapore

Wenling Wu
Chinese Academy of Sciences
Beijing, China

Huaxiong Wang
Nanyang Technological University
Singapore, Singapore

ISSN 0302-9743 ISSN 1611-3349 (electronic)
Lecture Notes in Computer Science
ISBN 978-3-030-62575-7 ISBN 978-3-030-62576-4 (eBook)
https://doi.org/10.1007/978-3-030-62576-4

LNCS Sublibrary: SL4 – Security and Cryptology

This Springer imprint is published by the registered company Springer Nature Switzerland AG
The registered company address is: Gewerbestrasse 11, 6330 Cham, Switzerland

Preface

This volume contains the papers presented at the 14th International Conference on Provable and Practical Security (ProvSec 2020), held during November 29 – December 1, 2020. The conference was planned to take place in Singapore. Due to the global COVID-19 pandemic, the conference changed to an online format, hosted by the Strategic Centre for Research in Privacy-Preserving Technologies & Systems (SCRIPTS) at Nanyang Technological University, Singapore.

The first ProvSec conference was held in 2007. Until 2018, ProvSec conferences focused on "Provable Security." In 2019, "Practical Security" was added into the theme to enrich the scope of the conference. This year, we continued to promote the area of "Practical Security," in order to bring together security researchers and practitioners.

The Program Committee consisted of 65 members from all over the world. In response to the call for papers, 59 papers were submitted to the conference. The papers were reviewed in a double-blind manner. Each paper was carefully evaluated by three to five reviewers, and then discussed among the Program Committee. Finally, 20 papers were selected for presentation at the conference. Based on the reviews and votes by Program Committee members, the following paper was given the Best Paper Award, with a prize of EUR 1,000 generously sponsored by Springer:

"Group Signature without Random Oracles from Randomizable Signatures," by Remi Clarisse and Olivier Sanders.

We were also delighted to welcome five keynote talks from Ronald Cramer (CWI, The Netherlands), Tetsu Iwata (Nagoya University, Japan), Chris Mitchell (Royal Holloway, University of London, UK), Mike Rosulek (Oregon State University, USA), and Yu Yu (Shanghai Jiao Tong University, China).

ProvSec 2020 would not have been possible without the contributions of the many volunteers who freely gave their time and expertise. We would like to thank the members of the Program Committee and the external reviewers for their substantial work in evaluating the papers. We thank the local organizers for their tremendous efforts in planning and executing this online event. Last but not least, we would like to express our gratitude to all invited speakers and all authors who submitted papers to ProvSec 2020.

November 2020

Khoa Nguyen
Wenling Wu
Kwok Yan Lam
Huaxiong Wang

Organization

Program Chairs

Khoa Nguyen	Nanyang Technological University, Singapore
Wenling Wu	Chinese Academy of Sciences, China

General Chairs

Kwok Yan Lam	Nanyang Technological University, Singapore
Huaxiong Wang	Nanyang Technological University, Singapore

Local Organizers

Eric Low Yang Chiang	Nanyang Technological University, Singapore
Jenn Ong	Nanyang Technological University, Singapore
Alice Yan Sin Yee	Nanyang Technological University, Singapore

Program Committee

Elena Andreeva	Technical University of Denmark, Denmark
Man Ho Au	The University of Hong Kong, Hong Kong
Joonsang Baek	University of Wollongong, Australia
Shi Bai	Florida Atlantic University, USA
Rishiraj Bhattacharyya	NISER, India
Jie Chen	East China Normal University, China
Hua Chen	Chinese Academy of Sciences, China
Céline Chevalier	Université Paris 2, France
Cheng-Kang Chu	Huawei, Singapore
Chitchanok Chuengsatiansup	The University of Adelaide, Australia
Yi Deng	Chinese Academy of Sciences, China
Dung Hoang Duong	University of Wollongong, Australia
Keita Emura	NICT, Japan
Xiong Fan	University of Maryland, USA
Junqing Gong	East China Normal University, China
Swee-Huay Heng	Multimedia University, Malaysia
Qiong Huang	South China Agricultural University, China
Xinyi Huang	Fujian Normal University, China
Tetsu Iwata	Nagoya University, Japan
David Jao	University of Waterloo, Canada
Sabyasachi Karati	NISER, India
Shuichi Katsumata	AIST, Japan

Xu Ke	Singapore Management University, Singapore
Jooyoung Lee	KAIST, South Korea
Hyung Tae Lee	JeonBuk National University, South Korea
Yang Li	The University of Electro-Communications, Japan
Changlu Lin	Fujian Normal University, China
Joseph Liu	Monash University, Australia
Zhen Liu	Shanghai Jiao Tong University, China
Dongxi Liu	CSIRO, Australia
Shengli Liu	Shanghai Jiao Tong University, China
Chris Mitchell	Royal Holloway, University of London, UK
Kirill Morozov	University of North Texas, USA
Fabrice Mouhartem	IIT Madras, India
Khoa Nguyen	Nanyang Technological University, Singapore
Federico Pintore	University of Oxford, UK
Baodong Qin	Xi'an University of Posts and Telecommunications, China
Somindu C. Ramanna	IIT Kharagpur, India
Amin Sakzad	Monash University, Australia
Olivier Sanders	Orange Labs, France
Jae Hong Seo	Hanyang University, South Korea
Daniel Slamanig	Austrian Institute of Technology, Austria
Shi-Feng Sun	Monash University, Australia
Willy Susilo	University of Wollongong, Australia
Paweł Szałachowski	SUTD, Singapore
Katsuyuki Takashima	Mitsubishi Electric, Japan
Atsushi Takayasu	NICT, Japan
Benjamin Hong Meng Tan	A*STAR, Singapore
Ni Trieu	Arizona State University, USA
Viet Cuong Trinh	Hong Duc University, Vietnam
Lei Wang	Shanghai Jiao Tong University, China
Liping Wang	Chinese Academy of Sciences, China
Weiqiang Wen	University of Rennes 1, CNRS, IRISA, France
Wenling Wu	Chinese Academy of Sciences, China
Keita Xagawa	NTT, Japan
Yanhong Xu	University of Calgary, Canada
Haiyang Xue	Chinese Academy of Sciences, China
Rupeng Yang	Hong Kong Polytechnic University, Hong Kong
Chung-Huang Yang	National Kaohsiung Normal University, Taiwan
Guomin Yang	University of Wollongong, Australia
Yong Yu	Shaanxi Normal University, China
Zhenfei Zhang	Algorand
Jiang Zhang	Chinese Academy of Sciences, China
Liangfeng Zhang	ShanghaiTech University, China
Jun Zhao	Nanyang Technological University, Singapore

External Reviewers

Behzad Abdolmaleki
Ang Chen
Xin Chen
Valerio Cini
Nan Cui
Dipayan Das
Pratish Datta
Rafael Dowsley
Sabyasachi Dutta
Shengyuan Feng
Adela Georgescu
Satrajit Ghosh
Hui Guo
Shuai Han
Keisuke Hara
Yiming Li
Jinhui Liu
Xiangyu Liu
Xueqiao Liu
Yanyan Liu
Xingye Lu
Jiazhuo Lyu
Mimi Ma
Sha Ma
Shunli Ma
Pratyay Mukherjee
Sayantan Mukherjee
Bo Pang
Tran Phuong
Sourav Sen Gupta
Vishal Sharma
Junbin Shi
Kazumasa Shinagawa
Fang Song
Ehsan Hesamifard
Zhengan Huang
Li Huilin
Dingding Jia
Yanxue Jia
Haodong Jiang
Shabnam Kasra Kermanshahi
Akinori Kawachi
Sunpill Kim
Takeshi Koshiba
Shangqi Lai
Hyeonbum Lee
Hongbo Li
Xinyu Li
Yannan Li
Erkan Tairi
Syhyuan Tan
Yangguang Tian
Ivan Tjuawinata
Jianfeng Wang
Luping Wang
Yuling Wang
Yuntao Wang
Yohei Watanabe
Shengmin Xu
Takashi Yamakawa
Jun Yan
Zuoxia Yu
Xingliang Yuan
Ming Zeng
Peng Zhang
Yang Zhao
Cong Zuo

Contents

Signature Schemes

Group Signature Without Random Oracles from Randomizable Signatures

Rémi Clarisse[1,2] and Olivier Sanders[1(✉)]

[1] Orange Labs, Applied Crypto Group, Cesson-Sévigné, France
olivier.sanders@orange.com
[2] Univ Rennes, CNRS, IRMAR - UMR 6625, 35000 Rennes, France

Abstract. Group signature is a central tool for privacy-preserving protocols, ensuring authentication, anonymity and accountability. It has been massively used in cryptography, either directly or through variants such as direct anonymous attestations. However, it remains a complex tool, especially if one wants to avoid proving security in the random oracle model.

In this work, we propose a new group signature scheme proven secure without random oracles which significantly decreases the complexity in comparison with the state-of-the-art. More specifically, we halve both the size and the computational cost compared to the most efficient alternative in the same model. Moreover, our construction is also competitive against the most efficient ones in the random oracle model.

Our construction is based on a tailored combination of two popular signatures, which avoids the explicit use of encryption schemes or zero-knowledge proofs while signing. It is flexible enough to achieve security in different models and is thus suitable for most contexts.

1 Introduction

Group Signature, introduced by Chaum and van Heyst [17], enables members of a group to sign on behalf of the group. The point is that the signature is anonymous, *i.e.* it cannot be traced back to its issuer, except for a specific entity, the opening authority, which can "open" any valid group signature.

Related Works. Combining seemingly contradictory properties such as authentication and anonymity has proved tricky, the first really practical solution being provided by Ateniese *et al.* [2]. Few years later, Bellare, Micciancio and Warinschi [5] proposed the first security model (BMW model) for static group signature, which was later extended to the case of dynamic group signature by Bellare, Shi and Zhang [6] (BSZ model). Besides providing a way to assess existing schemes, these seminal works have introduced a generic construction that has become the implicit framework for most of the following group signatures.

Informally, a group member of this generic construction receives from a so-called group manager a certificate (a digital signature) τ on his public key

K. Nguyen et al. (Eds.): ProvSec 2020, LNCS 12505, pp. 3–23, 2020.
https://doi.org/10.1007/978-3-030-62576-4_1

pk when he joins the group. To compute a group signature on some message m, he first generates a digital signature σ on m (using the corresponding signing key sk) and then encrypts σ and τ. Finally, he provides a non-interactive zero-knowledge (NIZK) proof that every element is well formed. This three-steps approach is usually known as Sign-Encrypt-Prove (SEP) in the literature.

The strength of the SEP paradigm is that it is based on standard cryptographic primitives for which many instantiations exist. Unfortunately, it leads to quite complex constructions because of the security requirements placed on each building block, but primarily because of the complexity of the resulting NIZK proof. Indeed, the signer must prove, without revealing σ and τ, that the group signature is a valid encryption of the signature σ that has been generated using keys certified by the group manager. Such a statement is difficult to prove and this becomes worse if one wants to achieve security without relying on the random oracle model (ROM). Indeed, NIZK proofs are much more complex outside this setting and even by using the Groth-Sahai methodology [24], group signatures still contain dozens of elements (see *e.g.* [23]).

A natural question arising from this observation is whether it is possible to construct more efficient schemes by using a different paradigm. Bichsel *et al.* [7] proposed an interesting answer to this question. They indeed introduced a very efficient alternative, at the cost of a slightly weaker notion of anonymity. This allows them to circumvent the result of Abdalla and Warinschi [1] and thus to avoid encryption. More specifically, their idea was to remove encryption by using re-randomizable [14] certificates τ and by merging σ with the NIZK proofs, leading to a signature of knowledge. The resulting construction is very efficient (see Table 4 at the end of the paper) and can be further improved by instantiating it with the randomizable signature scheme of Pointcheval and Sanders (PS) [28].

Another alternative based on equivalence-class signature [21] has recently been proposed by Derler and Slamanig [19]. It shares commonalities with [7], such as the absence of explicit encryption, but manages to achieve full anonymity at the cost of increased complexity. Unfortunately, both [7] and [19] inherently rely on signature of knowledge and so rather fit the random oracle model.

Very recently, Backes *et al.* [3] proposed a different framework based on a new primitive called signatures with flexible public keys. It yields secure constructions without random oracles with improved efficiency compared to the state-of-the-art in this setting. However, the resulting group signatures are three times larger than the ones in the ROM and require more computations to be generated.

More generally, designers of group signature schemes are confronted with the choice of either proving security without random oracles or favoring efficiency by relying on the random oracle model whose limits are known [16].

Our Contribution. In this work, we propose a new group signature scheme avoiding the ROM that halves the size and the computational complexity compared to the state-of-the-art [3]. More specifically, our group signature only consists of 2304 bits which makes it very competitive, even against constructions in the ROM (see Sect. 5 for more details).

As [3,7,19], our construction departs from the SEP framework and heavily relies on the randomizability of its components. However, contrarily to those works that assemble different building blocks (digital signature, NIZK, etc.) and so achieve some level of genericity, we are here interested in optimizing the combination to avoid NIZK proofs in the signature, so as to get the best possible efficiency.

Our work results from the observation that the equivalence-class signature of Fuchsbauer, Hanser and Slamanig (FHS) [21] nicely interacts with the Pointcheval and Sanders (PS) signature scheme [28]. More specifically, assuming very slight modifications of the FHS public key and of the PS signatures, we are able to merge the verification equations of FHS signatures with the one of PS signatures. Such a merge is crucial for our construction: it indeed means that it is no longer necessary to provide a NIZK proof that the signatures are valid and related. Thus, verifying our group signatures is essentially verifying FHS signatures.

Intuitively, we modify the PS signature scheme in such a way that each signature is of the form $(g^r, g^{y \cdot r} X^{r/h_m})$ where g^y is the user's secret key, r is a random scalar, h_m is a public element that depends on the message m to be signed and X is a public element. Leaving out the term in X, one can note that each signature contains a different representative of the same projective equivalence class as (g, g^y) and so it is quite easy, given a FHS signature on this pair, to prove that the PS signature was generated using certified keys.

Our group signature thus only consists of a PS signature and a FHS one which are both re-randomizable, leading to an anonymity proof under the DDH assumption. Moreover, we can prove that a non-registered user cannot generate a valid group signature unless he is able to forge FHS signatures. We only pay the price for our tailored construction in the proof of non-frameability, where we want to prove that no one can issue a forged group signature that can be traced back to an honest user. Indeed, we would like to directly rely on the security of PS signatures but this is impossible due to the modifications we introduced: a PS signature is not enough to answer adversary queries in our security proof. However, we show that we can tweak the original assumption underlying the security of PS signatures to suit our construction and so that we can rely on similar arguments to prove non-frameability.

While being non-generic, our construction remains flexible enough to comply with different group signature models. Interestingly, the different variants we consider achieve the same efficiency with respect to the group signature but mostly differ in the registration procedure. This concretely means that the most suitable setting can be chosen without any impact on the group signature itself. This also allows us in Table 4 to fairly compare our construction with the most relevant ones of the state-of-the-art and so to highlight the benefits of our group signature in all cases.

Organisation. We describe in Sect. 2 the building blocks that we need to construct our group signature. The Sect. 3 recalls the standard security model of group signatures. We describe our construction in Sect. 4 and compare it with the most relevant alternatives of the state-of-the-art in Sect. 5.

2 Preliminaries

Notations. The identity element of a group $\mathbb{G}$ is denoted $1_{\mathbb{G}}$ and $\mathbb{G}^*$ means $\mathbb{G}\backslash\{1_{\mathbb{G}}\}$. If the group $\mathbb{G}$ is of order p, then we may say interchangeably that $a \in \mathbb{Z}/p\mathbb{Z}$ or that a is a scalar. For a finite set X, the notation $x \xleftarrow{\$} X$ means that x is an element of X uniformly sampled.

2.1 Bilinear Groups

Definition 1. *Bilinear groups are a set of three groups $\mathbb{G}_1$, $\mathbb{G}_2$, and $\mathbb{G}_T$ of order p along with a map, called pairing, $e : \mathbb{G}_1 \times \mathbb{G}_2 \rightarrow \mathbb{G}_T$ that is*

- *bilinear: for any $g \in \mathbb{G}_1, \widetilde{g} \in \mathbb{G}_2$, and $a, b \in \mathbb{Z}/p\mathbb{Z}$, $e(g^a, \widetilde{g}^b) = e(g, \widetilde{g})^{ab}$;*
- *non-degenerate: for any $g \in \mathbb{G}_1^*$ and $\widetilde{g} \in \mathbb{G}_2^*$, $e(g, \widetilde{g}) \neq 1_{\mathbb{G}_T}$;*
- *efficient: for any $g \in \mathbb{G}_1$ and $\widetilde{g} \in \mathbb{G}_2$, $e(g, \widetilde{g})$ can be efficiently computed.*

We will only consider bilinear groups of prime order with *type*-3 pairings, *i.e.* there is no efficiently computable homomorphism between $\mathbb{G}_1$ and $\mathbb{G}_2$. We stress that this yields the most efficient parameters [25]. To highlight the differences between $\mathbb{G}_1$ and $\mathbb{G}_2$, we will denote elements of the latter with a tilde (*e.g.* $\widetilde{g}$).

2.2 Digital Signature

A digital signature scheme Σ is defined by four algorithms:

- `Setup`(1^λ): Outputs public parameters pp for security parameter λ.
- `Keygen`(pp): On input pp, outputs signing and verification keys $(\mathsf{sk}, \mathsf{pk})$.
- `Sign`(sk, m): Outputs a signature σ of message m under signing key sk.
- `Verify`(pk, m, σ): On input verification key pk, message m and its alleged signature σ, outputs 1 if σ is a valid signature on m under pk, and 0 otherwise.

The standard security notion for a signature scheme is *existential unforgeability under chosen message attacks* (EUF-CMA) [22]: it means that it is hard, even given access to a signing oracle, to output a valid pair (m, σ) for a message m never asked to the signing oracle.

PS Signature. In [28], Pointcheval and Sanders propose a *randomizable* signature scheme, *i.e.* a scheme enabling to derive re-randomized versions σ' of any valid signature σ. An interesting feature of their signatures is that one cannot link σ and σ' without knowing the corresponding message. They describe several versions of their signature scheme, offering different features. In this work we will use their variant supporting aggregation because it enables to decrease the size of the public key but we will not use this aggregation feature.

- `Setup`(1^λ): Outputs the parameters *pp* containing the description of type-3 bilinear groups $(\mathbb{G}_1, \mathbb{G}_2, \mathbb{G}_T, e)$ along with a set of generators $(g, \widetilde{g}) \in \mathbb{G}_1 \times \mathbb{G}_2$ and a pair $(X, \widetilde{X}) \leftarrow (g^x, \widetilde{g}^x)$ for some random scalar x.
- `Keygen`(pp): Generates a random scalar y and sets $(\mathsf{sk}, \mathsf{pk})$ as $(g^y, \widetilde{Y} = \widetilde{g}^y)$.
- `Sign`(sk, m): On message m, generates a signature $(\sigma_1, \sigma_2) \leftarrow (g^r, X^r \cdot g^{r \cdot y \cdot m})$ for some random scalar r.
- `Verify`$(\mathsf{pk}, m, (\sigma_1, \sigma_2))$: Accepts signature (σ_1, σ_2) on m if the following equality holds: $e(\sigma_1, \widetilde{X} \cdot \widetilde{Y}^m) = e(\sigma_2, \widetilde{g})$.

One can note that anyone can re-randomize a signature by raising σ_1 and σ_2 to the same power t. The PS signature scheme is proven EUF-CMA-secure under a LRSW assumption customized for type-3 pairing, that we recall in Subsect. 2.3.

FHS Signature. In [21], Fuchsbauer, Hanser and Slamanig introduce a signature on equivalence-class for the following equivalence relation on tuples in $\mathbb{G}_1^n$: $(M_1, \ldots, M_n)$ is in the same equivalence class as $(N_1, \ldots, N_n)$ if there exists a scalar a such that $N_i = M_i^a$ for all $i \in [1, n]$. In this paper, we will only consider the case $n = 2$.

- `Setup`(1^λ): Outputs parameters *pp* containing the description of type-3 bilinear groups $(\mathbb{G}_1, \mathbb{G}_2, \mathbb{G}_T, e)$, with generators $(g, \widetilde{g}) \in \mathbb{G}_1 \times \mathbb{G}_2$.
- `Keygen`(pp): Generates two random scalars α_1 and α_2 and sets sk as (α_1, α_2) and pk as $(\widetilde{A}_1, \widetilde{A}_2) = (\widetilde{g}^{\alpha_1}, \widetilde{g}^{\alpha_2})$.
- `Sign`$(\mathsf{sk}, (M_1, M_2))$: Selects a random scalar t and computes the signature $(\tau_1, \tau_2, \widetilde{\tau}) \leftarrow ((M_1^{\alpha_1} M_2^{\alpha_2})^t, g^{1/t}, \widetilde{g}^{1/t})$ on the representative $(M_1, M_2) \in \mathbb{G}_1^2$.
- `Verify`$(\mathsf{pk}, (M_1, M_2), (\tau_1, \tau_2, \widetilde{\tau}))$: Accepts $(\tau_1, \tau_2, \widetilde{\tau}) \in \mathbb{G}_1^2 \times \mathbb{G}_2$, a signature on (M_1, M_2), if $e(\tau_1, \widetilde{\tau}) = e(M_1, \widetilde{A}_1) \cdot e(M_2, \widetilde{A}_2)$ and $e(\tau_2, \widetilde{g}) = e(g, \widetilde{\tau})$ hold.

We note that the signature $(\tau_1, \tau_2, \widetilde{\tau})$ is only valid on the representative (M_1, M_2). However, we can easily derive a signature on other representatives (M_1^r, M_2^r) of the same equivalence class, while re-randomizing the signature, by generating a random scalar t' and computing $(\tau_1^{r \cdot t'}, \tau_2^{1/t'}, \widetilde{\tau}^{1/t'})$.

2.3 Computational Assumptions

SXDH Assumption. For $i \in \{1, 2\}$, the DDH problem is hard in $\mathbb{G}_i$ if, given $(g, g^x, g^y, g^z) \in \mathbb{G}_i^4$, it is hard to distinguish whether $z = x \cdot y$ or z is random. The SXDH assumption holds if DDH is hard in both $\mathbb{G}_1$ and $\mathbb{G}_2$.

PS Assumption. Pointcheval and Sanders [28] introduce "Assumption 1", here referred to as PS assumption, to prove the security of their construction.

PS Assumption: Let $(p, \mathbb{G}_1, \mathbb{G}_2, \mathbb{G}_T, e)$ be a bilinear group setting of type-3, with g (resp. $\widetilde{g}$) a generator of $\mathbb{G}_1$ (resp. $\mathbb{G}_2$). For $(\widetilde{X} = \widetilde{g}^x, \widetilde{Y} = \widetilde{g}^y)$, where x and y are random scalars, we define the oracle $\mathcal{O}(m)$ on input $m \in \mathbb{Z}/p\mathbb{Z}$ that chooses a random $r \in \mathbb{Z}/p\mathbb{Z}$ and outputs the pair $P = (g^r, g^{r(x+m \cdot y)})$. Given $(g, g^y, \widetilde{g}, \widetilde{X}, \widetilde{Y})$ and unlimited access to this oracle, no adversary can efficiently generate $(m^*, g^r, g^{r(x+m^* \cdot y)})$, with $r \neq 0$, for a new scalar m^*, not asked to $\mathcal{O}$.

MPS Assumption. As we explain in the introduction, we would like to directly rely on the PS assumption but this is not possible. In particular, in our group signature construction, the user incorporates parts of the group signature in the message to be signed. This is done by using a suitable map h that must be taken into account by the assumption. We therefore introduce a variant of the PS assumption that we call MPS assumption (M stands for modified).

MPS Assumption: Let $(p, \mathbb{G}_1, \mathbb{G}_2, \mathbb{G}_T, e)$ a bilinear group setting of type-3, with g (resp. $\widetilde{g}$) a generator of $\mathbb{G}_1$ (resp. $\mathbb{G}_2$), and $h : \{0,1\}^* \to \mathbb{Z}/p\mathbb{Z}$ a function. For random scalars x, y and z, we define the oracle $\mathcal{O}(m)$ on input $m \in \mathbb{Z}/p\mathbb{Z}$ that picks random $r, s \in \mathbb{Z}/p\mathbb{Z}$ and outputs the tuple $P = (s, \widetilde{g}^{r \cdot s}, g^r, g^{r \cdot z}, g^{r(x+t \cdot y)})$ with $t = h(\widetilde{g}^{r \cdot s} || g^r || m)$. Given $(g, g^y, g^z, g^{z \cdot x}, \widetilde{g}, \widetilde{X}, \widetilde{Y})$ and unlimited access to this oracle, no adversary can efficiently generate $(t^*, g^r, g^{r(x+t^* \cdot y)})$ with $r \neq 0$ and a value t^* different from those involved in the answers from $\mathcal{O}$.

The validity of the output can easily be checked thanks to the pairing e: $e(g^{r(x+t^* \cdot y)}, \widetilde{g}) \stackrel{?}{=} e(g^r, \widetilde{X} \cdot \widetilde{Y}^{t^*})$. We note that the adversary's goal is still to output a valid PS signature but it now has access to additional elements that do not seem helpful to create forgeries, as we discuss below. A proof that the MPS assumption holds in the generic group model is given in the full version [18].

Remark 1.
- Our new oracle still returns a PS signature $(g^r, g^{r(x+ty)})$ but on a scalar $t = h(\widetilde{g}^{r \cdot s} || g^r || m)$ instead of m. However, we define much harder success conditions for the adversary: it can only win if the scalar t used in its forgery is different from the ones used by $\mathcal{O}$ (in particular a forgery on a new message m^* is not valid if it leads to an already used t). Intuitively, this rules out any strategy based on the properties of h (such as collisions). We will therefore assume (and prove in the generic group model) that the MPS assumption holds for *any*[1] function $h : \{0,1\}^* \to \mathbb{Z}/p\mathbb{Z}$. From the security point of view, this therefore does not change anything compared to an assumption where $\mathcal{O}$ would return $(g^r, g^{r(x+my)})$.
- This slight modification induces another one: we now need to provide the pair $(g^z, g^{z \cdot x})$, for some random scalar z, in the assumption. In [28], this pair is exactly a signature on 0 and so is directly generated by the reduction in the security proof by running $\mathcal{O}$ on 0. This is no longer possible here, and we then need to explicitly add these elements in the definition of the assumption. In any case, this does not provide more power to the adversary than in the PS assumption.
- The element $g^{r \cdot z}$ is the only one involving the secret z in P. It seems therefore useless to combine it with the other elements of P to derive a new valid tuple.
- The last difference with the PS assumption is the pair $(s, \widetilde{g}^{r \cdot s})$ that must be added to the oracle answers. However, we note that $\widetilde{g}^{r \cdot s}$ is an element of $\mathbb{G}_2$ and so is intuitively useless to forge a PS signature $(g^r, g^{r(x+ty)}) \in \mathbb{G}_1^2$, thanks to the asymmetry of the pairing. The same holds true for s that is not one of the secret values used to compute the PS signature.

[1] We nevertheless note that the hardness of the corresponding problem depends on the function h. For example, if h is constant then no adversary can succeed as soon as it makes (at least) one query to $\mathcal{O}$.

3 Group Signature

For completeness, we recall here the security model for dynamic group signature from the BSZ model [6]. We introduce some minor syntactic changes and discuss popular variants of the original security notions introduced by Bellare *et al.* [6]. A reader familiar with group signature can safely jump to Remark 2.

Syntax. A group signature scheme is defined by the following algorithms that involve three types of entities: a group manager, an opening authority and users. Each of the latter is identified by a public index $i \in \mathbb{N}^*$.

- $\texttt{Setup}(1^\lambda)$: Outputs public parameters pp for security parameter λ.
- $\texttt{UKeygen}(pp)$: Returns a user's key pair $(\mathsf{sk}, \mathsf{pk})$ on public parameter pp. We assume that pk is public and anyone can get an authentic copy of it.
- $\texttt{OKeygen}(pp)$: Returns the opening authority's key pair $(\mathsf{osk}, \mathsf{opk})$ under pp.
- $\texttt{GKeygen}(pp)$: Returns the group manager's key pair $(\mathsf{gsk}, \mathsf{gpk})$ along with a public register $\mathbf{Reg}$, on public parameters pp.
- $\texttt{Join}$: This is a two-party interactive protocol between the group manager and a user i who wants to join the group. The input of the former is $(\mathsf{gsk}, \mathbf{Reg}, \mathsf{opk}, \mathsf{pk}_i)$ whereas the user takes as input $(\mathsf{gpk}, \mathsf{opk}, \mathsf{sk}_i)$. If the protocol does not fail, then the user gets a group signing key usk_i whereas the group manager updates $\mathbf{Reg}$. Else, both parties return $\perp$.
- $\texttt{Sign}(\mathsf{usk}_i, m)$: Returns a group signature σ of m under signing key usk_i.
- $\texttt{Verify}(\mathsf{gpk}, \sigma, m)$: On input the group manager's public key, a group signature σ and a message m, returns a bit $b \in \{0, 1\}$.
- $\texttt{Open}(\mathsf{osk}, \mathsf{gpk}, \mathbf{Reg}, \sigma, m)$: On input the opening authority's secret key, the group manager's public key, the register $\mathbf{Reg}$, a group signature σ and a message m, returns either 0, $\perp$ or an index $i \in \mathbb{N}^*$ along with a proof π.
- $\texttt{Judge}(\mathsf{gpk}, \mathbf{Reg}, \sigma, m, i, \pi)$: On input the group manager's public key, the register $\mathbf{Reg}$, a group signature σ, a message m, an index $i \in \mathbb{N}^*$ and a proof π, returns a bit $b \in \{0, 1\}$.

Security Model. A group signature should achieve *correctness*, *anonymity*, *traceability* and *non-frameability*. We refer to [6] for a formal definition of correctness, but informally it means that any user who has joined the group should be able to produce valid signatures σ (*i.e.* one for which Verify outputs 1) on any message m. Moreover, it should be possible to open such signatures, *i.e.* to recover the identity i of the signer, and to produce publicly verifiable proofs that user i has indeed issued these signatures.

Anonymity requires that group signatures should be anonymous, except for the opening authority. Traceability requires that no one can produced a valid signature that cannot be traced back to some user through the Open procedure. Finally, non-frameability means that no one can be falsely accused of having produced a signature. The corresponding security games, outlined in Fig. 1, make use of the following oracles:

$\mathsf{Exp}^{an}_{\mathcal{A}}(1^\lambda)$ – Anonymity Security Game

1. $pp \leftarrow \mathtt{Setup}(1^\lambda)$
2. $(\mathsf{osk}, \mathsf{opk}) \leftarrow \mathtt{OKeygen}(pp)$
3. $(\mathsf{gsk}, \mathsf{gpk}) \leftarrow \mathtt{GKeygen}(pp)$
4. $b \xleftarrow{\$} \{0,1\}$, $\mathbb{O} \leftarrow \{\mathcal{O}\mathtt{Add}, \mathcal{O}\mathrm{J}_U, \mathcal{O}\mathtt{Cor}, \mathcal{O}\mathtt{Sign}, \mathcal{O}\mathtt{Open}, \mathcal{O}\mathtt{Ch}_b\}$
5. $b^* \leftarrow \mathcal{A}^{\mathbb{O}}(\mathsf{gsk}, \mathsf{opk})$
6. If $\mathcal{O}\mathtt{Open}$ is queried on the output of $\mathcal{O}\mathtt{Ch}_b$, then return 0
7. Return $(b = b^*)$

$\mathsf{Exp}^{tra}_{\mathcal{A}}(1^\lambda)$ – Traceability Security Game

1. $pp \leftarrow \mathtt{Setup}(1^\lambda)$
2. $(\mathsf{osk}, \mathsf{opk}) \leftarrow \mathtt{OKeygen}(pp)$
3. $(\mathsf{gsk}, \mathsf{gpk}) \leftarrow \mathtt{GKeygen}(pp)$
4. $(\sigma, m) \leftarrow \mathcal{A}^{\mathcal{O}\mathtt{Add}, \mathcal{O}\mathrm{J}_{GM}, \mathcal{O}\mathtt{Cor}, \mathcal{O}\mathtt{Sign}}(\mathsf{gpk}, \mathsf{osk})$
5. If $\bot \leftarrow \mathtt{Open}(\mathsf{osk}, \mathsf{gpk}, \mathbf{Reg}, \sigma, m)$, then return 1
6. If $(i, \pi) \leftarrow \mathtt{Open}(\mathsf{osk}, \mathsf{gpk}, \mathbf{Reg}, \sigma, m)$ and $0 \leftarrow \mathtt{Judge}(\mathsf{gpk}, \mathbf{Reg}, \sigma, m, i, \pi)$, then return 1
7. Return 0

$\mathsf{Exp}^{nf}_{\mathcal{A}}(1^\lambda)$ – NF Security Game

1. $pp \leftarrow \mathtt{Setup}(1^\lambda)$
2. $(\mathsf{osk}, \mathsf{opk}) \leftarrow \mathtt{OKeygen}(pp)$
3. $(\mathsf{gsk}, \mathsf{gpk}) \leftarrow \mathtt{GKeygen}(pp)$
4. $(\sigma, m, i, \pi) \leftarrow \mathcal{A}^{\mathcal{O}\mathtt{Add}, \mathcal{O}\mathrm{J}_U, \mathcal{O}\mathtt{Cor}, \mathcal{O}\mathtt{Sign}}(\mathsf{gsk}, \mathsf{osk})$
5. If $\mathcal{O}\mathtt{Sign}$ returned σ, then return 0
6. If i is corrupt, then return 0
7. Return $\mathtt{Judge}(\mathsf{gpk}, \mathbf{Reg}, \sigma, m, i, \pi)$

Fig. 1. Security games for group signature

- $\mathcal{O}\mathtt{Add}(i)$ is an oracle that can be used to add a new user i. It then runs $\mathtt{UKeygen}(pp)$ to get $(\mathsf{sk}_i, \mathsf{pk}_i)$ and returns pk_i. If i has already been used in a previous query, then it returns $\bot$.
- $\mathcal{O}\mathrm{J}_U(i)$ is an oracle that plays the user's side of the $\mathtt{Join}$ protocol. It can be used by an adversary $\mathcal{A}$ playing the role of a corrupt group manager. It returns $\bot$ if i has already joined the group or if user i does not exist.
- $\mathcal{O}\mathtt{Cor}(i)$ is an oracle that returns all the secret keys of the user i. The user i is then said to be *corrupt.* Any non-corrupt user is considered *honest.*
- $\mathcal{O}\mathrm{J}_{GM}()$ is the counterpart of the $\mathcal{O}\mathrm{J}_U$ oracle that can be used by a corrupt user to join the group.
- $\mathcal{O}\mathtt{Sign}(i, m)$ is an oracle that returns $\mathtt{Sign}(\mathsf{usk}_i, m)$, provided that i is an honest user that has already joined the group.
- $\mathcal{O}\mathtt{Open}(\sigma, m)$ is an oracle that returns $\mathtt{Open}(\mathsf{osk}, \mathsf{gpk}, \mathbf{Reg}, \sigma, m)$.
- $\mathcal{O}\mathtt{Ch}_b(i_0, i_1, m)$ is an oracle that takes as inputs the index of two honest users and returns $\mathtt{Sign}(\mathsf{usk}_{i_b}, m)$.

Let $\mathcal{A}$ be a probabilistic polynomial adversary. A group signature scheme is

- anonymous if $\mathtt{Adv}^{an}(\mathcal{A}) = |\Pr[\mathsf{Exp}^{an}_{\mathcal{A}}(1^\lambda) = 1] - 1/2|$ is negligible for any $\mathcal{A}$;
- traceable if $\mathtt{Adv}^{tra}(\mathcal{A}) = \Pr[\mathsf{Exp}^{tra}_{\mathcal{A}}(1^\lambda) = 1]$ is negligible for any $\mathcal{A}$;
- non-frameable if $\mathtt{Adv}^{nf}(\mathcal{A}) = \Pr[\mathsf{Exp}^{nf}_{\mathcal{A}}(1^\lambda) = 1]$ is negligible for any $\mathcal{A}$.

The security model introduced by Bellare, Shi and Zhang [6] places no restriction on the $\mathcal{O}\mathtt{Cor}$ queries in the anonymity experiment. This means that the adversary is allowed to corrupt the "challenge" users (*i.e.* those that are involved in $\mathcal{O}\mathtt{Ch}$ queries). This corresponds to the strongest notion of anonymity, sometimes called *full anonymity* or *CCA-2 anonymity* (see *e.g.* [19]), where anonymity holds even if the users' secret keys are leaked.

Remark 2. The BSZ model [6] defines strong security properties that are sufficient in most contexts. However, it may be possible in some situations to relax some of them, usually leading to more efficient constructions. This is particularly true for the anonymity property for which popular variants exist, such as *CPA anonymity* [8,13] or *selfless anonymity* [7,9,28]. The former removes the oracle $\mathcal{O}\mathtt{Open}$ in the anonymity game but the users remain anonymous even if their secret keys leak. Contrarily, selfless anonymity allows $\mathcal{O}\mathtt{Open}$ queries but users are no longer anonymous when their secret keys leak. These two notions are incomparable and so fit different contexts. The construction we describe in the next section achieves both of them. Interestingly, it also achieves full anonymity in the model introduced by Bellare, Micciancio and Warinschi [5] (BMW model), where the group manager is also the opening authority.

4 Our Group Signature

4.1 The Construction

Intuition. A group signature usually contains two kinds of digital signatures that we will denote by σ and τ. The first one is issued on the message to be signed by the user using his own key pair $(\mathsf{usk}, \mathsf{upk})$. Intuitively, the unforgeability of the digital signature ensures that no adversary is able to produce a forged group signature which can be traced back to upk (non-frameability). The second one is issued by the group manager on usk (or upk) to differentiate key pairs of group members from those of unregistered users. Here, unforgeability ensures that only users that have joined the group can issue group signature, which is necessary to achieve traceability.

If non-frameability and traceability were the only two conditions expected from a group signature, then the latter would simply be $(\tau, \sigma, \mathsf{upk}, m)$. However, this cannot work when anonymity is also required so the standard practice has been to encrypt/commit at least τ and upk and then provide zero-knowledge proofs that these elements are well-formed.

The work of Bichsel *et al.* [7] has shown that we can do better when τ is randomizable. Indeed, in such a case there is no need to encrypt τ, the latter can simply be re-randomized and sent unencrypted, leading to significant gains in efficiency. Their group signature can only achieve a weaker selfless anonymity notion in the ROM, but it seems a reasonable price to pay in view of the benefits.

Despite its novelty, [7] still shares commonalities with the standard framework of the BSZ model [6]. There is indeed still a modular composition of two signatures τ and σ with a proof of knowledge. The latter two can be merged (leading to a signature of knowledge) using the Fiat-Shamir heuristic [20] in the ROM, but the spirit remains the same. Modular systems are interesting since they can leverage any advance in the construction of their building blocks. For example, the scheme of [7] can straightforwardly be improved by using PS signatures [28] to instantiate τ, instead of Camenisch-Lysyanskaya signatures [14] in the original construction. Unfortunately, the complexity of a modular construction is the sum of all its parts, so a natural question is whether it is possible to improve efficiency by optimizing the combination of the different building blocks for some specific instantiations.

In this section we construct the most efficient group signature without random oracles by noticing that FHS equivalence-class signatures [21] nicely interact with PS signatures [28]. Indeed let us recall the latter, and more specifically its variant designed to support aggregation. A (non-aggregated) signature on a message m in this case is given by $(\sigma_1, \sigma_2) = (g^r, X^r(g^{y \cdot m})^r)$ where r is some random scalar, $X = g^x$ is a public element and y is the signer's secret key. One can note that we can alternatively define σ_2 as $\sigma_2^{1/m} = X^{r/m}(g^y)^r$: any adversary able to forge such a signature can trivially be converted into an adversary against the original PS-signature scheme.

Therefore, any signature issued by a user will be of the form $(\sigma_1, \sigma_2) = (g^r, X^{r/m}(g^y)^r)$. If we applied the standard methodology here, we would provide a signature τ on y (or g^y) and then prove in a zero-knowledge way that τ is valid on the key that has been used to generate (σ_1, σ_2). However, we can do better if we directly use the FHS-signature scheme [21].

Indeed, for all r, if we discard the term $X^{r/m}$ in σ_2, it only remains $(g^r, g^{y \cdot r})$ which are different representatives of the same equivalent class. Thus, if we provide a FHS signature on $(g^r, g^{r \cdot y})$ one can *directly* check that (σ_1, σ_2) was generated using a certified key, without any proof of knowledge. Anonymity of the resulting construction simply follows from the ability to re-randomize FHS signature while changing the representative of the class.

It then only remains to explain how to remove $X^{r/m}$. Recall that a FHS signature on $(g^r, g^{r \cdot y})$ is a tuple $(\tau_1, \tau_2, \widetilde{\tau})$ such that

$$e(\tau_1, \widetilde{\tau}) = e(g^r, \widetilde{A}_1) \cdot e(g^{r \cdot y}, \widetilde{A}_2) \qquad \text{and} \qquad e(\tau_2, \widetilde{g}) = e(g, \widetilde{\tau}),$$

where $(\widetilde{A}_1, \widetilde{A}_2) = (\widetilde{g}^{\alpha_1}, \widetilde{g}^{\alpha_2})$ is the public key. Assume that we add $\widetilde{B} = \widetilde{X}^{\alpha_2}$ to this public key ($\widetilde{X} = \widetilde{g}^x$ is a part of the public key of the PS-signature scheme). Then, $e(\sigma_1, \widetilde{A}_1) \cdot e(\sigma_2, \widetilde{A}_2) \cdot e(\sigma_1, \widetilde{B}^{-1/m}) = e(g^r, \widetilde{A}_1) \cdot e(g^{y \cdot r}, \widetilde{A}_2) = e(\tau_1, \widetilde{\tau})$, and the second equation remains unchanged. This means that we can check the validity of both FHS and PS signatures at essentially the cost of verifying a FHS signature. Moreover, the fact that we merge the verification of these signatures makes zero-knowledge proofs unnecessary. Concretely, this means that our group signature only consists of $(\sigma_1, \sigma_2, \tau_1, \tau_2, \widetilde{\tau})$, *i.e.* four elements of $\mathbb{G}_1$ and one element of $\mathbb{G}_2$, and can be verified with merely two pairing equations.

Interestingly, the fact that we avoid the classical signature of knowledge of y allows to achieve both CPA anonymity and selfless anonymity. Indeed, schemes based on randomizable signatures (see *e.g.* [14,28]) are usually proven anonymous under the DDH assumption in $\mathbb{G}_1$. Therefore, to enable opening, they usually force the users to provide some "trapdoor" $\widetilde{g}^y \in \mathbb{G}_2$ that allows the opening authority to break DDH on their specific signatures. When y is part of the user's signing key usk (which is necessary for a signature of knowledge of y), leakage of the latter means that the adversary can recover y and thus $\widetilde{g}^y$. Anonymity can then no longer hold in this case leading to the selfless anonymity notion.

In our case, we note that $g^y \in \mathbb{G}_1$ is enough to issue group signatures, meaning that users can discard y after generating their keys. In case usk leaks, the adversary now recovers g^y, which is useless to break DDH. We can thus retain some level of anonymity (at least CPA anonymity) in this case.

The Protocol. We now formalize the previous intuition by describing the algorithms constituting our scheme. As we explain above, we manage to avoid NIZK proofs and explicit encryption in our signature. However, we still need such primitives for some algorithms such as `Join` and `Open`. Fortunately, the latter are in practice subject to less constraints that `Sign` as they have less impact on the user's experience (in particular because they are run far less often than `Sign`). Our construction therefore also makes use of a public key encryption scheme Γ and of a NIZK proof system. The latter will concretely be the Groth-Sahai proof system [24] that allows to prove most common relations in bilinear groups by using a common reference string *crs*. Additional details on these two primitives are provided in the full version [18].

- `Setup`(1^λ): Let $(\mathbb{G}_1, \mathbb{G}_2, \mathbb{G}_T, e)$ be the description of type-3 bilinear groups of prime order p, this algorithm first selects $g \xleftarrow{\$} \mathbb{G}_1^*$ and $\widetilde{g} \xleftarrow{\$} \mathbb{G}_2^*$, and then computes $(X, \widetilde{X}) \leftarrow (g^x, \widetilde{g}^x)$ for some random scalar x. It also generates the public parameters pp_Σ for a digital signature scheme[2] Σ and selects a hash function $h : \{0,1\}^* \rightarrow \mathbb{Z}/p\mathbb{Z}$. Finally, it generates a common reference string *crs* for the Groth-Sahai proof system [24] in the SXDH setting and then sets the public parameters as $pp = (\mathbb{G}_1, \mathbb{G}_2, \mathbb{G}_T, e, g, \widetilde{g}, X, \widetilde{X}, crs, pp_\Sigma, h)$.
- `UKeygen`(pp): The user defines his own key pair as $(\mathsf{sk}, \mathsf{pk}) \leftarrow \Sigma.$`Keygen`$(pp_\Sigma)$.
- `OKeygen`(pp): The opening authority generates a key pair $(\mathsf{osk}, \mathsf{opk})$ for a public key encryption scheme Γ.
- `GKeygen`(pp): The group manager selects two random scalars α_1 and α_2 and then computes $(\widetilde{A}_1, \widetilde{A}_2, \widetilde{B}) \leftarrow (\widetilde{g}^{\alpha_1}, \widetilde{g}^{\alpha_2}, \widetilde{X}^{\alpha_2})$. He then initializes a public register **Reg** and returns $(\mathsf{gsk}, \mathsf{gpk}) \leftarrow ((\alpha_1, \alpha_2), (\widetilde{A}_1, \widetilde{A}_2, \widetilde{B}))$.
- `Join`: To join the group, a user i first selects two random scalars, u and y, and computes $(g^u, g^{u \cdot y})$ along with $C \leftarrow \Gamma.$`Encrypt`$(\mathsf{opk}, \widetilde{g}^y)$. He then generates a NIZK proof π that C encrypts an element $\widetilde{g}^y \in \mathbb{G}_2$ such that $e(g^u, \widetilde{g}^y) = e(g^{u \cdot y}, \widetilde{g})$. Finally, he generates $\mu \leftarrow \Sigma.$`Sign`$(\mathsf{sk}_i, (g^u || g^{u \cdot y} || C || \pi))$ and sends it, along with $(g^u, g^{u \cdot y}, C, \pi)$, to the group manager.
  Upon receiving these elements, the group manager checks the validity of the proof π and that $\Sigma.$`Verify`$(\mathsf{pk}_i, \mu, (g^u || g^{u \cdot y} || C || \pi)) = 1$. If π and μ are both valid, then he stores $(g^u, g^{u \cdot y}, C, \pi, \mathsf{pk}_i, \mu)$ in **Reg**$[i]$, generates a $t \xleftarrow{\$} \mathbb{Z}/p\mathbb{Z}$ and returns $\tau_1' \leftarrow ((g^u)^{\alpha_1} (g^{u \cdot y})^{\alpha_2})^t$, $\tau_2 \leftarrow g^{1/t}$ and $\widetilde{\tau} \leftarrow \widetilde{g}^{1/t}$.

[2] Any EUF-CMA signature scheme can be selected here, without any impact on the complexity of the group signatures.

Finally, the user computes $\tau_1 \leftarrow (\tau_1')^{1/u}$ and sets $\mathsf{usk}_i = (\tau_1, \tau_2, \widetilde{\tau}, g^y)$.

- $\texttt{Sign}(\mathsf{usk}_i, m)$: To sign a message m, the user first selects two random scalars r and s, and generates the following elements:

$$\tau_1' \leftarrow \tau_1^{r \cdot s}, \quad (\tau_2', \widetilde{\tau}') \leftarrow (\tau_2^{1/s}, \widetilde{\tau}^{1/s}), \quad (\sigma_1, \sigma_2) \leftarrow (g^r, X^{r/h(\widetilde{\tau}'||\sigma_1||m)} \cdot (g^y)^r).$$

The group signature σ on m is then defined as $\sigma = (\tau_1', \tau_2', \widetilde{\tau}', \sigma_1, \sigma_2)$.

- $\texttt{Verify}(\mathsf{gpk}, \sigma, m)$: To verify a group signature σ on m, one checks that none of its elements is $1_{\mathbb{G}_1}$ or $1_{\mathbb{G}_2}$ and that the following equalities hold:

$$e(\sigma_1, \widetilde{A}_1 \widetilde{B}^{-1/h(\widetilde{\tau}||\sigma_1||m)}) \cdot e(\sigma_2, \widetilde{A}_2) = e(\tau_1, \widetilde{\tau}) \quad \text{and} \quad e(\tau_2, \widetilde{g}) = e(g, \widetilde{\tau}),$$

in which case one outputs 1. Otherwise, one returns 0.

- $\texttt{Open}(\mathsf{osk}, \mathsf{gpk}, \sigma, m)$: Before opening a signature, the opening authority first checks that it is valid. Otherwise, he returns 0. By using its secret key osk, the opening authority has the ability to decrypt any ciphertext C_i stored in $\mathbf{Reg}[i]$ and thus recover the elements $\widetilde{g}^{y_i} \in \mathbb{G}_2$ for all registered users. He can then check, for each of them, whether the following equality holds:

$$e(\sigma_2, \widetilde{g}) \cdot e(\sigma_1, \widetilde{X}^{-1/h(\widetilde{\tau}||\sigma_1||m)}) = e(\sigma_1, \widetilde{g}^{y_i}).$$

If there is no match, then the opening authority returns $\perp$. Otherwise, let j be the corresponding user. The opening authority recovers the data $(g^{u_j}, g^{u_j \cdot y_j}, C_j, \pi_j, \mathsf{pk}_j, \mu_j)$ stored in $\mathbf{Reg}[j]$, commits to $\widetilde{g}^{y_j}$ and then outputs j along with a Groth-Sahai proof π that:

$$e(\sigma_2, \widetilde{g}) \cdot e(\sigma_1, \widetilde{X}^{-1/h(\widetilde{\tau}||\sigma_1||m)}) = e(\sigma_1, \widetilde{g}^{y_j}) \quad \text{and} \quad e(g^{u_j \cdot y_j}, \widetilde{g}) = e(g^{u_j}, \widetilde{g}^{y_j}).$$

- $\texttt{Judge}(\mathsf{gpk}, \sigma, m, i, \pi)$: To verify an opening, one checks that π is valid, $\texttt{Verify}(\mathsf{gpk}, \sigma, m) = 1$ and $\Sigma.\texttt{Verify}(\mathsf{pk}_i, \mu_i, (g^{u_i}||g^{u_i \cdot y_i}||C_i||\pi_i)) = 1$. If all conditions are satisfied, then one returns 1. Otherwise, one returns 0.

Correctness. First note that at the end of the $\texttt{Join}$ protocol, the user gets a FHS equivalence-class signature [21] on the representative (g, g^y). Indeed, $(\tau_1, \tau_2, \widetilde{\tau}) = ((g^{\alpha_1} g^{y \cdot \alpha_2})^t, g^{1/t}, \widetilde{g}^{1/t})$. To issue a group signature on m, the user first re-randomizes $(\tau_1, \tau_2, \widetilde{\tau})$ using s while updating the representative to $(g^r, g^{r \cdot y})$. The resulting tuple $(\tau_1', \tau_2', \widetilde{\tau}')$ is $((g^{r \cdot \alpha_1} g^{r \cdot y \cdot \alpha_2})^{t \cdot s}, g^{1/(t \cdot s)}, \widetilde{g}^{1/(t \cdot s)})$ and is still a FHS signature on the same equivalent class. He then generates a pair (σ_1, σ_2) where $(\sigma_1, \sigma_2^{m'})$ is a PS signature [28] on $m' = h(\widetilde{\tau}'||\sigma_1||m)$ using the same randomness r. Therefore, such a group signature satisfies:

$$\begin{aligned} e\left(\sigma_1, \widetilde{A}_1 \widetilde{B}^{-1/m'}\right) \cdot e(\sigma_2, \widetilde{A}_2) &= e\left(g^r, \widetilde{g}^{\alpha_1 - \frac{x \cdot \alpha_2}{m'}}\right) \cdot e\left(g^{r(\frac{x}{m'} + y)}, \widetilde{g}^{\alpha_2}\right), \\ &= e(g, \widetilde{g})^{r(\alpha_1 + y \cdot \alpha_2)} = e(\tau_1', \widetilde{\tau}'), \end{aligned}$$

and $e(\tau_2', \widetilde{g}) = e(g^{1/(t \cdot s)}, \widetilde{g}) = e(g, \widetilde{g}^{1/(t \cdot s)}) = e(g, \widetilde{\tau}')$.

Remark 3. Group signatures following the classical Sign-Encrypt-Prove framework usually provide an efficient opening procedure. Indeed, the opening authority knows the corresponding decryption key and so can decrypt the ciphertext included in the group signature and then identify the signer. Unfortunately, there is no equivalent for constructions without encryption and in particular there is no longer a "master" key that the opening authority can use to break anonymity.

Constructions based on randomizable signatures [7,19] circumvent this issue by forcing each user to provide to the opening authority a way to open their signatures. Concretely, during the `Join` protocol, each user must transmit some elements depending on their secret keys to this authority. Unfortunately this requirement does not fit the BSZ model [6] where `Join` is a two-party protocol between the user and the group manager. There are then two ways to solve this problem. Either we add the opening authority as an acting party in `Join` or we require that the user sends these elements to the group manager. The first solution is conceptually the simplest but modifies the original BSZ model. The second one does not but requires additional primitives to ensure security. Indeed, the user cannot transmit such elements in clear (otherwise the group manager could break anonymity) so he must send them encrypted and prove (in a zero-knowledge way) that the resulting ciphertext is well-formed.

In this paper we choose to describe the most complex (second) solution since one can easily derive from it a group signature scheme complying with the first option. We will then need an IND-CCA2 secure public key encryption scheme that is compatible with NIZK proofs. In practice, one can choose for instance [27] that nicely interacts with Groth-Sahai proofs [24]. We note that efficiency is not really a concern here since this step of the `Join` protocol has no impact on the group signatures themselves.

Remark 4. We note that the security model of Bellare *et al.* [6] already assumes a trusted `Setup` phase, so our construction perfectly fits this model on this point. However, this does not explain how to generate the public parameters in real-world conditions. In practice, it would be natural that the opening authority generates them. Regarding security, it would only be problematic for non-frameability if corruption of this entity occurred *before* `Setup`, but this is excluded by the model of [6]. We can also mitigate the risks by relying on a cooperative generation of the parameters, as in [15].

4.2 Security Results

Theorem 1. *Our group signature is:*

- *traceable under the EUF-CMA security of the FHS signature scheme;*
- *non-frameable under the* MPS *assumption, the collision-resistance of the function* h *and the EUF-CMA security of* Σ*;*
- *CPA anonymous under the* SXDH *assumption and the IND-CCA2 of* Γ*;*
- *selfless anonymous if it is non-frameable, if* Γ *is IND-CCA2 secure and if the* SXDH *assumption holds;*

– *fully anonymous, with merged opening authority and group manager, if it is traceable and if the* SXDH *assumption holds.*

Theorem 1 shows that our scheme retains some security properties (namely CPA security) even when users' secret keys are leaked, contrarily to the ones of [7,28]. The fact that selfless anonymity depends on the non-frameability may seem surprising but this is due to the special opening process that the reduction $\mathcal{R}$ uses in our security proof. Informally, $\mathcal{R}$ is able to open all signatures but the ones generated by the "challenge" user. To circumvent this problem $\mathcal{R}$ stores all the signatures it has produced on behalf of this user so that it will be able to recognize them if they are later submitted to the $\mathcal{O}\mathtt{Open}$ oracle. However, this works as long as the adversary is unable to forge signatures for this user, hence the non-frameability requirement.

The last statement of the theorem shows that we can achieve the strongest notion of anonymity if we additionally assume that the opening authority is also the group manager, as in the model of Bellare, Micciancio and Warinschi [5].

The theorem is proved below, except the part regarding non-frameability that we only provide in the full version of this work [18] due to space limitation.

Proof of Anonymity. Our proofs of CPA anonymity and selfless anonymity are very similar and only differ by one game. We will then consider an adversary against "anonymity" without specifying which property we consider except in Game 5 where the distinction is necessary. We discuss the case of full anonymity in Remark 5.

Let $\mathcal{A}$ be an adversary against the anonymity of our construction succeeding with probability ε. We define a sequence of games to show that this advantage is negligible. For each Game i we define $\mathtt{Adv}_i = |\mathtt{Pr}(S_i) - 1/2|$, where S_i is the event "$\mathcal{A}$ succeeds in Game i". We additionally define $\mathtt{Adv}_{\mathsf{SXDH}}$ as the advantage against the SXDH problem.

Game 1. Our first game is exactly the one of anonymity of Fig. 1 where the reduction $\mathcal{R}$ generates normally all the secret values and so is able to answer any oracle query. By definition, we have $\mathtt{Adv}_1 = \varepsilon$.

Game 2. In our second game, $\mathcal{R}$ selects a random index $i^* \in [1, q_A]$, where q_A is a bound on the number of $\mathcal{O}\mathtt{Add}$ queries. $\mathcal{R}$ proceeds as usual but aborts if $\mathcal{A}$ queries (i_0, i_1, m) to the $\mathcal{O}\mathtt{Ch}$ oracle with $i_b \neq i^*$. The advantage of $\mathcal{A}$ in this new game is then at least $\frac{\varepsilon}{q_A}$.

Game 3. In the third game, $\mathcal{R}$ generates a simulated common reference string crs and simulates all the zero-knowledge proofs. Any change in the behaviour of $\mathcal{A}$ can then be used against the zero-knowledge property of these proofs, which rely on SXDH in our setting. Therefore, $\mathtt{Adv}_3 \geq \mathtt{Adv}_2 - \mathtt{Adv}_{\mathsf{SXDH}}$.

Game 4. In the fourth game, $\mathcal{R}$ sets opk as the public key of a IND-CCA 2 experiment. It then uses the decryption oracle to decrypt the ciphertext C_i stored in $\mathbf{Reg}[i]$ for all users i and so can answer any query as usual. However, upon receiving the $\mathcal{O}\mathrm{J}_U$ query on i^* (this query necessarily occurs because of Game 2), it proceeds normally except that it generates C as an encryption of a random element of $\mathbb{G}_2$ and simulates the proof. A change in the behaviour of $\mathcal{A}$ would imply an attack against the IND-CCA2 security of Γ, so we get $\mathtt{Adv}_4 \geq \mathtt{Adv}_3 - \mathtt{Adv}_{\mathsf{IND-CCA2}}$.

Game 5. In the fifth game, $\mathcal{R}$ stores every signature it generates on behalf of i^* in some register $\mathbf{Sig}$. Upon receiving a $\mathtt{Open}$ query for some pair (σ, m), it first checks whether $\sigma \in \mathbf{Sig}$ in which case it returns i^* along with a simulated proof. Otherwise, it returns $\mathtt{Open}(\sigma, m)$.

We note that Game 5 is the same as Game 4 when we consider CPA anonymity since there is no $\mathcal{O}\mathtt{Open}$ query in this case. For selfless anonymity, a difference only occurs when the adversary manages to submit a forged signature that can be traced back to i^*. However, such an adversary can straightforwardly be converted into an adversary against non-frameability. We then have $\mathtt{Adv}_5 \geq \mathtt{Adv}_4 - \mathtt{Adv}^{nf}$.

Game 6. In the sixth game, $\mathcal{R}$ proceeds as in the previous game except that it answers to the $\mathcal{O}\mathtt{Ch}$ query by returning a signature generated using a random key. The advantage of $\mathcal{A}$ can then only be 0. We prove below that the Games 5 and 6 cannot be distinguished under the SXDH assumption and we then have $\mathtt{Adv}_6 \geq \mathtt{Adv}_5 - \mathtt{Adv}_{\mathsf{SXDH}}$.

Proof (of indistinguishability between anonymity Games 5 and 6). $\mathcal{R}$ receives a DDH challenge (g, g^a, g^b, g^z) in $\mathbb{G}_1$ and must then decide whether $z = a \cdot b$. It will then act as if $y = a$ for the secret key usk_{i^*} of user i^*. This is not a problem since g^a is sufficient to issue group signatures and to join the group since Game 4. Moreover Game 5 ensures $\mathcal{R}$ is able to answer any $\mathcal{O}\mathtt{Open}$ query, even without knowing $\widetilde{g}^a$.

To answer the $\mathcal{O}\mathtt{Ch}$ query for a message m, it selects a random scalar t and computes a group signature σ as follows:

- $\tau_1 \leftarrow ((g^b)^{\alpha_1} \cdot (g^z)^{\alpha_2})^t$;
- $(\tau_2, \widetilde{\tau}) \leftarrow (g^{1/t}, \widetilde{g}^{1/t})$;
- $(\sigma_1, \sigma_2) \leftarrow (g^b, (g^b)^{x/h(\widetilde{\tau}||\sigma_1||m)} \cdot (g^z))$.

In any case, σ is a valid group signature on m, *i.e.* $\mathtt{Verify}(\mathsf{gpk}, \sigma, m)$ outputs the bit 1. If $z = a \cdot b$, then σ s a valid signature issued by user i^* and $\mathcal{A}$ is still playing Game 5. Else, σ is a signature issued with a random key, independent of a and $\mathcal{A}$ is playing Game 6. Any change of behavior of $\mathcal{A}$ between these two games can then be used against the DDH assumption in $\mathbb{G}_1$ and so against the SXDH assumption. □

We get the following result, which proves both CPA anonymity and selfless anonymity of our construction:

- $\varepsilon/q_A \leq 2\ \mathsf{Adv}_{\mathsf{SXDH}} + \mathsf{Adv}_{\mathsf{IND-CCA2}}$ for any adversary succeeding against CPA anonymity with probability ε;
- $\varepsilon/q_A \leq 2\ \mathsf{Adv}_{\mathsf{SXDH}} + \mathsf{Adv}_{\mathsf{IND-CCA2}} + \mathsf{Adv}^{nf}$ for any adversary succeeding against selfless anonymity with probability ε.

Remark 5. Let us now consider the case where the group manager and the opening authority are merged, as in the BMW model [5]. As explained in Remark 3, the use of IND-CCA2 encryption during the Join protocol is only necessary when the opening authority is not involved in this process, which is no longer the case here. We can then discard Γ and remove Game 4 in the security proof.

In Game 5, $\mathcal{R}$ proceeds as follows. It still stores the signatures generated on behalf of i^* in **Sig** but now answers $\mathcal{O}\mathtt{Open}$ queries on (σ, m) as follows:

- if $\sigma \in \mathbf{Sig}$, then it returns i^* along with a simulated proof π;
- if $\mathtt{Open}(\sigma, m)$ returns (i, π) or 0, then it forwards this answer to the adversary;
- if $\mathtt{Open}(\sigma, m)$ returns $\perp$, then it returns i^* along with a simulated proof π.

We note that a problem only occurs in the third case if the adversary managed to submit a group signature that cannot be traced back to a registered user. However, this would mean that $\mathcal{A}$ is a valid adversary against traceability, which is unlikely. All the other games remain unchanged so $\varepsilon/q_A \leq 2\ \mathsf{Adv}_{\mathsf{SXDH}} + \mathsf{Adv}^{tra}$ for any adversary succeeding against full anonymity with probability ε in BMW [5].

Proof of Traceability. We prove that any untraceable group signature can be used to construct a forgery against the FHS equivalence-class signature scheme. More specifically, let $\mathcal{A}$ be an adversary against traceability succeeding with probability ε, then $\mathcal{A}$ can be converted into an adversary succeeding against the EUF-CMA security of FHS signature with the same probability.

Technically, $\mathcal{A}$ can succeed by returning a valid signature σ on m that either foils the opening process or that can be opened but for which it is impossible to produce a valid proof of opening. We can exclude the latter in our construction because of the correctness and of the soundness of Groth-Sahai proofs.

Our reduction $\mathcal{R}$ generates the public parameters as usual except that it does not discard x after generating X and $\widetilde{X}$. It then gets the public key $\widetilde{A}_1$ and $\widetilde{A}_2$ from the EUF-CMA challenger and sets gpk as $(\widetilde{A}_1, \widetilde{A}_2, \widetilde{A}_2^x)$. By using its signing oracle, it is able to handle Join query so the simulation is perfect. At the end of the game, $\mathcal{A}$ then outputs with probability ε an untraceable group signature σ on m. If we parse σ as $(\tau_1, \tau_2, \widetilde{\tau}, \sigma_1, \sigma_2)$, this means that:

(1) $e(\sigma_1, \widetilde{A}_1 \widetilde{B}^{-1/h(\widetilde{\tau}||\sigma_1||m)}) \cdot e(\sigma_2, \widetilde{A}_2) = e(\tau_1, \widetilde{\tau})$;
(2) $e(\tau_2, \widetilde{g}) = e(g, \widetilde{\tau})$;
(3) $e(\sigma_2, \widetilde{g}) \cdot e(\sigma_1, \widetilde{X}^{-1/h(\widetilde{\tau}||\sigma_1||m)}) \neq e(\sigma_1, \widetilde{g}^{y_i})$ for all $\widetilde{g}^{y_i}$ stored (encrypted).

Equation (1.) is equivalent to: $e(\sigma_1, \widetilde{A}_1) \cdot e(\sigma_2 \cdot \sigma_1^{-x/h(\widetilde{\tau}||\sigma_1||m)}, \widetilde{A}_2) = e(\tau_1, \widetilde{\tau})$, which means (together with equation (2.)) that $(\tau_1, \tau_2, \widetilde{\tau})$ is a valid FHS signature on $(\sigma_1, \sigma_2 \cdot \sigma_1^{-x/h(\widetilde{\tau}||\sigma_1||m)})$. However, $(\tau_1, \tau_2, \widetilde{\tau})$ will be considered as a valid forgery only if $(\sigma_1, \sigma_2 \cdot \sigma_1^{-x/h(\widetilde{\tau}||\sigma_1||m)})$ does not belong to the equivalence class of a message submitted to the signing oracle.

Let $\mathcal{S} = \{(h_i, h_i^{y_i})\}_{i=1}^q$, for $h_i \in \mathbb{G}_1$ be the set of queried messages. All these messages were involved in a `Join` query during which the group manager received (and stored) $\widetilde{g}^{y_i}$ (encrypted). Therefore, if (μ_1, μ_2) belongs to the equivalent class of an element of $\mathcal{S}$, then there exists $i \in [1, q]$ such that $e(\mu_1, \widetilde{g}^{y_i}) = e(\mu_2, \widetilde{g})$.

Let us then assume that $(\sigma_1, \sigma_2 \cdot \sigma_1^{-x/h(\widetilde{\tau}||\sigma_1||m)})$ satisfies the previous condition, *i.e.* that there is i such that: $e(\sigma_1, \widetilde{g}^{y_i}) = e(\sigma_2 \cdot \sigma_1^{-x/h(\widetilde{\tau}||\sigma_1||m)}, \widetilde{g})$. We then have $e(\sigma_1, \widetilde{g}^{y_i}) = e(\sigma_2, \widetilde{g}) \cdot e(\sigma_1^{-x/h(\widetilde{\tau}||\sigma_1||m)}, \widetilde{g}) = e(\sigma_2, \widetilde{g}) \cdot e(\sigma_1, \widetilde{X}^{-1/h(\widetilde{\tau}||\sigma_1||m)})$, which contradicts equation (3.). The pair $(\sigma_1, \sigma_2 \cdot \sigma_1^{-x/h(\widetilde{\tau}||\sigma_1||m)})$ has then never been signed, nor any representative of the same equivalence class, which means that $(\tau_1, \tau_2, \widetilde{\tau})$ along with $(\sigma_1, \sigma_2 \cdot \sigma_1^{-x/h(\widetilde{\tau}||\sigma_1||m)})$ is a valid forgery against the EUF-CMA security of the FHS scheme.

5 Efficiency Comparison

We compare the signing algorithm of our scheme with the ones of other constructions of the state-of-the-art. All of them are proven under interactive assumptions (or directly in the generic group model) so we do not take this point into account in our comparison. In Table 4, we enumerate the number of expensive operations, *i.e.* exponentiations in $\mathbb{G}_1$, $\mathbb{G}_2$ and $\mathbb{G}_T$ (denoted by e_1, e_2 and e_T respectively). Regarding signing cost, our scheme is the most efficient one whenever computing $3\mathsf{e}_1 + 1\mathsf{e}_2$ is cheaper than computing $1\mathsf{e}_T$.

To compare these operations, we choose a common metric. We aim at the 128-bit security. Following the incentive of Barbulescu and Duquesne [4], we select Barreto-Lynn-Scott curves with $k = 12$ that now seem more appropriate than Barreto-Naehrig ones, considering the recent attacks on pairings [26]. Moreover, they are getting involved in more implementations, *e.g.* in Zexe [12], a ledger-based system, and in ZCash [11] for zk-SNARKs.

Like in [4], we select a prime $q \equiv 3 \pmod 4$ and construct the tower of fields:

$$\mathbb{F}_{q^2} = \frac{\mathbb{F}_q[U]}{(U^2+1)}, \qquad \mathbb{F}_{q^6} = \frac{\mathbb{F}_{q^2}[V]}{(V^3 - U - 1)} \qquad \text{and} \qquad \mathbb{F}_{q^{12}} = \frac{\mathbb{F}_{q^6}[W]}{(W^2 - V)}.$$

This choice yields the costs in Table 1, where $\mathbf{m}$ is the cost of one multiplication in $\mathbb{F}_q$ (we make the rough assumption that squaring is the same cost as multiplying in $\mathbb{F}_q$). The last line of Table 1 represents costs in the so-called cyclotomic subgroup $\mathbb{G}_{\Phi_{12}(q)} \subset \mathbb{F}_{q^{12}}$ of order $\Phi_{12}(q)$ (where $\Phi_{12}(q)$ is the 12th cyclotomic polynomial evaluated at q, see [4]). This is of interest to us since $\mathbb{G}_T \subset \mathbb{G}_{\Phi_{12}(q)}$ and squaring in $\mathbb{G}_{\Phi_{12}(q)}$ are twice faster.

For simplicity, we take our BLS12 curve in the short Weierstrass model, that is $y^2 = x^3 + b$ with $b \in \mathbb{F}_q$, and use the Jacobian coordinate system: representing

Table 1. Costs of arithmetic operations in the tower extension as in [4]

Field	Mult. (M)	Squaring (S)
$\mathbb{F}_q$	$\mathbf{m}$	$\mathbf{m}$
$\mathbb{F}_{q^2}$	$3\,\mathbf{m}$	$2\,\mathbf{m}$
$\mathbb{F}_{q^{12}}$	$54\,\mathbf{m}$	$36\,\mathbf{m}$
$\mathbb{G}_{\Phi_{12}(q)}$	$54\,\mathbf{m}$	$18\,\mathbf{m}$

(x, y) as (X, Y, Z) and satisfying the equations $x = X/Z^2$ and $y = Y/Z^3$. This is the most efficient for pairings, without changing models (see [10]): it takes 11 field multiplications and 5 field squarings to add two distinct points and 2 field multiplications and 5 field squarings to double a point. After converting squarings to multiplications (see Table 1), we end up with Table 2. Note that a point in $\mathbb{G}_2$ is on the degree-6 twist curve, *i.e.* over $\mathbb{F}_{q^2}$.

Table 2. Costs of arithmetic operations in the pairing groups $\mathbb{G}_1/\mathbb{F}_q$ and $\mathbb{G}_2/\mathbb{F}_{q^2}$, when modeling the curve with a short Weierstrass equation and using Jacobian coordinates

Group	Addition	Doubling
	$11M + 5S$	$2M + 5S$
$\mathbb{G}_1$	$16\,\mathbf{m}$	$7\,\mathbf{m}$
$\mathbb{G}_2$	$43\,\mathbf{m}$	$16\,\mathbf{m}$

Now, to compare exponentiation, let n be a positive integer. Think of n as one of the random scalars in our `Sign` procedure. A double-and-add algorithm will, on average, double $\log_2 n$ times and add $(\log_2 n)/2$ times. It means, for instance, that an exponentiation by n in $\mathbb{G}_1$ costs $15(\log_2 n)$ field multiplications. In the following, we bound n by p (the order of $\mathbb{G}_1$, $\mathbb{G}_2$ and $\mathbb{G}_T$) and so get Table 3, where $\mathbf{k} = \log_2 p$.

Table 3. Upper-bounded cost of one group exponentiation

Group	$\mathbb{G}_1$	$\mathbb{G}_2$	$\mathbb{G}_T$
Cost	$15\mathbf{k} \cdot \mathbf{m}$	$38\mathbf{k} \cdot \mathbf{m}$	$45\mathbf{k} \cdot \mathbf{m}$

Using BLS12 curves leads to a 256-bit representation of scalars and at least 384-bit (resp. 768-bit) for the elements of $\mathbb{G}_1$ (resp. $\mathbb{G}_2$). We summarize our comparison in Table 4, indicating if the constructions follow the BMW model [5] or the BSZ one [6] (see Sect. 3). We note that [19] also considers outlying properties, such as opening soundness, that have no impact on the group signature itself. The last line of the table corresponds to our construction where the opening authority and the group manager are merged, which impacts security but not efficiency.

Table 4. Efficiency and security comparisons using BLS12 curves ($\mathbf{m}$ represents the cost of one multiplication in the base field of the curve and $\mathbf{k} = \lceil \log_2 p \rceil$)

Scheme	Size in bit	Cost in grp. exp.	Cost with BLS12	ROM?	GS model	Anonymity
BCNSW [7]	1664	$3\ \mathsf{e}_1 + 1\ \mathsf{e}_T$	$90\mathbf{k} \cdot \mathbf{m}$	Yes	BMW	Selfless
PS [28]	1280	$2\ \mathsf{e}_1 + 1\ \mathsf{e}_T$	$75\mathbf{k} \cdot \mathbf{m}$	Yes	BMW	Selfless
DS [19]	2816	$5\ \mathsf{e}_1 + 1\ \mathsf{e}_2$	$113\mathbf{k} \cdot \mathbf{m}$	Yes	BSZ	CPA
DS* [19]	4608	$5\ \mathsf{e}_1 + 6\ \mathsf{e}_2$	$303\mathbf{k} \cdot \mathbf{m}$	Yes	BSZ	Full
BHKS [3]	4992	$9\ \mathsf{e}_1 + 2\ \mathsf{e}_2$	$211\mathbf{k} \cdot \mathbf{m}$	No	BMW	Full
Ours	2304	$5\ \mathsf{e}_1 + 1\ \mathsf{e}_2$	$113\mathbf{k} \cdot \mathbf{m}$	No	BSZ	CPA & Selfless
Ours*	2304	$5\ \mathsf{e}_1 + 1\ \mathsf{e}_2$	$113\mathbf{k} \cdot \mathbf{m}$	No	BMW	Full

If we focus on constructions without random oracles, our group signature outperforms the recent construction of [3]: it halves both the signature size and the signature cost. We also note that it is competitive against the most efficient construction [28] in the random oracle model (ROM). Indeed, while the signature size remains larger (double the size), the computational cost is quite similar and, more importantly, our signer no longer needs to perform operation in $\mathbb{G}_T$ and so, does not need to implement the arithmetic in $\mathbb{F}_{q^{12}}$, which is noticeable.

We would like to add that this comparison was made targeting the 128-bit security level. At higher security levels, BLS12 curves might not be relevant anymore. For instance, at 256 bits of security, the authors from [10] choose a BLS24 curve and different curve models for $\mathbb{G}_1$ and $\mathbb{G}_2$, thus satisfying the condition $3\mathsf{e}_1 + 1\mathsf{e}_2 < 1\mathsf{e}_T$. In that case, our group signature scheme is computationally the most efficient, even compared to the best alternative in the ROM [28].

6 Conclusion

In this paper, we have introduced the most efficient group signature scheme proved secure without random oracles. Our construction is based on a tailored combination of the PS signature scheme and the FHS equivalence-class signature scheme, leading to a group signature consisting only of four elements in $\mathbb{G}_1$ and one in $\mathbb{G}_2$. Its security mostly relies on the one of these signature schemes which have been widely used in cryptographic protocols, although we need to adapt the proof of PS signature to fit our construction.

Our scheme halves both the size and the computational cost compared to the most efficient alternative in the same model. It also significantly closes the gap with constructions in the ROM, showing that we can avoid this model without dramatically increasing complexity.

Acknowledgements. The authors are grateful for the support of the ANR through project ANR-16-CE39-0014 PERSOCLOUD and project ANR-18-CE-39-0019-02 MobiS5.

References

1. Abdalla, M., Warinschi, B.: On the minimal assumptions of group signature schemes. In: Lopez, J., Qing, S., Okamoto, E. (eds.) ICICS 2004. LNCS, vol. 3269, pp. 1–13. Springer, Heidelberg (2004). https://doi.org/10.1007/978-3-540-30191-2_1
2. Ateniese, G., Camenisch, J., Joye, M., Tsudik, G.: A practical and provably secure coalition-resistant group signature scheme. In: Bellare, M. (ed.) CRYPTO 2000. LNCS, vol. 1880, pp. 255–270. Springer, Heidelberg (2000). https://doi.org/10.1007/3-540-44598-6_16
3. Backes, M., Hanzlik, L., Kluczniak, K., Schneider, J.: Signatures with flexible public key: introducing equivalence classes for public keys. In: Peyrin, T., Galbraith, S. (eds.) ASIACRYPT 2018, Part II. LNCS, vol. 11273, pp. 405–434. Springer, Cham (2018). https://doi.org/10.1007/978-3-030-03329-3_14
4. Barbulescu, R., Duquesne, S.: Updating key size estimations for pairings. J. Cryptology **32**(4), 1298–1336 (2019). https://doi.org/10.1007/s00145-018-9280-5
5. Bellare, M., Micciancio, D., Warinschi, B.: Foundations of group signatures: formal definitions, simplified requirements, and a construction based on general assumptions. In: Biham, E. (ed.) EUROCRYPT 2003. LNCS, vol. 2656, pp. 614–629. Springer, Heidelberg (2003). https://doi.org/10.1007/3-540-39200-9_38
6. Bellare, M., Shi, H., Zhang, C.: Foundations of group signatures: the case of dynamic groups. In: Menezes, A. (ed.) CT-RSA 2005. LNCS, vol. 3376, pp. 136–153. Springer, Heidelberg (2005). https://doi.org/10.1007/978-3-540-30574-3_11
7. Bichsel, P., Camenisch, J., Neven, G., Smart, N.P., Warinschi, B.: Get shorty via group signatures without encryption. In: Garay, J.A., De Prisco, R. (eds.) SCN 2010. LNCS, vol. 6280, pp. 381–398. Springer, Heidelberg (2010). https://doi.org/10.1007/978-3-642-15317-4_24
8. Boneh, D., Boyen, X., Shacham, H.: Short group signatures. In: Franklin, M. (ed.) CRYPTO 2004. LNCS, vol. 3152, pp. 41–55. Springer, Heidelberg (2004). https://doi.org/10.1007/978-3-540-28628-8_3
9. Boneh, D., Shacham, H.: Group signatures with verifier-local revocation. In: ACM CCS (2004)
10. Bos, J.W., Costello, C., Naehrig, M.: Exponentiating in pairing groups. In: Lange, T., Lauter, K., Lisoněk, P. (eds.) SAC 2013. LNCS, vol. 8282, pp. 438–455. Springer, Heidelberg (2014). https://doi.org/10.1007/978-3-662-43414-7_22
11. Bowe, S.: BLS12-381: New zk-SNARK Elliptic Curve Construction (2017). https://electriccoin.co/blog/new-snark-curve/
12. Bowe, S., Chiesa, A., Green, M., Miers, I., Mishra, P., Wu, H.: Zexe: enabling decentralized private computation. IACR Cryptology ePrint Archive (2018)
13. Boyen, X., Waters, B.: Compact group signatures without random oracles. In: Vaudenay, S. (ed.) EUROCRYPT 2006. LNCS, vol. 4004, pp. 427–444. Springer, Heidelberg (2006). https://doi.org/10.1007/11761679_26
14. Camenisch, J., Lysyanskaya, A.: Signature schemes and anonymous credentials from bilinear maps. In: Franklin, M. (ed.) CRYPTO 2004. LNCS, vol. 3152, pp. 56–72. Springer, Heidelberg (2004). https://doi.org/10.1007/978-3-540-28628-8_4
15. Canard, S., Pointcheval, D., Sanders, O., Traoré, J.: Divisible E-cash made practical. In: PKC (2015)
16. Canetti, R., Goldreich, O., Halevi, S.: On the random-oracle methodology as applied to length-restricted signature schemes. In: Naor, M. (ed.) TCC 2004. LNCS, vol. 2951, pp. 40–57. Springer, Heidelberg (2004). https://doi.org/10.1007/978-3-540-24638-1_3

17. Chaum, D., van Heyst, E.: Group signatures. In: Davies, D.W. (ed.) EUROCRYPT 1991. LNCS, vol. 547, pp. 257–265. Springer, Heidelberg (1991). https://doi.org/10.1007/3-540-46416-6_22
18. Clarisse, R., Sanders, O.: Group Signature without Random Oracles from Randomizable Signatures (full version of this work). IACR Cryptol. ePrint Arch., 2018–1115 (2020)
19. Derler, D., Slamanig, D.: Highly-efficient fully-anonymous dynamic group signatures. In: ASIACCS (2018)
20. Fiat, A., Shamir, A.: How to prove yourself: practical solutions to identification and signature problems. In: Odlyzko, A.M. (ed.) CRYPTO 1986. LNCS, vol. 263, pp. 186–194. Springer, Heidelberg (1987). https://doi.org/10.1007/3-540-47721-7_12
21. Fuchsbauer, G., Hanser, C., Slamanig, D.: Structure-preserving signatures on equivalence classes and constant-size anonymous credentials. J. Cryptol. **32**(2), 498–546 (2019)
22. Goldwasser, S., Micali, S., Rivest, R.L.: A digital signature scheme secure against adaptive chosen-message attacks. SIAM J. Comput. **17**(2), 281–308 (1988)
23. Groth, J.: Fully anonymous group signatures without random oracles. In: Kurosawa, K. (ed.) ASIACRYPT 2007. LNCS, vol. 4833, pp. 164–180. Springer, Heidelberg (2007). https://doi.org/10.1007/978-3-540-76900-2_10
24. Groth, J., Sahai, A.: Efficient non-interactive proof systems for bilinear groups. In: Smart, N. (ed.) EUROCRYPT 2008. LNCS, vol. 4965, pp. 415–432. Springer, Heidelberg (2008). https://doi.org/10.1007/978-3-540-78967-3_24
25. Guillevic, A.: Comparing the pairing efficiency over composite-order and prime-order elliptic curves. In: Jacobson, M., Locasto, M., Mohassel, P., Safavi-Naini, R. (eds.) ACNS 2013. LNCS, vol. 7954, pp. 357–372. Springer, Heidelberg (2013). https://doi.org/10.1007/978-3-642-38980-1_22
26. Kim, T., Barbulescu, R.: Extended tower number field sieve: a new complexity for the medium prime case. In: Robshaw, M., Katz, J. (eds.) CRYPTO 2016, Part I. LNCS, vol. 9814, pp. 543–571. Springer, Heidelberg (2016). https://doi.org/10.1007/978-3-662-53018-4_20
27. Libert, B., Peters, T., Joye, M., Yung, M.: Non-malleability from malleability: simulation-sound quasi-adaptive NIZK proofs and CCA2-secure encryption from homomorphic signatures. In: Nguyen, P.Q., Oswald, E. (eds.) EUROCRYPT 2014. LNCS, vol. 8441, pp. 514–532. Springer, Heidelberg (2014). https://doi.org/10.1007/978-3-642-55220-5_29
28. Pointcheval, D., Sanders, O.: Short randomizable signatures. In: Sako, K. (ed.) CT-RSA 2016. LNCS, vol. 9610, pp. 111–126. Springer, Cham (2016). https://doi.org/10.1007/978-3-319-29485-8_7

Constant-Size Lattice-Based Group Signature with Forward Security in the Standard Model

Sébastien Canard[1], Adela Georgescu[2,3](✉), Guillaume Kaim[1,2], Adeline Roux-Langlois[2], and Jacques Traoré[1]

[1] Orange Labs, Applied Crypto Group, Caen, France
[2] Univ Rennes, CNRS, IRISA, Rennes, France
adela.georgescu@irisa.fr
[3] Department of Computer Science, University of Bucharest, Bucharest, Romania

Abstract. One important property of group signatures is forward-security, which prevents an attacker in possession of a group signing key to forge signatures produced in the past. In case of exposure of one group member's signing key, group signatures lacking forward-security need to invalidate all group public and secret keys (by re-initializing the whole system) but also invalidate all previously issued group signatures. Most of the existing forward-secure group signatures (FS-GS) are built from number-theoretic security assumptions which are vulnerable to quantum computers. The only post-quantum secure FS-GS scheme is built from lattices by Ling et al. (PQCrypto 19) in the random oracle model, following the classical framework of encrypt-then-prove, thus using non-interactive zero-knowledge (NIZK) proofs. In this work, we achieve the first FS-GS from lattices in the standard model. Our starting point is the group signature of Katsumada and Yamada (Eurocrypt 19) which replaces NIZK by attribute-based signatures (ABS), thus removing the need for random oracles. We first modify the underlying ABS of Tsabary (TCC 17) to equip it with forward-security property. We then prove that by plugging it back in the group signature framework of Katsumada and Yamada (Eurocrypt 19), we can design a FS-GS scheme secure in the standard model with public key and signature size constant in the number of users. Our constant size is achieved by relying on complexity leveraging, which further implies relying on the subexponential hardness of the Short Integers Solution (SIS) assumption.

1 Introduction

Group signatures were introduced as a new type of signatures by Chaum and van Heyst [CvH91] in 1991 and they were designed to allow only members of a group to sign messages while the identity of the signer remains hidden for the verifier (anonymity). The latter can only ensure that a member belonging to the group has signed the message. Moreover this property guarantees the unlinkability as well, preventing anyone to detect that two group signatures have been generated

K. Nguyen et al. (Eds.): ProvSec 2020, LNCS 12505, pp. 24–44, 2020.
https://doi.org/10.1007/978-3-030-62576-4_2

by the same group member. Nevertheless, if necessary, the signature can be opened by an entity called group manager who holds some secret information and reveals the identity of the signer (traceability). These features make group signatures very useful for real life applications including e-commerce systems, anonymous online communications and trusted hardware attestations.

From their beginning until now, a great variety of constructions for group signatures have been proposed, addressing different needs: in the random oracle model [CL04,BBS04] or standard model [BW06,Gro07], supporting static groups [BMW03], dynamic groups [BSZ05] or partially dynamic groups and constructions based on different theoretical assumptions such as RSA [ACJT00], or pairings [BBS04] for standard assumptions.

As for post-quantum constructions, there is a vast literature concerning group signatures based on lattices, some of them being designed to support most of the important properties listed above. Among them there are group signatures in the static model [GKV10,CNR12,LLLS13,NZZ15,LNW15,LLNW16], [LNWX18,BCN18,dPLS18], in the dynamic model where users have the flexibility to join and leave the group [LNWX17], achieving partially dynamicity by means of verifier-local revokability [LLNW14] (where new users can not join the group but they can leave it being revoked), or using other tools to achieve partial dynamicity [LLM+16,LMN16]. Concerning the random oracle model (ROM) and the standard model, all of the existing lattice-based group signature schemes are in the ROM except the construction by Katsumata and Yamada [KY19]. We can further notice that the recent construction of non-interactive zero-knowledge proof of knowledge (or NIZKPoK or NIZK) for all NP from [PS19] combined with [BMW03] can be adapted in a group signature scheme in the standard model in a straightforward manner (but very inefficiently as we explain in the next subsection).

Forward-security [Son01,NHF09,LY10] is an important additional security property sometimes considered in group signature constructions. Concerning lattices, to the best of our knowledge there is one such construction in the ROM model [LNWX19]. This property cuts the time into periods t and prevents attackers from forging group signatures pertaining to past time periods $t' < t$, even if a secret group signing key is revealed at the current time period. As explained in Song [Son01], in the context of group signatures, exposure of secret signing keys is more damaging since an adversary being in the possession of a member's group signing key can produce signatures on behalf of the whole group, but still remaining anonymous. As a consequence, all the public and secret keys of the group need to be regenerated and all previously generated group signatures have to be rendered invalid. We note that the solution to these problems is adding a forward-secure mechanism to group signatures as was previously done first for key exchange protocols [Gün89,DvOW92] and then for digital signatures [BM99,IR01], symmetric-key encryption [BY03] and public key encryption systems [CHK03]. This property aims to protect past use of private keys even if an adversary breaks-in at the current moment of time. When entering a new time period t, a new secret key related to t is computed from the previous secret key related to $t-1$ through a one-way key evolution algorithm, the latter one being deleted promptly afterwards.

1.1 Our Contribution

Our main achievement in this paper is a lattice-based forward-secure group signature scheme without NIZK in the standard model with public key and signature size constant (independent) on the number of users. We note that this is the first of its kind in the standard model as the only existing construction [LNWX19] for group signatures from lattices achieving forward-security is in the random oracle model. Our group signature corresponds to the transformation of the lattice-based group signature from [KY19] using the idea from [LNWX19] to obtain forward-security.

The main building block of our transformation is a lattice-based forward-secure attribute-based signature scheme (FS-ABS) that we introduce later in this paper as a novelty. We mention that there is a previous general construction of FS-ABS due to [YLH+12] which combines the general primitive of credential bundles (which can be instantiated with forward-secure digital signatures) and non-interactive witness-indistinguishable (NIWI) proofs. Using this framework one can achieve lattice-based FS-ABS as long as one can build forward-secure digital signature and NIWI from lattices, but, to the best of our knowledge, there is no construction in the lattice-settings for any of them. Therefore, we believe that our construction of lattice-based FS-ABS is of self-interest.

We mention that our group signature scheme satisfies CCA-selfless-anonymity (inherited from the base group signature scheme of [KY19]), a relaxation of the CCA-full-anonymity, since the adversary is not in possession of all the secret keys: he is missing the secret keys of the two members, whose identities compose the challenge. As for the traceability property, we show that our scheme achieves forward-secure traceability.

As already explained in [KY19], group signatures from lattices in the standard model can be achieved also by using the recent proposal for NIZK for all NP from LWE [PS19] (published shortly after [KY19]) instead of the ABS. The difference is that the ABS that we employ in our group signature scheme relies only on the hardness of SIS, avoiding the potentially stronger LWE assumption on which the NIZK mentioned above relies, leading to a potentially heavier group signature construction. Another drawback of a potential instantiation of group signatures using [PS19] is that the latter one relies on fully homomorphic encryption for evaluating circuits making it very costly in time efficiency.

1.2 Overview of the Building Blocks for Our Construction

In order to have all the elements needed to give a technical overview of our scheme, we start by describing three existing constructions: the group signature scheme of [KY19], the ABS proposed by Tsabary [Tsa17], and finally, the forward-secure mechanism of the group signature construction of [LNWX19].

Group Signature Scheme without NIZK. The starting point of our work is the recent lattice-based group signature scheme without NIZK in the standard model [KY19]. Previous to this construction, all works on group signatures were relying on the Sign-Encrypt-Prove framework defined by Bellare, Micciancio and Warinschi [BMW03]. In this framework, to sign a message M, a user encrypts both his certificate received from the group manager and a digital signature on M. Finally, he proves in non-interactive zero-knowledge that every element is well formed. Until recently (2019), constructing NIZK from lattices for any NP language was a long-standing open problem and by that time Katsumata and Yamada [KY19] proposed a group signature scheme that by-passed the utilization of NIZK by replacing it with *indexed* attribute-based signature scheme (ABS). Their idea is based on the fact that for group signatures the needed NIZK is in the common reference string (CRS) model and, in the context of group signatures, it resembles to *designated-prover* NIZK (DP-NIZK) where there is a proving key k_P that needs to be kept secret (and thus is not known to the verifier, assuring zero-knowledge) and a verification key k_V which is public. Anyway, simply replacing NIZK in the CRS model with DP-NIZK is not enough since it trivially breaks anonymity. The breakthrough idea of Katsumata and Yamada was to view ABS as DP-NIZK. In attribute-based signatures, a signer with an attribute x is provided a secret key sk_x from the authority and can anonymously sign a message associated with a policy C using his secret key, if and only if, his attribute satisfies the policy C. In particular, the signature hides the attribute (anonymity) and users can not collude to pull their attributes together if none of the attributes satisfies the policy associated to the message (unforgeability). Now, an ABS can be seen as a DP-NIZK by the following association: the attribute x is seen as a witness w and the ABS signing key sk_x can be set as the proving key k_P of the DP-NIZK. Thus proving that w is a valid witness to a statement s i.e. $(s, w) \in \mathcal{R}$ for the NP relation $\mathcal{R}$ resorts to, firstly prepare a circuit $C_s(w) = \mathcal{R}(s, w)$ that has the statement s hard-wired into it, secondly sign a message associated with the policy C_s using the proving key $k_P = sk_x$ and finally output the signature as the NIZK proof π. Anonymity and unforgeability of the ABS assure the zero-knowledge property and soundness respectively.

Having shown a way of substituting the NIZK with ABS, it remains to indicate how to use ABS to construct group signature. We briefly explain, in the following, the general framework from [KY19]. The group manager issues for user i a key K_i of a secret key encryption (SKE) scheme and an ABS signing key $sk_{i||K_i}$ where $i||K_i$ is seen as an attribute. To sign a message M, the group member i encrypts his identity under K_i obtaining $\mathsf{ct}_i = \mathsf{SKE.Enc}(K_i, i)$ and creates an attribute-based signature for some policy C_{ct_i} which serves as a NIZK proof of the fact that ct_i encrypts the identity. The circuit C_{ct_i} has the statement ct_i hardwired such that $C_{\mathsf{ct}_i}(i||K_i) := (i = \mathsf{SKE.Dec}(K_i, \mathsf{ct}_i))$. The traceability property of the group signature holds from unforgeability of ABS and anonymity holds from anonymity of the ABS and semantic security of the SKE.

As for the instantiation of the ABS from lattices, [KY19] gives two possible solutions: the first one uses the ABS proposed by Tsabary [Tsa17] proven secure under the SIS assumption and the second one is an indexed ABS designed by them, relying also on the SIS assumption. The need for the second construction is explained by the problems encountered when trying to plug the first construction into a group signature. Tsabary's scheme achieves selective unforgeability which is not enough for security purposes of group signatures. Adaptiveness is the required property and can be easily achieved via complexity leveraging with the drawback that this approach requires a subexponential security loss. We remark that in [KY19] they emphasize that they don't really need adaptiveness but rather something complementary to selectiveness called co-selective unforgeability. Unfortunately, we can not achieve this property directly, without complexity leveraging (see Sect. 3.3 for more details). The two different ABS constructions give two different group signature schemes with the following properties:

(i) Tsabary's ABS gives rise to a group signature scheme with public key and signature size constant (independent) in the number of users and whose security relies on the hardness of LWE with polynomial approximation factor and subexponential hardness of SIS with polynomial approximation factor.
(ii) The second ABS gives rise to a group signature scheme with public key and signature size linear in the number of users whose security relies on the hardness of LWE and SIS with polynomial approximation factors.

Attributed Based Signature from Constrained Signature of Tsabary. The main building block of our group signature is an Attribute Based Signature scheme. In the following we briefly explain the ABS developped in Tsabary's paper. First of all, the construction in Tsabary's paper is not really an *attribute-based signature* but rather a *key-policy constrained signature* or simply *constrained signature*. We note that the other flavour of constrained signatures, as defined in [Tsa17], called *message-policy constrained signature* is equivalent to attribute-based signatures. In constrained signatures, a signing key sk_f is associated with a policy $f : \{0,1\}^* \to \{0,1\}$, called the constraint, and a key sk_f can sign a message $x \in \{0,1\}^*$ only if the message satisfies the policy i.e. $f(x) = 0$. In attribute-based signatures each key is associated with an attribute $x \in \{0,1\}^*$ and a key sk_x can sign a policy f only if the attribute satisfies the policy i.e. $f(x) = 0$. A constrained signature can be easily transformed into an attribute-based signature using universal circuits (which we denote U_x) as briefly explained in [KY19] (but not done there), transformation that we apply in Sect. 3 and that we sketch below.

The ABS scheme (as well as the original constrained signature of [Tsa17]) is built from lattice trapdoors. The verification key vk consists of a uniformly sampled matrix $\overrightarrow{\mathbf{A}} = [\mathbf{A}_1\|...\|\mathbf{A}_\ell] \in \mathbb{Z}_q^{n\times(m\times\ell)}$ (with ℓ the input size of the circuit C) and a close to uniform matrix $\mathbf{A} \in \mathbb{Z}_q^{n\times p}$ while the master signing key msk is a trapdoor for $\mathbf{A}$ denoted $\mathbf{A}_{\gamma_0}^{-1}$. The signing key sk_{x_i} is associated to an user i (we prefer the simplified version of this notation even though it would be clearer to use $sk_{U_{x_i}}$ as notation) and to an universal circuit U_{x_i} (which has the attribute hard-wired and takes as input the policy (circuit) and a message). The secret key sk_{x_i} is a trapdoor $[\mathbf{A}\|\mathbf{A}_{x_i}]_\gamma^{-1}$ where $\mathbf{A}_{x_i} = \overrightarrow{\mathbf{A}} \cdot \mathbf{H}_{U_{x_i}} \in \mathbb{Z}_q^{n\times m}$ is computed from $\overrightarrow{\mathbf{A}}$ and U_{x_i} using the function EvalF. This function, associated with a function EvalFX, allows to compute $\mathbf{H}_{U_{x_i}} = \mathsf{EvalF}(U_{x_i}, \overrightarrow{\mathbf{A}})$, and $\mathbf{H}_{U_{x_i},\mathbf{x}} = \mathsf{EvalFX}(U_{x_i}, \mathbf{x}, \overrightarrow{\mathbf{A}})$ both in $\mathbb{Z}^{(\ell m)\times m}$ and of bounded norm such that $(\overrightarrow{\mathbf{A}} - \mathbf{x}\otimes\mathbf{G})\cdot \mathbf{H}_{U_{x_i},\mathbf{x}} = \overrightarrow{\mathbf{A}} \cdot \mathbf{H}_{U_{x_i}} - U_{x_i}(\mathbf{x})\mathbf{G} \mod q$, where $\mathbf{G}$ is the gadget matrix. Then, the manager can easily generate the secret key sk_{x_i} using it's own trapdoor $\mathbf{A}_{\gamma_0}^{-1}$. A valid signature for a message M, a circuit C and an attribute x_i is a short vector σ such that $[\mathbf{A}\|\overrightarrow{\mathbf{A}} - x_i\otimes\mathbf{G}]\cdot\sigma = \mathbf{0} \mod q$. We note that for every tuple (C, M, x_i), a trapdoor $[\mathbf{A}\|\overrightarrow{\mathbf{A}} - x_i\otimes\mathbf{G}]_{\gamma'}^{-1}$ can be derived from $[\mathbf{A}\|\overrightarrow{\mathbf{A}} - U_{x_i}(C, M)\mathbf{G}]_{\gamma'}^{-1}$ when $U_{x_i}(C, M) = C(x_i) = 0$.

We remark that, at this stage, the unforgeability of the ABS can be easily broken, as explained in [KY19] because the message is not bounded to the signature (both signature and verification just ignore the message) and a valid signature for a pair of policy and message (C, M) is also valid for (C, M') for $M \neq M'$. Therefore, in the security game, we can not allow signature queries and following the idea of [KY19], we use the fact that a scheme that is unforgeable only when the adversary can not make signature queries can be generically transformed into a scheme that is unforgeable even when the adversary is allowed to make signature queries. In short, the idea in [KY19] is to answer the signing queries using the secret key of a dummy user which does not exist in the real system. We will need to partition the set of all possible message-policy pairs into a challenge set and a controlled set (using admissible hash functions) with the hope that the adversary asks queries that fall into the controlled set to which the challenger can answer with the help of the dummy key. We also hope that the attacker outputs a forgery in the challenge set to allow the simulator to solve a hard problem.

Forward Secure Group Signature of [LNWX19]**.** Recall that for achieving forward-secure group signature, one needs a one-way key evolving mechanism for deriving secret keys for every period of time. Let us now briefly explain this mechanism following the idea of [LNWX19]. Let $T = 2^d$ be the total number of time periods, the time periods are represented in a binary tree, where each time period is a leaf of the tree. Each user secret key for a time period t is then associated with a sub-tree of depth d which uniquely defines the time period t. Let z be a binary string (corresponding to a time period) of lenth d_z. The set $\text{Nodes}_{(t\leftarrow T-1)}$ contains nodes for which bases (trapdoors) are derived at a current period of time t and which allow to compute subsequent keys in the key update algorithm using the bonsai tree technique [CHKP10]. Each user will have associated a matrix corresponding to period time $z \in \text{Nodes}_{(t\leftarrow T-1)}$: $\mathbf{A}_{x_i,z} = [\mathbf{A}\|\mathbf{A}_{x_i}\|\mathbf{T}_1^{z[1]}\|\cdots\|\mathbf{T}_{d_z}^{z[d_z]}]$ where the last d_z matrices corresponding to the bits of d_z are public. Therefore, the group signing key of user i at time t is $\{\mathbf{S}_{i\|z}, z \in \text{Nodes}_{(t\leftarrow T-1)}\}$ which satisfies $\mathbf{A}_{x_i,z}\cdot\mathbf{S}_{i\|z} = \mathbf{0} \bmod q$. The user is then able to compute all possible $\mathbf{S}_{i\|t}$ by employing $\mathbf{S}_{i\|z}$ if z is an ancestor of t where t is the binary representation of a period of time. The basis delegation technique allows users to compute trapdoor matrices for all the descendent nodes in the set $\text{Nodes}_{(t\leftarrow T-1)}$ and therefore to compute all the subsequent signing keys.

1.3 Our Construction

We are now able to better explain our contribution. We start from the constrained signature of Tsabary, we transform it in an ABS (according to [KY19] suggestion) as previously explained, we equip it with forward-security (following the mechanism of [LNWX19]), then plug it into the group signature of [KY19]. Thus we achieve the first forward-secure group signature from lattices without NIZK in the standard model having public key and signature size independent of the number of users for which we managed to prove forward-secure traceability and CCA-selfless anonymity. The drawback is that the security assumption on which the GS scheme relies is SIS with subexponential hardness.

Our main building block is then a forward secure Attribute Based Signature which is built using the idea from [LNWX19] having as starting point Tsabary's constrained signature. As explained in [LNWX19], the advantage of this method is that it incurs only logarithmic dependency on T. Therefore our construction achieves signature size and public key size constant in N and logarithmic in T. We note that [LNWX19] applied it directly for building forward-secure group signature (FS-GS) while we need to apply it first on our ABS to get forward-secure attribute-based signatures (FS-ABS). Indeed, in an encrypt-then-prove paradigm for group signatures, the transformation of [LNWX19] into a forward secure group signature is independent of the encryption scheme and of the NIZK scheme used to prove the membership. This is because the group secret key of a user does not appear as input in the NIZK proof but is embedded in a ciphertext on which the proof is performed. Instead, the paradigm on which we build our construction uses an ABS to prove that the user belongs to the group, and the ABS secret key is a direct component of the group secret key of a user. This means that if we want to update the group secret key of a user, we need to update the ABS secret key as well.

From this observation and the fact that the ABS built by Tsabary [Tsa17] is based on lattice trapdoors which fit perfectly with bonsai trees, we can then adapt the forward security mechanism of [LNWX19] to the ABS derived from [Tsa17], and use the resulting ABS to get forward-secure group signature scheme. We note that if we try to apply the same technique for the second ABS from [KY19] (also built from lattice trapdoors) we can not get forward-security. The problem is that the design of ABS forces us to keep the initial secret key derived by the master authority for every user in order to be able to compute all the other subsequent keys for the following periods of time. This means that an adversary who gains access to a secret key for a certain period of time, would be able to compute the secret keys for all periods of time (including previous ones).

The main difficulty encountered when trying to add forward security to the ABS derived from [Tsa17] is then the way to deal with the trapdoors for each of the time periods. This includes the trapdoors considered in the ABS construction as well as in the simulation. Moreover this modification induces a new time parameter t, that has to be handled in the unforgeability proof. Indeed, the construction of [Tsa17] has been designed to only consider a fixed matrix $\mathbf{A}$ and a vector of matrices $\overrightarrow{\mathbf{A}}$ linked to the attribute to generate and verify signatures. But now we add log t additional matrices in order to integrate the time parameter, in a similar way to [LNWX19]. This transformation implies that the secret keys have to be modified according to the time period considered. It means that a trapdoor update mechanism needs to be built from the trapdoor construction of Tsabary, using tools introduced in the bonsai tree mechanism [CHKP10], and the time component has to be dealt with in the different queries from the simulation-based proof.

Finally, as we apply forward-secure property to an attribute-based construction in our case, we also have to handle an additional component which is the attribute. A naive adaptation from the transformation of [LNWX19] (on a group signature) to our construction (an attribute based signature) would not be secure. Indeed, we have to deal with two types of trapdoor: the trapdoor inherent to the ABS construction derived from [Tsa17], and the trapdoors given by the matrices linked to the time parameter. In the security proof of the ABS scheme, we need to simulate these two types of trapdoors according to each other, and according to the time period considered, in order to be able to answer all the queries of an attacker. At the same time, we expect all these trapdoors to vanish when the forgery of the attacker is outputted, in order to be able to conclude the simulation and then to argue about the security reduction getting a solution to a hard problem.

Related Work. The only previous work on forward-secure group signature schemes from lattices is the work of [LNWX19] in the random oracle model using NIZK achieving signature size $\tilde{O}(\lambda(\log N + \log T))$ and group public key size $\tilde{O}(\lambda^2(\log N + \log T))$. Our scheme is constant in the number of group members and logarithmic in the number of time periods i.e. $\tilde{O}(\lambda \log T)$ and group public key size $\tilde{O}(\lambda^2 \log T)$. Their scheme satisfies full-anonymity and forward-secure traceability under SIS and LWE hardness.

Open Problems. One open problem would be to achieve a group signature scheme with the same properties without relying on complexity leveraging (that we need to employ in the underlying ABS). Another open problem would be to upgrade the anonymity property from selfless anonymity to full anonymity.

2 Preliminaries

2.1 Lattices and Trapdoors

In this paper we use several values defined as follows: λ is the security parameter and n, m and $q \geq 2$ are integers such that $n = \text{poly}(\lambda)$ and $m \geq n\lceil \log q \rceil$. The discrete Gaussian distribution $\mathcal{D}_{\mathbb{Z}^m,\tau}$ over $\mathbb{Z}^m$ with parameter τ is the distribution where the probability of all $\mathbf{x}$ is proportional to $e^{-\pi\|\mathbf{x}\|/\tau^2}$. The norm of a matrix $\mathbf{A} = [\mathbf{a}_1, \ldots, \mathbf{a}_m] \in \mathbb{Z}_q^{n\times m}$, is denoted $\|\mathbf{A}\| = \max_j \|\mathbf{a}_j\|, j \in [m]$, and it is the maximum of the Euclidean norm of its vectors.

Lattices. For a matrix $\mathbf{A} \in \mathbb{Z}_q^{n\times m}$ and $\mathbf{u} \in \mathbb{Z}_q^n$ that admits a solution to the equation $\mathbf{A}\cdot\mathbf{x} = \mathbf{u} \bmod q$, define the m-dimensional lattice: $\Lambda^\perp(\mathbf{A}) = \{\mathbf{x} \in \mathbb{Z}^m : \mathbf{A}\cdot\mathbf{x} = \mathbf{0} \bmod q\} \subseteq \mathbb{Z}^m$, and the coset $\Lambda_{\mathbf{u}}^\perp(\mathbf{A}) = \{\mathbf{x} \in \mathbb{Z}^m : \mathbf{A}\cdot\mathbf{x} = \mathbf{u} \bmod q\}$.

We briefly remind the SIS assumption and its hardness.

Definition 1 ($\mathrm{SIS}_{n,q,B,m}$). *Given a uniformly chosen matrix $\mathbf{A} \in \mathbb{Z}_q^{n\times m}$, find nonzero integer vector $\mathbf{s} \in \mathbb{Z}^m$ such that $\|\mathbf{s}\|_\infty \leq B$ and $\mathbf{A}\cdot\mathbf{s} = \mathbf{0} \mod q$. $\mathrm{SIS}_{n,q,B,m}$ is hard if for any adversary $\mathcal{A}$, the probability to solve* SIS *is negligible, i.e. it is bounded by negl(λ).* $\mathrm{SIS}_{n,q,B,m}$ *is sub-exponentially hard if the probability to solve* SIS *is bounded by $2^{-O(n^\epsilon)}\cdot negl(\lambda)$ for some constant $0 < \epsilon < 1$.*

Trapdoors. For all $\mathbf{v} \in \mathbb{Z}_q^n$, $\mathbf{A}_{\gamma_0}^{-1}(\mathbf{v})$ is the random variable with discrete gaussian distribution $D_{\mathbb{Z}^m,\gamma_0}$ conditioned on $\mathbf{A}\cdot\mathbf{A}_{\gamma_0}^{-1}(\mathbf{v}) = \mathbf{v} \bmod q$. A γ_0-trapdoor for $\mathbf{A}$ allows a procedure that can sample from $\mathbf{A}_{\gamma_0}^{-1}(\mathbf{v})$ in time poly$(n, m, \log q)$ for any $\mathbf{v} \in \mathbb{Z}_q^n$. By overloading notation we denote a γ_0-trapdoor for $\mathbf{A}$ by $\mathbf{A}_{\gamma_0}^{-1}$.

We define the gadget matrix $\mathbf{G}$ based on the vector $\mathbf{g} \in \mathbb{Z}_q^k$ whose entries are the power of two $\mathbf{g}^t := [1 \quad 2 \quad 4 \quad \cdots \quad 2^{k-1}]$ and $k = \lceil \log q \rceil$. The matrix $\mathbf{G}$ is the diagonal concatenation of $\mathbf{g}$ n times, i.e. $\mathbf{G} = \mathbf{g} \otimes \mathbf{I}_n \in \mathbb{Z}_q^{n\times nk}$.

Lemma 1 (Trapdoor generation [Ajt96, MP12]**).** *There exists an efficient procedure, that we call* TrapGen$(1^n, 1^m, q)$*, with an efficiently computable value $m_0 = O(n \log q)$ such that for all $m \geqslant m_0$ outputs a pair $(\mathbf{A}, \mathbf{A}_{\gamma_0}^{-1})$, where $\mathbf{A} \in \mathbb{Z}_q^{n\times m}$ is at negligible distance from uniform and $\mathbf{A}_{\gamma_0}^{-1}$ is a γ_0-trapdoor for $\mathbf{A}$ with $\gamma_0 = O(\sqrt{n \log q \log n})$.*

Lemma 2 (Leftover Hash Lemma [HILL99]**).** *Let $m, n, q \geqslant 1$ be integers such that $m \geqslant 4n \log q$ and q prime. Let $\mathbf{A} \xleftarrow{\$} \mathbb{Z}_q^{m\times n}$, $\mathbf{r} \xleftarrow{\$} \{0,1\}^m$, then $(\mathbf{A}, \mathbf{Ar})$ is at negligible statistical distance from uniform distribution on $\mathbb{Z}_q^{m\times n} \times \mathbb{Z}_q^n$.*

2.2 Delegation Functions

During different time periods, a signer will need to delegate some lattice trapdoor from a previous period to a next one. We make use of the following lemmas.

Lemma 3 (Trapdoor extension [ABB10, MP12]**).** *Let $\in \mathbb{Z}_q^{n\times m}$ be a matrix with trapdoor $\mathbf{M}_\gamma^{-1}$ and $\mathbf{N} \in \mathbb{Z}_q^{n\times p}$ a matrix such that $\mathbf{M} = \mathbf{NS}$ mod q where $\mathbf{S} \in \mathbb{Z}_q^{p\times m}$ with $s_1(\mathbf{S})$ its largest singular value. Then we can use $(\mathbf{M}_\gamma^{-1}, \mathbf{S})$ to sample from $\mathbf{N}_{\gamma'}^{-1}$ for any $\gamma' \geq \gamma \cdot s_1(\mathbf{S})$.*

Lemma 4 ([CHKP10, Lemma 3.2])**.** *There is a deterministic polynomial-time algorithm* ExtBasis *with the following properties: given an arbitrary $\mathbf{A} \in \mathbb{Z}_q^{n\times m}$ whose columns generate the entire group $\mathbb{Z}_q^n$, an arbitrary basis $\mathbf{S} \in \mathbb{Z}^{m\times m}$ of $\Lambda^\perp(\mathbf{A})$, and an arbitrary $\bar{\mathbf{A}} \in \mathbb{Z}_q^{n\times \bar{m}}$,* ExtBasis$(\mathbf{S}, \mathbf{A}' = \mathbf{A}\|\bar{\mathbf{A}})$ *outputs a basis $\mathbf{S}'$ of $\Lambda^\perp(\mathbf{A}') \subseteq \mathbb{Z}^{m+\bar{m}}$ such that $\|\tilde{\mathbf{S}}'\| = \|\tilde{\mathbf{S}}\|$. Moreover the same holds even for any permutation of the columns of $\mathbf{A}'$.*

There exists a function RandBasis developed by [CHKP10], which verifies the following lemma:

Lemma 5 **([CHKP10, Lemma 3.3]).** *Let* $\mathbf{S}$ *be a basis of a* m*-dimensional integer lattice* Λ *and a parameter* $s \geq \|\tilde{\mathbf{S}}\| \cdot \omega(\sqrt{\log n})$*. The algorithm* RandBasis$(\mathbf{S}, s)$ *outputs a new basis* $\mathbf{S}'$ *of* Λ *such that, with overwhelming probability,* $\mathbf{S}'$ *verifies* $\|\mathbf{S}'\| \leqslant s \cdot \sqrt{m}$*. Moreover, for any two basis* $\mathbf{S}_0, \mathbf{S}_1$ *of the same lattice and any* $s \geqslant \max\{\|\tilde{\mathbf{S}}_0\|, \|\tilde{\mathbf{S}}_1\|\} \cdot \omega(\sqrt{\log n})$*, the outputs of* RandBasis$(\mathbf{S}_0, s)$ *and* RandBasis$(\mathbf{S}_1, s)$ *are within* negl(n) *statistical distance.*

We further need an important property of lattice trapdoors [ABB10, MP12]:

Lemma 6. *For* $\mathbf{A} \in \mathbb{Z}_q^{n\times p}$ *and* $\mathbf{R} \in \mathbb{Z}_q^{p\times m}$ *with* $m = n\lceil \log q \rceil$*, one can compute* $[\mathbf{A}\|\mathbf{AR} + \mathbf{G}]_\gamma^{-1}$ *for* $\gamma = O(\sqrt{mp}\,\|\mathbf{R}\|_\infty)$*.*

2.3 Evaluation Functions

In order to generate or check the validity of a signature, we need to execute some evaluation of a function with a set of lattices as input. The output of this evaluation is 1 if the function evaluated on an attribute x is not valid and 0 if the evaluation is correct. We use the notations and definition of the evaluation functions developed by Tsabary [Tsa17]. Moreover we denote $[x_1\mathbf{G}|\cdots|x_\ell\mathbf{G}]$ by $\mathbf{x} \otimes \mathbf{G}$ with $\mathbf{x} = (x_1, \cdots, x_\ell) \in \{0,1\}^\ell$.

Theorem 1 **([Tsa17, Theorem 2.7]).** *There exist efficient deterministic algorithms* EvalF *and* EvalFX *such that for all* $n, q, \ell \in \mathbb{N}$*,* $m = n\lceil \log q \rceil$*, and for any sequence of matrices* $\overrightarrow{\mathbf{A}} = (\mathbf{A}_1, \cdots, \mathbf{A}_l) \in (\mathbb{Z}_q^{n\times m})^\ell$*, for any depth* d *boolean circuit* $f : \{0,1\}^\ell \to \{0,1\}$ *and for every* $\mathbf{x} = (x_1, \cdots, x_\ell) \in \{0,1\}^\ell$*, the outputs* $\mathbf{H}_f = \mathsf{EvalF}(f, \overrightarrow{\mathbf{A}})$*, and* $\mathbf{H}_{f,\mathbf{x}} = \mathsf{EvalFX}(f, \mathbf{x}, \overrightarrow{\mathbf{A}})$ *are in* $\mathbb{Z}^{(\ell m)\times m}$ *and it holds that* $\|\mathbf{H}_f\|_\infty, \|\mathbf{H}_{f,\mathbf{x}}\|_\infty \leqslant (2m)^d$ *and* $(\overrightarrow{\mathbf{A}} - \mathbf{x} \otimes \mathbf{G}) \cdot \mathbf{H}_{f,\mathbf{x}} = \overrightarrow{\mathbf{A}} \cdot \mathbf{H}_f - f(\mathbf{x})\mathbf{G} \mod q$*.*

2.4 Building Blocks for Our Construction

As in [KY19], we employ **secret key encryption** (SKE) and **one-time signature** (OTS), both from lattices, in order to build our group signature scheme. We use the SKE scheme based on LWE from [KY19], which is a secret key variant of [Reg05] and the OTS scheme from [Moh10]

Admissible hash functions represent a family of hash functions introduced in [BB04], which allows to separate the input space into two sets, the challenge set and the controlled set. In practice, in a simulation-based game, a simulator owning a dummy key can answer to queries in the controlled set but not in the challenge set, and the adversary is expected to make his forgery in the challenge set, allowing the simulator to solve a hard problem.

We fit in the definition of admissible hash functions given in [KY19].

3 Forward-Secure Indexed Attribute-Based Signature Scheme from Lattices

As already explained in the introduction, we replace the ABS scheme in the general construction of [KY19] with a forward-secure indexed ABS. We start by giving the definition and the security requirements of a forward-secure indexed attribute based signature. We note that the ABS scheme supports multiple users since it is designed as a building block for group signature scheme.

The starting point of our scheme is the constrained signature of [Tsa17]. We first adapt it into an indexed attribute-based signature, by including an index i into the attribute x, following the idea of [KY19]. Moreover we extend this construction to a forward-secure attribute-based signature scheme, by applying a transformation similar to [LNWX19]. The idea of this transformation is that we consider a pair of matrices $\mathbf{T}_j^b, b \in \{0,1\}$ for every bit j of the time period t considered. Then by concatenating these matrices $\mathbf{T}_j^b$ to the public key of [Tsa17], we can include a time period t into the verification key and the signatures. The technical difficulty that arises when using this transformation into the Tsabary's construction is simulating the secret keys for each period of time and for each user, without possessing the master secret key. This can be done by using "dummy" secret keys which vanish when the signature is made for an identity and a time period chosen selectively by the adversary at the beginning of the game, allowing the simulator to solve a hard problem (which is the SIS problem). We then get a new forward-secure attribute-based signature scheme which is independent of the number of users N, and only logarithmic on the total number of periods T.

3.1 Framework and Security Properties

We denote $\{\mathcal{C}_\lambda\}_{\lambda \in \mathbb{N}}$ the set of circuits with domain $\{0,1\}^{k(\lambda)}$ and range $\{0,1\}$. We bound the size of every circuit in $\{\mathcal{C}_\lambda\}$ by $k_c = \text{poly}(\lambda)$. We also denote the space of messages as $\{\mathcal{M}_\lambda\}_{\lambda \in \mathbb{N}}$, for which we bound the size elements by $k_m = \text{poly}(\lambda)$. Usually we simplify notation and just denote these spaces $\mathcal{C}$ and $\mathcal{M}$. We then define the forward-secure indexed attribute-based signature scheme for the circuit class $\mathcal{C}$:

Definition 2. *A forward-secure indexed attribute-based signature (FSI-ABS) scheme consists of the following algorithms:*

$\mathsf{ABS.Setup}(1^\lambda, 1^N, 1^T)$ *The setup algorithm takes as input λ the security parameter, N the size of the index space and T the number of time periods, given in unary form, and it outputs a master public key* mpk *and a master secret key* msk.

$\mathsf{ABS.KeyGen}(\mathsf{msk}, i, x_i)$ *The key generation algorithm takes as input the master secret key* msk, *an index $i \in [N]$ and the attribute $x_i \in \{0,1\}^k$. It outputs $\mathsf{sk}_{x_i,0}$, the initial secret key associated to x_i.*

$\mathsf{ABS.KeyUpdate}(\mathsf{mpk}, i, \mathsf{sk}_{x_i,t}, t+1)$ *The key update algorithm takes as input the master secret key* msk, *an index of an user i as well as its secret key for the time t, $\mathsf{sk}_{x_i,t}$. It updates this key $\mathsf{sk}_{x_i,t}$ for the next time period $t+1$ and outputs $\mathsf{sk}_{x_i,t+1}$.*

$\mathsf{ABS.Sign}(\mathsf{mpk}, \mathsf{sk}_{x_i,t}, C, M, t)$ *The signing algorithm takes as input the master public key* mpk, *a secret key $\mathsf{sk}_{x_i,t}$ for the current period of time t, a circuit*

$C \in \mathcal{C}_\lambda$, a message $M \in \mathcal{M}_\lambda$ and a time period t and it outputs an attribute-based signature σ if $C(x_i) = 0$.

$\mathsf{ABS.Verify}(\mathsf{mpk}, C, M, \sigma, t)$ *The verification algorithm takes as input the master public key* mpk, *the circuit C, the message M, the attribute-based signature σ and the time period t. This algorithm outputs* Valid *if the signature σ is valid for the time period t and* Invalid *otherwise.*

For a FSI-ABS scheme, we require *correctness* and two security properties: *perfect-privacy* and *forward-secure policy-selective unforgeability.* Perfect privacy captures the idea that the attribute used to sign a message must remain anonymous. The unforgeability property says that even if users collude they can not forge a signature on a message associated with a policy if none of the attributes satisfies the policy. We note that we can not achieve selective unforgeability directly, but we start from no-signing-query and apply a transformation using admissible hash functions to obtain selective unforgeability. We explain this in more detail at the end of this section.

3.2 Construction of FSI-ABS Scheme from Lattices

We adapt the constrained signature developed by Tsabary [Tsa17] to a forward-secure attribute-based signature scheme. As explained by Katsumata and Yamada [KY19], the signature scheme of Tsabary is not an attribute-based signature but a constrained signature. It means that in the constrained signature, a user does not sign a circuit but an attribute. Then the role of the attribute and the circuit are exchanged compared to an actual attribute-based signature scheme. However, as explained in [KY19], we can turn a constrained signature into an attribute-based signature: we consider a constraint space composed of all d-depth bounded circuit $\mathcal{F}_d = \{f : \{0,1\}^\ell \to \{0,1\}\}$, with $\ell = \text{poly}(\lambda)$, then a constraint f can be seen as a universal circuit $U(\cdot,\cdot,x)$ (that we denote $U_x(\cdot,\cdot)$), which takes as input the circuit-message pair (C, M) (seen as a string of size ℓ).

Our contribution is to build a forward-secure attribute-based signature scheme meaning that the lifetime of the scheme is divided into $T = 2^d$ discrete periods. To represent the time periods we use a binary tree (Fig. 1), then each time period t is associated with a leaf $\mathsf{Bin}(t)$. Following [BSSW06], for $j \in [d+1]$, we define a time period's "second sibling at depth j". Intuitively, it corresponds to the right neighbour at depth j of each node on the path from the root to the leaf $\mathsf{Bin}(t)$.

$$\mathsf{Sibling}(j,t) = \begin{cases} (1) & \text{if } j = 1 \text{ and } \mathsf{Bin}(t)[j] = 0 \\ (\mathsf{Bin}(t)[1], ..., \mathsf{Bin}(t)[j-1], 1) & \text{if } 1 < j \leq d \text{ and } \mathsf{Bin}(t)[j] = 0 \\ \perp & \text{if } 1 \leqslant j \leq d \text{ and } \mathsf{Bin}(t)[j] = 1 \\ \mathsf{Bin}(t) & \text{if } j = d+1 \end{cases} .$$

We also define node set $\text{Nodes}_{(t \to T-1)}$ to be $\{\mathsf{Sibling}(1,t), ..., \mathsf{Sibling}(d+1,t)\}$. The goal of this set is to uniquely define the path to each leaf of the tree.

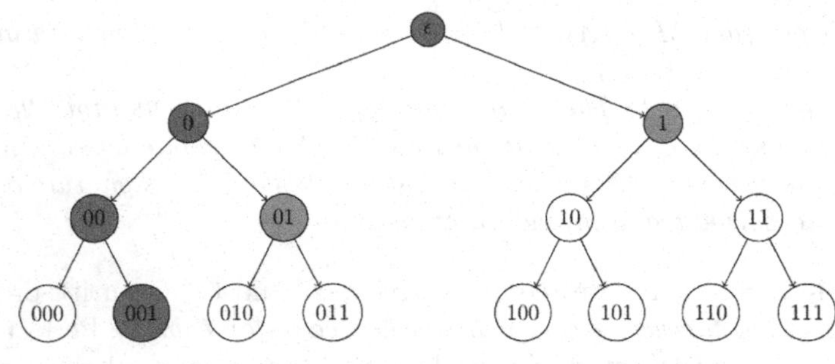

Fig. 1. A binary tree with time periods T = 2^3. In order to fill the set $\text{Nodes}_{(t \to T-1)}$ we begin with the leaf Bin(t) that we add in the set $\text{Nodes}_{(t \to T-1)}$, together with its sibling (which is its right neighbour), if it exists. Then recursively, we go up in the tree to the parent of the node considered (coloured in red), and we add its sibling (coloured in orange) to the set $\text{Nodes}_{(t \to T-1)}$ (still if it exists). We keep going this way, until we reach the root of the binary tree. We stop then and output the corresponding list $\text{Nodes}_{(t \to T-1)}$. On the path from node ϵ to the leaf node (001) we then have $\text{Nodes}_{(1 \to 7)} = \{(1), (01), \perp, (001)\}$. (Color figure online)

We consider also a function called bitstr which takes as input a message-circuit pair (C, M) and which outputs its input seen as a string of bits. Then $\mathsf{bitstr} : \{0,1\}^{k_c} \times \{0,1\}^{k_m} \mapsto \{0,1\}^{\ell}$, such that

$$\mathsf{bitstr}(C, M) = \{C_1, \cdots, C_{k_c}, M_1, \cdots, M_{k_m}\}.$$

Selection of Parameters. Given the security parameter λ, the parameters m_0, p, γ_0 and τ_s are chosen according to TrapGen algorithm, $T = 2^d$ is chosen as a power of 2, for $d \in \mathbb{N}$, and is the number of time periods considered, and ℓ is the size of input of the circuit. We choose parameters τ_u and B by referring to Theorem 1. Finally s_j is dictated also by Lemma 3. Then we set:

- $m = 4n\lceil \log q \rceil$, $m_0 = O(n \log q) \geqslant 4n \log q$,
- $p = \max\{m_0, (n+1)\lceil \log q \rceil + 2\lambda\}$,
- $\gamma_0 = O(\sqrt{n \lceil \log q \rceil \log n})$,
- $\tau_s = \max\{\sqrt{p} \cdot \ell \cdot 2^d m^{1.5+d}, \gamma_0\}$,
- $\tau_u = \tau_s \cdot \sqrt{\ell} \cdot 2^d m^{0.5+d}$,
- $B = \tau_u \sqrt{(1+d) \cdot p + \ell \cdot m}$,
- $s_j = \mathcal{O}(\sqrt{nd \log q})^{j+1} \cdot \omega(\sqrt{\log n})^{j+1}$ for $j \in [d]$.

ABS.Setup($1^\lambda, 1^N, 1^T$) On input the security parameter 1^λ, 1^N where N is the number of indexes $i \in [N]$ and 1^T where T is the number of time periods $T = 2^d$ for some $d \in \mathbb{N}$, it sets the parameters n, m, p, q, γ_0 to be polynomial in λ. Then, it generates:

- uniform matrix $\overrightarrow{\mathbf{A}} = [\mathbf{A}_1 \| ... \| \mathbf{A}_\ell] \xleftarrow{\$} \mathbb{Z}_q^{n \times \ell m}$,
- $(\mathbf{A}, \mathbf{A}_{\gamma_0}^{-1}) \leftarrow \mathsf{TrapGen}(1^n, 1^p, q)$, with $\mathbf{A} \in \mathbb{Z}_q^{n \times p}$ and $\mathbf{A}_{\gamma_0}^{-1}$ its trapdoor,

- $2d$ matrices $\mathbf{T}_j^b \xleftarrow{\$} \mathbb{Z}_q^{n\times p}$ for all $j \in [d]$ and $b \in \{0,1\}$.

The algorithm outputs: $\mathsf{mpk} = (\mathbf{A}, \overrightarrow{\mathbf{A}}, \{\mathbf{T}_j^b\}_{j\in[d],b\in\{0,1\}})$ and $\mathsf{msk} = (\mathbf{A}_{\gamma_0}^{-1})$.

ABS.KeyGen(msk, i, x_i) On input the master secret key msk, the index $i \in [N]$ and the attribute $x_i \in \{0,1\}^k$, it computes U_{x_i}, $\mathbf{H}_{U_{x_i}} = \mathsf{EvalF}(U_{x_i}, \overrightarrow{\mathbf{A}}) \in \mathbb{Z}_q^{\ell m\times m}$ as defined in Theorem 1 and $\mathbf{A}_{x_i} = \overrightarrow{\mathbf{A}} \cdot \mathbf{H}_{U_{x_i}} \in \mathbb{Z}_q^{n\times m}$. Then, it uses $\mathbf{A}_{\gamma_0}^{-1}$ to compute $\mathbf{R}_{x_i} = [\mathbf{A}\|\mathbf{A}_{x_i}]^{-1}$. Then it determines the set $\text{Nodes}_{(0\to T-1)}$ and for $z \in \text{Nodes}_{(0\to T-1)}$:
  - if $z = \perp$, set $\mathsf{sk}_{x_i}[z] = \perp$,
  - else it denotes d_z as the bit-length of z, with $d_z \leqslant d$, and computes the matrix: $\mathbf{A}_{x_i,z} = [\mathbf{A}\|\mathbf{A}_{x_i}\|\mathbf{T}_1^{\mathsf{Bin}(z)[1]}\|\cdots\|\mathbf{T}_{d_z}^{\mathsf{Bin}(z)[d_z]}] \in \mathbb{Z}_q^{n\times((d_z+1)p+m)}$, then it computes: $\mathbf{R}_{x_i,z} \leftarrow \text{RandBasis}(\text{ExtBasis}(\mathbf{R}_{x_i}, \mathbf{A}_{x_i,z}), s_{d_z})$, and set $\mathsf{sk}_{x_i}[z] = \mathbf{R}_{x_i,z}$,

  Finally we get: $\mathsf{sk}_{x_i,0} = \{\mathsf{sk}_{x_i}[z], z \in \text{Nodes}_{(0\to T-1)}\}$.

ABS.KeyUpdate($\mathsf{mpk}, i, \mathsf{sk}_{x_i,t}, t+1$) First parse the set $\mathsf{sk}_{x_i,t} = \{\mathsf{sk}_{x_i}[z], z \in \text{Nodes}_{(t\to T-1)}\}$ and determine the set $\text{Nodes}_{(t+1\to T-1)}$.
  For $z' \in \text{Nodes}_{(t+1\to T-1)}$:
  - if $z' = \perp$, set $\mathsf{sk}_{x_i}[z'] = \perp$.
  - Otherwise, there exists exactly one $z \in \text{Nodes}_{(t\to T-1)}$ which is a prefix of z' i.e. $z' = z\|y$. There are two possibilities here:
    1. if $z' = z$ then $\mathsf{sk}_{x_i}[z'] = \mathsf{sk}_{x_i}[z]$,
    2. if $z' = z\|y$ for some non-empty y, then z is an ancestor of z', and from $\mathsf{sk}_{x_i}[z] = \mathbf{R}_{x_i,z}$ it can delegate a basis
       $\mathbf{R}_{x_i,z'} \leftarrow \text{RandBasis}(\text{ExtBasis}(\mathbf{R}_{x_i,z}, \mathbf{A}_{x_i,z'}), s_{d_{z'}})$, and set
       $\mathsf{sk}_{x_i}[z'] = \mathbf{R}_{x_i,z'}$.

  Finally output $\mathsf{sk}_{x_i,t+1} = \{\mathsf{sk}_{x_i}[z'], z' \in \text{Nodes}_{(t+1\to T-1)}\}$.

ABS.Sign($\mathsf{mpk}, \mathsf{sk}_{x_i,t}, C, M, t$) First compute $\mathbf{x} = \mathsf{bitstr}(C, M)$. If $U_{x_i}(\mathbf{x}) = C(x_i) \neq 0$ output $\perp$. Otherwise, first compute $\mathbf{H}_{U_{x_i},\mathbf{x}} = \mathsf{EvalFX}(U_{x_i}, \mathbf{x}, \overrightarrow{\mathbf{A}}) \in \mathbb{Z}_q^{\ell m\times m}$, as defined in Theorem 1, such that $(\overrightarrow{\mathbf{A}} - \mathbf{x}\otimes\mathbf{G}) \cdot \mathbf{H}_{U_{x_i},\mathbf{x}} = \overrightarrow{\mathbf{A}} \cdot \mathbf{H}_{U_{x_i}} - U_{x_i}(\mathbf{x})\mathbf{G} = \mathbf{A}_{x_i}$ as $U_{x_i}(\mathbf{x}) = 0$.
  Compute $\overrightarrow{\mathbf{B}_t} = [\mathbf{A}\|\overrightarrow{\mathbf{A}} - \mathbf{x}\otimes\mathbf{G}\|\mathbf{T}_1^{\mathsf{Bin}(t)[1]}\|\cdots\|\mathbf{T}_d^{\mathsf{Bin}(t)[d]}] \in \mathbb{Z}_q^{n\times((d+1)p+\ell m)}$, and

$$\mathbf{S}_i = \begin{bmatrix} \mathbf{I}_p & & & & \\ & \mathbf{H}_{U_{x_i},\mathbf{x}} & & & \\ & & \mathbf{I}_p & & \\ & & & \cdots & \\ & & & & \mathbf{I}_p \end{bmatrix} \in \mathbb{Z}_q^{((d+1)p+\ell m)\times((d+1)p+m)}.$$

  We then have $\overrightarrow{\mathbf{B}_t} \cdot \mathbf{S}_i = [\mathbf{A}\|\mathbf{A}_{x_i}\|\mathbf{T}_1^{\mathsf{Bin}(t)[1]}\|\cdots\|\mathbf{T}_d^{\mathsf{Bin}(t)[d]}] = \mathbf{A}_{x_i,t}$. Since $\mathsf{sk}_{x_i,t}$ contains a trapdoor for $\mathbf{A}_{x_i,t}$, we can apply the trapdoor extension from Lemma 3 to obtain $\mathbf{B}_{\tau_u}^{-1} = [\overrightarrow{\mathbf{B}_t}]^{-1} = [\mathbf{A}\|\overrightarrow{\mathbf{A}} - \mathbf{x}\otimes\mathbf{G}\|\mathbf{T}_1^{\mathsf{Bin}(t)[1]}\|\cdots\|\mathbf{T}_d^{\mathsf{Bin}(t)[d]}]_{\tau_u}^{-1}$, where $\mathbf{A} = \mathbf{A}_{x_i,t}$, $\mathbf{B} = \overrightarrow{\mathbf{B}_t}$ and $\mathbf{S} = \mathbf{S}_i$ using $\mathsf{sk}_{x_i,t} = [\mathbf{A}_{x_i,t}]_{\tau_s}^{-1}$.

  Then the signer has a trapdoor for $\overrightarrow{\mathbf{B}_t}$ and he can compute $\sigma_{\mathbf{x},t} \xleftarrow{\$} \overrightarrow{\mathbf{B}_t}^{-1}(\mathbf{0})$.

ABS.Verify($\mathsf{mpk}, C, M, \sigma_{\mathbf{x},t}, t$). First, compute $\mathbf{x} = \mathsf{bitstr}(C, M)$ and then check that:

- $[\mathbf{A}\|\overrightarrow{\mathbf{A}} - \mathbf{x} \otimes \mathbf{G}\|\mathbf{T}_1^{\mathsf{Bin}(t)[1]}\| \cdots \|\mathbf{T}_d^{\mathsf{Bin}(t)[d]}] \cdot \sigma_{\mathbf{x},t} = \mathbf{0}$,
- $\|\sigma_{\mathbf{x},t}\|_\infty \leqslant B$.

If the verification passes, then output Valid, if not, output Invalid.

3.3 Security Proofs

Lemma 7. *Our ABS scheme is perfectly private.*[1]

Lemma 8. *Our ABS satisfies forward-secure no-signing-query unforgeability assuming* $\mathsf{SIS}_{n,q,B',m'}$ *is hard, with* $B' = (\ell(m+d)+1)B$ *and* $m' = (d+1)p+\ell \cdot m$.

What we prove in this theorem is a weak property of unforgeability, where an attacker is prohibited to make signing queries. Indeed, we do not include the message to be signed in the different steps of the signature process and note that if the attacker would be able to perform some signature query on a circuit message pair (C, M) and get σ, he could just output the valid signature σ but on a pair (C, M') with $M' \neq M$ and win the unforgeability game.

However, in the context in which we intend to use the attribute-based signature, namely the group signature, this property of unforgeability is not enough. We note that they face the same problem in [KY19] and introduce a reduction from a (co-)selective unforgeable ABS to a no-signing-query ABS, using as a tool the admissible hash function. Adapting in the same way as their construction, we get a stronger unforgeability property, namely selective unforgeability.

With the above lemma and the no-signing to selective transformation of [KY19], we prove that the attribute-based signature derived from the constrained signature of Tsabary [Tsa17] is forward-secure policy-selective unforgeable where the adversary chooses its target circuit-message pair (C^*, M^*) for the forgery at the beginning of the game. But still this security notion is not enough for our group signature scheme, we need adaptive security and we can only achieve it by utilizing complexity leveraging as suggested in [KY19]. We have to randomly guess (C^*, M^*) in the reduction from selective to adaptive security. Let us evaluate the reduction loss (as done in [KY19]): the length of the message M^* is bounded by poly(λ) and a circuit C^* can be described by ovk and ct which can be seen as binary strings with length poly$(\lambda, \log N)$ inducing a reduction loss of $2^{-\mathrm{poly}(\lambda, \log N)}$. To account for the loss in advantage we need to enlarge the dimension n of the scheme to be poly$(\lambda, \log N)^{1/\epsilon}$ where ϵ is some constant in $(0, 1)$ requiring subexponential hardness of the SIS problem. As mentioned in the introduction, co-selective unforgeability (where the adversary has to make all the key queries at the beginning of the game but he can choose the target policy adaptively) would be enough for our scheme but we can not achieve it directly since in the unforgeability game we need to target policy associated to the forgery to be chosen at the beginning of the game so that we can build the public matrix for which we solve the SIS problem.

Lemma 9. *Our ABS satisfies FS adaptive unforgeability under the subexponential hardness of SIS.*

[1] All the proofs can be found on the full version.

4 Forward-Secure Group Signature Scheme

In this section we present the construction of our forward-secure group signature (FS-GS) scheme from lattices.

We use the model of forward-secure group signature scheme formalized in [NHF09] and [LNWX19] and we give the definition below.

Definition 3. *A forward-secure group signature scheme consists of the following algorithms:*

$\mathsf{GS.KeyGen}(1^\lambda, 1^N, 1^T)$ *is a randomized algorithm taking as input a security parameter λ, number of users N and number of time periods T. Its output consists of a group public key* gpk*, an opening key* gok *and a set of initial user secret keys* $\{\mathsf{gsk}_{i,0}\}_{i\in[N]}$.

$\mathsf{GS.KeyUpdate}(\mathsf{gpk}, \mathsf{gsk}_{i,t}, i, t+1)$ *is a randomized algorithm that takes as input the group public key* gpk*, the secret key* $\mathsf{gsk}_{i,t}$ *of user i at time t, a user i and a time period $t+1$ and outputs* $\mathsf{gsk}_{i,t+1}$*, the secret signing key of user i at time $t+1$.*

$\mathsf{GS.Sign}(\mathsf{gpk}, \mathsf{gsk}_{i,t}, i, M, t)$ *takes as input the group public key* gpk*, the ith user secret key* $\mathsf{gsk}_{i,t}$ *at time t, the index i of the user, a message $M \in \{0,1\}^*$ and the current time interval t and outputs a group signature Σ.*

$\mathsf{GS.Verify}(\mathsf{gpk}, M, \Sigma, t)$ *takes as input the group public key* gpk*, a message M, a signature Σ and the time period t. It outputs either* Valid *or* Invalid. Valid *indicates that Σ is a valid signature on M at time period t w.r.t* gpk.

$\mathsf{GS.Open}(\mathsf{gpk}, \mathsf{gok}, M, \Sigma, t)$ *takes as input the group public key* gpk*, the opening key* gok*, a message M, a signature Σ and time interval t and outputs an identity or* Invalid *if it fails to identify the signer.*

We require two security properties: forward-secure traceability and CCA-selfless anonymity.

4.1 Forward-Secure Group Signature from Lattices

We now describe our lattice-based FS-GS scheme which employs the FSI-ABS scheme given in the previous section and which satisfies CCA-selfless anonymity and traceability. As the ABS used is forward-secure, we show that the group signature is also forward-secure, so we consider that the lifetime of the scheme is divided into T time periods. When entering a new period of time, a new secret key is computed from the current one and afterwards the current key is deleted promptly.

GS.KeyGen$(1^\lambda, 1^N, 1^T)$ On input security parameter λ, the number of group members N and the total number of time periods $T = 2^d$, the algorithms works as follows: First sample $\mathsf{pp} \leftarrow \mathsf{SKE.Setup}(1^\lambda)$ and $(\mathsf{mpk}, \mathsf{msk}) \leftarrow \mathsf{ABS.Setup}(1^\lambda, 1^N, 1^T)$, then, for $i \in [N]$, sample $K_i \leftarrow \mathsf{SKE.Gen}(\mathsf{pp})$ and compute $sk_{x_i,0}$ as $sk_{i||K_i,0} \leftarrow \mathsf{ABS.KeyGen}(\mathsf{msk}, i, i||K_i)_{i\in[N]}$.
Output $\mathsf{gpk} = (\mathsf{pp}, \mathsf{mpk}), \mathsf{gok} = \{K_i\}_{i\in[N]}, \mathsf{gsk}_{i,0} = (i, K_i, \mathsf{sk}_{i||K_i,0})$.

GS.KeyUpdate($\mathsf{gpk}, \mathsf{gsk}_{i,t}, i, t+1$) It calls the key update algorithm of the ABS and returns $\mathsf{gsk}_{i,t+1} = (i, K_i, \mathsf{ABS.KeyUpdate}(\mathsf{mpk}, i, \mathsf{sk}_{t,i}, t+1))$.

GS.Sign($\mathsf{gpk}, \mathsf{gsk}_{i,t}, i, M, t$) In order to sign a message, the user samples $(\mathsf{ovk}, \mathsf{osk}) \leftarrow \mathsf{OTS.KeyGen}(1^\lambda)$ and computes the encryption of his identity under the key K_i as $\mathsf{ct} \leftarrow \mathsf{SKE.Enc}(K_i, i||\mathsf{ovk})$. Then, he computes

$$\sigma \leftarrow \mathsf{ABS.Sign}(\mathsf{mpk}, \mathsf{sk}_{i||K_i}, C[\mathsf{ovk}, \mathsf{ct}], M, t),$$

where the circuit $C[\mathsf{ovk}, \mathsf{ct}]$ is defined as follows:

$$C[\mathsf{ovk}, \mathsf{ct}](i||K_i)$$

Hardwired constants: a verification key ovk of OTS and ciphertext ct of SKE

- Retrieve $i \in [N]$ and K_i from the input. If this is impossible, return 1.
- Compute $\mathsf{SKE.Dec}(K_i, \mathsf{ct}) = i'||\mathsf{ovk}'$. If $i' = i$ and $\mathsf{ovk}' = \mathsf{ovk}$ output 0. Otherwise, output 1.

Finally run $\tau \leftarrow \mathsf{OTS.Sign}(\mathsf{osk}, M||\sigma)$.
The signature consists of $\Sigma = (\mathsf{ct}, \mathsf{ovk}, \sigma, \tau)$.

GS.Verify($\mathsf{gpk}, M, \Sigma, t$). On input gpk, a message M, a group signature Σ on M and a period time t, check that $\mathsf{ABS.Verify}(\mathsf{mpk}, C[\mathsf{ovk}, \mathsf{ct}], M, \sigma, t) = \mathsf{Valid}$ and $\mathsf{OTS.Verify}(\mathsf{ovk}, \tau, M||\sigma) = \mathsf{Valid}$; if one of these verification condition does not hold, return Invalid. Otherwise return Valid.

GS.Open($\mathsf{gpk}, \mathsf{gok}, M, \Sigma, t$). First run **GS.Verify**($\mathsf{gpk}, M, \Sigma, t$) and return Invalid if the verification result does not hold. Otherwise, parse $\Sigma \rightarrow (\mathsf{ct}, \mathsf{ovk}, \sigma, \tau)$. Since the manager does not know the identity of the user who produced the signature, he has to find it by trial and error, i.e. he computes $d_i \leftarrow \mathsf{SKE.Dec}(K_i, \mathsf{ct})$ for $i \in [N]$ and outputs the smallest index i such that $d_i \neq \mathsf{Invalid}$. If there is no such i, return Invalid.

4.2 Security

Correctness. The correctness of the FS-GS scheme follows directly from the correctness of OTS, ABS and SKE.

Theorem 2 (Traceability). *If ABS is forward-secure (adaptively) unforgeable and SKE has key-robustness then the group signature scheme constructed above has the forward-secure traceability property.*

The following theorem addresses the CCA-selfless anonymity of the above GS scheme. We omit the proof and mention that it is a straightforward adaptation of the CCA-selfless anonymity proof from [KY19, Th. 5].

Theorem 3 (CCA-selfless anonymity). *If ABS is perfectly private and adaptive unforgeable, OTS is strongly unforgeable and SKE is IND-CCA secure and key-robust, then GS constructed as above is CCA-selfless anonymous.*

Acknowledgements. This work is supported by the European Union PROMETHEUS project (Horizon 2020 Research and Innovation Program, grant 780701) and by the french Programme "Investissement d'Avenir" under the national project RISQ P141580-2660001/DOS0044216.

References

[ABB10] Agrawal, S., Boneh, D., Boyen, X.: Lattice basis delegation in fixed dimension and shorter-ciphertext hierarchical IBE. In: Rabin, T. (ed.) CRYPTO 2010. LNCS, vol. 6223, pp. 98–115. Springer, Heidelberg (2010). https://doi.org/10.1007/978-3-642-14623-7_6

[ACJT00] Ateniese, G., Camenisch, J., Joye, M., Tsudik, G.: A practical and provably secure coalition-resistant group signature scheme. In: Bellare, M. (ed.) CRYPTO 2000. LNCS, vol. 1880, pp. 255–270. Springer, Heidelberg (2000). https://doi.org/10.1007/3-540-44598-6_16

[Ajt96] Ajtai, M.: Generating hard instances of lattice problems (extended abstract). In: STOC, pp. 99–108. ACM (1996)

[BB04] Boneh, D., Boyen, X.: Secure identity based encryption without random oracles. In: Franklin, M. (ed.) CRYPTO 2004. LNCS, vol. 3152, pp. 443–459. Springer, Heidelberg (2004). https://doi.org/10.1007/978-3-540-28628-8_27

[BBS04] Boneh, D., Boyen, X., Shacham, H.: Short group signatures. In: Franklin, M. (ed.) CRYPTO 2004. LNCS, vol. 3152, pp. 41–55. Springer, Heidelberg (2004). https://doi.org/10.1007/978-3-540-28628-8_3

[BCN18] Boschini, C., Camenisch, J., Neven, G.: Floppy-sized group signatures from lattices. In: Preneel, B., Vercauteren, F. (eds.) ACNS 2018. LNCS, vol. 10892, pp. 163–182. Springer, Cham (2018). https://doi.org/10.1007/978-3-319-93387-0_9

[BM99] Bellare, M., Miner, S.K.: A forward-secure digital signature scheme. In: Wiener, M. (ed.) CRYPTO 1999. LNCS, vol. 1666, pp. 431–448. Springer, Heidelberg (1999). https://doi.org/10.1007/3-540-48405-1_28

[BMW03] Bellare, M., Micciancio, D., Warinschi, B.: Foundations of group signatures: formal definitions, simplified requirements, and a construction based on general assumptions. In: Biham, E. (ed.) EUROCRYPT 2003. LNCS, vol. 2656, pp. 614–629. Springer, Heidelberg (2003). https://doi.org/10.1007/3-540-39200-9_38

[BSSW06] Boyen, X., Shacham, H., Shen, E., Waters, B.: Forward-secure signatures with untrusted update. In: ACM Conference on Computer and Communications Security, pp. 191–200. ACM (2006)

[BSZ05] Bellare, M., Shi, H., Zhang, C.: Foundations of group signatures: the case of dynamic groups. In: Menezes, A. (ed.) CT-RSA 2005. LNCS, vol. 3376, pp. 136–153. Springer, Heidelberg (2005). https://doi.org/10.1007/978-3-540-30574-3_11

[BW06] Boyen, X., Waters, B.: Compact group signatures without random oracles. In: Vaudenay, S. (ed.) EUROCRYPT 2006. LNCS, vol. 4004, pp. 427–444. Springer, Heidelberg (2006). https://doi.org/10.1007/11761679_26

[BY03] Bellare, M., Yee, B.: Forward-security in private-key cryptography. In: Joye, M. (ed.) CT-RSA 2003. LNCS, vol. 2612, pp. 1–18. Springer, Heidelberg (2003). https://doi.org/10.1007/3-540-36563-X_1

[CHK03] Canetti, R., Halevi, S., Katz, J.: A forward-secure public-key encryption scheme. In: Biham, E. (ed.) EUROCRYPT 2003. LNCS, vol. 2656, pp. 255–271. Springer, Heidelberg (2003). https://doi.org/10.1007/3-540-39200-9_16

[CHKP10] Cash, D., Hofheinz, D., Kiltz, E., Peikert, C.: Bonsai trees, or how to delegate a lattice basis. In: Gilbert, H. (ed.) EUROCRYPT 2010. LNCS, vol. 6110, pp. 523–552. Springer, Heidelberg (2010). https://doi.org/10.1007/978-3-642-13190-5_27

[CL04] Camenisch, J., Lysyanskaya, A.: Signature schemes and anonymous credentials from bilinear maps. In: Franklin, M. (ed.) CRYPTO 2004. LNCS, vol. 3152, pp. 56–72. Springer, Heidelberg (2004). https://doi.org/10.1007/978-3-540-28628-8_4

[CNR12] Camenisch, J., Neven, G., Rückert, M.: Fully anonymous attribute tokens from lattices. In: Visconti, I., De Prisco, R. (eds.) SCN 2012. LNCS, vol. 7485, pp. 57–75. Springer, Heidelberg (2012). https://doi.org/10.1007/978-3-642-32928-9_4

[CvH91] Chaum, D., van Heyst, E.: Group signatures. In: Davies, D.W. (ed.) EUROCRYPT 1991. LNCS, vol. 547, pp. 257–265. Springer, Heidelberg (1991). https://doi.org/10.1007/3-540-46416-6_22

[dPLS18] del Pino, R., Lyubashevsky, V., Seiler, G.: Lattice-based group signatures and zero-knowledge proofs of automorphism stability. In: ACM Conference on Computer and Communications Security, pp. 574–591. ACM (2018)

[DvOW92] Diffie, W., van Oorschot, P.C., Wiener, M.J.: Authentication and authenticated key exchanges. Des. Codes Cryptogr. **2**(2), 107–125 (1992)

[GKV10] Gordon, S.D., Katz, J., Vaikuntanathan, V.: A group signature scheme from lattice assumptions. In: Abe, M. (ed.) ASIACRYPT 2010. LNCS, vol. 6477, pp. 395–412. Springer, Heidelberg (2010). https://doi.org/10.1007/978-3-642-17373-8_23

[Gro07] Groth, J.: Fully anonymous group signatures without random oracles. In: Kurosawa, K. (ed.) ASIACRYPT 2007. LNCS, vol. 4833, pp. 164–180. Springer, Heidelberg (2007). https://doi.org/10.1007/978-3-540-76900-2_10

[Gün89] Günther, C.G.: An identity-based key-exchange protocol. In: Quisquater, J.-J., Vandewalle, J. (eds.) EUROCRYPT 1989. LNCS, vol. 434, pp. 29–37. Springer, Heidelberg (1990). https://doi.org/10.1007/3-540-46885-4_5

[HILL99] Håstad, J., Impagliazzo, R., Levin, L.A., Luby, M.: A pseudorandom generator from any one-way function. SIAM J. Comput. **28**(4), 1364–1396 (1999)

[IR01] Itkis, G., Reyzin, L.: Forward-secure signatures with optimal signing and verifying. In: Kilian, J. (ed.) CRYPTO 2001. LNCS, vol. 2139, pp. 332–354. Springer, Heidelberg (2001). https://doi.org/10.1007/3-540-44647-8_20

[KY19] Katsumata, S., Yamada, S.: Group signatures without NIZK: from lattices in the standard model. In: Ishai, Y., Rijmen, V. (eds.) EUROCRYPT 2019. LNCS, vol. 11478, pp. 312–344. Springer, Cham (2019). https://doi.org/10.1007/978-3-030-17659-4_11

[LLLS13] Laguillaumie, F., Langlois, A., Libert, B., Stehlé, D.: Lattice-based group signatures with logarithmic signature size. In: Sako, K., Sarkar, P. (eds.) ASIACRYPT 2013. LNCS, vol. 8270, pp. 41–61. Springer, Heidelberg (2013). https://doi.org/10.1007/978-3-642-42045-0_3

[LLM+16] Libert, B., Ling, S., Mouhartem, F., Nguyen, K., Wang, H.: Signature schemes with efficient protocols and dynamic group signatures from lattice assumptions. In: Cheon, J.H., Takagi, T. (eds.) ASIACRYPT 2016. LNCS, vol. 10032, pp. 373–403. Springer, Heidelberg (2016). https://doi.org/10.1007/978-3-662-53890-6_13

[LLNW14] Langlois, A., Ling, S., Nguyen, K., Wang, H.: Lattice-based group signature scheme with verifier-local revocation. In: Krawczyk, H. (ed.) PKC 2014. LNCS, vol. 8383, pp. 345–361. Springer, Heidelberg (2014). https://doi.org/10.1007/978-3-642-54631-0_20

[LLNW16] Libert, B., Ling, S., Nguyen, K., Wang, H.: Zero-knowledge arguments for lattice-based accumulators: logarithmic-size ring signatures and group signatures without trapdoors. In: Fischlin, M., Coron, J.-S. (eds.) EUROCRYPT 2016. LNCS, vol. 9666, pp. 1–31. Springer, Heidelberg (2016). https://doi.org/10.1007/978-3-662-49896-5_1

[LMN16] Libert, B., Mouhartem, F., Nguyen, K.: A lattice-based group signature scheme with message-dependent opening. In: Manulis, M., Sadeghi, A.-R., Schneider, S. (eds.) ACNS 2016. LNCS, vol. 9696, pp. 137–155. Springer, Cham (2016). https://doi.org/10.1007/978-3-319-39555-5_8

[LNW15] Ling, S., Nguyen, K., Wang, H.: Group signatures from lattices: simpler, tighter, shorter, ring-based. In: Katz, J. (ed.) PKC 2015. LNCS, vol. 9020, pp. 427–449. Springer, Heidelberg (2015). https://doi.org/10.1007/978-3-662-46447-2_19

[LNWX17] Ling, S., Nguyen, K., Wang, H., Xu, Y.: Lattice-based group signatures: achieving full dynamicity with ease. In: Gollmann, D., Miyaji, A., Kikuchi, H. (eds.) ACNS 2017. LNCS, vol. 10355, pp. 293–312. Springer, Cham (2017). https://doi.org/10.1007/978-3-319-61204-1_15

[LNWX18] Ling, S., Nguyen, K., Wang, H., Xu, Y.: Constant-size group signatures from lattices. In: Abdalla, M., Dahab, R. (eds.) PKC 2018. LNCS, vol. 10770, pp. 58–88. Springer, Cham (2018). https://doi.org/10.1007/978-3-319-76581-5_3

[LNWX19] Ling, S., Nguyen, K., Wang, H., Xu, Y.: Forward-secure group signatures from lattices. In: Ding, J., Steinwandt, R. (eds.) PQCrypto 2019. LNCS, vol. 11505, pp. 44–64. Springer, Cham (2019). https://doi.org/10.1007/978-3-030-25510-7_3

[LY10] Libert, B., Yung, M.: Dynamic fully forward-secure group signatures. In: AsiaCCS, pp. 70–81. ACM (2010)

[Moh10] Mohassel, P.: One-time signatures and chameleon hash functions. In: Biryukov, A., Gong, G., Stinson, D.R. (eds.) SAC 2010. LNCS, vol. 6544, pp. 302–319. Springer, Heidelberg (2011). https://doi.org/10.1007/978-3-642-19574-7_21

[MP12] Micciancio, D., Peikert, C.: Trapdoors for lattices: simpler, tighter, faster, smaller. In: Pointcheval, D., Johansson, T. (eds.) EUROCRYPT 2012. LNCS, vol. 7237, pp. 700–718. Springer, Heidelberg (2012). https://doi.org/10.1007/978-3-642-29011-4_41

[NHF09] Nakanishi, T., Hira, Y., Funabiki, N.: Forward-secure group signatures from pairings. In: Shacham, H., Waters, B. (eds.) Pairing 2009. LNCS, vol. 5671, pp. 171–186. Springer, Heidelberg (2009). https://doi.org/10.1007/978-3-642-03298-1_12

[NZZ15] Nguyen, P.Q., Zhang, J., Zhang, Z.: Simpler efficient group signatures from lattices. In: Katz, J. (ed.) PKC 2015. LNCS, vol. 9020, pp. 401–426. Springer, Heidelberg (2015). https://doi.org/10.1007/978-3-662-46447-2_18

[PS19] Peikert, C., Shiehian, S.: Noninteractive zero knowledge for NP from (plain) learning with errors. In: Boldyreva, A., Micciancio, D. (eds.) CRYPTO 2019. LNCS, vol. 11692, pp. 89–114. Springer, Cham (2019). https://doi.org/10.1007/978-3-030-26948-7_4

[Reg05] Regev, O.: On lattices, learning with errors, random linear codes, and cryptography. In: STOC, pp. 84–93. ACM (2005)

[Son01] Song, D.X.: Practical forward secure group signature schemes. In: ACM Conference on Computer and Communications Security, pp. 225–234. ACM (2001)

[Tsa17] Tsabary, R.: An equivalence between attribute-based signatures and homomorphic signatures, and new constructions for both. In: Kalai, Y., Reyzin, L. (eds.) TCC 2017. LNCS, vol. 10678, pp. 489–518. Springer, Cham (2017). https://doi.org/10.1007/978-3-319-70503-3_16

[YLH+12] Yuen, T.H., Liu, J.K., Huang, X., Au, M.H., Susilo, W., Zhou, J.: Forward secure attribute-based signatures. In: Chim, T.W., Yuen, T.H. (eds.) ICICS 2012. LNCS, vol. 7618, pp. 167–177. Springer, Heidelberg (2012). https://doi.org/10.1007/978-3-642-34129-8_15

A Lattice-Based Provably Secure Multisignature Scheme in Quantum Random Oracle Model

Masayuki Fukumitsu[1(✉)] and Shingo Hasegawa[2]

[1] Faculty of Information Media, Hokkaido Information University, Nishi-Nopporo 59-2, Ebetsu, Hokkaido 069-8585, Japan
fukumitsu@do-johodai.ac.jp

[2] Graduate School of Information Sciences, Tohoku University, 41 Kawauchi, Aoba-ku, Sendai, Miyagi 980-8576, Japan
shingo.hasegawa.b7@tohoku.ac.jp

Abstract. The multisignature schemes are attracted to utilize in some cryptographic applications such as the blockchain. Though the lattice-based constructions of multisignature schemes exist as quantum-secure multisignature, a multisignature scheme whose security is proven in the *quantum* random oracle model (QROM), rather than the classical random oracle model (CROM), is not known.

In this paper, we propose a first lattice-based multisignature scheme whose security is proven in QROM. The difficultly of proving the security in QROM than CROM is how to program the random oracle in the security proof. Although our proposed scheme is based on the Dilithium-QROM signature whose security is proven in QROM, their proof technique cannot be directly applied to the multisignature setting. To solve the problems in the security proof, we develop several proof techniques in QROM. First, we employ the searching query technique by Targi and Unruh to convert the Dilithium-QROM into the multisignature setting. For the second, we develop a new programming technique in QROM, since the conventional programming techniques seem not to work in the multisignature setting of QROM. We combine the programming technique by Unruh with the one by Liu and Zhandry. The new technique enables us to program the random oracle in QROM and to construct the signing oracle in the security proof.

Keywords: Lattice cryptography · Multisigature · Quantum random oracle model · CRYSTALS-Dilithium

1 Introduction

The multisignature scheme [16] is a variant of digital signature schemes in a sense that a group of signers can prove their authenticity of a single message. One of the advantages is that these can reduce the size of an issued *multisignature*

K. Nguyen et al. (Eds.): ProvSec 2020, LNCS 12505, pp. 45–64, 2020.
https://doi.org/10.1007/978-3-030-62576-4_3

compared with that of all signatures generated by each signer individually. This property is suitable for IoT devices, and the multisignature schemes are recently employed in the blockchain to realize a transaction by a multi-user.

Although many multisignature schemes were proposed, most of them are based on the discrete logarithm assumption or the integer factoring assumption. Such schemes have the threat by quantum computers, because Shor [24] presented the quantum algorithm for breaking these assumptions. The lattice-based multisignature schemes are one of the promising candidates for quantum-resistant multisignature schemes. El Bansarkhani and Sturm [10] proposed the first lattice-based multisignature scheme for the constant number of signers. Their multisignature scheme is based on a lattice-based standard signature scheme by Güneysu, Lyubashevsky and Pöppelmann (GLP) [15], which is a Fiat-Shamir-type signature scheme [11], and its security is proven from the Ring Short Integer Solution assumption. Fukumitsu and Hasegawa [13] recently enhanced their multisignature scheme concerning the tightness of security reduction. The main idea of their construction is replacing the GLP signature scheme part with the Abdalla-Fouque-Lyubashevsky-Tibouchi (AFLT) signature scheme [1] which is known as a tightly-secure Fiat-Shamir-type signature scheme from the Ring Learning with Errors assumption.

The security of these lattice-based multisignature schemes was proven only in the classical random oracle model (CROM). In CROM, an adversary is supposed to obtain any hash value from the random oracle, but a classical query is only allowed. In order to show that the schemes have the security against quantum computers, an adversary should enable quantum queries to the random oracle. Boneh, Dagdelen, Fischlin, Lehmann, Schaffner and Zhandry [5] proposed the quantum random oracle model (QROM). In this model, an adversary can quantum query to the random oracle. The security of several cryptographic schemes e.g. [5,8,19,20,25–28] has been proven in this model, however, there is no multisignature scheme that is provably secure in QROM.

1.1 Our Contribution

Overview. We proposed a first multisignature scheme which is provably secure in QROM. The construction of our scheme is started with replacing the AFLT signature scheme part of the Fukumitsu-Hasegawa multisignature scheme with a variant of the candidates of the post-quantum cryptographic standard [22], the Dilithium-QROM [19]. The Dilithium-QROM achieves the provable security in QROM under the Modulo-LWE assumption. We aim to prove the plain-public key (ppk) security of our proposed scheme in QROM. The ppk security [4] considered as the standard security notion of the multisignature scheme, and it means that on a given challenge public key $\mathbf{pk}^*$, any probabilistic polynomial-time (PPT), especially quantum polynomial-time (QPT), adversary $\mathcal{A}$ cannot forge a new multisignature σ^* under a group of signers which contains the signer owning $\mathbf{pk}^*$ beyond negligible probability. During that, $\mathcal{A}$ can adaptively obtain multisignatures under an arbitrary chosen pairs of a message μ and a group of signers which contains the signer owning $\mathbf{pk}^*$ from the signing oracle simulated by a challenger, where the challenger plays the role of the signer owning $\mathbf{pk}^*$ while $\mathcal{A}$ does that of the co-signers.

Proof Technique. The main idea of proving the security of our proposed multisignature scheme is employing the proof technique by Kiltz, Lyubashevsky and Schaffner [19]. They proved the security of the Fiat-Shamir-type signature scheme in QROM. Their main feature is to naturally extend the security proof in CROM by [1,17], which is called a *lossy ID technique*, to the QROM case. The result suggests that the security proof given in CROM by the lossy ID technique can be converted to the one in QROM. On the other hand, the security of the original scheme [13] of our proposed scheme was proven by using the lossy ID technique. Therefore, we expect that we can prove the security of our multisignature scheme in QROM by extending the security proof by [19] to the multisignature scheme case. However, such a natural extension of [19] seems not to work well. We then describe the details of the problems and their solutions.

We first briefly recap the structure of Fiat-Shamir-type signature schemes and the security proof by [19]. A signature generated by such types consists of a pair (w, z) such that z is determined by using a hash value $c = H_2(w, \mu)$ of the first component w and a message μ and a secret key of a signer. Their proof is divided into three steps. In the first step, the signing oracle in the security game is replaced with a simulator that no longer uses a secret key. In order to achieve the security in QROM, all signatures which are replied to $\mathcal{A}$ from the signing oracle are determined at the beginning of the game by utilizing a random function. In the second step, a public key given to $\mathcal{A}$ is switched into a "lossy" one which intuitively means a public key that has no corresponding secret key. In the third step, they evaluate the upper bound of the winning probability of the "changed" game at the previous steps. Then, they convert the challenger of the changed game into an unbounded algorithm that solves the generic search problem with bounded probabilities (GSPB) [19]. They also showed that any unbounded quantum algorithm solves GSPB with negligible probability. These imply that the winning probability of the original security game is almost bounded by the probability of distinguishing the distribution of a regular public key and that of a lossy public key.

According to these steps, we attempt to prove the security of the proposed multisignature scheme. Namely, we shall construct a simulator of the signing oracle and evaluate the security game with respect to a lossy public key by converting the challenger of the changed game into an algorithm for solving GSPB. However, it turns out that two problems obstruct the naive application of [19] to our multisignature case, and we have to overcome them to succeed in the security proof.

The first one is how to search queries to the random oracle by $\mathcal{A}$ in the QROM case. Intuitively says, a multisignature during our signing protocol consists of the summation $(\boldsymbol{w}, \boldsymbol{z}) = \sum (\boldsymbol{w}_v, \boldsymbol{z}_v)$ of all solo signatures $(\boldsymbol{w}_v, \boldsymbol{z}_v)$ of the Dilithium-QROM issued by all signers individually. Following the signing protocols by [10,13], each signer broadcasts the hash value $\boldsymbol{g}_v = H_0(\boldsymbol{w}_v)$ of $\boldsymbol{w}_v$ to the co-signers before broadcasting $\boldsymbol{w}_v$. By utilizing this process, we aims to construct a simulator which recovers each of $\boldsymbol{w}_v$ from $\boldsymbol{g}_v$ as in [10,13] before broadcasting $\boldsymbol{w}_v$. In the CROM case, this is done by using the hash table of H_0. However, this technique cannot be immediately utilized in the QROM case as mentioned in [5,28]. This is because hash queries and these responses in QROM are in superposition, and then recording such values to the hash table is in general difficult. To solve this problem, we employ the technique by Targi and Unruh [25] which is used to prove the security of a variant of the Fujisaki-Okamoto transformation [12] in QROM. They overcame the difficultly by simulating the random oracle using an efficiently invertible function, i.e. a polynomial. Namely, it recovers a hash query to the random oracle by computing the root of the polynomial. Note that since the polynomial has multiple roots, to determine a hash query from the multiple roots, they utilize a one-way injection of a public key encryption scheme under fixed public key and randomness. To employ their method, we involve a one-way injective function in our signing protocol. We also note that the post-quantum public-key encryption schemes and the one-way injective functions such as [6,14,23] can be adapted as a one-way injective function.

The second one is how one can program the hash values in QROM. The simulator of the signing oracle, which plays the role of the signer owning $\mathbf{pk}^*$, is required to issue a solo signature of the Dilithium-QROM without the secret key corresponding to $\mathbf{pk}^*$. Recall that [19] succeeded in constructing such a simulator by determining the signatures of all messages queried by $\mathcal{A}$ at the beginning of the game. However, this technique cannot be applied immediately in our case. This is because in the signing protocol of the multisignature scheme, a multisignature $(\boldsymbol{w}, \boldsymbol{z})$ is issued by combining each of solo signatures $(\boldsymbol{w}_v, \boldsymbol{z}_v)$ from all co-signers which are played by $\mathcal{A}$, and hence the simulator no longer issues all multisignatures up-front. In order to resolve this problem, we employ a programing technique proposed by Unruh [26]. Their technique supports to program a hash value on H_2 of an input value which is known just before the programming. Although their technique seems to be suitable in our case, it requires that an input value to be hashed by H_2 must be determined just before the programming by using fresh random coins. On the other hand, the input values $\boldsymbol{w}$ and μ are determined before broadcasting $\boldsymbol{w}_v$ in our construction, and hence these values include no fresh random coin. This is a new problem to be addressed. For this new problem, we combine the programming technique by Liu and Zhandry [20]. Their technique realizes the programming of an arbitrary value as a hash value. By using the technique by [20], the fresh random coins are programmed as a hash value given by employing a new hash function H_1, and then the technique by [26] can be applied to our multisignature case by adding the fresh random coins as the input value of H_2. Our new programming technique which combines the two conventional techniques [20,26] enables us to construct the simulator in the multisiganture case even in QROM, and then realizes the natural extension of the security proof in CROM into the QROM.

1.2 Future Works

We employ a new cryptographic assumption called the *rMLWE assumption* which is a lattice analog of the rDCK assumption [3] to simulate the signing oracle. Showing the validity of the new assumption or removing it from the security proof is an important future work.

Another important future work is concerning the parameters of our multisignature scheme. Although we will show the bound and the relationship among the parameters in Table 1, the concrete recommended values have not been discussed. We will determine them so that our proposed scheme takes significance in the real world.

2 Preliminaries

Let $\mathcal{A}$ be an algorithm. $y \leftarrow \mathcal{A}(x)$ means that $\mathcal{A}$ outputs y on input x when $\mathcal{A}$ is deterministic. When $\mathcal{A}$ is probabilistic, we denote this by $y \leftarrow \mathcal{A}(x; r)$, where r is an internal coin of $\mathcal{A}$. And then, $\mathcal{A}(x)$ is a random variable over the choice of r. For any Boolean formula B, $\neg B$ means that B does not satisfied. Let $\mathbb{N}$ be the set of natural numbers. A function ϵ in κ is said to be negligible if for any polynomial p, there exists $\kappa_0 \in \mathbb{N}$ such that $\epsilon(\kappa) < 1/p(\kappa)$ for any $\kappa \geq \kappa_0$.

Let $\mathbb{Z}$, $\mathbb{Z}_n$ and $\mathbb{F}_q$ be the ring of integers, that of residues and the finite field over q respectively, where $n \in \mathbb{N}$, and q is a prime or a power of 2. Consider a finite set X. For a probabilistic distribution D over X, $x \in_D X$ means that x is chosen according to D. $x \in_{\mathrm{U}} X$ means that x is chosen uniformly at random from X. Let Uni be a probabilistic algorithm that outputs $x \in_{\mathrm{U}} X$ on a given set X. Although the length of the representation of X may be beyond polynomial in a security parameter, we use Uni only in unbounded algorithms in this paper. For any real number $0 \leq \lambda \leq 1$, B_λ is the Bernoulli distribution, namely $\Pr_{x \in_{B_\lambda} \{0,1\}}[x = 1] = \lambda$. For a set X, $|X|$ stands for the number of elements in X, while $|a|$ does for the absolute value of a for any number a.

2.1 Quantum Computation

The state $|\psi\rangle$ of n qubits is expressed by $|\psi\rangle = \sum_{s \in \{0,1\}^n} \alpha_s |s\rangle$, where each of α_s is a complex number such that $\sum_{s \in \{0,1\}^n} |\alpha_s|^2 = 1$. And, $\{|s\rangle\}_{s \in \{0,1\}^n}$ is called *computational basis*. The qubit is said to be *in superposition* if there exists $s \in \{0,1\}^n$ such that $0 < |\alpha_s| < 1$, whereas it is *classical* otherwise. Any string $s \in \{0,1\}^n$ can be measured in the computational basis with probability $|\alpha_s|^2$. The evolution of a quantum system in a state $|\psi\rangle$ is defined by using a unitary matrix U of size $2^n \times 2^n$. For the detail, please refer to a textbook such as [21].

Consider an oracle $\mathcal{O}$ which returns an m-bit string on input n-bit string. Following [5], the quantum access to $\mathcal{O}$ is expressed by a unitary matrix $U_{\mathcal{O}}$ which maps $|x\rangle|\psi\rangle$ to $|x\rangle|\psi \oplus \mathcal{O}(x)\rangle$, where $x \in \{0,1\}^n$, $\psi \in \{0,1\}^m$ and $\oplus$ denotes the bitwise exclusive-or operation. For an quantum algorithm $\mathcal{A}$, $\mathcal{A}^{|\mathcal{O}\rangle}$ means that $\mathcal{A}$ is allowed to access the oracle $\mathcal{O}$ in superposition.

We recall the generic search problem with bounded probabilities (GSPB) which is defined in [19] (Fig. 1). Intuitively, the adversary $\mathcal{A} = (\mathcal{A}_1, \mathcal{A}_2)$ in the GSPB game aims to find a string $x \in X$ such that $g(x) = 1$. Here, $\mathcal{A}$ can declare the probability $\lambda(x)$ that $g(x) = 1$ for each $x \in X$ under the constraint that $\lambda(x) < \lambda$ for some designated $0 \leq \lambda \leq 1$, and then the challenge $\mathcal{C}$ determines the function $g(x)$ according to $B_{\lambda(x)}$ for each $x \in X$.

$\mathbf{Exp}^{\mathsf{GSPB}}_{\lambda,\mathcal{A}}(\kappa)$

(1) $(\{\lambda(x)\}_{x \in X}, \mathrm{st}) \leftarrow \mathcal{A}_1(1^\kappa)$
(2) return 0 if $\exists x \in X$ s.t. $\lambda(x) > \lambda$.
(3) For each $x \in X$, set $g(x) \in_{B_{\lambda(x)}} \{0,1\}$
(4) $x \leftarrow \mathcal{A}_2^{|g\rangle}(\mathrm{st})$
(5) return $g(x)$

Fig. 1. The generic search problem with bounded probabilities $0 \leq \lambda \leq 1$

$\mathbf{Exp}^{\mathsf{Reprog}}_{\mathfrak{D},\mathfrak{R},b',\mathcal{A}}(\kappa)$

(1) $H \in_{\mathrm{U}} \mathsf{Fun}(\mathfrak{D}, \mathfrak{R})$.
(2) $\mathrm{st}_0 \leftarrow \mathcal{A}_0^{|H\rangle}(1^\kappa)$.
(3) $(w, \mathrm{st}_c) \leftarrow \mathcal{A}_C(\mathrm{st}_0)$.
(4) $c = H(w)$ if $b' = 1$, or $c \in_{\mathrm{U}} \mathfrak{R}$ and set $H(w) = c$ otherwise.
(5) return $\mathcal{A}_2^{|H\rangle}(c, \mathrm{st}_c)$.

Fig. 2. The reprogram problem in QROM

Lemma 1 ([19, Lemma 2.1], **Generic Search Problem with Bounded Probabilities).** *For any real number $0 \leq \lambda \leq 1$, and any unbounded quantum algorithm $\mathcal{A} = (\mathcal{A}_1, \mathcal{A}_2)$ making at most Q queries to $g : X \to \{0,1\}$, we have* $\Pr\left[\mathbf{Exp}^{\mathsf{GSPB}}_{\lambda,\mathcal{A}}(\kappa) = 1\right] \leq 8\lambda(Q+1)^2$.

2.2 Quantum Random Oracle Model

In this subsection, we explain the notion of the quantum random oracle model and the ways to simulate it. Let $\mathsf{Fun}(\mathfrak{D}, \mathfrak{R})$ be the set of all functions $H : \mathfrak{D} \to \mathfrak{R}$. Then, the *quantum random oracle model (QROM)* is a security model in which any adversary $\mathcal{A}$ obtains hash values from the random oracle by accessing the oracle in superposition. For a hash function $H \in \mathsf{Fun}(\mathfrak{D}, \mathfrak{R})$, we write $\mathcal{A}^{|H\rangle}$ to denote that $\mathcal{A}$ can access the random oracle H in superposition.

It is known that there are several ways to simulate the random oracle. We recall the techniques of replacing the random oracle with several functions, and that of involving the compressed oracle proposed by [28].

The first way to simulate the random oracle is to replace the random oracle with a random function $H \in_{\mathrm{U}} \mathsf{Fun}(\mathfrak{D}, \mathfrak{R})$. In this way, a challenger selects H at the beginning of the security game, and replies $H(x)$ on a given query x in superposition. The random oracle is simulated perfectly by this technique, because the uniformly random choice of a function from $\mathsf{Fun}(\mathfrak{D}, \mathfrak{R})$ implies that the hash value $H(x)$ is uniformly distributed over $\mathfrak{R}$ for any value x. The following lemma says that we can replace a hash value with a random value even in QROM. Namely, we can use the programming technique with random values in this simulation. The *collision-entropy* [26] of a random variable X is defined by $-\log \Pr[X = X']$, where X' is a random variable X' which is independent of X, but has the same distribution.

Lemma 2 ([26]). *Let* $\mathfrak{D}$, $\mathfrak{R}$ *be finite sets, and let* $\mathcal{A} = (\mathcal{A}_0, \mathcal{A}_C, \mathcal{A}_2)$ *be an algorithm such that* $\mathcal{A}_0$ *and* $\mathcal{A}_2$ *are quantum algorithms which can access the random oracle, and* $\mathcal{A}_C$ *is a probabilistic classical algorithm. Assume that* $\mathcal{A}_C(\mathrm{st}_0)$ *has collision-entropy at least* ι *for any input* st_0. *For* $\mathbf{Exp}^{\mathsf{Reprog}}_{\mathfrak{D},\mathfrak{R},b',\mathcal{A}}$ *depicted in Fig. 2, and the number* q_A *of queries by* $\mathcal{A}_0$, *we have*

$$\left|\Pr\left[\mathbf{Exp}^{\mathsf{Reprog}}_{\mathfrak{D},\mathfrak{R},0,\mathcal{A}}(1^\kappa) = 1\right] - \Pr\left[\mathbf{Exp}^{\mathsf{Reprog}}_{\mathfrak{D},\mathfrak{R},1,\mathcal{A}}(1^\kappa) = 1\right]\right| \le (4 + \sqrt{2})\sqrt{q_A}2^{-\iota/4}.$$

Moreover, the following lemma guarantees that H can be replaced with a $2Q$-wise independent function in the simulation of the random oracle.

Lemma 3 ([27]). *Let* $\mathcal{A}$ *be a quantum algorithm, which can access the random oracle in superposition at most* Q *times. Then, a simulator of the random oracle which uses a function* $H \in_{\mathrm{U}} \mathsf{Fun}(\{0,1\}^n, \{0,1\}^m)$ *is perfectly indistinguishable from the one which uses a* $2Q$*-wise independent function from* $\mathcal{A}$. *A random polynomial* f_{2Q} *of degree* $2Q$ *over the finite field* $\mathbb{F}_{2^m}$ *is* $2Q$*-wise independent.*

Note that the root of f_{2Q} can be computed in polynomial-time.

The second way to replace the random oracle is the use of the compressed oracle [28]. The concept of compressed oracles was introduced to simulate the random oracle as in the case of the classical ROM. Namely, a database of all pairs of a random oracle query and its hash value is utilized in the simulation. We now briefly recall the notion of the compressed Fourier oracle and the compressed phase oracle, respectively. For the detail, please refer to the papers such as [20,28]. Consider that $\mathfrak{R} = \{0,1\}^\theta$, and a superposition of databases D which contains pairs (x, y) of an input and an output of a hash function H. Hence, $(x, y) \in D$ means that $H(x) = y$. At the beginning of a security game, D is initialized to a pure state over empty databases. For each query, the *compressed Fourier oracle* returns its hash value in superposition after operating $D \oplus (x, y)$. The operation $D \oplus (x, y)$ is defined in the following way:

- D if $y = 0$,
- $D \cup \{(x, y)\}$ else if $y \neq 0 \wedge D(x) = \perp$,
- $D \setminus \{(x, y)\}$ else if there exists x such that $D(x) = y' \wedge y + y' \equiv 0 \pmod{2^\theta}$, or
- $D \setminus \{(x, y)\} \cup \{(x, y + y')\}$ otherwise.

The *compressed phase oracle* is intuitively obtained by applying the quantum Fourier transformation to D. And any QPT algorithm can simulate both the compressed Fourier oracle and the compressed phase oracle in the straightforward way as follows.

Lemma 4 ([28]). *Let $\mathcal{A}$ be a quantum algorithm which makes queries to a random oracle $H : \mathfrak{D} \to \{0,1\}^n$, and outputs tuples $(x_1, \ldots, x_k, y_1, \ldots, y_k, z)$. Let R be a collection of such tuples. Suppose that with probability p, $\mathcal{A}$ outputs a tuple such that (1) the tuple is in R and (2) for all i, $H(x_i) = y_i$. Now consider running $\mathcal{A}$ with each of the compressed Fourier oracle and the compressed phase oracle, and suppose that the database D is measured after $\mathcal{A}$ produces its output. Let p' be the probability that the conditions (1) and (2) hold in this running case. Then, we have $\sqrt{p} \leq \sqrt{p'} + \sqrt{k/2^n}$.*

Liu and Zhandry [20] recently introduced a new compressed oracle, which is called *almost compressed Fourier oracle*, by combining the compressed Fourier oracle with the compressed phase oracle. In the use of the almost compressed Fourier oracle, some points are called *special points*, and they are dealt with the (uncompressed) phase oracle. On the other hand, other points are dealt with the compressed Fourier oracle. As a programming technique on the almost compressed Fourier oracle, the following lemma holds. This lemma can be extended to a case for several special points as noted in [20].

Lemma 5 ([20, Corollary 7]). *Consider a random oracle which maps an element in $\{0,1\}^n$ into the one in $\{0,1\}^n$. Assume that an adversary $\mathcal{A}$ is interacting with a simulator of an almost compressed phase oracle where the i-th oracle query x^* is regarded as the special point. Instead of appending $\sum_y |y\rangle$ into the database for the i-th query, $|r\rangle$ for randomly chosen r is appended. Then, $\mathcal{A}$ and the simulator continue the running, and eventually the simulator measures the output registers. Then, $\mathcal{A}$ cannot distinguish such a replacement.*

More precisely, consider the following situation. Let S be a set of all possible entire states w of $\mathcal{A}$ and compressed database $D \cup \{(x^*, r)\}$. We define a measurement $P_0 = \sum_{(w, D\cup\{x^*,r\})\in S} |w, D \cup \{(x^*, r)\}\rangle\langle w, D \cup \{(x^*, r)\}|$ and $P_1 = I - P_0$. Let γ be the probability that the measurement gives 0 in the game where $\sum_y |y\rangle$ is appended into D as the hash value of x^*, and γ' be the one where $|r\rangle$ is appended. Then, we have $\gamma = \gamma'$.

2.3 Lattice

Consider $q, n \in \mathbb{N}$. Let R and R_q be the rings $\mathbb{Z}[X]/(X^n + 1)$ and $\mathbb{Z}_q/(X^n + 1)$, respectively. An element $a = \sum_{i=0}^{n-1} a_i x^i$ in R or R_q is represented by its coefficients vector $(a_0, a_1, \ldots, a_{n-1})$. Regular font letters stand for elements in R or R_q, while bold font letters stand for vectors and matrices over R or R_q.

For $\alpha \in \mathbb{N}$, $r = x \bmod {}^{+}\alpha$ denotes the ordinary residue of the division over α, namely $0 \leq r < \alpha$, while $r = x \bmod {}^{\pm}\alpha$ does the *centered* residue such that $-\alpha/2 < r \leq \alpha/2$ when α is even, or $-(\alpha-1)/2 \leq r \leq (\alpha-1)/2$ otherwise. Hereafter, each element x in $\mathbb{Z}_q$ including coefficients of $a \in R_q$ is represented by the centered residue instead of the ordinary one. For any $r \in \mathbb{Z}_q$, $\|r\|_\infty$ is defined by $|r \bmod {}^{\pm}q|$. By using this notation, any element $r = x \bmod {}^{\pm}\alpha$ satisfies that $\|r\|_\infty \leq \alpha/2$ for any natural number $\alpha \leq q$ and integer x. The L^∞-norm and the L^2-norm of a polynomial $a = (a_0, a_1, \ldots, a_{n-1}) \in R_q$ are represented by

$\|a\|_\infty = \max_{0\leq i\leq n-1}\|a_i\|_\infty$ and $\|a\|_2 = \sqrt{\sum_{i=0}^{n-1}\|a_i\|_\infty^2}$, respectively. The L^∞-norm and the L^2-norm of a vector $\boldsymbol{a} = (a_1,\ldots,a_\ell) \in R_q^\ell$ for any $\ell \in \mathbb{N}$ are represented by $\|\boldsymbol{a}\|_\infty = \max_{1\leq i\leq \ell}\|a_i\|_\infty$ and $\|\boldsymbol{a}\|_2 = \sqrt{\sum_{i=1}^{\ell}\|a_i\|_\infty^2}$, respectively. For any $\eta \in \mathbb{N}$, let S_η be a set of all elements $a \in R$ such that $\|a\|_\infty \leq \eta$.

Consider $k,\ell \in \mathbb{N}$, a probability distribution D over R_q. For any polynomial T_{MLWE} and any function ϵ_{MLWE}, the $(T_{\mathrm{MLWE}},\epsilon_{\mathrm{MLWE}},D)$*-Modulo-LWE assumption* ($(T_{\mathrm{MLWE}},\epsilon_{\mathrm{MLWE}},D)$-MLWE assumption) states that for any QPT adversary $\mathcal{A}$ whose running time is at most T_{MLWE}, it holds that $\left|P_0^{\mathrm{MLWE}} - P_1^{\mathrm{MLWE}}\right| \leq \epsilon_{\mathrm{MLWE}}(\kappa)$ for any κ, where

$$P_0^{\mathrm{MLWE}} = \Pr\left[\mathcal{A}(\boldsymbol{A},\boldsymbol{t}) = 1 : \boldsymbol{A} \in_{\mathrm{U}} R_q^{k\times\ell}, \boldsymbol{s}_1, \in_D R_q^\ell, \boldsymbol{s}_2 \in_D R_q^k, \boldsymbol{t} = \boldsymbol{A}\boldsymbol{s}_1 + \boldsymbol{s}_2\right],$$
$$P_1^{\mathrm{MLWE}} = \Pr\left[\mathcal{A}(\boldsymbol{A},\boldsymbol{t}) = 1 : \boldsymbol{A} \in_{\mathrm{U}} R_q^{k\times\ell}, \boldsymbol{t} \in_{\mathrm{U}} R_q^k\right].$$

We also consider another assumption which is an analog of the rejected-DCK assumption [3] to the MLWE case. For any polynomial T_{rMLWE}, any function $\epsilon_{\mathrm{rMLWE}}$ and any constants γ' and β, the $(T_{\mathrm{rMLWE}},\epsilon_{\mathrm{rMLWE}},D,\gamma',\beta)$*-rejected-MLWE assumption* ($(T_{\mathrm{rMLWE}},\epsilon_{\mathrm{rMLWE}},D,\gamma',\beta)$-rMLWE assumption) states that for any QPT adversary $\mathcal{A}$ whose running time is at most T_{rMLWE}, it holds that $\left|P_0^{\mathrm{rMLWE}} - P_1^{\mathrm{rMLWE}}\right| \leq \epsilon_{\mathrm{rMLWE}}(\kappa)$ for any κ, where

$$P_0^{\mathrm{rMLWE}} = \Pr\left[\mathcal{A}(\boldsymbol{A},\boldsymbol{w},c) = 1 : \begin{array}{l} \boldsymbol{A} \in_{\mathrm{U}} R_q^{k\times\ell}, \boldsymbol{s} \in_D R_q^\ell, \\ \boldsymbol{y} \in_{\mathrm{U}} S_{\gamma'-1}^\ell, \\ \boldsymbol{w} = \boldsymbol{A}\boldsymbol{y}, c \in_{\mathrm{U}} \mathcal{CH} \end{array} \mid \boldsymbol{y} + c\boldsymbol{s} \geq \gamma' - \beta\right],$$

$$P_1^{\mathrm{rMLWE}} = \Pr\left[\mathcal{A}(\boldsymbol{A},\boldsymbol{w},c) = 1 : \begin{array}{l} \boldsymbol{A} \in_{\mathrm{U}} R_q^{k\times\ell}, \boldsymbol{s} \in_D R_q^\ell, \\ \boldsymbol{y} \in_{\mathrm{U}} S_{\gamma'-1}^\ell, \\ \boldsymbol{w} \in_{\mathrm{U}} R_q^k, c \in_{\mathrm{U}} \mathcal{CH} \end{array} \mid \boldsymbol{y} + c\boldsymbol{s} \geq \gamma' - \beta\right].$$

2.4 Multisignature Scheme

We now introduce the notion of the multisignature and its security. A *multisignature scheme* consists of the following four tuples $(\mathsf{Setup},\mathsf{KGen},\mathsf{Sig},\mathsf{Ver})$. Setup and KGen are PPT algorithms. $\mathsf{Setup}(1^\kappa)$ returns a system parameter $\mathbf{pp}$ on a security parameter κ. Each signer generates a pair $(\mathbf{sk},\mathbf{pk})$ of a secret key $\mathbf{sk}$ and a public key $\mathbf{pk}$ by $\mathsf{KGen}(\mathbf{pp})$. The signing process can be done by running the designated multiparty protocol during multiple signers to issue a signature σ on a message μ and a set PK of public keys. Each signer executes the interactive polynomial-time algorithm $\mathsf{Sig}(\mathbf{pp},\mathbf{sk},\mathsf{PK},\mu)$ in order to execute this protocol. Ver is a deterministic polynomial-time algorithm which returns 1 on input $(\mathbf{pp},\mathsf{PK},\mu,\sigma)$ if σ is a valid signature for (PK,μ).

Correctness. Let $\mathsf{MSig} = (\mathsf{Setup},\mathsf{KGen},\mathsf{Sig},\mathsf{Ver})$ be a multisignature scheme. For any $\mathbf{pp} \leftarrow \mathsf{Setup}(1^\kappa)$ and any message μ, consider the situation where for each $1 \leq v \leq U$, a v-th signer generates own key pair $(\mathbf{sk}_v,\mathbf{pk}_v) \leftarrow \mathsf{KGen}(\mathbf{pp})$, executes $\mathsf{Sig}(\mathbf{pp},\mathbf{sk}_v,\mathsf{PK},\mu)$ in order to run the protocol, and then obtains a signature σ, where $\mathsf{PK} = \{\mathbf{pk}_u\}_{u=1}^U$. MSig satisfies the *correctness* if it always holds $\mathsf{Ver}(\mathbf{pp},\mathsf{PK},\mu,\sigma) = 1$.

Init $\mathcal{C}$ generates $\mathbf{pp} \leftarrow \mathsf{Setup}(1^\kappa)$ and $\mathcal{C}$'s key pair $(\mathbf{pk}^*, \mathbf{sk}^*) \leftarrow \mathsf{KGen}(\mathbf{pp})$. Then $\mathcal{C}$ sends $(\mathbf{pp}, \mathbf{pk}^*)$ to $\mathcal{F}$.

Sign For a query $(\mu^{(i)}, \mathsf{PK}^{(i)})$ of a message $\mu^{(i)}$ and a public key set $\mathsf{PK}^{(i)} = \left\{\mathbf{pk}_u^{(i)}\right\}_{u=1}^{U}$ including $\mathbf{pk}^*$, $\mathcal{C}$ runs the protocol by playing the role of the signer which generates $\mathbf{pk}^*$ and then returns a multisignature $\sigma^{(i)}$ to $\mathcal{F}$. We assume without loss of generality that $\mathbf{pk}_1^{(i)} = \mathbf{pk}^*$. Here, $\mathcal{F}$ plays the role of the co-signers.

Challenge For a final output $(\mathsf{PK}^*, \mu^*, \sigma^*)$ of $\mathcal{F}$, $\mathcal{F}$ is said to *win this game* if the following conditions hold:
(1) $\mathbf{pk}^* \in \mathsf{PK}^*$,
(2) (μ^*, PK^*) is not queried in **Sign** phase, and
(3) $\mathsf{Ver}(\mathbf{pp}, \mathsf{PK}^*, \mu^*, \sigma^*) = 1$.

Fig. 3. The description of the ppk game

Security. The plain public key (ppk) security [4] for multisignatures is defined by the ppk game between the challenger $\mathcal{C}$ and the forger $\mathcal{F}$ (Fig. 3).

Definition 6. *Let T be a polynomial, ϵ be a function and U be the number of signers. A multisignature scheme* MSig *with U signers is (T, U, ϵ, Q_S)*-ppk secure *if for any forger $\mathcal{F}$ running in time T which makes at most Q_S queries in* **Sign** *phase, the probability that $\mathcal{F}$ wins the ppk game is ϵ.*

Especially, MSig *is said to be* $(T, U, \epsilon, Q_S, Q_0, Q_1, \ldots)$-ppk secure in QROM *if* MSig *is (T, U, ϵ, Q_S)-ppk secure and the number of queries to the random oracle H_i is at most Q_i for all i.*

3 A Dilithium-Based Multisignature Scheme

We propose a multisignature scheme which is based on the Dilithium-QROM signature scheme [19]. In their scheme, several supporting algorithms are employed to optimize efficiency. We start by introducing such several supporting algorithms in the next subsection.

Table 1. Parameters of the proposed multisignature scheme, where $\boldsymbol{A}$, $\boldsymbol{t}$, $\boldsymbol{w}_\mathsf{H}$, $\boldsymbol{s}_1$, $\boldsymbol{s}_2$ and H_1 will be defined in Fig. 5.

U	# of signers	constant
q	ring modulus	$q \equiv 5 \pmod 8$
n	ring dimension	
(k, ℓ)	dimension of matrix $\boldsymbol{A}$	$\ell \leq k$
d	dropped bit from $\boldsymbol{t}$	$46 \cdot 2^{d-1} \leq \gamma,\ 2^d < 4U(\gamma' - \beta) - 4$
γ	max. coefficient of $\boldsymbol{w}_\mathsf{H}$	$q > 4U\gamma,\ q \equiv 1 \pmod{2U\gamma}$, $2\beta \ll 2\gamma \leq \sqrt{q/2}/U$
γ'	$\approx$ max. sig. coefficient	$2\beta \ll 2\gamma' \leq \sqrt{q/2}$
η	max. coefficients of $\boldsymbol{s}_1, \boldsymbol{s}_2$	
β	$\beta = 46\eta$	$\forall c \in \mathcal{CH}, \forall s \in S_\eta, \lVert cs \rVert_\infty < \beta$
θ	length of hash values of H_1	polynomial

3.1 Supporting Algorithms

The basic strategy of the Dilithium-QROM signature scheme to reduce the key size and the signature size is to ignore the residues of values by dividing them by some designated even number $\alpha < q$. In order to apply such a strategy to a signature scheme, the Dilithium-QROM signature scheme employs several supporting algorithms which are summarized in Fig. 4.

$\mathsf{Power2Round}_q(r \in \mathbb{Z}_q, d \in \mathbb{N})$:
(1) $r = r \bmod {}^{+}q$.
(2) $r_{\mathsf{L}} = r \bmod {}^{\pm}2^d$.
(3) return $(r - r_{\mathsf{L}})/2^d$.

$\mathsf{UseHint}_q(h \in \{0,1\}, r \in \mathbb{Z}_q, \alpha \in 2\mathbb{N})$:
(1) $m = (q-1)/\alpha$.
(2) $(r_{\mathsf{H}}, r_{\mathsf{L}}) \leftarrow \mathsf{Decompose}_q(r, \alpha)$.
(3) return r_{H} if $h = 0$.
(4) return $(r_{\mathsf{H}} + 1) \bmod {}^{+}m$ if $r_{\mathsf{L}} > 0$.
(5) return $(r_{\mathsf{H}} - 1) \bmod {}^{+}m$ if $r_{\mathsf{L}} \leq 0$.

$\mathsf{MakeHint}_q(z \in \mathbb{Z}_q, r \in \mathbb{Z}_q, \alpha \in 2\mathbb{N})$:
(1) $r_{\mathsf{H}} \leftarrow \mathsf{HighBits}_q(r, \alpha)$.
(2) $v_{\mathsf{H}} \leftarrow \mathsf{HighBits}_q(r + z, \alpha)$.
(3) return 0 if $r_{\mathsf{H}} = v_{\mathsf{H}}$, or 1 otherwise.

$\mathsf{Decompose}_q(r \in \mathbb{Z}_q, \alpha \in 2\mathbb{N})$:
(1) $r = r \bmod {}^{+}q$.
(2) $r_{\mathsf{L}} = r \bmod {}^{\pm}\alpha$.
(3) return $(r_{\mathsf{H}}, r_{\mathsf{L}}) = (0, r_{\mathsf{L}} - 1)$ if $r - r_{\mathsf{L}} = q - 1$.
(4) $r_{\mathsf{H}} = (r - r_{\mathsf{L}})/\alpha$.
(5) return $(r_{\mathsf{H}}, r_{\mathsf{L}})$.

$\mathsf{HighBits}_q(r \in \mathbb{Z}_q, \alpha \in 2\mathbb{N})$:
(1) $(r_{\mathsf{H}}, r_{\mathsf{L}}) \leftarrow \mathsf{Decompose}_q(r, \alpha)$
(2) return r_{H}

$\mathsf{LowBits}_q(r \in \mathbb{Z}_q, \alpha \in 2\mathbb{N})$:
(1) $(r_{\mathsf{H}}, r_{\mathsf{L}}) \leftarrow \mathsf{Decompose}_q(r, \alpha)$
(2) return r_{L}

Fig. 4. Supporting algorithms [9]

We note that the supporting algorithms can be applied to vectors or polynomials rather than scalars, by applying each of these elements in the vectors. For example, $\mathsf{Decompose}_q(a, \alpha)$ for $a = (a_0, a_1, \ldots, a_{n-1}) \in R_q$ means that $\mathsf{Decompose}_q$ is applied to each coefficients of a with the same modulus α. Namely, $\mathsf{Decompose}_q(a, \alpha) = (\mathsf{Decompose}_q(a_0, \alpha), \ldots, \mathsf{Decompose}_q(a_{n-1}, \alpha))$. We can employ the same manner for a vector over R_q. For a vector $\boldsymbol{h} = (h_0, \ldots, h_{n-1}) \in \{0,1\}^n$, $\mathsf{UseHint}_q(\boldsymbol{h}, a, \alpha)$ means $(\mathsf{UseHint}_q(h_0, a_0, \alpha), \ldots, \mathsf{UseHint}_q(h_{n-1}, a_{n-1}, \alpha))$. $\mathsf{MakeHint}_q$ is also applied to the same manner.

3.2 Proposed Scheme

We present our Dilithium-based multisignature scheme in this subsection. We set $\mathcal{CH} = \{c \in R \mid \|c\|_\infty = 1 \wedge \|c\|_2 = \sqrt{46}\}$, and consider the number U of signers and parameters $(q, n, k, \ell, d, \gamma, \gamma', \eta, \beta, \theta)$ which are defined as Table 1. Let Sam be an algorithm which outputs a matrix $\boldsymbol{A} \in_{\mathrm{U}} R_q^{k \times \ell}$ on input $\varrho \in \{0,1\}^{256}$. And, let H_0, H_1 and H_2 be functions that $H_0 : \mathfrak{D}_0 \to \mathfrak{R}_0$, $H_1 : \mathfrak{D}_1 \to \{0,1\}^\theta$ and $H_2 : \mathfrak{D}_2 \to \mathcal{CH}$, respectively. We use a one-way injective function OW.

$\mathsf{Setup}(1^\kappa)$ returns $\varrho \in_{\mathrm{U}} \{0,1\}^{256}$.

$\mathsf{KGen}(\varrho)$ returns a key pair $(\mathbf{sk}_v, \mathbf{pk}_v)$ which is computed as follows:
(1) $\boldsymbol{A} = \mathsf{Sam}(\varrho)$.
(2) $\mathbf{sk}_v = (\boldsymbol{s}_{v,1}, \boldsymbol{s}_{v,2}) \in_{\mathrm{U}} S_\eta^\ell \times S_\eta^k$.
(3) $\boldsymbol{t}_v = \boldsymbol{A}\boldsymbol{s}_{v,1} + \boldsymbol{s}_{v,2}$.
(4) decomposite $\boldsymbol{t}_v$ into $(\boldsymbol{t}_{v,\mathsf{H}}, \boldsymbol{t}_{v,\mathsf{L}})$ according to $\mathsf{Power2Round}_q$ such that $\boldsymbol{t}_v = 2^d \cdot \boldsymbol{t}_{v,\mathsf{H}} + \boldsymbol{t}_{v,\mathsf{L}}$.
(5) $\mathbf{pk}_v = (\boldsymbol{t}_{v,\mathsf{H}}, \boldsymbol{t}_{v,\mathsf{L}})$.

$\mathsf{Ver}(\varrho, \mathsf{PK}, \mu, (\boldsymbol{w}_{\mathsf{H}}, \boldsymbol{z}, \boldsymbol{h}))$ returns 1 if the following holds, where $\boldsymbol{A} = \mathsf{Sam}(\varrho)$, $\mathsf{PK} = \{\mathbf{pk}_u\}_{u=1}^U$, $\mathbf{pk}_u = (\boldsymbol{t}_{u,\mathsf{H}}, \boldsymbol{t}_{u,\mathsf{L}})$, $\tau_u = H_1(\mathbf{pk}_u, \boldsymbol{w}_{\mathsf{H}}, \mathsf{PK}, \mu)$ and $c_u = H_2(\mathbf{pk}_u, \boldsymbol{w}_{\mathsf{H}}, \mathsf{PK} \setminus \{\mathbf{pk}_u\}, \mu, \tau_u)$, for each $1 \le u \le U$:
(a) $\|\boldsymbol{z}\|_\infty < U(\gamma' - \beta)$.
(b) $\boldsymbol{w}_{\mathsf{H}} = \mathsf{UseHint}_q(\boldsymbol{h}, \boldsymbol{x}, 2U\gamma)$, where $\boldsymbol{x} = \boldsymbol{A}\boldsymbol{z} - 2^d \sum_{u=1}^U c_u \boldsymbol{t}_{u,\mathsf{H}}$.

$\mathsf{Sig}(\varrho, \mathsf{PK}, \mathbf{sk}_v, \mu)$ returns $\sigma = (\boldsymbol{w}_{\mathsf{H}}, \boldsymbol{z}, \boldsymbol{h})$ on the message μ under the public key set $\mathsf{PK} = \{\mathbf{pk}_u\}_{u=1}^U$ by running the following protocol, where $\mathbf{pk}_u = (\boldsymbol{t}_{u,\mathsf{H}}, \boldsymbol{t}_{u,\mathsf{L}})$ for each $1 \le u \le U$. The following protocol is described in the viewpoint of the signer owning the public key $\mathbf{pk}_v$ which corresponds to $\mathbf{sk}_v$. If the time of the iteration exceeds E which is the expected time of the iteration, it returns $\sigma = \perp$.

1st stage proceed to the followings, and then broadcast $(\boldsymbol{g}_v, \boldsymbol{p}_v)$ to the co-signers:
(1.1) $\boldsymbol{A} = \mathsf{Sam}(\varrho)$; $\boldsymbol{y}_v \in_{\mathrm{U}} S_{\gamma'-1}^\ell$; $\boldsymbol{w}_v = \boldsymbol{A}\boldsymbol{y}_v$.
(1.2) $\boldsymbol{g}_v = H_0(\boldsymbol{w}_v)$; $\boldsymbol{p}_v = \mathsf{OW}_{\boldsymbol{g}_v}(\boldsymbol{w}_v)$.

2nd stage After receiving $\{(\boldsymbol{g}_u, \boldsymbol{p}_u)\}_{u \ne v}$, broadcast $\boldsymbol{w}_v$ to the co-signers.

3rd stage After receiving $\{\boldsymbol{w}_u\}_{u \ne v}$, proceed as follows, and then broadcast $\boldsymbol{z}_v$ to the co-signers:
(3.1) abort if $\neg(\boldsymbol{g}_u = H_0(\boldsymbol{w}_u) \wedge \boldsymbol{p}_u = \mathsf{OW}_{\boldsymbol{g}_u}(\boldsymbol{w}_u))$ for some $u \ne v$.
(3.2) $\boldsymbol{w} = \sum_{u=1}^U \boldsymbol{w}_u$; $\boldsymbol{w}_{\mathsf{H}} = \mathsf{HighBits}_q(\boldsymbol{w}, 2U\gamma)$.
(3.3) $\tau_v = H_1(\mathbf{pk}_v, \boldsymbol{w}_{\mathsf{H}}, \mathsf{PK}, \mu)$.
(3.4) $c_v = H_2(\mathbf{pk}_v, \boldsymbol{w}_{\mathsf{H}}, \mathsf{PK} \setminus \{\mathbf{pk}_v\}, \mu, \tau_v)$.
(3.5) $\boldsymbol{z}_v = \boldsymbol{y}_v + c_v \boldsymbol{s}_{v,1}$.
(3.6) restart if $\neg(\|\boldsymbol{z}_v\|_\infty < \gamma' - \beta)$.

4th stage After receiving $\{\boldsymbol{z}_u\}_{u \ne v}$, proceed as follows:
(4.1) $\boldsymbol{z} = \sum_{u=1}^U \boldsymbol{z}_u$.
(4.2) restart if $\neg\left(\left\|\mathsf{LowBits}_q\left(\boldsymbol{A}\boldsymbol{z} - \sum_{u=1}^U c_u \boldsymbol{t}_u, 2U\gamma\right)\right\|_\infty < U(\gamma - \beta)\right)$.
(4.3) $\boldsymbol{h} = \mathsf{MakeHint}_q\left(-\sum_{u=1}^U c_u \boldsymbol{t}_{u,\mathsf{L}}, \boldsymbol{A}\boldsymbol{z} - 2^d \sum_{u=1}^U c_u \boldsymbol{t}_{u,\mathsf{H}}, 2U\gamma\right)$.

Fig. 5. Proposed multisignature scheme

The proposed multisignature scheme is given in Fig. 5. In the full version of this paper, we show the correctness of our multisignature scheme, and evaluate the expected time E of iterations. Especially, we estimate that the restart probabilities ω_1 and ω_2 in (3.6) and (4.2) are $1 - e^{-n\ell\beta/\gamma'}$ and $1 - e^{-nk\beta/\gamma}$, respectively. This can be done in the same way as in [18, Lemma 4.4].

3.3 Security

We now show the security proof of the proposed multisignature scheme.

Theorem 7. *Let $(q, n, k, \ell, d, \gamma, \gamma', \eta, \beta, \theta)$ be parameters as in Table 1, and let* OW *be a one-way injective function such that any QPT adversary breaks* *the one-wayness with probability at most ϵ_{OW}. Assume that the $(T_{\mathrm{MLWE}}, \epsilon_{\mathrm{MLWE}}, \mathsf{Uni}(S_\eta))$-MLWE assumption and $(T_{\mathrm{rMLWE}}, \epsilon_{\mathrm{rMLWE}}, \mathsf{Uni}(S_\eta), \gamma', \beta)$-rMLWE assumption hold. Then, the proposed multisignature signature scheme is $(T, U, \epsilon, Q_S, Q_0, Q_1, Q_2)$-ppk secure in QROM, where*

$$
\begin{aligned}
&T = T_{\mathrm{MLWE}} - \mathrm{poly} = T_{\mathrm{rMLWE}} - \mathrm{poly}, \\
&\epsilon < \epsilon_{\mathrm{MLWE}} + \frac{2\sqrt{Q_1}}{2^{\theta/2}} + \frac{Q_S E(4+\sqrt{2})\sqrt{Q_2 + (Q_S E - 1)U}}{2^{\theta/4}} + Q_S E \epsilon_{\mathrm{rMLWE}} \\
&\quad + 8 \cdot \left(\frac{1}{|\mathcal{CH}|} + 2|\mathcal{CH}|^2 \left(\frac{32U^2\gamma'\gamma}{q} \right)^{kn} \right) \cdot (Q_2 + Q_S U E + 1)^2 + \epsilon_{\boldsymbol{w}_{\mathsf{H}}} + \epsilon_{\mathsf{OW}} + \mathrm{negl}.
\end{aligned}
$$

Here, $\epsilon_{\boldsymbol{w}_{\mathsf{H}}}$ denotes the probability that $\boldsymbol{w}_{\mathsf{H}} = \mathsf{HighBits}_q\left(\boldsymbol{A}\boldsymbol{y} + \sum_{u=2}^{U} \boldsymbol{w}_u, 2U\gamma\right)$ over the choices of $\boldsymbol{A} \in_{\mathrm{U}} R_q^{k\times\ell}$ and $\boldsymbol{y} \in_{\mathrm{U}} S_{\gamma'-1}^{\ell}$ for any $\boldsymbol{w}_{\mathsf{H}}$ which would be output by $\mathsf{HighBits}_q(\boldsymbol{w}, 2U\gamma)$ and any fixed set $\{\boldsymbol{w}_u\}_{u=2}^{U}$.

For the probability $\epsilon_{\boldsymbol{w}_{\mathsf{H}}}$, the following lemma holds. The proof is given in the full paper. This is shown as in that of [18, Lemma 4.7].

Lemma 8. *It holds that*

$$
\epsilon_{\boldsymbol{w}_{\mathsf{H}}} \leq \frac{1}{(2\gamma'-1)^{n\ell}} + \left(\frac{(4U\gamma+1)(4\gamma'+1)}{q} \right)^{nk}.
$$

Proof (Theorem 7). The theorem is proven by the hybrid argument. Let $\mathcal{F}$ be a forger against the proposed multisignature scheme. We denote by Win_k the event that $\mathcal{F}$ wins $\mathbf{Game}_k$ for each $0 \leq k \leq 6$ except $k = 5$, and $\mathsf{Win}_{5,t}$ the event that $\mathcal{F}$ wins $\mathbf{Game}_{5,t}$ for each $0 \leq t \leq Q_s E$. Note that proofs of Lemma 9, 10 and 11, which will be appeared in this proof, are given in the full version of this paper.

$\mathbf{Game}_0$ *(ppk game with simulating the random oracles).* This game coincides with the ppk game of the proposed multisignature scheme as in Fig. 6. Here, the hash functions H_0 and H_2 are simulated by random functions, whereas H_1 is done by the almost compressed Fourier oracle. As mentioned in Subsect. 2.2, the random oracles are perfectly simulated by using random functions H_0 and H_2. Since H_1 is simulated by the almost compressed random oracle with the database D, there is a possibility that some tuple $(\mathbf{pk}, \boldsymbol{w}_{\mathsf{H}}, \mathsf{PK}, \mu)$ is not contained in D, but $H_1(\mathbf{pk}, \boldsymbol{w}_{\mathsf{H}}, \mathsf{PK}, \mu) = \tau$ for some τ in the case where H_1 is a perfectly random function. It follows from Lemma 4 and the $(T, U, \epsilon, Q_S, Q_0, Q_1, Q_2)$-ppk security of the proposed multisignature scheme that $\sqrt{\epsilon} \leq \sqrt{\Pr[\mathsf{Win}_0]} + \sqrt{Q_1/2^{\theta}}$. Since $\epsilon \leq 1$, we have

$$
\Pr[\mathsf{Win}_0] \geq \left(\sqrt{\epsilon} - \sqrt{\frac{Q_1}{2^{\theta}}} \right)^2 = \epsilon + \frac{Q_1}{2^{\theta}} - 2\sqrt{\frac{Q_1}{2^{\theta}} \cdot \epsilon} \geq \epsilon - 2\sqrt{\frac{Q_1}{2^{\theta}}}. \quad (1)
$$

Init $\mathcal{C}$ proceeds as follows:

(1) $H_0 \in_U \mathsf{Fun}(\mathfrak{D}_0, \mathfrak{R}_0)$;

(2) $H_2 \in_U \mathsf{Fun}(\mathfrak{D}_2, \mathcal{CH})$.

(3) $\varrho \leftarrow \mathsf{Setup}(1^\kappa)$.

(4) $(\mathbf{sk}^*, \mathbf{pk}^*) \leftarrow \mathsf{KGen}(\varrho)$, where $\mathbf{sk}^* = (\boldsymbol{s}_1^*, \boldsymbol{s}_2^*)$ and $\mathbf{pk}^* = (\boldsymbol{t}_\mathsf{H}^*, \boldsymbol{t}_\mathsf{L}^*)$.

(5) send $(\varrho, \mathbf{pk}^*)$ to $\mathcal{F}$.

H_0 **oracle** On $|\boldsymbol{w}\rangle|\psi\rangle$, reply $|\boldsymbol{w}\rangle|\psi \oplus H_0(\boldsymbol{w})\rangle$.

H_1 **oracle** On $|\mathbf{pk}, \boldsymbol{w}_\mathsf{H}, \mathsf{PK}, \mu\rangle|\tau\rangle$, reply the hash value by using a database D.

H_2 **oracle** On $|\chi\rangle|\psi\rangle$, reply $|\chi\rangle|\psi \oplus H_2(\chi)\rangle$, where $\chi = (\mathbf{pk}, \boldsymbol{w}_\mathsf{H}, P, \mu, \tau)$.

Challenge Given $(\mathsf{PK}^*, \mu^*, \sigma^*)$ by $\mathcal{F}$, $\mathcal{C}$ returns 1 if the followings hold, where $\mathsf{PK}^* = \{\mathbf{pk}_u^*\}_{u=1}^U$, $\sigma^* = (\boldsymbol{w}_\mathsf{H}^*, \boldsymbol{z}^*, \boldsymbol{h}^*)$, and for each $1 \le u \le U$, $\mathbf{pk}_u^* = (\boldsymbol{t}_{u,\mathsf{H}}^*, \boldsymbol{t}_{u,\mathsf{L}}^*)$, $\tau_u^* = H_1(\mathbf{pk}_u^*, \boldsymbol{w}_\mathsf{H}^*, \mathsf{PK}^*, \mu^*)$, and $c_u^* = H_2(\mathbf{pk}_u^*, \boldsymbol{w}_\mathsf{H}^*, \mathsf{PK}^* \setminus \{\mathbf{pk}_u^*\}, \mu^*, \tau_u^*)$:

- $\mathbf{pk}^* \in \mathsf{PK}^*$,
- (μ^*, PK^*) does not queried,
- σ^* is valid, i.e.
  (a) $\|\boldsymbol{z}^*\|_\infty < U(\gamma' - \beta)$, and
  (b) $\boldsymbol{w}_\mathsf{H}^* = \mathsf{UseHint}_q(\boldsymbol{h}^*, \boldsymbol{x}^*, 2U\gamma)$, where $\boldsymbol{x}^* = \boldsymbol{A}\boldsymbol{z}^* - 2^d \sum_{u=1}^U c_u^* \boldsymbol{t}_{u,\mathsf{H}}^*$.

Sign When $\mathcal{F}$ makes an i-th query $(\mathsf{PK}^{(i)}, \mu^{(i)})$ of a set $\mathsf{PK}^{(i)} = \{\mathbf{pk}_u^{(i)}\}_{u=1}^U$ and a message $\mu^{(i)}$ such that $\mathbf{pk}_1^{(i)} = \mathbf{pk}^*$, $\mathcal{C}$ finally returns $\sigma^{(i)} = (\boldsymbol{w}_\mathsf{H}^{(i)}, \boldsymbol{z}^{(i)}, \boldsymbol{h}^{(i)})$ after running the following protocol, where $\mathbf{pk}_u^{(i)} = (\boldsymbol{t}_{u,\mathsf{H}}^{(i)}, \boldsymbol{t}_{u,\mathsf{L}}^{(i)})$ for each $2 \le u \le U$:

1st stage proceed as follows, and then send $(\boldsymbol{g}_1^{(i)}, \boldsymbol{p}_1^{(i)})$ to $\mathcal{F}$:

(1.1) $\boldsymbol{A} = \mathsf{Sam}(\varrho)$; $\boldsymbol{y}_1^{(i)} \in_U S_{\gamma'-1}^\ell$; $\boldsymbol{w}_1^{(i)} = \boldsymbol{A}\boldsymbol{y}_1^{(i)}$.

(1.2) $\boldsymbol{g}_1^{(i)} = H_0(\boldsymbol{w}_1^{(i)})$; $\boldsymbol{p}_1^{(i)} = \mathsf{OW}_{\boldsymbol{g}_1^{(i)}}(\boldsymbol{w}_1^{(i)})$.

2nd stage After receiving $\{(\boldsymbol{g}_u^{(i)}, \boldsymbol{p}_u^{(i)})\}_{u=2}^U$, send $\boldsymbol{w}_1^{(i)}$ to $\mathcal{F}$.

3rd stage After receiving $\{\boldsymbol{w}_u^{(i)}\}_{u=2}^U$, proceed as follows, and then send $\boldsymbol{z}_1^{(i)}$ to $\mathcal{F}$:

(3.1) abort if $\neg(\boldsymbol{g}_u^{(i)} = H_0(\boldsymbol{w}_u^{(i)}) \wedge \boldsymbol{p}_u^{(i)} = \mathsf{OW}_{\boldsymbol{g}_u^{(i)}}(\boldsymbol{w}_u^{(i)}))$ for some $2 \le u \le U$.

(3.2) $\boldsymbol{w}^{(i)} = \sum_{u=1}^U \boldsymbol{w}_u^{(i)}$; $\boldsymbol{w}_\mathsf{H}^{(i)} = \mathsf{HighBits}_q(\boldsymbol{w}^{(i)}, 2U\gamma)$.

(3.3) $\tau_1^{(i)} = H_1(\mathbf{pk}^*, \boldsymbol{w}_\mathsf{H}^{(i)}, \mathsf{PK}^{(i)}, \mu^{(i)})$.

(3.4) $c_1^{(i)} = H_2(\mathbf{pk}^*, \boldsymbol{w}_\mathsf{H}^{(i)}, \mathsf{PK}^{(i)} \setminus \{\mathbf{pk}^*\}, \mu^{(i)}, \tau_1^{(i)})$.

(3.5) $\boldsymbol{z}_1^{(i)} = \boldsymbol{y}_1^{(i)} + c_1^{(i)} \boldsymbol{s}_1^*$.

(3.6) restart if $\neg(\|\boldsymbol{z}_1^{(i)}\|_\infty < \gamma' - \beta)$.

4th stage After receiving $\{\boldsymbol{z}_u^{(i)}\}_{u=2}^U$, proceed as follows:

(4.1) $\boldsymbol{z}^{(i)} = \sum_{u=1}^U \boldsymbol{z}_u^{(i)}$.

(4.2) restart if $\neg(\|\mathsf{LowBits}_q(\boldsymbol{A}\boldsymbol{z}^{(i)} - \sum_{u=1}^U c_u^{(i)} \boldsymbol{t}_u^{(i)}, 2U\gamma)\|_\infty < U(\gamma - \beta))$.

(4.3) $\boldsymbol{h}^{(i)} = \mathsf{MakeHint}_q(-\sum_{u=1}^U c_u^{(i)} \boldsymbol{t}_{u,\mathsf{L}}^{(i)}, \boldsymbol{A}\boldsymbol{z}^{(i)} - 2^d \sum_{u=1}^U c_u^{(i)} \boldsymbol{t}_{u,\mathsf{H}}^{(i)}, 2U\gamma)$.

Fig. 6. Game_0

Game$_1$. At (1) of **Init** phase, $\mathcal{C}$ chooses H_0 uniformly at random from a set of all polynomials of degree $2(Q_0 + Q_S UE)$, instead of $H_0 \in_U \mathsf{Fun}(\mathfrak{D}_0, \mathfrak{R}_0)$. Since $\mathcal{F}$ makes at most Q_0 queries, and $\mathcal{C}$ computes at most UE hash values of H_0 for each signing oracle query, it follows from Lemma 3 that

$$\Pr[\mathsf{Win}_1] = \Pr[\mathsf{Win}_0]. \tag{2}$$

2nd stage After receiving $\{(\boldsymbol{g}_u^{(i)}, \boldsymbol{p}_u^{(i)})\}_{u=2}^{U}$, proceed as follows, and then send $\boldsymbol{w}_1^{(i)}$ to $\mathcal{F}$:

(2.1) for each $2 \le u \le U$,

(2.1a) compute the roots $\{\boldsymbol{r}_{u,j}^{(i)}\}_j$ of $H_0 - \boldsymbol{g}_u^{(i)}$,

(2.1b) find $\boldsymbol{r}_u^{(i)} \in \{\boldsymbol{r}_{u,j}^{(i)}\}_j$ such that $\boldsymbol{p}_u^{(i)} = \mathsf{OW}_{\boldsymbol{g}_u^{(i)}}(\boldsymbol{r}_u^{(i)})$, and

(2.1c) abort if there is no such $\boldsymbol{r}_u^{(i)}$.

(2.2) $\boldsymbol{w}^{(i)} = \boldsymbol{w}_1^{(i)} + \sum_{u=2}^{U} \boldsymbol{r}_u^{(i)}$.

(2.3) $\boldsymbol{w}_{\mathsf{H}}^{(i)} = \mathsf{HighBits}_q(\boldsymbol{w}^{(i)}, 2U\gamma)$.

(2.4) $\tau_1^{(i)} = H_1(\mathbf{pk}^*, \boldsymbol{w}_{\mathsf{H}}^{(i)}, \mathsf{PK}^{(i)}, \mu^{(i)})$.

(2.5) $c_1^{(i)} = H_2(\mathbf{pk}^*, \boldsymbol{w}_{\mathsf{H}}^{(i)}, \mathsf{PK}^{(i)} \setminus \{\mathbf{pk}^*\}, \mu^{(i)}, \tau_1^{(i)})$.

3rd stage After receiving $\{\boldsymbol{w}_u^{(i)}\}_{u=2}^{U}$, proceed as follows, and then send $\boldsymbol{z}_1^{(i)}$ to $\mathcal{F}$:

(3.1) abort if $\neg(\boldsymbol{r}_u^{(i)} = \boldsymbol{w}_u^{(i)})$ for some $2 \le u \le U$.

(3.2) $\boldsymbol{z}_1^{(i)} = \boldsymbol{y}_1^{(i)} + c_1^{(i)} \boldsymbol{s}_1^*$.

(3.3) restart if $\neg(\left\|\boldsymbol{z}_1^{(i)}\right\|_\infty < \gamma' - \beta)$.

Fig. 7. Description of **Game**$_2$ changed from **Game**$_1$

Game$_2$. In this game, $c_1^{(i)}$ is computed at **2nd stage** in **Sign** phase, instead of **3rd stage** in **Game**$_1$. In order to accomplish this change, $\boldsymbol{w}_{\mathsf{H}}^{(i)}$ is also required to be computed at **2nd stage**. Hence, **2nd stage** and **3rd stage** in **Sign** phase are replaced with Fig. 7.

Before showing the relationship between Win_1 and Win_2, we note the process (2.1a). As mentioned in Subsect. 2.2, the roots of the polynomials of degree $2(Q_0 + Q_S UE)$ can be computed in polynomial time, and hence the process (2.1a) can be done in polynomial time.

Assume that $\mathcal{C}$ does not abort at (2.1c) on **Game**$_2$. In this case, the injectivity of OW implies that the condition $\boldsymbol{r}_u^{(i)} = \boldsymbol{w}_u^{(i)}$ checked in (3.1) on **Game**$_2$ is equivalent to the condition $\boldsymbol{g}_u^{(i)} = H_0(\boldsymbol{w}_u^{(i)}) \wedge \boldsymbol{p}_u^{(i)} = \mathsf{OW}_{\boldsymbol{g}_u^{(i)}}(\boldsymbol{w}_u^{(i)})$ checked in (3.1) on **Game**$_1$. Thus we can consider that $\mathcal{C}$ also does not abort in (3.1) on **Game**$_2$ under the assumption that $\mathcal{C}$ does not abort at (2.1c).

We now evaluate the abort probability in (2.1c) on **Game**$_2$. To proceed to **Sign** phase, $\mathcal{F}$ must send a set $\left\{\left(\boldsymbol{g}_u^{(i)}, \boldsymbol{p}_u^{(i)}\right)\right\}_{u=2}^{U}$ to $\mathcal{C}$, such that there exist $\boldsymbol{w}_u^{(i)}$'s which satisfy $\boldsymbol{g}_u^{(i)} = H_0\left(\boldsymbol{w}_u^{(i)}\right)$ and $\boldsymbol{p}_u^{(i)} = \mathsf{OW}_{\boldsymbol{g}_u^{(i)}}\left(\boldsymbol{w}_u^{(i)}\right)$. It follows from the injectivity of OW that there is at most one $\boldsymbol{w}_u^{(i)}$ for each i and u. Therefore there must exist $\boldsymbol{r}^{(i)}$ which satisfies $\boldsymbol{p}_u^{(i)} = \mathsf{OW}_{\boldsymbol{g}_u^{(i)}}\left(\boldsymbol{r}_u^{(i)}\right)$, and hence we can consider that $\mathcal{C}$ never abort in (2.1c).

We have

$$\Pr[\mathsf{Win}_2] = \Pr[\mathsf{Win}_1], \tag{3}$$

Game$_3$. At (2.4) during each execution of **Sign** in this game, $\mathcal{C}$ is changed to abort if D have already contained the tuple $\left(\mathbf{pk}^*, \boldsymbol{w}_{\mathsf{H}}^{(i)}, \mathsf{PK}^{(i)}, \mu^{(i)}\right)$. Otherwise, $\left(\mathbf{pk}^*, \boldsymbol{w}_{\mathsf{H}}^{(i)}, \mathsf{PK}^{(i)}, \mu^{(i)}\right)$ is regarded as a special point on the almost compressed

Fourier oracle, and then $\mathcal{C}$ appends $\sum_{\tau_1^{(i)}} \left|\tau_1^{(i)}\right\rangle$ into the database D as the hash value of $\left(\mathbf{pk}^*, \boldsymbol{w}_{\mathsf{H}}^{(i)}, \mathsf{PK}^{(i)}, \mu^{(i)}\right)$.

In order to evaluate the abort probability due to the change in **Game**$_3$, we focus on the probability that $\mathcal{F}$ finds $\boldsymbol{w}_{\mathsf{H}}^{(i)}$ before querying $\left(\mathbf{pk}^*, \boldsymbol{w}_{\mathsf{H}}^{(i)}, \mathsf{PK}^{(i)}, \mu^{(i)}\right)$. There are two ways that $\mathcal{F}$ finds $\boldsymbol{w}_{\mathsf{H}}^{(i)}$.

The first one is to find it from $\boldsymbol{g}_1^{(i)}$ and $\boldsymbol{p}_1^{(i)}$, because $\boldsymbol{g}_1^{(i)}$ and $\boldsymbol{p}_1^{(i)}$ are computed from $\boldsymbol{w}_1^{(i)}$. Since H_0 is a polynomial of degree $2(Q_0+Q_SUE)$ and its coefficients are hidden to $\mathcal{F}$, it is difficult for $\mathcal{F}$ to determine $\boldsymbol{w}_1^{(i)}$ from H_0 [25]. Moreover, it follows from the one-wayness of OW that such a vector also cannot be determined from OW. Therefore, the abort probability due to these reasons is at most $\epsilon_{\mathsf{OW}}+$ negl.

The second one is that $\boldsymbol{w}_{\mathsf{H}}^{(i)}$ has been found at the process (2.3) for a randomly chosen $\boldsymbol{y}_1^{(i)} \in_{\mathrm{U}} S_{\gamma'-1}^{\ell}$ and any $\left\{\boldsymbol{w}_u^{(i)}\right\}_{u=2}^{U}$ given from $\mathcal{F}$. This can be evaluated by the probability $\epsilon_{\boldsymbol{w}_{\mathsf{H}}}$ that $\boldsymbol{w}_{\mathsf{H}} = \mathsf{HighBits}_q\left(\boldsymbol{A}\boldsymbol{y} + \sum_{u=2}^{U} \boldsymbol{w}_u, 2U\gamma\right)$ holds for any $\boldsymbol{w}_{\mathsf{H}}$ which would be output by $\mathsf{HighBits}_q(\boldsymbol{w}, 2U\gamma)$ and any fixed set $\{\boldsymbol{w}_u\}_{u=2}^{U}$, where the probability is taken over the choices of $\boldsymbol{A} \in_{\mathrm{U}} R_q^{k\times\ell}$ and $\boldsymbol{y} \in_{\mathrm{U}} S_{\gamma'-1}^{\ell}$.

Then we have

$$|\Pr[\mathsf{Win}_3] - \Pr[\mathsf{Win}_2]| \leq \epsilon_{\mathsf{OW}} + \epsilon_{\boldsymbol{w}_{\mathsf{H}}} + \text{negl}, \tag{4}$$

Game$_4$. At (2.4) during each execution of **Sign** in this game, $\mathcal{C}$ is changed to appends $\left|\tau_1^{(i)}\right\rangle$ for $\tau_1^{(i)} \in_{\mathrm{U}} \{0,1\}^{\theta}$ into the database as the hash value of $\left(\mathbf{pk}^*, \boldsymbol{w}_{\mathsf{H}}^{(i)}, \mathsf{PK}^{(i)}, \mu^{(i)}\right)$, instead of $\sum_{\tau_1^{(i)}} \left|\tau_1^{(i)}\right\rangle$ in **Game**$_3$. From Lemma 5, this change does not affect the probability of the measurement of D. Then we have

$$\Pr[\mathsf{Win}_4] = \Pr[\mathsf{Win}_3]. \tag{5}$$

Game$_{5,t}$. In this game, we consider the process (2.5) of **Sign**. **Sign** phase is queried at most Q_s times by $\mathcal{F}$. Moreover, for each query by $\mathcal{F}$, the process (2.5) is executed at most E times. Then the total number of the execution of (2.5) during the game is at most Q_sE. Fix an index $0 \leq t \leq Q_sE$. In **Game**$_{5,t}$, on the k-th execution of (2.5) for $1 \leq k \leq t$, $\mathcal{C}$ sets the hash value $c_1^{(i)}$ as follows: chooses $c_1^{(i)} \in_{\mathrm{U}} \mathcal{CH}$ and set $H_2\left(\mathbf{pk}^*, \boldsymbol{w}_{\mathsf{H}}^{(i)}, \mathsf{PK}^{(i)} \setminus \{\mathbf{pk}^*\}, \mu^{(i)}, \tau_1^{(i)}\right) = c_1^{(i)}$.

When $t=0$, the replacement on $c_1^{(i)}$ does not happen, and hence we have

$$\Pr[\mathsf{Win}_{5,0}] = \Pr[\mathsf{Win}_4]. \tag{6}$$

Otherwise, we employ Lemma 2 to evaluate the difference between the probability of $\mathsf{Win}_{5,t}$ and that of $\mathsf{Win}_{5,t+1}$. We construct an algorithm $\mathcal{A} = (\mathcal{A}_0, \mathcal{A}_C, \mathcal{A}_2)$ depicted in Fig. 8. Observe that $\mathbf{Exp}^{\mathsf{Reprog}}_{\mathfrak{D}_2,\mathcal{CH},1,\mathcal{A}}$ and $\mathbf{Exp}^{\mathsf{Reprog}}_{\mathfrak{D}_2,\mathcal{CH},0,\mathcal{A}}$ coincide with **Game**$_{5,t}$ and **Game**$_{5,t+1}$, respectively. Since $\mathcal{F}$ queries to H_2 at

$\mathcal{A}_0(1^\kappa)$ executes $\mathbf{Game}_{5,t}$ by playing the role of $\mathcal{C}$ and interacting with $\mathcal{F}$ just until the $(t+1)$-th execution of (2.1c), and then returns st $=$ $\left(H_0, \mathbf{sk}^*, \mathbf{pk}^*, \mathsf{PK}^{(i)}, \mu^{(i)}, \boldsymbol{y}_1^{(i)}, \boldsymbol{w}_1^{(i)}, \left\{\boldsymbol{g}_u^{(i)}\right\}_{u=1}^U, \left\{\boldsymbol{p}_u^{(i)}\right\}_{u=1}^U, \left\{\boldsymbol{r}_u^{(i)}\right\}_{u=2}^U\right)$.

$\mathcal{A}_C(\text{st})$ executes (2.2), (2.3) and (2.4) on the $(t+1)$-th execution, and then outputs $\left(\mathbf{pk}^*, \boldsymbol{w}_{\mathsf{H}}^{(i)}, \mathsf{PK}^{(i)} \setminus \{\mathbf{pk}^*\}, \mu^{(i)}, \tau_1^{(i)}\right)$ and st.

$\mathcal{A}_2(c_1^{(i)}, \text{st})$ executes $\mathbf{Game}_{5,t}$ until the end, and then returns $\mathcal{C}$'s final output.

Fig. 8. Adversary $\mathcal{A}$ of the reprogram problem from $\mathbf{Game}_{5,t}$

1st stage proceed as follows, and then send $(\boldsymbol{g}_1^{(i)}, \boldsymbol{p}_1^{(i)})$ to $\mathcal{F}$:
(1.1) $\boldsymbol{A} = \mathsf{Sam}(\varrho)$.
(1.2) $c_1^{(i)} \in_{\text{U}} \mathcal{CH}$.
(1.3) $\boldsymbol{z}_1^{(i)} \in_{\text{U}} S^{\ell}_{\gamma'-\beta-1}$.
(1.4) $\nu \in_{B_{\omega_1}} \{0,1\}$, where $\omega_1 = 1 - e^{-n\ell\beta/\gamma'}$.
(1.5) $\boldsymbol{w}_1^{(i)} = \boldsymbol{A}\boldsymbol{z}_1^{(i)} - c_1^{(i)}(\boldsymbol{t}^* - \boldsymbol{s}_2^*)$ if $\nu = 0$, or $\boldsymbol{w}_1^{(i)} \in_{\text{U}} R_q$ otherwise.
(1.6) $\boldsymbol{g}_1^{(i)} = H_0(\boldsymbol{w}_1^{(i)})$; $\boldsymbol{p}_1^{(i)} = \mathsf{OW}_{\boldsymbol{g}_1^{(i)}}(\boldsymbol{w}_1^{(i)})$.

2nd stage After receiving $\{(\boldsymbol{g}_u^{(i)}, \boldsymbol{p}_u^{(i)})\}_{u=2}^U$, proceeds as follows, and then send $\boldsymbol{w}_1^{(i)}$ to $\mathcal{F}$:
(2.1) for each $2 \le u \le U$,
(2.1a) compute the roots $\{\boldsymbol{r}_{u,j}^{(i)}\}_j$ of $H_0 - \boldsymbol{g}_u^{(i)}$,
(2.1b) find $\boldsymbol{r}_u^{(i)} \in \{\boldsymbol{r}_{u,j}^{(i)}\}_j$ such that $\boldsymbol{p}_u^{(i)} = \mathsf{OW}_{\boldsymbol{g}_u^{(i)}}(\boldsymbol{r}_u^{(i)})$,
(2.1c) abort if there is no such $\boldsymbol{r}_u^{(i)}$.
(2.2) $\boldsymbol{w}^{(i)} = \boldsymbol{w}_1^{(i)} + \sum_{u=2}^U \boldsymbol{r}_u^{(i)}$.
(2.3) $\boldsymbol{w}_{\mathsf{H}}^{(i)} = \mathsf{HighBits}_q(\boldsymbol{w}^{(i)}, 2U\gamma)$.
(2.4) abort if D has already contained $(\mathbf{pk}^*, \boldsymbol{w}_{\mathsf{H}}^{(i)}, \mathsf{PK}^{(i)}, \mu^{(i)})$.
(2.5) $\tau_1^{(i)} \in_{\text{U}} \{0,1\}^\theta$; append $((\mathbf{pk}^*, \boldsymbol{w}_{\mathsf{H}}^{(i)}, \mathsf{PK}^{(i)}, \mu^{(i)}), \tau_1^{(i)})$ to D.
(2.6) set $H_2(\mathbf{pk}^*, \boldsymbol{w}_{\mathsf{H}}^{(i)}, \mathsf{PK}^{(i)} \setminus \{\mathbf{pk}^*\}, \mu^{(i)}, \tau_1^{(i)}) = c_1^{(i)}$.

3rd stage After receiving $\{\boldsymbol{w}_u^{(i)}\}_{u=2}^U$, proceed as follows, and then send $\boldsymbol{z}_1^{(i)}$ to $\mathcal{F}$:
(3.1) abort if $\neg(\boldsymbol{r}_u^{(i)} = \boldsymbol{w}_u^{(i)})$ for some $2 \le u \le U$.
(3.2) restart if $\nu = 1$.

Fig. 9. Description of $\mathbf{Game}_6$ changed from $\mathbf{Game}_{5,Q_sE}$

most Q_2 times and $\mathcal{C}$ acted by $\mathcal{A}_0$ queries at most tU times, the number of access H_2 by $\mathcal{A}_0$ is at most $Q_2 + tU$. The uniform choice of $\tau_1^{(i)}$ over $\{0,1\}^\theta$ by $\mathcal{A}_C$ at (2.4) implies that the collision-entropy can be evaluated by θ.

Then, for $0 \le t \le Q_sE - 1$, it follows from Lemma 2 that

$$|\Pr[\mathsf{Win}_{5,t+1}] - \Pr[\mathsf{Win}_{5,t}]| \le (4+\sqrt{2})\sqrt{Q_2 + tU}\,2^{-\theta/4}. \tag{7}$$

$\mathbf{Game}_6$. In this game, the way of generating $\left(\boldsymbol{w}_{\mathsf{H}}^{(i)}, c_1^{(i)}, \boldsymbol{z}_1^{(i)}\right)$ is changed. Concretely, **1st stage**, **2nd stage** and **3rd stage** in **Sign** phase are replaced with Fig. 9. The following lemma shows the relationship between Win_{5,Q_sE} and Win_6.

This proof is based on that of [18, Lemma 4.3] for the case $\nu = 0$, and that of [2, Theorem 5] for the case $\nu = 1$[1].

Lemma 9. *It holds that*

$$|\Pr[\mathsf{Win}_6] - \Pr[\mathsf{Win}_{5,Q_sE}]| \le Q_S E \epsilon_{\text{rMLWE}}. \tag{8}$$

Game$_7$. In this game, (1.5) of **1st stage** in **Sign** phase is replaced with $\boldsymbol{w}_1^{(i)} = \boldsymbol{A}\boldsymbol{z}_1^{(i)} - c_1^{(i)}(\boldsymbol{t}^* - \boldsymbol{s}^{(i)})$ where $\boldsymbol{s}^{(i)} \in_{\mathrm{U}} S_\eta^k$ instead of $\boldsymbol{w}_1^{(i)} = \boldsymbol{A}\boldsymbol{z}_1^{(i)} - c_1^{(i)}(\boldsymbol{t}^* - \boldsymbol{s}_2^*)$, if $\nu = 0$. The following lemma guarantees that this change does not affect.

Lemma 10. *It holds that*

$$\Pr[\mathsf{Win}_7] = \Pr[\mathsf{Win}_6]. \tag{9}$$

Game$_8$. In this game, $\mathbf{pk}^* = (\boldsymbol{t}_1^*, \boldsymbol{t}_0^*)$ is generated in a way that $\boldsymbol{t}^* = 2^d \cdot \boldsymbol{t}_1^* + \boldsymbol{t}_0^*$ for $\boldsymbol{t}^* \in_{\mathrm{U}} R_q^k$, instead of $\boldsymbol{t}^* = \boldsymbol{A}\boldsymbol{s}_1^* + \boldsymbol{s}_2^*$ in **Init** phase. Therefore, we have

$$|\Pr[\mathsf{Win}_8] - \Pr[\mathsf{Win}_7]| \le \epsilon_{\text{MLWE}}. \tag{10}$$

The Upper Bound of Winning Probability of **Game**$_8$. We evaluate the upper bound of the winning probability of **Game**$_8$ by using the GSPB game. The winning probability is evaluated by the following lemma. We can prove the lemma by the combination of the proofs of [19, Theorem 3.4] and [18, Lemma 4.5].

Lemma 11. *It holds that*

$$\Pr[\mathsf{Win}_8] < 8 \cdot \left(\frac{1}{|\mathcal{CH}|} + 2|\mathcal{CH}|^2\left(\frac{32U^2\gamma'\gamma}{q}\right)^{kn}\right) \cdot (Q_2 + Q_S U E + 1)^2. \tag{11}$$

Thus, we have

$$\begin{aligned}\epsilon < \epsilon_{\text{MLWE}} + \frac{2\sqrt{Q_1}}{2^{\theta/2}} + \frac{Q_S E(4+\sqrt{2})\sqrt{Q_2 + (Q_S E - 1)U}}{2^{\theta/4}} + Q_S E \epsilon_{\text{rMLWE}} \\ + 8 \cdot \left(\frac{1}{|\mathcal{CH}|} + 2|\mathcal{CH}|^2\left(\frac{32U^2\gamma'\gamma}{q}\right)^{kn}\right) \cdot (Q_2 + Q_S U E + 1)^2 + \epsilon_{w_{\mathsf{H}}} + \epsilon_{\mathsf{OW}} + \text{negl}.\end{aligned}$$

The proof is completed. □

Acknowledgements. We would like to thank anonymous reviewers for their valuable comments and suggestions. We are also grateful to Akira Takahashi for his fruitful comments on the security proof. This work was supported in part by JSPS KAKENHI Grant Numbers JP18K11288 and JP19K20272.

[1] [7] pointed out that $\boldsymbol{w}_1^{(i)}$ in the case where $\mathcal{C}$ restarts should be simulated strictly. We employ a method by [2,3] to deal with the case.

References

1. Abdalla, M., Fouque, P.A., Lyubashevsky, V., Tibouchi, M.: Tightly secure signatures from lossy identification schemes. J. Cryptol. **29**(3), 597–631 (2016). https://doi.org/10.1007/s00145-015-9203-7
2. Barthe, G., et al.: Masking the GLP lattice-based signature scheme at any order. Cryptology ePrint Archive, Report 2018/381 (2018). https://eprint.iacr.org/2018/381
3. Barthe, G., et al.: Masking the GLP lattice-based signature scheme at any order. In: Nielsen, J.B., Rijmen, V. (eds.) EUROCRYPT 2018. LNCS, vol. 10821, pp. 354–384. Springer, Cham (2018). https://doi.org/10.1007/978-3-319-78375-8_12
4. Bellare, M., Neven, G.: Multi-signatures in the plain public-key model and a general forking lemma. In: Proceedings of the 13th ACM Conference on Computer and Communications Security, CCS 2006, pp. 390–399. ACM, New York (2006). https://doi.org/10.1145/1180405.1180453
5. Boneh, D., Dagdelen, Ö., Fischlin, M., Lehmann, A., Schaffner, C., Zhandry, M.: Random oracles in a quantum world. In: Lee, D.H., Wang, X. (eds.) ASIACRYPT 2011. LNCS, vol. 7073, pp. 41–69. Springer, Heidelberg (2011). https://doi.org/10.1007/978-3-642-25385-0_3
6. de Castro, A.: Quantum one-way permutation over the finite field of two elements. Quantum Inf. Process. **16**(6) (2017). https://doi.org/10.1007/s11128-017-1599-6
7. Damågrd, I., Orlandi, C., Takahashi, A., Tibouchi, M.: Two-round n-out-of-n and multi-signatures and trapdoor commitment from lattices. Cryptology ePrint Archive, Report 2020/1110 (2020). https://eprint.iacr.org/2020/1110
8. Don, J., Fehr, S., Majenz, C., Schaffner, C.: Security of the Fiat-Shamir transformation in the quantum random-oracle model. In: Boldyreva, A., Micciancio, D. (eds.) CRYPTO 2019. LNCS, vol. 11693, pp. 356–383. Springer, Cham (2019). https://doi.org/10.1007/978-3-030-26951-7_13
9. Ducas, L., et al.: CRYSTALS-Dilithium: a lattice-based digital signature scheme. IACR Trans. Cryptogr. Hardware Embed. Syst. **2018**(1), 238–268 (2018). https://doi.org/10.13154/tches.v2018.i1.238-268
10. El Bansarkhani, R., Sturm, J.: An efficient lattice-based multisignature scheme with applications to bitcoins. In: Foresti, S., Persiano, G. (eds.) CANS 2016. LNCS, vol. 10052, pp. 140–155. Springer, Cham (2016). https://doi.org/10.1007/978-3-319-48965-0_9
11. Fiat, A., Shamir, A.: How to prove yourself: practical solutions to identification and signature problems. In: Odlyzko, A.M. (ed.) CRYPTO 1986. LNCS, vol. 263, pp. 186–194. Springer, Heidelberg (1987). https://doi.org/10.1007/3-540-47721-7_12
12. Fujisaki, E., Okamoto, T.: Secure integration of asymmetric and symmetric encryption schemes. J. Cryptol. **26**(1), 80–101 (2013)
13. Fukumitsu, M., Hasegawa, S.: A tightly-secure lattice-based multisignature. In: Proceedings of the 6th on ASIA Public-Key Cryptography Workshop, APKC 2019, pp. 3–11. ACM, New York (2019). https://doi.org/10.1145/3327958.3329542. http://doi.acm.org/10.1145/3327958.3329542
14. Gentry, C., Peikert, C., Vaikuntanathan, V.: Trapdoors for hard lattices and new cryptographic constructions. In: Proceedings of the Fortieth Annual ACM Symposium on Theory of Computing, STOC 2008, pp. 197–206. ACM, New York (2008). https://doi.org/10.1145/1374376.1374407. http://doi.acm.org/10.1145/1374376.1374407

15. Güneysu, T., Lyubashevsky, V., Pöppelmann, T.: Practical lattice-based cryptography: a signature scheme for embedded systems. In: Prouff, E., Schaumont, P. (eds.) CHES 2012. LNCS, vol. 7428, pp. 530–547. Springer, Heidelberg (2012). https://doi.org/10.1007/978-3-642-33027-8_31
16. Itakura, K., Nakamura, K.: A public-key cryptosystem suitable for digital multisignature. NEC Res. Dev. **71**, 1–8 (1983)
17. Katz, J., Wang, N.: Efficiency improvements for signature schemes with tight security reductions. In: Proceedings of the 10th ACM Conference on Computer and Communications Security, CCS 2003, pp. 155–164. ACM, New York (2003). https://doi.org/10.1145/948109.948132
18. Kiltz, E., Lyubashevsky, V., Schaffner, C.: A concrete treatment of Fiat-Shamir signatures in the quantum random-oracle model. Cryptology ePrint Archive, Report 2017/916 (2017). https://eprint.iacr.org/2017/916
19. Kiltz, E., Lyubashevsky, V., Schaffner, C.: A concrete treatment of Fiat-Shamir signatures in the quantum random-oracle model. In: Nielsen, J.B., Rijmen, V. (eds.) EUROCRYPT 2018. LNCS, vol. 10822, pp. 552–586. Springer, Cham (2018). https://doi.org/10.1007/978-3-319-78372-7_18
20. Liu, Q., Zhandry, M.: Revisiting post-quantum Fiat-Shamir. In: Boldyreva, A., Micciancio, D. (eds.) CRYPTO 2019. LNCS, vol. 11693, pp. 326–355. Springer, Cham (2019). https://doi.org/10.1007/978-3-030-26951-7_12
21. Nielsen, M.A., Chuang, I.L.: Quantum Computation and Quantum Information. Cambridge University Press, Cambridge (2000)
22. NIST: Post-quantum cryptography (2017). https://csrc.nist.gov/Projects/Post-Quantum-Cryptography. Accessed 17 Nov 2019
23. Peikert, C., Waters, B.: Lossy trapdoor functions and their applications. In: Proceedings of the Fortieth Annual ACM Symposium on Theory of Computing, STOC 2008, pp. 187–196. ACM, New York (2008). https://doi.org/10.1145/1374376.1374406. http://doi.acm.org/10.1145/1374376.1374406
24. Shor, P.W.: Polynomial-time algorithms for prime factorization and discrete logarithms on a quantum computer. SIAM Rev. **41**(2), 303–332 (1999). https://doi.org/10.1137/S0036144598347011
25. Targhi, E.E., Unruh, D.: Post-quantum security of the Fujisaki-Okamoto and OAEP transforms. In: Hirt, M., Smith, A. (eds.) TCC 2016. LNCS, vol. 9986, pp. 192–216. Springer, Heidelberg (2016). https://doi.org/10.1007/978-3-662-53644-5_8
26. Unruh, D.: Non-interactive zero-knowledge proofs in the quantum random oracle model. In: Oswald, E., Fischlin, M. (eds.) EUROCRYPT 2015. LNCS, vol. 9057, pp. 755–784. Springer, Heidelberg (2015). https://doi.org/10.1007/978-3-662-46803-6_25
27. Zhandry, M.: Secure identity-based encryption in the quantum random oracle model. In: Safavi-Naini, R., Canetti, R. (eds.) CRYPTO 2012. LNCS, vol. 7417, pp. 758–775. Springer, Heidelberg (2012). https://doi.org/10.1007/978-3-642-32009-5_44
28. Zhandry, M.: How to record quantum queries, and applications to quantum indifferentiability. In: Boldyreva, A., Micciancio, D. (eds.) CRYPTO 2019. LNCS, vol. 11693, pp. 239–268. Springer, Cham (2019). https://doi.org/10.1007/978-3-030-26951-7_9

Achieving Pairing-Free Aggregate Signatures using Pre-Communication between Signers

Kaoru Takemure[1,2(✉)], Yusuke Sakai[2], Bagus Santoso[1], Goichiro Hanaoka[2], and Kazuo Ohta[1,2]

[1] The University of Electro-Communications, Tokyo, Japan
[2] National Institute of Advanced Industrial Science and Technology (AIST), Tokyo, Japan

Abstract. Most aggregate signature schemes are relying on pairings, but high computational and storage costs of pairings limit the feasibility of those schemes in practice. Zhao proposed the first pairing-free aggregate signature scheme (AsiaCCS 2019). However, the security of Zhao's scheme is based on the hardness of a newly introduced non-standard computational problem. The recent impossibility results of Drijvers et al. (IEEE S&P 2019) on two-round pairing-free multi-signature schemes whose security based on the standard discrete logarithm (DL) problem has strengthened the view that constructing a pairing-free aggregate signature scheme which is proven secure based on standard problems such as DL problem is indeed a challenging open problem.

In this paper, we offer a novel solution to this open problem. We introduce a new paradigm of aggregate signatures, i.e., aggregate signatures with an additional *pre-communication* stage. In the pre-communication stage, each signer interacts with the aggregator to agree on a specific random value *before deciding messages to be signed.* We also discover that the impossibility results of Drijvers et al. apply if the adversary can decide the whole randomness part of any individual signature. Based on the new paradigm and our discovery of the applicability of the impossibility result, we propose a pairing-free aggregate signature scheme such that any individual signature includes a random nonce which can be freely generated by the signer. We prove the security of our scheme based on the hardness of the *standard DL problem.* As a trade-off, in contrast to the plain public-key model, which Zhao's scheme uses, we employ a more restricted key setup model, i.e., the knowledge of secret-key model.

Keywords: Aggregate Signatures · Pre-Communication · Knowledge of Secret Key Model · Rogue-Key Attack

1 Introduction

Boneh et al. [8] introduced the concept of *aggregate signatures*, in which individual signatures on different messages generated by n signers are combined by

K. Nguyen et al. (Eds.): ProvSec 2020, LNCS 12505, pp. 65–84, 2020.
https://doi.org/10.1007/978-3-030-62576-4_4

any party acting as an *aggregator* into a single signature with the length shorter than the total length of n individual signatures. The aggregate signature scheme proposed in [8] requires bilinear map computations using pairings in the verification step, and the security of the scheme is based on the hardness of the pairing-based Diffie-Hellman assumption.

However, from the perspective of practical implementation and security guarantee, it is much preferable if we can avoid the pairings completely. First, the pairing computation is still relatively quite costly. Since most pairing-based schemes require pairing computations in verification, for the situation where the verifiers are lightweight devices, such schemes might not be suitable. In addition, recently, large cryptanalytic effort, such as [15,19], revealed a new weakness of pairing based problems, and in a subsequent paper by Guillevic [15], it was shown that we need to make the field size of the group used for pairing $\approx 75\%$ larger than the initial recommendation of the parameter for 128-bit security.

Recently, Zhao proposed an aggregate signature scheme based on the sigma protocol which does not require pairing computation at all [32]. However, the security of his scheme is based on the hardness of a non-standard computational problem, i.e., the *non-malleable discrete logarithm (NMDL)* assumption, which is newly introduced by Zhao in the same paper.

Therefore, constructing an aggregate signature scheme with the following properties is a very important open problem from the practical and theoretical points of view: (1) *pairing-free*, i.e., the scheme does not rely on pairing computations or pairing-based assumption, and (2) provably secure based on well-established standard assumptions, e.g., standard discrete logarithm problem. The aim of this paper is to propose a solution to this open problem. For simplicity, we will focus only on pairing-free schemes here afterward.

1.1 Properties of Aggregate Signatures and Multi-signatures

Another cryptographic primitive which is closely related to aggregate signatures is *multi-signatures*. In a multi-signature scheme, the combined signature must be the combination of signatures on the *same* message, while in an aggregate signature scheme, the combined signature can be the combination of signatures on *different* messages. We will show below several properties related to the signature generating procedure and the security, which most aggregate signatures and multi-signatures have in common.

Stages in Combining Signatures. Here, we unify the representation of signature generating procedures in most (pairing-free) multi-signatures and aggregate signatures into a sequence of three stages.[1]

- *Stage I (Offline Stage).* In this stage, each signer performs the necessary interactive communication with other signers before deciding the message to be signed.

[1] It should be noted that an aggregate signature schemes or a multi-signature do not have to have all the three stages.

Table 1. Comparison among Pairing-Free Multi-signature and Aggregate Signature Schemes

	Multi signatures			Aggregate signatures	
	BN(-IAS) [5]	CoSi [10,29]	mBCJ [2,10]	Zhao [32]	PCAS
#rounds in Stage I	0	0	0	0	1
Non-interactive message decision in Stage II	No	No	No	Yes	**Yes**
#rounds in Stage III	3	2	2	1	1
#allowed concurrent signing queries	poly(n)	log(n)	poly(n)	poly(n)	**poly(n)**
Security Assumption	DL	OMDL	DL	NMDL	**DL**
Key-Setup Model	plain PK	KOSK	KV	plain PK	KOSK

* PCAS is our proposed scheme. The first row and the third row indicate the number of interactive communication between signers in Stage I and Stage III respectively. The second row indicates whether the message decision in Stage II is carried *without* any interaction between signers. The fourth row indicates the maximum number of concurrent signing queries which is allowed without breaking the security of the scheme. Here, n indicates the number of signers. DL, OMDL, NMDL indicate the standard discrete logarithm problem, one-more discrete logarithm problem, and non-malleable discrete logarithm problem [32], respectively. We describe the notions of the key-setup model mentioned at the final row in the paragraph *Attacks and Key-Setup Model* in Sect. 1.1.

- *Stage II (Message Decision Stage).* In this stage, signers decide the message they will individually sign and eventually include in the final combined signature. In the case of multi-signatures, since all signatures to combine have to be signatures on one single same message, it is almost natural that the signers communicate to each other *interactively* to decide the message to be signed in this stage. In the case of aggregate signatures, generally, a signer does not need to share the message with other signers.
- *Stage III (Online Stage).* In this stage, signers share specific values related to the messages decided in Stage II to others via interactive communication.

Research Question. We compare several pairing-free multi-signature and aggregate signature schemes in Table 1. Notice that most pairing-free multi-signature schemes require more than one communication round in the online stage (Stage III), while they achieve provable security based on the hardness of standard computational problems [2,5,29]. On the other hand, the pairing-free aggregate signature scheme, Zhao's scheme only requires a single communication round in the online stage, while it achieves provable security using the hardness of newly introduced non-standard computational problems. Our question here is as follows.

> *"Is it possible to construct a new scheme which achieves the best of the two worlds: (1) one communication round in Stage III, and (2) provable security based on the hardness of standard computational problems ?"*

Aggregate Signatures based on Multi-signatures. In a multi-signature scheme, signatures on the same message are combined into the final signature. However, one can easily tweak the scheme such that the combined signature will be a signature on multiple different messages decided by different signers. In Stage II, via an interactive message decision process, each signer can send an individual message to all other signers and then combine all different individual messages into one single message by simple concatenation. This single message will be the message to be signed which is agreed by all signers. In [5], Bellare and Neven introduced this concept as *Interactive Aggregate Signatures (IAS).*

Attacks and Key-Setup Model. In both multi-signatures and aggregate signatures, one should consider an attack scenario which is called the *rogue-key attack.* In a rogue-key attack, an attacker generates public keys dishonestly and tries to forge a combined signature involving such dishonest keys. In general, we can guarantee the security of the scheme against the rogue-key attacks using the following two basic strategies. The first is (i) *to prove directly that there exists no rogue-key attack*, and the second is (ii) *to exclude rogue-key attacks by a specific key registration protocol.* These two approaches are formally modeled by (i) *the plain public-key (PK) model* [5] and (ii) *the knowledge of secret keys (KOSK) model* [6,21], respectively.

(i) *The plain PK model* is the model without any assumption in the key setup. In the security model, an adversary can freely choose all cosigners' public keys excluding at least one honest signer's key.
(ii) *The KOSK model* is the model where all signers need to prove the validity of their public key. In the security model, an adversary can freely pick all cosigners' public keys, but it must output the secret keys corresponding to these public keys. In practice, the KOSK model can be implemented using one of the following models: (1) a *trusted setup* model [25], in which a dedicated key registration protocol is needed to be executed by each signer, (2) the *key verification* (KV) model [2], and (3) the *proof-of-possession* (PoP) model [27], where each signer submits a certificate to prove possession of a secret key.

1.2 Our Contributions

In this paper, we propose a new paradigm for constructing aggregate signature which we call *aggregate signatures with pre-communication* (*AS with PreCom*). We propose an aggregate signature scheme based on the new paradigm, which we name PCAS, and proved its security based on the standard discrete logarithm (DL) assumption in the KOSK model using a random oracle. We show the comparison of PCAS with other *pairing-free* multi-signature and aggregate signature schemes in Table 1 (We also show the performance comparison among aggregate signature scheme and related schemes in Table 2 in Sect. 4).

Most aggregate signature schemes (either with pairings or without pairings) do not have any interactive round between signers in Stage I. In contrast, an aggregate signature scheme with pre-communication, have one interactive round in Stage I before the message deciding stage (Stage II). We believe that this drawback only has minor effects on the practical use. As shown in Table 1, PCAS still keeps the most important feature of aggregate signatures, i.e., any signer is allowed to choose their individual message to be signed without interacting with other signers in Stage II. Moreover, one should notice that the total number of interactive rounds in PCAS, i.e., two, is the lowest number of interactive rounds that the multi-signature schemes (either with pairing or without pairing) can ever achieve in theory and these multi-signature schemes are being used widely in real-world practice today [11].

Comparison to Zhao's Aggregate Signature Scheme. As opposed to Zhao's aggregate signature scheme [32] which is proven based on a non-standard computational problem NMDL, our proposed aggregate signature scheme PCAS is proven secure under the standard discrete-logarithm (DL) assumption. To prove the security of our scheme, we assume the KOSK model as the key-setup model.[2] Although the KOSK model is more costly compared to the plain PK model, there are several practical methods for implementing the KOSK model as mentioned in the previous section.

PCAS achieves a smaller signature size than the signature size in Zhao's scheme [32]. Concretely, let n be the number of individual signatures to combine. For λ-bit security, in Zhao's scheme the combined signature includes n group elements whose total size is about $2\lambda n$ bits, while in PCAS the combined signature includes a random string with the total size of λn bits.

Circumventing Impossibility Results of Drijvers et al. [10]. In [10] Drijvers et al. showed attacks against several two-round multi-signature schemes and also show the impossibility of proving the security of those schemes. Since our proposed aggregate signature scheme bears a resemblance to CoSi scheme [29], one of the multi-signature schemes covered in [10], one may wonder whether the impossibility results of Drijvers et al. are applicable to our proposed scheme. However, as shown in a more detailed explanation at Sect. 5, the random value t which is freshly chosen by the signer in every signature query, is actually sufficient for our proposed scheme to avoid the impossibility results. Concretely, the root of the impossibility results is the adversary's ability to force the honest signer to use a specific hash value c of the adversary's choice in the response to a signature query. This ability is eliminated by the random value t, which makes the adversary unable to predict the challenge c that the honest signer will use since c is computed depending on the value of t in our scheme. For more detail, see the full version of this paper.

1.3 Difficulty and Our Techniques

The Schnorr digital signature scheme [28] built from the Schnorr identification by the Fiat-Shamir transform [12] is used in many applications as well as ours because of the small computational complexity and well-established security. Let q be a prime integer, g be a generator of a cyclic group G with order q,

[2] The KOSK model is essential because there is a *sub-exponential* attack against this scheme in the plain PK model by using k-sum algorithm as in [10]. For more detail of this attack, see the full version of this paper.

X be a public key, m be a message, (R, s) is a signature on m, and H be a hash function $H : \{0,1\}^* \rightarrow Z_q$. The verification formula of the Schnorr signature scheme is $R = g^s X^{-c}$ where c is the value such that $c = H(R, X, m)$.[3] We can aggregate the formula because of the linearity. More specifically, for all $i = 1, \ldots, n$, when each signer $\mathcal{S}_i$ (with public key X_i) submits a signature (R_i, s_i) on a message m_i, one can compress all signatures into $(\widetilde{R}, \tilde{s})$ where $\widetilde{R} = \prod_{i=1}^n R_i$ and $\tilde{s} = \sum_{i=1}^n s_i \mod q$. Then the verification formula is $\widetilde{R} = g^{\tilde{s}} \prod_{i=1}^n X_i^{c_i}$ where $c_i = H(R_i, X_i, m_i)$.[4]

However, there are three difficulties in extending the Schnorr digital signature scheme to multi-signatures or aggregate signatures by the above compression.

First, (I) *all signers need to share* $\widetilde{R}$ *before generating a signature.* On the Schnorr signature, a signer inputs R_i to the hash function to generate c_i. If an aggregator compresses all signers' R_i into $\widetilde{R}$, a verifier cannot know R_i and cannot compute c_i. Thus we need to replace R_i with $\widetilde{R}$ in the input of the hash function, but in that case, then all signers require $\widetilde{R}$ for generating signatures.

Second, (II) *by sharing* $\widetilde{R}$*, a reduction fails to simulate the honest signer in the security proof.* In the Schnorr signature scheme, the reduction simulates the signing oracle by the honest-verifier zero-knowledge property of the sigma protocol and the random oracle. In detail, the reduction chooses s and c at uniformly random from Z_q, computes $R \leftarrow g^s X^{-c}$, sets $H(R, X, m) \leftarrow c$ in the random oracle table, and return (R, s) as a signature. If $H(R, X, m)$ is predefined by hash queries, the reduction cannot set $H(R, X, m) \leftarrow c$ and cannot complete this simulation. In the case that the input R of the hash function is changed to $\widetilde{R}$, the reduction can compute $\widetilde{R}$ only after an adversary outputs all cosigners' R_i. Thus an adversary can know $\widetilde{R}$ before the reduction knows it, and can prevent the reduction from setting $H(\widetilde{R}, X, m) \leftarrow c$ in the random oracle table by making a hash query $(\widetilde{R}, X, m)$.

Third, (III) *it is hard to compute the solution of the DL problem from forgeries because of the term related to cosigners.* Recall that the verification formula is $\widetilde{R} = g^{\tilde{s}} \prod_i X_i^{-c_i}$. Let $\bar{X}$ be an instance of the DL problem the reduction tries to solve. For simplicity, we assume the restricted case where the k-th signer is the honest signer ($X_k = \bar{X}$) and a forger assigns distinct group elements to cosigners' key. [5] The reduction uses the rewinding technique and obtains the two formulae $\widetilde{R} = g^{\tilde{s}} \prod_i X_i^{-c_i}$ and $\widetilde{R}' = g^{\tilde{s}'} \prod_i X_i^{-c_i'}$ where $\widetilde{R} = \widetilde{R}'$, and $c_k \neq c_k'$. When the reduction tries to extract the discrete logarithm of $\bar{X}$ by dividing the above two formulae, it can obtain

$$\bar{X}^{c_k - c_k'} = g^{\tilde{s} - \tilde{s}'} \prod_{i \neq k} X_i^{-c_i + c_i'}. \tag{1}$$

[3] For the convenience of considering multiple users, we added the public key to the input of the hash function.

[4] If we set $m_1 = m_2 = \cdots = m_n$, then we can see it as multi-signatures.

[5] In [5], Bellare and Neven consider the case where there are several public keys with the same values.

However, notice here that the term $\prod_{i \neq k} X_i^{-c_i+c'_i}$ related to cosigners becomes the barrier for the reduction to extract the discrete logarithm of $\bar{X}$.

Next, we show how Bellare-Neven multi-signature scheme [5] circumvents the above difficulties. First, note that in a multi-signature scheme, all signers who participate will generate signatures on the same message and are allowed to interact with each other in the signing procedure. For (I), all signers share $\{R_i\}_i$ in the signing protocol and compute $\widetilde{R}$. For (II), each signer generates a commitment to R_i by using a hash function and sends the commitment to all other signers, before it sends R_i. By this, in the security proof, when the reduction receives all cosigners' commitments to $\{R_i\}_i$, it can compute $\widetilde{R}$ by searching all cosigners' R_i in the random oracle table simulating the hash function before the adversary knows $\widetilde{R}$. For (III), the reduction programs the random oracle carefully as follows. For the hash query $(\widetilde{R}, X_k, L, m)$ where L is the list of the signers' public keys, the reduction fixes $H(\widetilde{R}, X_i, L, m)$ to the random value for all $i \neq k$ *before* it defines $H(\widetilde{R}, X_k, L, m)$. By this careful programming of a random oracle, the reduction can make the situation that $c_i = c'_i$ holds for $i \neq k$ in Eq. (1) and can cancel out the term $\prod_{i \neq k} X_i^{-c_i+c'_i}$ related to cosigners. Then it can extract the solution to the problem as $(\tilde{s} - \tilde{s}')/(c_k - c'_k) \mod q$ without cosigners' secret key. Thus, this scheme can be proved secure in the *plain PK model.*

Unfortunately, these techniques to circumvent the three difficulties (I)-(III) are effective only for multi-signatures, not for aggregate signatures. Recall that the techniques to circumvent (I) and (II) require the communication in the signing phase. Applying them to aggregate signatures will automatically destroy the advantage of aggregate signatures over multi-signatures, i.e., the freedom of the signers to sign their own chosen message individually without sharing it with other signers beforehand. And the technique to circumvent (III) is simply impossible to apply on aggregate signatures. This technique works *only if* all messages in the signatures to be combined are fixed *before* the rewinding point in the security proof. However, in aggregate signatures, the cosigners controlled by the adversary always have the freedom to change the messages in the signatures to be combined any time, *even after* the rewinding point. Therefore, we need to explore other approaches to overcome the above three difficulties in aggregate signatures.

We overcome the three difficulties as follows. For (I), noticing that $\widetilde{R}$ is pre-communicable, we introduce the pre-communication and exclude the communication in the signing protocol. For (II), we resolve the difficulty by adding the random value t_i generated by the signer in the signing phase to the input of the hash function to produce c_i. In more details, each c_i is computed as $c_i \leftarrow H(\widetilde{R}, X_i, t_i, m_i)$ and a set of t_i is included in a aggregate signature as $(\widetilde{R}, \tilde{s}, \{t_i\}_i)$. Consequently, thanks to t_i, the reduction can succeed in simulating the honest signer no matter how cleverly the adversary behaves, because the adversary should guess the random value t_i. For (III), we use the KOSK model. By this, the reduction can obtain cosigners' secret keys x_i for $i \neq k$ and compute the discrete logarithm of $\prod_{i \neq k} X_i^{-c_i + c'_i}$ in Eq. (1). Therefore it can extract a solution to the DL problem as $(\tilde{s} - \tilde{s}' - \sum_{i \neq k} x_i(c_i - c'_i))/(c_k - c'_k) \mod q$.[6]

1.4 Related Work

Boneh et al. suggested the idea of aggregate signatures and proposed the first aggregate signature scheme using pairing [8]. Bellare et al. showed that the aggregate signature scheme [8] is secure even if the restriction of different pairs of a public key and a message between all signers is eliminated [4]. There are many pairing-based aggregate signature schemes [1,7,16,17,21,23,26].

Lysyanskaya et al. introduced a notion of sequential aggregate signatures, where signers sequentially generate a signature on his message by using previous signers' messages and signatures and provided the first sequential aggregate signature scheme built from the RSA assumption [22]. After that, pairing-based sequential aggregate signature schemes [13,20,21] and pairing-free sequential aggregate signature schemes [3,9,26] were proposed.

Gentry and Ramzan proposed the first aggregate signature in the synchronized setting [14], and Ahn et al. formalized the synchronized aggregate signatures, in which signatures generated in the same period can be compressed into an aggregate signature. Hohenberger and Waters provided an RSA-based synchronized aggregate signature scheme [18]. We can implement an AS with PreCom scheme using a synchronized aggregate signature scheme as follows. In a PreCom phase, the signers can agree on the time period by pre-communication. A restriction of this approach is that the number of the signatures the signers can issue is bounded at the setup time. Our proposed scheme does not have such a restriction.

Identity-based aggregate signatures [7,14,17,30] are the aggregate signatures in which each signer is assigned an ID and creates a signature by using a secret key that a private key generator generates by the master secret key and the signer's ID. Bellare and Neven proposed a DL-based multi-signature scheme and mentioned the applicability of multi-signatures to (interactive) aggregates signature [5]. This application presupposes that signers can share messages.

Zhao proposed an aggregate signature scheme for blockchain applications [32]. This scheme is asynchronous and constructed from general elliptic curves. He stated that the proposed scheme is more applicable to blockchain applications than pairing-based aggregate signatures for the system complexity and the verification speed. His scheme is an extension of the Γ-signature [31] to aggregate signatures. Though the signature size linearly depends on the number of signers, this scheme is proved secure in the plain PK model and requires no communication between signers for signing. The security of this scheme is based on the non-malleable discrete logarithm (NMDL) assumption. This assumption

[6] Here, we implicitly assumed the same restriction as we assumed in Sect. 1.3 for discussing Bellare-Neven's approach to the difficulty (III). However, this restriction can be removed in the actual proof of this proposed scheme. For detail, see the security model in Sect. 3.1.

is only justified in the generic group model [24] with random oracles, where an adversary is allowed to query both of the random oracle and the generic group oracle.

2 Preliminaries

2.1 Notation

For a prime integer q, we denote the ring of integers modulo q by Z_q and the multiplicative group of Z_q by Z_q^*. Let G be a cyclic group of order q and let g be a generator of G. For a set A, we write $a \xleftarrow{\$} A$ to mean that a is chosen at uniformly random from A. For a probabilistic algorithm B, we write $b \leftarrow \mathcal{B}(\beta_1, \ldots; \rho)$ to mean that B on inputs $\beta_1, \ldots$ and random tape ρ outputs b, and $b \xleftarrow{\$} \mathcal{B}(\beta_1, \ldots)$ to mean that ρ is chosen at uniformly random and let $b \leftarrow \mathcal{B}(\beta_1, \ldots; \rho)$.

2.2 Hardness Assumption

We now recall the definition of the discrete logarithm assumption.

Definition 1 (Discrete Logarithm Assumption). *For (G, g, q), let $\mathcal{E}$ be a PPT algorithm that is given y chosen at uniformly random from G. We say that $\mathcal{E}$ (t, ε)-breaks DL if $\mathcal{E}$ runs in time at most t and outputs x such that $y = g^x$ with probability at least ε.*

3 Aggregate Signatures with Pre-Communication

3.1 Definition

In this paper, particularly, we introduce a model where, before signing, each signer communicates with the aggregator and shares information in advance, which we hereafter call helper information. Note that communication in this model is the one-to-one communication between a signer and the aggregator. We now describe the definition of aggregate signature (AS) with pre-communication (PreCom) below. We illustrate pre-communication and aggregation in Fig. 1.

Definition 2 (AS with PreCom). *An AS with PreCom consists of the following five algorithms and one protocol. Let n be the number of signers and let i be the index of a signer.*

Setup$(1^\lambda) \rightarrow pp$. *The public parameter generation algorithm takes as input a security parameter 1^λ, then outputs a public parameter pp.*

KeyGen$(pp) \rightarrow (pk, sk)$. *The key generation algorithm takes as input a public parameter pp, then outputs a public key pk and a secret key sk.*

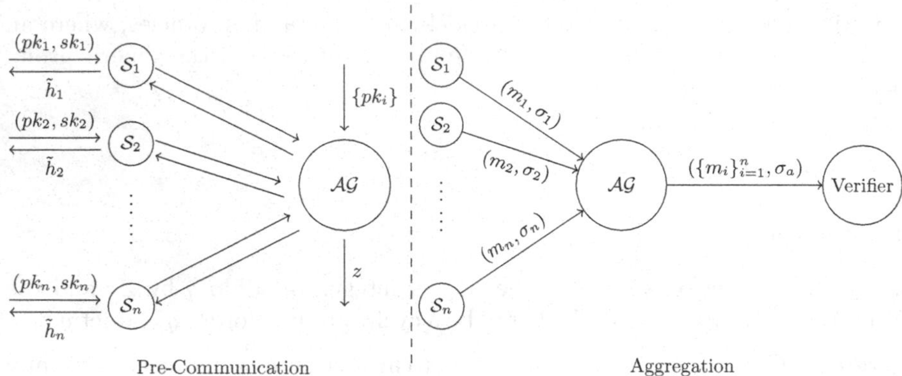

Fig. 1. Aggregate Signature with Pre-Communication: The arrows that denote the communication are simplified to one round communication as in the proposed scheme in this paper. In our model, we do not restrict the number of rounds to one.

PreCom$\langle \mathcal{S}_1(pk_1, sk_1), \ldots, \mathcal{S}_n(pk_n, sk_n), \mathcal{AG}(\{pk_i\}_{i=1}^n)\rangle \rightarrow (\tilde{h}_1, \ldots, \tilde{h}_n, z)$**.** *The pre-communication protocol is executed between each signer $\mathcal{S}_i$ with input a public key pk_i and a secret key sk_i and an aggregator $\mathcal{AG}$ with input all the signers' public keys $\{pk_i\}_{i=1}^n$. After the protocol terminates, each $\mathcal{S}_i$ and $\mathcal{AG}$ obtain $\tilde{h}_i$ and z as helper information, respectively.*

Sign$(pp, pk, sk, \tilde{h}, m) \rightarrow \sigma$**.** *The signing algorithm takes as input a public parameter pp, a public key pk, a secret key sk, helper information $\tilde{h}$, and a message m, then outputs a signature σ.*

Agg$(pp, z, \{(pk_i, m_i, \sigma_i)\}_{i=1}^n) \rightarrow \sigma_a$**.** *The aggregation algorithm takes as input a public parameter pp, helper information z, and a set of all signers' public keys, messages, and signatures $\{(pk_i, m_i, \sigma_i)\}_{i=1}^n$, then outputs an aggregate signature σ_a.*

AggVer$(pp, \{(pk_i, m_i)\}_{i=1}^n, \sigma_a) \rightarrow \{0, 1\}$**.** *The aggregate signature verification algorithm takes as input a public parameter pp, a set of all signers' public keys and messages $\{(pk_i, m_i)\}_{i=1}^n$, and an aggregate signature σ_a, then outputs 0 (REJECT) or 1 (ACCEPT).*

For any set of messages $\{m_i\}_{i=1}^n$, if all signers and an aggregator behave honestly, then $\Pr[\textbf{AggVer}(pp, \{(pk_i, m_i)\}_{i=1}^n, \sigma_a) = 1] = 1$ *holds.*

Security Model of AS with PreCom. Below, we show the definition of existential unforgeability under the chosen-message attack to AS with PreCom in the random oracle model and knowledge of secret key (KOSK) model [6,21]. This security definition requires that it be infeasible to forge aggregate signatures involving at least one honest signer. In the security model here, as a forger $\mathcal{F}$, we consider aggregators who corrupt signers except for one honest signer. Also the forger $\mathcal{F}$ can execute the pre-communication and the aggregation protocols with an honest signer several times, and after that, it tries to output a forgery. Then the forger $\mathcal{F}$ can arbitrarily choose the corrupted cosigners' public keys even though it must output secret keys corresponding to these public keys. This restriction is called the KOSK model.

Formally, the security model here is defined by the three-phase game of the following.

Setup. The challenger chooses the parameter $pp \xleftarrow{\$} \mathbf{Setup}(1^\lambda)$ and the key pair $(pk, sk) \xleftarrow{\$} \mathbf{KeyGen}(pp)$. It runs a forger $\mathcal{F}$ on input pk and pp.

Signing Queries. The challenger receives (j, i_j) as *a PreCom signing query*. The challenger and $\mathcal{F}$ execute the pre-communication protocol **PreCom** $\langle \mathcal{S}_1(pk_1, sk_1), \ldots, \mathcal{S}_n(pk_n, sk_n), \mathcal{AG}(\{pk_i\}_{i=1}^n)\rangle \rightarrow (\tilde{h}_1, \ldots, \tilde{h}_n, z)$ where the challenger behaves as $\mathcal{S}_{i_j}(pk, sk)$ and all the other parties are controlled by $\mathcal{F}$. Then, the challenger obtains the helper information $\tilde{h}_{i_j}$ and stores this information with the PreCom signing query. The challenger receives (j, m') as *a message signing query.* It reads out $\tilde{h}_{i_j}$ and computes $\sigma'_j \leftarrow \mathbf{Sign}(pp, pk, sk, \tilde{h}_{i_j}, m')$. The challenger returns σ'_j to $\mathcal{F}$. $\mathcal{F}$ is allowed to concurrently make any number of above queries where it is allowed to make only one message signing query per one PreCom signing query.[7]

Output. After $\mathcal{F}$ terminates, it outputs n key pairs $\{(pk_i, sk_i)\}_{i=1}^n$, a set of messages $\{m_i^*\}_{i=1}^n$, and a forgery σ_a^* where the following holds.
- $\{pk_i\}_{i=1}^n$ is distinct to each other.
- $pk \in \{pk_i\}_{i=1}^n$.
- sk_k is $\perp$ where k is such that $pk_k = pk$.

If $\mathbf{AggVer}(pp, \{(pk_i, m_i^*)\}_{i=1}^n, \sigma_a^*) = 1$ is true and m_i^* has never been queried where i is such that $pk_i = pk$, then $\mathcal{F}$ is said to succeed in forgery.

Definition 3 (Unforgeability in KOSK Model for AS with PreCom). *Let N be a maximum number of cosigners being involved in the forgery. We say that $\mathcal{F}$ $(t, q_S, q_H, N, \varepsilon)$-break AS with PreCom if $\mathcal{F}$ runs in at most t time, makes at most q_S signing queries and at most q_H random oracle queries, and succeeds in forgery in the above game with probability at least ε. For an AS scheme with PreCom, if there are no $\mathcal{F}$ that $(t, q_S, q_H, N, \varepsilon)$-breaks it, we say the scheme is $(t, q_S, q_H, N, \varepsilon)$-secure.*

3.2 Our AS Scheme with PreCom (PCAS)

In this section, we propose the AS scheme with PreCom PCAS based on the discrete logarithm assumption in the random oracle model and the KOSK model. This scheme is an extension of the Schnorr signature scheme to aggregate signatures. We introduce the pre-communication to solve the difficulty (I) in Sect. 1.3 without the communication in the signing phase.

[7] This restriction is essential. If this restriction is omitted, there is an attack against our proposed scheme. See Remark 1 for more detail.

The Algorithms and Protocol of PCAS**.** Below, we now show the algorithms and protocol of PCAS.

Setup$(1^\lambda) \rightarrow pp$**.** It chooses (G, q, g), a hash function $H : \{0,1\}^* \rightarrow Z_q$, and a parameter κ, then outputs $pp = (G, q, g, H, \kappa)$.

KeyGen$(pp) \rightarrow (pk, sk)$**.** It computes $x \xleftarrow{\$} Z_q$ and $X \leftarrow g^x$, then outputs the public key $pk = X$ and the secret key $sk = x$.

PreCom$\langle \mathcal{S}_1(pk_1, sk_1), \ldots, \mathcal{S}_n(pk_n, sk_n), \mathcal{AG}(\{pk_i\}_{i=1}^n)\rangle \rightarrow (\tilde{h}_1, \ldots, \tilde{h}_n, z)$**.** For all $i \in [1, n]$, firstly, each signer $\mathcal{S}_i$ computes $r_i \xleftarrow{\$} Z_q$ and $R_i \leftarrow g^{r_i}$ and sends R_i to the aggregator. The aggregator generates $\widetilde{R} \leftarrow \prod_{i=1}^n R_i$ from given $\{R_i\}_{i=1}^n$, and returns $\widetilde{R}$ to all the signers. Each signer $\mathcal{S}_i$ and the aggregator store $\tilde{h}_i = (r_i, \widetilde{R})$ and $z = \widetilde{R}$ as the helper information, respectively.

Sign$(pp, pk, sk, \tilde{h}, m) \rightarrow \sigma$**.** It chooses a value $t \xleftarrow{\$} \{0,1\}^\kappa$ at uniformly random, computes $c \leftarrow H(\widetilde{R}, X, t, m)$ and $s \leftarrow cx + r \mod q$, then outputs $\sigma = (s, t)$ as a signature.

Agg$(pp, z, \{(pk_i, m_i, \sigma_i)\}_{i=1}^n) \rightarrow \sigma_a$**.** It computes $\tilde{s} \leftarrow \sum_{i=1}^n s_i \mod q$, then outputs the aggregate signature $\sigma_a = (\tilde{s}, \{t_i\}_{i=1}^n, \widetilde{R})$.

AggVer$(pp, \{(pk_i, m_i)\}_{i=1}^n, \sigma_a) \rightarrow \{0,1\}$**.** If $\{pk_i\}_{i=1}^n$ are not distinct to each other, it outputs 0. For all $i \in [1, n]$, it computes $c_i \leftarrow H(\widetilde{R}, X_i, t_i, m_i)$. If $\widetilde{R} = g^{\tilde{s}} \prod_{i=1}^n X_i^{-c_i}$ holds, then outputs 1. Otherwise outputs 0.

For the verification formula, it holds that $g^{\tilde{s}} \prod_{i=1}^n X_i^{-c_i} = g^{\sum x_i c_i + r_i} g^{\sum -x_i c_i} = g^{\sum r_i} = \widetilde{R}$. Thus, an aggregate signature is accepted with probability 1 when it is generated honestly.

Remark 1. Note that already used helper information cannot be reused because the adversary can obtain two distinct signatures generated from the same helper information and extract a secret key by exploiting the special soundness property. Moreover, in the aggregation phase, if several signers fail to participate in this phase, the protocol terminates, and it should be restarted from pre-communication.

The Security of PCAS**.** We should overcome two difficulty (II) and (III) in Sect. 1.3 to prove PCAS secure. (For more detail, see Sect. 1.3).

To overcome the difficulty (II), we add the random value t to the input of a hash function which produces c. We explain how this t enables us to simulate the signing oracle. Towards this end, let us review how to simulate the honest signer for the Schnorr signature. Firstly, the reduction receives m' from a forger as a signing query, randomly chooses (c, s) and computes $R \leftarrow g^s X^{-c}$ where X is the honest signer's public key. After that, it sets $H(R, X, m') \leftarrow c$ in the random oracle table and return (R, s) as a valid signature to a forger. In this case, $H(R, X, m')$ is not predefined with overwhelming probability because R is a fresh random value generated by the reduction. For PCAS, the reduction needs to set $H(\widetilde{R}, X, t, m') \leftarrow c$ in the random oracle table. Although a forger can decide $\widetilde{R}$ and m', it cannot obtain t until the reduction return (s, t). Therefore, the reduction can set $H(\widetilde{R}, X, t, m') \leftarrow c$ between receiving $\widetilde{R}$ and m' from a forger and returning (s, t).

To overcome the difficulty (III), we consider the KOSK model. By this, the reduction can make use of the cosigners' secret keys to extract the solution to the DL problem. Moreover, the KOSK model is essential for PCAS because there is a rogue-key attack in the plain PK model. We describe this attack in the full version of this paper.

The following theorem states that PCAS is secure under the discrete logarithm assumption in the random oracle model and the KOSK model.

Theorem 1. *If there is a forger $\mathcal{F}$ that $(t, q_S, q_H, N, \varepsilon)$-breaks* PCAS, *then there is an algorithm $\mathcal{B}$ that (t', ε')-breaks DL such that*

$$\varepsilon' \geqq \frac{\varepsilon^2}{q_H+1} - \frac{2q_S(2q_H+q_S-1)}{(q_H+1)2^{\kappa+1}} - \frac{1}{q}, \qquad t' \leqq 2t + 2q_S t_{exp} + O(q_H + q_S + 1),$$

where t_{exp} is the time for an exponentiation in G and we assume that $\kappa = \lambda$.

Proof. We first show the construction of the algorithm $\mathcal{B}$ which can solve the DL problem using the forger $\mathcal{F}$. $\mathcal{B}$ is given an instance of the DL problem Y and a parameter (G, q, g).

To construct $\mathcal{B}$, let $\mathcal{A}$ be the algorithm as follows. On inputs (G, q, g, Y), $h_1, \ldots, h_{q_H+1} \in Z_q$, and a random tape ρ, $\mathcal{A}$ runs $\mathcal{F}$ on inputs (G, q, g) and Y as an honest signer's public key. It initializes counters $ctr_1 = 1, ctr_2 = 0$ and tables $T[\cdot]$, $L[\cdot]$ to be empty, where $T[\cdot]$ is a random oracle table and $L[\cdot]$ is a table that stores helper information of PreCom for signing queries. It responds to $\mathcal{F}$'s hash queries and signing queries as follows.

Hash Query *H(Q)*. A query Q is parsed as $Q = (\widetilde{R}, X, t, m)$. In the case that $X = Y$, $\mathcal{A}$ lets $T[Q] = h_{ctr_1}$ and $ctr_1 \leftarrow ctr_1 + 1$ if $T[Q]$ is undefined. In the case that $X \neq Y$, $\mathcal{A}$ lets $c \xleftarrow{\$} Z_q, T[Q] \leftarrow c$ if $T[Q]$ is undefined. It returns $T[Q]$.

Signing Query. Firstly, when $\mathcal{A}$ receives the signal to start PreCom, it sets $ctr_2 \leftarrow ctr_2 + 1$, chooses $s', c' \xleftarrow{\$} Z_q$, computes $R' \leftarrow g^{s'} X_k^{-c'}$, and sends R' to $\mathcal{F}$. After that, when $\mathcal{A}$ is given $\widetilde{R}'$ from $\mathcal{F}$, $\mathcal{A}$ assigns $L[ctr_2] \leftarrow (s', c', \widetilde{R}')$. When receiving a query (m', J), $\mathcal{A}$ sets $M' \leftarrow M' \cup \{m'\}$ and reads $L[J]$. It returns $\perp$ to $\mathcal{F}$ if $L[J]$ is empty. $\mathcal{A}$ chooses $t' \xleftarrow{\$} \{0,1\}^\kappa$ and sets $Q' = (\widetilde{R}', Y, t', m')$. It sets *bad* $\leftarrow$ *true* and halts with output $\perp$ if $T[Q']$ is already defined. Otherwise it assigns $T[Q'] \leftarrow c'$, empties $L[J]$ and returns (s', t') to $\mathcal{F}$.

Finally, $\mathcal{F}$ outputs $\{X_i^*\}_{i=1}^{n^*}$ which is the set of public keys including Y, $\{x_i^*\}_{i\in[1,n^*]\setminus\{k\}}$ which is the set of secret keys corresponding to the public keys except X_k such that $Y = X_k$, the set of messages $\{m_i^*\}_{i=1}^{n^*}$, and a forgery $(\tilde{s}^*, \{t_i^*\}_{i=1}^{n^*}, \widetilde{R}^*)$. $\mathcal{A}$ checks whether $m_k^* \notin M'$ and $\mathbf{AggVer}(pp, \{(X_i^*, m_i)\}_{i=1}^{n^*}, (\tilde{s}^*, \{t_i^*\}_{i=1}^{n^*}, \widetilde{R}^*)) = 1$ holds, and it outputs $\perp$ if not. Otherwise $\mathcal{A}$ outputs

$(I, \{(X_i, x_i)\}_{i \in [1,n] \setminus \{k\}}, (\tilde{s}^*, \{c_i^*\}_{i=1}^{n^*}, \widetilde{R}^*))$ where $c_i^* = T[\widetilde{R}^*, X_i, t_i^*, m_i^*]$ and I is the index such that $h_I = T[\widetilde{R}^*, Y, t_k^*, m_k^*]$.

$\mathcal{B}$ obtains the following two sequences by rewinding $\mathcal{A}$ according to the Bellare-Neven general forking Lemma [5].

$$(I^{(1)}, \{(X_i^{(1)}, x_i^{(1)})\}_{i \in [1,n^{(1)}] \setminus \{k^{(1)}\}}, (\tilde{s}^{(1)}, \{c_i^{(1)}\}_{i=1}^{n^{(1)}}, \widetilde{R}^{(1)}))$$
$$(I^{(2)}, \{(X_i^{(2)}, x_i^{(2)})\}_{i \in [1,n^{(2)}] \setminus \{k^{(2)}\}}, (\tilde{s}^{(2)}, \{c_i^{(2)}\}_{i=1}^{n^{(2)}}, \widetilde{R}^{(2)}))$$
$$\text{s.t. } \widetilde{R}^{(1)} = \widetilde{R}^{(2)} \wedge I^{(1)} = I^{(2)} \wedge c_{k^{(1)}}^{(1)} \neq c_{k^{(2)}}^{(2)}$$

Since the above sequences satisfy the verification formula, we have

$$\widetilde{R}^{(1)} = g^{\tilde{s}^{(1)}} \prod_{i=1}^{n^{(1)}} X_i^{(1)^{-c_i^{(1)}}} \quad \text{and} \quad \widetilde{R}^{(2)} = g^{\tilde{s}^{(2)}} \prod_{i=1}^{n^{(2)}} X_i^{(2)^{-c_i^{(2)}}}.$$

By $\widetilde{R}^{(1)} = \widetilde{R}^{(2)}$, dividing the above two equations gives

$$Y^{c_1^{(1)} - c_1^{(2)}} = g^{\tilde{s}^{(1)} - \tilde{s}^{(2)}} \prod_{i \in [1,n^{(1)}] \setminus \{k^{(1)}\}} X_i^{(1)^{-c_i^{(1)}}} \prod_{i \in [1,n^{(2)}] \setminus \{k^{(2)}\}} X_i^{(2)^{c_i^{(2)}}}.$$

Therefore, finally $\mathcal{B}$ outputs the following as the solution to the instance Y of the DL problem.

$$y \leftarrow \frac{\tilde{s}^{(1)} - \tilde{s}^{(2)} - \sum_{i \in [1,n^{(1)}] \setminus \{k^{(1)}\}} x_i^{(1)} c_i^{(1)} + \sum_{i \in [1,n^{(2)}] \setminus \{k^{(2)}\}} x_i^{(2)} c_i^{(2)}}{c_{k^{(1)}}^{(1)} - c_{k^{(2)}}^{(2)}} \mod q \tag{2}$$

$\mathcal{B}$ succeeds in outputting y if and only if it succeeds in forking $\mathcal{A}$. Let *frk* be the probability of succeeding in forking $\mathcal{A}$, and then the success probability ε' of $\mathcal{B}$ is equal to *frk*. Let *acc* be the probability that $\mathcal{A}$ outputs the sequence. We have

$$acc = \Pr[bad \neq true \wedge \mathcal{F} succeed] \geqq \Pr[\mathcal{F} succeed] - \Pr[bad = true].$$

The event $bad = true$ happens when $\mathcal{A}$ cannot set $H(\widetilde{R}', X, t', m') \leftarrow c'$ in the random oracle table due to a predefined $H(\widetilde{R}', X, t', m')$. $\mathcal{F}$ can cause this event by guessing t' which is the part of a signature that the signing oracle returns. How $\mathcal{F}$ maximizes the probability of causing this event is as follows. Firstly, for a hash query $Q_k = (\widetilde{R}', X, t', m')$, $\mathcal{F}$ fixes $\widetilde{R}', X$, and m' and queries q_H times with t' different from each other. After that, $\mathcal{F}$ makes q_S signing queries by using $\widetilde{R}', X$, and m'. Let Hit_f be the event that $bad = true$ is happened in the fth time signing query. Note that one new row in the random oracle table is created every time $\mathcal{F}$ makes signing query. Then $\Pr[bad = true]$ is bounded as follows.

$$\begin{aligned} \Pr[bad = true] &= \Pr[\mathsf{Hit}_1 \vee \mathsf{Hit}_2 \vee \ldots \vee \mathsf{Hit}_{q_S}] \\ &\leqq \Pr[\mathsf{Hit}_1] + \Pr[\mathsf{Hit}_2] + \ldots + \Pr[\mathsf{Hit}_{q_S}] \\ &\leqq \frac{q_H}{2^\kappa} + \frac{q_H + 1}{2^\kappa} + \ldots + \frac{q_H + q_S - 1}{2^\kappa} = \frac{q_S(2q_H + q_S - 1)}{2^{\kappa+1}}. \end{aligned}$$

Thus we obtain

$$acc \geqq \varepsilon - \frac{q_S(2q_H + q_S - 1)}{2^{\kappa+1}}.$$

By the Bellare-Neven general forking lemma [5], we have

$$\begin{aligned}\varepsilon' = frk &\geqq acc\left(\frac{acc}{q_H+1} - \frac{1}{q}\right) \geqq \frac{acc^2}{q_H+1} - \frac{1}{q}\\ &= \frac{1}{q_H+1}\left(\varepsilon - \frac{q_S(2q_H+q_S-1)}{2^{\kappa+1}}\right)^2 - \frac{1}{q}\\ &\geqq \frac{\varepsilon^2}{q_H+1} - \frac{2q_S(2q_H+q_S-1)}{(q_H+1)2^{\kappa+1}} - \frac{1}{q}.\end{aligned}$$

The running time t' of $\mathcal{B}$ is twice as the running time t of $\mathcal{F}$ plus $O(q_H+q_S+1)$ time needed to answer hash queries plus $2q_S t_{exp}$ time because each signing query involves two exponentiation in G. □

The Restriction on the Public Keys. For PCAS, all signers' public keys need to be distinct from each other. The reason is as follows: in the security proof, if several cosigners are having the same public key as an honest signer, the denominator of Eq. (2) is $\sum_{i\in[1,n^{(1)}] \text{ s.t. } Y=X_i^{(1)}} c_i^{(1)} - \sum_{i\in[1,n^{(2)}] \text{ s.t. } Y=X_i^{(2)}} c_i^{(2)}$. In this situation, we cannot know whether this denominator is not equal to 0 only from condition $c_1^{(1)} \neq c_1^{(2)}$.

On the KOSK Model and Its Implementation. We used the KOSK model in the security proof for simplicity and necessity. In practice, a possible way to implement the KOSK model is to use a proof-of-possession (PoP). The security of this implementation depends on the security of PoP. For example, we may consider the case of using the Schnorr signature [28] as PoP. More specifically, if a signer is required to include the PoP signed by his secret key in his public key, then, in the security game, a forger outputs the PoP signed by the secret keys behind the cosigners' public keys, not the secret keys. Since the set of the cosigners' secret keys is necessary for the proof of Theorem 1, proving the security of PCAS with this PoP is not trivial. A possible way to prove such a scheme secure is applying Bagherzandi-Cheon-Jarecki generalized forking lemma [2].

4 Performance Comparison among Aggregate Signature Scheme and Related Schemes

In this section, we compare the proposed aggregate signature scheme with pre-communication PCAS with the Zhao's aggregate signature scheme [32] and the Bellare-Neven interactive aggregate signature scheme BN-IAS [5]. These schemes are constructed based on the Schnorr signature scheme [28]. Note that we suppose the situation that these schemes are used for the same purpose of compressing signatures on different messages into a compact signature. Then, we focus on

Table 2. Performance Comparison among Aggregate Signature Scheme and Related Schemes

Scheme	BN-IAS [5]	Zhao [32]	PCAS
Type	IAS	standard AS	AS with PreCom
No sharing Messages	No	Yes	Yes
Communication Complexity	$(\lvert M\rvert + l_0 + \lvert G\rvert + \lvert Z_q\rvert) \times n(n-1)$	$2n\lvert Z_q\rvert$	$n(2\lvert G\rvert + \lvert Z_q\rvert + \kappa)$
Signature Size	$\lvert Z_q\rvert + \lvert G\rvert$	$\lvert Z_q\rvert + n\lvert G\rvert$	$\lvert Z_q\rvert + \lvert G\rvert + n\kappa$
Assumption	DL	NMDL	DL
Key Setup	plain PK	plain PK	KOSK
Restriction in Aggregation	No Restriction	Distinct (pk,m)	Distinct pk
Withdrawal	No	Yes	No

* The row 1 and 2 indicate pairing-free aggregate signature (AS) scheme and related schemes. In row 4 and 5, $|M|$, $|Z_q|$ and $|G|$ indicate the size of a element in $|M|$, Z_q, and G. Also. n denotes the number of signers, and ℓ_0 and κ are specific parameters on each scheme. Especially, the bit-length of κ is as same as the security parameter in general. The row 6 and 7 show that the assumption and the key-setup model (cf., the notion of models in Sect. 1.1) in which each scheme is proved secure, where DL and NMDL indicate the discrete logarithm assumption and non-malleable DL assumption [32]. The row 8 shows the restriction of all signers' public keys and/or messages to be accepted in the verification. The final row shows the possibility of a continuation of the procedure in the case where signers disappear before the aggregation phase.

sharing messages, communication complexity, withdrawal, the key setup model, assumptions, and the size of the aggregate signature for the comparison. Table 2 summarizes this comparison.

Necessity of Sharing Messages. On the above purpose, BN-IAS is the multi-signature scheme used as an aggregate signature scheme. More detail, this scheme generates a combined signature on different messages by seeing a set of signers' messages as one message. Then, all players need to execute the interactive protocols in Stage II in Sect. 1.1.

PCAS and Zhao's scheme need not share messages between all signers. Especially, PCAS requires interactive protocol as PreCom, however, this interaction is executed in Stage I. Thus, it achieves no sharing messages. Zhao's scheme has the standard construction of the aggregate signature, so it has no interaction protocol.

Communication Complexity. Firstly, let n be the number of signers, and $|M|$ be the size of a message M. Moreover, we consider the communication complexity including the cost of one-shot communication from signers to an aggregator for submitting a signature.

For BN-IAS, all signers need to share messages before the signing phase. Also, the signing protocol requires three-round communication between every two signers. Therefore, this scheme requires $n(n-1)/2$ channels, and the total communication complexity per channel is $2|M| + 2l_0 + 2|G| + 2|Z_q|$ where l_0 is the bit-length of the range of the hash function to produce the commitment to commitment element on the Schnorr signature scheme. The total communication complexity in aggregation protocol is $n(n-1)(|M| + l_0 + |G| + |Z_q|)$.

PCAS needs one bidirectional communication to share helper information between signers and the aggregator in the pre-communication phase. Hence this scheme requires n channels, and the total communication complexity per channel is $2|G|+|Z_q|+\kappa$. Then the total communication complexity is $n(2|G|+|Z_q|+\kappa)$.

Zhao's scheme has no interactive protocol, so there are only communications for submitting signatures. Then this scheme requires n channels, and the total communication complexity is $2n|Z_q|$.

The Size of an Aggregate Signature. The size of a signature of BN-IAS is $|Z_q|+|G|$, and hence it is independent of n. The signature size of PCAS is $|Z_q| + |G| + n\kappa$ and the signature size of Zhao's scheme is $|Z_q|+n|G|$. Notably, both sizes depend on n. We can pick κ to be equal to the security parameter λ because we should consider only target collisions for the hash function in the proof of Theorem 1. Also, We can have $\kappa \leqq |G|$ because the order of G is about $2^{2\lambda}$ in general. Therefore PCAS can achieve a smaller signature size than Zhao's scheme.

Key Setup Model, Assumptions, and Acceptable Condition. We proved PCAS secure under the DL assumption in the KOSK model and the random oracle model. This scheme needs to use a PoP to prove the correct generation of a public key in practical due to the KOSK model. BN-IAS was proved secure under the DL assumption in the random oracle model and the plain PK model. Zhao's scheme was proved secure under the NMDL assumption in the random oracle model and the plain PK model. Zhao also showed the hardness of the NMDL problem in the generic group model [24] and the random oracle model.

BN-IAS has no restrictions on public keys and messages, namely, we may include duplicate public keys and messages in aggregation. In Zhao's scheme, an aggregate signature is not accepted when all signers' pairs of a public key and a message are not distinct to each other. In PCAS, the aggregate signature can be accepted at least every public keys should be distinct.

Withdrawal. BN-IAS must halt and restart a signing protocol when some signers disappear in the signing phase. Also, PCAS must halt and restart a signing protocol when some signers fail to participate in an aggregation phase. On the other hand, Zhao's scheme can continue the process in such a situation because each signer generates a signature without any communication.

5 How to Avoid Drijvers et al.'s Impossibility

Drijvers et al. showed that several multi-signature schemes claimed to be secure are in fact insecure by both concrete attacks and meta-reductions demonstrating the impossibility of proving their security [10]. Because all of such schemes are based on the Schnorr identification or extensions thereof, one may wonder if their attacks or meta-reduction arguments are applicable or not to our schemes and, if not, may want to know the reason for the inapplicability. In particular, the CoSi scheme [29], which is one of the targets of these attacks and meta-reductions is quite similar to our PCAS scheme and is essentially the PCAS scheme without t. Therefore, it seems to be reasonable that our PCAS scheme is a target of (a natural extension of) these attacks and meta-reductions.

We discover that the meta-reductions of Drijvers et al. apply to any multi-signature or aggregate signature scheme based on sigma protocol, e.g., Schnorr identification scheme, with the following properties: (1) the challenge of each signer depends solely on the message to be signed and the combined commitment, and (2) a malicious aggregator can control the values of the combined commitment. Exploiting the above properties, a meta-reduction algorithm can somehow rewind any reduction algorithm which simulates an honest signer and *force* the honest signer to use different challenges of the malicious aggregator's choice. Thus, if the reduction simulates the honest signer perfectly, the meta-reduction algorithm obtains two distinct individual signatures based on two different combined commitments but the same fixed individual commitment from the honest signer. The special soundness property of sigma protocol enables the meta-reduction algorithm to break the hardness of underlying computational problem and thus the impossibility holds.

For the PCAS scheme, this structure is eliminated by introducing a random value of t. The point is that t is chosen by the honest signer *after an aggregator broadcasting the combined commitment.* Due to this t, a malicious aggregator cannot force the honest signer to use the challenge of the malicious aggregator's choice.

In the full version of this paper, we elaborate more on the above-outlined weakness of the PCAS scheme without t from the viewpoints of both concrete attacks and meta-reduction arguments. Furthermore, we explain how this weakness was overcome by the introduction of the random value t.

6 Conclusion

In this paper, we propose a new paradigm *pre-communication* and the PCAS scheme which is constructed based on this new paradigm and proved secure under the standard DL assumption and the KOSK model. By presenting the concrete rogue-key attack, we state that the KOSK model is essential for PCAS. Moreover, we explain that we avoided Drijvers et al.'s attacks and impossibility results.

In practice, PCAS need proof-of-possession (PoP) because of their security in the KOSK model. Therefore to analyze the security of schemes equipped with a concrete PoP is an important open question.

Acknowledgments. This paper is based on results obtained from a project commissioned by the New Energy and Industrial Technology Development Organization (NEDO). This work was supported by JST CREST Grant Number JPMJCR19F6, Japan. This work was supported by JSPS KAKENHI Grant Numbers JP18H01438, JP18H03238, JP18H05289, JP18K11292, JP18K11293, JP18K18055, JP19H01109. We are grateful to an anonymous reviewer, who pointed out subtleties in the security definition of aggregate signatures with pre-communication.

References

1. Ahn, J.H., Green, M., Hohenberger, S.: Synchronized aggregate signatures: new definitions, constructions and applications. In: CCS 2010, pp. 473–484 (2010)
2. Bagherzandi, A., Cheon, J.H., Jarecki, S.: Multisignatures secure under the discrete logarithm assumption and a generalized forking lemma. In: CCS 2008, pp. 449–458 (2008)
3. El Bansarkhani, R., Mohamed, M.S.E., Petzoldt, A.: MQSAS - a multivariate sequential aggregate signature scheme. In: Bishop, M., Nascimento, A.C.A. (eds.) ISC 2016. LNCS, vol. 9866, pp. 426–439. Springer, Cham (2016). https://doi.org/10.1007/978-3-319-45871-7_25
4. Bellare, M., Namprempre, C., Neven, G.: Unrestricted aggregate signatures. In: Arge, L., Cachin, C., Jurdziński, T., Tarlecki, A. (eds.) ICALP 2007. LNCS, vol. 4596, pp. 411–422. Springer, Heidelberg (2007). https://doi.org/10.1007/978-3-540-73420-8_37
5. Bellare, M., Neven, G.: Multi-signatures in the plain public-key model and a general forking lemma. In: CCS 2006, pp. 390–399 (2006)
6. Boldyreva, A.: Threshold signatures, multisignatures and blind signatures based on the gap-diffie-hellman-group signature scheme. In: Desmedt, Y.G. (ed.) PKC 2003. LNCS, vol. 2567, pp. 31–46. Springer, Heidelberg (2003). https://doi.org/10.1007/3-540-36288-6_3
7. Boldyreva, A., Gentry, C., O'Neill, A., Yum, D.H.: Ordered multisignatures and identity-based sequential aggregate signatures, with applications to secure routing. In: CCS 2007, pp. 276–285 (2007)
8. Boneh, D., Gentry, C., Lynn, B., Shacham, H.: Aggregate and verifiably encrypted signatures from bilinear maps. In: Biham, E. (ed.) EUROCRYPT 2003. LNCS, vol. 2656, pp. 416–432. Springer, Heidelberg (2003). https://doi.org/10.1007/3-540-39200-9_26
9. Brogle, K., Goldberg, S., Reyzin, L.: Sequential aggregate signatures with lazy verification from trapdoor permutations. In: Wang, X., Sako, K. (eds.) ASIACRYPT 2012. LNCS, vol. 7658, pp. 644–662. Springer, Heidelberg (2012). https://doi.org/10.1007/978-3-642-34961-4_39
10. Drijvers, M., et al.: On the security of two-round multi-signatures. In: IEEE S&P 2019, pp. 1084–1101 (2019)
11. Drijvers, M., Gorbunov, S., Neven, G., Wee, H.: Pixel: multi-signatures for consensus. In: IACR Cryptology ePrint Archive 2019, p. 514 (2019)
12. Fiat, A., Shamir, A.: How to prove yourself: practical solutions to identification and signature problems. In: CRYPTO 1986, pp. 186–194 (1986)
13. Fischlin, M., Lehmann, A., Schröder, D.: History-free sequential aggregate signatures. In: Visconti, I., De Prisco, R. (eds.) SCN 2012. LNCS, vol. 7485, pp. 113–130. Springer, Heidelberg (2012). https://doi.org/10.1007/978-3-642-32928-9_7
14. Gentry, C., Ramzan, Z.: Identity-based aggregate signatures. In: Yung, M., Dodis, Y., Kiayias, A., Malkin, T. (eds.) PKC 2006. LNCS, vol. 3958, pp. 257–273. Springer, Heidelberg (2006). https://doi.org/10.1007/11745853_17
15. Guillevic, A.: A short-list of pairing-friendly curves resistant to special TNFS at the 128-bit security level. In: Kiayias, A., Kohlweiss, M., Wallden, P., Zikas, V. (eds.) PKC 2020. LNCS, vol. 12111, pp. 535–564. Springer, Cham (2020). https://doi.org/10.1007/978-3-030-45388-6_19
16. Hohenberger, S., Koppula, V., Waters, B.: Universal signature aggregators. In: Oswald, E., Fischlin, M. (eds.) EUROCRYPT 2015. LNCS, vol. 9057, pp. 3–34. Springer, Heidelberg (2015). https://doi.org/10.1007/978-3-662-46803-6_1

17. Hohenberger, S., Sahai, A., Waters, B.: Full domain hash from (leveled) multilinear maps and identity-based aggregate signatures. In: Canetti, R., Garay, J.A. (eds.) CRYPTO 2013. LNCS, vol. 8042, pp. 494–512. Springer, Heidelberg (2013). https://doi.org/10.1007/978-3-642-40041-4_27
18. Hohenberger, S., Waters, B.: Synchronized aggregate signatures from the RSA assumption. In: Nielsen, J.B., Rijmen, V. (eds.) EUROCRYPT 2018. LNCS, vol. 10821, pp. 197–229. Springer, Cham (2018). https://doi.org/10.1007/978-3-319-78375-8_7
19. Kim, T., Barbulescu, R.: Extended tower number field sieve: a new complexity for the medium prime case. In: Robshaw, M., Katz, J. (eds.) CRYPTO 2016. LNCS, vol. 9814, pp. 543–571. Springer, Heidelberg (2016). https://doi.org/10.1007/978-3-662-53018-4_20
20. Lee, K., Lee, D.H., Yung, M.: Sequential aggregate signatures made shorter. In: Jacobson, M., Locasto, M., Mohassel, P., Safavi-Naini, R. (eds.) ACNS 2013. LNCS, vol. 7954, pp. 202–217. Springer, Heidelberg (2013). https://doi.org/10.1007/978-3-642-38980-1_13
21. Lu, S., Ostrovsky, R., Sahai, A., Shacham, H., Waters, B.: Sequential aggregate signatures and multisignatures without random oracles. In: Vaudenay, S. (ed.) EUROCRYPT 2006. LNCS, vol. 4004, pp. 465–485. Springer, Heidelberg (2006). https://doi.org/10.1007/11761679_28
22. Lysyanskaya, A., Micali, S., Reyzin, L., Shacham, H.: Sequential aggregate signatures from trapdoor permutations. In: Cachin, C., Camenisch, J.L. (eds.) EUROCRYPT 2004. LNCS, vol. 3027, pp. 74–90. Springer, Heidelberg (2004). https://doi.org/10.1007/978-3-540-24676-3_5
23. Ma, D., Tsudik, G.: Extended abstract: forward-secure sequential aggregate authentication. In: S&P 2007, pp. 86–91 (2007)
24. Maurer, U.M.: Abstract models of computation in cryptography. In: IMA 2005, pp. 1–12 (2005)
25. Micali, S., Ohta, K., Reyzin, L.: Accountable-subgroup multisignatures: extended abstract. In: CCS 2001, pp. 245–254 (2001)
26. Neven, G.: Efficient sequential aggregate signed data. In: Smart, N. (ed.) EUROCRYPT 2008. LNCS, vol. 4965, pp. 52–69. Springer, Heidelberg (2008). https://doi.org/10.1007/978-3-540-78967-3_4
27. Ristenpart, T., Yilek, S.: The power of proofs-of-possession: securing multiparty signatures against rogue-key attacks. In: Naor, M. (ed.) EUROCRYPT 2007. LNCS, vol. 4515, pp. 228–245. Springer, Heidelberg (2007). https://doi.org/10.1007/978-3-540-72540-4_13
28. Schnorr, C.: Efficient identification and signatures for smart cards. In: CRYPTO 1989, pp. 239–252 (1989)
29. Syta, E., et al.: Keeping authorities "honest or bust" with decentralized witness cosigning. In: S&P 2016, pp. 526–545 (2016)
30. Xu, J., Zhang, Z., Feng, D.: ID-based aggregate signatures from bilinear pairings. In: Desmedt, Y.G., Wang, H., Mu, Y., Li, Y. (eds.) CANS 2005. LNCS, vol. 3810, pp. 110–119. Springer, Heidelberg (2005). https://doi.org/10.1007/11599371_10
31. Yao, A.C., Zhao, Y.: Online/offline signatures for low-power devices. IEEE Trans. Inf. Forensics Secur. **8**(2), 283–294 (2013)
32. Zhao, Y.: Practical aggregate signature from general elliptic curves, and applications to blockchain. In: AsiaCCS, 2019, pp. 529–538 (2019)

Short Lattice Signatures in the Standard Model with Efficient Tag Generation

Kaisei Kajita[1(✉)], Kazuto Ogawa[1], Koji Nuida[2], and Tsuyoshi Takagi[2]

[1] Japan Broadcasting Corporation, 1-10-11, Kinuta, Setagaya-ku, Tokyo, Japan
kajita.k-bu@nhk.or.jp

[2] The University of Tokyo, 7-3-1, Hongo, Bunkyo-ku, Tokyo, Japan

Abstract. We propose new short signature schemes under the ring-SIS assumption in the standard model. Specifically, by revisiting an existing construction in [Ducas and Micciancio, CRYPTO 2014], we demonstrate efficient lattice-based signatures with improved tag generation. We firstly construct a scheme under mild security condition that is existentially unforgeable against random message attack with auxiliary information. We then convert the mildly secure scheme to a fully secure scheme by applying a trapdoor commitment scheme. Our schemes enable the generation of tags from messages and the collision of multiple tags, which improves reduction loss. Our schemes have short signature sizes of $O(1)$ and achieves tighter reduction loss than that of Ducas et al.'s scheme. In accordance with two kinds of parameter set for tag generation, we get two signature schemes with different properties of reduction loss and verification key size. One of our schemes has tighter reduction and as the same size verification key of $O(\log n)$ as that of Ducas et al.'s scheme, where n is the security parameter. Another scheme achieves much tighter reduction loss of $O(\frac{Q}{n})$ for the sake of verification size of $O(n)$, where Q is the number of signing queries.

Keywords: Digital signatures · Ring-SIS assumption · Security reduction · Trapdoor commitment

1 Introduction

1.1 Background

Digital signatures are one of the most fundamental cryptographic primitives that guarantee authenticity of electronic documents and are an indispensable component of our digital infrastructure. When using digital signatures, each signer has a pair of keys consisting of one secret (signing) and one public (verification) key. A signer signs a document with the secret key, and the document's authenticity is publicly verifiable with the public key.

K. Ogawa—He is on loan to National Institute of Information and Communications Technology.

K. Nguyen et al. (Eds.): ProvSec 2020, LNCS 12505, pp. 85–102, 2020.
https://doi.org/10.1007/978-3-030-62576-4_5

The performance of cryptographic primitives, such as digital signatures, can be evaluated using *reduction loss* relative to a difficult problem. Reduction loss is the gap in difficulty between breaking the cryptographic primitive and solving the difficult problem. When there is approximately no reduction loss (i.e., when breaking the cryptographic primitive is at least as difficult as solving the difficult problem), the digital signature scheme is called *tightly secure*. The reduction loss can have a dramatic impact on the scheme's parameters. Lowering the reduction loss of a cryptosystem is important because this enables security parameters to be made as small as necessary without compromising security.

The model of signature schemes with a random oracle is called the *random oracle model*. It is an ideal framework for discussing the security of cryptosystems, replacing the execution of the hash function $H(\cdot)$ with a query to a random oracle, whose output is uniformly random. In general, a signature scheme in the *standard model* (i.e., without a random oracle) is superior to that in the random oracle model under the same condition. Here, we now discuss digital signature schemes in the standard model.

In 1994, Peter Shor showed that quantum computers can efficiently solve the integer factorization problem and the discrete logarithm problem [20]. *Post-Quantum Cryptography (PQC)*, which is believed to be resistant to an attack from a quantum computer, is studied around the world. Lattice-based cryptography is one type of PQC. Cryptosystems based on lattice problems have been increasing since the original work of Ajtai [2,3]. One great concern in this area is the need for a more efficient post-quantum digital signature scheme. The construction of an efficient lattice-based scheme under the standard assumption (i.e., general assumption such as the one-wayness of trapdoor permutation or more specific assumption such as the RSA assumption, the CDH assumption, or the Short Integer Solution assumption) with tight reduction loss in the standard model is desirable.

1.2 Related Works

The direct constructions of lattice signatures were presented by Lyubashevsky et al. [16] and Gentry et al. [13]. Lyubashevsky proposed a provably secure one-time signature scheme in the standard model. Gentry et al. constructed a signature scheme in the random oracle model that employs a sampling algorithm from Gaussian distribution. Both schemes achieved *short* signatures consisting of a single lattice vector.

We give a comparison of post-quantum signature schemes in the standard model in Table 1. In 2010, Cash et al. [9] provides with the first lattice-based signature scheme in the standard model applying chameleon hash function with reduction loss of $O(nQ)$ in reduction, where n is the security parameter and Q is the number of signing queries. Boyen [7] proposed the *vanishing trapdoor* technique and constructed a short signature scheme in the standard model with reduction loss of $O(nQ)$ in reduction. In 2013, Böhl et al. [6] formulated the *confined guessing* technique. Their scheme has verification and signing keys of size $O(1)$ in the standard model with reduction loss of $O(nQ)$ in reduction,

Table 1. Signature schemes under the (ring) SIS assumption in the standard model: n is the security parameter; β is the SIS parameter: Q is the number of signing queries; and $\epsilon, \delta, \ell, \alpha$, and c are parameters for each scheme. For proposed scheme 1, the parameter for tag generation is $C_i = 2^{\lfloor \alpha c^i \rfloor}$, and that for proposed scheme 2 is $C_i = 2^i$. The unit of size in SIS assumption is $\mathbb{Z}_q^n$ and that in the ring-SIS assumption is $\mathcal{R}_q$.

Scheme	$\lvert vk \rvert$	$\lvert sk \rvert$	$\lvert sig \rvert$	Reduction loss	Assumption	β
CHKP10 [9]	$O(n)$	$O(n)$	$O(n)$	$O(nQ)$	SIS	$\Omega(n^2)$
Boyen10 [7]	$O(n)$	$O(1)$	$O(1)$	$O(nQ)$	SIS	$\Omega(n^{7/2})$
BHJKSS13 [6]	$O(1)$	$O(1)$	$O(\log n)$	$O(nQ)$	SIS	$\Omega(n^{5/2})$
BKKP15 [5]	$O(1)$	$O(1)$	$O(n)$	$O(1)$	SIS	$\Omega(n^{3/2})$
Alperin15 [4]	$O(1)$	$O(1)$	$O(1)$	$O(nQ)$	SIS	$\Omega(n^{11/2}\delta^{2\delta})$
BL16 [8]	$O(n)$	$O(1)$	$O(1)$	$O(n)$	SIS+PRF	$\Omega(n^{7/2}\ell^{4c})$
DM14 [11]	$O(\log n)$	$O(1)$	$O(1)$	$O\left(\left(\frac{Q^2}{\epsilon}\right)^c\right)$	ring-SIS	$\Omega(n^{7/2})$
Proposed scheme 1	$O(\log n)$	$O(1)$	$O(1)$	$O\left(\left(\frac{Q}{n}\right)^c\right)$	ring-SIS	$\Omega(n^{7/2})$
Proposed scheme 2	$O(n)$	$O(1)$	$O(1)$	$O\left(\frac{Q}{n}\right)$	ring-SIS	$\Omega(n^{7/2})$

but longer signatures, of size $O(\log n)$. In 2014, a new short-signature framework using the confined guessing and vanishing trapdoor techniques was proposed by Ducas et al. [11]. Ducas et al.'s scheme has relatively short verification keys of $O(\log n)$ with reduction loss of $O(\left(\frac{Q^2}{\epsilon}\right)^c)$ for an arbitrary constant $c > 1$ and adversarial advantage ϵ.

Ducas et al. focus on a certain tag set and adjust the size of tag set so that one tag collision occurs. In the confined guessing technique, the simulator can solve a difficult problem by embedding the problem in the tag where the collision occurs, so the size of the tag set greatly affects the efficiency of the reduction loss. Therefore, efficient tag generation is important in signature schemes that use confined guessing. A short-signature scheme with almost tight security in the standard model using pseudorandom functions was proposed by Boyen et al. [8] in 2016. Their signature scheme eliminates the reduction loss's dependency on the number of adversary's queries, but their verification key is large, and a pseudorandom function is used in their scheme. A tightly secure signature scheme with short keys in the standard model was proposed by Blazy et al. [5], but its signature size is large. A signature scheme that has short signatures and keys was proposed by Alperin [4], but their reduction loss is loose.

Despite these outstanding works, lattice-based signature schemes that have short signatures and keys and tight reduction loss in the standard model remain unknown.

1.3 Contributions

We revisit Ducas et al. signature scheme [11] which employs the confined guessing technique [6]. We improve the tag generation method of [6,11]. Regarding a monotonically increasing parameter C_i for tag generation, each tag set is constructed as $\{0,1\}^{C_i}$ in [11]. The number of elements in the tag sets directly lead to reduction loss in the security proof when using confined guessing because a challenger embeds a challenge problem into a certain target tag and hopes an adversary forges a signature with corresponding the target tag. We consider multiple tag collisions, which enable tag sets to be made smaller and to enhance the probability that a tag from a forged signature corresponds with the target tag.

In addition, we consider a security model, existential unforgeability against extended random message attack (EUF-XRMA), which enables us to generate tags from random messages. Each tag can be related to a single message, so our signature scheme is regarded as a non-rerandomizable signature [14]. Hofheinz et al. shows that re-randomizable signatures has a bound of reduction loss of $O(Q)$ [14]. We then achieve a fully secure model, existential unforgeability against chosen message attacks (EUF-CMA), which secures signatures by applying the conversion technique proposed by Abe et al. [1] using trapdoor commitments. As a result, our construction (proposed scheme 1 in Table 1) has a tighter reduction loss of $O\left(\left(\frac{Q}{n}\right)^{c}\right)$ than that of Ducas et al.'s signatures, where n is the security parameter, which has the same size of verification key as that of Ducas et al.'s signatures.

Moreover, by choosing parameter C_i carefully, we achieve tighter reduction loss of $O(\frac{Q}{n})$ at the cost of verification key size of $O(n)$ (proposed scheme 2 in Table 1). Our signature schemes can be easily switched between proposed scheme 1 and 2 changing the value of tag-generation parameter C_i.

As a result, our signature scheme has a short signature size of $O(1)$ and achieves a relatively short verification key size of $O(\log n)$ and reduction loss of $O\left(\left(\frac{Q}{n}\right)^{c}\right)$ in reduction when $C_i = \lfloor \alpha c^i \rfloor$, where $c > 1$ and $\alpha \geq \frac{1}{c-1}$, or achieves a verification key size of $O(n)$ and reduction loss of $O(\frac{Q}{n})$ in reduction when $C_i = i$.

2 Preliminaries

Notation: If S is a set, $a \stackrel{\$}{\leftarrow} S$ denotes sampling a at uniformly random from S. $\mathsf{negl}(n)$ denotes an unspecified function $f(n)$ such that $f(n) = n^{-\omega(1)}$, meaning that such a function is negligible in n. For a probabilistic polynomial-time (PPT) algorithm $\mathcal{A}$, we write $y \leftarrow \mathcal{A}(x)$ to denote the experiment of running $\mathcal{A}$ for a given x, selecting an inner coin r uniformly from an appropriate domain, and assigning the results of this experiment to the variable y, i.e. $y = \mathcal{A}(x;r)$. Let $X = \{X_n\}_{n\in\mathbb{N}}$ and $Y = \{Y_n\}_{n\in\mathbb{N}}$ be probability ensembles such that each X_n and Y_n are random variables over $\{0,1\}^n$. The statistical distance between X_n and Y_n is $\mathsf{Dist}(X_n, Y_n) := \frac{1}{2}\sum_{s\in\{0,1\}^n} |\Pr[X_n = s] - \Pr[Y_n = s]|$. We write $X \equiv Y$ if $\mathsf{Dist}(X_n, Y_n) = 0$. We sometimes use a short notation $(\mathbf{A}, \mathbf{B})$ for the result of vertically stacking two matrices $\mathbf{A}$ and $\mathbf{B}$. We write # to denote the number of elements. Let g be real valued functions, we sometimes use a notation of $\tilde{O} = O(g(n) \log^k g(n))$ for some k. We denote $||\mathbf{x}|| = \sqrt{\sum_i x_i^2}$ as the Euclidean norm.

$\mathsf{Expt}_{\mathsf{SIG},\mathcal{A}}^{\text{EUF-CMA}}(n)$:
$(vk, sk) \leftarrow \mathsf{KGen}(1^n)$;
$(m^*, \sigma^*) \leftarrow \mathcal{A}^{\mathsf{Sign}_{sk}(\cdot)}(vk)$
If $m^* \in \mathcal{Q}_m$, then return 0
Return $\mathsf{Vrfy}(vk, m^*, \sigma^*)$.

Fig. 1. Experiment with EUF-CMA.

$\mathsf{Expt}_{\mathsf{SIG},\mathcal{A}}^{\text{EUF-XRMA}}(n)$:
$(vk, sk) \leftarrow \mathsf{KGen}(1^n)$;
$gk \leftarrow \mathsf{Setup}(1^n)$
For $\forall i \in [Q]$,
$(m_i, \rho_i) \leftarrow \mathsf{MsgGen}(gk)$;
$\sigma_i \leftarrow \mathsf{Sign}_{sk}(m_i)$
$(m^*, \sigma^*) \leftarrow \mathcal{A}(vk, \{m_i, \sigma_i, \rho_i\}_{i=1}^{Q})$
If $m^* \in \mathcal{Q}_m$, then return 0
Return $\mathsf{Vrfy}(vk, m^*, \sigma^*)$.

Fig. 2. Experiment with EUF-XRMA. The Setup algorithm is a PPT algorithm that takes as input a security parameter 1^n and outputs gk.

2.1 Digital Signatures

A digital signature scheme is given by a triple, $\mathsf{SIG} = (\mathsf{KGen}, \mathsf{Sign}, \mathsf{Vrfy})$, of PPT Turing machines, where for every sufficiently large $n \in \mathbb{N}$, the key-generation algorithm KGen takes as input security parameter 1^n and outputs a pair of verification and signing keys, (vk, sk). Here, let $\mathcal{M}_n$ be message space. The signing algorithm Sign takes as input (vk, sk) and a message $m \in \mathcal{M}_n$ and produces a signature σ. The verification algorithm Vrfy takes as input vk, m, and σ, and outputs a verification result bit. For correctness, $\mathsf{Vrfy}(vk, m, \sigma) = 1$, where $\sigma = \mathsf{Sign}(sk, m)$, must hold for any (vk, sk) pair generated with $KGen(1^n)$ and for any $m \in \mathcal{M}_n$.

2.2 Security Classes

EUF-CMA: A digital signature scheme SIG is considered existentially unforgeable against adaptively chosen-message attack (EUF-CMA) [12] if for any adversary $\mathcal{A}$, $\mathsf{Adv}_{\mathsf{SIG},\mathcal{A}}^{\text{EUF-CMA}}(n) := \Pr[\mathsf{Expt}_{\mathsf{SIG},\mathcal{A}}^{\text{EUF-CMA}}(n) = 1] = \mathsf{negl}(n)$, where $\mathsf{Expt}_{\mathsf{SIG},\mathcal{A}}^{\text{EUF-CMA}}(n)$ is defined in Fig. 1. $\mathsf{Sign}_{sk}(\cdot)$ is a signing oracle with respect to sk that takes as input m, returns $\sigma \stackrel{\$}{\leftarrow} \mathsf{Sign}_{sk}(m)$ and records m to a message list $\mathcal{Q}_m$, which is initially an empty list.

EUF-XRMA: A SIG is considered existentially unforgeable against extended random-message attack (EUF-XRMA) [1] with respect to the message generator MsgGen, a PPT algorithm that takes as input a message-generation key gk and outputs m and ρ, if for any $\mathcal{A}$ and any positive integer Q, $\mathsf{Adv}^{\text{EUF-XRMA}}_{\mathsf{SIG},\mathcal{A}}(n) := \Pr[\mathsf{Expt}^{\text{EUF-XRMA}}_{\mathsf{SIG},\mathcal{A}}(n) = 1] = \mathsf{negl}(n)$, where $\mathsf{Expt}^{\text{EUF-XRMA}}_{\mathsf{SIG},\mathcal{A}}(n)$ is defined in Fig. 2, and $\mathcal{Q}_m = \{m_1, \ldots, m_Q\}$.

2.3 Lattice and Gaussian

A full-rank n-dimensional lattice is the set $\Lambda = \{\mathbf{Bz} : \mathbf{z} \in \mathbb{Z}^n\}$ of all integers combinations of n basis vectors $\mathbf{B} = [\mathbf{b}_1, \ldots, \mathbf{b}_n] \in \mathbb{Z}_q^{n\times n}$. For positive integers n and q, let $\mathbf{A} \in \mathbb{Z}_q^{n\times n}$ be arbitrary and define the following full-rank n-dimensional q-ary lattices:

$$\Lambda^{\perp}(\mathbf{A}) = \{\mathbf{z} \in \mathbb{Z}^n : \mathbf{Az} = 0 \mod q\},$$
$$\Lambda(\mathbf{A}) = \{\mathbf{z} \in \mathbb{Z}^n : \exists \mathbf{s} \in \mathbb{Z}_q^n \text{ s.t. } \mathbf{z} = \mathbf{A}^t\mathbf{s} \mod q\}.$$

For any $\mathbf{u} \in \mathbb{Z}_q^n$, define the coset (or shifted lattice) $\Lambda_{\mathbf{u}}^{\perp}(\mathbf{A}) = \{\mathbf{z} \in \mathbb{Z}^n : \mathbf{Az} = \mathbf{u} \mod q\}$.

We consider lattice problems restricted to ideal lattices [18]. We focus on rings of the form $\mathcal{R} = \mathbb{Z}[X]/\Phi_n(X)$ or $\mathcal{R}_q = (\mathcal{R}/q\mathcal{R})$, where n is a power of 2, q is an integer, and $\Phi_n(X) = X^n + 1$ is the cyclotomic polynomial of degree n [17]. For our construction, we require that $\Phi_n(X)$ does not split into low degree polynomials modulo the prime factors of q. More specifically, we choose $q = 3^k$. Note that the lattice dimensions and polynomial orders are the same for the sake of simplicity. The geometric quality of a matrix $\mathbf{A} \in \mathbb{R}^{m\times n}$ is measured by its spectral norm $s_1 = \sup_{\mathbf{x}} ||\mathbf{Ax}||/||\mathbf{x}||$ for every $\mathbf{x} \in \Lambda$.

The n-dimensional Gaussian function $\rho_s : \mathcal{R}^n \to (0, 1]$ is defined as $\rho_s(\mathbf{x}) = \exp(-\pi \cdot ||\mathbf{x}/s||^2)$ for a variance s. For any countable $X \subset \mathcal{R}^n$, let $\rho(X) = \sum_{\mathbf{x}\in X} \rho_s(\mathbf{x})$. The discrete Gaussian distribution $D_{\Lambda,s}$ over a lattice Λ is defined as $D_{\Lambda,s}(\mathbf{x}) = \rho_s(\mathbf{x})/\rho_s(\Lambda)$ for all $\mathbf{x} \in \Lambda$. The discrete Gaussian distribution over n-dimensional row vectors of ring $D_{\mathcal{R},s} := D^n_{\mathbb{Z},s}$ is defined by identifying the ring $\mathcal{R}$ with $\mathbb{Z}^n$ under the coefficient embedding. The discrete Gaussian distribution over the ring $\mathbf{x} \leftarrow D_{\mathcal{R},s}$ is sub-Gaussian of parameter s.

Then we define the ring-SIS problem as follows.

Definition 1. *In the small integer solution over rings problem* (ring-SIS$_{w,q,\beta}$)*, one is given a matrix $A \in \mathcal{R}_q^{1\times w}$ and asked to find a non-zero vector $\mathbf{x} \in \Lambda_q^{\perp}(\mathbf{A})$ such that $||\mathbf{x}|| \leq \beta$.*

2.4 Lattice Trapdoor

W define lattice trapdoors as follows on the basis of Ducas et al.'s signature [11]. For modulus $q = 3^k$ and $n \times n$ identity matrix $\mathbf{I}_n$, we define the gadget matrix $\mathbf{G} = [\mathbf{I}_n | 3\mathbf{I}_n | \ldots | 3^{k-1}\mathbf{I}_n] \in \mathbb{Z}_q^{n\times kn}$. Because $\mathbf{I}_n$ corresponds with the ring element $1 \in \mathcal{R}_q$, the gadget matrix $\mathbf{G}$ can be regarded as a row vector of the ring elements: $\mathbf{G} = [1, 3, \ldots 3^{k-1}] \in \mathcal{R}_q^{1\times k}$.

Definition 2. *For any* $\mathbf{A} \in \mathcal{R}_q^{1\times(w+k)}$*, and invertible* $\mathbf{H} \in \mathcal{R}_q^{1\times 1}$*, a* **G***-trapdoor for* $\mathbf{A}$ *with* $\mathbf{H}$ *is a matrix* $\mathbf{S} \in \mathcal{R}_q^{w\times k}$ *such that* $\mathbf{A}\begin{bmatrix}\mathbf{S}\\ \mathbf{I}_k\end{bmatrix} = \mathbf{HG}$.

The quality of a **G**-trapdoor **S** is measured by the spectral norm $s_1(\mathbf{S})$. If $\mathbf{S} \leftarrow D_{\mathcal{R},s}^{w\times k}$, then we have $s_1(\mathbf{S}) = s\sqrt{n}\cdot O(\sqrt{w} + \sqrt{k} + \omega(\sqrt{\log n}))$ with overwhelming probability. Let $\mathcal{U}_w$ be the uniform distribution over w-dimensional ring elements. We introduce the following theorem.

Theorem 1 ([11]). *There is a polynomial time algorithm* $\mathsf{GenTrap}(\mathbf{A}', \mathbf{H}, s)$ *that on inputting a matrix* $\mathbf{A}' \in \mathcal{R}_q^{1\times w}$, $\mathbf{H} \in \mathcal{R}_q$*, with parameter* $s > \omega(\sqrt{\ln nw})$*, outputs a matrix* $\mathbf{A}'' \in \mathcal{R}_q^{1\times k}$ *and a* **G***-trapdoor* $\mathbf{S} \in \mathcal{R}_q^{w\times k}$ *for* $\mathbf{A} = [\mathbf{A}', \mathbf{A}'']$ *with* $\mathbf{H} \in \mathcal{R}_q$ *such that* $s_1(\mathbf{S}) = s\cdot O(\sqrt{w} + \sqrt{k} + \omega(\sqrt{\log n}))$*. In addition, if* $w \geq 2(\lceil \log_2 q\rceil + 1)$*, then with overwhelming probability over the choice of* $\mathbf{A}' \leftarrow \mathcal{U}_w$*, the distribution of* $\mathbf{A}''$ *is statistically close to uniform.*

We introduce the following lemma that any linear combination of **S** is also **G**-trapdoor. For any matrix $X \in \mathcal{R}$, we write the sub-matrix as $X_{[i]}$.

Lemma 1 ([11]). *For* $i = 0, \ldots, d$*, let* $\mathbf{S}_{[i]} \in \mathcal{R}_q^{w\times k}$ *be a* **G***-trapdoor for* $[\mathbf{A}, \mathbf{A}_{[i]}]$ *with* $\mathbf{H}_{[i]} \in \mathcal{R}_q$*, where* $\mathbf{A}_{[i]} \in \mathcal{R}_q^{1\times k}$*. Then, any linear combination* $\mathbf{S} = \sum_i y_i \cdot \mathbf{S}_{[i]}$ *with* $y_i \in \mathcal{R}_q$ *is a* **G***-trapdoor for* $[\mathbf{A}, \sum_i y_i \mathbf{A}_{[i]}]$ *with* $\mathbf{H} = \sum_i y_i \mathbf{H}_{[i]}$.

Let us introduce a sampling algorithm from [19].

Definition 3. *There is an efficient algorithm* $\mathsf{SampleD}(\mathbf{A}, \mathbf{u}_0, \mathbf{S}, s)$ *that, on inputting a matrix* $\mathbf{A} \in \mathcal{R}_q^{1\times(w+k)}$*, a syndrome* $\mathbf{u}_0 \in \mathcal{R}_q$*, a* **G***-trapdoor* $\mathbf{S} \in \mathcal{R}_q^{w\times k}$ *for* $\mathbf{A}$ *with invertible* $\mathbf{H} \in \mathcal{R}_q$*, and parameter* $s = \omega(\sqrt{\log n})\cdot s_1(\mathbf{S})$*, produces a sample statistically close to the distribution* $D_{\Lambda^{\perp}_{\mathbf{u}_0}(\mathbf{A}),s}$*, where* $D_{\Lambda^{\perp}_{\mathbf{u}_0}(\mathbf{A}),s}$ *is the discrete Gaussian distribution whose variance is* s *and center is* $\mathbf{u}_0$.

2.5 Trapdoor Commitments

We define a trapdoor commitment scheme [10]. Let $\mathsf{TCOM} = (\mathsf{KGen}^{\mathsf{tc}}, \mathsf{Com}^{\mathsf{tc}}, \mathsf{TCom}^{\mathsf{tc}}, \mathsf{TCol}^{\mathsf{tc}})$ be a tuple of the following four algorithms. $\mathsf{KGen}^{\mathsf{tc}}$ is a PPT algorithm that takes as a input security parameter 1^n and outputs a pair of keys, one public and one trapdoor $(pk, tk) \leftarrow \mathsf{KGen}^{\mathsf{tc}}(1^n)$. $\mathsf{Com}^{\mathsf{tc}}$ is a PPT algorithm that takes as input pk and m, selects a random $r \leftarrow \mathsf{COIN}$' in which $r \in \mathbb{Z}_q$, and outputs a commitment $\mu = \mathsf{Com}^{\mathsf{tc}}_{pk}(m; r)$. $\mathsf{TCom}^{\mathsf{tc}}$ is a PPT algorithm that takes as input 1^n and tk, and outputs $(\mu, \chi) \leftarrow \mathsf{TCom}^{\mathsf{tc}}_{tk}(1^n)$, where χ is auxiliary information. $\mathsf{TCol}^{\mathsf{tc}}$ is a deterministic polynomial-time algorithm that takes as input tk, μ, χ and m, and outputs r such that $\mu = \mathsf{Com}^{\mathsf{tc}}_{pk}(m; r)$. The construction of lattice-based commitment schemes [15] is used implicitly in this paper.

3 Mildly Secure Scheme

We firstly demonstrate the generation method of tag to construct EUF-XRMA secure signature scheme.

3.1 Tags

We define the sets of tag prefixes $\mathcal{T}_i = \{0,1\}^{C_i}$, where C_i is a monotonically increasing constant for $i = \{1, \ldots, d\}$ and $d < n$. In our proposed scheme 1, the parameter C_i is the same as Ducas et al.'s, $C_i = \lfloor \alpha c^i \rfloor$, where $c > 1$ and $\alpha \geq \frac{1}{c-1}$. On the other hand, in our proposed scheme 2, $C_i = i$.

We identify each tag prefix $t = [t_0, \ldots, t_{i-1}] \in \mathcal{T}_i$ with a corresponding ring element $t(X) = \sum_{j<i} t_j X^j \in \mathcal{R}_q$ with binary coefficients $t_j \in \{0,1\}$. We demonstrate the following lemma to prove the security of our signature scheme later in this paper.

Lemma 2. *Let $Q = 2^{O(n)}$ and $\psi = \Omega(n)$. If $\#\mathcal{T} > \frac{2eQ}{\psi+1}$,*

$$\Pr[(\psi+1)\text{-fold}] := \Pr[\exists i_1, \ldots, i_{\psi+1} \in [Q] \text{s.t.} t_{i_1} = \cdots = t_{i_{\psi+1}}]$$

is exponentially small in n, where $t_1, \ldots, t_Q$ are independently and uniformly chosen from $\mathcal{T}$ and e denotes the base of the natural logarithm.

Proof. We compute the probability of $\Pr[(\psi+1)\text{-fold}]$ where $\psi+1$ tags are same from Q elements. We then apply the Stirling's approximation and asymptotically estimate the probability.

$$\begin{aligned}
&\Pr[\exists i_1, \ldots, i_{\psi+1} \in [Q] \text{ s.t } t_{i_1} = \cdots = t_{i_{\psi+1}}] \\
&\leq \binom{Q}{\psi+1} \left(\frac{1}{\#\mathcal{T}}\right)^{\psi} \\
&= \frac{Q \cdot (Q-1) \cdots (Q-\psi)}{(\psi+1)!} \left(\frac{1}{\#\mathcal{T}}\right)^{\psi} \\
&\leq \frac{Q^{\psi+1}}{(\psi+1)!} \left(\frac{1}{\#\mathcal{T}}\right)^{\psi} \\
&\leq \frac{Q^{\psi+1}}{\sqrt{2\pi(\psi+1)}} \left(\frac{e}{\psi+1}\right)^{\psi+1} \left(\frac{1}{\#\mathcal{T}}\right)^{\psi} \quad \cdots (*) \\
&= \frac{e \cdot Q}{\sqrt{2\pi(\psi+1)} \cdot (\psi+1)} \left(\frac{e \cdot Q}{\#\mathcal{T}(\psi+1)}\right)^{\psi}.
\end{aligned}$$

Inequality $(*)$ holds by Stirling's approximation

$$\sqrt{2\pi x} \left(\frac{x}{e}\right)^x \leq x! \leq e\sqrt{x} \left(\frac{x}{e}\right)^x.$$

From $\psi = O(n)$ and $Q = 2^{O(n)}$,

$$\frac{e \cdot Q}{\sqrt{2\pi(\psi+1)} \cdot (\psi+1)} = \frac{2^{O(n)}}{O(n^{3/2})}$$

Now, we set $\#\mathcal{T} > \frac{2eQ}{\psi+1}$ and $\frac{e \cdot Q}{n(\psi+1)} < \frac{1}{2}$. $\frac{e \cdot Q}{\sqrt{2\pi(\psi+1)} \cdot (\psi+1)}$ is a power of 2 order in n. Hence, $\Pr[(\psi+1)\text{-fold}]$ is exponentially small in n. □

The lemma above is a generalized birthday bound lemma, which often appears in the literature with ψ as a constant number, including [6]. In this case, ψ is not constant and Q is an exponential number, which lead to somewhat different results than those in [6,11]. In addition, by using Stirling's approximation with suitable parameter selection, we obtain the results given above.

3.2 Construction

We propose a signature scheme SIG_0. We prove later in this paper that SIG_0 is EUF-XRMA secure with respect to MsgGen under the ring-SIS assumption. SIG_0 is similar to the non-adaptively secure signature scheme in [11]. The main differences between SIG_0 and Ducas et al.'s scheme are the generation of tags from messages and the enabling of multiple tag collisions in SIG_0. In an EUF-XRMA game, it is supposed that random messages are given. The EUF-XRMA game does not enables tags to be sent with signatures because all tags can be generated from messages when generating the signature. We describe our signature scheme SIG_0 in Fig. 4. Let k be an arbitrary system parameter. We let $w = 2\lceil \log_2 q \rceil + 2$, $q = 3^k$, and $s = n^{3/2} \cdot \omega(\log n)^{3/2}$ for system parameters. For any full tag $t \in \mathcal{T} = \mathcal{T}_d$ and $i < d$, we write $t_{\leq i} \in \mathcal{T}_i$ for its prefix of length i, and $t_{[i]}$ for the (ring) difference $t_{\leq i}(X) - t_{\leq i-1}(X) \in \mathcal{R}_q$. Let the algorithm BtoR in Sign be a function that converts an nk bits string into a k-dimension vector in $\mathcal{R}_q$. We note that to sign a message m, SIG_0 generates $\{t_{\leq 1}, \ldots, t_{\leq d}\}$ and $\{t_{[1]}, \ldots, t_{[d]}\}$, from m. Figure 3 is an example that shows mod operations $t_{\leq i} = m \mod C_i$ when $C_i = i$. Then $t_{[i]}$ is obtained by computed the difference $t_{\leq i}(X) - t_{\leq i-1}(X)$. Both our schemes and Ducas et al. signature scheme employ the confined guessing technique proposed by Böhl et al. by embedding tags, whose each domain varies in size, into public keys.

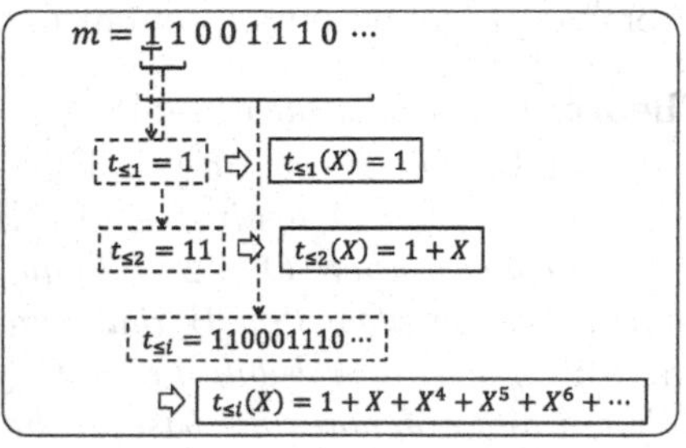

Fig. 3. An example of tags when $C_i = i$

Correctness: The correctness of the scheme is verified as follows. Because $s = n^{3/2} \cdot \omega(\log n)^{3/2}$, the signature $\boldsymbol{\sigma}$ produced during the signature generation process follows the distribution $D_{\Lambda_{\mathbf{u}}^{\perp}(\mathbf{A}_t),s}$ and has a length of at most $s\sqrt{n(w \times k)}$ with overwhelming probability. Thus, the signature $\boldsymbol{\sigma}$ is accepted by the verification algorithm.

Two Results of Efficiency: We propose two results of efficiency by altering parameter C_i for the tag set $\mathcal{T}_i = \{0,1\}^{C_i}$. If $C_i = \lfloor \alpha c^i \rfloor$, i.e. the same as Ducas et al.'s signatures, we achieve slightly tighter reduction of $O((\frac{Q}{n})^c)$ in reduction with verification keys of $O(\log n)$. If $C_i = i$, we achieve tighter reduction of $O(\frac{Q}{n})$ at the cost of verification key size of $O(n)$.

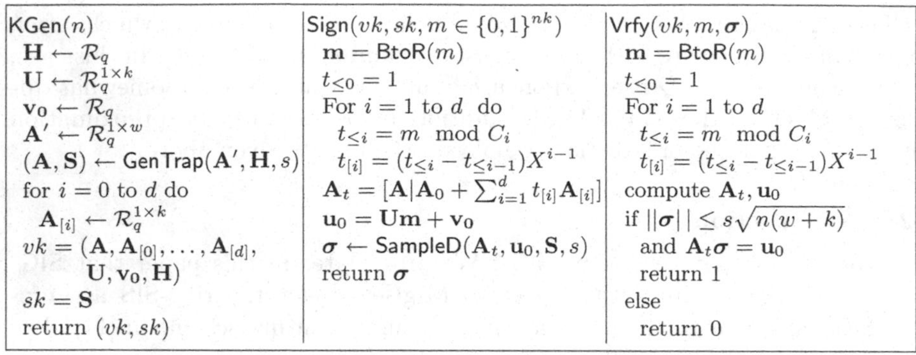

$\mathsf{KGen}(n)$	$\mathsf{Sign}(vk, sk, m \in \{0,1\}^{nk})$	$\mathsf{Vrfy}(vk, m, \boldsymbol{\sigma})$
$\mathbf{H} \leftarrow \mathcal{R}_q$	$\mathbf{m} = \mathsf{BtoR}(m)$	$\mathbf{m} = \mathsf{BtoR}(m)$
$\mathbf{U} \leftarrow \mathcal{R}_q^{1\times k}$	$t_{\leq 0} = 1$	$t_{\leq 0} = 1$
$\mathbf{v}_0 \leftarrow \mathcal{R}_q$	For $i = 1$ to d do	For $i = 1$ to d
$\mathbf{A}' \leftarrow \mathcal{R}_q^{1\times w}$	$t_{\leq i} = m \mod C_i$	$t_{\leq i} = m \mod C_i$
$(\mathbf{A}, \mathbf{S}) \leftarrow \mathsf{GenTrap}(\mathbf{A}', \mathbf{H}, s)$	$t_{[i]} = (t_{\leq i} - t_{\leq i-1})X^{i-1}$	$t_{[i]} = (t_{\leq i} - t_{\leq i-1})X^{i-1}$
for $i = 0$ to d do	$\mathbf{A}_t = [\mathbf{A} \vert \mathbf{A}_0 + \sum_{i=1}^{d} t_{[i]}\mathbf{A}_{[i]}]$	compute $\mathbf{A}_t, \mathbf{u}_0$
$\mathbf{A}_{[i]} \leftarrow \mathcal{R}_q^{1\times k}$	$\mathbf{u}_0 = \mathbf{U}\mathbf{m} + \mathbf{v}_0$	if $\vert\vert\boldsymbol{\sigma}\vert\vert \leq s\sqrt{n(w+k)}$
$vk = (\mathbf{A}, \mathbf{A}_{[0]}, \ldots, \mathbf{A}_{[d]},$	$\boldsymbol{\sigma} \leftarrow \mathsf{SampleD}(\mathbf{A}_t, \mathbf{u}_0, \mathbf{S}, s)$	and $\mathbf{A}_t\boldsymbol{\sigma} = \mathbf{u}_0$
$\mathbf{U}, \mathbf{v}_0, \mathbf{H})$	return $\boldsymbol{\sigma}$	return 1
$sk = \mathbf{S}$		else
return (vk, sk)		return 0

Fig. 4. SIG_0: EUF-XRMA secure signature scheme under ring-SIS assumption.

3.3 Security Analysis

To prove our theorems later in this paper, we define $(m, \chi) \leftarrow \mathsf{MsgGen}$ in the EUF-XRMA experiment using a standard trapdoor commitment scheme based on lattices. Let $(m, \chi) \leftarrow \mathsf{MsgGen}$ be the algorithm that runs $(\mu, \chi) \leftarrow \mathsf{TCom}_{tk}^{\mathsf{tc}}(1^n)$ and outputs a commitment μ as a message m.

Theorem 2. *Under the* ring-SIS$_{w,q,\beta}$ *assumption for* $\beta = \tilde{O}(n^{7/2})$, *the signature scheme* SIG_0 *for* $C_i = \lfloor \alpha c^i \rfloor$ *is* EUF-XRMA *secure. More precisely, if there exists an attacker* $\mathcal{A}$ *against* EUF-XRMA$_{\mathsf{SIG}_0}$ *that runs in time* T, *makes at most* Q *queries where* $Q = 2^{O(n)}$ *and succeeds with probability* $\epsilon \geq 2^{-O(n)}$, *then there exists an algorithm* $\mathcal{B}$ *that runs in time* $T' = T + poly(n)$, *and solves* ring-SIS$_{w,q,\beta}$ *with probability* $\epsilon' = \Omega((\frac{\psi+1}{4eQ})^c) \cdot \epsilon$, *where* ψ *is the number of tag-collision and* e *denotes the base of the natural logarithm.*

The security proof of Theorem 2 is approximately the same as Ducas et al.'s security proof without the tag generation method and adversary's condition. We give the full proof of Theorem 2 in Appendix A. Here, we give its sketch.

Proof Sketch. The simulator $\mathcal{B}$ receives a ring-SIS challenge and gets Q messages from MsgGen. Then, $\mathcal{B}$ generates tags from the messages: $t_{\leq i}^{(j)} = m^{(j)} \mod 2^{\lfloor \alpha c^i \rfloor}$ for $j = 1, \ldots, Q$. First, $\mathcal{B}$ sets the target tag set $\mathcal{T}_{i^*}$. We denote the event $(\psi+1)$-fold happening be $Pr[(\psi+1)\text{-fold}^{\text{real}}]$. Here, $Pr[(\psi+1)\text{-fold}^{\text{real}}]$ and $Pr[(\psi+1)\text{-fold}^{\text{ideal}}]$ are statistically indistinguishable. $\mathcal{B}$ randomly chooses $t_{\leq i^*}^* \xleftarrow{\$} \mathcal{T}_{i^*}$, set $\mathcal{M}' := \{m \vert t_{\leq i^*}^* = t_{\leq i^*}^{(j)}\}$. If $\#\mathcal{M}' \geq \psi + 1$, $\mathcal{B}$ aborts. In accordance with Lemma 2, $\mathcal{B}$ chooses $\#\mathcal{T}_{i^*}$ such that $\#\mathcal{T}_{i^*-1} < \frac{2eQ}{\psi+1} < \#\mathcal{T}_{i^*}$. From $C_i = \lfloor \alpha c^i \rfloor$ for $c > 1$ and $\alpha \geq \frac{1}{c-1}$, $\alpha c^i \leq C_i + 1$ holds. Then,

$$C_{i^*} \leq \alpha c^{i^*} = c\alpha c^{i^*-1} \leq c(C_{i^*-1} + 1).$$

$\mathcal{B}$ sets $\#\mathcal{T}_{i^*}$ as

$$\#\mathcal{T}_{i^*} = 2^{C_{i^*}} \leq 2^{c(C_{i^*-1}+1)} = (2 \cdot 2^{C_{i^*-1}})^c \leq \left(\frac{4eQ}{\psi+1}\right)^c.$$

Let t^* in $\mathcal{T}_{i^*}$ be the target tag and embed the hint for solving the ring-SIS challenge in it. After $\mathcal{B}$ feeds all information, messages, signatures, and tags as auxiliary information, the adversary $\mathcal{A}$ returns the forgery $\boldsymbol{\sigma}^\diamond$ for a fresh message $m^\diamond$. If the tag $t^\diamond$ for the forgery corresponds the target tag t^*, $\mathcal{B}$ can solve the ring-SIS challenge. Therefore, the success probability $\epsilon' \geq \frac{1}{\#\mathcal{T}_{i^*}}\epsilon = \Omega(\left(\frac{\psi+1}{4eQ}\right)^c)\epsilon$.

If $C_i = i$, the following theorem holds.

Theorem 3. *Under the* ring-SIS$_{w,q,\beta}$ *assumption for* $\beta = \tilde{O}(n^{7/2})$, *the signature scheme* SIG_0 *for* $C_i = i$ *is* EUF-XRMA *secure. More precisely, if there exists an attacker* A *against* EUF-XRMA$_{\mathsf{SIG}_0}$ *that runs in time* T, *makes at most* Q *queries where* $Q = 2^{O(n)}$, *and succeeds with probability* $\epsilon = 2^{-O(n)}$, *then there exists an algorithm* $\mathcal{B}$ *that runs in time* $T' = T + poly(n)$, *and solves* ring-SIS$_{w,q,\beta}$ *with probability* $\epsilon' = \Omega(\frac{\psi}{Q}) \cdot \epsilon$, *where* ψ *is the number of tag collisions.*

The proof of Theorem 3 is the same as that of Theorem 2 without the tag set's parameter. $\mathcal{B}$ sets $\#\mathcal{T}_{i^*} = 2^{i^*} \leq 2 \cdot 2^{i^*-1} = 2\mathcal{T}_{i^*-1} \leq \frac{4eQ}{\psi+1}$. After all simulation, $\mathcal{B}$ can solve the ring-SIS challenge with success probability $\epsilon' \geq \frac{1}{\#\mathcal{T}_{i^*}}\epsilon = \Omega\left(\frac{\psi+1}{4eQ}\right)\epsilon$.

4 Fully Secure Scheme

In this section, we demonstrate the construction of a fully EUF-CMA secure scheme from SIG_0 by applying the trapdoor commitment TCOM. We call TCOM a trapdoor commitment scheme if the following conditions hold.

4.1 Conditions of TCOM

Hiding. For the pk generated with $\mathsf{KGen}^{\mathsf{tc}}(1^n)$, and any $m, m' \in \mathcal{M}_n$, *statistical hiding* holds if the following ensembles are statistically indistinguishable in n:

$$\left\{(\mu, m, r) \mid \mu = \mathsf{Com}^{\mathsf{tc}}_{pk}(m; r); r \leftarrow \mathsf{COIN}'\right\}$$
$$\overset{s}{\approx}\left\{(\mu', m', r') \mid \mu' = \mathsf{Com}^{\mathsf{tc}}_{pk}(m'; r'); r' \leftarrow \mathsf{COIN}'\right\}.$$

Computational Binding. For any polynomial-time adversary $\mathcal{A}$,

$$\epsilon^{\mathrm{bind}} := \Pr\left[\begin{array}{l}(m_1, m_2, r_1, r_2) \leftarrow \mathcal{A}(pk);\\ (pk, tk) \leftarrow \mathsf{KGen}^{\mathsf{tc}}(1^n) :\\ \mathsf{Com}^{\mathsf{tc}}_{pk}(m_1; r_1) = \mathsf{Com}^{\mathsf{tc}}_{pk}(m_2; r_2) \wedge (m_1 \neq m_2)\end{array}\right]$$
$$= \mathsf{negl}(n).$$

$\mathsf{KGen}(n)$	$\mathsf{Sign}(vk, sk, m \in \{0,1\}^{nk})$	$\mathsf{Vrfy}(vk, m, \boldsymbol{\sigma}, r)$
$\mathbf{H} \leftarrow \mathcal{R}_q$	$r \leftarrow \mathsf{COIN}^{\mathsf{com}}$	$\mu = \mathsf{Com}^{\mathsf{tc}}_{pk}(m; r)$
$\mathbf{U} \leftarrow \mathcal{R}_q^{1\times k}$	$\mu = \mathsf{Com}^{\mathsf{tc}}_{pk}(m; r)$	$\boldsymbol{\mu} = \mathsf{BtoR}(\mu)$
$\mathbf{v}_0 \leftarrow \mathcal{R}_q$	$\boldsymbol{\mu} = \mathsf{BtoR}(\mu)$	$t_{\leq 0} = 1$
$\mathbf{A}' \leftarrow \mathcal{R}_q^{1\times w}$	$t_{\leq 0} = 1$	For $i = 1$ to d
$(\mathbf{A}, \mathbf{S}) \leftarrow \mathsf{GenTrap}(\mathbf{A}', \mathbf{H}, s)$	For $i = 1$ to d do	$t_{\leq i} = \mu \mod C_i$
for $i = 0$ to d do	$t_{\leq i} = \mu \mod C_i$	$t_{[i]} = (t_{\leq i} - t_{\leq i-1})X^{i-1}$
$\mathbf{A}_{[i]} \leftarrow \mathcal{R}_q^{1\times k}$	$t_{[i]} = (t_{\leq i} - t_{\leq i-1})X^{i-1}$	Compute $\mathbf{A}_t, \mathbf{u}_0$
$(tk, pk) \leftarrow \mathsf{KGen}^{\mathsf{tc}}(n)$	$\mathbf{A}_t = [\mathbf{A} \vert \mathbf{A}_0 + \sum_{i=1}^{d} t_{[i]}\mathbf{A}_{[i]}]$	if $\vert\vert\boldsymbol{\sigma}\vert\vert \leq s\sqrt{n(w+k)}$
$vk = (\mathbf{A}, \mathbf{A}_{[0]}, \ldots, \mathbf{A}_{[d]},$	$\mathbf{u}_0 = \mathbf{U}\boldsymbol{\mu} + \mathbf{v}_0$	and $\mathbf{A}_t\boldsymbol{\sigma} = \mathbf{u}_0$
$\mathbf{U}, \mathbf{v}_0, \mathbf{H})$	$\boldsymbol{\sigma} \leftarrow \mathsf{SampleD}(\mathbf{A}_t, \mathbf{u}_0, \mathbf{S}, s)$	return 1
$sk = \mathbf{S}$	return $(\boldsymbol{\sigma}, r)$	else
return (vk, sk, pk, tk)		return 0

Fig. 5. SIG_1: EUF-CMA-secure signature scheme with TCOM

Trapdoor Property. The algorithm $\mathsf{KGen}^{\mathsf{tc}}$ for generating pk also outputs a trapdoor tk. There is an efficient algorithm $\mathsf{TCom}^{\mathsf{tc}}$ that, on inputting tk, pk, outputs a commitment μ, and an algorithm $\mathsf{TCol}^{\mathsf{tc}}$ that, on inputting any m, produces r such that $\mu = \mathsf{Com}^{\mathsf{tc}}_{pk}(m; r)$. The distribution of μ computed by $\mathsf{TCom}^{\mathsf{tc}}$ is statistically indistinguishable from that of commitments computed by $\mathsf{Com}^{\mathsf{tc}}$,

$$\Big\{(\mu, m, r) \mid \mu = \mathsf{Com}^{\mathsf{tc}}_{pk}(m; r); r \leftarrow \mathsf{COIN}'\Big\}$$
$$\overset{\mathrm{s}}{\approx}\Big\{(\mu, m, r) \mid (\mu, \chi) \leftarrow \mathsf{TCom}^{\mathsf{tc}}_{tk}(1^n); r = \mathsf{TCol}^{\mathsf{tc}}_{tk}(\mu, \chi, m)\Big\}.$$

4.2 Construction

Let SIG_1 be a signature scheme constructed by applying TCOM to SIG_0. We describe it in Fig. 5. In the signing and verification algorithms of SIG_1, commitments μ are regarded as messages. The correctness of the signature scheme SIG_1 can be demonstrated in the same way as that of SIG_0.

4.3 Security Analysis

We demonstrate that SIG_1 is EUF-CMA secure with TCOM by constructing the adversary $\mathcal{B}^{\mathrm{bind}}$ which breaks the computational binding of TCOM, or the adversary $\mathcal{B}^{\mathrm{euf-xrma}}_{\mathsf{SIG}_0}$ which breaks the EUF-XRMA security.

Theorem 4. *If* $\mathsf{TCOM} = (\mathsf{KGen}^{\mathsf{tc}}, \mathsf{Com}^{\mathsf{tc}}, \mathsf{TCom}^{\mathsf{tc}}, \mathsf{TCol}^{\mathsf{tc}})$ *is a trapdoor commitment and* SIG_0 *is* EUF-XRMA *secure, then* SIG_1 *is* EUF-CMA *secure.*

Proof. Let $\mathcal{B}^{\text{EUF-XRMA}}_{\mathsf{SIG}_0}$ be the adversary that can break EUF-XRMA security of SIG_0, and let $\mathcal{B}^{\text{bind}}$ be the adversary that can break computational binding for TCOM. Let $\mathcal{A}^{\text{EUF-CMA}}_{\mathsf{SIG}_1}$ be the adversary that can break EUF-CMA security of SIG_1. Let $\epsilon^{\text{EUF-XRMA}}_{\mathsf{SIG}_0} = \mathsf{Adv}^{\text{EUF-XRMA}}_{\mathsf{SIG}_0,\mathcal{B}}(n)$ be an advantage of $\mathcal{B}^{\text{EUF-XRMA}}_{\mathsf{SIG}_0}$, ϵ^{bind} be an advantage of $\mathcal{B}^{\text{bind}}$, and $\epsilon^{\text{EUF-CMA}}_{\mathsf{SIG}_1} = \mathsf{Adv}^{\text{EUF-CMA}}_{\mathsf{SIG}_1,\mathcal{A}}(n)$ be an advantage of $\mathcal{A}^{\text{EUF-CMA}}_{\mathsf{SIG}_1}$. We write $\mathcal{B}^{\text{EUF-XRMA with } \mathsf{TCOM}}_{\mathsf{SIG}_0}$ as the adversary against EUF-XRMA security with TCOM of SIG_0. We write the verification key and signing key of SIG_1 as (vk, sk) and those of SIG_0 as (vk_0, sk_0). From the view of $\mathcal{A}^{\text{EUF-CMA}}_{\mathsf{SIG}_1}$, $\mathcal{B}^{\text{EUF-XRMA}}_{\mathsf{SIG}_0}$ and $\mathcal{B}^{\text{bind}}$ are statistically indistinguishable. Now, we show that if $\mathcal{A}^{\text{EUF-CMA}}_{\mathsf{SIG}_1}$ that can break EUF-CMA security of SIG_1 exists, then $\mathcal{B}^{\text{EUF-XRMA with } \mathsf{TCOM}}_{\mathsf{SIG}_0}$ or $\mathcal{B}^{\text{bind}}$ exists.

Setup: We consider $\mathsf{TCom}^{\mathsf{tc}}_{tk}$ as MsgGen of EUF-XRMA. Then, commitments are generated with auxiliary information such that $(\mu_i, r'_i) \leftarrow \mathsf{TCom}^{\mathsf{tc}}_{tk}(1^n)$. The adversary $\mathcal{B}^{\text{EUF-XRMA with } \mathsf{TCOM}}_{\mathsf{SIG}_0}$ receives the verification key vk_0, commitments μ_i, and signatures $\boldsymbol{\sigma}_i$ of SIG_0 for $1 \leq i \leq Q$ and auxiliary information $\rho_i = (pk, tk, r'_i)$, where pk is the public key, tk is the trapdoor key for TCOM, and commitment μ_i satisfies $\mu_i = \mathsf{Com}_{pk}(x_i; r'_i)$ for $x_i \in \mathcal{M}_n$. $\mathcal{B}^{\text{EUF-XRMA with } \mathsf{TCOM}}_{\mathsf{SIG}_0}$ sets $vk = (vk_0, pk)$ and sends vk to $\mathcal{A}^{\text{EUF-CMA}}_{\mathsf{SIG}_1}$.

Signing: $\mathcal{A}^{\text{EUF-CMA}}_{\mathsf{SIG}_1}$ makes Q signing queries. For $1 \leq i \leq Q$, $\mathcal{A}^{\text{EUF-CMA}}_{\mathsf{SIG}_1}$ gives a message m_i to $\mathcal{B}^{\text{EUF-XRMA with } \mathsf{TCOM}}_{\mathsf{SIG}_0}$. Then $\mathcal{B}^{\text{EUF-XRMA with } \mathsf{TCOM}}_{\mathsf{SIG}_0}$ computes $r_i = \mathsf{TCol}^{\mathsf{tc}}_{tk}(\mu_i, \chi_i, m_i)$, where r_i satisfies $\mu_i = \mathsf{Com}^{\mathsf{tc}}_{pk}(m_i; r_i)$. According to the statistical hiding property of trapdoor commitments, from the view of $\mathcal{A}^{\text{EUF-CMA}}_{\mathsf{SIG}_1}$, the r that is generated by both COIN' and $\mathsf{TCol}^{\mathsf{tc}}_{tk}$ are statistically indistinguishable. $\mathcal{B}^{\text{EUF-XRMA with } \mathsf{TCOM}}_{\mathsf{SIG}_0}$ then returns $(\boldsymbol{\sigma}_i, r_i)$ corresponding to m_i. Here, the signatures that $\mathcal{B}^{\text{EUF-XRMA with } \mathsf{TCOM}}_{\mathsf{SIG}_0}$ first received as input are regarded as that of SIG_1 since messages can be just replaced by commitments.

Forgery of $\mathcal{A}^{\text{EUF-CMA}}_{\mathsf{SIG}_1}$*:* $\mathcal{B}^{\text{EUF-XRMA with } \mathsf{TCOM}}_{\mathsf{SIG}_0}$ receives a forgery $(m^*, \boldsymbol{\sigma}^*, r^*)$ of SIG_1 from $\mathcal{A}^{\text{EUF-CMA}}_{\mathsf{SIG}_1}$, where $m^* \notin \{m_1, \ldots, m_q\}$. $\mathcal{B}^{\text{EUF-XRMA with } \mathsf{TCOM}}_{\mathsf{SIG}_0}$ then computes commitment $\mu^* = \mathsf{Com}^{\mathsf{tc}}_{pk}(m^*; r^*)$.

Case 1: breaking EUF-XRMA *security of* SIG_0. In this case that $\mu^* \notin \{\mu_1, \ldots, \mu_Q\}$, $\mathcal{B}^{\text{EUF-XRMA with } \mathsf{TCOM}}_{\mathsf{SIG}_0}$ outputs $(\mu^*, \boldsymbol{\sigma}^*)$. This means the adversary succeeds in breaking EUF-XRMA with TCOM security of SIG_0. This goes against the fact that any adversary who breaks the EUF-XRMA security of SIG_0 does not exists in Theorem 2.

Case 2: breaking computational binding. In this case that $\mu^* \in \{\mu_1, \ldots, \mu_Q\}$, $\mathcal{B}^{\text{bind}}$ outputs (m^*, r^*, m_i, r_i) such that $(\mu^* = \mu_i) \cap (m^* \neq m_i)$ for $1 \leq i \leq Q$. This means $\mathcal{B}^{\text{EUF-XRMA with } \mathsf{TCOM}}_{\mathsf{SIG}_0}$ succeeds in breaking computational binding for trapdoor commitment as $\mathcal{B}^{\text{bind}}$.

Analysis: Supposed that SIG_1 is EUF-CMA secure. Then $\mathcal{B}^{\text{EUF-XRMA with } \mathsf{TCOM}}_{\mathsf{SIG}_0}$ breaks EUF-XRMA security when $\mu^* \notin \{\mu_1, \ldots, \mu_q\}$ or $\mathcal{B}^{\text{bind}}$ breaks computational binding for trapdoor commitments when $\mu^* \in \{\mu_1, \ldots, \mu_Q\}$. Therefore

$\epsilon_{\mathsf{SIG}_1}^{\text{EUF-CMA}}$ is bounded by sum of $\epsilon_{\mathsf{SIG}_0}^{\text{EUF-XRMA}}$ and ϵ^{bind}. Hence,

$$\epsilon_{\mathsf{SIG}_1}^{\text{EUF-CMA}} \leq \epsilon^{\text{bind}} + \epsilon_{\mathsf{SIG}_0}^{\text{EUF-XRMA}}.$$

□

Table 2. The comparison between Proposed scheme and DM14

Scheme	Tag collisions	$\lvert\mathcal{T}_i\rvert$	d	$\lvert vk\rvert$	Reduction loss
DM14	1	$2^{\lfloor \alpha c^i \rfloor}$	$\lceil \log_c(\log_2(\frac{2Q^2}{\epsilon}))\rceil$	$O(\log n)$	$(\frac{4Q^2}{\epsilon})^c$
Proposed scheme 1	ψ	$2^{\lfloor \alpha c^i \rfloor}$	$\lceil \log_c(\log_2(\frac{2eQ}{\psi+1}))\rceil$	$O(\log n)$	$(\frac{4eQ}{\psi+1})^c$
Proposed scheme 2	ψ	2^i	$\lceil \log_2(\frac{2eQ}{\psi+1})\rceil$	$O(n)$	$\frac{4eQ}{\psi+1}$

5 Reduction Loss

We discuss the reduction loss in this section. We denote ϵ_m, ϵ_{nur}, $\epsilon_{t^\diamond=t^*}$, and $\epsilon_{\mathbf{w}=0}$ as follows: ϵ_m is the probability that events $\#\mathcal{M}' \geq \psi+1$ occur and is exponentially small; $\epsilon_{nur} = 1/2^{\Omega(n)}$ is the advantage of $\mathcal{A}$ that distinguishes between uniformly random distributed tags and simulated tags; $\epsilon_{t^\diamond=t^*}$ is the probability that $t^\diamond$ corresponds to the the target tag t^*, that is, $1/\#\mathcal{T}_{i^*}$; and $\epsilon_{\mathbf{w}=0}$ is the probability that the ring-SIS solution $\mathbf{w}=0$.

For the advantage of the ring-SIS problem $\epsilon^{\text{ring}-\text{SIS}}$, in accordance with to Theorems 2 and 3,

$$\epsilon^{\text{ring}-\text{SIS}} \geq (1-\epsilon_m-\epsilon_{nur})\cdot\epsilon\cdot\epsilon_{t^\diamond=t^*}(1-\epsilon_{\mathbf{z}=0}).$$

Therefore, because $\epsilon \geq \epsilon^{\mathsf{euf\text{-}cma}} - \epsilon^{\text{bind}}$ from Theorem 4, where $\epsilon^{\mathsf{euf\text{-}cma}}$ is the advantage of EUF-CMA security of SIG_1 of,

$$\epsilon^{\text{ring}-\text{SIS}} = \mathcal{O}\left(\frac{1}{\#\mathcal{T}^{(j^*)}}\right)\cdot\epsilon = \mathcal{O}\left(\frac{1}{\#\mathcal{T}^{(j^*)}}\right)\cdot\left(\epsilon^{\mathsf{euf\text{-}cma}} - \epsilon^{\text{bind}}\right).$$

If $C_i = \lfloor \alpha c^i \rfloor$,

$$\epsilon^{\mathsf{euf\text{-}cma}} = \mathcal{O}\left(\left(\frac{Q}{n}\right)^c\right)\cdot\epsilon^{\text{ring}-\text{SIS}} + \epsilon^{\text{bind}},$$

if $C_i = i$,

$$\epsilon^{\mathsf{euf\text{-}cma}} = \mathcal{O}\left(\frac{Q}{\psi}\right)\cdot\epsilon^{\text{ring}-\text{SIS}} + \epsilon^{\text{bind}}.$$

The advantage of computational binding can be reduced to the ring-SIS problem. The whole reduction loss to the ring-SIS problem is $O\left(\frac{Q}{\psi}\right)$ if $C_i = i$ or $O\left(\left(\frac{Q}{\psi}\right)^c\right)$ if $C_i = \lfloor \alpha c^i \rfloor$. The reduction loss is related to ψ and Q. There is an asymptotic relation between them, $\psi = \log(Q)$. The modification of tag generation and evaluation of the probability of tag collisions can eliminate the parameter ϵ from the reduction loss of Ducas et al.'s signature scheme, $O\left(\left(\frac{Q^2}{\epsilon}\right)^c\right)$. We show the detailed comparison in Table 2.

6 Conclusion

We have developed signature schemes that have a tighter reduction loss than that of Ducas et al.'s signature [11] and have small signing keys and signatures under the standard assumption in the standard model. Our proposed methods are based on [11]. In Ducas et al.'s signatures, tags are used, but the tag construction method uses a random value unrelated to the message. In our method, tags are associated with messages because we consider the EUF-XRMA game where random messages are given with auxiliary information. We then convert our scheme with EUF-XRMA security to a scheme with EUF-CMA security applying trapdoor commitments to auxiliary information. Our signature schemes can be easily switched between proposed scheme 1 and 2 changing the value of tag-generation parameter C_i. Because the reduction loss can have a dramatic impact on the scheme's parameters, the tighter reduction loss is, the faster computations of signature generation and verification are.

As a result, our signature scheme has a short signature size of $O(1)$, achieves a relatively short verification key size of $O(\log n)$, and reduction loss of $O\left(\left(\frac{Q^2}{\epsilon}\right)^c\right)$ in reduction when the parameter for tag generation $C_i = \lfloor \alpha c^i \rfloor$ (proposed scheme 1). Alternately, it achieves a verification key size of $O(n)$ and reduction loss of $O\left(\frac{Q}{n}\right)$ in reduction when $C_i = i$ (proposed scheme 2).

A Proof of Theorem 2

Proof. Suppose that there exists a PPT $\mathcal{A}$ against SIG_0 and MsgGen. We demonstrate that we can construct an algorithm $\mathcal{B}$ that uses $\mathcal{A}$ as an internal sub-algorithm to solve the ring-SIS problem.

Setup: $\mathcal{B}$ receives a ring-SIS challenge $A' \in \mathcal{R}_q^{1\times w}$. $\mathcal{B}$ then runs MsgGen to receive $\{m^{(j)}, \{t_{[i]}^{(j)}\}_{i=0}^{d}\}_{j=1}^{Q} \leftarrow \mathsf{MsgGen}(1^n)$ as follows. Let us define $\mathcal{M} := \{m^{(j)}\}_{j=1}^{Q}$ and $\mathcal{T}_i := \{0,1\}^{C_i}$ for $i = 0, \ldots, d$. For $j = 1, \ldots, Q$, $\mathcal{B}$ chooses message $m^{(j)} \in \{0,1\}^{nk}$ uniformly at random. Then, for $i = 0, \ldots, d$ and $c > 1$, let

$$t_{\le i}^{(j)} = \begin{cases} 0 & \text{if } i = 0 \\ m^{(j)} \mod C_i & \text{if } i \ge 1 \end{cases}$$
$$t_{[i]}^{(j)} = t_{\le i}^{(j)}(X) - t_{\le i-1}^{(j)}(X) \in \mathcal{R}_q$$

$\mathcal{B}$ sets i^* to be as small as possible such that $i^* > \lfloor (2eQ)/(\psi+1) \rfloor$. If $\#\mathcal{T}_{i^*} > \lfloor (2eQ)/(\psi+1) \rfloor$, the probability that event $(\psi+1)$-fold occurs is exponentially small if Q tags are independently and uniformly chosen from $\mathcal{T}_{i^*}$, due to Lemma 2. Let us denote by $(\psi+1)\text{-fold}^{\text{real}}$ the event that $(\psi+1)$-fold happens on some tag in $\mathcal{T}_{i^*}$ when $t_{\le i^*}^{(j)}$ are chosen according to the distribution of MsgGen. Here we show that the statistical distance between the distribution of tags computed by the signed message and the uniform distribution is negligible.

Claim. $\Pr[(\psi+1)\text{-fold}^{\text{real}}] = \Pr[(\psi+1)\text{-fold}^{\text{ideal}}] + 2^{-O(n)}$.

Proof of Claim. Let m be a message outputted by MsgGen, which is distributed over R_q. By construction , the distribution of $t^* = m \mod C_i$ is statistically close to the uniform distribution over T_{i^*}, where C_i is the tag generation parameter, e.g., $C_i = 2^i$. Its distance is bounded by $2^{-O(n)}$. Although independent Q messages are considered, the distance should be still $2^{-O(n)}$. □

$\mathcal{B}$ randomly chooses $t^*_{\leq i^*} \xleftarrow{\$} \mathcal{T}_{i^*}$. $\mathcal{B}$ can solve the ring-SIS problem when $\mathcal{A}$ outputs a forged pair $(m^\diamond, \boldsymbol{\sigma}^\diamond)$ such that $t^*_{\leq i^*} = m^\diamond \mod C_{i^*}$. Let

$$\mathcal{M}' := \{m \in \mathcal{M} | t^*_{\leq i^*} = t^{(j)}_{\leq i^*}\}.$$

If $\#\mathcal{M}' \geq \psi + 1$, $\mathcal{B}$ aborts; otherwise, it sets the verification key parameters as follows:

$$\mathbf{H}_{[i]} = \begin{cases} 0 \in \mathcal{R}_q & \text{if i} > \text{i}^*, \\ 1 \in \mathcal{R}_q & \text{if } 1 \leq \text{i} \leq \text{i}^*, \\ -t^*_{\leq i^*} & \text{if i} = 0. \end{cases}$$

For $s' = \omega(\sqrt{\log n})$, $\mathcal{B}$ runs $(\mathbf{A}_{[i]}, \mathbf{S}_{[i]}) \leftarrow \mathsf{GenTrap}(\mathbf{A}', \mathbf{H}_{[i]}, s')$. From Lemma 1, because we have $\mathbf{H}_t = \mathbf{H}_{[0]} + \sum_{i=1}^{d} t_{[i]}\mathbf{H}_{[i]} = -t^*_{[i^*]} + \sum_{i=1}^{i^*} t_{[i]} = -t^*_{\leq i^*} + t_{\leq i^*}$, $\mathbf{A}_t \begin{bmatrix} \mathbf{S}_t \\ \mathbf{I} \end{bmatrix} = \mathbf{H}_t\mathbf{G}$ holds for

$$\mathbf{S}_t = \mathbf{S}_{[0]} + \sum_{i=1}^{d} t_{[i]}\mathbf{S}_{[i]},$$
$$\mathbf{H}_t = -t^*_{\leq i^*} + t_{\leq i^*},$$
$$\mathbf{A}_t = [\mathbf{A}' | \mathbf{A}_{[0]} + \sum_{i=1}^{d} t_{[i]}\mathbf{A}_{[i]}].$$

Simulation of Signatures: If $t^*_{\leq i^*} \neq t^{(j)}_{\leq i^*}$, $\mathcal{B}$ can run the signing algorithm $\boldsymbol{\sigma}^{(j)} \leftarrow \mathsf{Sign}(sk, m^{(j)})$ because $\mathbf{H}_t = -t^*_{\leq i^*} + t_{\leq i^*} \neq 0$. Otherwise, because $\mathbf{H}_t = -t^*_{\leq i^*} + t_{\leq i^*} = 0$ holds, $\mathcal{B}$ chooses $\boldsymbol{\sigma}^{(j)} \leftarrow D^{w+k}_{\mathcal{R}_q, s}$. Then $\mathcal{B}$ chooses $m^{(j^*)}$ at random from $\mathcal{M}'$ and sets $m^* = m^{(j^*)}$. For the chosen j^*, $\mathcal{B}$ sets $\boldsymbol{\sigma}^* = \boldsymbol{\sigma}^{(j^*)}$.

Generation of Verification Key: To exploit a forgery, $\mathcal{B}$ chooses $\mathbf{S_U} \leftarrow D^{w \times k}_{\mathcal{R}, s'}$. The spectrum norm of $\mathbf{S_U}$ satisfies $s_1(\mathbf{S_U}) = \sqrt{n} \cdot \omega(\log n)$. Then we have $\mathbf{U} = \mathbf{A}'\mathbf{S_U}$. In addition, $\mathcal{B}$ chooses $\mathbf{v_0} \leftarrow \mathcal{R}_q$ and sets $vk = (\mathbf{A}', \mathbf{A}_{[0]}, \ldots, \mathbf{A}_{[d]}, \mathbf{U}, \mathbf{v_0})$. Here, these simulated keys are indistinguishable from real keys.

$\mathcal{B}$ feeds $(vk, \{m^{(j)}, \boldsymbol{\sigma}^{(j)}, \{t^{(j)}_{[i]}\}_{i=0}^{d}\}_{j=1}^{Q})$ to $\mathcal{A}$.

$\mathcal{A}$'s Forgery: Given $(vk, \{m^{(j)}, \boldsymbol{\sigma}^{(j)}, \{t^{(j)}_{[i]}\}_{i=0}^{d}\}_{j=1}^{Q})$ from $\mathcal{B}$, $\mathcal{A}$ generates a forged signature $(m^\diamond, \boldsymbol{\sigma}^\diamond)$ and feeds it to $\mathcal{B}$.

Exploiting the Forgery: $\mathcal{A}$ outputs a forgery $\boldsymbol{\sigma}^\diamond$ for some message $m^\diamond$ of its choice with a probability of at least ϵ. The simulator hope that $t^\diamond_{\leq i^*} = t^*_{\leq i^*}$ is fulfilled with probability $1/|\mathcal{T}_{i^*}|$. If $t^\diamond_{\leq i^*} \neq t^*_{\leq i^*}$, $\mathcal{B}$ aborts. Otherwise, $\mathcal{B}$ computes $\mathbf{A}^\diamond_{\mathbf{t}}$, $u^\diamond_0$ and gets $\boldsymbol{\sigma} \leftarrow \mathsf{SampleD}(\mathbf{A}_t, u_0, \mathbf{S}, s)$. Because $\mathbf{A}_{t^\diamond}\boldsymbol{\sigma}^\diamond = u^\diamond_0$ holds, $\mathcal{B}$ has $\mathbf{v_0} = \mathbf{A}_{t^\diamond}\boldsymbol{\sigma}^\diamond - u^\diamond_0$. Similarly for $\boldsymbol{\sigma}^*$, $\mathcal{B}$ has $\mathbf{v_0} = \mathbf{A}_{t^*}\boldsymbol{\sigma}^*_1 - u^*_0$. Therefore, $\mathbf{A}_{t^*}\boldsymbol{\sigma}^* - u^*_0 = \mathbf{A}_{t^\diamond}\boldsymbol{\sigma}^\diamond - u^\diamond_0$. Because the condition $t^\diamond_{\leq i^*} = t^*_{\leq i^*}$ ensures $\mathbf{H}_{t^*} = \mathbf{H}_{t^\diamond} = 0$, we derive

$$[\mathbf{A}| - \mathbf{A}\mathbf{S}_{t^*}| - \mathbf{A}\mathbf{S}_{\mathbf{U}}] \cdot \begin{bmatrix} \boldsymbol{\sigma}^*_u \\ \boldsymbol{\sigma}^*_\ell \\ m^* \end{bmatrix} = \mathbf{v_0} = [\mathbf{A}| - \mathbf{A}\mathbf{S}_{t^\diamond}| - \mathbf{A}\mathbf{S}_{\mathbf{U}}] \cdot \begin{bmatrix} \boldsymbol{\sigma}^\diamond_u \\ \boldsymbol{\sigma}^\diamond_\ell \\ m^\diamond \end{bmatrix},$$

where $\boldsymbol{\sigma} = (\boldsymbol{\sigma}_u, \boldsymbol{\sigma}_\ell)$ for the computation. In particular we obtain $\mathbf{A}\mathbf{w} = \mathbf{0}$ for

$$\mathbf{w} = (\boldsymbol{\sigma}^*_u - \boldsymbol{\sigma}^*_\ell - (\mathbf{S}_{t^*} \cdot \boldsymbol{\sigma}^\diamond_u - \mathbf{S}_{t^\diamond} \cdot \boldsymbol{\sigma}^\diamond_\ell) - \mathbf{S}_{\mathbf{U}}(m^* - m^\diamond)).$$

Because $\mathbf{w}$ has at least $\omega(n)$ min-entropy, the probability of $\mathbf{w} = \mathbf{0}$ is $2^{-\Omega(n)}$.

Size of the Extracted Ring-SIS Solution: Because $\mathbf{s}^*$ and $\mathbf{s}^\diamond$ are valid signatures,

$$||\mathbf{s}^*||, ||\mathbf{s}^\diamond|| \leq n^2 w \cdot \omega(\log n)^{3/2}.$$

Additionally, $s_1(\mathbf{S}_t) \leq n^3/2 \cdot \omega(\log n)$ for any tag $t \in \mathcal{T}$, and

$$||m^*||, ||m^\diamond|| \leq O(\sqrt{nk})$$
$$\mathbf{S}_{\mathbf{U}} \leq \sqrt{n} \cdot \omega(\log n).$$

Combining all these bounds, we obtain

$$||\mathbf{w}|| \leq n^{7/2} \cdot \log n \cdot \omega(\log n)^{3/2}.$$

□

References

1. Abe, M., Chase, M., David, B., Kohlweiss, M., Nishimaki, R., Ohkubo, M.: Constant-size structure-preserving signatures: generic constructions and simple assumptions. J. Cryptol. **29**(4), 833–878 (2016). https://doi.org/10.1007/s00145-015-9211-7
2. Ajtai, M.: Generating hard instances of lattice problems. In: STOC, pp. 99–108. ACM (1996)
3. Ajtai, M., Dwork, C.: A public-key cryptosystem with worst-case/average-case equivalence. In: STOC, pp. 284–293. ACM (1997)
4. Alperin-Sheriff, J.: Short signatures with short public keys from homomorphic trapdoor functions. In: Katz, J. (ed.) PKC 2015. LNCS, vol. 9020, pp. 236–255. Springer, Heidelberg (2015). https://doi.org/10.1007/978-3-662-46447-2_11
5. Blazy, O., Kakvi, S.A., Kiltz, E., Pan, J.: Tightly-secure signatures from chameleon hash functions. In: Katz, J. (ed.) PKC 2015. LNCS, vol. 9020, pp. 256–279. Springer, Heidelberg (2015). https://doi.org/10.1007/978-3-662-46447-2_12

6. Böhl, F., Hofheinz, D., Jager, T., Koch, J., Seo, J.H., Striecks, C.: Practical signatures from standard assumptions. In: Johansson, T., Nguyen, P.Q. (eds.) EUROCRYPT 2013. LNCS, vol. 7881, pp. 461–485. Springer, Heidelberg (2013). https://doi.org/10.1007/978-3-642-38348-9_28
7. Boyen, X.: Lattice mixing and vanishing trapdoors: a framework for fully secure short signatures and more. In: Nguyen, P.Q., Pointcheval, D. (eds.) PKC 2010. LNCS, vol. 6056, pp. 499–517. Springer, Heidelberg (2010). https://doi.org/10.1007/978-3-642-13013-7_29
8. Boyen, X., Li, Q.: Towards tightly secure lattice short signature and ID-based encryption. In: Cheon, J.H., Takagi, T. (eds.) ASIACRYPT 2016, Part II. LNCS, vol. 10032, pp. 404–434. Springer, Heidelberg (2016). https://doi.org/10.1007/978-3-662-53890-6_14
9. Cash, D., Hofheinz, D., Kiltz, E., Peikert, C.: Bonsai trees, or how to delegate a lattice basis. In: Gilbert, H. (ed.) EUROCRYPT 2010. LNCS, vol. 6110, pp. 523–552. Springer, Heidelberg (2010). https://doi.org/10.1007/978-3-642-13190-5_27
10. Damgård, I.: Efficient concurrent zero-knowledge in the auxiliary string model. In: Preneel, B. (ed.) EUROCRYPT 2000. LNCS, vol. 1807, pp. 418–430. Springer, Heidelberg (2000). https://doi.org/10.1007/3-540-45539-6_30
11. Ducas, L., Micciancio, D.: Improved short lattice signatures in the standard model. In: Garay, J.A., Gennaro, R. (eds.) CRYPTO 2014. LNCS, vol. 8616, pp. 335–352. Springer, Heidelberg (2014). https://doi.org/10.1007/978-3-662-44371-2_19
12. Goldwasser, S., Micali, S., Rivest, R.L.: A digital signature scheme secure against adaptive chosen-message attacks. J. Comput. **17**(2), 281–308 (1988)
13. Gentry, C., Peikert, C., Vaikuntanathan, V.: Trapdoors for hard lattices and new cryptographic constructions. In: STOC, pp. 197–206. ACM (2008)
14. Hofheinz, D., Jager, T., Knapp, E.: Waters signatures with optimal security reduction. In: Fischlin, M., Buchmann, J., Manulis, M. (eds.) PKC 2012. LNCS, vol. 7293, pp. 66–83. Springer, Heidelberg (2012). https://doi.org/10.1007/978-3-642-30057-8_5
15. Kawachi, A., Tanaka, K., Xagawa, K.: Concurrently secure identification schemes based on the worst-case hardness of lattice problems. In: Pieprzyk, J. (ed.) ASIACRYPT 2008. LNCS, vol. 5350, pp. 372–389. Springer, Heidelberg (2008). https://doi.org/10.1007/978-3-540-89255-7_23
16. Lyubashevsky, V., Micciancio, D.: Asymptotically efficient lattice-based digital signatures. In: Canetti, R. (ed.) TCC 2008. LNCS, vol. 4948, pp. 37–54. Springer, Heidelberg (2008). https://doi.org/10.1007/978-3-540-78524-8_3
17. Lyubashevsky, V., Micciancio, D., Peikert, C., Rosen, A.: SWIFFT: a modest proposal for FFT hashing. In: Nyberg, K. (ed.) FSE 2008. LNCS, vol. 5086, pp. 54–72. Springer, Heidelberg (2008). https://doi.org/10.1007/978-3-540-71039-4_4
18. Micciancio, D.: Generalized compact knapsacks, cyclic lattices, and efficient one-way functions. In: Computational Complexity Conference (CCC), vol. 16, no. 4, pp. 365–411. Schloss Dagstuhl (2007)
19. Micciancio, D., Peikert, C.: Trapdoors for lattices: simpler, tighter, faster, smaller. In: Pointcheval, D., Johansson, T. (eds.) EUROCRYPT 2012. LNCS, vol. 7237, pp. 700–718. Springer, Heidelberg (2012). https://doi.org/10.1007/978-3-642-29011-4_41
20. Shor, P.W.: Algorithms for quantum computation: discrete logarithms and factoring. In: FOCS, pp. 124–134. IEEE (1994)

One-Time Delegation of Unlinkable Signing Rights and Its Application

Takashi Nishide(✉)

University of Tsukuba, Tsukuba, Japan
nishide@risk.tsukuba.ac.jp

Abstract. Delegation of signing rights can be useful to promote effective resource sharing and smooth cooperation among participants in distributed systems, and in many situations, we often need restricted delegation such as one-timeness and unlinkability rather than simple full delegation. Particularly, one-timesness cannot be achieved just by deploying cryptographic measures, and one needs to resort to some form of tamper-proofness or the assistance from external cloud servers for "key-disabling". In this work, we extend the latter such that a delegatee can sign a message without the delegator's involvement with the assumption that there exists at least one honest cloud server with secure erasure to achieve one-timeness. In this setting, if the delegator just shares their signing key between the delegatee and cloud servers, it may be problematic. It is because in the worst case, the delegator cannot know whether or not a signing key theft occurred because the signatures generated illegally are indistinguishable from the ones generated legally. To solve this, first we propose an efficient one-time delegation scheme of Okamoto-Schnorr signing. Further we combine the basic delegation scheme with anonymous credentials such that the delegator can detect the signing key theft even if one-time delegation is broken while also achieving unlinkability for both the delegator and cloud servers. Further we show its application to an e-cash scheme, which can prevent double-spending.

Keywords: Signature · Delegation · Anonymous credential · E-cash

1 Introduction

Delegation of rights to services and resources is old (e.g., [10]), but still relevant in distributed applications (e.g., [36,40]), and it can often be realized via delegation of *signing* rights. Signing rights are unlinkable if a delegatee can sign a message unlinkably, where "unlinkably" means that when a delegator delegated their signing rights to multiple delegatees, no entities including the delegator can know which delegatee signed a message from its resulting signature as in group signatures [6]. This type of delegation is useful in applications needing privacy-preserving access control. Further we consider one-time delegation, where "one-time" means that a delegator outsources their one-time signing capability. More specifically, after the delegator outsources their signing capability to

K. Nguyen et al. (Eds.): ProvSec 2020, LNCS 12505, pp. 103–123, 2020.
https://doi.org/10.1007/978-3-030-62576-4_6

the delegatee, the following properties hold without the delegator's involvement: (1) a delegatee can sign a message, (2) the verifier can verify the signature, and (3) the delegatee is prevented from signing more than once rather than detected after the fact. This type of one-timeness is often useful for electronic one-show tokens such as e-cash. In this work, we aim for such one-time delegation of unlinkable signing rights. In general, we cannot achieve one-timeness just by deploying cryptographic measures, and one viable approach is to resort to tamper-proofness such as smartcards (e.g., [12,27],[13, Sect. 6.3],[8]), one-time programs (OTPs) [33], or trusted execution environments (TEEs) (e.g., [35,40]). However, such hardware-based solutions may sometimes be undesirable due to various side-channel attacks or cumbersome to use or deploy in practice (e.g., as pointed out in [17]). As a practical alternative to achieve one-timeness (except a feasibility result using quantum objects [2]), there is another line of research, e.g., [17,29,38,39] (called *password-authenticated server-aided signatures* in [17]). In this line of research, roughly speaking, signing operations are made more secure by employing threshold signing and external clouds (or hardware devices), so that signatures can be generated only when the original signer authenticates to the clouds and cooperate with the clouds having shares of a signing key. Such a technique can make one-time delegation possible by letting a delegator secret-share the signing key between a delegatee and clouds, and the clouds erase the shares (i.e., key-disabling or rate-limiting the signing requests) after the delegatee accessed the clouds for signing operations. However, such an existing approach may be insufficient in the context of delegation (where a delegatee is also a potential adversary) due to the following: When one-timeness is broken in the worst case (i.e., a delegatee signed more than once illegally, given only the one-time signing right, e.g., via cloud breaches), it would be desirable for the delegator to be able to detect the fact from the generated and collected signatures. However, the existing works do not enable the delegator to detect it because all the signing rights use the same key and the signatures generated illegally are indistinguishable from the legal ones. This drawback may deter the delegators from relying on such delegation because no perfect protection against cloud breaches exists. Further, simply using different signing keys for each delegation may make it difficult to realize delegation of unlinkable signing rights.

Our Contributions. We propose efficient delegation of signing rights such that it is one-time, unlinkable for clouds as well as the delegator and *multi-run-detectable* even if one-timeness is broken, which means that the delegator can know the fact that one-time signing right was exerted more than once illegally from the generated and collected signatures[1]. To this end, we extend the existing approach using one cloud (e.g., [17,29]) to the setting with multiple clouds and Okamoto-Schnorr blind signatures, and combine it with anonymous credentials such that no master signing key needs to be shared among the delegatee and the clouds. In the setting of one cloud, the delegatee does not need to check the validity of the response from the cloud because it can be checked by verifying

[1] As in e-cash schemes, we believe that it is a natural assumption that the signatures generated by the delegatees are eventually collected by the delegator.

the resulting signature, but in our setting of multiple clouds, we need an efficient way of checking the validity of each response, and for that, we use a variant of the MACs based on secret sharing in [28]. Further we show a natural application of our one-time delegation to e-cash where double-spending is prevented and even if one-timeness is broken, double-spenders are identified. Our scheme does not require clouds to interact with each other, so will enjoy easy deployment as well.

Other Related Work. Group signatures (e.g., [6,34]) and its generalized version (also called anonymous proxy signatures, e.g., [31][2]) can also be viewed as delegation of unlinkable signing rights, but one-timeness has not been much explored. In the area of (delegatable) anonymous credentials (e.g., [9,21,23,31,42]), there exists a notion called k-times credential (e.g., [3,14,43]), which allows a user to show a credential unlinkably up to k times, but the user is not prevented from showing the same credential more than k times (although identified after $k+1$ showings). Revocation of anonymous credentials is possible (e.g., [1,16]). For example, in [1], revocation is realized with accumulators that maintain non-revoked or revoked users in an anonymous way efficiently, and in [16], an attribute in the credential corresponds to an expiration date, and the credential issuer puts update values for each non-revoked user on a public bulletin board periodically such that only a non-revoked user can retrieve their corresponding value and update their credential for the new time period. Although this kind of revocation is useful in many situations, it will be insufficient for our purpose because we need revocation immediately after one showing of the credential.

The systems like [36,40] also address delegation of credentials such as passwords and signing keys with TEEs[3]. In, e.g., [40], a delegator just sends their credential to a TEE residing on the delegatee's computer (or TEE on the centrally brokered system) such that the delegatee can later use the delegated credential inside the TEE with appropriate authentication. Compared with [36,40], our approach (1) avoids putting the (master) signing key of a delegator directly in clouds, and (2) tries to reduce the reliance on TEEs by using distributed clouds such that the security is guaranteed even if part of clouds are corrupted.

We construct e-cash by applying our one-time delegation scheme. In the offline e-cash model [26], a bank does not need to be involved in the payment, but double-spending can only be detected without being prevented. In the online e-cash model [22–24], double-spending is prevented by the bank being online to be involved in the payment. Our e-cash scheme based on one-time delegation can also prevent double-spending without the online bank in the payment, but with

---

[2] In anonymous proxy signatures, anyone can act as a group manager by delegating its signing rights to others who can then unlinkably sign, and in addition, received rights can be re-delegated.

[3] One-timeness is not a main theme in [36,40], but it will be possible if the delegator specifies a delegation policy enforcing one-timeness for TEEs.

the increased communication overhead due to payers' access to clouds[4], which we believe can be alleviated, e.g., by the emerging 5G technology. In the e-cash scheme of [12,13], a tamper-proof device such as smartcards (sometimes called *observer* [25]) is issued and delivered to a user by the bank. Roughly speaking, one-timeness is realized by the fact that spending e-cash needs the assistance of the device (i.e., part of computation needs to be done by the device holding partial secret values, and the device is supposed to refuse to reuse the same e-cash). Although the scheme in [12,13] is efficient, as pointed out in e.g., [5], its core building block, blind signature, does not have a proof of security, and the exculpability property is not achieved when applied to e-cash.

2 Preliminaries

Notation. We use $\lambda \in \mathbb{N}$ as a security parameter. We assume a random oracle (RO) which can be viewed as an idealized hash function, and denote it by $H\colon \{0,1\}^* \rightarrow \{0,1\}^{2\lambda}$ (actually the range varies according to the context). We denote string concatenation by $\|$.

Bilinear Groups. Bilinear groups consist of three cyclic groups $\mathbb{G}_1$, $\mathbb{G}_2$, and $\mathbb{G}_T$ of prime order p, and have a bilinear pairing $e\colon \mathbb{G}_1 \times \mathbb{G}_2 \rightarrow \mathbb{G}_T$ with the properties: (1) $\forall g \in \mathbb{G}_1$, $\widetilde{g} \in \mathbb{G}_2$ and $a, b \in \mathbb{Z}_p$, $e(g^a, \widetilde{g}^b) = e(g, \widetilde{g})^{ab}$, (2) $\forall g \neq 1_{\mathbb{G}_1}$ and $\widetilde{g} \neq 1_{\mathbb{G}_2}$, $e(g, \widetilde{g}) \neq 1_{\mathbb{G}_T}$, (3) the pairing e can be computed efficiently. In this work, we use type-3 pairings where DDH holds in both $\mathbb{G}_1$ and $\mathbb{G}_2$ [32][5].

Okamoto-Schnorr (OS) ***Signature.*** The OS signature scheme [41] is obtained by applying the Fiat-Shamir transform [30] to the OS proof of knowledge, and the OS scheme enjoys witness indistinguishability[6]. The construction is given in Fig. 1. We also show the OS blind signatures used in Sect. 3. In the OS blind signature scheme, OS.KeyGen and OS.Vrfy remain the same, but OS.Sign is replaced with OS.SigIssue protocol between a signer $\mathcal{S}$ and user $\mathcal{U}$ (Fig. 1).

Proof of Knowledge for Pedersen Commitment. We show a proof of knowledge (PK) of the discrete logarithm representation in a Pedersen commitment in Fig. 2, which is a Σ protocol and can be viewed as a generalization of the Schnorr proof of knowledge. We assume that the protocol in Fig. 2 is made non-interactive in the RO model by applying the Fiat-Shamir transform [30], and use the Camenisch-Stadler [18] notation such as $\mathsf{PK}\{(x_1, \ldots, x_k)\colon h = g_1^{x_1} \cdots g_k^{x_k}\}$ to denote this non-interactive zero-knowledge proof of knowledge of $(x_1, \ldots, x_k)$. Similarly we use the notation $\mathsf{SPK}\{(x_1, \ldots, x_k)\colon h = g_1^{x_1} \cdots g_k^{x_k}\}(m)$ to denote the signature on m (i.e., signature based on a PK like OS signatures).

It is well known that, for this PK, there exist a knowledge extractor $\mathcal{E}_\Sigma$ able to extract witnesses and zero-knowledge simulator $\mathcal{S}_\Sigma$ able to generate indistinguishable views by controlling the RO, which are used in security proofs.

[4] In the context of online e-cash, our approach can be viewed as the bank's outsourcing double-spending checks securely to the clouds.

[5] Type-3 pairings are considered to be the most efficient [32,42].

[6] We need this property in the proof of Theorem 2, and this is why we need OS instead of plain "Schnorr".

- $\mathsf{OS.KeyGen}(1^\lambda) \to (sk, pk)$: Choose a prime p, cyclic group $\mathbb{G}$ of order p, and generators $g, h \in \mathbb{G}$. The secret (signing) key sk is $(x_1, x_2) \in \mathbb{Z}_p^2$, and public key is $pk = (g,\ h,\ p,\ y)$ where $y = g^{x_1} h^{x_2}$.
- $\mathsf{OS.Sign}(sk,\ m \in \{0,1\}^*) \to (c, z_1, z_2)$: Choose random $r_1, r_2 \in \mathbb{Z}_p$, and compute
  $$s \leftarrow g^{r_1} h^{r_2},\ c \leftarrow H(s \parallel m),\ z_i \leftarrow r_i - c \cdot x_i \bmod p \text{ for } i = 1, 2$$
  where $H\colon \{0,1\}^* \to \mathbb{Z}_p$ is modeled as an RO. The signature is $(c,\ z_1,\ z_2)$.
- $\mathsf{OS.Vrfy}(pk, m, (c, z_1, z_2))$: Check whether $c \stackrel{?}{=} H(g^{z_1} h^{z_2} y^c \parallel m)$, and if it holds, the output is 1, and otherwise 0.
- $\mathsf{OS.SigIssue}(\mathcal{S}(x_1, x_2),\ \mathcal{U}(pk, m))$: // for blind signatures
  1. $\mathcal{S}$ chooses random $r_1, r_2 \in \mathbb{Z}_p$, and sends $s \leftarrow g^{r_1} h^{r_2}$ to $\mathcal{U}$.
  2. $\mathcal{U}$ computes $c' \leftarrow H(s \cdot g^{\alpha_1} h^{\alpha_2} y^{\beta} \parallel m)$ with random $\alpha_1, \alpha_2, \beta \in \mathbb{Z}_p$, and sends $c \leftarrow c' - \beta \bmod p$ to $\mathcal{S}$ [6)].
  3. $\mathcal{S}$ sends $z_i \leftarrow r_i - c \cdot x_i \bmod p$ (for $i = 1, 2$) to $\mathcal{U}$.
  4. If $s = g^{z_1} h^{z_2} y^c$ does not hold, $\mathcal{U}$ aborts, and otherwise $\mathcal{U}$ computes $z_i' \leftarrow z_i + \alpha_i \bmod p$ for $i = 1, 2$, and the signature on m is $(c',\ z_1',\ z_2')$.

Fig. 1. Okamoto-Schnorr (Blind) Signature ([6]Here we can see that $\mathcal{U}$ randomizes $g^{r_1} h^{r_2}$ and $c'(= H(s \cdot g^{\alpha_1} h^{\alpha_2} y^{\beta} \parallel m))$. We note that the hash function is computed by $\mathcal{U}$ instead of $\mathcal{S}$ in OS blind signatures.)

Authenticated Secret Sharing. We explain the MACs we use in the context of secret sharing (see Sect. 3.1). This was proposed in [28], and it enables us to efficiently check whether a reconstructed secret is correct. In Fig. 3, we show the case where parties P_1, P_2 additively secret-share two secrets r, x, and reconstruct a linear combination $z = c'r + cx \bmod p$ of r and x (where c', c are known to P_1, P_2). In Sect. 3.1, we use a variant of this where first the delegator distributes the shares of secrets, MAC key, and MAC tags, and later the delegatee can check whether the shares sent by clouds are correct in reconstructing a secret.

- **Inputs:** A prover $\mathcal{P}$ has commitment $h = \prod_{i=1}^{k} g_i^{x_i}$ and gives the zero-knowledge proof of knowledge of $\{x_i \in \mathbb{Z}_p\}_{1 \le i \le k}$ to a verifier $\mathcal{V}$.
- **Auxiliary inputs:** The commitment h and generators $g_1, \ldots, g_k$ are public information and known to $\mathcal{V}$.
- **The protocol:**
  1. $\mathcal{P}$ chooses random $r_i \in \mathbb{Z}_p$ and sends $R \leftarrow \prod_{i=1}^{k} g_i^{r_i}$ to $\mathcal{V}$.
  2. $\mathcal{V}$ sends random $c \in \mathbb{Z}_p$ to $\mathcal{P}$.
  3. $\mathcal{P}$ computes and sends $z_i \leftarrow r_i + c \cdot x_i \bmod p$ to $\mathcal{V}$.
  4. If $Rh^c = \prod_{i=1}^{k} g_i^{z_i}$ holds, $\mathcal{V}$ accepts the proof, and otherwise rejects.

Fig. 2. Proof of knowledge for Pedersen commitment

Anonymous Credential. An anonymous credential scheme (e.g., [5,42]) consists of the following algorithms:

- **Inputs:** The secrets r, x, MAC key α, and MAC tags αr, αx are additively secret-shared as
  $r = r_1 + r_2 \bmod p$, $x = x_1 + x_2 \bmod p$, $\alpha = \alpha_1 + \alpha_2 \bmod p$,
  $\alpha \cdot r = m_1^{(r)} + m_2^{(r)} \bmod p$, $\alpha \cdot x = m_1^{(x)} + m_2^{(x)} \bmod p$ where p is a prime and the shares with subscript i are held by P_i.
- **Output:** P_1 and P_2 reconstruct $z = c'r + cx \bmod p$ if the MAC verification is successful, and otherwise abort.
- **The protocol:**
  1. Each P_i publishes its share $z_i = c'r_i + cx_i \bmod p$ of z (we note that malicious P_i may publish incorrect z_i).
  2. Each P_i computes a candidate value $z' = z_1 + z_2 \bmod p$ of z.
  3. Each P_i computes $v_i = \alpha_i z' - (c'm_i^{(r)} + cm_i^{(x)}) \bmod p$, and publishes the commitment of v_i, $\mathsf{Com}(v_i)$.
  4. Each P_i publishes the opening of $\mathsf{Com}(v_i)$, and checks whether $v_1 + v_2 \stackrel{?}{=} 0 \bmod p$. If $v_1 + v_2 = 0 \bmod p$, each P_i accepts z' as a correctly reconstructed value, and otherwise aborts.

Fig. 3. Reconstruction of secret in authenticated secret sharing [28]

- $\mathsf{AC.Setup}(1^\lambda) \rightarrow \mathsf{params}$: Generate public parameters params.
- $\mathsf{AC.IKeyGen}(\mathsf{params}, w) \rightarrow (\mathsf{pk}_\mathcal{I}, \mathsf{sk}_\mathcal{I})$: Generate a public key $\mathsf{pk}_\mathcal{I}$ and secret key $\mathsf{sk}_\mathcal{I}$ of the credential issuer $\mathcal{I}$ where w is the number of attributes. We implicitly assume that $\mathsf{pk}_\mathcal{I}$ includes params, and $\mathsf{sk}_\mathcal{I}$ includes $\mathsf{pk}_\mathcal{I}$.
- $\mathsf{AC.CredIssue}(\mathcal{I}(\mathsf{sk}_\mathcal{I}), \mathcal{U}(\mathsf{att}_\mathcal{U}))$ is an *issuance protocol* between $\mathcal{I}$ and $\mathcal{U}$. At the end of the protocol, $\mathcal{U}$ obtains the credential $\mathsf{cr}_\mathcal{U}$ on attributes $\mathsf{att}_\mathcal{U}$.
- $\mathsf{AC.CredShow}(\mathcal{U}(\mathsf{att}_\mathcal{U}, \mathsf{cr}_\mathcal{U}), \mathcal{V}(\mathsf{pk}_\mathcal{I}))$ is a *show protocol* between $\mathcal{U}$ and a verifier $\mathcal{V}$. At the end of the protocol, if the $\mathsf{cr}_\mathcal{U}$ is a valid credential on $\mathsf{att}_\mathcal{U}$ issued by $\mathcal{I}$, $\mathcal{V}$ accepts the fact that $\mathcal{U}$ possesses the valid $\mathsf{cr}_\mathcal{U}$. If necessary, $\mathcal{U}$ can also disclose part of $\mathsf{att}_\mathcal{U}$ to $\mathcal{V}$ in this protocol.

Ideal Functionality $\mathcal{F}_{\text{CA}}$. We assume a public key infrastructure where the delegator and clouds register their public keys, modeled by $\mathcal{F}_{\text{CA}}$ [20].

Ideal Functionality $\mathcal{F}_{\text{AUTH}}$. We assume parties communicate via authenticated (but public) channels modeled by $\mathcal{F}_{\text{AUTH}}$ [19].

3 One-Time Delegation of Okamoto-Schnorr Signing

Basic Idea. We consider one-time delegation of Okamoto-Schnorr (OS) signing. Here the OS signing key itself is shared among the delegatee and clouds, so it is not multi-run-detectable, but this serves as an important building block for one-time multi-run-detectable delegation scheme in Sect. 4. Conceptually one-time delegation can be viewed as if a delegator hands a delegatee a signing program that can be run only once with a message to be signed. Making abstraction of how such a signing program is implemented for now, we call it an OS signing one-time

Algorithm 1. $[\mathsf{OS.BSign}(x_1, x_2, r_1, r_2, \bar{m})]_{\mathrm{otp}}$

Require: $m \in \{0,1\}^*$, $\langle g, h, y = g^{x_1}h^{x_2}, p, s = g^{r_1}h^{r_2}, \{[r_i - \bar{c} \cdot x_i \bmod p]_{\mathrm{otp}}\}_{i=1}^{2}\rangle$
Ensure: signature (c', z_1', z_2') on m specified by $\mathsf{E}_{\mathrm{otp}}$ under the public key y
1: $\mathsf{E}_{\mathrm{otp}}$ chooses random $\alpha_1, \alpha_2, \beta \in \mathbb{Z}_p$, and computes $c' \leftarrow H(s \cdot g^{\alpha_1}h^{\alpha_2}y^{\beta} \parallel m)$
2: $\mathsf{E}_{\mathrm{otp}}$ computes $c \leftarrow c' - \beta \bmod p$
3: $\mathsf{E}_{\mathrm{otp}}$ runs $z_i \leftarrow [r_i - \bar{c} \cdot x_i \bmod p]_{\mathrm{otp}}$ with clouds by substituting c for $\bar{c}$ for $i = 1, 2$
4: $\mathsf{E}_{\mathrm{otp}}$ computes $z_i' \leftarrow z_i + \alpha_i \bmod p$ for $i = 1, 2$, and obtains (c', z_1', z_2')

program (OTP), and running the OTP actually involves interaction between the delegatee and clouds, but does not need interaction with the delegator (i.e., the delegator can be offline when the OTP is run). In this context, we call a delegator an OTP generator $\mathsf{G}_{\mathrm{otp}}$, and a delegatee an OTP executor $\mathsf{E}_{\mathrm{otp}}$. We consider how to construct the OS signing OTP (sOTP) from the algorithm $\mathsf{OS.Sign}(sk, m)$ (Fig. 1). To make the computation performed in the OTP as small as possible, we avoid simply embedding the whole computation of $\mathsf{OS.Sign}(sk, m)$ including the hash function into the OTP, and embed only the computation part $z_i \leftarrow r_i - cx_i \bmod p$ into the OTP, thus leading to much better efficiency. Here an input variable of an OTP specified by $\mathsf{E}_{\mathrm{otp}}$ is denoted by, e.g., $\bar{m}$, and a hardcoded secret variable is denoted as is. If we let $[f]_{\mathrm{otp}}$ denote the OTP of f, the OTP of $\mathsf{OS.Sign}(sk, m)$ can be like a tuple $[\mathsf{OS.Sign}(sk, \bar{m})]_{\mathrm{otp}} = \langle g, h, y, p, s, \{[r_i - \bar{c} \cdot x_i \bmod p]_{\mathrm{otp}}\}_{i=1}^{2}\rangle$ where $y = g^{x_1}h^{x_2}$, $s = g^{r_1}h^{r_2}$, $\bar{c} \leftarrow H(s \parallel \bar{m})$. I.e., $\mathsf{E}_{\mathrm{otp}}$ specifies the variable $\bar{m}$ and obtains the output by: (1) compute $c \leftarrow H(s \parallel m)$, (2) run $[r_i - \bar{c} \cdot x_i \bmod p]_{\mathrm{otp}}$ by substituting c for $\bar{c}$ for $i = 1, 2$. We can notice that actually this can be viewed as an OS *blind* signing operation because the hash calculation is not done by the signer (OTP). Therefore, the randomization of $s = g^{r_1}h^{r_2}$ and the hash value c is also possible as $\mathcal{U}$ does in $\mathsf{OS.SigIssue}$ (Fig. 1). As a result, the basic building block for an OS sOTP $[\mathsf{OS.BSign}(x_1, x_2, r_1, r_2, \bar{m})]_{\mathrm{otp}}$ is Algorithm 1.

3.1 Instantiating OS Signing OTP with Clouds

Now we focus on $[r_i - \bar{c} \cdot x_i \bmod p]_{\mathrm{otp}}$ in the OS signing OTP (sOTP), and consider how to instantiate this OTP with clouds. The basic idea is simple and efficient. The main part $[r_i - \bar{c} \cdot x_i \bmod p]_{\mathrm{otp}}$ is just computing $r_i - cx_i \bmod p$ with input c specified later by $\mathsf{E}_{\mathrm{otp}}$, so $\mathsf{G}_{\mathrm{otp}}$ can secret-share $\{r_i, x_i\}_{i=1}^{2}$ with the delegatee $\mathsf{E}_{\mathrm{otp}}$ and clouds, and let them compute $r_i - cx_i \bmod p$ distributively[7] with the shares and let the clouds erase the shares later. Although corrupted clouds will not erase the shares correctly, one-timesness can be achieved if there exists at least one honest cloud with secure erasure. We construct our protocol such that $\mathsf{E}_{\mathrm{otp}}$ needs to authenticate to clouds by using a password in running an sOTP. First we define the ideal functionality $\mathcal{F}_{\mathrm{otp}}^{\mathrm{BOS}}$ (Fig. 4) corresponding to our real protocol, which allows $\mathsf{E}_{\mathrm{otp}}$ to specify c and compute $r_i - cx_i \bmod p$ for $i = 1, 2$ only once, and for $\mathcal{F}_{\mathrm{otp}}^{\mathrm{BOS}}$, we assume the following:

[7] No interaction among clouds is needed here thanks to the simplicity of OS signing.

1. `OTP Generation Request`. On input (OTP-GENREQ, *sid*, G_{otp}, *pwd*) from E_{otp}:
   - Record (otpgen-req, *sid*, $\mathsf{E}_{otp}, \mathsf{G}_{otp}$, *pwd*).
   - Send (OTP-GENREQ, *sid*, $\mathsf{E}_{otp}, \mathsf{G}_{otp}$) to $\mathcal{S}$. Upon receiving ok from $\mathcal{S}$, output (OTP-GENREQ, *sid*, E_{otp}) to G_{otp}.
2. `OTP Generation`. On input (OTP-GEN, *sid*, E_{otp}, g, h, p, x_1, x_2) from G_{otp}:
   - Look up a record (otp-genreq, *sid*, $\mathsf{E}_{otp}, \mathsf{G}_{otp}$, *pwd*)[8)].
   - Choose random $r_1, r_2 \in \mathbb{Z}_p$ and record (otp, *sid*, $\mathsf{E}_{otp}, \mathsf{G}_{otp}$, *pwd*, p, x_1, x_2, r_1, r_2, *run-flg*), where *run-flg* = not-run. Delete (otp-genreq, *sid*, $\mathsf{E}_{otp}, \mathsf{G}_{otp}$, *pwd*).
   - If E_{otp} is corrupted, send (OTP-GEN-LEAK1, *sid*, $\mathsf{G}_{otp}, \mathsf{E}_{otp}, g, h, p, g^{x_1}h^{x_2}, g^{r_1}h^{r_2}$) to $\mathcal{S}$. If at least one S_j is corrupted, send (OTP-GEN-LEAK2, *sid*, G_{otp}, p) to $\mathcal{S}$.
   - Send (OTP-GEN, *sid*, $\mathsf{G}_{otp}, \mathsf{E}_{otp}$) to $\mathcal{S}$. Upon receiving ok from $\mathcal{S}$, output (OTP, *sid*, G_{otp}) to E_{otp}. For each S_j, send (OTP-GEN, *sid*, $\mathsf{G}_{otp}, \mathsf{S}_j$) to $\mathcal{S}$. Upon receiving ok from $\mathcal{S}$, output (OTP-SHARE, *sid*, G_{otp}) to each S_j.
3. `Running OTP`. On input (OTP-RUN, *sid*, $\{qid_j\}_{j=1}^m$, *pwd'*, c') from E_{otp}:
   - Look up records (otp, *sid*, E_{otp}, $*$, *pwd*, p, x_1, x_2, r_1, r_2, *run-flg*).
   - If the record (otp-running, *sid*, E_{otp}) already exists, wait until it is deleted.
   - Record (otp-running, *sid*, E_{otp}).
   - Set *ath-flg* $\leftarrow$ pwdok, $rslt_i \leftarrow r_i - c'x_i \bmod p$ for $i = 1, 2$ if *pwd* = *pwd'*, and otherwise *ath-flg* $\leftarrow$ pwdwrong, $rslt_i \leftarrow \perp$. Initialize *otp-finish* $\leftarrow$ true.
   - // OTP was already run
     If *run-flg* = run, output (OTP-RUN, *sid*, $\{qid_j\}_{j=1}^m, \perp$) to E_{otp}
   - Else, if E_{otp} is corrupted, output (OTP-RUN, *sid*, $\{qid_j\}_{j=1}^m$, $\{rslt_i\}_{i=1}^2$) to E_{otp} // OTP can be run
   - Else, if no S_j is corrupted, // E_{otp} is honest
     - send (OTP-RUN, *sid*, $\{qid_j\}_{j=1}^m$, E_{otp}) to $\mathcal{S}$. Upon receiving ok from $\mathcal{S}$, output (OTP-RUN, *sid*, $\{qid_j\}_{j=1}^m$, $\{rslt_i\}_{i=1}^2$) to E_{otp}
   - Else, send (OTP-RUN-LEAK, *sid*, $\{qid_j\}_{j=1}^m$, E_{otp}, c', *ath-flg*) to $\mathcal{S}$[9)], set *otp-finish* $\leftarrow$ false, and record (otp-running-wait-share, *sid*, $\{qid_j\}_{j=1}^m$, E_{otp}, c', *ath-flg*). // E_{otp} is honest and at least one of $\{\mathsf{S}_j\}_{j=1}^m$ is corrupted
   - If *otp-finish* = true and *ath-flg* = pwdok, update the record (otp, *sid*, E_{otp}, $*$, *pwd*, p, x_1, x_2, r_1, r_2, *run-flg*) such that *run-flg* $\leftarrow$ run.
   - If *otp-finish* = true, delete (otp-running, *sid*, E_{otp}).
4. `Corrupted Server Proceeds`. On input (OTP-SH-PROC, *sid*, $\{qid_j\}_{j=1}^m$, E_{otp}, *sh-flg*) from $\mathcal{S}$ where *sh-flg* $\in$ {correct-sh, $\perp$}:
   - Look up records (otp, *sid*, E_{otp}, $*$, *pwd*, p, x_1, x_2, r_1, r_2, *run-flg*), (otp-running, *sid*, E_{otp}), (otp-running-wait-share, *sid*, $\{qid_j\}_{j=1}^m$, E_{otp}, c', *ath-flg*).
   - Initialize $rslt_i \leftarrow \perp$ for $i = 1, 2$.
   - // At least one S_j is honest, so if the password is wrong, E_{otp} cannot
     // obtain the correct result. Note that $\mathcal{S}$ can ignore *ath-flg* if it wants.
     If *ath-flg* = pwdok and *sh-flg* = correct-sh, $rslt_i \leftarrow r_i - c'x_i \bmod p$ for $i = 1, 2$.
   - Send (OTP-RUN, *sid*, $\{qid_j\}_{j=1}^m$, E_{otp}) to $\mathcal{S}$. Upon receiving ok from $\mathcal{S}$, output (OTP-RUN, *sid*, $\{qid_j\}_{j=1}^m$, $\{rslt_i\}_{i=1}^2$) to E_{otp}.
   - If *ath-flg* = pwdok, update the record (otp, *sid*, E_{otp}, $*$, *pwd*, p, x_1, x_2, r_1, r_2, *run-flg*) such that *run-flg* $\leftarrow$ run. Delete (otp-running-wait-share, *sid*, $\{qid_j\}_{j=1}^m, \mathsf{E}_{otp}, c'$, *ath-flg*), (otp-running, *sid*, E_{otp}).

Fig. 4. $\mathcal{F}_{otp}^{BOS}$ for OS Signing OTP ("//" means comments and "$*$" is a wildcard)([8]When we say that a functionality "looks up a record", we mean that if the record is not found, the functionality just ignores the input. [9]In this case, $\mathcal{S}$ can only prevent E_{otp} from obtaining correct shares by responding with incorrect shares.)

- The existence of clouds $\{\mathsf{S}_j\}_{j=1}^m$ is public information.
- An (ideal) adversary (i.e., simulator) $\mathcal{S}$ is static (i.e., non-adaptive).
- *sid* is a common globally unique session ID both $\mathsf{G}_{\mathrm{otp}}$ and $\mathsf{E}_{\mathrm{otp}}$ have previously agreed upon (i.e., each OTP has its own unique *sid*) as in [17].
- qid_j is a common globally unique query ID both S_j and $\mathsf{E}_{\mathrm{otp}}$ have previously agreed upon each time $\mathsf{E}_{\mathrm{otp}}$ tries to retrieve a share from S_j as in [17].

Then we give the full description of OTP generation and OTP execution in Fig. 5, 6 respectively. For password authentication, we extend the method in [17] such that $\mathsf{E}_{\mathrm{otp}}$ can specify the password for multiple clouds. To let the simulation-based security proof go through, here we need to use additive secret sharing rather than Shamir's secret sharing[8] as in [17,38,39]. We explain the overview of how to adapt and embed the MAC scheme in [28] into our construction such that $\mathsf{E}_{\mathrm{otp}}$ can check the correctness of the shares sent by the clouds. Suppose the cloud S_j holds the shares $\{r'_{i,j},\ x'_{i,j}\}_{i=1}^2$, and sends $\{r'_{i,j} - c'x'_{i,j} \bmod p\}_{i=1}^2$ to $\mathsf{E}_{\mathrm{otp}}$ in response to c' specified by $\mathsf{E}_{\mathrm{otp}}$. First we outline the process for $\mathsf{G}_{\mathrm{otp}}$.

1. $\mathsf{G}_{\mathrm{otp}}$ chooses a random MAC key $\alpha^{(j)} \in \mathbb{Z}_p$ and prepares its additive sharing $\alpha^{(j)} = \alpha^{(j)}_{\mathsf{E}_{\mathrm{otp}}} + \alpha^{(j)}_{\mathsf{S}_j} \bmod p$.
2. $\mathsf{G}_{\mathrm{otp}}$ prepares the additive sharings of MAC tags $\{\alpha^{(j)}r'_{i,j},\ \alpha^{(j)}x'_{i,j}\}_{i=1}^2$ $\{\alpha^{(j)}r'_{i,j} = m^{(j,r'_i)}_{\mathsf{E}_{\mathrm{otp}}} + m^{(j,r'_i)}_{\mathsf{S}_j} \bmod p,\ \ \alpha^{(j)}x'_{i,j} = m^{(j,x'_i)}_{\mathsf{E}_{\mathrm{otp}}} + m^{(j,x'_i)}_{\mathsf{S}_j} \bmod p\}_{i=1}^2$
3. $\mathsf{G}_{\mathrm{otp}}$ sends $\langle \alpha^{(j)}_{\mathsf{S}_j}, \{r'_{i,j}, x'_{i,j}, m^{(j,r'_i)}_{\mathsf{S}_j}, m^{(j,x'_i)}_{\mathsf{S}_j}\}_{i=1}^2\rangle$ to S_j, and $\langle \alpha^{(j)}_{\mathsf{E}_{\mathrm{otp}}}, \{m^{(j,r'_i)}_{\mathsf{E}_{\mathrm{otp}}}, m^{(j,x'_i)}_{\mathsf{E}_{\mathrm{otp}}}\}_{i=1}^2\rangle$ to $\mathsf{E}_{\mathrm{otp}}$.

Next we outline the protocol between S_j and $\mathsf{E}_{\mathrm{otp}}$ running an sOTP.

1. Given c' by $\mathsf{E}_{\mathrm{otp}}$[9], for $i = 1, 2$, S_j computes $z'_{i,j} = r'_{i,j} - c'x'_{i,j} \bmod p$ and similarly $v_{i,\mathsf{S}_j} = \alpha^{(j)}_{\mathsf{S}_j} z'_{i,j} - (m^{(j,r'_i)}_{\mathsf{S}_j} - c' \cdot m^{(j,x'_i)}_{\mathsf{S}_j}) \bmod p$, and sends $\{z'_{i,j},\ v_{i,\mathsf{S}_j}\}_{i=1}^2$ to $\mathsf{E}_{\mathrm{otp}}$.
2. For $i = 1, 2$, $\mathsf{E}_{\mathrm{otp}}$ computes $v^{(j)}_{i,\mathsf{E}_{\mathrm{otp}}} = \alpha^{(j)}_{\mathsf{E}_{\mathrm{otp}}} z'_{i,j} - (m^{(j,r'_i)}_{\mathsf{E}_{\mathrm{otp}}} - c' \cdot m^{(j,x'_i)}_{\mathsf{E}_{\mathrm{otp}}})$, and checks whether $v^{(j)}_{i,\mathsf{E}_{\mathrm{otp}}} + v_{i,\mathsf{S}_j} \stackrel{?}{=} 0 \bmod p$. If 0, $\mathsf{E}_{\mathrm{otp}}$ accepts $\{z'_{i,j}\}_{i=1}^2$, and otherwise aborts.

For malicious S_j to cheat here such that $\mathsf{E}_{\mathrm{otp}}$ accepts $z'_{i,j} + \Delta = r'_{i,j} - c'x'_{i,j} + \Delta$ (where $\Delta \neq 0$), S_j needs to compute the following v^*_{i,S_j} by guessing $\alpha^{(j)}_{\mathsf{E}_{\mathrm{otp}}}$

[8] The adversarial $\mathsf{E}_{\mathrm{otp}}$ can send different c's to $\{\mathsf{S}_j\}_{j=1}^m$ in Step 3 of Fig. 6 maliciously because we do not require $\{\mathsf{S}_j\}_{j=1}^m$ to coordinate with each other to reject such requests (because we tried to keep the protocol as simple as possible). This makes the use of Shamir's secret sharing non-trivial in terms of the simulation in the proof.

[9] We note that the value c' does not need to be hidden from $\{\mathsf{S}_j\}_{j=1}^m$ because it is randomized in OS blind signing.

We assume the following:

- $\mathsf{G}_{\mathsf{otp}}$ has a signing key $(x_1, x_2) \in \mathbb{Z}_p^2$ and public key $y = g^{x_1} h^{x_2}$ with a group $\mathbb{G}$ of prime order p and generator $g, h \in \mathbb{G}$.
- Each cloud is denoted by S_j where $1 \leq j \leq m$.
- $\mathsf{G}_{\mathsf{otp}}$ and each S_j register their public keys $pk_{\mathsf{G}_{\mathsf{otp}}}$, pk_{S_j} with $\mathcal{F}_{\text{CA}}$ at the beginning of the protocol.
- $\mathsf{G}_{\mathsf{otp}}$ and $\mathsf{E}_{\mathsf{otp}}$ have already agreed upon generating an sOTP.
- The communication between parties is done via $\mathcal{F}_{\text{AUTH}}$.

1. On input ($\mathsf{OTP\text{-}GENREQ}$, *sid*, $\mathsf{G}_{\mathsf{otp}}$, *pwd*), $\mathsf{E}_{\mathsf{otp}}$ chooses random $seed \in \{0,1\}^\lambda$, and generates $\{salt_j,\ h_j\}_{j=1}^m$ such that
   $salt_j \leftarrow H(seed \parallel \mathsf{S}_j)$, $\ h_j \leftarrow H(salt_j \parallel pwd)$.
   $\mathsf{E}_{\mathsf{otp}}$ obtains $pk_{\mathsf{G}_{\mathsf{otp}}}$, $\{pk_{\mathsf{S}_j}\}_{j=1}^m$ from $\mathcal{F}_{\text{CA}}$, and sends $(sid, \mathsf{Enc}(pk_{\mathsf{G}_{\mathsf{otp}}}, pk_{\mathsf{E}_{\mathsf{otp}}}, \{\mathsf{Enc}(pk_{\mathsf{S}_j}, h_j)\}_{j=1}^m))$ to $\mathsf{G}_{\mathsf{otp}}$ where $\mathsf{Enc}(pk, m)$ denotes the ciphertext of m under the key pk.
2. $\mathsf{G}_{\mathsf{otp}}$ decrypts and receives $(sid, pk_{\mathsf{E}_{\mathsf{otp}}}, \{\mathsf{Enc}(pk_{\mathsf{S}_j}, h_j)\}_{j=1}^m)$ from $\mathsf{E}_{\mathsf{otp}}$ and outputs ($\mathsf{OTP\text{-}GENREQ}$, *sid*, $\mathsf{E}_{\mathsf{otp}}$).
   On input ($\mathsf{OTP\text{-}GEN}$, *sid*, $\mathsf{E}_{\mathsf{otp}}$, g, h, p, x_1, x_2), $\mathsf{G}_{\mathsf{otp}}$ chooses random $r_1, r_1 \in \mathbb{Z}_p$, generates $s = g^{r_1} h^{r_2}$, and splits $\{r_i,\ x_i\}_{i=1}^2$ into $r_i = r_i' + r_i'' \bmod p$, $x_i = x_i' + x_i'' \bmod p$ at random.
3. To (m, m)-secret-share $\{r_i',\ x_i'\}_{i=1}^2$ among $\{\mathsf{S}_j\}_{j=1}^m$, $\mathsf{G}_{\mathsf{otp}}$ generates the random shares $\{r_{i,j}',\ x_{i,j}'\}_{i=1,2}^{1 \leq j \leq m}$ such that
   $$r_i' = \sum_{j=1}^m r_{i,j}' \bmod p \ \text{ and } \ x_i' = \sum_{j=1}^m x_{i,j}' \bmod p \ \text{ for } i = 1, 2.$$
4. For $1 \leq j \leq m$, $\mathsf{G}_{\mathsf{otp}}$ chooses random MAC keys $\{\alpha^{(j)} \in \mathbb{Z}_p\}_{j=1}^m$, and prepares the following additive sharings at random:
   $\alpha^{(j)} = \alpha_{\mathsf{E}_{\mathsf{otp}}}^{(j)} + \alpha_{\mathsf{S}_j}^{(j)} \bmod p$,
   $\alpha^{(j)} r_{i,j}' = m_{\mathsf{E}_{\mathsf{otp}}}^{(j,r_i')} + m_{\mathsf{S}_j}^{(j,r_i')} \bmod p$, $\alpha^{(j)} x_{i,j}' = m_{\mathsf{E}_{\mathsf{otp}}}^{(j,x_i')} + m_{\mathsf{S}_j}^{(j,x_i')} \bmod p$ for $i = 1, 2$.
5. $\mathsf{G}_{\mathsf{otp}}$ obtains $\{pk_{\mathsf{S}_j}\}_{j=1}^m$ from $\mathcal{F}_{\text{CA}}$, and sends to each S_j
   $(sid, \mathsf{Enc}(pk_{\mathsf{S}_j}, h_j), \mathsf{Enc}(pk_{\mathsf{S}_j}, \langle \alpha_{\mathsf{S}_j}^{(j)}, \{r_{i,j}', x_{i,j}', m_{\mathsf{S}_j}^{(j,r_i')}, m_{\mathsf{S}_j}^{(j,x_i')}\}_{i=1}^2 \rangle))$.
6. An OS sOTP P is as follows:
   $$P = \langle sid, g, h, \underbrace{y}_{g^{x_1} h^{x_2}}, p, \underbrace{s}_{g^{r_1} h^{r_2}}, \{r_i'', x_i''\}_{i=1}^2, \{\alpha_{\mathsf{E}_{\mathsf{otp}}}^{(j)}\}_{j=1}^m, \{m_{\mathsf{E}_{\mathsf{otp}}}^{(j,r_i')}, m_{\mathsf{E}_{\mathsf{otp}}}^{(j,x_i')}\}_{i=1,2}^{1 \leq j \leq m} \rangle$$
   $\mathsf{G}_{\mathsf{otp}}$ sends $(sid, \mathsf{Enc}(pk_{\mathsf{E}_{\mathsf{otp}}}, P))$ to $\mathsf{E}_{\mathsf{otp}}$.
7. S_j receives $(sid, \mathsf{Enc}(pk_{\mathsf{S}_j}, h_j), \mathsf{Enc}(pk_{\mathsf{S}_j}, \langle \alpha_{\mathsf{S}_j}^{(j)}, \{r_{i,j}', x_{i,j}', m_{\mathsf{S}_j}^{(j,r_i')}, m_{\mathsf{S}_j}^{(j,x_i')}\}_{i=1}^2 \rangle))$ from $\mathsf{G}_{\mathsf{otp}}$, stores $\langle sid, h_j, \alpha_{\mathsf{S}_j}^{(j)}, \{r_{i,j}', x_{i,j}', m_{\mathsf{S}_j}^{(j,r_i')}, m_{\mathsf{S}_j}^{(j,x_i')}\}_{i=1}^2 \rangle$, and outputs ($\mathsf{OTP\text{-}SHARE}$, *sid*, $\mathsf{G}_{\mathsf{otp}}$).
8. $\mathsf{E}_{\mathsf{otp}}$ receives $(sid, \mathsf{Enc}(pk_{\mathsf{E}_{\mathsf{otp}}}, P))$ from $\mathsf{G}_{\mathsf{otp}}$, stores $(seed, P)$[12)], and outputs (OTP, *sid*, $\mathsf{G}_{\mathsf{otp}}$).

Fig. 5. Protocol for Generating an OS Signing OTP ([12]We assume that *pwd* exists only in $\mathsf{E}_{\mathsf{otp}}$'s brain (not stored in $\mathsf{E}_{\mathsf{otp}}$'s computer).)

unknown to S_j, but the probability that the guess is correct is only $1/p$.

$$\begin{aligned} v^*_{i,\mathsf{S}_j} &= -v^{(j)}_{i,\mathsf{E}_{\mathrm{otp}}} = -(\alpha^{(j)}_{\mathsf{E}_{\mathrm{otp}}}(r'_{i,j} - c'x'_{i,j} + \Delta) - (m^{(j,r'_i)}_{\mathsf{E}_{\mathrm{otp}}} - c' \cdot m^{(j,x'_i)}_{\mathsf{E}_{\mathrm{otp}}})) \\ &= -\alpha^{(j)}_{\mathsf{E}_{\mathrm{otp}}}\Delta + \alpha^{(j)}_{\mathsf{S}_j}(r'_{i,j} - c'x'_{i,j}) - (m^{(j,r'_i)}_{\mathsf{S}_j} - c'm^{(j,x'_i)}_{\mathsf{S}_j}) \end{aligned}$$

Although discrete-log based commitments can also be used to check the response $\{z'_{i,j}\}^2_{i=1}$ from S_j here, the above MACs are much more efficient in that $\mathsf{E}_{\mathrm{otp}}$ needs only modular addition/multiplication rather than exponentiations.

- In this protocol for running an OS sOTP, $\mathsf{E}_{\mathrm{otp}}$ interacts with each S_j.
- $\mathsf{E}_{\mathrm{otp}}$ has an OS sOTP P (Fig. 5) and is given input c' where c' is computed as $c \leftarrow H(s{\cdot}g^{\alpha_1}h^{\alpha_2}y^{\beta} \parallel m)$, $c' \leftarrow c{-}\beta \bmod p$ with s in P, random $\alpha_1, \alpha_2, \beta \in \mathbb{Z}_p$[14], and message $m \in \{0,1\}^*$ to be signed.

1. On input (OTP-RUN, *sid*, $\{qid_j\}^m_{j=1}$, *pwd*, c'), to retrieve a share from each S_j, $\mathsf{E}_{\mathrm{otp}}$ computes, for authentication,
$$ath_j \leftarrow H(sid \parallel qid_j \parallel \overbrace{H(\underbrace{H(seed \parallel \mathsf{S}_j)}_{salt_j} \parallel pwd)}^{h_j}),$$
and sends (*sid*, qid_j, $\mathsf{Enc}(pk_{\mathsf{S}_j}, pk_{\mathsf{E}_{\mathrm{otp}}}, c', ath_j)$) to each S_j.
2. Each S_j decrypts and obtains (*sid*, qid_j, $pk_{\mathsf{E}_{\mathrm{otp}}}$, c', ath_j) from $\mathsf{E}_{\mathrm{otp}}$. If S_j does not have a data tuple corresponding to *sid* or it does not hold that $ath_j = H(sid \parallel qid_j \parallel h_j)$, S_j sets $rslt_i \leftarrow \perp$ for $i = 1, 2$. Otherwise S_j computes, for $i = 1, 2$,
$z'_{i,j} \leftarrow r'_{i,j} - c' \cdot x'_{i,j} \bmod p, \quad v_{i,\mathsf{S}_j} \leftarrow \alpha^{(j)}_{\mathsf{S}_j} z'_{i,j} - (m^{(j,r'_i)}_{\mathsf{S}_j} - c' \cdot m^{(j,x'_i)}_{\mathsf{S}_j}) \bmod p,$
erases $\langle sid, h_j, \alpha^{(j)}_{\mathsf{S}_j}, \{r'_{i,j}, x'_{i,j}, m^{(j,r'_i)}_{\mathsf{S}_j}, m^{(j,x'_i)}_{\mathsf{S}_j}\}^2_{i=1}\rangle$ [15]since it is no longer needed, and sets $rslt_i \leftarrow \langle z'_{i,j}, v_{i,\mathsf{S}_j}\rangle$. S_j sends (*sid*, qid_j, $\mathsf{Enc}(pk_{\mathsf{E}_{\mathrm{otp}}}, \{rslt_i\}^2_{i=1})$) to $\mathsf{E}_{\mathrm{otp}}$.
3. If $\mathsf{E}_{\mathrm{otp}}$ decrypts and receives $\{rslt_i\}^2_{i=1}$ from S_j and $rslt_i \neq \perp$, $\mathsf{E}_{\mathrm{otp}}$ computes
$v^{(j)}_{i,\mathsf{E}_{\mathrm{otp}}} = \alpha^{(j)}_{\mathsf{E}_{\mathrm{otp}}} z'_{i,j} - (m^{(j,r'_i)}_{\mathsf{E}_{\mathrm{otp}}} - c' \cdot m^{(j,x'_i)}_{\mathsf{E}_{\mathrm{otp}}}) \bmod p,$
and verifies $v^{(j)}_{i,\mathsf{E}_{\mathrm{otp}}} + v_{i,\mathsf{S}_j} \stackrel{?}{=} 0 \bmod p$ for $i = 1, 2$. If the verification fails or $rslt_i = \perp$, $\mathsf{E}_{\mathrm{otp}}$ outputs (OTP-RUN, *sid*, $\{qid_j\}^m_{j=1}$, $\perp$).
Otherwise $\mathsf{E}_{\mathrm{otp}}$ has $\{z'_{i,j}\}^{1\le j\le m}_{i=1,2}$, computes, for $i = 1, 2$,
$z'_i = r_i - c'x_i = (\sum^m_{j=1} z'_{i,j}) + (r''_i - c'x''_i) \bmod p,$
and outputs (OTP-RUN, *sid*, $\{qid_j\}^m_{j=1}$, $\{z'_i\}^2_{i=1}$).

Fig. 6. Protocol for Running an OS Signing OTP ([14]This randomizability makes the resulting signature unlinkable even for the clouds as well as the delegator because c' (visible to the clouds) is independent of the signature. [15]We assume that while a thread running in S_j is accessing a data tuple $\langle sid, h_j, \alpha^{(j)}_{\mathsf{S}_j}, \{r'_{i,j}, x'_{i,j}, m^{(j,r'_i)}_{\mathsf{S}_j}, m^{(j,x'_i)}_{\mathsf{S}_j}\}^2_{i=1}\rangle$, the access to this tuple (with tuple ID *sid*) by other threads is prevented with appropriate mutual exclusion.)

Theorem 1. *The protocol in Fig. 5, 6 securely realizes the functionality* $\mathcal{F}_{\mathrm{otp}}^{\mathrm{BOS}}$ *(Fig. 4) in the* $(\mathcal{F}_{\mathrm{CA}}, \mathcal{F}_{\mathrm{AUTH}})$*-hybrid and RO model, assuming that the static adversary corrupts* $\mathsf{E}_{\mathrm{otp}}$ *and at most* $(m-1)$ *clouds and the unforgeability of the MAC scheme based on authenticated secret sharing.*

We prove the above theorem in the full version by following the ideal/real simulation paradigm. In the proof, basically we show that there exists a simulator $\mathcal{S}$ that interacts with $\mathcal{F}_{\mathrm{otp}}^{\mathrm{BOS}}$ and the adversary $\mathcal{A}$ and can generate an indistinguishable view for $\mathcal{A}$ by using only leakage from $\mathcal{F}_{\mathrm{otp}}^{\mathrm{BOS}}$ without knowing $\{r_i, x_i\}_{i=1}^2$.

4 One-Time Multi-Run-Detectable Delegation Based on Anonymous Credentials

Now we construct a one-time multi-run-detectable delegation scheme of unlinkable signing rights with OS sOTPs and anonymous credentials (ACs) such that a delegator does not need to embed their master signing key directly into the OTP. First we construct a one-time AC (OAC) scheme, in which the credential issuer can issue a one-time unlinkable credential which can be shown to a verifier only once based on our OTPs. As an underlying AC scheme, we use the PS scheme [42], which consists of the following:
– randomizable blind signatures with the message space of multiple attributes,
– zero-knowledge proof of knowledge of a signature.

Key Idea to combine* OS *sOTP and* PS *scheme: In the PS scheme, the credential requestor $\mathcal{U}$ obtains a blind signature on the commitment to $\mathsf{att}_{\mathcal{U}}$ in the issuance protocol, and in the show protocol, gives a zero-knowledge proof of knowledge of $\mathsf{att}_{\mathcal{U}}$. In our OAC scheme, the issuer adds hidden extra random attributes $a_{1,\mathrm{otp}}, a_{2,\mathrm{otp}} \in \mathbb{Z}_p$ to the commitment before signing it, and also hands an OS sOTP including $\{a_{i,\mathrm{otp}}\}_{i=1}^2$ to $\mathcal{U}$[10]. As a result, $\mathcal{U}$ is forced to use the sOTP to prove knowledge of a signature in the show protocol because $\mathcal{U}$ cannot know $\{a_{i,\mathrm{otp}}\}_{i=1}^2$ directly, and thus it leads to a one-time credential.

Building on the PS scheme and the above idea, our construction is given in Fig. 7. The main differences between the PS scheme and ours are:

- how to issue a credential in $\mathsf{OAC.CredIssue}_{\mathrm{otp}}$,
- part of the prover's process

is replaced with a run of an OS sOTP.
Although an OS sOTP is run in $\mathsf{OAC.CredShow}_{\mathrm{otp}}$, the prover's process is the same as that of the PS scheme. Thus it is sufficient for us to prove that $\mathsf{OAC.CredIssue}_{\mathrm{otp}}$ is a blind signature scheme, i.e., its blindness and unforgeability with the following theorem (the proof is given in the full version).

[10] $\{a_{i,\mathrm{otp}}\}_{i=1}^2$ corresponding to a signing key in the OS scheme are fresh random and used only once in our OAC, so the attack [7] on OS blind signatures does not apply here because [7] needs concurrent $\mathsf{polylog}(\lambda)$ signing queries with the same signing key.

- $\mathsf{OAC.Setup_{otp}}(1^\lambda)$: generate public parameters $\mathsf{params} = (p, \mathbb{G}_1, \mathbb{G}_2, \mathbb{G}_T, e)$ of a type-3 bilinear group.
- $\mathsf{OAC.IKeyGen_{otp}}(\mathsf{params}, w)$: choose generators $g \in \mathbb{G}_1$, $\widetilde{g} \in \mathbb{G}_2$ and random values $(x, y_1, \ldots, y_w, y_{1,\mathrm{otp}}, y_{2,\mathrm{otp}}, y_{\mathsf{s}}) \in \mathbb{Z}_p^{w+4}$, and compute $(X, Y_1, \ldots, Y_w, Y_{1,\mathrm{otp}}, Y_{2,\mathrm{otp}}, Y_{\mathsf{s}}) \leftarrow (g^x, g^{y_1}, \ldots, g^{y_w}, g^{y_{1,\mathrm{otp}}}, g^{y_{2,\mathrm{otp}}}, g^{y_{\mathsf{s}}})$, $(\widetilde{X}, \widetilde{Y}_1, \ldots, \widetilde{Y}_w, \widetilde{Y}_{1,\mathrm{otp}}, \widetilde{Y}_{2,\mathrm{otp}}, \widetilde{Y}_{\mathsf{s}}) \leftarrow (\widetilde{g}^x, \widetilde{g}^{y_1}, \ldots, \widetilde{g}^{y_w}, \widetilde{g}^{y_{1,\mathrm{otp}}}, \widetilde{g}^{y_{2,\mathrm{otp}}}, \widetilde{g}^{y_{\mathsf{s}}})$ where $\mathsf{pk}_{\mathcal{I}} = (g, \{Y_i\}_{i=1}^w, Y_{1,\mathrm{otp}}, Y_{2,\mathrm{otp}}, Y_{\mathsf{s}}, \widetilde{g}, \widetilde{X}, \{\widetilde{Y}_i\}_{i=1}^w, \widetilde{Y}_{1,\mathrm{otp}}, \widetilde{Y}_{2,\mathrm{otp}}, \widetilde{Y}_{\mathsf{s}})$ and $\mathsf{sk}_{\mathcal{I}} = X$. The values $(Y_i, \widetilde{Y}_i)$ are related to attribute i, and $(g, \widetilde{g})$ are said to be related to dummy attribute 0.
- $\mathsf{OAC.CredIssue_{otp}}(\mathcal{I}(\mathsf{sk}_{\mathcal{I}}), \mathcal{U}(\mathsf{att}_{\mathcal{U}}))$ is the following protocol between $\mathcal{I}$ and $\mathcal{U}$.
  1. To obtain a signature on the attributes $\mathsf{att}_{\mathcal{U}} = (a_1, \ldots, a_w) \in \mathbb{Z}_p^w$, $\mathcal{U}$ generates $C \leftarrow g^r \cdot Y_{\mathsf{s}}^{s_{\mathcal{U}}} \cdot \prod_{i=1}^w Y_i^{a_i}$ with random $r, s_{\mathcal{U}} \in \mathbb{Z}_p$, and sends C to $\mathcal{I}$.
  2. $\mathcal{U}$ gives to $\mathcal{I}$ the following proof of knowledge PK (Fig. 2) regarding C [16], $\mathsf{PK}\{(r, s_{\mathcal{U}}, a_1, \ldots, a_w) \colon C = g^r \cdot Y_{\mathsf{s}}^{s_{\mathcal{U}}} \cdot \prod_{i=1}^w Y_i^{a_i}\}$.
  3. If the PK regarding C is valid, $\mathcal{I}$ chooses random values $u, a_{1,\mathrm{otp}}, a_{2,\mathrm{otp}}, r_{1,\mathrm{otp}}, r_{2,\mathrm{otp}}\ s_{\mathcal{I}} \in \mathbb{Z}_p$, and sends $\mathcal{U}$ the following: $\sigma' = (\sigma'_1, \sigma'_2) = (g^u, (X \cdot C \cdot Y_{1,\mathrm{otp}}^{a_{1,\mathrm{otp}}} \cdot Y_{2,\mathrm{otp}}^{a_{2,\mathrm{otp}}} \cdot Y_{\mathsf{s}}^{s_{\mathcal{I}}})^u)$, OTP, $P = \langle \{\widetilde{Y}_{i,\mathrm{otp}}\}_{i=1}^2, \widetilde{Y}_{1,\mathrm{otp}}^{a_{1,\mathrm{otp}}} \cdot \widetilde{Y}_{2,\mathrm{otp}}^{a_{2,\mathrm{otp}}}, s_{\mathcal{I}}, p, \widetilde{Y}_{1,\mathrm{otp}}^{r_{1,\mathrm{otp}}} \cdot \widetilde{Y}_{2,\mathrm{otp}}^{r_{2,\mathrm{otp}}}, \{[r_{i,\mathrm{otp}} - \bar{c} \cdot a_{i,\mathrm{otp}} \bmod p]_{\mathrm{otp}}\}_{i=1}^2 \rangle$
  4. $\mathcal{U}$ obtains the signature σ on $(\mathsf{att}_{\mathcal{U}}, a_{1,\mathrm{otp}}, a_{2,\mathrm{otp}}, \mathsf{sn})$ where $\mathsf{sn} = s_{\mathcal{U}} + s_{\mathcal{I}}$ as
  $$\sigma = (\sigma_1, \sigma_2) = (\sigma'_1, \sigma'_2/{\sigma'_1}^r) = (g^u, (X \cdot Y_{1,\mathrm{otp}}^{a_{1,\mathrm{otp}}} \cdot Y_{2,\mathrm{otp}}^{a_{2,\mathrm{otp}}} \cdot Y_{\mathsf{s}}^{\mathsf{sn}} \cdot \prod_{i=1}^{w} Y_i^{a_i})^u).$$

  The signature on $(\mathsf{att}_{\mathcal{U}}, a_{1,\mathrm{otp}}, a_{2,\mathrm{otp}}, \mathsf{sn})$ can be verified as $\sigma_1 \neq 1_{\mathbb{G}_1}$ and $e(\sigma_1, \widetilde{X} \cdot \widetilde{Y}_{1,\mathrm{otp}}^{a_{1,\mathrm{otp}}} \cdot \widetilde{Y}_{2,\mathrm{otp}}^{a_{2,\mathrm{otp}}} \cdot \widetilde{Y}_{\mathsf{s}}^{\mathsf{sn}} \cdot \prod_{i=1}^w \widetilde{Y}_i^{a_i}) \stackrel{?}{=} e(\sigma_2, \widetilde{g})$.
  By viewing $\sigma = (\sigma_1, \sigma_2)$ as a signature on $(0, \mathsf{att}_{\mathcal{U}}, a_{1,\mathrm{otp}}, a_{2,\mathrm{otp}}, \mathsf{sn})$ where the first entry is the value of dummy attribute 0, $\mathcal{U}$ can randomize σ to obtain another fresh signature on $(t, \mathsf{att}_{\mathcal{U}}, a_{1,\mathrm{otp}}, a_{2,\mathrm{otp}}, \mathsf{sn})$ by computing new $\sigma \leftarrow (\sigma_1^s, (\sigma_1^t \cdot \sigma_2)^s)$ with random $s, t \in \mathbb{Z}_p$. We note that the portion corresponding to $(\mathsf{att}_{\mathcal{U}}, a_{1,\mathrm{otp}}, a_{2,\mathrm{otp}}, \mathsf{sn})$ cannot be changed.
  $\langle \sigma, (t, \mathsf{att}_{\mathcal{U}}, a_{1,\mathrm{otp}}, a_{2,\mathrm{otp}}, \mathsf{sn}), P \rangle$ corresponds to the credential $\mathsf{cr}_{\mathcal{U}}$.
- $\mathsf{OAC.CredShow_{otp}}(\mathcal{V}(\mathsf{pk}_{\mathcal{I}}, \sigma, \mathsf{sn}), \mathcal{U}(\mathsf{cr}_{\mathcal{U}}))$ is a show protocol between $\mathcal{U}$ and verifier $\mathcal{V}$. What $\mathcal{U}$ does is to prove knowledge of a (randomized) signature σ. Since the verification of the randomized signature $\sigma = (\sigma_1, \sigma_2)$ on $(t, \mathsf{att}_{\mathcal{U}}, a_{1,\mathrm{otp}}, a_{2,\mathrm{otp}}, \mathsf{sn})$ can be done as $e(\sigma_1, \widetilde{X} \cdot \widetilde{g}^t \cdot \widetilde{Y}_{1,\mathrm{otp}}^{a_{1,\mathrm{otp}}} \cdot \widetilde{Y}_{2,\mathrm{otp}}^{a_{2,\mathrm{otp}}} \cdot \widetilde{Y}_{\mathsf{s}}^{\mathsf{sn}} \cdot \prod_{i=1}^w \widetilde{Y}_i^{a_i}) \stackrel{?}{=} e(\sigma_2, \widetilde{g})$, this verification can also be viewed as
  $$e(\sigma_1, \widetilde{g})^t \cdot \prod_{i=1}^{2} e(\sigma_1, \widetilde{Y}_{i,\mathrm{otp}})^{a_{i,\mathrm{otp}}} \cdot e(\sigma_1, \widetilde{Y}_{\mathsf{s}})^{\mathsf{sn}} \cdot \prod_{i=1}^{w} e(\sigma_1, \widetilde{Y}_i)^{a_i} \stackrel{?}{=} \frac{e(\sigma_2, \widetilde{g})}{e(\sigma_1, \widetilde{X})},$$
  so with bases $\{e(\sigma_1, \widetilde{g}), \{e(\sigma_1, \widetilde{Y}_{i,\mathrm{otp}})\}_{i=1}^2, e(\sigma_1, \widetilde{Y}_{\mathsf{s}}), \{e(\sigma_1, \widetilde{Y}_i)\}_{i=1}^w\}$, giving the following PK leads to proving knowledge of a signature:
  $$\mathsf{PK}\{(t, a_1, \ldots, a_w, a_{1,\mathrm{otp}}, a_{2,\mathrm{otp}}, \mathsf{sn}) \colon e(\sigma_2, \widetilde{g})/\{e(\sigma_1, \widetilde{X}) \cdot e(\sigma_1, \widetilde{Y}_{\mathsf{s}})^{\mathsf{sn}}\} = e(\sigma_1, \widetilde{g})^t \cdot \prod_{i=1}^{w} e(\sigma_1, \widetilde{Y}_i)^{a_i} \cdot \prod_{i=1}^{2} e(\sigma_1, \widetilde{Y}_{i,\mathrm{otp}})^{a_{i,\mathrm{otp}}}\}.$$
  Here $\mathcal{V}$ requires $\mathcal{U}$ to disclose sn, and $\mathcal{U}$ runs the OS sOTP P [17].

Fig. 7. One-Time Anonymous Credential Scheme ([16]Depending on applications, $\mathcal{U}$ can send part of $\mathsf{att}_{\mathcal{U}}$ in the clear to $\mathcal{I}$, and $\mathcal{I}$ will judge that $\mathcal{U}$ is qualified as the portion of $\mathsf{att}_{\mathcal{U}}$. In the underlying non-blind PS multi-message signature [42, Sect. 4.2], these clear $\mathsf{att}_{\mathcal{U}}$ corresponds to multiple messages. [17]The details of how running an OTP is combined with a (signature based on a) PK can be found in Fig. 10, which is similar to this PK of a signature.)

Theorem 2. *The OAC scheme in Fig. 7 is one-time, blind, and unforgeable based on the security of OTPs and the underlying* PS *scheme in the RO model.*

Now we can see that the OAC scheme in Fig. 7 can be turned into an sOTP because the PK in $\mathsf{OAC.CredShow}_{\mathrm{otp}}$ can be turned into an SPK as OS signatures by using the Fiat-Shamir transform. Thus the credential issuer and holder can be viewed as a delegator and delegatee respectively. The value sn in $\mathsf{OAC.CredIssue}_{\mathrm{otp}}$ cannot be changed by $\mathcal{U}$ in $\mathsf{OAC.CredShow}_{\mathrm{otp}}$ because of the unforgeability of the PS scheme, and needs to be disclosed in the resulting signature, so if the delegator finds more than one same sn in the collected signatures, the delegator can detect the fact that an sOTP was run more than once, thus achieving multi-run-detectability (if necessary, the delegator can announce that sn is blocked). The PS scheme and OS sOTPs are unlinkable because of randomizability, so our resulting sOTP also enjoys unlinkability for both the delegator and clouds.

5 E-Cash Based on Signing OTPs

Building on our sOTPs based on OACs (Fig. 7), we construct an e-cash scheme. In the traditional e-cash originating from [22], the following protocols exist:

- Withdraw protocol: A user $\mathcal{U}$ communicates with bank $\mathcal{B}$, and receives electronic data (called *e-coin*), and $\mathcal{B}$ debits $\mathcal{U}$'s account the corresponding value.
- Spend protocol: $\mathcal{U}$ spends an e-coin by sending it to a merchant $\mathcal{M}$.
- Deposit protocol: $\mathcal{M}$ deposits the e-coin spent by $\mathcal{U}$ to $\mathcal{B}$, and $\mathcal{B}$ credits the corresponding amount to the $\mathcal{M}$'s account.

Employing our sOTP, our EC (Fig. 8, 9) prevents double-spending[11] and further identifies a double-spender even if sOTPs are broken. We adopt the elegant framework [15] such that $\mathcal{B}$ can issue an e-coin including an sOTP and user's ID in the Withdraw protocol without embedding its master signing key, and two signatures originating from the same e-coin (collected in the Deposit protocol) can reveal the user's ID. The scheme in [13, Sect. 6.3] takes a similar approach, but the double-spender's secret key is revealed, so "exculpability" is not achieved (i.e., $\mathcal{B}$ can frame users), while ours reveals only the double-spender's public key according to [15], thus achieving exculpability. Following the e-cash security model [11,15,37], we give the proofs in the full version, and discuss the additional possible extensions.

Batch Spending. What happens in the Spend protocol can be viewed as:
- $\mathcal{U}_i$ has an e-coin that can be viewed as a kind of public key certified by $\mathcal{B}$.
- $\mathcal{U}_i$ signs the message from $\mathcal{M}_j$ with e-coin, and sends the signature to $\mathcal{M}_j$.
- Then the value of the e-coin is transferred to $\mathcal{M}_j$.

[11] Our e-cash is somewhat incomparable to existing e-cash since we assume there exist distributed partially trusted clouds as in [17,29], while other schemes do not.

- $\mathsf{EC.Setup}(1^\lambda)$ is the same as $\mathsf{OAC.Setup_{otp}}(1^\lambda)$, and $\mathcal{B}$ obtains $\mathsf{params} = (p,\ \mathbb{G}_1,\ \mathbb{G}_2,\ \mathbb{G}_T,\ e)$.
- $\mathsf{EC.BKeyGen}(\mathsf{params})$: first run $\mathsf{OAC.IKeyGen}(\mathsf{params},\ 3)$, and $\mathcal{B}$ obtain the signing key $\mathsf{sk}_\mathcal{B} = X$, and partial public key $\mathsf{ppk}_\mathcal{B} = (\mathsf{params},\ g,\ g_\mathsf{v},\ g_\mathsf{u},\ f_\mathsf{u},\ g_{1,\mathrm{otp}},\ g_{2,\mathrm{otp}},\ g_\mathsf{s},\ \widetilde{g},\ \widetilde{X},\ \widetilde{g}_\mathsf{v},\ \widetilde{g}_\mathsf{u},\ \widetilde{f}_\mathsf{u},\ \widetilde{g}_{1,\mathrm{otp}},\widetilde{g}_{2,\mathrm{otp}},\widetilde{g}_\mathsf{s})$. Next $\mathcal{B}$ computes an additional key $H(\mathsf{ppk}_\mathcal{B}) \to g_{\mathsf{u}'} \in \mathbb{G}_1$ with an appropriate hash function $H : \{0,1\}^* \to \mathbb{G}_1$,and lets $\mathsf{pk}_\mathcal{B} = (\mathsf{ppk}_\mathcal{B},\ g_{\mathsf{u}'})$.
- $\mathsf{EC.UKeyGen}(\mathsf{params},\ \mathsf{pk}_\mathcal{B})$: $\mathcal{U}_i$ chooses their secret key $\mathsf{sk}_{\mathcal{U}_i} \in \mathbb{Z}_p$ for EC and resultant public keys $(\mathsf{pk}_{\mathcal{U}_i} = g_\mathsf{u}^{\mathsf{sk}_{\mathcal{U}_i}},\ \mathsf{pk}'_{\mathcal{U}_i} = g_{\mathsf{u}'}^{\mathsf{sk}_{\mathcal{U}_i}})$. Moreover $\mathcal{U}_i$ generates $\mathsf{PK}\{(\mathsf{sk}_{\mathcal{U}_i}) : \mathsf{pk}_{\mathcal{U}_i} = g_\mathsf{u}^{\mathsf{sk}_{\mathcal{U}_i}} \wedge \mathsf{pk}'_{\mathcal{U}_i} = g_{\mathsf{u}'}^{\mathsf{sk}_{\mathcal{U}_i}}\}$ and a signature $\sigma(\mathsf{pk}_{\mathcal{U}_i},\ \mathsf{pk}'_{\mathcal{U}_i})$ on $(\mathsf{pk}_{\mathcal{U}_i},\ \mathsf{pk}'_{\mathcal{U}_i})$ under their PKI key $\mathsf{pk}^{(\mathrm{pki})}_{\mathcal{U}_i}$, and sends $(\mathsf{pk}_{\mathcal{U}_i},\ \mathsf{pk}'_{\mathcal{U}_i},\ \mathsf{pk}^{(\mathrm{pki})}_{\mathcal{U}_i},\ \sigma(\mathsf{pk}_{\mathcal{U}_i},\ \mathsf{pk}'_{\mathcal{U}_i}),\ \mathsf{PK})$ to $\mathcal{B}$ [19)], which stores them in the user DB.
- $\mathsf{EC.Withdraw}(\mathcal{B}(\mathsf{sk}_\mathcal{B},\ \mathsf{pk}_{\mathcal{U}_i}),\ \mathcal{U}_i(\mathsf{sk}_{\mathcal{U}_i},\ \mathsf{pk}_\mathcal{B}))$ is the following protocol between $\mathcal{B}$ and $\mathcal{U}_i$ where $\mathcal{U}_i$ obtains an e-coin corresponding to v dollars [20)].
  1. $\mathcal{U}_i$ sends $v,\ \mathsf{pk}_{\mathcal{U}_i},\ \mathsf{pk}'_{\mathcal{U}_i}$ to $\mathcal{B}$, and also gives $\mathsf{PK}\{(\mathsf{sk}_{\mathcal{U}_i}) : \mathsf{pk}_{\mathcal{U}_i} = g_\mathsf{u}^{\mathsf{sk}_{\mathcal{U}_i}}\}$ (Fig. 2) [21)]. $\mathcal{B}$ rejects the request if $\mathsf{pk}_{\mathcal{U}_i}$ is not found in the user DB.
  2. $\mathcal{U}_i$ chooses random $r,\ s_{\mathcal{U}_i},\ \omega_\mathsf{u} \in \mathbb{Z}_p$, computes the following commitment C, and gives the following PK to $\mathcal{B}$.
     $\mathsf{PK}\{(r,\ s_{\mathcal{U}_i},\ \omega_\mathsf{u}) : C = g^r \cdot g_\mathsf{s}^{s_{\mathcal{U}_i}} \cdot f_\mathsf{u}^{\omega_\mathsf{u}}\}$
  3. If the PK is valid, $\mathcal{B}$ chooses random $u,\ s_\mathcal{B},\ x_{1,\mathrm{otp}}, x_{2,\mathrm{otp}}, r_{1,\mathrm{otp}}, r_{2,\mathrm{otp}} \in \mathbb{Z}_p$, computes
     $C' \leftarrow C \cdot \mathsf{pk}_{\mathcal{U}_i} \cdot g_\mathsf{v}^v \cdot g_\mathsf{s}^{s_\mathcal{B}} \cdot g_{1,\mathrm{otp}}^{x_{1,\mathrm{otp}}} \cdot g_{2,\mathrm{otp}}^{x_{2,\mathrm{otp}}} = g^r \cdot g_\mathsf{v}^v \cdot g_\mathsf{s}^{s_\mathcal{B}+s_{\mathcal{U}_i}} \cdot g_\mathsf{u}^{\mathsf{sk}_{\mathcal{U}_i}} \cdot f_\mathsf{u}^{\omega_\mathsf{u}} \cdot g_{1,\mathrm{otp}}^{x_{1,\mathrm{otp}}} \cdot g_{2,\mathrm{otp}}^{x_{2,\mathrm{otp}}}$,
     $\sigma' \leftarrow (\sigma'_1,\ \sigma'_2) = (g^u,\ (X \cdot C')^u)$,
     and generates the OTP P as follows
     $P = \langle \widetilde{g}_{1,\mathrm{otp}},\ \widetilde{g}_{2,\mathrm{otp}},\ \widetilde{g}_{1,\mathrm{otp}}^{x_{1,\mathrm{otp}}} \cdot \widetilde{g}_{2,\mathrm{otp}}^{x_{2,\mathrm{otp}}},\ p,\ \widetilde{g}_{2,\mathrm{otp}}^{r_{2,\mathrm{otp}}} \cdot \widetilde{g}_{2,\mathrm{otp}}^{r_{2,\mathrm{otp}}},$
     $\{[r_{i,\mathrm{otp}} - \bar{c} \cdot x_{i,\mathrm{otp}} \bmod p]_\mathrm{otp}\}_{i=1}^2\rangle$.
     $\mathcal{B}$ sends $\sigma',\ s_\mathcal{B},\ P$ to $\mathcal{U}_i$, and debits $\mathcal{U}_i$'s account v dollars.
  4. $\mathcal{U}_i$ obtains the signature σ'' on $(v,\ \mathsf{sn},\ \mathsf{sk}_{\mathcal{U}_i},\ \omega_\mathsf{u},\ x_{1,\mathrm{otp}},\ x_{2,\mathrm{otp}})$ where $\mathsf{sn} = s_\mathcal{B} + s_{\mathcal{U}_i}$ (called *serial number*) as
     $\sigma'' = (\sigma''_1,\ \sigma''_2) = (\sigma'_1,\ \sigma'_2/\sigma'^{\,r}_1)$, which can be verified as
     $e(\sigma''_1,\ \widetilde{X} \cdot \widetilde{g}_\mathsf{v}^v \cdot \widetilde{g}_\mathsf{s}^\mathsf{sn} \cdot \widetilde{g}_\mathsf{u}^{\mathsf{sk}_{\mathcal{U}_i}} \cdot \widetilde{f}_\mathsf{u}^{\omega_\mathsf{u}} \cdot \widetilde{g}_{1,\mathrm{otp}}^{x_{1,\mathrm{otp}}} \cdot \widetilde{g}_{2,\mathrm{otp}}^{x_{2,\mathrm{otp}}}) \stackrel{?}{=} e(\sigma''_2,\ \widetilde{g})$.
     $\mathcal{U}_i$ can obtain a randomized signature σ_co on $(t,\ v,\ \mathsf{sn},\ \mathsf{sk}_{\mathcal{U}_i},\ \omega_\mathsf{u},\ x_{1,\mathrm{otp}},\ x_{2,\mathrm{otp}})$ with random $s,\ t \in \mathbb{Z}_p$ and computing, $\sigma_\mathsf{co} = (\sigma_1^s,\ (\sigma_1^t \cdot \sigma_2)^s)$.
     The obtained e-coin co consists of $(\sigma_\mathsf{co},\ t,\ v,\ \mathsf{sn},\ \mathsf{sk}_{\mathcal{U}_i},\ \omega_\mathsf{u},\ P)$.

Fig. 8. E-Cash based on signing OTPs (1/2) ([19]We take the approach similar to group signatures in [42]. This is needed to identify the user in the real world when disputes related to double-spending occur. [20]We define $\mathsf{EC.Withdraw}$ such that $\mathcal{U}_i$ can specify v, but in practice, v may be a constant or chosen from a set of predefined e-coin denominations to reduce linkability.)

- $\mathsf{EC.Spend}(\mathcal{M}_j(\mathsf{pk}_\mathcal{B}, \sigma_{\mathsf{co}}, v, \mathsf{sn}), \mathcal{U}_i(\mathsf{pk}_\mathcal{B}, \mathsf{co}))$ is the following protocol between a merchant $\mathcal{M}_j$ who has a signing key pair $(\mathsf{sk}_{\mathcal{M}_j}, \mathsf{pk}_{\mathcal{M}_j})$ and $\mathcal{U}_i$ where $\mathcal{U}_i$ spends an e-coin co corresponding to v dollars.
  1. $\mathcal{M}_j$ sends $\mathsf{pk}_{\mathcal{M}_j}$, info_j to $\mathcal{U}_i$ where info_j is a random bit string.
  2. $\mathcal{U}_i$ computes $c_{\mathsf{ds}} \leftarrow H(\mathsf{pk}_{\mathcal{M}_j} \parallel \mathsf{info}_j)$ called *double-spending challenge* where H is a hash function (modeled as an RO), and the following commitments $\mathsf{Com}_{\mathsf{co}} \leftarrow e(\sigma_2, \widetilde{g})/e(\sigma_1, \widetilde{X} \cdot \widetilde{g}_{\mathsf{v}}^{v} \cdot \widetilde{g}_{\mathsf{s}}^{\mathsf{sn}})$ (for proof of knowledge of a signature) $= e(\sigma_1, \widetilde{g})^t \cdot e(\sigma_1, \widetilde{g}_{\mathsf{u}})^{\mathsf{sk}_{\mathcal{U}_i}} \cdot e(\sigma_1, \widetilde{f}_{\mathsf{u}})^{\omega_{\mathsf{u}}} \cdot e(\sigma_1, \widetilde{g}_{1,\mathrm{otp}})^{x_{1,\mathrm{otp}}} \cdot e(\sigma_1, \widetilde{g}_{2,\mathrm{otp}})^{x_{2,\mathrm{otp}}}$, $\mathsf{Com}_{\mathsf{ds}} \leftarrow g_{\mathsf{u}'}^{\mathsf{sk}_{\mathcal{U}_i}} \cdot (g_{\mathsf{u}'}^{\omega_{\mathsf{u}}})^{c_{\mathsf{ds}}} = g_{\mathsf{u}'}^{\mathsf{sk}_{\mathcal{U}_i}} \cdot (g_{\mathsf{u}'}^{c_{\mathsf{ds}}})^{\omega_{\mathsf{u}}}$ (called *double-spending tag*) and generates the following signature $\sigma(\sigma_{\mathsf{co}}, v, \mathsf{sn}, \mathsf{Com}_{\mathsf{ds}}, \mathsf{pk}_{\mathcal{M}_j}, \mathsf{info}_j)$ on $(\sigma_{\mathsf{co}}, v, \mathsf{sn}, \mathsf{Com}_{\mathsf{ds}}, \mathsf{pk}_{\mathcal{M}_j}, \mathsf{info}_j)$ (Sect. 2) by using the OTP P as well, and sends $(\sigma_{\mathsf{co}}, v, \mathsf{sn}, \sigma(\sigma_{\mathsf{co}}, v, \mathsf{sn}, \mathsf{Com}_{\mathsf{ds}}, \mathsf{pk}_{\mathcal{M}_j}, \mathsf{info}_j))$ to $\mathcal{M}_j$:
     $\sigma(\sigma_{\mathsf{co}}, v, \mathsf{sn}, \mathsf{Com}_{\mathsf{ds}}, \mathsf{pk}_{\mathcal{M}_j}, \mathsf{info}_j) = \mathsf{SPK}\{(t, \mathsf{sk}_{\mathcal{U}_i}, \omega_{\mathsf{u}}, x_{1,\mathrm{otp}}, x_{2,\mathrm{otp}}) :$
     $\mathsf{Com}_{\mathsf{co}} = e(\sigma_1, \widetilde{g})^t e(\sigma_1, \widetilde{g}_{\mathsf{u}})^{\mathsf{sk}_{\mathcal{U}_i}} e(\sigma_1, \widetilde{f}_{\mathsf{u}})^{\omega_{\mathsf{u}}} e(\sigma_1, \widetilde{g}_{1,\mathrm{otp}})^{x_{1,\mathrm{otp}}} e(\sigma_1, \widetilde{g}_{2,\mathrm{otp}})^{x_{2,\mathrm{otp}}}$
     $\wedge\, \mathsf{Com}_{\mathsf{ds}} = g_{\mathsf{u}'}^{\mathsf{sk}_{\mathcal{U}_i}} \cdot (g_{\mathsf{u}'}^{c_{\mathsf{ds}}})^{\omega_{\mathsf{u}}}\}(\sigma_{\mathsf{co}}, v, \mathsf{sn}, \mathsf{Com}_{\mathsf{ds}}, \mathsf{pk}_{\mathcal{M}_j}, \mathsf{info}_j)$. [22]
  3. $\mathcal{M}_j$ accepts the e-coin if $\sigma(\sigma_{\mathsf{co}}, v, \mathsf{sn}, \mathsf{Com}_{\mathsf{ds}}, \mathsf{pk}_{\mathcal{M}_j}, \mathsf{info}_j)$ is a valid signature, and stores the following tuple which will be deposited later
     $\mathsf{dpst} = \langle \sigma_{\mathsf{co}}, v, \mathsf{sn}, \mathsf{Com}_{\mathsf{ds}}, \mathsf{pk}_{\mathcal{M}_j}, \mathsf{info}_j, \sigma(\sigma_{\mathsf{co}}, v, \mathsf{sn}, \mathsf{Com}_{\mathsf{ds}}, \mathsf{pk}_{\mathcal{M}_j}, \mathsf{info}_j)\rangle$
     where sn is the serial number of this e-coin.
- $\mathsf{EC.Deposit}(\mathsf{dpst})$: $\mathcal{B}$ does the following after receiving from $\mathcal{M}_j$, $\mathsf{dpst} = \langle \sigma_{\mathsf{co}}, v, \mathsf{sn}, \mathsf{Com}_{\mathsf{ds}}, \mathsf{pk}_{\mathcal{M}_j}, \mathsf{info}_j, \sigma(\sigma_{\mathsf{co}}, v, \mathsf{sn}, \mathsf{Com}_{\mathsf{ds}}, \mathsf{pk}_{\mathcal{M}_j}, \mathsf{info}_j)\rangle$.
  1. If $\sigma(\sigma_{\mathsf{co}}, v, \mathsf{sn}, \mathsf{Com}_{\mathsf{ds}}, \mathsf{pk}_{\mathcal{M}_j}, \mathsf{info}_j)$ in dpst is invalid, $\mathcal{B}$ rejects the deposit.
  2. If the verification is successful and the serial number sn is fresh in the deposit DB, $\mathcal{B}$ requires $\mathcal{M}_j$ to send a signature $\sigma_{\mathcal{M}_j}(\mathsf{dpst})$ on dpst under $\mathsf{pk}_{\mathcal{M}_j}$. If $\sigma_{\mathcal{M}_j}(\mathsf{dpst})$ is invalid, $\mathcal{B}$ rejects the deposit, and otherwise $\mathcal{B}$ stores $(\mathsf{dpst}, \sigma_{\mathcal{M}_j}(\mathsf{dpst}))$ in the deposit DB, and credits v dollars to $\mathcal{M}_j$'s account.
  3. If a tuple exists in the deposit DB which has the same sn, $\mathsf{pk}_{\mathcal{M}_j}$, info_j as dpst, $\mathcal{B}$ rejects this invalid deposit (i.e., $\mathcal{M}_j$ is cheating).
  4. If $\mathsf{dpst}' = \langle \sigma'_{\mathsf{co}}, v', \mathsf{sn}, \mathsf{Com}'_{\mathsf{ds}}, \mathsf{pk}_{\mathcal{M}'_j}, \mathsf{info}'_j, \sigma(\sigma'_{\mathsf{co}}, v', \mathsf{sn}, \mathsf{Com}'_{\mathsf{ds}}, \mathsf{pk}_{\mathcal{M}'_j}, \mathsf{info}'_j)\rangle$ exists in the deposit DB which has the same sn as dpst, but different $\mathsf{pk}_{\mathcal{M}'_j}$ or info'_j [23], then $\mathcal{B}$ can have the proof $\Pi_{\mathsf{ds}} = (\mathsf{dpst}, \mathsf{dpst}')$ which can be used to identify the double-spender's public key in EC.Identify.
- $\mathsf{EC.Identify}(\mathsf{params}, \mathsf{pk}_\mathcal{B}, \Pi_{\mathsf{ds}})$: $\mathcal{B}$ identifies a double-spender as follows:
  1. If dpst and dpst′ in Π_{ds} have the same serial number, $\mathcal{B}$ obtains the double-spending tags $(\mathsf{Com}_{\mathsf{ds}}, c_{\mathsf{ds}})$, $(\mathsf{Com}'_{\mathsf{ds}}, c'_{\mathsf{ds}})$ from Π_{ds}.
  2. The double-spender's public key $\mathsf{pk}'_{\mathsf{ds}}$ can be computed as
     $\mathsf{pk}'_{\mathsf{ds}} = (\mathsf{Com}_{\mathsf{ds}}^{c'_{\mathsf{ds}}} / \mathsf{Com}'^{\,c_{\mathsf{ds}}}_{\mathsf{ds}})^{1/(c'_{\mathsf{ds}} - c_{\mathsf{ds}})}$.
- $\mathsf{EC.VrfyGuilt}(\mathsf{params}, \mathsf{pk}_\mathcal{B}, \mathsf{sn}, \mathsf{pk}'_{\mathsf{ds}}, \Pi_{\mathsf{ds}})$: anyone can publicly verify the proof Π_{ds} that the user with $\mathsf{pk}'_{\mathsf{ds}}$ is guilty of double-spending the e-coin whose serial number is sn. The verification can be done by $\mathsf{EC.Identify}(\mathsf{params}, \mathsf{pk}_\mathcal{B}, \Pi_{\mathsf{ds}}) \stackrel{?}{=} \mathsf{pk}'_{\mathsf{ds}}$.

Fig. 9. E-Cash based on signing OTPs (2/2) ([22]This includes proofs of knowledge of equality of discrete logs $(\mathsf{sk}_{\mathcal{U}_i}, \omega_{\mathsf{u}})$ [27], and its full description is given in Fig. 10. [23]If this occurs, it means the adversary ran an OTP more than once by breaking the security of OTPs. In this case, it is possible to distribute a list of blocked sn.)

Hence, e.g., if $\mathcal{U}_i$ has e-coins $\sigma_{\mathsf{co}_1}, \sigma_{\mathsf{co}_2}$ corresponding to v_1, v_2 dollars respectively, and signs σ_{co_1} by σ_{co_2}, then we can think that the value v_2 in σ_{co_2} is transferred to σ_{co_1}, and that signing a message with σ_{co_1} yields $v_1 + v_2$ dollars. This way of thinking can reduce the number of signatures that need to be generated during the Spend protocol, and we give the overview of this method (which we call *batch spending*) as follows:

- Suppose $\mathcal{U}_i$ has e-coins, e.g., $\sigma_{\mathsf{co}_1}, \sigma_{\mathsf{co}_2}, \sigma_{\mathsf{co}_3}$ corresponding to v_1, v_2, v_3 dollars respectively, and wants to spend $v_1 + v_2 + v_3$ dollars for $\mathcal{M}_j$.
- Then $\mathcal{U}_i$ signs σ_{co_1} with $\sigma_{\mathsf{co}_2}, \sigma_{\mathsf{co}_3}$ in advance, obtaining 2 signatures on σ_{co_1}.
- In the Spend protocol with $\mathcal{M}_j$, $\mathcal{U}_i$ signs the message from $\mathcal{M}_j$ with σ_{co_1}, and sends 3 signatures to $\mathcal{M}_j$.
- $\mathcal{M}_j$ verifies the 2 signatures on σ_{co_1}, and another signature generated by σ_{co_1}[12]. If all the verifications are successful and the amount of e-coins suffices, $\mathcal{M}_j$ accepts the e-coins.
- Similarly $\mathcal{B}$ also verifies all the signatures in the Deposit protocol, and checks freshness of all the serial numbers.

As we can see, $\mathcal{U}_i$ has only to generate 1 signature during the Spend protocol although actually it spends 3 e-coins. To sign σ_{co_1} with σ_{co}, as in Step 2 of EC.Spend (Fig. 9), a double-spending challenge $c_{\mathsf{ds}} \in \mathbb{Z}_p$ is necessary, for which $H(\sigma_{\mathsf{co}_1})$ can be used here. To make the difference clear between the signature on the double-spending tag (i.e., $\sigma(\sigma_{\mathsf{co}}, v, \mathsf{sn}, \mathsf{Com}_{\mathsf{ds}}, \mathsf{pk}_{\mathcal{M}_j}, \mathsf{info}_j)$ in Fig. 9) and signature on the e-coin, we modify the hash calculation of $(*)$ (Fig. 10) by adding a simple tag as

$$c = H(R_1 \parallel R_2 \parallel \sigma_{\mathsf{co}} \parallel v \parallel \mathsf{sn} \parallel \mathsf{Com}_{\mathsf{ds}} \parallel 0 \parallel \mathsf{pk}_{\mathcal{M}_j} \parallel \mathsf{info}_j)$$
$$\text{(case of signature on } (\sigma_{\mathsf{co}}, v, \mathsf{sn}, \mathsf{Com}_{\mathsf{ds}}, \mathsf{pk}_{\mathcal{M}_j}, \mathsf{info}_j)),$$
$$c = H(R_1 \parallel R_2 \parallel \sigma_{\mathsf{co}} \parallel v \parallel \mathsf{sn} \parallel \mathsf{Com}_{\mathsf{ds}} \parallel 1 \parallel \sigma_{\mathsf{co}_1})$$
$$\text{(case with additional e-coin } \sigma_{\mathsf{co}_1}).$$

Thus if $\mathcal{B}$ or $\mathcal{M}_j$ receives a signature with $H(R_1 \parallel R_2 \parallel \sigma_{\mathsf{co}} \parallel v \parallel \mathsf{sn} \parallel \mathsf{Com}_{\mathsf{ds}} \parallel 1 \parallel \sigma_{\mathsf{co}_1})$, $\mathcal{B}$ or $\mathcal{M}_j$ also requires another signature by σ_{co_1} to accept the e-coins.

Transferring E-Coin. By further extending batch spending, $\mathcal{U}_i$ can transfer an e-coin to another, but with somewhat less anonymity as mentioned later. In batch spending, $\mathcal{U}_i$ signs its own e-coins, whereas, in transferring $\mathcal{U}_i$'s e-coin σ_{co_i} to another e-coin σ_{co_j} of $\mathcal{U}_j$, $\mathcal{U}_i$ signs σ_{co_j} with σ_{co_i}, and the value of σ_{co_i} is transferred to σ_{co_j}. Here the value of σ_{co_j} can be zero. To receive the transfer of many e-coins, we assume that $\mathcal{U}_j$ can obtain e-coins whose values are zero (i.e., they function as placeholders of the transferred e-coins) from $\mathcal{B}$ for free in advance. In this case, however, we have incomplete anonymity in the following sense: Suppose $\mathcal{U}_i$ transferred σ_{co_i} to σ_{co_j}, and the several transfers continued, and the e-coin originating from σ_{co_i} returned to $\mathcal{U}_i$, then $\mathcal{U}_i$ can recognize that

[12] More exactly $\mathcal{M}_j$ will also need to check that the serial numbers of $\sigma_{\mathsf{co}_1}, \sigma_{\mathsf{co}_2}, \sigma_{\mathsf{co}_3}$ are all different.

$\mathcal{U}_i$ used to hold the e-coin. To obtain complete anonymity, the technique from [4] may be applicable, but its efficient instantiation will be non-trivial.

– In Fig. 9, $\mathcal{U}_i$ generates the following SPK in spending v dollars with serial number sn by running sOTP P,
$\sigma(\sigma_{\mathsf{co}}, v, \mathsf{sn}, \mathsf{Com}_{\mathsf{ds}}, \mathsf{pk}_{\mathcal{M}_j}, \mathsf{info}_j) = \mathsf{SPK}\{(t, \mathsf{sk}_{\mathcal{U}_i}, \omega_{\mathsf{u}}, x_{1,\mathrm{otp}}, x_{2,\mathrm{otp}}) :$

$$\mathsf{Com}_{\mathsf{co}} = e(\sigma_1, \widetilde{g})^t e(\sigma_1, \widetilde{g}_{\mathsf{u}})^{\mathsf{sk}_{\mathcal{U}_i}} e(\sigma_1, \widetilde{f}_{\mathsf{u}})^{\omega_{\mathsf{u}}} e(\sigma_1, \widetilde{g}_{1,\mathrm{otp}})^{x_{1,\mathrm{otp}}} e(\sigma_1, \widetilde{g}_{2,\mathrm{otp}})^{x_{2,\mathrm{otp}}}$$
$$\wedge\ \mathsf{Com}_{\mathsf{ds}} = g_{\mathsf{u}'}^{\mathsf{sk}_{\mathcal{U}_i}} \cdot (g_{\mathsf{u}'}^{c_{\mathsf{ds}}})^{\omega_{\mathsf{u}}}\}(\sigma_{\mathsf{co}}, v, \mathsf{sn}, \mathsf{Com}_{\mathsf{ds}}, \mathsf{pk}_{\mathcal{M}_j}, \mathsf{info}_j),$$

where $c_{\mathsf{ds}} = H(\mathsf{pk}_{\mathcal{M}_j} \parallel \mathsf{info}_j)$,

$$P = \langle \widetilde{g}_{1,\mathrm{otp}}, \widetilde{g}_{2,\mathrm{otp}}, \widetilde{g}_{1,\mathrm{otp}}^{x_{1,\mathrm{otp}}} \cdot \widetilde{g}_{2,\mathrm{otp}}^{x_{2,\mathrm{otp}}}, p, \widetilde{g}_{1,\mathrm{otp}}^{r_{1,\mathrm{otp}}} \cdot \widetilde{g}_{2,\mathrm{otp}}^{r_{2,\mathrm{otp}}}, \{[r_{i,\mathrm{otp}} - \bar{c} \cdot x_{i,\mathrm{otp}} \bmod p]_{\mathrm{otp}}\}_{i=1}^{2}\rangle.$$

1. $\mathcal{U}_i$ chooses random $\alpha_1, \alpha_2, \beta, \beta_1, \beta_2, \beta_3 \in \mathbb{Z}_p$ and computes
$R \leftarrow \widetilde{g}_{1,\mathrm{otp}}^{r_{1,\mathrm{otp}}} \cdot \widetilde{g}_{2,\mathrm{otp}}^{r_{2,\mathrm{otp}}} \cdot \widetilde{g}_{1,\mathrm{otp}}^{\alpha_1} \cdot \widetilde{g}_{2,\mathrm{otp}}^{\alpha_2} \cdot (\widetilde{g}_{1,\mathrm{otp}}^{x_{1,\mathrm{otp}}} \cdot \widetilde{g}_{2,\mathrm{otp}}^{x_{2,\mathrm{otp}}})^{\beta}$
$R_1 \leftarrow e(\sigma_1, \widetilde{g})^{\beta_1} \cdot e(\sigma_1, \widetilde{g}_{\mathsf{u}})^{\beta_2} \cdot e(\sigma_1, \widetilde{f}_{\mathsf{u}})^{\beta_3} \cdot e(\sigma_1, R)\ (= e(\sigma_1, \widetilde{g}^{\beta_1} \cdot \widetilde{g}_{\mathsf{u}}^{\beta_2} \cdot \widetilde{f}_{\mathsf{u}}^{\beta_3} \cdot R))$
$R_2 \leftarrow g_{\mathsf{u}'}^{\beta_2} \cdot (g_{\mathsf{u}'}^{c_{\mathsf{ds}}})^{\beta_3}$ (here $g_{\mathsf{u}'}$ and $g_{\mathsf{u}'}^{c_{\mathsf{ds}}}$ are bases of the commitment)
$c \leftarrow H(R_1 \parallel R_2 \parallel \sigma_{\mathsf{co}} \parallel v \parallel \mathsf{sn} \parallel \mathsf{Com}_{\mathsf{ds}} \parallel \mathsf{pk}_{\mathcal{M}_j} \parallel \mathsf{info}_j)$ $(*)$
$z_1 \leftarrow \beta_1 - c \cdot t \bmod p,\ z_2 \leftarrow \beta_2 - c \cdot \mathsf{sk}_{\mathcal{U}_i} \bmod p,\ z_3 \leftarrow \beta_3 - c \cdot \omega_{\mathsf{u}} \bmod p$
$z_4 \leftarrow r_{1,\mathrm{otp}} - (c - \beta) \cdot x_{1,\mathrm{otp}} + \alpha_1 \bmod p$ (run with sOTP P)
$z_5 \leftarrow r_{2,\mathrm{otp}} - (c - \beta) \cdot x_{2,\mathrm{otp}} + \alpha_2 \bmod p$ (run with sOTP P)
where $\{r_{i,\mathrm{otp}} - (c - \beta) \cdot x_{i,\mathrm{otp}}\}_{i=1}^{2}$ can be obtained from P by inputting $c - \beta$ (this is the same randomization as OS.BSign of Algorithm 1).
2. The signature $\sigma(\sigma_{\mathsf{co}}, v, \mathsf{sn}, \mathsf{Com}_{\mathsf{ds}}, \mathsf{pk}_{\mathcal{M}_j}, \mathsf{info}_j)$ consists of $(c, z_1, z_2, z_3, z_4, z_5)$ and can be verified by
$c \stackrel{?}{=} H(e(\sigma_1, \widetilde{g})^{z_1} \cdot e(\sigma_1, \widetilde{g}_{\mathsf{u}})^{z_2} \cdot e(\sigma_1, \widetilde{f}_{\mathsf{u}})^{z_3} \cdot e(\sigma_1, \widetilde{g}_{1,\mathrm{otp}})^{z_4} \cdot e(\sigma_1, \widetilde{g}_{2,\mathrm{otp}})^{z_5} \cdot \mathsf{Com}_{\mathsf{co}}^{c}$
$\parallel g_{\mathsf{u}'}^{z_2} \cdot (g_{\mathsf{u}'}^{c_{\mathsf{ds}}})^{z_3} \cdot \mathsf{Com}_{\mathsf{ds}}^{c} \parallel \sigma_{\mathsf{co}} \parallel v \parallel \mathsf{sn} \parallel \mathsf{Com}_{\mathsf{ds}} \parallel \mathsf{pk}_{\mathcal{M}_j} \parallel \mathsf{info}_j).$

Fig. 10. Signature based on Proof of Knowledge (SPK) in Our E-Cash

Acknowledgments. The author thanks Jacob Schuldt for his valuable comments on the early draft and anonymous reviewers of Financial Cryptography'20 and ProvSec'20 for their helpful comments. This work was supported in part by JSPS KAKENHI Grant Number 20K11807.

References

1. Acar, T., Chow, S.S.M., Nguyen, L.: Accumulators and U-Prove revocation. In: Sadeghi, A.-R. (ed.) FC 2013. LNCS, vol. 7859, pp. 189–196. Springer, Heidelberg (2013). https://doi.org/10.1007/978-3-642-39884-1_15
2. Amos, R., Georgiou, M., Kiayias, A., Zhandry, M.: One-shot signatures and applications to hybrid quantum/classical authentication. In: STOC, pp. 255–268 (2020)

3. Au, M.H., Susilo, W., Mu, Y.: Constant-size dynamic k-TAA. In: De Prisco, R., Yung, M. (eds.) SCN 2006. LNCS, vol. 4116, pp. 111–125. Springer, Heidelberg (2006). https://doi.org/10.1007/11832072_8
4. Baldimtsi, F., Chase, M., Fuchsbauer, G., Kohlweiss, M.: Anonymous transferable e-cash. In: Katz, J. (ed.) PKC 2015. LNCS, vol. 9020, pp. 101–124. Springer, Heidelberg (2015). https://doi.org/10.1007/978-3-662-46447-2_5
5. Baldimtsi, F., Lysyanskaya, A.: Anonymous credentials light. In: CCS, pp. 1087–1098. ACM (2013)
6. Bellare, M., Shi, H., Zhang, C.: Foundations of group signatures: the case of dynamic groups. In: Menezes, A. (ed.) CT-RSA 2005. LNCS, vol. 3376, pp. 136–153. Springer, Heidelberg (2005). https://doi.org/10.1007/978-3-540-30574-3_11
7. Benhamouda, F., Lepoint, T., Orrù, M., Raykova, M.: On the (in) security of ROS. Cryptology ePrint Archive, Report 2020/945 (2020)
8. Bichsel, P., Camenisch, J., Groß, T., Shoup, V.: Anonymous credentials on a standard Java card. In: CCS, pp. 600–610. ACM (2009)
9. Blömer, J., Bobolz, J.: Delegatable attribute-based anonymous credentials from dynamically malleable signatures. In: Preneel, B., Vercauteren, F. (eds.) ACNS 2018. LNCS, vol. 10892, pp. 221–239. Springer, Cham (2018). https://doi.org/10.1007/978-3-319-93387-0_12
10. Borisov, N., Brewer, E.A.: Active certificates: a framework for delegation. In: NDSS (2002)
11. Bourse, F., Pointcheval, D., Sanders, O.: Divisible e-cash from constrained pseudorandom functions. In: Galbraith, S.D., Moriai, S. (eds.) ASIACRYPT 2019. LNCS, vol. 11921, pp. 679–708. Springer, Cham (2019). https://doi.org/10.1007/978-3-030-34578-5_24
12. Brands, S.: Untraceable off-line cash in wallet with observers. In: Stinson, D.R. (ed.) CRYPTO 1993. LNCS, vol. 773, pp. 302–318. Springer, Heidelberg (1994). https://doi.org/10.1007/3-540-48329-2_26
13. Brands, S.: Rethinking public key infrastructures and digital certificates: building in privacy. MIT Press (2000)
14. Camenisch, J., Hohenberger, S., Kohlweiss, M., Lysyanskaya, A., Meyerovich, M.: How to win the clone wars: efficient periodic n-times anonymous authentication. In: CCS, pp. 201–210. ACM (2006)
15. Camenisch, J., Hohenberger, S., Lysyanskaya, A.: Compact e-cash. In: Cramer, R. (ed.) EUROCRYPT 2005. LNCS, vol. 3494, pp. 302–321. Springer, Heidelberg (2005). https://doi.org/10.1007/11426639_18
16. Camenisch, J., Kohlweiss, M., Soriente, C.: Solving revocation with efficient update of anonymous credentials. In: Garay, J.A., De Prisco, R. (eds.) SCN 2010. LNCS, vol. 6280, pp. 454–471. Springer, Heidelberg (2010). https://doi.org/10.1007/978-3-642-15317-4_28
17. Camenisch, J., Lehmann, A., Neven, G., Samelin, K.: Virtual smart cards: how to sign with a password and a server. In: Zikas, V., De Prisco, R. (eds.) SCN 2016. LNCS, vol. 9841, pp. 353–371. Springer, Cham (2016). https://doi.org/10.1007/978-3-319-44618-9_19
18. Camenisch, J., Stadler, M.: Efficient group signature schemes for large groups. In: CRYPTO, pp 410–424. Springer (1997)
19. R. Canetti. Universally composable security: a new paradigm for cryptographic protocols. Cryptology ePrint Archive, Report 2000/067 (2000)
20. Canetti, R.: Universally composable signature, certification, and authentication. In: CSFW, pp. 219–233. IEEE (2004)

21. Chase, M., Lysyanskaya, A.: On signatures of knowledge. In: Dwork, C. (ed.) CRYPTO 2006. LNCS, vol. 4117, pp. 78–96. Springer, Heidelberg (2006). https://doi.org/10.1007/11818175_5
22. Chaum, D.: Blind signatures for untraceable payments. In: Chaum, D., Rivest, R.L., Sherman, A.T. (eds.) Advances in Cryptology, pp. 199–203. Springer, Boston, MA (1983). https://doi.org/10.1007/978-1-4757-0602-4_18
23. Chaum, D.: Security without identification: transaction systems to make big brother obsolete. Commun. ACM **28**(10), 1030–1044 (1985)
24. Chaum, D.: Online cash checks. In: Quisquater, J.-J., Vandewalle, J. (eds.) EUROCRYPT 1989. LNCS, vol. 434, pp. 288–293. Springer, Heidelberg (1990). https://doi.org/10.1007/3-540-46885-4_30
25. Chaum, D.: Achieving electronic privacy. Sci. Am. **267**(2), 96–101 (1992)
26. Chaum, D., Fiat, A., Naor, M.: Untraceable electronic cash. In: Goldwasser, S. (ed.) CRYPTO 1988. LNCS, vol. 403, pp. 319–327. Springer, New York (1990). https://doi.org/10.1007/0-387-34799-2_25
27. Chaum, D., Pedersen, T.P.: Wallet databases with observers. In: Brickell, E.F. (ed.) CRYPTO 1992. LNCS, vol. 740, pp. 89–105. Springer, Heidelberg (1993). https://doi.org/10.1007/3-540-48071-4_7
28. Damgård, I., Pastro, V., Smart, N., Zakarias, S.: Multiparty computation from somewhat homomorphic encryption. In: Safavi-Naini, R., Canetti, R. (eds.) CRYPTO 2012. LNCS, vol. 7417, pp. 643–662. Springer, Heidelberg (2012). https://doi.org/10.1007/978-3-642-32009-5_38
29. Everspaugh, A., Chaterjee, R., Scott, S., Juels, A., Ristenpart, T.: The Pythia PRF service. In: USENIX Security Symposium, pp. 547–562 (2015)
30. Fiat, A., Shamir, A.: How to prove yourself: practical solutions to identification and signature problems. In: Odlyzko, A.M. (ed.) CRYPTO 1986. LNCS, vol. 263, pp. 186–194. Springer, Heidelberg (1987). https://doi.org/10.1007/3-540-47721-7_12
31. Fuchsbauer, G.: Commuting signatures and verifiable encryption. In: Paterson, K.G. (ed.) EUROCRYPT 2011. LNCS, vol. 6632, pp. 224–245. Springer, Heidelberg (2011). https://doi.org/10.1007/978-3-642-20465-4_14
32. Galbraith, S.D., Paterson, K.G., Smart, N.P.: Pairings for cryptographers. Dis Appl. Math. **156**(16), 3113–3121 (2008)
33. Goldwasser, S., Kalai, Y.T., Rothblum, G.N.: One-time programs. In: Wagner, D. (ed.) CRYPTO 2008. LNCS, vol. 5157, pp. 39–56. Springer, Heidelberg (2008). https://doi.org/10.1007/978-3-540-85174-5_3
34. Groth, J.: Fully anonymous group signatures without random oracles. In: Kurosawa, K. (ed.) ASIACRYPT 2007. LNCS, vol. 4833, pp. 164–180. Springer, Heidelberg (2007). https://doi.org/10.1007/978-3-540-76900-2_10
35. Kaptchuk, G., Miers, I., Green, M.: Giving state to the stateless: augmenting trustworthy computation with ledgers. In: NDSS (2019)
36. Kurnikov, A., Paverd, A., Mannan, M., Asokan, N.: Keys in the clouds: auditable multi-device access to cryptographic credentials. In: ARES, pp. 40:1–40:10. ACM (2018)
37. Libert, B., Ling, S., Nguyen, K., Wang, H.: Zero-knowledge arguments for lattice-based PRFs and applications to e-cash. In: Takagi, T., Peyrin, T. (eds.) ASIACRYPT 2017. LNCS, vol. 10626, pp. 304–335. Springer, Cham (2017). https://doi.org/10.1007/978-3-319-70700-6_11
38. MacKenzie, P., Reiter, M.K.: Delegation of cryptographic servers for capture-resilient devices. Distrib. Comput. **16**(4), 307–327 (2003)

39. Marcedone, A., Pass, R., Shelat, A.: Minimizing trust in hardware wallets with two factor signatures. In: Goldberg, I., Moore, T. (eds.) FC 2019. LNCS, vol. 11598, pp. 407–425. Springer, Cham (2019). https://doi.org/10.1007/978-3-030-32101-7_25
40. Matetic, S., Schneider, M., Miller, A., Juels, A., Capkun, S.: DelegaTEE: Brokered delegation using trusted execution environments. In: USENIX Security Symposium, pp. 1387–1403 (2018)
41. Okamoto, T.: Provably secure and practical identification schemes and corresponding signature schemes. In: Brickell, E.F. (ed.) CRYPTO 1992. LNCS, vol. 740, pp. 31–53. Springer, Heidelberg (1993). https://doi.org/10.1007/3-540-48071-4_3
42. Pointcheval, D., Sanders, O.: Short randomizable signatures. In: Sako, K. (ed.) CT-RSA 2016. LNCS, vol. 9610, pp. 111–126. Springer, Cham (2016). https://doi.org/10.1007/978-3-319-29485-8_7
43. Teranishi, I., Sako, K.: k-Times anonymous authentication with a constant proving cost. In: Yung, M., Dodis, Y., Kiayias, A., Malkin, T. (eds.) PKC 2006. LNCS, vol. 3958, pp. 525–542. Springer, Heidelberg (2006). https://doi.org/10.1007/11745853_34

Watermarkable Signature with Computational Function Preserving

Kyohei Sudo[1(✉)], Masayuki Tezuka[1], Keisuke Hara[1,2], Yusuke Yoshida[1], and Keisuke Tanaka[1]

[1] Tokyo Institute of Technology, Tokyo, Japan
{sudo.k.ac,tezuka.m.ac,hara.k.am,yoshida.y.aw}@m.titech.ac.jp, keisuke@c.titech.ac.jp

[2] National Institute of Advanced Industrial Science and Technology (AIST), Tokyo, Japan

Abstract. Software watermarking enables one to embed some information called "mark" into a program while preserving its functionality, and to read it from the program. As a definition of function preserving, Cohen et al. (STOC 2016) proposed statistical function preserving which requires that the input/output behavior of the marked circuit is identical almost everywhere to that of the original unmarked circuit. They showed how to construct watermarkable cryptographic primitives with statistical function preserving, including pseudorandom functions (PRFs) and public-key encryption from indistinguishability obfuscation. Recently, Goyal et al. (CRYPTO 2019) introduced more relaxed definition of function preserving for watermarkable signature. Watermarkable signature embeds a mark into a signing circuit of digital signature. The relaxed function preserving only requires that the marked signing circuit outputs valid signatures. They provide watermarkable signature with the relaxed function preserving only based on (standard) digital signature.

In this work, we introduce an intermediate notion of function preserving for watermarkable signature, which is called *computational function preserving*. Then, we examine the relationship among our computational function preserving, relaxed function preserving by Goyal et al., and statistical function preserving by Cohen et al. Furthermore, we propose a generic construction of watermarkable signature scheme satisfying computational function preserving based on public key encryption and (standard) digital signature.

1 Introduction

1.1 Backgrounds

Digital Watermarking. Digital watermarking is a technology to embed some special information called a mark into digital objects such as images, movies, music files, or programs. Digital watermarking is required to satisfy two basic requirements. One is function preserving that guarantees a marked object should not be significantly different from the original object. The other is unremovability

K. Nguyen et al. (Eds.): ProvSec 2020, LNCS 12505, pp. 124–144, 2020.
https://doi.org/10.1007/978-3-030-62576-4_7

that guarantees it should be difficult for malicious entities to remove the mark from a marked object without damaging the object itself.

A critical application of digital watermarking is copyright protection. Let us consider a situation where we distribute a digital object to unspecified users. In order to prevent the users from distributing the digital object illegally, we can embed user's name in the digital object by using digital watermarking. Due to the function preserving of digital watermarking, it is ensured that the marked object has almost same functionality with the original unmarked object. If we find a digital object copied by some user, we can extract the embedded mark from the marked object to identify the user.

In cryptography, watermarking schemes were proposed for pseudorandom functions [4,6,10,11,16–18], encryption schemes [6,8,18], and digital signature schemes [6,8,18]. In particular, these studies treat an algorithm as a circuit and aim to embed a mark in the function evaluation circuit for watermarkable pseudorandom functions, in the decryption circuit for watermarkable encryption schemes, and in the signing circuit for watermarkable signature schemes.

In particular, a watermarkable signature consists of setup, mark, and extraction algorithm, in addition to the usual key-generation, signing, and verification algorithm of digital signature. The mark algorithm embeds a mark to the signing circuit determined by a signing key. The extraction algorithm extracts the mark from the marked circuit.

Variation of Function Preserving. The first formal definition for watermarking was given by Barak, Goldreich, Impagliazzo, Rudich, Sahai, Vadhan, and Yang [2,3]. They proposed a security notion called perfect function preserving which requires that the input/output behavior of the marked circuit is identical to that of the original unmarked circuit. They showed an impossibility result that assuming indistinguishability obfuscation (iO), a watermarking scheme which satisfies perfect function preserving cannot exist.

Cohen, Holmgren, Nishimaki, Vaikuntanathan, and Wichs[6,7,15] relaxed perfect function preserving and proposed statistical function preserving which requires that the input/output behavior of the marked circuit is identical almost everywhere to that of the original unmarked circuit. They constructed watermarkable pseudorandom functions with statistical function preserving by using indistinguishability obfuscation (iO). They mentioned the existence of a watermarkable encryption scheme and signature scheme with statistical function preserving under the existence of iO and injective one-way functions. These constructions were presented in [15] which are based on the public key encryption scheme and the signature scheme constructed from iO.

The recent work by Goyal, Kim, Manohar, Waters, and Wu [8] further relaxed the requirement of function preserving for watermarkable signature and encryption. For watermarkable signature, the function preserving by Goyal et al. only requires that a marked circuit still produces valid signatures. This requirement allows signatures output by the original signing circuit and by a marked signing circuit to be apparently different. For a watermarkable encryption scheme, the function preserving by Goyal et al. only requires that a marked circuit can decrypt ciphertexts. This requirement allows the output of decryption by a marked decryption circuit to differ from the output of decryption by the original decryption circuit on invalid ciphertexts. These relaxations for function preserving allow us to obtain various watermarkable public key primitives from more reasonable assumptions. Actually, they constructed a watermarkable signature scheme from digital signature and a watermarkable (attribute-based) encryption scheme from delegatable attribute-based encryption and mixed functional encryption.

Motivation. Watermarkable schemes are expected to make the marked objects as similar as possible to the original. From this perspective, function preserving by Goyal et al. seems to be too relaxed since this property allows that input/output behavior of the marked circuits and that of the original circuits to be distinguishable. Here, a natural question arises:

> *Is there a reasonable definition of function preserving between statistical function preserving and function preserving by Goyal et al. ?*

1.2 Our Contributions

Based on the above motivation, we firstly define *computational* function preserving, which requires the input/output behavior of the marked object is computationally indistinguishable to that of the original object.

Secondly, we study the relationship between our definition for watermarkable signature and that of Goyal et al. [8]. Moreover, we extend the definition of computational function preserving into general watermarkable primitive, and investigate the relations between our computational function preserving and statistical function preserving proposed by Cohen et al. [6].

Finally, we construct watermarkable signature satisfying computational function preserving based on public key encryption and (standard) digital signature.

Computational Function Preserving for Watermarkable Signature. As the most important difference from previous works, we introduce *computational function preserving* for watermarkable signature. Informally, computational function preserving requires that "the input/output behavior of marked and original circuits are computationally indistinguishable". See Sect. 2 for the details.

In order to see the usefulness of computational function preserving, let us consider the following typical application of watermarkable signature. When the original signer wishes to delegate his/her signing rights to others, the original signer puts the delegated signer's identity as a part of the mark embedded into the signing circuit, and gives the marked circuits to the delegated signers. When a marked signing circuit leaked illegally, the source of the leak can be identified from the extracted mark.

If the watermarkable signature only satisfies the function preserving by Goyal et al., even identities of the honest delegated signers may be revealed from signatures generated by the marked signing circuits. Actually, their watermarkable signature scheme allows anyone to see the mark from signatures. This seems undesirable for honest delegated signers. Computational function preserving guarantees delegated signer's privacy.

Note that it seems difficult to achieve computational function preserving with public extraction. Because, in watermarkable cryptographic primitives, the embedded mark is extracted from outputs of the marked circuit. If a watermarking scheme supports public extraction, anyone can see the mark from the marked circuit.

In Sect. 4, we see the relations on function preserving of watermarkable primitives. Firstly, we focus on watermarkable signature and examine the relations between our computational function preserving of watermarkable signature and the function preserving by Goyal et al. [8]. There, we see that our computational function preserving implies function preserving by Goyal et al.

Next, we investigate the relations on function preserving for general watermarkable primitives. Cohen et al. [6] gave a statistical function preserving for general watermarkable primitives. In order to see the relations, we abstract our computational function preserving for watermarkable signature to one supporting general watermarkable primitives. Then, we provide the relations between this computational function preserving and statistical function preserving of general watermarkable primitive by Cohen et al. As a result, we show that our computational function preserving is incomparable with the statistical function preserving by Cohen et al.

Redefining Watermarkable Signature. We replace the extraction algorithm with an opening algorithm. The extraction algorithm takes an extract key, a verification key and a marked circuit, and outputs a mark that is embedded in the circuit. The difference between these algorithms, an opening algorithm only takes as input the output of the marked circuit instead of circuit itself. Remember the application of watermarkable signature we mentioned above, the original signer puts the delegated signer's identity as a part of the mark embedded into the signing circuit. The opening algorithm do not require the leaked circuit itself. The source of the leak can be identified only from the output of the leaked circuit. Note that the extraction algorithm can be made from the opening algorithm. In Sect. 4 we see the relations among our definition, definition by Cohen et al. [6], and Goyal et al. [8] which we recall in Appendix B.

In previous works, unremovability is defined with the extraction algorithm. Due to the modification of the syntax, we also modify the definition of unremovability. In our definition, similar to the definition by Goyal et al., we consider collusion of parties. That is, an adversary is allowed to collect polynomial number of marked circuits. Additionally, we allow the adversary to get signatures generated by marked circuits that are not corrupted. It almost covers the security of unforgeability, which ensures that the watermarkable signature is unforgeable as a digital signature. Unlike the existing definitions of watermarkable signature, our definition does not explicitly require unforgeability. See discussions on unforgeability in Sect. 4 for the details.

Our Construction. We give an overview of our construction of watermarkable signature satisfying computational function preserving in Sect. 3. Our construction of watermarkable signature is based on the watermarkable signature scheme by Goyal et al. [8]. The construction by Goyal et al. is in the public extraction setting where anyone can extract a mark from a marked circuit. In contrast, our construction is in the secret extraction setting that requires an extract key is needed to extract a mark from a marked circuit.

Now, we briefly explain an overview of our construction. Let $\mathcal{M}$ be a message space and $\mathcal{T}$ a mark space for a watermarkable signature scheme, $\mathsf{PKE} = (\mathsf{PKE.Gen}, \mathsf{PKE.Enc}, \mathsf{PKE.Dec})$ a public key encryption scheme and $\mathsf{DS} = (\mathsf{DS.Gen}, \mathsf{DS.Sign}, \mathsf{DS.Verify})$ a digital signature scheme.

- As a setup, we generate $(\mathsf{ek}, \mathsf{dk})$ by running $\mathsf{PKE.Gen}$. ek is used to encrypt a mark and dk is needed to extract a mark. ek is published and dk is sent to a party who allowed to extract a mark from a marked circuit.
- The original signing key $\mathsf{sk_{WM}}$ and verification key $\mathsf{vk_{WM}}$ consist of $\mathsf{sk_{WM}} = (\mathsf{ek}, \mathsf{sk}_1, \mathsf{sk}_2, w = (\mathsf{vk}_2, c, \sigma_1))$ and $\mathsf{vk_{WM}} = \mathsf{vk}_1$. ek is generated by a setup procedure, $(\mathsf{vk}_1, \mathsf{sk}_1)$ and $(\mathsf{vk}_2, \mathsf{sk}_2)$ is generated by $\mathsf{DS.Gen}$. c is a ciphertext of a symbol $\perp$ which represents "unmarked". σ_1 is a signature computed by $\sigma_1 \leftarrow \mathsf{DS.Sign}(\mathsf{sk}_1, (\mathsf{vk}_2, c))$. We explain roles of elements of $\mathsf{sk_{WM}}$. sk_2 is used to sign a message. $w = (\mathsf{vk}_2, c, \sigma_1)$ is a certificate that links vk_2 and c. This implies that $\perp$ and vk_2 are linked. sk_1 is used to generate a marked circuit. More specifically, sk_1 is used to generate certificates.
- By using $\mathsf{sk_{WM}}$, a signature σ on a message $m \in \mathcal{M}$ is computed as $\sigma = (w, \sigma_2)$ where $\sigma_2 \leftarrow \mathsf{DS.Sign}(\mathsf{sk}_2, m)$.
- A circuit C_τ with an embedded mark $\tau \in \mathcal{T}$ is generated from $\mathsf{sk_{WM}}$ as follows. First, compute $(\mathsf{vk}'_2, \mathsf{sk}'_2)$ by running $\mathsf{DS.Gen}$ and a ciphertext $c' \leftarrow \mathsf{PKE.Enc}(\mathsf{ek}, \tau)$. Then, generate a new certificate $w' = (\mathsf{vk}'_2, c', \sigma'_1)$ where $\sigma'_1 \leftarrow \mathsf{DS.Sign}(\mathsf{sk}_1, (\mathsf{vk}'_2, c'))$. w' links τ and vk'_2. Finally, generate a marked circuit $C_\tau(\cdot) := (w' = (\mathsf{vk}'_2, c', \sigma'_1), \mathsf{DS.Sign}(\mathsf{sk}'_2, \cdot))$.
- A verification of a pair m and $\sigma = (\mathsf{vk}_2, c, \sigma_1, \sigma_2)$ can be done by checking $\mathsf{DS.Verify}(\mathsf{vk}_1, (\mathsf{vk}_2, c), \sigma_1) = 1$ and $\mathsf{DS.Verify}(\mathsf{vk}_2, m, \sigma_2) = 1$.
- Extraction of a mark from $\sigma = (\mathsf{vk}_2, c, \sigma_1, \sigma_2)$ can be done by compute a mark $\tau = \mathsf{PKE.Dec}(\mathsf{dk}, c)$.

Computational function preserving of our scheme is followed by the indistinguishability of PKE. We explain intuition why our construction satisfies unremovability. To simplify our explanation, we consider a non-collusion setting. That is, we consider the case where an adversary has only one marked circuit and tries to change or remove the embedded mark in the marked circuit without breaking its functionality. We assume that the adversary can get a valid signature on any message output by any marked circuit and the original signing circuit via oracle queries. To change or remove the embedded mark, the adversary changes a certificate w embedded in the marked circuit. We can consider two strategies for the adversary. One strategy is that the adversary forges a new certificate and embeds it into a forged circuit. However, by the unforgeability of DS, it is hard for the adversary to generate such a new certificate. The other strategy is that the adversary queries a message $\tilde{m}$ for the original signing circuit or marked circuits, gets a signature $\tilde{\sigma} = (\tilde{w}, \tilde{\sigma}_2) = ((\tilde{\mathsf{vk}}_2, \tilde{c}, \tilde{\sigma}_1), \tilde{\sigma}_2)$, embeds $\tilde{w}$ into a forged circuit. However, the adversary does not know $\tilde{\mathsf{sk}}_2$. Therefore, it is hard to change or remove the embedded mark from the marked circuit without breaking its functionality.

Our construction also supports unremovability in a collusion setting where the adversary can get marked circuits by oracle queries. See Sect. 2 for definition of unremovability in the collusion setting.

1.3 Related Works

We briefly review several studies related to watermarking. One of the earliest works related to watermarking is due to Naccache, Shamir, and Stern [12]. They treated the problem of "copy-righting" public-key encryption schemes in a setting that is similar to traitor tracing [5]. They gave a method for tracking different copies of functionally equivalent algorithms containing a sort of marks. However, this security is not sufficient for watermarking since it does not guarantee unremovability.

Barak et al. [2,3] firstly formalize a watermarking scheme and its security definition in a simulation based manner. Then, they gave an impossibility result for general-purpose program watermarking by using impossibility results of general-purpose program obfuscation [2,3]. General-purpose program watermarking (resp. obfuscation) is a watermarking scheme (resp., obfuscation) that can be applied to any program.

Hopper, Molnar, and Wagner [9] proposed a game-based security for watermarking schemes. They also introduce a notion of secret extraction watermarking. In this setting, to extract the embedded mark the marked object, we need secret information called an extract key. However, they did not provide any concrete constructions.

Nishimaki [13,14] proposed watermarking schemes for lossy trapdoor functions. Security of a construction in [13] (resp., [14]) is based on the decisional linear (DLIN) (resp., the symmetric external Diffie-Hellman (SXDH)) assumption. However, the author considered weaker security and restrictions on the adversary's capabilities.

Cohen et al. [6] formalized a notion of statistical function preserving. They also formalized a watermarkable signature and watermarkable encryption. They gave a construction of watermarkable pseudorandom functions by using iO in the public extraction setting. They also showed an impossibility result that watermarking is impossible for any class of learnable functions.

After the work of Cohen et al., one of main line of watermarking researches is how to build watermarkable pseudorandom functions with statistical function preserving scheme from weaker assumptions such as lattice-based assumptions by Kim and Wu [10,11] or an existence of CCA-secure encryption by Quach, Wichs, and Zirdelis [16].

Another line of watermarking researches is how to build watermarkable primitives with stronger security.

Yang, Au, Lai, Xu, and Yu [17] improved watermarkable pseudorandom functions in [6]. They achieved public extraction and security which require that only an entity who holds the mark key should be able to embed a mark into a program.

They also proposed a collusion resistant watermarking scheme for pseudorandom functions and encryption scheme in [18]. They mentioned the existence of a collusion resistant watermarkable signature scheme. They did not provide a concrete collusion resistant watermarkable signature scheme in [18].

Some studies focus on watermarking for public key primitives. Baldimtsi, Kiayias, and Samari [1] showed how to watermark public key cryptographic primitives. However, they consider a stateful setting and a modified security model where a trusted watermarking authority generates both original and marked circuits. Watermarkable signature schemes and (attribute) encryption schemes has been proposed in [8]. These constructions achieves collusion resistance security.

1.4 Road Map

In Sect. 2, we describe our definition of watermarkable signature. In Sect. 3, we construct a watermarkable signature scheme and give brief security proofs. In Sect. 4, we explain features of our definition in comparison with previous works. In Appendix A, we recall the definition of public encryption and digital signature. In Appendix B, we provide existing definitions of watermarkable signature.

1.5 Notations

In this paper, we use the following notations. Let λ be the security parameter. A function $f : \mathbb{N} \to \mathbb{R}^+$ is negligible in λ if $f(\lambda) \leq 2^{-\omega(\log \lambda)}$. If function f is negligible in λ, we denote $f(\lambda) \leq \mathsf{negl}(\lambda)$. PPT stands for probabilistic polynomial time. For a finite set S, $s \leftarrow S$ denotes choosing an element s from S uniformly at random. For an integer n, $[n]$ denotes the set $\{1, \ldots, n\}$. For an algorithm $\mathcal{A}$, $y \leftarrow \mathcal{A}(x)$ denotes that the algorithm $\mathcal{A}$ outputs y on input x.

2 Watermarkable Signature

We introduce a new definition of watermarkable signature. A watermarkable signature scheme consists of a setup algorithm, mark algorithm, and opening algorithm, in addition to the usual key-generation, signing, and verification algorithm of digital signature. The mark algorithm embeds a mark to the signing circuit determined by a signing key. Instead of a extraction algorithm, the opening algorithm extracts the mark from an output of the marked circuit. We discuss features of this definition in Sect. 4.

Definition 1 (Watermarkable Signature). *A watermarkable signature scheme* WMSS *with a message space* $\mathcal{M}$ *and a mark space* $\mathcal{T}$ *is a tuple of PPT algorithms* $(\mathsf{WMSetup}, \mathsf{SigSetup}, \mathsf{Sign}, \mathsf{Verify}, \mathsf{Mark}, \mathsf{Open})$.

- $\mathsf{WMSetup}(1^\lambda) \rightarrow (\mathsf{wpp}, \mathsf{mk}, \mathsf{xk})$: Given a security parameter 1^λ as input, the watermark setup algorithm outputs a watermark public parameter wpp, a mark key mk, and an extract key xk.
- $\mathsf{SigSetup}(\mathsf{wpp}) \rightarrow (\mathsf{vk}, \mathsf{sk})$: Given a watermark public parameter wpp as input, the signing setup algorithm outputs a verification key vk and signing key sk.
- $\mathsf{Sign}(\mathsf{sk}, m) \rightarrow \sigma$: Given a signing key sk and a message m as input, the signing algorithm outputs a signature σ.
- $\mathsf{Verify}(\mathsf{vk}, m, \sigma) \rightarrow 0/1$: Given a verification key vk, a message m, and a signature σ as input, the verification algorithm outputs 0 or 1.
- $\mathsf{Mark}(\mathsf{mk}, \mathsf{sk}, \tau) \rightarrow C_\tau$: Given a mark key mk, a signing key sk, and a mark τ, the marking algorithm outputs a marked circuit C_τ.
- $\mathsf{Open}(\mathsf{xk}, \mathsf{vk}, \sigma) \rightarrow \tau/\bot$: Given an extract key xk, a verification key vk and a signature σ as input, the opening algorithm outputs a mark or the invalid symbol $\bot$.

For functionality and security of WMSS, we define correctness, meaningfulness, function preserving, and unremovability.

WMSS is correct if it is correct as a digital signature scheme.

Definition 2 (Correctness). WMSS *satisfies correctness if for any public parameter* wpp *and message* $m \in \mathcal{M}$*,*

$$\Pr\left[\mathsf{Verify}(\mathsf{vk}, m, \sigma) = 1 : \begin{array}{l}(\mathsf{vk}, \mathsf{sk}) \leftarrow \mathsf{SigSetup}(\mathsf{wpp}),\\ \sigma \leftarrow \mathsf{Sign}(\mathsf{sk}, m)\end{array}\right] = 1$$

holds.

If WMSS is meaningful, when opening a signature generated by the unmarked signing algorithm, its output should be invalid.

Definition 3 (Meaningfulness). WMSS *satisfies meaningfulness if for all* $m \in \mathcal{M}$*,*

$$\Pr\left[\mathsf{Open}(\mathsf{xk}, \mathsf{vk}, \sigma) = \bot : \begin{array}{l}(\mathsf{wpp}, \mathsf{mk}, \mathsf{xk}) \leftarrow \mathsf{WMSetup}(1^\lambda),\\ (\mathsf{vk}, \mathsf{sk}) \leftarrow \mathsf{SigSetup}(\mathsf{wpp}),\\ \sigma \leftarrow \mathsf{Sign}(\mathsf{sk}, m)\end{array}\right] = 1$$

holds.

In WMSS, marked circuits should preserve the *functionality* of the original signing algorithm. We interpret this requirement as "marking circuits does not change how their behavior looks like". In other words, marked circuits work as indistinguishably the same as unmarked circuits.

Definition 4 (Computational Function Preserving). *We define the computational function preserving for* WMSS *by the following game between a challenger and a PPT adversary* $\mathcal{A}$*.*

1. *The challenger runs* $(\mathsf{wpp}, \mathsf{mk}, \mathsf{xk}) \leftarrow \mathsf{WMSetup}(1^\lambda)$, $(\mathsf{vk}, \mathsf{sk}) \leftarrow \mathsf{SigSetup}(\mathsf{wpp})$, *and gives* $(\mathsf{wpp}, \mathsf{vk})$ *to* $\mathcal{A}$. *Then,* $\mathcal{A}$ *outputs a mark* τ.
2. *The challenger runs* $C_\tau \leftarrow \mathsf{Mark}(\mathsf{mk}, \mathsf{sk}, \tau)$, *samples* $b \leftarrow \{0,1\}$, *and sets* $C_b := C_\tau(\cdot)$, $C_{b\oplus 1} := \mathsf{Sign}(\mathsf{sk}, \cdot)$.
3. *The adversary* $\mathcal{A}$, *given oracle access to the signing circuits* $C_0(\cdot)$, $C_1(\cdot)$, *and the marking oracle* $\mathsf{Mark}(\mathsf{mk}, \mathsf{sk}, \cdot)$, *outputs a bit* b'.

A WMSS *satisfies the function preserving if for all PPT adversaries* $\mathcal{A}$,

$$\mathsf{Adv}^{\mathsf{func}}_{\mathsf{WMSS},\mathcal{A}}(\lambda) := \left| \Pr[b = b'] - \frac{1}{2} \right| \leq \mathsf{negl}(\lambda)$$

holds.

Computational function preserving is hard to be compatible with public extraction. As far as we know, in watermarking schemes, embedded mark is extracted by outputs of the marked circuit. If a watermarking scheme supports public extraction, anyone can extract embedded mark from the marked circuit. Due to the reason above, we consider WMSS in the secret extraction setting.

Intuitively, unremovability of WMSS guarantees that it is hard to remove a mark from a signature while remaining valid. The following definition satisfies collusion resistance since the adversary can obtain multiple marked circuits. Furthermore, the adversary is allowed to carry out chosen message attacks on not only the unmarked signing circuits but also marked circuits.

Definition 5 (Unremovability). *The unremovability for* WMSS *is defined by the following game between a challenger and a PPT adversary* $\mathcal{A}$.

1. *The challenger runs* $(\mathsf{wpp}, \mathsf{mk}, \mathsf{xk}) \leftarrow \mathsf{WMSetup}(1^\lambda)$, $(\mathsf{vk}, \mathsf{sk}) \leftarrow \mathsf{SigSetup}(\mathsf{wpp})$ *and initializes a list* $Q_{sign} \leftarrow \{\}$, $Q_{mark} \leftarrow \{\}$, *an array* A, *a counter* $i := 0$. *The challenger gives* $(\mathsf{wpp}, \mathsf{mk}, \mathsf{xk}, \mathsf{vk})$ *to* $\mathcal{A}$.
2. *Throughout the entire game,* $\mathcal{A}$ *is given access to the following oracles.*
   - *Signing oracle* $\mathsf{Sign}(\mathsf{sk}, \cdot)$*: Given an input* m, *the signing oracle runs* $\sigma \leftarrow \mathsf{Sign}(\mathsf{sk}, m)$, *updates* $Q_{sign} \leftarrow Q_{sign} \cup \{(m, \sigma)\}$, $Q_{mark} \leftarrow Q_{mark} \cup \{\bot\}$, *and returns* σ *to* $\mathcal{A}$.
   - *Make circuit oracle* $\mathsf{MakeCircuit}(\cdot)$*: Given an input* τ, *the make circuit oracle runs* $C_\tau \leftarrow \mathsf{Mark}(\mathsf{mk}, \mathsf{sk}, \tau)$, *updates* $\mathsf{A}[i][1] \leftarrow \tau$, $\mathsf{A}[i][2] \leftarrow C_\tau$, $i := i + 1$. *This oracle returns nothing to* $\mathcal{A}$.
   - *Watermark-signing oracle* $\mathsf{WMSign}(\cdot, \cdot)$*: Given an input* (i, m), *the watermark-signing oracle gets* $C \leftarrow \mathsf{A}[i][2]$ *and runs* $\sigma \leftarrow C(m)$, *updates* $Q_{sign} \leftarrow Q_{sign} \cup \{(m, \sigma)\}$, *and returns* σ *to* $\mathcal{A}$.
   - *Reveal circuit oracle* $\mathsf{RevealCircuit}(\cdot)$*: Given an input* i, *the watermark-sining oracle gets* $\tau \leftarrow \mathsf{A}[i][1]$, $C_\tau \leftarrow \mathsf{A}[i][2]$, *updates* $Q_{mark} \leftarrow Q_{mark} \cup \{\tau\}$, *and returns* C_τ *to* $\mathcal{A}$.
3. $\mathcal{A}$ *outputs a forgery* (m^*, σ^*).

A WMSS *satisfies the unremovability if for all PPT adversaries* $\mathcal{A}$*,*

$$\begin{aligned}&\mathsf{Adv}^{\mathsf{unr}}_{\mathsf{WMSS},\mathcal{A}}(\lambda)\\&:= \Pr\left[\begin{array}{l}\mathsf{Open}(\mathsf{xk},\mathsf{vk},\sigma^*) \notin Q_{mark} \wedge \mathsf{Verify}(\mathsf{vk},m^*,\sigma^*) = 1\\ \wedge\, (m^*,\sigma^*) \notin Q_{sign}\end{array}\right] \leq \mathsf{negl}(\lambda)\end{aligned}$$

holds.

Remark 1. If WMSS satisfies unremovability, then the algorithm Open satisfies correctness. Specifically, for any $\tau \in \mathcal{T}$ and $m \in \mathcal{M}$, the following holds.

$$\Pr\left[\mathsf{Open}(\mathsf{xk},\mathsf{vk},C(m)) \neq \tau : \begin{array}{l}(\mathsf{wpp},\mathsf{mk},\mathsf{xk}) \leftarrow \mathsf{WMSetup}(1^\lambda),\\ (\mathsf{sk},\mathsf{vk}) \leftarrow \mathsf{SigSetup}(1^\lambda,\mathsf{wpp}),\\ C \leftarrow \mathsf{Mark}(\mathsf{mk},\mathsf{sk},\tau)\end{array}\right] \leq \mathsf{negl}(\lambda)$$

3 Construction

In this section, we show how to construct a watermark signature scheme from a digital signature scheme and public-key encryption scheme. We show the construction of our watermarkable signature scheme WMSS in Fig. 1.

3.1 Correctness and Security Proof

In this section, we show that our watermarkable signature scheme WMSS satisfies correctness and security properties.

Theorem 1. *If* DS *satisfies correctness, then* WMSS *satisfies correctness.*

By construction, it is easy to see that correctness of WMSS is followed by correctness of DS.

Theorem 2. *If* PKE *satisfies correctness, then* WMSS *satisfies meaningfulness.*

By construction, it is easy to see that meaningfulness of WMSS is followed by correctness of PKE.

Theorem 3. *If* PKE *satisfies* IND-CPA *security, then* WMSS *satisfies computational function preserving.*

Proof of Theorem 3. Let $\mathcal{A}$ be any PPT adversary that attacks the computational function preserving of WMSS. Then, by using $\mathcal{A}$, we construct a PPT adversary $\mathcal{B}$ that attacks the variant of IND-CPA security described in Appendix A.1 of PKE as follows.

1. Upon receiving a public key ek from the challenger, $\mathcal{B}$ sets wpp = ek, generates $(\mathsf{vk}_1,\mathsf{sk}_1) \leftarrow \mathsf{DS.Gen}(1^\lambda)$, and gives a security parameter 1^λ, wpp, and $\mathsf{vk}_{\mathsf{WM}} = \mathsf{vk}_1$ to $\mathcal{A}$.

$\mathsf{WMSetup}(1^\lambda)$: $(\mathsf{ek}, \mathsf{dk}) \leftarrow \mathsf{PKE.Gen}(1^\lambda)$ Output $(\mathsf{wpp}, \mathsf{mk}, \mathsf{xk}) = (\mathsf{ek}, \bot, \mathsf{dk})$	$\mathsf{SigSetup}(\mathsf{wpp})$: Parse wpp as ek $(\mathsf{sk}_1, \mathsf{vk}_1) \leftarrow \mathsf{DS.Gen}(1^\lambda)$ $(\mathsf{sk}_2, \mathsf{vk}_2) \leftarrow \mathsf{DS.Gen}(1^\lambda)$ $c \leftarrow \mathsf{PKE.Enc}(\mathsf{ek}, \bot)$ $\sigma_1 \leftarrow \mathsf{DS.Sign}(\mathsf{sk}_1, (\mathsf{vk}_2, c))$ Output $(\mathsf{sk}_{\mathsf{WM}}, \mathsf{vk}_{\mathsf{WM}}) =$ $((\mathsf{ek}, \mathsf{sk}_1, \mathsf{sk}_2, \mathsf{vk}_2, c, \sigma_1), \mathsf{vk}_1)$
$\mathsf{Mark}(\mathsf{mk}, \mathsf{sk}_{\mathsf{WM}}, \tau)$: Parse $\mathsf{sk}_{\mathsf{WM}}$ as $((\mathsf{ek}, \mathsf{sk}_1, \mathsf{sk}_2, \mathsf{vk}_2, c), \sigma_1)$ $(\mathsf{sk}'_2, \mathsf{vk}'_2) \leftarrow \mathsf{DS.Gen}(1^\lambda)$ $c' \leftarrow \mathsf{PKE.Enc}(\mathsf{ek}, \tau)$ $\sigma'_1 \leftarrow \mathsf{DS.Sign}(\mathsf{sk}_1, (\mathsf{vk}'_2, c'))$ $\mathsf{sk}'_{\mathsf{WM}} := (\mathsf{sk}'_2, \mathsf{vk}'_2, c', \sigma'_1)$ Output the following circuit $C(\mathsf{sk}'_{\mathsf{WM}}, \cdot)$ $C(\mathsf{sk}'_{\mathsf{WM}}, m)$: Parse $\mathsf{sk}'_{\mathsf{WM}}$ as $(\mathsf{sk}'_2, \mathsf{vk}'_2, c', \sigma'_1)$ $\sigma'_2 \leftarrow \mathsf{DS.Sign}(\mathsf{sk}'_2, m)$ Output $\sigma = (\mathsf{vk}'_2, c', \sigma'_1, \sigma'_2)$	$\mathsf{Sign}(\mathsf{sk}_{\mathsf{WM}}, m)$: Parse $\mathsf{sk}_{\mathsf{WM}}$ as $((\mathsf{ek}, \mathsf{sk}_1, \mathsf{sk}_2, \mathsf{vk}_2, c), \sigma_1)$ $\sigma_2 \leftarrow \mathsf{DS.Sign}(\mathsf{sk}_2, m)$ Output $\sigma = (\mathsf{vk}_2, c, \sigma_1, \sigma_2)$
$\mathsf{Open}(\mathsf{xk}, \mathsf{vk}_{\mathsf{WM}}, \sigma)$: Parse σ as $(\mathsf{vk}_2, c, \sigma_1, \sigma_2)$ $\tau \leftarrow \mathsf{PKE.Dec}(\mathsf{dk}, c)$ Output τ	$\mathsf{Verify}(\mathsf{vk}_{\mathsf{WM}}, m, \sigma)$: Parse $\mathsf{vk}_{\mathsf{WM}}$ as vk_1 Parse σ as $(\mathsf{vk}_2, c, \sigma_1, \sigma_2)$ If $\mathsf{DS.Verify}(\mathsf{vk}_1, (\mathsf{vk}_2, c), \sigma_1) = 1$ and $\mathsf{DS.Verify}(\mathsf{vk}_2, m, \sigma_2) = 1$, Output 1 else Output 0

Fig. 1. Construction of watermarkable signature scheme.

2. When $\mathcal{A}$ outputs a mark τ, $\mathcal{B}$ makes a challenge query $(m_0, m_1) = (\tau, \bot)$ and gets a challenge ciphertext (c_0, c_1). Then, $\mathcal{B}$ generates $(\mathsf{vk}_2, \mathsf{sk}_2) \leftarrow \mathsf{DS.Gen}(1^\lambda)$ and $(\mathsf{vk}'_2, \mathsf{sk}'_2) \leftarrow \mathsf{DS.Gen}(1^\lambda)$, and computes $\sigma_1 \leftarrow \mathsf{DS.Sign}(\mathsf{sk}_1, (\mathsf{vk}_2, c_0))$ and $\sigma'_1 \leftarrow \mathsf{DS.Sign}(\mathsf{sk}_1, (\mathsf{vk}'_2, c_1))$.
3. $\mathcal{B}$ answers an $\mathcal{A}$'s oracle query as follows.
   - When $\mathcal{A}$ makes a query m for a signing circuit C_0(*resp.*, C_1), $\mathcal{B}$ computes σ_2(*resp.*, σ'_2) $\leftarrow \mathsf{DS.Sign}(\mathsf{sk}_2$(*resp.*, sk'_2)$, m)$ and returns $(\mathsf{vk}_2, c_0, \sigma_1, \sigma_2)$ (*resp.*, $(\mathsf{vk}'_2, c_1, \sigma'_1, \sigma'_2)$) to $\mathcal{A}$.
   - When $\mathcal{A}$ makes a circuit generation query τ, $\mathcal{B}$ generates $(\widetilde{\mathsf{vk}}_2, \widetilde{\mathsf{sk}}_2) \leftarrow \mathsf{DS.Gen}(1^\lambda)$ and computes $c \leftarrow \mathsf{PKE.Enc}(\mathsf{ek}, \tau)$ and $\sigma \leftarrow \mathsf{DS.Sign}(\mathsf{sk}_1, (\widetilde{\mathsf{vk}}_2, c))$. Then, $\mathcal{B}$ sets $\mathsf{sk}_{\mathsf{WM}} = (\widetilde{\mathsf{sk}}_2, \widetilde{\mathsf{vk}}_2, c, \sigma)$ and returns $C(\mathsf{sk}_{\mathsf{WM}}, \cdot) := (\widetilde{\mathsf{vk}}_2, c, \sigma, \mathsf{DS.Sign}(\widetilde{\mathsf{sk}}_2, \cdot))$ to $\mathcal{A}$.
4. When $\mathcal{A}$ finally outputs a bit $b' \in \{0, 1\}$, $\mathcal{B}$ returns b' to its challenger.

We can see that $\mathcal{B}$ perfectly simulates the game of computational function preserving in which the challenge bit for $\mathcal{A}$ is the same as that in the game between the challenger and $\mathcal{B}$. Moreover, $\mathcal{B}$ just finally returns $\mathcal{A}$'s output b'.

Therefore, $\mathsf{Adv}^{\mathsf{func}}_{\mathsf{WMSS},\mathcal{A}}(\lambda) = \mathsf{Adv}^{\mathsf{ind\text{-}cpav}}_{\mathsf{PKE},\mathcal{B}}(\lambda)$ holds. Since PKE satisfies IND-CPA security, we have $\mathsf{Adv}^{\mathsf{func}}_{\mathsf{WMSS},\mathcal{A}}(\lambda) = \mathsf{negl}(\lambda)$, and thus WMSS satisfies computational function preserving. □
(Theorem 3)

Theorem 4. *If* DS *satisfies* sEUF-CMA *security and* PKE *satisfies correctness, then* WMSS *satisfies unremovability.*

Due to the space limitation, we now give only an intuition of this proof here. The formal proof will be given in the full version of this paper.

Let $\mathcal{A}$ be an adversary of unremovability for WMSS and (m^*, σ^*) be a forgery output by $\mathcal{A}$. To satisfy $(m^*, \sigma^*) \notin \mathcal{Q}_{sign}$, $\mathcal{A}$ is not allowed to output an answer of the signing oracle or watermark-signing oracle. When $\mathcal{A}$ queries to reveal circuit oracle and gets a marked circuit C, by correctness of PKE, $\mathcal{A}$ is not allowed to output $(m^*, C(m^*))$ such that satisfying $\mathsf{Open}(\mathsf{xk}, \mathsf{vk}, \sigma^*) \notin \mathcal{Q}_{mark}$. In this setting, $\mathcal{A}$ has three strategies.

One is reusing a verification key, a ciphertext of mark and their signature from signing oracle, and forging signature of m^*. Namely, $\mathcal{A}$ queries m to its signing or watermark-signing oracle and gives an answer $(\mathsf{vk}, c, \sigma_1, \sigma_2)$, outputs $(m^*, (\mathsf{vk}, c, \sigma_1, \sigma_2^*))((m^*, \sigma_2^*) \neq (m, \sigma_2))$. In this case, by the sEUF-CMA security of DS, the advantage of $\mathcal{A}$ is negligible.

Another one is reusing a verification key, a ciphertext of mark and their signature from watermark-signing oracle, and forging signature of m^*. In this case, as the first one, by the sEUF-CMA security of DS, the advantage of $\mathcal{A}$ is negligible.

The other is computing a verification key, a ciphertext of mark and signature of m^*, and forging signature of a verification key and a ciphertext. Namely, $\mathcal{A}$ computes $(\mathsf{vk}, \mathsf{sk}) \leftarrow \mathsf{DS.Gen}(1^\lambda)$, $c \leftarrow \mathsf{PKE.Enc}(\mathsf{ek}, \tau)(\mathsf{wpp} = \mathsf{ek})$, signs $\sigma_2 \leftarrow \mathsf{DS.Sign}(\mathsf{sk}, m^*)$, and outputs $(m^*, (\mathsf{vk}, c, \sigma_1^*, \sigma_2))$. Also in this case, by the sEUF-CMA security of DS, the advantage of $\mathcal{A}$ is negligible.

4 Relation with Previous Definitions of Watermarking

In this section, to clarify the features of our definition, we discuss the relationship between our definition and that of Cohen et al. [6] and Goyal et al. [8] which we recall in Appendix B.

On the Syntax. Our definition of watermarkable signature is basically based on Definition 9 proposed by Goyal et al. [8] in which we can mark a signing circuit with multiple marks by the marking algorithm. This is in contrast to Definition 15 proposed by Cohen et al. [6], in which no marking algorithm is employed, instead, a mark is embedded into a circuit when generating signing and verification keys.

The most characteristic point of our definition is that we introduced the opening algorithm instead of extraction algorithm. Previous definitions of watermarking schemes have an extraction algorithm which on input a marked circuit, output the embedded mark. Clearly, we can construct a trivial extraction algorithm from an opening algorithm just by running the circuit for some input message and execute the opening for the output of the circuit.

On the Correctness and Meaningfulness. As for the functionality of watermarkable signature, we defined correctness and meaningfulness. These properties ensure that "signatures generated by unmarked signing key are valid" and "opening a signature output by (unmarked) signing algorithm should be invalid" respectively.

Previous works explicitly require "when extracting a marked circuit, the mark should be correctly extracted" as a part of the correctness (Definition 10, 16) and "no mark can be extracted from any circuit chosen independently of the public parameter or mark key" as a part of the meaningfulness (Definition 11). We do not require correctness for the Open algorithm like the former property because unremovability implies this correctness. Unremovability also implies following property. For any fixed set, a message m and a signature σ, choosing independently from watermarking or signature parameters, the provability that σ is a valid signature for m and $\mathsf{Open}(\mathsf{xk}, \mathsf{vk}, \sigma)$ outputs any marks except $\perp$ is negligible.

On the Unremovability. Due to the modification of the syntax, our definition of unremovability differs from that of previous works. Originally, unremovability is defined with the extraction algorithm, where the goal of the adversary is to work out a ϵ-good circuit from which a novel mark is extracted. ϵ-good means that, for ϵ fraction of the domain, behavior of the circuit is the same as the unmarked signing algorithm (Definition 18), or output of the circuit is valid (Definition 14). If the watermarkable signature scheme, which has sufficient large message space, satisfies our unremovability, then it satisfies the unremovability defined with the trivial extraction algorithm, for any small but noticeable ϵ-good in the latter sense, which is the best we can hope for a watermarkable primitive.

Similar to Goyal et al., we consider collusion of adversaries in the definition of unremovability. Specifically, Goyal et al. give the adversary access to the mark oracle so that the adversary can collect multiple marked circuits. In our definition, the adversary can collect marked circuits through access to the make-circuit and the reveal-circuit oracles. Moreover, our definition allows the adversary to see signatures generated by marked circuits that are not corrupted. This makes the definition of unremovability stronger so that it almost covers the security of unforgeability as explained next.

On (Omission of) Unforgeability. Unlike the existing definitions of watermarkable signature, our definition does not explicitly require unforgeability which ensures that the watermarkable signature is unforgeable as a digital signature. This is because our definition of unremovability almost captures such unforgeability. Specifically, when the adversary does not use the reveal-circuit oracle in the game of unremovability, the game corresponds to that of unforgeability.

Cohen et al. defined a selective unforgeability (Definition 17), that is, the adversary chooses a message on which try to forge a signature at the first step of the game. Definition 13 by Goyal et al. as well as ours captures strongly existential unforgeability (sEUF) where the adversary output the target message at the last step.

A shortcoming of Definition 13 is that only the signing oracle is provided to the adversary. In our definition, the adversary has access to not only the signing oracle but also the make-circuit oracle and the watermark signing oracle. Thus we can capture the situations where the adversary can see signatures generated from not only the unmarked circuit but also marked circuits.

In Definition 13, the watermark authority could be malicious, which means that the adversary can choose the public parameter, mark-key, and extract-key. Only this feature is not covered by our definition of unremovability, however, we can explicitly add such a definition of unforgeability. We can prove our scheme to be unforgeable in a very similar way as the case of the unremovability.

On the Function Preserving of Watermarkable Signatures. On the function preserving, we firstly examine the relations between the function preserving of our watermarkable signature and one of Goyal et al.'s watermarkable signature [8]. At first, we recall the definition of function preserving for Goyal et al.'s watermarkable signature [8]. Informally, their definition requires only that a marked signing key still produces valid signatures which verify with respect to the original verification key. In other words, this definition does not guarantee an input/output behavior with respect to watermarked signing keys. The formal definition is described in Appendix B. We can see that our computational function preserving defined in Sect. 2 is stronger than the Goyal et al.'s function preserving. Specifically, we have the following statement.

Theorem 5. *If watermarkable signature satisfies correctness and computational function preserving, then it satisfies function preserving.*

On the Function Preserving of General Watermarkable Primitives. Next, we investigate the relations about function preserving on general watermarkable primitives. Based on our definition for watermarkable signature, we firstly introduce the definition of computational function preserving for general watermarkable primitives.

A (general) watermarkable primitive with a mark space $\mathcal{T}$ is a tuple of the following four PPT algorithms $(\mathsf{WMSetup}, \mathsf{Gen}, \mathsf{Mark}, \mathsf{Extract})$.

- $\mathsf{WMSetup}(1^\lambda) \to (\mathsf{wpp}, \mathsf{mk}, \mathsf{xk})$: Given a security parameter 1^λ as input, the watermark setup algorithm outputs a watermark public parameter wpp, a mark key mk, and an extract key xk.
- $\mathsf{Gen}(\mathsf{wpp}) \to (\mathsf{pk}, C)$: Given a watermark public parameter wpp as input, the circuit generation algorithm outputs a public key pk and a circuit C.
- $\mathsf{Mark}(\mathsf{mk}, C, \tau) \to C_\tau$: Given a mark key mk, a circuit C, and a mark τ as input, the marking algorithm outputs a marked circuit C_τ.

- $\mathsf{Extract}(\mathsf{xk}, \mathsf{pk}, C_\tau) \to \tau/\bot$: Given an extract key xk, a public key pk, and a marked circuit C_τ, the extraction algorithm outputs a mark τ or $\bot$.

We define the computational function preserving for a watermarkable primitive as follows.

Definition 6 (Computational Function Preserving for a Watermarkable Primitive). *A watermarkable primitive* $(\mathsf{WMSetup}, \mathsf{Gen}, \mathsf{Mark}, \mathsf{Extract})$ *satisfies computational function preserving if there exists a negligible function* $\mathsf{negl}(\cdot)$ *for any PPT adversary* $\mathcal{A} = (\mathcal{A}_1, \mathcal{A}_2)$,

$$\left| \Pr\left[b = b' : \begin{array}{l} (\mathsf{wpp}, \mathsf{mk}, \mathsf{xk}) \leftarrow \mathsf{WMSetup}(1^\lambda), \\ (\mathsf{pk}, C) \leftarrow \mathsf{Gen}(\mathsf{wpp}), (\tau, \mathsf{st}_1) \leftarrow \mathcal{A}_1(\mathsf{wpp}, \mathsf{pk}), \\ C_\tau \leftarrow \mathsf{Mark}(\mathsf{mk}, C, \tau), b \leftarrow \{0,1\}, \\ C_b := C_\tau, C_{b \oplus 1} := C \\ b' \leftarrow \mathcal{A}_2^{C_0(\cdot), C_1(\cdot), \mathsf{Mark}(\mathsf{mk}, C, \cdot)}(\mathsf{st}_1) \end{array} \right] - \frac{1}{2} \right| \leq \mathsf{negl}(\lambda),$$

where $C_0(\cdot)(resp., C_1(\cdot))$ *is a circuit evaluation oracle that, given an input* x*, outputs* $C_0(x)$ $(resp., C_1(x))$ *and* $\mathsf{Mark}(\mathsf{mk}, C, \cdot)$ *is a circuit generation oracle that, given a mark* τ *as input, outputs a marked circuit* $C_\tau(\cdot) \leftarrow \mathsf{Mark}(\mathsf{mk}, C, \tau)$.

Then, we see the relations between this computational function preserving and statistical function preserving of Cohen et al.'s general watermarkable primitive [6]. Next, we recall the definition of statistical function preserving for a general watermarkable primitive defined in [6]. Intuitively, their definition captures a situation where the input/output behavior of the marked circuit is statistically close to that of the original circuit when we embed any mark into a circuit over the honest setup. The formal definition is given as follows.

Definition 7 (Statistical Function Preserving for a Watermarkable Primitive). *A watermarkable primitive satisfies statistical function preserving for a circuit class* $\{C\}_\lambda$ *if there exists a negligible function* $\mathsf{negl}(\cdot)$ *for any circuit* $C \in \{C\}_\lambda$*, input* x*, and* $\tau \in \mathcal{T}$,

$$\Pr\left[C(x) = C_\tau(x) : \begin{array}{l} (\mathsf{wpp}, \mathsf{mk}, \mathsf{xk}) \leftarrow \mathsf{WMSetup}(1^\lambda), \\ C_\tau \leftarrow \mathsf{Mark}(\mathsf{mk}, C, \tau) \end{array} \right] \geq 1 - \mathsf{negl}(\lambda).$$

At first glance, since their definition satisfies a statistical property while our definition only satisfies a computational property, it seems that their definition implies ours. However, we can see that the above statistical function preserving does not imply our computational function preserving. This is because, in our definition, a marked circuit can be chosen after generating a watermark public parameter, a mark key, and an extract key, and an adversary can choose a challenge mark after seeing a watermarkable public parameter. In general, it is important to consider such an adaptive security for cryptographic primitives capturing a standard security requirement in real-world applications.

(For example, in a signature setting, our definition can capture an existential unforgeability while the above definition only captures weak existential unforgeability.) Actually, we can extend the above statistical function preserving into ideal one supporting an adaptive security as follows.

Definition 8 ("Ideal" Statistical Function Preserving). *A watermarkable primitive satisfies "ideal" statistical function preserving if there exists a negligible function* $\mathsf{negl}(\cdot)$ *for any computationally unbounded adversary* $\mathcal{A} = (\mathcal{A}_1, \mathcal{A}_2)$,

$$\Pr\left[C(x') = C_\tau(x') : \begin{array}{l} (\mathsf{wpp}, \mathsf{mk}, \mathsf{xk}) \leftarrow \mathsf{WMSetup}(1^\lambda), \\ (\mathsf{pk}, C) \leftarrow \mathsf{Gen}(\mathsf{wpp}), (\tau, \mathsf{st}_1) \leftarrow \mathcal{A}_1(\mathsf{wpp}), \\ C_\tau \leftarrow \mathsf{Mark}(\mathsf{mk}, C, \tau), \\ x' \leftarrow \mathcal{A}_2^{C(\cdot), C_\tau(\cdot), \mathsf{Mark}(\mathsf{mk}, C, \cdot)}(\mathsf{st}_1) \end{array}\right] \geq 1 - \mathsf{negl}(\lambda),$$

where $C(\cdot)$*(resp.,* $C_\tau(\cdot)$*) is a circuit evaluation oracle that, given an input* x*, outputs* $C(x)$*(resp.,* $C_\tau(x)$*).* $\mathcal{A}$ *is allowed to access* $C(\cdot)$*(resp.,* $C_\tau(\cdot)$*) only polynomial times.* $\mathsf{Mark}(\mathsf{mk}, C, \cdot)$ *is a circuit generation oracle that, given a mark* τ *as input, outputs a marked circuit* $C_\tau(\cdot) \leftarrow \mathsf{Mark}(\mathsf{mk}, C, \tau)$.

It is easy to see that the above ideal statistical function preserving implies our computational function preserving. However, we do not know how to obtain a watermarkable primitive satisfying this ideal statistical function preserving. On the other hand, as shown in Sect. 3, we can obtain a watermarkable signature scheme satisfying computational function preserving by requiring only PKE and (standard) signature both of which are basic cryptographic primitives.

5 Conclusions

We reorganize the definition of watermarkable signature recently proposed by Goyal et al. [8] and introduce a new security notion called *computational function preserving* for it. Then, we can see that our computational function preserving defined in Sect. 2 is stronger than the function preserving by Goyal et al. . Moreover, we extend the definition of computational function preserving into general watermarkable primitive setting, then also investigate the relationships between our computational function preserving and statistical function preserving proposed by Cohen et al. [6]. In addition, we propose a watermarkable signature scheme satisfying computational function preserving based on public key encryption and (standard) digital signature.

Acknowledgements. A part of this work was supported by NTT Secure Platform Laboratories, JST OPERA JPMJOP1612, JST CREST JPMJCR14D6, JSPS KAKENHI JP16H01705, JP17H01695, JP19J22363, JP20J14338.

A Basic Cryptographic Primitives

A.1 Public Key Encryption

A public key encryption scheme PKE with a message space $\mathcal{M}$ is a tuple of PPT algorithms ($\mathsf{PKE.Gen}$, $\mathsf{PKE.Enc}$, $\mathsf{PKE.Dec}$).

- $\mathsf{PKE.Gen}(1^\lambda) \to (\mathsf{ek}, \mathsf{dk})$: Given a security parameter 1^λ as input, the key generation algorithm outputs a encryption/decryption key pair $(\mathsf{ek}, \mathsf{dk})$.
- $\mathsf{PKE.Enc}(\mathsf{ek}, m) \to c$: Given an encryption key ek and a plaintext m as input, the encryption algorithm outputs a ciphertext c.
- $\mathsf{PKE.Dec}(\mathsf{dk}, c) \to m/\bot$: Given a decryption key dk and a ciphertext c as input, the decryption algorithm outputs a message m or invalid symbol $\bot$.

Correctness PKE satisfies correctness if for all $m \in \mathcal{M}$, $\Pr[\mathsf{PKE.Dec}(\mathsf{dk}, c) = m : (\mathsf{ek}, \mathsf{dk}) \leftarrow \mathsf{PKE.Gen}(1^\lambda), c \leftarrow \mathsf{PKE.Enc}(\mathsf{ek}, m)] = 1$ holds.

variant of IND-CPA For any PPT adversary $\mathcal{A}$,

$$\mathsf{Adv}^{\mathsf{ind\text{-}cpav}}_{\mathsf{PKE},\mathcal{A}} := \left| \Pr\left[b = b' : \begin{array}{c} (\mathsf{ek}, \mathsf{dk}) \leftarrow \mathsf{PKE.Gen}(1^\lambda), (m_0, m_1) \leftarrow \mathcal{A}(\mathsf{ek}), \\ b \leftarrow \{0,1\}, c_b \leftarrow \mathsf{PKE.Enc}(\mathsf{ek}, m_0), \\ c_{b \oplus 1} \leftarrow \mathsf{PKE.Enc}(\mathsf{ek}, m_1), b' \leftarrow \mathcal{A}(c_0, c_1) \end{array} \right] - \frac{1}{2} \right|$$

is $\mathsf{negl}(\lambda)$. This security is equivalent to the general one.

A.2 Digital Signature

A digital signature scheme DS with a message space $\mathcal{M}$ is a tuple of PPT algorithms ($\mathsf{DS.Gen}$, $\mathsf{DS.Sign}$, $\mathsf{DS.Verify}$).

- $\mathsf{DS.Gen}(1^\lambda) \to (\mathsf{vk}, \mathsf{sk})$: Given a security parameter 1^λ as input, the key generation algorithm outputs a verification/signing key pair $(\mathsf{vk}, \mathsf{sk})$.
- $\mathsf{DS.Sign}(\mathsf{sk}, m) \to \sigma$: Given a signing key sk and a message m as input, the signing algorithm outputs a signature σ.
- $\mathsf{DS.Verify}(\mathsf{vk}, m, \sigma) \to 0/1$: Given a verification key vk, a message m, and a signature σ as input, the verification algorithm outputs 0 or 1.

Correctness DS satisfies correctness if for all $m \in \mathcal{M}$, $\Pr[\mathsf{DS.Verify}(\mathsf{vk}, m, \sigma) = 1 : (\mathsf{vk}, \mathsf{sk}) \leftarrow \mathsf{DS.Gen}(1^\lambda), \sigma \leftarrow \mathsf{DS.Sign}(\mathsf{sk}, m)] = 1$

sEUF-CMA The sEUF-CMA security for DS is defined by the following game between a challenger and a PPT adversary $\mathcal{A}$.

1. The challenger runs $(\mathsf{vk}, \mathsf{sk}) \leftarrow \mathsf{DS.Gen}(1^\lambda)$, initializes a list $Q \leftarrow \{\}$, and gives vk to $\mathcal{A}$.
2. Throughout the entire game, $\mathcal{A}$ is given access to signing oracle $\mathsf{DS.Sign}(\mathsf{sk}, \cdot)$. Given an input m, the signing oracle runs $\sigma \leftarrow \mathsf{DS.Sign}(\mathsf{sk}, m)$, updates $Q \leftarrow Q \cup \{(m, \sigma)\}$, and returns σ to $\mathcal{A}$
3. $\mathcal{A}$ outputs a forgery (m^*, σ^*).

DS satisfies the sEUF-CMA security if for all PPT adversaries $\mathcal{A}$, $\mathsf{Adv}^{\mathsf{unf}}_{\mathsf{DS},\mathcal{A}} := \Pr[\mathsf{DS.Verify}(\mathsf{vk}, m^*, \sigma^*) = 1 \wedge (m^*, \sigma^*) \notin Q] \leq \mathsf{negl}(\lambda)$ holds.

B Watermarkable Signature in Previous Works

To compare with watermarkable signature in previous works, we describe formal definitions of watermarkable signature proposed by Goyal et al. [8] and Cohen et al. [6].

B.1 Definition by Goyal et al. [8]

Definition 9 (Watermarkable Signature). *A watermarkable signature scheme with a message space $\mathcal{M}$ and a mark space $\mathcal{T}$ is a tuple of PPT algorithms* $(\mathsf{WMSetup}, \mathsf{SigSetup}, \mathsf{Sign}, \mathsf{Verify}, \mathsf{Mark}, \mathsf{Extract})$.

- $\mathsf{WMSetup}(1^\lambda) \to (\mathsf{wpp}, \mathsf{mk}, \mathsf{xk})$
- $\mathsf{SigSetup}(1^\lambda, \mathsf{wpp}) \to C$
- $\mathsf{Sign}(\mathsf{sk}, m) \to \sigma$
- $\mathsf{Verify}(\mathsf{vk}, m, \sigma) \to 0/1$
- $\mathsf{Mark}(\mathsf{mk}, \mathsf{sk}, \tau) \to C_\tau$
- $\mathsf{Extract}(\mathsf{xk}, \mathsf{vk}, C_\tau) \to \tau/\bot$

Definition 10 (Correctness). *For any $m \in \mathcal{M}$ and $\tau \in \mathcal{T}$,*

$$\Pr\left[\begin{array}{l}\mathsf{Verify}(\mathsf{vk}, m, C(m)) \neq 1 \vee \\ \mathsf{Extract}(\mathsf{xk}, \mathsf{vk}, C) \neq \tau\end{array} : \begin{array}{l}(\mathsf{wpp}, \mathsf{mk}, \mathsf{xk}) \leftarrow \mathsf{WMSetup}(1^\lambda), \\ (\mathsf{sk}, \mathsf{vk}) \leftarrow \mathsf{SigSetup}(1^\lambda, \mathsf{wpp}), \\ C \leftarrow \mathsf{Mark}(\mathsf{mk}, \mathsf{sk}, \tau)\end{array}\right] \leq \mathsf{negl}(\lambda)$$

holds.

Definition 11 (Meaningfulness). *Meaningfulness requires the following two properties holds.*

1. For all fixed circuits $C : \mathcal{M} \to \mathbb{SIG}$[1],

$$\Pr\left[\mathsf{Extract}(\mathsf{xk}, \mathsf{vk}, C) \neq \bot : \begin{array}{l}(\mathsf{wpp}, \mathsf{mk}, \mathsf{xk}) \leftarrow \mathsf{WMSetup}(1^\lambda), \\ (\mathsf{sk}, \mathsf{vk}) \leftarrow \mathsf{SigSetup}(1^\lambda, \mathsf{wpp})\end{array}\right] \leq \mathsf{negl}(\lambda)$$

2.

$$\Pr\left[\mathsf{Extract}(\mathsf{xk}, \mathsf{vk}, \mathsf{Sign}(\mathsf{sk}, \cdot)) \neq \bot : \begin{array}{l}(\mathsf{wpp}, \mathsf{mk}, \mathsf{xk}) \leftarrow \mathsf{WMSetup}(1^\lambda), \\ (\mathsf{sk}, \mathsf{vk}) \leftarrow \mathsf{SigSetup}(1^\lambda, \mathsf{wpp})\end{array}\right] \leq \mathsf{negl}(\lambda)$$

Definition 12 (Function Preserving). *For any $m \in \mathcal{M}$ and $\tau \in \mathcal{T}$,*

$$\Pr\left[\mathsf{Verify}(\mathsf{vk}, m, C(m)) = 0 : \begin{array}{l}(\mathsf{wpp}, \mathsf{mk}, \mathsf{xk}) \leftarrow \mathsf{WMSetup}(1^\lambda), \\ (\mathsf{sk}, \mathsf{vk}) \leftarrow \mathsf{SigSetup}(1^\lambda, \mathsf{wpp}), \\ C \leftarrow \mathsf{Mark}(\mathsf{mk}, \mathsf{sk}, \tau)\end{array}\right] \leq \mathsf{negl}(\lambda)$$

holds.

---

[1] $\mathbb{SIG}$ is a signature space for the watermarkable signature scheme.

Definition 13 (Unforgeability). *For any PPT adversary $\mathcal{A}$,*

$$\Pr\left[\mathsf{Verify}(\mathsf{vk}, m^*, \sigma^*) = 1 \wedge m \in \mathcal{Q} : \begin{array}{l} \mathsf{wpp} \leftarrow \mathcal{A}(1^\lambda), \\ (\mathsf{vk}, \mathsf{sk}) \leftarrow \mathsf{SigSetup}(1^\lambda, \mathsf{wpp}), \\ (m^*, \sigma^*) \leftarrow \mathcal{A}^{\mathsf{Sign}(\mathsf{sk}, \cdot)}(\mathsf{vk}) \end{array}\right] \leq \mathsf{negl}(\lambda)$$

holds, where $\mathcal{Q} \subseteq \mathcal{M}$ is the set of messages $\mathcal{A}$ submitted to the signing oracle.

Definition 14 (Unremovability). *For any PPT adversary $\mathcal{A}$,*

$$\Pr\left[\mathsf{Extract}(\mathsf{xk}, \mathsf{vk}, C^*) \notin \mathcal{Q} : \begin{array}{l} (\mathsf{wpp}, \mathsf{mk}, \mathsf{xk}) \leftarrow \mathsf{WMSetup}(1^\lambda), \\ (\mathsf{vk}, \mathsf{sk}) \leftarrow \mathsf{SigSetup}(1^\lambda, \mathsf{wpp}), \\ C^* \leftarrow \mathcal{A}^{\mathsf{Sign}(\mathsf{sk}, \cdot)\mathsf{Mark}(\mathsf{mk}, \mathsf{vk}, \cdot)}(1^\lambda, \mathsf{wpp}, \mathsf{vk}) \end{array}\right] \leq \mathsf{negl}(\lambda)$$

holds, where $\mathcal{Q} \subseteq \mathcal{M}$ is the set of messages $\mathcal{A}$ submitted to the Mark oracle. $\mathcal{A}$ is said to be ϵ-unremovable admissible if the circuit C^* it outputs is an ϵ-good signer for key vk*. Here we say that C^* is an ϵ-good signer circuit for key* vk *if the following* $\Pr[\mathsf{Verify}(\mathsf{vk}, m, C^*(m)) = 1 : m \leftarrow \mathcal{M}] \geq \epsilon$ *holds.*

B.2 Definition by Cohen et al. [6]

Definition 15 (Watermarkable Signature). *A watermarkable signature scheme with a message space $\mathcal{M}$ and a mark space $\mathcal{T}$ is tuple of PPT algorithms* (WMSetup, SigSetup, Sign, Verify, Extract).

- $\mathsf{WMSetup}(1^\lambda) \to (\mathsf{mk}, \mathsf{xk})$
- $\mathsf{SigSetup}(1^\lambda, \mathsf{mk}, \tau) \to (\mathsf{vk}, \mathsf{sk})$
- $\mathsf{Sign}(\mathsf{sk}, m) \to \sigma$
- $\mathsf{Verify}(\mathsf{vk}, m, \sigma) \to 0/1$
- $\mathsf{Extract}(\mathsf{xk}, \mathsf{vk}, \mathsf{DS.Sign}_{\mathsf{sk}}) \to \tau/\bot$

Definition 16 (Correctness). *For any $\lambda \in \mathbb{N}$, $m \in \mathcal{M}$, and $\tau \in \mathcal{T}$,*

$$\Pr\left[\begin{array}{l} \mathsf{Verify}(\mathsf{vk}, m, C(m)) \neq 1 \vee \\ \mathsf{Extract}(\mathsf{xk}, \mathsf{vk}, C) \neq \tau \end{array} : \begin{array}{l} (\mathsf{wpp}, \mathsf{mk}, \mathsf{xk}) \leftarrow \mathsf{WMSetup}(1^\lambda), \\ (\mathsf{sk}, \mathsf{vk}) \leftarrow \mathsf{SigSetup}(1^\lambda, \mathsf{wpp}), \\ C \leftarrow \mathsf{Mark}(\mathsf{mk}, \mathsf{sk}, \tau) \end{array}\right] \leq \mathsf{negl}(\lambda)$$

holds.

Definition 17 ((Selective) Unforgeability). *For any PPT adversary $\mathcal{A}$,*

$$\Pr\left[\mathsf{Verify}(\mathsf{vk}, m^*, \sigma^*) = 1 : \begin{array}{l} m^* \leftarrow \mathcal{A}(1^\lambda), (\mathsf{mk}, \mathsf{xk}) \leftarrow \mathsf{WMSetup}(1^\lambda), \\ (\mathsf{vk}, \mathsf{sk}) \leftarrow \mathsf{SigSetup}(1^\lambda, \mathsf{mk}, \tau), \\ \sigma^* \leftarrow \mathcal{A}^{\mathsf{Sign}_{m^*}(\mathsf{sk}, \cdot)}(\mathsf{vk}, \mathsf{xk}) \end{array}\right] \leq \mathsf{negl}(\lambda)$$

holds where $\mathsf{Sign}_{m^*}(\mathsf{sk}, \cdot)$ is an oracle that signs any message except for m^*.

Definition 18 (Unremovability). *For any PPT adversary $\mathcal{A}$ and for any mark τ,*

$$\Pr\left[\begin{array}{l} C^* \approx_\epsilon \mathsf{Sign}_{\mathsf{sk}} \ \wedge \\ \mathsf{Extract}(\mathsf{xk}, \mathsf{vk}, C^*) \neq \tau \end{array} : \begin{array}{c} (\mathsf{mk}, \mathsf{xk}) \leftarrow \mathsf{WMSetup}(1^\lambda), \\ (\mathsf{vk}, \mathsf{sk}) \leftarrow \mathsf{SigSetup}(1^\lambda, \mathsf{mk}, \tau), \\ C^* \leftarrow \mathcal{A}(1^\lambda, \mathsf{sk}, \mathsf{xk}) \end{array}\right] \leq \mathsf{negl}(\lambda)$$

holds, where $C^* \approx_\epsilon \mathsf{Sign}_{\mathsf{sk}}$ denotes C^* and $\mathsf{Sign}_{\mathsf{sk}}$ agree on ϵ fraction of their inputs.

References

1. Baldimtsi, F., Kiayias, A., Samari, K.: Watermarking public-key cryptographic functionalities and implementations. In: Nguyen, P., Zhou, J. (eds.) ISC 2017. LNCS, vol. 10599, pp. 173–191. Springer, Cham (2017). https://doi.org/10.1007/978-3-319-69659-1_10
2. Barak, B., et al.: On the (im)possibility of obfuscating programs. In: Kilian, J. (ed.) CRYPTO 2001. LNCS, vol. 2139, pp. 1–18. Springer, Heidelberg (2001). https://doi.org/10.1007/3-540-44647-8_1
3. Barak, B., et al.: On the (im)possibility of obfuscating programs. J. ACM **59**(2), 6:1–6:48 (2012)
4. Boneh, D., Lewi, K., Wu, D.J.: Constraining pseudorandom functions privately. In: Fehr, S. (ed.) PKC 2017, Part II. LNCS, vol. 10175, pp. 494–524. Springer, Heidelberg (2017). https://doi.org/10.1007/978-3-662-54388-7_17
5. Chor, B., Fiat, A., Naor, M.: Tracing traitors. In: Desmedt, Y.G. (ed.) CRYPTO 1994. LNCS, vol. 839, pp. 257–270. Springer, Heidelberg (1994). https://doi.org/10.1007/3-540-48658-5_25
6. Cohen, A., Holmgren, J., Nishimaki, R., Vaikuntanathan, V., Wichs, D.: Watermarking cryptographic capabilities. In: ACM, STOC 2016, pp. 1115–1127 (2016)
7. Cohen, A., Holmgren, J., Vaikuntanathan, V.: Publicly verifiable software watermarking. IACR Cryptology ePrint Archive, 2015:373 (2015)
8. Goyal, R., Kim, S., Manohar, N., Waters, B., Wu, D.J.: Watermarking public-key cryptographic primitives. In: Boldyreva, A., Micciancio, D. (eds.) CRYPTO 2019, Part III. LNCS, vol. 11694, pp. 367–398. Springer, Cham (2019). https://doi.org/10.1007/978-3-030-26954-8_12
9. Hopper, N., Molnar, D., Wagner, D.: From weak to strong watermarking. In: Vadhan, S.P. (ed.) TCC 2007. LNCS, vol. 4392, pp. 362–382. Springer, Heidelberg (2007). https://doi.org/10.1007/978-3-540-70936-7_20
10. Kim, S., Wu, D.J.: Watermarking cryptographic functionalities from standard lattice assumptions. In: Katz, J., Shacham, H. (eds.) CRYPTO 2017, Part I. LNCS, vol. 10401, pp. 503–536. Springer, Cham (2017). https://doi.org/10.1007/978-3-319-63688-7_17
11. Kim, S., Wu, D.J.: Watermarking PRFs from lattices: stronger security via extractable PRFs. In: Boldyreva, A., Micciancio, D. (eds.) CRYPTO 2019, Part III. LNCS, vol. 11694, pp. 335–366. Springer, Cham (2019). https://doi.org/10.1007/978-3-030-26954-8_11
12. Naccache, D., Shamir, A., Stern, J.P.: How to copyright a function? In: Imai, H., Zheng, Y. (eds.) PKC 1999. LNCS, vol. 1560, pp. 188–196. Springer, Heidelberg (1999). https://doi.org/10.1007/3-540-49162-7_14

13. Nishimaki, R.: How to watermark cryptographic functions. In: Johansson, T., Nguyen, P.Q. (eds.) EUROCRYPT 2013. LNCS, vol. 7881, pp. 111–125. Springer, Heidelberg (2013). https://doi.org/10.1007/978-3-642-38348-9_7
14. Nishimaki, R.: How to watermark cryptographic functions by bilinear maps. IEICE Trans. Fundam. Electron. Commun. Comput. Sci. **102–A**(1), 99–113 (2019)
15. Nishimaki, R., Wichs, D.: Watermarking cryptographic programs against arbitrary removal strategies. IACR Cryptology ePrint Archive, 2015:344 (2015)
16. Quach, W., Wichs, D., Zirdelis, G.: Watermarking PRFs under standard assumptions: public marking and security with extraction queries. In: Beimel, A., Dziembowski, S. (eds.) TCC 2018, Part II. LNCS, vol. 11240, pp. 669–698. Springer, Cham (2018). https://doi.org/10.1007/978-3-030-03810-6_24
17. Yang, R., Au, M.H., Lai, J., Xu, Q., Yu, Z.: Unforgeable watermarking schemes with public extraction. In: Catalano, D., De Prisco, R. (eds.) SCN 2018. LNCS, vol. 11035, pp. 63–80. Springer, Cham (2018). https://doi.org/10.1007/978-3-319-98113-0_4
18. Yang, R., Au, M.H., Lai, J., Xu, Q., Yu, Z.: Collusion resistant watermarking schemes for cryptographic functionalities. In: Galbraith, S.D., Moriai, S. (eds.) ASIACRYPT 2019, Part I. LNCS, vol. 11921, pp. 371–398. Springer, Cham (2019). https://doi.org/10.1007/978-3-030-34578-5_14

Privacy-Preserving Authentication for Tree-Structured Data with Designated Verification in Outsourced Environments

Fei Zhu[1(✉)], Xun Yi[1], Sharif Abuadbba[2], Ibrahim Khalil[1], Xu Yang[1], Surya Nepal[2], and Xinyi Huang[3(✉)]

[1] School of Science, RMIT University, Melbourne, Australia
{fei.zhu,xun.yi,ibrahim.khalil,xu.yang}@rmit.edu.au

[2] CSIRO Data61, Sydney, Australia
{sharif.abuadbba,surya.nepal}@data61.csiro.au

[3] School of Mathematics and Informatics, Fujian Normal University, Fuzhou, China
xyhuang81@gmail.com

Abstract. Nowadays, the use of database outsourcing is on the rise. Since the service provider may not be fully trusted, a crucial requirement in outsourced data sharing is therefore to ensure that users can verify the integrity and authenticity of their query results. In outsourced healthcare data sharing, because the data contains sensitive information, an equally significant issue is to guarantee that the sharing process does not lead to any information leakages. Though some privacy-preserving authentication solutions have been presented to address these issues, unfortunately, none of them consider the risk of privacy leakage during the dissemination of authenticated healthcare data. That is, the queried data may be leaked by the user since any third party getting hold of a signed data would be convinced of its validity. In other words, for privacy concerns, we need a secure mechanism to ensure that only a specific receiver can check the integrity and authenticity of shared outsourced data.

To address the these concerns, in our work, we propose a privacy-preserving authentication scheme with designated verification for tree-structured data (i.e., XML-based healthcare records). We provide the formal definition and related security properties of our scheme. We further put forward our concrete construction and prove its security under the standard cryptographic assumption in the random oracle model. The comparison analysis of theory and practice shows that our scheme provides stronger privacy protection than existing schemes while having the shortest key length and signature size. Therefore, our construction is efficient and practical for outsourced environments.

Keywords: Privacy-preserving authentication · Outsourced environments · Trees · Privacy · Data sharing

K. Nguyen et al. (Eds.): ProvSec 2020, LNCS 12505, pp. 145–165, 2020.
https://doi.org/10.1007/978-3-030-62576-4_8

1 Introduction

Database outsourcing [25] is a popular trend in the fast-growing cloud computing paradigm. In a typical outsourced database (ODB) model, the data owner outsources his local data to the powerful cloud service provider (SP), and the SP answers users' queries on behalf of the data owner. The ODB model not only provides a flexible solution for resource-constrained users to maintain their database services, but also enables the SP to take advantage of the concentration on professional resources. Although this promising service model has numerous advantages, it poses many challenges to data security and privacy since the SP may not be fully trusted and may tamper with the contents of the database for some purpose. The situation is further aggravated if the outsourced data (such as healthcare, biological, and financial data) contains sensitive information that cannot be disclosed. Therefore, in addition to the need for an effective data authentication scheme to guarantee that users can verify the integrity and authenticity of their query results, a significant requirement is to make sure that the authentication process does not lead to any information leakages. Because tree structure (such as XML-based example) [2,9,13,15,17] is one of the most extensively used data organization structures, a fundamental but vital requirement is to design the specific authentication techniques for trees in the ODB model. Moreover, as shown in Fig. 1, since anyone who obtains the signed query result can easily verify its authenticity [23], the user can simply send the tree-signature pair to any interested third-party verifier (i.e., the external entity beyond the OBD model). What's even worse is this signed query result can be further leaked to an unlimited number of third party verifiers [27], thus posing a serious privacy threat to the data owner. For privacy concerns, how to prevent the authenticated query result from being leaked by the user is also crucial.

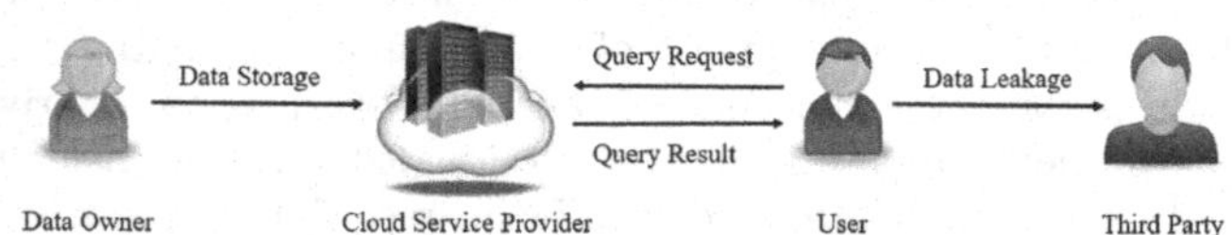

Fig. 1. Data Leakage in the ODB model.

Take the following scenario borrowed from [2,13,15] as an example. As shown in Fig. 2, the tree T stands for an individual's XML-based healthcare record; the tree structure may be publicly known, and the record is signed by the individual (i.e., the data owner Alice) and remotely stored in a database server. Suppose that siblings nodes $a6$, $a7$ and $a8$ refer to some different diseases such as cancer, HIV test, and kidney failure she has suffered from during her life, and the order between them represents the temporal order in which she suffered from the diseases. Assume that a researcher (i.e., the user Bob) makes a query for the healthcare database on a specific group of diseases (see the shaded part) that

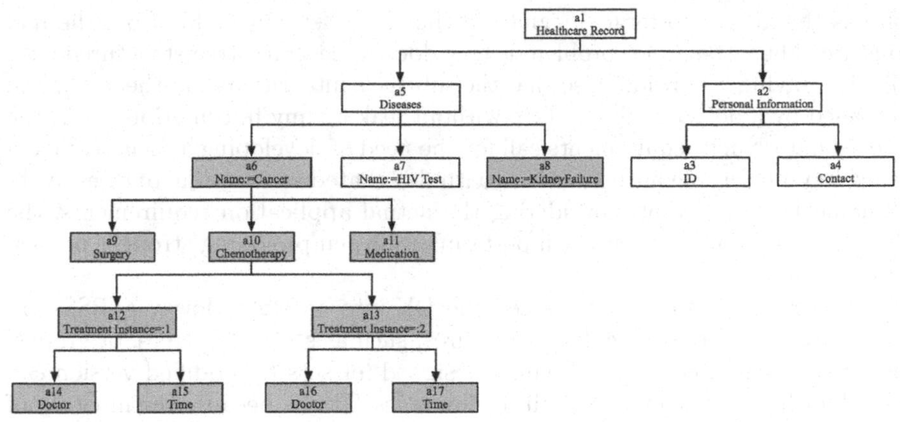

Fig. 2. The tree representation of a XML-based healthcare record for an individual.

an individual may have suffered from, and the query result returned by the SP is represented as T_δ. Traditionally, the Merkle hash technique (MHT) [18] is used to assure the integrity of T_δ. However, the verification process needs some information (at least the hash value) about $a7$. Here, we refer the reader to [14] for the detailed example and related consequence of inference attacks. In all, because $a7$ is not part of T_δ, for privacy concerns, Bob cannot be allowed to infer any information about $a7$ in the received information. In the meantime, Bob should be capable of verifying the integrity and authenticity of T_δ.

Motivation. To address this issue, many researchers have deployed redactable signature schemes (RSSs) [10] into the area of authenticating tree-structured data [2,11–13,15–17,21]. This is due to the fact that an RSS allows the SP to delete some portions of the signed data and generate a valid signature for the remaining data without the signer's secret key. This homomorphic property in the RSS makes it differ from the traditional signature scheme on which any edit operation will destroy the integrity and authenticity of the retained data. Notably, in an RSS, the retained data and its signature do not leak any content information about deleted parts. Unfortunately, simply using an RSS is not enough in the aforementioned scenario. This is because it cannot prevent users from leaking the authenticated query result to an interested third party.

In the above scenario, for example, since the query result contains some sensitive information and Alice does not wish Bob to convince any third party (say Dave) the truth of the result (i.e., might reliably learn her disease), he is therefore not allowed to let Dave know this fact. Hence, what is needed is a designated verifier (DV) for the redacted version of the healthcare record. In other words, when redacting the healthcare record, Alice should be capable of defining the specified receiver Bob. In this case, although anyone can verify the integrity and authenticity of a leaked record, only Bob can be sure of its validity. This can be achieved by constructing the scheme in the following way: The DV

Bob has the ability to forge a signature that is indistinguishable from the real signature. Thus, the above problem is how does Alice sign a tree-structured data *once* (i.e., saving bandwidth), so that the subtree's integrity and authenticity can be verified by a designated user Bob without leaking any information about the removed data. Such requirements call for the need of developing a security model for 'privacy-preserving authentication with designated verification' of trees. Also, we should be aware that, considering the actual application requirements, the solution should not sacrifice much performance when providing stronger privacy protection.

The work in [5] firstly introduced the DV into an RSS. However, RSSs are usually designed for specific data structures, such as sets, lists, trees, or graphs. The scheme presented in [5] is mainly designed for sets (a modified version can be used for lists) but cannot be suitable for trees. This is because the integrity of sets only refers to content integrity, while trees also involve structural integrity. Motivated by these observations, in this work, we make use of the concept of universal designated verifier signatures (UDVSs) [23,27] and propose a practical privacy-preserving authentication scheme for trees with designated verification in outsourced healthcare data sharing.

Contributions. Previous solutions of RSS for trees cannot address the above privacy concern in outsourced healthcare data sharing. To achieve the aforementioned security and privacy protection requirements, in our work, we put forward an efficient privacy-preserving authentication scheme for trees with designated verification (DV-PPAT). More concretely, the scheme supports the integrity and authenticity verification of tree-structured data returned from the SP with designated verification. The framework of our DV-PPAT is described as follows: The data owner signs the original tree-structured data and uploads the tree-signature pair to a remote database server. Each time when a user wants to make a query for the stored data, the SP deletes some portions of the signed tree and generates a valid signature for the retained subtree independently. On this basis, the SP further computes a DV signature for the subtree and returns the new subtree-signature pair to the user. After receiving the subtree, only the user himself can verify its integrity and authenticity, and the verification process reveals nothing about the pruned nodes in the original tree. Our main contributions are as follows:

1. Existing tree-structured data authentication schemes (such as [12,16]) are inefficient and have the problem that the authenticated query result may be leaked by the user (i.e., the requester). We therefore propose a practical DV-PPAT scheme that can (i) support the integrity and authenticity verification of the retained subtree (i.e., the query result) returned by the SP without disclosing any sensitive information about the deleted part, and (ii) prevent the user from leaking the authenticated query result to any third party, making the third party believe that the user holds a valid signature. Notably, our scheme allows one to redact leaves and inner nodes.
2. Kundu et al. [12] presented the security definition of RSS for trees. We note that their definition does not appropriately capture the desired security

properties. For the first time, we formally define DV-PPAT and related security properties, including unforgeability and privacy-preserving properties such as privacy, transparency, and non-transferability. We further present the rigorous security proofs of our scheme under the standard cryptographic assumption in the random oracle (RO) model.

3. Our DV-PPAT scheme achieves stronger privacy protection (i.e., the non-transferability as defined in Sect. 4.2) than that of state-of-the-art schemes. In the meantime, our scheme does not sacrifice much performance. Instead, it has a shorter key length and signature size. Specifically, our signature size for the original tree T is similar to the scheme in [16], and it is about 23.4% of that of the scheme in [12]. Our signature size for the redacted tree T_δ is about 66.6% of that of the scheme in [16] and 93.7% of that of the scheme in [12]. Therefore, our proposed scheme is practical for outsourced healthcare data sharing.

1.1 Organization

The remaining paper is organized as the following: We describe the related work in Sect. 2 and give some required preliminaries in Sect. 3. Sect. 4 presents related definitions and security models of DV-PPAT. Section 5 presents our concrete construction and its security proofs. Section 6 evaluates the performance of our scheme and we conclude the paper in Sect. 7.

2 Related Work

Tree-structured data sharing over an untrusted server requires that both integrity and authenticity must be assured. To address this concern, many authentication techniques have been proposed in the literature. Assuring the integrity of tree-structured data is mainly carried by the MHT [18] introduced by Merkle in 1989. A drawback of such a technique is that a user who receives a shared subtree will also need to receive some private information about unshared nodes (such as the hash value) for verification [26]. Therefore, the schemes of the authenticated data structure (ADS) [7] derived from the MHT technology cannot also achieve confidentiality-preserving. Groß [8] proposed a third-party auditing system based on zero-knowledge (ZK) proof for topology graphs; however, the scheme cannot be used for data sharing and therefore cannot solve our problem. In 2008, Kundu and Bertino [13] firstly presented an RSS for trees and claimed that it guarantees both confidentiality and integrity. However, the scheme lacks formal security definitions and proofs. Subsequently, Brzuska et al. [2] revisited the work in [13], gave definitions and security models for RSS for trees, and also proposed a provably secure construction under standard cryptographic assumptions. Unfortunately, the scheme presented in [2] only allows to redact leaf nodes. Samelin et al. [22] proposed an RSS allowing to independently redact structure and content. It is worth mention that Samelin et al. [21] presented new attacks with respect to unforgeability, privacy, and transparency on the RSSs in

[2,13,21], and gave a flexible construction based on the initial idea in [13]. Kundu et al. [11,12] introduced the concept of secure names and proposed the secure naming scheme (SNS) in 2012. The SNS can assign 'secure names' to nodes such that these secure names can be used for verifying the order between the nodes efficiently without revealing any information about other nodes. On this basis, they used the underlying condensed-RSA scheme [20] and proposed an RSS for trees. However, their scheme requires a long signature size and a high communication cost. More importantly, as mentioned before, it cannot prevent users from sharing the authenticated query result to an external third party, which may cause the privacy of the data owner to be leaked. In 2018, the work in [12] was further extended by Liu et al. [16] to achieve redaction control. However, their construction is inefficient. At present, numerous integrity and authenticity authentication schemes with privacy protection have been proposed for trees in outsourced healthcare data sharing; however, none of them consider the risk that the shared data would be leaked by the user which will lead to severe privacy problems.

3 Preliminaries

We define some preliminaries used by our paper in this section.

General Notations. The set of positive integers $\{1, 2, \ldots\}$ is denoted as $\mathbb{N}$. We say a function $\xi : \mathbb{N} \rightarrow \mathbb{R}$ is negligible if for any positive polynomial $pol(\cdot)$ there exists $\lambda_0 \in \mathbb{N}$ for every $\lambda > \lambda_0$, the inequality $\xi(\lambda) < 1/p(\lambda)$ holds. We use the notation $x \stackrel{\$}{\leftarrow} \mathcal{S}$ to represent that the element x is chosen uniformly and randomly from the set $\mathcal{S}$.

Trees. A tree $T = (V, E)$ consists of a set of nodes $V \in \mathbb{N}$ and a set of edges $E \subseteq V \times V$. We use c_{u_i} and $e(u_i, u_j)$ to denote the content of an atomic data unit u_i and an edge from u_i to u_j respectively. Note that all edges in our scheme are directed. The fact that u_j precedes one of its siblings u_k in T is referred as $u_j \prec u_k$. We use $T_\delta = (V_\delta, E_\delta) \subseteq T = (V, E)$ to represent a subtree of T.

3.1 Complexity Assumption

Bilinear Mapping. Let $\mathbb{G}_1 =< g_1 >$ and $\mathbb{G}_2 =< g_2 >$ be two q-order cyclic groups, and $\mathbb{G}_T$ be a group with the same order. Let $\hat{e}$: $\mathbb{G}_1 \times \mathbb{G}_2 \rightarrow \mathbb{G}_T$ be a pairing with the following three properties:

1. Bilinearity: $\hat{e}({g_1}^\alpha, {g_2}^\beta) = \hat{e}(g_1, g_2)^{\alpha\beta}$ for every $\alpha, \beta \in \mathbb{Z}_q$.
2. Efficiency: For every $\alpha, \beta \in \mathbb{Z}_q$, $\hat{e}({g_1}^\alpha, {g_2}^\beta)$ is efficiently computable.
3. Non-degeneracy: $\hat{e}(g_1, g_2) \neq 1$.

Following [3,24], in this paper, we use the so called Type-2 pairing which exists an efficiently-computable isomorphism $\psi : \mathbb{G}_2 \rightarrow \mathbb{G}_1$.

Bilinear Diffie-Hellman (BDH) problem [19]: Given g_2, ${g_2}^\alpha$, ${g_2}^\beta \in \mathbb{G}_2$, and ${g_1}^\gamma \in \mathbb{G}_1$, where α, β, $\gamma \stackrel{\$}{\leftarrow} \mathbb{Z}_q^*$, compute $\hat{e}(g_1, g_2)^{\alpha\beta\gamma} \in \mathbb{G}_T$.

Let a BDH parameter generator $\mathsf{G}(1^\lambda)$ be a probabilistic polynomial time (p.p.t.) algorithm that taking as input 1^λ, and outputs a prime q and an admissible bilinear mapping $\hat{e}$: $\mathbb{G}_1 \times \mathbb{G}_2 \rightarrow \mathbb{G}_T$.

Definition 1. (BDH assumption). *For a p.p.t. adversary $\mathcal{F}$, we define his probability in solving the* BDH *problem as*

$$\Pr_{\mathscr{F}}^{\mathsf{BDH}} = \Pr\left[\mathcal{F}\begin{pmatrix} q, \mathbb{G}_1, \mathbb{G}_2, \hat{e} \\ g_2, {g_2}^{\alpha}, {g_2}^{\beta}, {g_1}^{\gamma} \end{pmatrix} = \hat{e}(g_1, g_2)^{\alpha\beta\gamma} \middle| \begin{array}{c} (q, \mathbb{G}_1, \mathbb{G}_2, \hat{e}) \leftarrow \mathsf{G}(1^\lambda), \\ g_1 \xleftarrow{\$} \mathbb{G}_1, g_2 \xleftarrow{\$} \mathbb{G}_2, \\ \alpha, \beta, \gamma \xleftarrow{\$} \mathbb{Z}_q^* \end{array}\right].$$

We say that the BDH *problem is hard if for any p.p.t. adversary $\mathcal{F}$ with negligible function ξ, $\Pr_{\mathscr{F}}^{\mathsf{BDH}} \leq \xi(\lambda)$.*

3.2 Secure Naming Scheme

In order to protect the order of siblings of a node in an ordered tree, similar to [16], we use an underlying secure naming scheme SNS=(NaGen, NaVerify), described as usual through its p.p.t. name generation and verification algorithms. Introduced by Kundu et al. in [11,12], the SNS can traverse an ordered tree $T = (V, E)$ bottom-up and assign *secure names* θ_{u_i} to all nodes $u_i \in T$. The aim of using secure names is to prove/disprove the order between a pair of nodes without leaking anything else about T (such as whether they are adjacent siblings, how many other siblings are between them).

Remark 1. In the early work of Kundu et al. such as in [13], they used the randomized traversal numbers as a building block to construct RSSs for trees. These works were further proven to be insecure in [2,21,22]. Later, Kundu et al. designed the SNS scheme and proposed new RSSs for trees. To the best of our knowledge, the SNS scheme has not been cracked so far. As stated by [22], it is a completely new construction not related to the original idea.

Definition 2. (SNS). *A* SNS=(NaGen, NaVerify) *is defined via the following two polynomial-time algorithms:*

- $\Theta \leftarrow \mathsf{NaGen}(1^\lambda, V)$*: On input the security parameter 1^λ, and nodes $V = \{u_i | 1 \leq i \leq n\}$, the algorithm outputs $\Theta = \{\theta_{u_i} | 1 \leq i \leq n\}$, where θ_{u_i} is the probabilistic secure name of u_i.*
- $\{0,1\} \leftarrow \mathsf{NaVerify}(1^\lambda, (u_i, \theta_{u_i}), (u_j, \theta_{u_j}))$*: On input the security parameter 1^λ, and two pairs (u_i, θ_{u_i}) and (u_j, θ_{u_j}), the algorithm outputs a verification decision $d \in \{0,1\}$.*

A SNS achieves name-transparency, i.e., anyone who has been given an ordered set of secure names $\Theta_\delta \subseteq \Theta$, can not infer whether $\Theta_\delta = \Theta$ or $\Theta_\delta \neq \Theta$. Please refer to [11,12] for its concrete construction and security proof.

4 Definitions of Our DV-PPAT

In previous work, Kundu et al. presented the definitions of RSS for trees in [12]. However, their model cannot capture the case where the authenticated query result should not be leaked by the verifier during the process of dissemination. To overcome this shortcoming, we propose the desirable model of DV-PPAT.

This section will devote to the formal definitions of DV-PPAT, including its syntax and security properties, such as unforgeability, privacy, transparency, and non-transferability.

4.1 Syntax of DV-PPAT

A DV-PPAT scheme consists of eight polynomial time algorithms, i.e., DV-PPAT= (ParaG, SigKG, VerKG, Sign, Verify, Redact, DeSign, DeVerify). Among them, ParaG, SigKG, and VerKG are used to generate system parameters, key pairs for the signer (i.e., the data owner) and the DV respectively. Sign is used by the signer to authentication a given tree T, and Verify is used to verify whether the received signature is valid. The SP uses Redact to obtain a signature for the subtree T_δ (i.e., the query result) and then uses DeSign to generate a DV signature for T_δ. DeVerify is used by the verifier to check whether the DV signature is valid. Following is the detailed syntax of DV-PPAT:

- $para \leftarrow \mathsf{ParaG}(1^\lambda)$: On input security parameter 1^λ, the probabilistic algorithm outputs common parameters $para$.
- $(x_s, y_s) \leftarrow \mathsf{SigKG}(para)$: On input common parameters $para$, the probabilistic algorithm returns a secret/public key pair (x_s, y_s) for the signer.
- $(x_v, y_v) \leftarrow \mathsf{VerKG}(para)$: On input common parameters $para$, the probabilistic algorithm returns a secret/public key pair (x_v, y_v) for the DV.
- $\sigma_T \leftarrow \mathsf{Sign}(x_s, T)$: The algorithm takes as input x_s and a tree $T = (V, E)$. It returns σ_T as the signature for T.
- $\{0,1\} \leftarrow \mathsf{Verify}(y_s, T, \sigma_T)$: The algorithm takes as input y_s, a tree T and its signature σ_T as input. It outputs a verification decision $d \in \{0,1\}$.
- $\sigma_{T_\delta} \leftarrow \mathsf{Redact}(y_s, T, \sigma_T, T'_\delta)$: The algorithm takes as input y_s, an original authenticated tree T and its signature σ_T, and a redaction subtree $T'_\delta = (V'_\delta, E'_\delta)$. It outputs a signature σ_{T_δ} for a retained tree $T_\delta = (V_\delta, E_\delta)$.
- $\sigma^{ds}_{T_\delta} \leftarrow \mathsf{DeSign}(y_s, y_v, T_\delta, \sigma_{T_\delta})$: The algorithm takes as input y_s and y_v, a retained tree T_δ and its signature σ_{T_δ}. It outputs a DV signature $\sigma^{ds}_{T_\delta}$ for T_δ.
- $\{0,1\} \leftarrow \mathsf{DeVerify}(y_s, x_v, T_\delta, \sigma^{ds}_{T_\delta})$: The algorithm takes as input y_s, x_v, a tree T and its DV signature $\sigma^{ds}_{T_\delta}$. The algorithm firstly generates a DV signature $\sigma^{\bar{ds}}_{T_\delta}$ for T_δ. To check whether $\sigma^{\bar{ds}}_{T_\delta}=\sigma^{ds}_{T_\delta}$ holds or not, it outputs a verification decision $d \in \{0,1\}$.

Consistency of DV-PPAT: In general, we require a DV-PPAT scheme should satisfy two consistency properties:

- Verify Consistency of Sign: The signature generated by Sign is accepted as valid by Verify. Thus, we have: $\Pr[\mathsf{Verify}(y_s, T, \mathsf{Sign}(x_s, T)) = 1] = 1$.
- DeVerify Consistency of DeSign: The DV signature produced by DeSign is accepted as valid by DeVerify. That is: $\Pr[\mathsf{DeVerify}(y_s, x_v, T_\delta, \mathsf{DeSign}(y_s, y_v, T_\delta, \sigma_{T_\delta})) = 1] = 1$.

4.2 Notions of Security for DV-PPAT

This section will define some security properties for DV-PPAT, including unforgeability and privacy-preserving properties such as privacy, transparency, and non-transferability.

Unforgeability. We define two types of unforgeability properties in DV-PPAT, i.e., σ_T-unforgeability and $\sigma_{T_\delta}^{ds}$-unforgeability. Intuitively, the former requires that no adaptive p.p.t. adversary has the ability to forge a valid signature σ_T for the original tree T under adaptive chosen message attack. The latter refers that without σ_T, no adaptive p.p.t. adversary can forge a valid DV signature $\sigma_{T_\delta}^{ds}$ for the redacted tree T_δ to convince any third party of this fact (i.e., holding such a valid $\sigma_{T_\delta}^{ds}$). It is clear that, since anyone who possesses $(y_s, y_v, T, \sigma_T, T'_\delta)$ is able to use Redact and DeSign to get $\sigma_{T_\delta}^{ds}$, the $\sigma_{T_\delta}^{ds}$-unforgeability implies the σ_T-unforgeability. Hence, we only formalize the property of $\sigma_{T_\delta}^{ds}$-unforgeability. Let $\mathcal{A}$ be an adaptive chosen message p.p.t. adversary. The goal of $\mathcal{A}$ is to forge a valid DV signature ${\sigma_{T_\delta}^{ds}}^*$ for a redacted tree ${T_\delta}^* = ({V_\delta}^*, {E_\delta}^*)$. The security model of DV-PPAT is defined via the following Unforgeability Experiment 4.2.1 between $\mathcal{A}$ and a challenger $\mathcal{C}$:

- Setup Phase: $\mathcal{C}$ runs ParaG to generate the common parameters *para*, then runs SigKG and VerKG to obtain the signer's secret/public key pair (x_s, y_s) and DV's secret/public key pair (x_v, y_v) respectively. $\mathcal{C}$ further provides $\mathcal{A}$ with $(para,\ y_s,\ y_v)$.
- Query Phase: Proceeding adaptively, $\mathcal{A}$ can request signatures with y_s on trees $T_i = (V_i, E_i)$ $(1 \le i \le n)$ of his choice. Each time when $\mathcal{C}$ responds to $\mathcal{A}$'s query, he runs the oracle Sign to obtain the signature σ_{T_i} for T_i and forwards (T_i, σ_{T_i}) to $\mathcal{A}$.
- Output Phase: Finally, $\mathcal{A}$ either concedes failure or forges a DV signature ${\sigma_{T_\delta}^{ds}}^*$ for a redacted tree ${T_\delta}^* = ({V_\delta}^*, {E_\delta}^*)$. $\mathcal{A}$ wins the above experiment if: (1) $\mathsf{DeVerify}(y_s, x_v, {T_\delta}^*, {\sigma_{T_\delta}^{ds}}^*) = 1$, and (2) ${T_\delta}^*$ is not a subtree of any tree that has been submitted as one of queries in Query Phase.

We define the advantage of $\mathcal{A}$ in winning the experiment 4.2.1 as $\mathsf{Adv}_{\mathcal{A},\mathsf{DV-PPAT}}^{euf-cma}(1^\lambda)$.

Definition 3. *A scheme* DV-PPAT$=$(ParaG, SigKG, VerKG, Sign, Verify, Redact, DeSign, DeVerify) *is existentially unforgeable under adaptive chosen message attack (EUF-CMA) if* $\mathsf{Adv}_{\mathcal{A},\mathsf{DV-PPAT}}^{euf-cma}(1^\lambda)$ *is negligible for any p.p.t. adversary* $\mathcal{A}$*, where* 1^λ *is the security parameter.*

Privacy and Transparency. There are three privacy-preserving properties, i.e., privacy, transparency, and non-transferability in DV-PPAT. Similar to the indistinguishability notion for an encryption scheme, the privacy for DV-PPAT refers that the DV should not be able to gain any knowledge about redacted parts without having access to them. The transparency for DV-PPAT requires that the DV cannot decide whether the received tree is the original one or the redacted version. As stated by Brzuska et al. in [2], this property is a stronger notion and subsumes privacy which only covers the contents of the deleted nodes. To avoid duplicate work, we only formally define transparency. Let $\mathcal{D}_1$ be an adaptive chosen message p.p.t. adversary. $\mathcal{D}_1$'s goal is to decide whether a given signature σ_T for tree T is directly generated by Sign or obtained by Redact. The transparency of DV-PPAT is defined via the following Transparency Experiment 4.2.2 between $\mathcal{D}_1$ and a challenger $\mathcal{C}$:

- Setup Phase: This step is similar to the Setup Phase in experiment 4.2.1, but eventually, $\mathcal{C}$ provides $\mathcal{D}_1$ with $(para, y_s, y_v, x_v)$.
- Query Phase 1: This step is the same as the Query Phase 1 in experiment 4.2.1.
- Challenge:
  (1) At the end of Query Phase 1, $\mathcal{D}_1$ selects two trees $T_0 = (V_0, E_0)$ and $T_1 = (V_1, E_1)$ such that $T_0 \subseteq T_1$ and sends them to $\mathcal{C}$.
  (2) $\mathcal{C}$ randomly flips a coin $c \in \{0, 1\}$. He runs Sign to generate the signature σ_{T_0} for T_0 in the case of $c = 0$. Otherwise, he uses Sign to obtain the signature σ_{T_1} for T_1 and runs Redact to produce the signature σ_{T_0} for T_0. $\mathcal{C}$ then forwards the challenge pair (T_0, σ_{T_0}) to $\mathcal{D}_1$.
- Query Phase 2: During this phase, $\mathcal{D}_1$ can make oracles Sign, Verify, and Redact queries as the same as in the Query Phase 1.
- Output Phase: At the end of this experiment, $\mathcal{D}_1$ outputs his guess c' and wins the experiment if $c' = c$.

We define the advantage of $\mathcal{D}_1$ in winning the experiment 4.2.2 as $\mathsf{Adv}^{euf-cma}_{\mathcal{D}_1,\mathsf{DV-PPAT}}(1^\lambda) = |\Pr[c' = c] - 1/2|$.

Definition 4. *A scheme* DV-PPAT=(ParaG, SigKG, VerKG, Sign, Verify, Redact, DeSign, DeVerify) *achieves the property of transparency if* $\mathsf{Adv}^{euf-cma}_{\mathcal{D}_1,\mathsf{DV-PPAT}}(1^\lambda)$ *is negligible for any p.p.t. adversary* $\mathcal{D}_1$*, where* 1^λ *is the security parameter.*

Non-transferability. The non-transferability for DV-PPAT refers that no DV can use the signature $\sigma^{ds}_{T_\delta}$ to convince a third party that the tree T_δ was originally signed by the signer. This property can be achieved because the DV has the ability to produce the signature $\sigma^{ds}_{T_\delta}$ by using his secret key. That is, even if he publishes his secret key to a third party, the third party cannot distinguish whether the $\sigma^{ds}_{T_\delta}$ was generated by the original signer or forged by the DV. Let $\mathcal{D}_2$ be an adaptive chosen message p.p.t. adversary. $\mathcal{D}_2$'s goal is to decide whether a given DV signature $\sigma^{ds}_{T_\delta}$ for tree T_δ is signed by the real signer or generated by the DV. The non-transferability of DV-PPAT is defined via the following Non-transferability Experiment 4.2.3 between $\mathcal{D}_2$ and a challenger $\mathcal{C}$:

- Setup Phase: This step is similar to the Setup Phase in experiment 4.2.2.
- Query Phase 1: Proceeding adaptively, $\mathcal{D}_2$ can make oracles Sign, Verify, Redact, DeSign, and DeVerify queries as his wish. Each time when responds to $\mathcal{D}_2$'s query, $\mathcal{C}$ proceeds as the real scheme to obtain the related value.
- Challenge:
  (1) At the end of Query Phase 1, $\mathcal{D}_2$ selects a tree T_δ and sends it to $\mathcal{C}$.
  (2) $\mathcal{C}$ randomly flips a coin $c \in \{0,1\}$. If $c = 0$, he executes DeSign to generate the DV signature $\sigma^{ds}_{T_\delta}$ for T_δ. Otherwise, he proceeds as DeVerify to generate a signature $\sigma^{\bar{ds}}_{T_\delta}$. $\mathcal{C}$ further provides $\mathcal{D}_2$ with the pair $(T_\delta, \sigma^{ds}_{T_\delta})$ or $(T_\delta, \sigma^{\bar{ds}}_{T_\delta})$ accordingly.
- Query Phase 2: During this phase, $\mathcal{D}_2$ can also make oracles queries as the same as in the Query Phase 1.
- Output Phase: At the end of this experiment, $\mathcal{D}_1$ outputs his guess c' and wins the experiment if $c' = c$.

We define the advantage of $\mathcal{D}_2$ in winning the experiment 4.2.3 as $\mathsf{Adv}^{euf-cma}_{\mathcal{D}_2,\mathsf{DV-PPAT}}(1^\lambda) = |\Pr[c' = c] - 1/2|$.

Definition 5. *A scheme* DV-PPAT=(ParaG, SigKG, VerKG, Sign, Verify, Redact, DeSign, DeVerify) *achieves non-transferability if* $\mathsf{Adv}^{euf-cma}_{\mathcal{D}_2,\mathsf{DV-PPAT}}(1^\lambda)$ *is negligible for any p.p.t. adversary* $\mathcal{D}_2$*, where* 1^λ *is the security parameter.*

5 Our Construction

This section provides a concrete DV-PPAT scheme by integrating the concept of RSS and UDVS. The scheme deploys the BGLS scheme in [1] and the work in [19] as building blocks. Similar to [11,12,16], we also make use of the efficient scheme SNS=(NaGen, NaVerify) as a primitive. However, to avoid duplication work, we omit its concrete description. Later, we give the detailed security analysis to DV-PPAT in a model where the hash function is a RO. For simplicity, let n and k be the number of nodes in the original tree T and the redacted tree T_δ respectively.

- ParaG(1^λ): Given a security parameter 1^λ, the algorithm chooses a Type-2 pairing $\hat{e}$: $\mathbb{G}_1 \times \mathbb{G}_2 \rightarrow \mathbb{G}_T$ such that all groups have the same order q. Let g_1 and g_2 be the generator of $\mathbb{G}_1$ and $\mathbb{G}_2$ respectively. Denote by $\psi : \mathbb{G}_2 \rightarrow \mathbb{G}_1$ the isomorphism satisfying $\psi(g_2) = g_1$ and $H(\cdot) : \{0,1\}^* \rightarrow \mathbb{G}_1$ the cryptographic hash function. The parameters are $para = (\hat{e}, q, g_1, g_2, \psi, h(\cdot))$.
- SigKG($para$): Given $para$, the signer chooses $x_s \xleftarrow{\$} \mathbb{Z}_q$, and computes $y_s \leftarrow {g_2}^{x_s} \in \mathbb{G}_2$. The signer's secret/public key pair is (x_s, y_s).
- VerKG($para$): Given $para$, the verifier chooses $x_v \xleftarrow{\$} \mathbb{Z}_q$, and computes $y_v \leftarrow {g_2}^{x_v} \in \mathbb{G}_2$. The verifier's secret/public key pair is (x_v, y_v).
- Sign(x_s, T): The signer uses this algorithm to sign a tree. The algorithm takes the signer's secret key x_s and a tree $T = (V, E)$ as input. It proceeds as the following:

1. Carry out a traversal on T and let c_{u_i} be the content of a node $u_i \in V$. Let $\theta_{u_i} \in \mathbb{Z}_q$ and $\theta_{p_{u_i}} \in \mathbb{Z}_q$ denote the secure names of u_i and its parent that are generated by NaGen.
2. For all $u_i \in V$ $(1 \leq i \leq n)$, it computes $h_{u_i} \leftarrow H(\theta_{p_{u_i}} || \theta_{u_i} || c_{u_i})$ and node signatures $\sigma_{u_i} \leftarrow (h_{u_i})^{x_s} \in \mathbb{G}_1$.
3. It computes $\sigma'_T \leftarrow \prod_{i=1}^{n} \sigma_{u_i}$, and returns $\sigma_T \leftarrow (\sigma'_T, \sigma_{u_i}, \Theta_T)$ as the signature for T, where $\Theta_T \leftarrow \{(\theta_{u_i}, \theta_{p_{u_i}}) | u_i \in V\}$ is the set of secure names of nodes and their respective parents in T.

- Verify(y_s, T, σ_T): The algorithm is processed by the SP. It takes the signer's public key y_s, a tree $T = (V, E)$ and its signature σ_T as input. It proceeds as follows:
  1. It parses σ_T as $(\sigma'_T, \sigma_{u_i}, \Theta_T)$.
  2. It computes $h_{u_i} \leftarrow H(\theta_{p_{u_i}} || \theta_{u_i} || c_{u_i})$ for each $u_i \in V$, and ensures $\hat{e}(g_2, \sigma'_T) = \hat{e}(\prod_{i=1}^{n} h_{u_i}, y_s)$ holds and rejects otherwise.
  3. It verifies the structural relationship of T: (i) Let u_i be the parent of u_j. It ensures $\theta_{u_i} = \theta_{p_{u_j}}$ holds and rejects otherwise. (ii) Let u_j and u_k are children of u_i, and let $u_j \prec u_k$. It ensures $u_j \prec u_k$ holds and rejects otherwise by using NaVerify.
- Redact$(y_s, T, \sigma_T, T'_\delta)$: The SP executes this algorithm to obtain a signature for the redacted tree. The algorithm takes as input the signer's public key y_s, a tree T and its signature σ_T, and a subtree T'_δ to be removed. Let $T_\delta = (V_\delta, E_\delta)$ be the redacted tree. To cut a subtree $T'_\delta = (V'_\delta, E'_\delta)$ from T and generate a signature σ_{T_δ} for T_δ, it proceeds as follows:
  1. It parses σ_T as $(\sigma'_T, \sigma_{u_i}, \Theta_T)$.
  2. If $T'_\delta = (V'_\delta, E'_\delta) \nsubseteq T = (V, E)$, it returns $\perp$ to indicate failure.
  3. Let $\Theta_{T_\delta} \leftarrow \{(\theta_{u_i}, \theta_{p_{u_i}}) | u_i \in V_\delta\}$ be the set of secure names of nodes and their respective parents in T_δ.
  4. It cuts the subtree $T'_\delta = (V'_\delta, E'_\delta)$ from T and computes $\sigma'_{T_\delta} \leftarrow \prod_{i=1}^{k} \sigma_{u_i}$.
  5. It returns $\sigma_{T_\delta} \leftarrow (\sigma'_{T_\delta}, \Theta_{T_\delta})$ as the signature for T_δ.
- DeSign$(y_s, y_v, T_\delta, \sigma_{T_\delta})$: The SP uses this algorithm to generate a DV signature for the redacted tree. The algorithm takes as input the signer's public key y_s, the verifier's public key y_v, a redacted tree T_δ and its signature σ_{T_δ}. It parses σ_{T_δ} as $(\sigma'_{T_\delta}, \Theta_{T_\delta})$, computes $\sigma_{T_\delta}^{ds'} \leftarrow \hat{e}(y_v, \sigma'_{T_\delta})$, and returns $\sigma_{T_\delta}^{ds} \leftarrow (\sigma_{T_\delta}^{ds'}, \Theta_{T_\delta})$ as the DV signature for T_δ.
- DeVerify$(y_s, x_v, T_\delta, \sigma_{T_\delta}^{ds})$: The algorithm is operated by the DV. It takes as input the signer's public key y_s, the DV's secret key x_v, a redacted tree T_δ and its DV signature $\sigma_{T_\delta}^{ds}$ and operates as follows:
  1. It parses $\sigma_{T_\delta}^{ds}$ as $(\sigma_{T_\delta}^{ds'}, \Theta_{T_\delta})$.
  2. It computes $h_{u_i} \leftarrow H(\theta_{p_{u_i}} || \theta_{u_i} || c_{u_i})$ for each $u_i \in V_\delta$, computes $\sigma_{T_\delta}^{\bar{ds}} \leftarrow \hat{e}({y_s}^{x_v}, \prod_{i=1}^{k} h_{u_i})$, and ensures $\sigma_{T_\delta}^{ds'} = \sigma_{T_\delta}^{\bar{ds}}$ holds and rejects otherwise.
  3. It operates as the step 3 in Verify to check the structural relationship of T_δ.

Remark 2. Following previous work on RSSs for trees, the Redact is directly designed for deriving a signature for the retained subtree. This might be a limitation when the output is a forest. One possible approach is to slightly modify the Sign: It computes $H(\theta_{u_i}||\theta_{u_j})$ for all edges $e(u_i, u_j)$ in T, signs these values, and sets them as part of our signature. In this way, the secure name of a parent node is no need to be included in the computation of the integrity verifier of a node u_i, because we directly sign the edge relationships. That is, h_{u_i} can be computed as $H(\theta_{u_i}||c_{u_i})$. However, this will sacrifice some performance for both the signing and verification of our scheme.

Consistency of DV-PPAT: Obviously, there are two consistency properties achieved by our proposed DV-PPAT scheme.

- Verify Consistency of Sign: To demonstrate the Verify consistency property of Sign, we note that if $\sigma_T \stackrel{def}{=} \prod_{i=1}^{n} \sigma_{u_i}$, and $\sigma_{u_i} \stackrel{def}{=} (h_{u_i})^{x_s}$, then

$$\hat{e}(g_2, \sigma'_T) = \hat{e}(g_2, \prod_{i=1}^{n} \sigma_{u_i}) = \hat{e}(g_2, \prod_{i=1}^{n} (h_{u_i})^{x_s})$$
$$= \hat{e}({g_2}^{x_s}, \prod_{i=1}^{n} h_{u_i}) = \hat{e}(y_s, \prod_{i=1}^{n} h_{u_i}).$$

- DeVerify Consistency of DeSign: To demonstrate the DeVerify consistency property of DeSign, we note that if $\sigma_{T_\delta}^{ds'} \stackrel{def}{=} \hat{e}(y_v, \sigma'_{T_\delta})$, $\sigma'_{T_\delta} \stackrel{def}{=} \prod_{i=1}^{k} \sigma_{u_i}$, $\sigma_{u_i} \stackrel{def}{=} (h_{u_i})^{x_s}$, and $\sigma_{T_\delta}^{\bar{ds}} \stackrel{def}{=} \hat{e}({y_s}^{x_v}, \prod_{i=1}^{k} h_{u_i})$, then

$$\sigma_{T_\delta}^{ds'} = \hat{e}(y_v, \sigma'_{T_\delta}) = \hat{e}(y_v, \prod_{i=1}^{k} \sigma_{u_i}) = \hat{e}({g_2}^{x_v}, \prod_{i=1}^{k} (h_{u_i})^{x_s})$$
$$= \hat{e}({g_2}^{x_s x_v}, \prod_{i=1}^{k} h_{u_i}) = \hat{e}({y_s}^{x_v}, \prod_{i=1}^{k} h_{u_i}) = \sigma_{T_\delta}^{\bar{ds}}.$$

5.1 Security Results

We analyze the security of our DV-PPAT scheme in this section.

Theorem 1. (Unforgeability of DV-PPAT). *Let $\mathcal{A}$ be a p.p.t. forger who can forge a valid signature of our scheme in the RO model with success probability* $\mathsf{Adv}_{\mathcal{A},\mathsf{DV\text{-}PPAT}}^{uf-cma}(1^\lambda)$ *under the security parameter 1^λ. In some polynomial time, he can make at most q_H hash queries to $H(\cdot)$ and q_S signing queries, then there exists another adversary $\mathcal{B}$ who can utilize $\mathcal{A}$ to solve an instance of* BDH *problem in $(\mathbb{G}_1, \mathbb{G}_2)$ with the success probability* $\mathsf{Adv}_{\mathcal{B}}^{\mathrm{BDH}}(1^\lambda) \geq 1/e(nq_S + n) \cdot \mathsf{Adv}_{\mathcal{A},\mathsf{DV\text{-}PPAT}}^{uf-cma}(1^\lambda)$*, where e is the base of natural logarithms.*

Proof. The proof is presented in Appendix A.

Theorem 2. (Transparency of DV-PPAT). *The proposed* DV-PPAT *is transparent against an adaptive chosen message p.p.t. adversary $\mathcal{D}_1$.*

Proof. We will show that the DV-PPAT is transparent via an experiment as defined in the Transparency Experiment 4.2.2, which is carried out by the interaction between an adaptive chosen message p.p.t. adversary $\mathcal{D}_1$ and a challenger $\mathcal{C}$.

At the beginning, $\mathcal{C}$ runs $\mathsf{ParaG}(1^\lambda)$ to generate the common parameters $para$, and runs SigKG and VerKG to obtain the secret/public key pairs (x_s, y_s) and (x_v, y_v) for the signer and the DV respectively. $\mathcal{C}$ then sends $(para, y_s, x_v, y_v)$ to $\mathcal{D}_1$. Note that in $\mathcal{D}_1$'s view, all the distributions are equal to the real construction. The subsequent experimental processes, i.e., Query Phase 1, Challenge, Query Phase 2, and Output Phase, are the same as the per defined experiment, thus omitted here for simplicity. Recall that $\mathcal{D}_1$'s goal is to decide whether a given signature σ_{T_0} for tree T_0 is directly generated by Sign or obtained by Redact.

Observe that the signing algorithm Sign in our scheme firstly computes candidate signatures for all nodes u_i in a tree and then compresses them into a single signature for the tree. This signing process is similar to generating an aggregate signature [1]. Also, note that our scheme deploys an underlying SNS proposed by Kundu et al. in [11] as a primitive; the scheme is efficient and proven to be name-transparent in the RO model. In SNS, random numbers are assigned to the secure names of u_i in T_c, where c is chosen uniformly and randomly from $\{0, 1\}$. These properties ensure that our Sign generates a uniformly distributed aggregate signature for T_c. Besides, deleting a random number from a uniformly distributed aggregate through the Redact will result in a uniformly distributed signature again. In such a case, $\mathcal{D}_1$ cannot output his guess for c better than at random, hence the probability for $c' = c$ is infinitely close to 1/2. In addition, if the redacted tree would have been signed directly, the distributions are still uniform, and $\mathcal{D}_1$ can also not output his guess $c' = c$ with a probability non-negligibly larger than 1/2. Therefore, in the information-theoretical sense, we have $\mathsf{Adv}^{euf-cma}_{\mathcal{D}_1,\mathsf{DV-PPAT}}(1^\lambda) = |\Pr[c' = c] - 1/2| = \xi$. □

Theorem 3. (Non-transferability of DV-PPAT). *Our* DV-PPAT *scheme is non-transferable against an adaptive chosen message p.p.t. adversary* $\mathcal{D}_2$.

Proof. We will show that our DV-PPAT scheme is perfectly non-transferable via an experiment as defined in the Non-transferability Experiment 4.2.3. The experiment is carried out by the interaction between an adaptive chosen message p.p.t. adversary $\mathcal{D}_2$ and a challenger $\mathcal{C}$.

At the beginning, $\mathcal{C}$ uses $\mathsf{ParaG}(1^\lambda)$ to generate the common parameters $para$, and runs SigKG and VerKG to produce the secret/public key pairs (x_s, y_s) and (x_v, y_v) for the signer and the DV respectively. $\mathcal{C}$ then sends $(para, y_s, x_v, y_v)$ to $\mathcal{D}_2$. Note that in $\mathcal{D}_2$'s view, all the distributions are equal to the real construction. The subsequent experimental processes, i.e., Query Phase 1, Challenge, Query Phase 2, and Output Phase, are the same as the per defined experiment, thus omitted here for simplicity. Recall that $\mathcal{D}_2$'s goal is to decide whether a given DV signature $\sigma^{ds}_{T_\delta}$ for tree T_δ is directly generated by the signer or the DV.

Observe that the DeVerify Consistency of DeSign in the proposed scheme ensures that the signature $\sigma^{ds}_{T_\delta}$ generated by DeSign is computational indistinguishable from the signature $\sigma_{T_\delta}^{\bar{ds}}$ generated by DeVerify, hence $\Pr[\sigma_{T_\delta}^{ds} = \sigma_{T_\delta}^{\bar{ds}}] = 1$. That is, $\mathcal{D}_2$ can also not output his guess $c' = c$ with a probability non-negligibly larger than 1/2. Therefore, in the information-theoretical sense, we have $\mathsf{Adv}_{\mathcal{D}_2,\mathsf{DV-PPAT}}^{euf-cma}(1^\lambda) = |\Pr[c' = c] - 1/2| = \xi$. □

6 Performance Evaluation

This section evaluates the practical efficiency of our scheme.

Comparison of Computational Costs. Let n and k be the number of nodes in the original tree T and the redacted tree T_δ respectively. Let notations t_m, t_e, t_d, t_i, t_h, and t_p be the time cost for a single modular multiplication, exponentiation, division, inversion, map-to-point hash, and pairing operations respectively. Both our scheme and the schemes in [12,16] are using the underlying SNS scheme which mainly involves some general hash operations and XOR operations, thus omitted. We summarize the evaluation of DV-PPAT and other related schemes [12,16] in the following Table 1.

Table 1. Comparison of computational costs

Scheme	Sign	Verify	Redact	DeSign	DeVerify
[12]	$O(n(t_e+t_m))$	$O(k(t_m)+t_e)$	$O(nt_m)$	\	\
[16]	$O(n(t_h+t_e+t_m)+t_p)$	$O(n(t_h+t_e+t_m+t_p))$	$O(n(t_h+t_m+t_p)+t_d)$	\	\
Our	$O(n(t_h+t_e+t_m))$	$O(n(t_h+t_m)+t_p)$	$O(kt_m)$	$O(t_p)$	$O(k(t_h+t_m)+t_e+t_p)$

We also built an experiment to roughly compare the time cost of our DV-PPAT with the other pairing-based scheme in [16]. We firstly quantify the time cost of serval cryptographic operations by using the PBC library (https://crypto.stanford.edu/pbc/, version 0.5.14) under the Ubuntu 18.04.4 LTS operating system with C programming language. Other information for the experiment environment are: Intel(R) Core(TM) $i5-8250$U CPU @ 1.60 GHz and 2.7 GB of RAM. As stated in [4], any Type 2 scheme can be converted to a Type 3 setting without loss of functionality, security, or efficiency. For the sake of simplicity, our tests use the MNT224 curve (providing an 96-bit security level) for pairings since it is the best Type 3 curve in PBC internals. Table 2 shows the average execution time of various operations after running 10 times. Due to space limits, we simply evaluate the time costs when $n = 1000, k = 500$ and $n = 2000, k = 1000$ respectively. The final result of our approximate comparison is presented in Table 3.

Table 2. Average time cost for serval cryptographic operations (in ms)

Operation	t_h	t_e	t_m	t_d	t_p
Time	0.123	8.074	0.023	0.027	9.375

Table 3. Comparison of time costs (in s)

Scheme		Sign	Verify	Redact	DeSign	DeVerify
$n = 1000$	[16]	16.343	17.641	4.761	\	\
$k = 500$	Our	8.220	0.165	0.011	0.009	0.090
$n = 2000$	[16]	32.660	35.236	9.521	\	\
$k = 1000$	Our	16.440	0.311	0.023	0.009	0.163

Table 4. Comparison of features

Scheme	Secret key length	Signature for T	Signature for T_δ	Complexity Problem	Structural Integrity	Non-leaves Redaction	Non-transferability Privacy
Kundu et al. [12]	≈ 1024-bit	$(2n+2)\|N\|$ ≈ 2050048-bit	$(2k+2)\|N\|$ ≈ 1026048-bit	**RSA**	yes	yes	no
Liu et al. [16]	≈ 160-bit	$(3n+2)\|\mathbb{G}_1\|$ ≈ 480320-bit	$(3k+2)\|\mathbb{G}_T\|$ ≈ 1441920-bit	**co-CDH**	yes	yes	no
Our scheme	≈ 160-bit	$(3n+1)\|\mathbb{G}_1\|$ ≈ 480160-bit	$(2k+1)\|\mathbb{G}_T\|$ ≈ 960960-bit	BDH	yes	yes	yes

As shown in these tables, the computation time of these two schemes increases linearly with the values of n and k, but overall, the time cost of our scheme is smaller than the scheme in [16]. Note that pairing operation is the most time-consuming operation of all operations. As we can see, to generate a DV signature $\sigma_{T_\delta}^{ds}$ for the redacted tree T_δ, the SP only needs one pairing operation. This is desirable since our DV-PPAT scheme can address privacy issues in the dissemination of tree-structured data without sacrificing much performance.

Comparison of Features. We also compare some features of the DV-PPAT with other related schemes [12,16] in terms of lengths of secret keys and signatures, the complexity problem, and functionality in Table 4. We use $|\mathbb{G}_1|$, $|\mathbb{G}_T|$, and $|N|$ to denote the length of groups $\mathbb{G}_1$, $\mathbb{G}_T$, and the RSA modulus N respectively. Recall that the 1024-bit key of RSA provides an 80-bit security level. To make a fair comparison, we here use the MNT160 curve (with embedding degree 6), which also provides an 80-bit security level. Based on this curve, the approximate number of bits to optimally represent an element of the group $\mathbb{G}_1$ and $\mathbb{G}_T$ are 160-bit and 960-bit respectively [6]. The table also shows the bit length of signatures for T and T_δ respectively when $n = 1000$ and $k = 500$.

As we can see, our signature size for T is similar to the scheme in [16], and it is about 23.4% of that of the scheme in [12]. In the meantime, our signature size for T_δ is about 66.6% of that of the scheme in [16] and 93.7% of that of the scheme in [12]. That is, our scheme has a shorter key length and signature size. It therefore saves substantial communication costs than others. Moreover, our scheme is the only one that can achieve the non-transferability privacy which provides stronger privacy protection.

In terms of security and efficiency, from the above analysis, we can see that our scheme is more desirable than related works for tree-structured data sharing in outsourced environments.

7 Conclusions

In this paper, we explore the issue of integrity and authenticity verification and privacy protection in the outsourced database model associated with the dissemination of authenticated tree-structured health data. To address this issue, we introduced a scheme DV-PPAT which allows the SP to share part of the authenticated tree-structured data to users on behalf of the data owner. Our scheme not only ensures the user can verify the integrity and authenticity of his queried results without disclosing any privacy of the data owner but also prevents the user from leaking the query results to any external third party. We prove that our scheme satisfies three privacy-preserving properties and is unforgeable under adaptive chosen message attack in the RO model, assuming that the BDH problem is hard. Finally, the performance evaluation demonstrates that our privacy-preserving authentication scheme is an efficient and practical solution for trees with designated verification in outsourced healthcare data sharing.

The problem of constructing a practical DV-PPAT scheme in multi-user setting is an interesting topic for future work.

Acknowledgment. We have no conflicts of interest to this work. We would like to thank the anonymous reviewers for their valuable comments.

Appendix A

Proof of Theorem 1. The proof is similar to [16,19]. Given $w \in \mathbb{G}_1$ and $g_2, u, v \in \mathbb{G}_2$, where $u = {g_2}^a, v = {g_2}^b$ and $w = {g_1}^c$ for some unknown $a, b, c \in \mathbb{Z}_q$, we will reveal how the adversary $\mathcal{B}$ can utilize the forger $\mathcal{A}$ to obtain the value $\hat{e}(g_1, g_2)^{abc}$.

- Setup Phase: $\mathcal{B}$ randomly chooses $r_1, r_2 \xleftarrow{\$} \mathbb{Z}_q$, and sets $y_s = u \cdot {g_2}^{r_1} \in \mathbb{G}_2$ and $y_v = v \cdot {g_2}^{r_2} \in \mathbb{G}_2$ as the signer's public key and the DV's public key respectively. $\mathcal{B}$ returns (g_2, y_s, y_v) to $\mathcal{A}$.
- Hash Queries: In this process, $\mathcal{A}$ has access to a hash oracle $H(\cdot)$ at any time. Note that $\mathcal{B}$ will act the oracle in our proof. To respond to $\mathcal{A}$'s queries, $\mathcal{B}$ maintains a list of tuples $L(m, h, d, c)$ (initially, $L(\cdot, \cdot, \cdot, \cdot) = \phi$) as explained below. Each time when $\mathcal{A}$ queries the hash oracle $H(\cdot)$ at a point $m \in \{0, 1\}^*$, $\mathcal{B}$ responds as the following:
  1. If m already exists in the L-list in some tuple (m_i, h_i, d_i, c_i) then $\mathcal{B}$ looks up on the list and responds with $H(m_i) = h_i \in \mathbb{G}_1$.
  2. Otherwise, $\mathcal{B}$ randomly flips a coin $c_i \in \{0, 1\}$, so that $\Pr[c = 0] = 1/(nq_S + n)$.

3. $\mathcal{B}$ randomly chooses $d_i \xleftarrow{\$} \mathbb{Z}_q$. If $c_i = 0$ holds, he computes $h_i \leftarrow w_i \cdot \psi(g_2)^{d_i} \in \mathbb{G}_1$; otherwise, he computes $h_i \leftarrow \psi(g_2)^{d_i} \in \mathbb{G}_1$.
4. $\mathcal{B}$ adds the item (m_i, h_i, d_i, c_i) into the L-list and answering $\mathcal{A}$'s query as $H(m_i) = h_i$.

Note that each time from the perspective of $\mathcal{A}$, h_i is uniform in $\mathbb{G}_2$ and hence its distribution is identical to the real construction.

- Signature Queries: Assume that a tree $T = (V, E)$ be a signing query requested by $\mathcal{A}$ under the signer's public key y_s. To respond to the query, $\mathcal{B}$ does as follows:
  1. Similar to our Sign, $\mathcal{B}$ carries out a traversal on T and generates secure names θ_{u_i} and $\theta_{p_{u_i}}$ for each node $u_i \in V$ and its parent respectively.
  2. $\mathcal{B}$ operates as Hash Queries to obtain a $h_i \in \mathbb{G}_1$ such that $H(m_i) = h_i$. Here we assume that (m_i, h_i, d_i, c_i) be the item in L-list corresponding to each node u_i. If $c_i = 0$ holds, $\mathcal{B}$ returns $\perp$ to indicate failure and terminates.
  3. If $c_i = 1$ for all $u_i \in V$ holds and hence $h_i \leftarrow \psi(g_2)^{d_i} \in \mathbb{G}_1$, $\mathcal{B}$ defines $\sigma_i = \psi(u)^{d_i} \cdot \psi(g_2)^{r_1 d_i} \in \mathbb{G}_1$. Observe that $\sigma_i = {h_i}^{a+r_1}$ and hence that σ_i is a valid signature on m_i under the public key $y_s = {g_2}^{a+r_1}$.
  4. $\mathcal{B}$ computes $\sigma'_T = \prod_{i=1}^{n} \sigma_i$ and returns $\sigma_T \leftarrow (\sigma'_T, \Theta_T)$ to $\mathcal{A}$, where $\Theta_T \leftarrow \{(\theta_{u_i}, \theta_{p_{u_i}}) | u_i \in V\}$.
- Output Phase: Eventually, $\mathcal{A}$ halts. $\mathcal{A}$ either outputs $\perp$ to indicate failure or forges a valid DV signature $\sigma_{T_\delta}^{ds'*}$ for a tree $T_\delta^* = (V_\delta^*, E_\delta^*)$ such that no node $u_i \in V_\delta^*$ $(1 \leq i \leq k)$ has been queried during the process of Signature Queries. Note that if there is no item (m_i, h_i, d_i, c_i) in the L-list containing nodes in V_δ^*, then $\mathcal{B}$ can easily operate as the Hash Queries to obtain these corresponding items by himself. Again, we stress that $\sigma_{T_\delta}^{ds'*}$ must be a valid signature; otherwise, $\mathcal{B}$ returns $\perp$ to indicate failure and terminates.

  $\mathcal{B}$ will not abort when $c_1 = 0$ and $c_i = 1$ $(2 \leq i \leq k)$. If $c_1 = 0$, we have $h_1 = w \cdot \psi(g_2)^{d_1}$. For $2 \leq i \leq k$, since $c_i = 1$, we have $h_i = \psi(g_2)^{d_i}$. Note that the signature $\sigma_{T_\delta}^{ds'*}$ must be successful verified by the DeVerify. That is, the equation $\sigma_{T_\delta}^{ds'*} = \hat{e}({y_s}^{x_v}, \prod_{i=1}^{k} h_i)$ holds. $\mathcal{B}$, therefore, computes

$$\begin{aligned}\sigma_{T_\delta}^{ds'*} &= \hat{e}({y_s}^{x_v}, h_1) \cdot \hat{e}({y_s}^{x_v}, \prod_{i=2}^{k} h_i) = \hat{e}({y_s}^{x_v}, w \cdot \psi(g_2)^{d_1}) \cdot \hat{e}({y_s}^{x_v}, \prod_{i=2}^{k} \psi(g_2)^{d_i}) \\ &= \hat{e}({y_s}^{x_v}, w \cdot {g_1}^{d_1}) \cdot \hat{e}({y_s}^{x_v}, \prod_{i=2}^{k} {g_1}^{d_i}).\end{aligned}$$

  $\mathcal{B}$ now constructs a value $\Delta = \{\hat{e}({y_s}^{x_v}, \prod_{i=2}^{k} {g_1}^{d_i}) \cdot \hat{e}(w, u^{r_2} \cdot v^{r_1} \cdot {g_2}^{r_1 r_2}) \cdot \hat{e}(u^{d_1}, \psi(y_v)) \cdot \hat{e}(v \cdot {g_2}^{r_2}, \psi(g_2)^{d_1 r_1})\}^{-1}$ and computes the required value

$\hat{e}(g_1, g_2)^{abc}$ as $\sigma_{T_\delta}^{ds'^*} \cdot \Delta$. This can be easily verified because:

$$\begin{aligned}\sigma_{T_\delta}^{ds'^*} \cdot \Delta =& \hat{e}({y_s}^{x_v}, w \cdot {g_1}^{d_1}) \cdot \hat{e}({y_s}^{x_v}, \prod_{i=2}^{k} {g_1}^{d_i}) \cdot \Delta \\ =& \hat{e}({y_s}^{x_v}, w \cdot {g_1}^{d_1}) \cdot \{\hat{e}(w, u^{r_2} \cdot v^{r_1} \cdot {g_2}^{r_1 r_2}) \cdot \hat{e}(u^{d_1}, \\ & \psi(y_v)) \cdot \hat{e}(v \cdot {g_2}^{r_2}, \psi(g_2)^{d_1 r_1})\}^{-1} \\ =& \hat{e}(g_1, g_2)^{abc}.\end{aligned}$$

This completes the description of $\mathcal{B}$. The running time needed for $\mathcal{B}$ consists of three parts, i.e., the running time needed for $\mathcal{A}$, $\mathcal{B}$'s responds to Hash Queries and Signature Queries, and the time for computing the final BDH solution.

We now analyze $\mathcal{B}$'s probability in solving the given instance of BDH problem in $(\mathbb{G}_1, \mathbb{G}_2)$ with the success probability $\mathsf{Adv}_{\mathcal{B}}^{\mathrm{BDH}}(1^\lambda)$. $\mathcal{B}$ will succeed if the following three events occur: (1) $\mathcal{B}$ does not abort in the Signature Queries phase (remark as Ev_1), (2) $\mathcal{A}$ successfully forges a valid DV signature $\sigma_{T_\delta}^{ds'^*}$ for tree $T_\delta^* = (V_\delta^*, E_\delta^*)$ (remark as Ev_2), and (3) Event Ev_2 occurs, and $c_1 = 0$ and $c_i = 1$ $(2 \leq i \leq k)$, where c_i is the c-component of the item containing m_i in the L-list (remark as Ev_1). Consequently, the success probability for $\mathcal{B}$ is $\mathsf{Adv}_{\mathcal{B}}^{\mathrm{BDH}}(1^\lambda)= \Pr[\mathrm{Ev}_1 \wedge \mathrm{Ev}_3]$. It further can be decomposed as $\Pr[\mathrm{Ev}_1 \wedge \mathrm{Ev}_3] = \Pr[\mathrm{Ev}_1] \cdot \Pr[\mathrm{Ev}_2|\mathrm{Ev}_1] \cdot \Pr[\mathrm{Ev}_3|\mathrm{Ev}_1 \wedge \mathrm{Ev}_2]$.

W.l.o.g., we assume that $\mathcal{A}$ queries the hash oracle $H(\cdot)$ and the signature of each message only once. Because the c-component of the item in the L-list is independent of $\mathcal{A}$'s view; when $\mathcal{A}$ makes q_S signature queries, the probability of Ev_1 occurs is $\Pr[\mathrm{Ev}_1] \geq 1 - 1/(nq_S + n)^{nq_S}$. Recall that in $\mathcal{A}$'s view, all the settings in our simulation are identical to the real construction. Since $\mathcal{B}$ did not abort in the simulation, all his responses to $\mathcal{A}$'s queries are valid. That is, the probability of $\mathcal{A}$'s forgery output in our RO model is at least $\mathsf{Adv}_{\mathcal{A},\mathsf{DV-PPAT}}^{uf-cma}(1^\lambda)= \xi$. Therefore, we have $\Pr[\mathrm{Ev}_2|\mathrm{Ev}_1] \geq \xi$. Note that c_i $(1 \leq i \leq k)$ are all independent of each other. If the event Ev_1 and Ev_2 happen, and $\mathcal{A}$ generates his forgery in the case that $c_1 = 0$ and $c_i = 1$ $(2 \leq i \leq k)$, then the probability $\Pr[\mathrm{Ev}_3|\mathrm{Ev}_1 \wedge \mathrm{Ev}_2] \geq (1 - 1/(nq_S + n))^{n-1} \cdot 1/(nq_S + n)$. Clearly, we have

$$\begin{aligned}\mathsf{Adv}_{\mathcal{B}}^{\mathrm{BDH}}(1^\lambda) =& \Pr[\mathrm{Ev}_1 \wedge \mathrm{Ev}_3] = \Pr[\mathrm{Ev}_1] \cdot \Pr[\mathrm{Ev}_2|\mathrm{Ev}_1] \cdot \Pr[\mathrm{Ev}_3|\mathrm{Ev}_1 \wedge \mathrm{Ev}_2] \\ \geq& (1 - 1/(nq_S + n)^{nq_S}) \cdot \xi \cdot (1 - 1/(nq_S + n))^{n-1} \cdot \\ & 1/(nq_S + n) \geq 1/e(nq_S + n) \cdot \xi \\ =& 1/e(nq_S + n) \cdot \mathsf{Adv}_{\mathcal{A},\mathsf{DV-PPAT}}^{uf-cma}(1^\lambda),\end{aligned}$$

as required, and hence completes the proof. □

References

1. Boneh, D., Gentry, C., Lynn, B., Shacham, H.: Aggregate and verifiably encrypted signatures from bilinear maps. In: Biham, E. (ed.) EUROCRYPT 2003. LNCS, vol. 2656, pp. 416–432. Springer, Heidelberg (2003). https://doi.org/10.1007/3-540-39200-9_26

2. Brzuska, C., et al.: Redactable signatures for tree-structured data: definitions and constructions. In: Zhou, J., Yung, M. (eds.) ACNS 2010. LNCS, vol. 6123, pp. 87–104. Springer, Heidelberg (2010). https://doi.org/10.1007/978-3-642-13708-2_6
3. Chatterjee, S., Hankerson, D., Knapp, E., Menezes, A.: Comparing two pairing-based aggregate signature schemes. Des. Codes Crypt. **55**(2–3), 141–167 (2010)
4. Chatterjee, S., Menezes, A.: On cryptographic protocols employing asymmetric pairings - the role of Ψ revisited. Discret. Appl. Math. **159**(13), 1311–1322 (2011)
5. Derler, D., Krenn, S., Slamanig, D.: Signer-anonymous designated-verifier redactable signatures for cloud-based data sharing. In: Foresti, S., Persiano, G. (eds.) CANS 2016. LNCS, vol. 10052, pp. 211–227. Springer, Cham (2016). https://doi.org/10.1007/978-3-319-48965-0_13
6. Ferrara, A.L., Green, M., Hohenberger, S., Pedersen, M.Ø.: Practical short signature batch verification. In: Fischlin, M. (ed.) CT-RSA 2009. LNCS, vol. 5473, pp. 309–324. Springer, Heidelberg (2009). https://doi.org/10.1007/978-3-642-00862-7_21
7. Goodrich, M.T., Tamassia, R., Triandopoulos, N.: Efficient authenticated data structures for graph connectivity and geometric search problems. Algorithmica **60**(3), 505–552 (2011)
8. Groß, T.: Efficient certification and zero-knowledge proofs of knowledge on infrastructure topology graphs. In: CCSW 2014, pp. 69–80. ACM (2014)
9. Hachicha, M., Darmont, J.: A survey of XML tree patterns. IEEE Trans. Knowl. Data Eng. **25**(1), 29–46 (2013)
10. Johnson, R., Molnar, D., Song, D., Wagner, D.: Homomorphic signature schemes. In: Preneel, B. (ed.) CT-RSA 2002. LNCS, vol. 2271, pp. 244–262. Springer, Heidelberg (2002). https://doi.org/10.1007/3-540-45760-7_17
11. Kundu, A., Atallah, M.J., Bertino, E.: Efficient leakage-free authentication of trees, graphs and forests. IACR Cryptology ePrint Archive **2012**, 36 (2012)
12. Kundu, A., Atallah, M.J., Bertino, E.: Leakage-free redactable signatures. In: CODASPY 2012, pp. 307–316. ACM (2012)
13. Kundu, A., Bertino, E.: Structural signatures for tree data structures. Proc. VLDB Endow. **1**(1), 138–150 (2008)
14. Kundu, A., Bertino, E.: How to authenticate graphs without leaking. In: EDBT 2010, pp. 609–620. ACM (2010)
15. Kundu, A., Bertino, E.: Privacy-preserving authentication of trees and graphs. Int. J. Inf. Secur. **12**(6), 467–494 (2013). https://doi.org/10.1007/s10207-013-0198-5
16. Liu, J., Ma, J., Zhou, W., Xiang, Y., Huang, X.: Dissemination of authenticated tree-structured data with privacy protection and fine-grained control in outsourced databases. In: Lopez, J., Zhou, J., Soriano, M. (eds.) ESORICS 2018. LNCS, vol. 11099, pp. 167–186. Springer, Cham (2018). https://doi.org/10.1007/978-3-319-98989-1_9
17. de Meer, H., Pöhls, H.C., Posegga, J., Samelin, K.: Redactable signature schemes for trees with signer-controlled non-leaf-redactions. In: Obaidat, M.S., Filipe, J. (eds.) ICETE 2012. CCIS, vol. 455, pp. 155–171. Springer, Heidelberg (2014). https://doi.org/10.1007/978-3-662-44791-8_10
18. Merkle, R.C.: A certified digital signature. In: Brassard, G. (ed.) CRYPTO 1989. LNCS, vol. 435, pp. 218–238. Springer, New York (1990). https://doi.org/10.1007/0-387-34805-0_21
19. Mihara, A., Tanaka, K.: Universal designated-verifier signature with aggregation. In: ICITA 2005, pp. 514–519. IEEE (2005)

20. Mykletun, E., Narasimha, M., Tsudik, G.: Signature bouquets: immutability for aggregated/condensed signatures. In: Samarati, P., Ryan, P., Gollmann, D., Molva, R. (eds.) ESORICS 2004. LNCS, vol. 3193, pp. 160–176. Springer, Heidelberg (2004). https://doi.org/10.1007/978-3-540-30108-0_10
21. Samelin, K., Pöhls, H.C., Bilzhause, A., Posegga, J., de Meer, H.: On structural signatures for tree data structures. In: Bao, F., Samarati, P., Zhou, J. (eds.) ACNS 2012. LNCS, vol. 7341, pp. 171–187. Springer, Heidelberg (2012). https://doi.org/10.1007/978-3-642-31284-7_11
22. Samelin, K., Pöhls, H.C., Bilzhause, A., Posegga, J., de Meer, H.: Redactable signatures for independent removal of structure and content. In: Ryan, M.D., Smyth, B., Wang, G. (eds.) ISPEC 2012. LNCS, vol. 7232, pp. 17–33. Springer, Heidelberg (2012). https://doi.org/10.1007/978-3-642-29101-2_2
23. Steinfeld, R., Bull, L., Wang, H., Pieprzyk, J.: Universal designated-verifier signatures. In: Laih, C.-S. (ed.) ASIACRYPT 2003. LNCS, vol. 2894, pp. 523–542. Springer, Heidelberg (2003). https://doi.org/10.1007/978-3-540-40061-5_33
24. Uzunkol, O., Kiraz, M.S.: Still wrong use of pairings in cryptography. Appl. Math. Comput. **333**, 467–479 (2018)
25. Wang, J., Chen, X., Huang, X., You, I., Xiang, Y.: Verifiable auditing for outsourced database in cloud computing. IEEE Trans. Comput. **64**(11), 3293–3303 (2015)
26. Zhu, F., Wu, W., Zhang, Y., Chen, X.: Privacy-preserving authentication for general directed graphs in industrial IoT. Inf. Sci. **502**, 218–228 (2019)
27. Zhu, F., Zhang, Y., Lin, C., Wu, W., Meng, R.: A universal designated multi-verifier transitive signature scheme. In: Chen, X., Lin, D., Yung, M. (eds.) Inscrypt 2017. LNCS, vol. 10726, pp. 180–195. Springer, Cham (2018). https://doi.org/10.1007/978-3-319-75160-3_12

Encryption Schemes and NIZKs

Semi-Adaptively Secure Offline Witness Encryption from Puncturable Witness PRF

Tapas Pal([✉]) and Ratna Dutta

Department of Mathematics, Indian Institute of Technology Kharagpur, Kharagpur 721302, India
tapas.pal@iitkgp.ac.in, ratna@maths.iitkgp.ernet.in

Abstract. In this work, we introduce the notion of *puncturable witness pseudorandom function* (pWPRF) which is a stronger variant of WPRF proposed by Zhandry, TCC 2016. The punctured technique is similar to what we have seen for puncturable PRFs and is capable of extending the applications of WPRF. Specifically, we construct a *semi-adaptively* secure *offline witness encryption* (OWE) scheme using a pWPRF, an indistinguishability obfuscation ($i\mathcal{O}$) and a symmetric-key encryption (SKE), which enables us to encrypt messages along with NP statements. We show that replacing $i\mathcal{O}$ with extractability obfuscation, the OWE turns out to be an *extractable offline witness encryption* scheme. To gain finer control over data, we further demonstrate how to convert our OWEs into *offline functional witness encryption* (OFWE) and *extractable* OFWE. All of our OWEs and OFWEs produce an optimal size ciphertext, in particular, encryption of a message is as small as the size of the message plus the security parameter multiplied with a constant, which is optimal for any public-key encryption scheme. On the other hand, in any previous OWE, the size of a ciphertext increases polynomially with the size of messages. Finally, we show that the WPRF of Pal et al. (ACISP 2019) can be extended to a pWPRF and an *extractable* pWPRF.

Keywords: Puncturable witness pseudorandom function · Offline witness encryption · Offline functional witness encryption · Obfuscation

1 Introduction

Witness Pseudorandom Function. The purpose of a pseudorandom function is to generate a pseudorandom value for an input $x \in \mathcal{X}$ using a secret-key. Zhandry [26] proposed an enhanced primitive called *witness pseudorandom function* (WPRF) which enables us to produce pseudorandom values corresponding to statements of an NP language L with a relation $R : \mathcal{X} \times \mathcal{W} \to \{0, 1\}$. If $x \in L$ then there exists a witness $w \in \mathcal{W}$ such that $R(x, w) = 1$, otherwise R maps to 0. In the setup of WPRF, we generate two keys: a secret function key fk and a public evaluation key ek. To compute a pseudorandom value $y \in \mathcal{Y}$ corresponding to

K. Nguyen et al. (Eds.): ProvSec 2020, LNCS 12505, pp. 169–189, 2020.
https://doi.org/10.1007/978-3-030-62576-4_9

a statement $x \in \mathcal{X}$, we use the secret function key fk. The same pseudorandom value y can only be recovered using the public evaluation key ek if we have a witness w such that $R(x, w) = 1$. The security of pseudorandomness is ensured by the fact that y is completely uniform over $\mathcal{Y}$ if $x \notin L$. In *extractable* WPRF, we relax the requirement by allowing x to be in L. However, in such a scenario, if an adversary can distinguish the honestly computed y from a uniformly chosen element of $\mathcal{Y}$ then we can extract a valid witness of x using an efficient extractor.

A list of cryptographic primitives have been realized from WPRF in [26] such as multiparty non-interactive key exchange without trusted setup, poly-many hardcore bits for one-way functions and secret sharing for monotone NP languages. More interestingly, WPRF directly implies a modern primitive called witness encryption (WE) [18] which encrypts messages with respect to a NP statement and a valid witness for the statement is capable of decrypting the ciphertext to the original message. Furthermore, one can construct a more refined variant of WE, termed as reusable WE [26], using WPRF. The main goal of reusable WE was to make the encryption algorithm relatively efficient and ciphertext size *optimal*, besides it provides security in chosen ciphertext attack model. On the other hand, extractable WPRF was used to build a fully distributed broadcast encryption [26] where the size of secret-keys, public-keys and ciphertexts are all poly-logarithmic in the number of users.

Our Contribution. Inspired by the applications of WPRF in [26], we are keen to build more advanced primitives from WPRF. It is desirable to begin with a relatively closer primitive such as offline witness encryption (OWE) [1] maintaining the same encryption efficiency of the reusable WE. An OWE is more preferable over the normal WE because the computationally hard work is shifted from the encryption algorithm by introducing an additional setup phase. Unfortunately, WPRF does not immediately achieve OWE or offline functional WE [8]. Existing OWEs [1,12,24] do not have optimal ciphertext size as in reusable WE of [26].

In this work, we extend the applications of WPRF by introducing a puncturing technique akin to puncturable pseudorandom function (pPRF) [25]. In the security model of normal WPRF, an adversary $\mathcal{A}$ is given access to an oracle $\mathsf{F}(\mathsf{fk}, \cdot)$ which on input $x \in \mathcal{X}$ of $\mathcal{A}$'s choice outputs a pseudorandom value corresponding to x. Naturally, $\mathcal{A}$ is restricted to query on the challenge statement x^* which is not in L. In our setting, instead of giving access to $\mathsf{F}(\mathsf{fk}, \cdot)$, $\mathcal{A}$ is provided with a punctured key fk_{x^*} which enables $\mathcal{A}$ to learn the pseudorandom value corresponding to any x except x^*. The WPRF is secure if $\mathcal{A}$ is unable to distinguish $\mathsf{F}(\mathsf{fk}, x^*)$ from a random element. We call this variant of WPRF a *puncturable* WPRF (pWPRF). In *extractable* pWPRF, we allow x^* to be in L. In that case, there exists an extractor $\mathcal{E}$ which outputs a witness of x^* with high probability and the run time of $\mathcal{E}$ depends on the distinguishing advantage of $\mathcal{A}$ between $\mathsf{F}(\mathsf{fk}, x^*)$ and a random element. A pWPRF having this extractability property is called *puncturable witness-extractable pseudorandom function* (pWEPRF).

Both WE and WPRF have been realized using various assumptions on multilinear maps [18,26], but recent attacks on multilinear maps [11,13] introduce threats on the security of those schemes. We bring the punctured program technique of PRF [25] in case of WPRF. The main idea is to build two equivalent programs P and P′ where P uses the secret-key oblivious to the adversary and P′ uses a punctured key available to the adversary. An important tool in this setup is indistinguishability obfuscation ($i\mathcal{O}$) [16]. We build following primitives using the additional punctured technique of WPRF:

- We build a semi-adaptively secure OWE scheme (Sect. 3) using a pWPRF, an $i\mathcal{O}$, a pseudorandom generator (PRG) and a symmetric key encryption (SKE) scheme. Our OWE is the first to achieve optimal ciphertext-size, namely $|m|+\text{poly}(\lambda)$ where $|m|$ is the size of message and λ is the security parameter.
- Replacing $i\mathcal{O}$ with extractability obfuscation ($e\mathcal{O}$) [8], we convert the OWE into an *extractable* OWE (EOWE) in Sect. 3. The ciphertext-size remains the same which is optimal for any public-key encryption scheme.
- In a plain OWE, a user having a valid witness can learn the whole message. This all-or-nothing type encryption may not be sufficient for applications where we need fine-grained access control over the data. In such a scenario, *offline functional* WE (OFWE), introduced by Boyle et al. [8], can be utilized as the user having a valid witness can now learn a function of the message and witness. In this work, we show that our techniques of achieving OWE can be extended to realize semi-adaptively secure OFWE and selectively secure *extractable* OFWE schemes (Sect. 4).

Finally, we show that the WPRF of [24] satisfies our definition of pWPRF (Sect. 5). In particular, we can construct pWPRF using a pPRF and an $i\mathcal{O}$. Furthermore, a pWEPRF can be achieved by replacing the $i\mathcal{O}$ with an $e\mathcal{O}$. We emphasize the implausibility results of [9,17] on $e\mathcal{O}$ or extractable WE do not have any impact on our $e\mathcal{O}$-based constructions as the results can only be applied for circuits with specific auxiliary inputs.

Feasibility of $i\mathcal{O}$. A natural question is why we build cryptographic primitives based on $i\mathcal{O}$ which is not yet realized from standard assumptions. Recent attacks on multilinear maps bring cryptographers attention to find new techniques to build $i\mathcal{O}$. Bitansky and Vaikunthanathan [7] and Ananth and Jain [3] developed a transformation that achieves $i\mathcal{O}$ assuming just functional encryption. Achieving such functional encryptions from smaller constant degree multilinear maps and special pseudorandom generators with certain locality properties has been discussed in [5,22,23]. New ideas were formalized in [2,4] to construct $i\mathcal{O}$ from bilinear maps and specific pseudorandom tools that are conjectured to be secure.

Recently, a very interesting and simple approach is developed by Brakerski et al. [10] that utilizes fully-homomorphic encryption (FHE) schemes [19,20] to get full fledge $i\mathcal{O}$. In particular, they proposed a new primitive called split FHE and showed that split FHE is sufficient for constructing $i\mathcal{O}$. The transformation is provably secure and relies on (heuristic but) appropriately defined oracle model. Note that, split FHE can be realized from existing FHEs (based on learning with errors problem [19,20]) and linearly homomorphic encryption schemes (such as Damgård-Jurik encryption scheme based on decisional composite residues problem [14]). In the view of recent developments, it is believed that the community will arrive at a practical construction of $i\mathcal{O}$ in the near future. On the other hand, we note that all existing constructions of WPRF and OWE are either built from multilinear maps vulnerable to practical attacks or depend on $i\mathcal{O}$.

Related Works. Zhandry [26] constructed WPRF from subset-sum Diffie-Hellman assumption related to multilinear maps. Getting a pseudorandom value using an evaluation key is computationally expensive as one need to apply a multilinear map with linearity much larger than the size of the NP relation. On the other hand, we extend the $i\mathcal{O}$-based WPRF of [24] into a puncturable WPRF to enhance the field of application. We note that, although obfuscation itself is a powerful assumption, a wide range of functionalities, including the function classes required in this work, can be efficiently realized using Trusted Execution Environments (TEEs), Intel's Software Guard Extensions (SGXs) [6,15].

Abusalah et al. [1] introduced OWE with the purpose of making encryption much more efficient than the existing WEs. However, the OWE of [1] is selectively secure and the size of ciphertexts are not promising as it contains a simulation sound non-interactive zero-knowledge proof along with two (public-key) encryptions of the same message. OWE with semi-adaptive security is built in [12] relying on $i\mathcal{O}$, but the size of ciphertext is not as compact as one would have wanted for lightweight devices. Our OWEs deliver semi-adaptive security with an optimal size ciphertext similar to the reusable WE of [26].

2 Preliminaries

Notations. We denote $\lambda \in \mathbb{N}$ by a security parameter. If $x \in \{0,1\}^*$, then we denote $|x|$ by size of the string x. For any set S, the notation $x \leftarrow S$ denotes the process of sampling x uniformly at random from the set S. Let Algo be a probabilistic polynomial time (PPT) algorithm, then $y \leftarrow \mathsf{Algo}(x)$ denotes the execution of Algo with an input x using a fresh randomness and assign the output to y. If the randomness, say r, is provided externally then we denote this execution by $y \leftarrow \mathsf{Algo}(x; r)$. We call $\{\mathcal{C}_\lambda\}$ as a family of polynomial sized circuits if there exists a fixed polynomial p such that $|C| < \mathsf{p}(\lambda)$ for any $C \in \mathcal{C}_\lambda$. We say $\mathsf{negl}: \mathbb{N} \to \mathbb{R}$ be a negligible function of λ if for every positive polynomial p, there exists an integer $n_\mathsf{p} \in \mathbb{N}$ such that $\mathsf{negl}(\lambda) < 1/\mathsf{p}(\lambda)$ for all $n > n_\mathsf{p}$.

2.1 Pseudorandom Generator

Definition 1. A pseudorandom generator (PRG) is a deterministic polynomial time algorithm PRG that on input a seed $s \in \{0,1\}^\lambda$ outputs a string of length $\ell(\lambda)$ such that the following holds:

- *expansion*: For every λ it holds that $\ell(\lambda) > \lambda$.
- *pseudorandomness*: For all PPT adversary $\mathcal{A}$ and $s \leftarrow \{0,1\}^\lambda, r \leftarrow \{0,1\}^{\ell(\lambda)}$ there exists a negligible function negl such that

$$\mathsf{Adv}_{\mathcal{A}}^{\mathsf{PRG}}(\lambda) = |\Pr[\mathcal{A}(1^\lambda, \mathsf{PRG}(s)) = 1] - \Pr[\mathcal{A}(1^\lambda, r) = 1]| < \mathsf{negl}(\lambda).$$

2.2 Puncturable Pseudorandom Function

Definition 2. A puncturable pseudorandom function (pPRF) is a tuple of PPT algorithms (Gen, PuncKey, Eval, PuncEval) defined as follows:

- $\mathsf{K} \leftarrow \mathsf{Gen}(1^\lambda)$: on input a security parameter λ, returns a secret-key K.
- $\mathsf{K}_x \leftarrow \mathsf{PuncKey}(\mathsf{K}, x)$: returns K_x, a punctured key for an element $x \in \mathcal{X}$.
- $y \leftarrow \mathsf{Eval}(\mathsf{K}, x)$: returns a pseudorandom value $y \in \mathcal{Y}$ for $x \in \mathcal{X}$.
- $\mathsf{PuncEval}(\mathsf{K}_x, x') \in \mathcal{Y} \cup \{\perp\}$: on input a punctured key K_x and an element $x' \in \mathcal{X}$, returns a pseudorandom value $y \in \mathcal{Y}$ if $x \neq x'$, otherwise returns $\perp$.

We note that, each of the above algorithms except Gen is a deterministic algorithm. The pPRF is said to be correct if the following holds:

- *correctness*: For all distinct pair of elements $x, x' \in \mathcal{X}^2$, $\mathsf{K} \leftarrow \mathsf{Gen}(1^\lambda)$, we require that $\Pr[\mathsf{Eval}(\mathsf{K}, x') = \mathsf{PuncEval}(\mathsf{PuncKey}(\mathsf{K}, x), x')] = 1$.

Definition 3. A puncturable pseudorandom function (pPRF) is said to be secure (or preserves pseudorandomness at punctured point) if, for all PPT adversary $\mathcal{A}$ and any $x \in \mathcal{X}$, $\mathsf{K} \leftarrow \mathsf{Gen}(1^\lambda)$, $\mathsf{K}_x \leftarrow \mathsf{PuncKey}(\mathsf{K}, x)$ there exists a negligible function negl such that

$$\mathsf{Adv}_{\mathcal{A}}^{\mathsf{pPRF}}(\lambda) = |\Pr[\mathcal{A}(1^\lambda, \mathsf{K}_x, \mathsf{Eval}(\mathsf{K}, x)) = 1] - \Pr[\mathcal{A}(1^\lambda, \mathsf{K}_x, y \leftarrow \mathcal{Y}) = 1]| < \mathsf{negl}(\lambda).$$

2.3 Symmetric Key Encryption

Definition 4. A symmetric key encryption (SKE) scheme is a tuple of PPT algorithms (Gen, Enc, Dec) defined as follows:

- $\mathsf{K} \leftarrow \mathsf{Gen}(1^\lambda)$: on input a security parameter λ, returns a key K.
- $c \leftarrow \mathsf{Enc}(\mathsf{K}, m)$: a deterministic algorithm that returns c, an encryption of the message $m \in \mathcal{M}$.
- $\mathsf{Dec}(\mathsf{K}, c) \in \mathcal{M} \cup \{\perp\}$: a deterministic algorithm that decrypts the ciphertext c and returns a message $m \in \mathcal{M}$, or $\perp$ if it fails.

The SKE is said to be correct if the following holds:

- *correctness*: For all $m \in \mathcal{M}$ and $\mathsf{K} \leftarrow \mathsf{Gen}(1^\lambda)$, we require that

$$\Pr[\mathsf{Dec}(\mathsf{K}, \mathsf{Enc}(\mathsf{K}, m)) = m] = 1$$

Definition 5. A symmetric key encryption SKE is said to satisfy ciphertext indistinguishability (CIND) security if, for all PPT adversary $\mathcal{A}$ and any pair of equal length messages (m_0, m_1) there exists a negligible function negl such that

$$\mathsf{Adv}_{\mathcal{A}}^{\mathsf{SKE}}(\lambda) = |\Pr[\mathcal{A}(1^\lambda, \mathsf{Enc}(\mathsf{K}, m_0)) = 1] - \Pr[\mathcal{A}(1^\lambda, \mathsf{Enc}(\mathsf{K}, m_1)) = 1]| < \mathsf{negl}(\lambda)$$

$x^* \leftarrow \mathcal{A}(1^\lambda)$
$(\mathsf{fk}, \mathsf{ek}) \leftarrow \mathsf{Gen}(1^\lambda, R)$
$\mathsf{fk}_{x^*} \leftarrow \mathsf{PuncKey}(\mathsf{fk}, x^*)$
$y_0 \leftarrow \mathsf{F}(\mathsf{fk}, x^*),\ y_1 \leftarrow \mathcal{Y}$
$b \leftarrow \{0,1\}$
$b' \leftarrow \mathcal{A}(\mathsf{ek}, \mathsf{fk}_{x^*}, y_b)$
return 1 if $(b' = b) \wedge (x^* \notin L)$

Fig. 1. $\mathsf{Expt}_{\mathcal{A}}^{\mathsf{pWPRF},R}(1^\lambda)$

$x^* \leftarrow \mathcal{A}(1^\lambda)$
$(\mathsf{pp_e}, \mathsf{pp_d}) \leftarrow \mathsf{Setup}(1^\lambda, R)$
$(m_0, m_1) \leftarrow \mathcal{A}(\mathsf{pp_e}, \mathsf{pp_d})$
$b \leftarrow \{0,1\}$
$\mathsf{c} \leftarrow \mathsf{Enc}(\mathsf{pp_e}, x^*, m_b)$
$b' \leftarrow \mathcal{A}(\mathsf{c})$
return 1 if $(b' = b) \wedge (x^* \notin L) \wedge (|m_0| = |m_1|)$

Fig. 2. $\mathsf{Expt}_{\mathcal{A}}^{\mathsf{OWE},R}(1^\lambda)$

2.4 Puncturable Witness Pseudorandom Function

Definition 6. A puncturable witness pseudorandom function (pWPRF) for an NP language L with a relation R is a tuple of PPT algorithms (Gen, F, PuncKey, PuncF, Eval) defined as follows:

- $(\mathsf{fk}, \mathsf{ek}) \leftarrow \mathsf{Gen}(1^\lambda, R)$: on input a security parameter λ and a relation circuit $R : \mathcal{X} \times \mathcal{W} \rightarrow \{0,1\}$, returns a secret function key fk and a public evaluation key ek.
- $y \leftarrow \mathsf{F}(\mathsf{fk}, x)$: returns a pseudorandom value $y \in \mathcal{Y}$ for $x \in \mathcal{X}$.
- $\mathsf{fk}_x \leftarrow \mathsf{PuncKey}(\mathsf{fk}, x)$: returns fk_x, a punctured key for an element $x \in \mathcal{X}$.
- $\mathsf{PuncF}(\mathsf{fk}_x, x') \in \mathcal{Y} \cup \{\perp\}$: on input a punctured key fk_x and an element $x' \in \mathcal{X}$, returns a pseudorandom value $y \in \mathcal{Y}$ if $x \neq x'$, otherwise returns $\perp$.
- $\mathsf{Eval}(\mathsf{ek}, x, w) \in \mathcal{Y} \cup \{\perp\}$: on input an evaluation key ek, an element $x \in \mathcal{X}$ and a witness $w \in \mathcal{W}$, returns an element $y \in \mathcal{Y}$, or $\perp$ if it fails.

We note that, each of the above algorithms except Gen is a deterministic algorithm. The pWPRF is said to be correct if the following properties hold:

- *correctness of* Eval: For all $x \in \mathcal{X}, w \in \mathcal{W}$ and $(\mathsf{fk}, \mathsf{ek}) \leftarrow \mathsf{Gen}(1^\lambda, R)$, we require that

$$\mathsf{Eval}(\mathsf{ek}, x, w) = \begin{cases} \mathsf{F}(\mathsf{fk}, x) & \text{if } R(x, w) = 1 \\ \perp & \text{if } R(x, w) = 0 \end{cases}$$

- *correctness of* PuncF: For all distinct pair of elements $x, x' \in \mathcal{X}^2$ and $(\mathsf{fk}, \mathsf{ek}) \leftarrow \mathsf{Gen}(1^\lambda, R)$, we require that

$$\Pr[\mathsf{F}(\mathsf{fk}, x') = \mathsf{PuncF}(\mathsf{PuncKey}(\mathsf{fk}, x), x')] = 1.$$

Note that, our definition of pWPRF is crafted in a similar fashion like Sahai and Waters [25] formalized pPRF from PRF. Instead of providing an oracle to learn $\mathsf{F}(\mathsf{fk}, x')$ as in the case of normal WPRF given by Zhandry [26], the adversary $\mathcal{A}$ can use a punctured key fk_x to compute the pseudorandom value $\mathsf{F}(\mathsf{fk}, x')$ by itself if $x \neq x'$. The security experiment $\mathsf{Expt}_{\mathcal{A}}^{\mathsf{pWPRF},R}(1^\lambda)$ of our pWPRF is defined in Fig. 1. We consider the selective model for our applications. At the last step of the experiment, the challenger verifies that $x^* \notin L$ which means our challenger is not efficient. In this context, we note that WEs, OWEs and WPRFs are defined in the same way and the definition has been proven useful in developing many interesting cryptographic primitives [1,18,21,26].

Definition 7. A puncturable witness pseudorandom function pWPRF for an NP language L with a relation R is said to be selectively secure if, for all PPT adversary $\mathcal{A}$, there exists a negligible function negl such that

$$\mathsf{Adv}_{\mathcal{A}}^{\mathsf{pWPRF},R}(\lambda) = |\Pr[\mathsf{Expt}_{\mathcal{A}}^{\mathsf{pWPRF},R}(1^\lambda) = 1] - \frac{1}{2}| < \mathsf{negl}(\lambda)$$

In extractable pWPRF, we allow the challenge statement x^* to be in L. Accordingly, we modify the security experiment defined in Fig. 1 (in particular, line 7) and rename it as $\mathsf{Expt}_{\mathcal{A}}^{\mathsf{pWEPRF},R}(1^\lambda)$.

Definition 8. A puncturable witness pseudorandom function is said to be extractable or puncturable witness-extractable pseudorandom function (pWEPRF) for an NP language L with a relation R, if for any PPT adversary $\mathcal{A}$ and any polynomial $\mathsf{p}_{\mathcal{A}}(\lambda)$ there exists a PPT extractor $\mathcal{E}$ and a polynomial $\mathsf{p}_{\mathcal{E}}$ such that

$$\mathsf{Adv}_{\mathcal{A}}^{\mathsf{pWEPRF},R}(\lambda) = |\Pr[\mathsf{Expt}_{\mathcal{A}}^{\mathsf{pWEPRF},R}(1^\lambda) = 1] - \frac{1}{2}| \geq \frac{1}{\mathsf{p}_{\mathcal{A}}(\lambda)}$$

$$\Rightarrow \Pr[w^* \leftarrow \mathcal{E}(1^\lambda, x^*) : R(x^*, w^*) = 1] \geq \frac{1}{\mathsf{p}_{\mathcal{E}}(\lambda)}$$

The extractability says that when the adversary can distinguish the honestly computed $y = \mathsf{F}(\mathsf{fk}, x^*)$ from a uniformly chosen element, then it must know a witness w^* satisfying $R(x^*, w^*) = 1$.

2.5 Offline Witness Encryption

Definition 9. An offline witness encryption (OWE) scheme for an NP language L with a relation R is a tuple of PPT algorithms (Setup, Enc, Dec) defined as follows:

- $(\mathsf{pp_e}, \mathsf{pp_d}) \leftarrow \mathsf{Setup}(1^\lambda, R)$: on input a security parameter λ and a relation $R : \mathcal{X} \times \mathcal{W} \rightarrow \{0, 1\}$, returns two public parameters $\mathsf{pp_e}$ for encryption and $\mathsf{pp_d}$ for decryption.
- $c \leftarrow \mathsf{Enc}(\mathsf{pp_e}, x, m)$: returns c, an encryption of the message $m \in \mathcal{M}$ with respect to the statement $x \in \mathcal{X}$.
- $\mathsf{Dec}(\mathsf{pp_d}, c, w) \in \mathcal{M} \cup \{\perp\}$: a deterministic algorithm that decrypts the ciphertext c using a witness $w \in \mathcal{W}$ and returns a message $m \in \mathcal{M}$, or $\perp$.

The OWE scheme is said to be correct if the following holds:

- *correctness*: For all $x \in \mathcal{X}$, $w \in \mathcal{W}$, $m \in \mathcal{M}$ and $(\mathsf{pp_e}, \mathsf{pp_d}) \leftarrow \mathsf{Setup}(1^\lambda, R)$, we require that

$$\Pr[\mathsf{Dec}(\mathsf{pp_d}, \mathsf{Enc}(\mathsf{pp_e}, x, m), w) = m : R(x, w) = 1] = 1$$

The semi-adaptive security experiment $\mathsf{Expt}_{\mathcal{A}}^{\mathsf{OWE},R}(1^\lambda)$ is defined in Fig. 2.

Definition 10. An offline witness encryption OWE for an NP language L with a relation R is said to be semi-adaptively secure if, for all PPT adversary $\mathcal{A}$, there exists a negligible function negl such that

$$\mathsf{Adv}_{\mathcal{A}}^{\mathsf{OWE},R}(\lambda) = |\Pr[\mathsf{Expt}_{\mathcal{A}}^{\mathsf{OWE},R}(1^\lambda) = 1] - \frac{1}{2}| < \mathsf{negl}(\lambda)$$

For extractable offline witness encryption we modify the experiment defined in Fig. 2 so that x^* may belong to L and rename it as $\mathsf{Expt}_{\mathcal{A}}^{\mathsf{EOWE},R}(1^\lambda)$.

Definition 11. An offline witness encryption OWE is said to be semi-adaptively secure extractable offline witness encryption (EOWE) for an NP language L with a relation R, if for any PPT adversary $\mathcal{A}$ and any polynomial $\mathsf{p}_{\mathcal{A}}(\lambda)$ there exists a PPT extractor $\mathcal{E}$ and a polynomial $\mathsf{p}_{\mathcal{E}}$ such that

$$\mathsf{Adv}_{\mathcal{A}}^{\mathsf{EOWE},R}(\lambda) = |\Pr[\mathsf{Expt}_{\mathcal{A}}^{\mathsf{EOWE},R}(1^\lambda) = 1] - \frac{1}{2}| \geq \frac{1}{\mathsf{p}_{\mathcal{A}}(\lambda)}$$
$$\Rightarrow \Pr[w^* \leftarrow \mathcal{E}(1^\lambda, x^*) : R(x^*, w^*) = 1] \geq \frac{1}{\mathsf{p}_{\mathcal{E}}(\lambda)}$$

2.6 Obfuscation

Definition 12. A PPT algorithm $i\mathcal{O}$ is said to be an indistinguishability obfuscator for a class of circuits $\{\mathcal{C}_\lambda\}$, if it satisfies the following properties:

- *Functionality*: For all security parameter $\lambda \in \mathbb{N}$, for all $C \in \mathcal{C}_\lambda$, for all inputs x, we require that

$$\Pr[\widetilde{C}(x) = C(x) : \widetilde{C} \leftarrow i\mathcal{O}(1^\lambda, C)] = 1$$

- *Indistinguishability*: For any PPT distinguisher $\mathcal{D}$, there exists a negligible function negl such that for all pair of circuits $C_0, C_1 \in \mathcal{C}_\lambda$ that compute the same function and are of same size, we require that

$$\mathsf{Adv}_{\mathcal{D}}^{i\mathcal{O}}(\lambda) = |\Pr[b \leftarrow \{0,1\}, \widetilde{C} \leftarrow i\mathcal{O}(1^\lambda, C_b) : \mathcal{D}(\widetilde{C}, C_0, C_1) = b] - \frac{1}{2}| < \mathsf{negl}(\lambda)$$

Definition 13. A PPT algorithm $e\mathcal{O}$ is said to be an extractability obfuscator for a class of circuits $\{\mathcal{C}_\lambda\}$, if it satisfies the following properties:

- *Functionality*: For all security parameter $\lambda \in \mathbb{N}$, for all $C \in \mathcal{C}_\lambda$, for all inputs x, we require that

$$\Pr[\widetilde{C}(x) = C(x) : \widetilde{C} \leftarrow e\mathcal{O}(1^\lambda, C)] = 1$$

- *Extractability*: For any PPT distinguisher $\mathcal{D}$ and polynomial $\mathsf{p}_{\mathcal{D}}(\lambda)$, there exists an extractor $\mathcal{E}$ and a polynomial $\mathsf{p}_{\mathcal{E}}$ such that for all pair of circuits $C_0, C_1 \in \mathcal{C}_\lambda$ that are of same size, for all auxiliary input $z \in \{0,1\}^*$, we require that

$$\mathsf{Adv}_{\mathcal{D}}^{e\mathcal{O}}(\lambda) = \left|\Pr[b \leftarrow \{0,1\}, \widetilde{C} \leftarrow e\mathcal{O}(1^\lambda, C_b) : \mathcal{D}(\widetilde{C}, C_0, C_1, z) = b] - \frac{1}{2}\right| \geq \frac{1}{\mathsf{p}_{\mathcal{D}}(\lambda)}$$

$$\Rightarrow \Pr[x \leftarrow \mathcal{E}(1^\lambda, C_0, C_1, z) : C_0(x) \neq C_1(x)] \geq \frac{1}{\mathsf{p}_{\mathcal{E}}(\lambda)}$$

3 Construction: (Extractable) Offline Witness Encryption

In this section, we describe our construction of $\mathsf{OWE} = (\mathsf{Setup}, \mathsf{Enc}, \mathsf{Dec})$ for an NP language L and a relation $R : \mathcal{X} \times \mathcal{W} \to \{0,1\}$. We consider the statement space $\mathcal{X}$ to be $\{0,1\}^\lambda$ (containing L) and $\mathcal{W} = \{0,1\}^n$ where n is a polynomial in the security parameter λ. The following primitives are utilized in our construction:

- A pseudorandom generator $\mathsf{PRG} : \{0,1\}^\lambda \to \{0,1\}^{2\lambda}$.
- A CIND secure symmetric key encryption $\mathsf{SKE} = (\mathsf{Gen}, \mathsf{Enc}, \mathsf{Dec})$.
- A $\mathsf{pWPRF} = (\mathsf{Gen}, \mathsf{F}, \mathsf{PuncKey}, \mathsf{PuncF}, \mathsf{Eval})$ for the NP language $L' = \{(x, v) : \exists u \in \{0,1\}^\lambda$ such that $\mathsf{PRG}(x \oplus u) = v\}$ with a relation $R' : \mathcal{X}' \times \mathcal{W}' \to \{0,1\}$. So, $R'((x,v), u) = 1$ if $\mathsf{PRG}(x \oplus u) = v$, 0 otherwise.
- An obfuscator $\mathcal{O}$ for the class of circuits $\mathcal{C}_\lambda$ required in the constructions. The only difference between the constructions of OWE and extractable OWE (EOWE) is that: $\mathcal{O}$ is an indistinguishability obfuscator ($i\mathcal{O}$) for OWE whereas $\mathcal{O}$ is an extractability obfuscator ($e\mathcal{O}$) for EOWE.

Our OWE construction is shown in Fig. 3 where we assume that the circuit $C[\mathsf{fk}] \in \mathcal{C}_\lambda$ and $\mathcal{O}$ is an $i\mathcal{O}$. For *correctness*, we need to verify that the same key $\mathsf{K} \leftarrow \mathsf{SKE.Gen}(1^\lambda; y)$ is generated during encryption and decryption of OWE. In particular, the same randomness y should be utilized in Enc as well as in Dec. Note that, we compute y using the $\mathsf{pWPRF.Eval}(\mathsf{ek}, (x, v), \cdot)$ with a witness u corresponding to the relation R'. While decrypting, by the correctness of Eval, we generate the same y inside the circuit $\widetilde{C}$ using $\mathsf{pWPRF.F}(\mathsf{fk}, (x, v))$ extracted from the ciphertext. Therefore, $\mathsf{SKE.Dec}(\mathsf{K}, c_s)$ returns the same message that was encrypted in Enc if $R(x, w) = 1$. Finally, we conclude the correctness by observing that $C[\mathsf{fk}]$ and $\widetilde{C}$ compute the same function because of the functionality of $i\mathcal{O}$. We skip the correctness of EOWE as it can be argued similarly.

Comparison: The ciphertext size of our OWEs is as compact as one can desire: excluding the instance, it is only $|c_s| + |v| = |m| + 2\lambda$ which is *optimal* for any public-key encryption. More precisely, the bit size of a ciphertext encrypting a λ-bit message is 3λ. Let us compare our ciphertext size with all existing OWEs

$\underline{\mathsf{Setup}(1^\lambda, R)}$:
1. $(\mathsf{fk}, \mathsf{ek}) \leftarrow \mathsf{pWPRF.Gen}(1^\lambda, R')$
2. $\widetilde{C} \leftarrow \mathcal{O}(1^\lambda, C[\mathsf{fk}])$
3. set $\mathsf{pp_e} = \mathsf{ek}$, $\mathsf{pp_d} = \widetilde{C}$
4. return $(\mathsf{pp_e}, \mathsf{pp_d})$

$\underline{\mathsf{Enc}(\mathsf{pp_e}, x, m)}$:
1. parse $\mathsf{pp_e} = \mathsf{ek}$
2. $u \leftarrow \{0,1\}^\lambda$, $v \leftarrow \mathsf{PRG}(x \oplus u)$
3. $y \leftarrow \mathsf{pWPRF.Eval}(\mathsf{ek}, (x, v), u)$
4. $\mathsf{K} \leftarrow \mathsf{SKE.Gen}(1^\lambda; y)$
5. $c_s \leftarrow \mathsf{SKE.Enc}(\mathsf{K}, m)$
6. return $c = (c_s, x, v)$

$\underline{C[\mathsf{fk}](c, w)}$
1. parse $c = (c_s, x, v)$
2. if $R(x, w) = 1$
3. $\quad y \leftarrow \mathsf{pWPRF.F}(\mathsf{fk}, (x, v))$
4. $\quad \mathsf{K} \leftarrow \mathsf{SKE.Gen}(1^\lambda; y)$
5. $\quad$ return $\mathsf{SKE.Dec}(\mathsf{K}, c_s)$
6. else
7. $\quad$ return $\perp$

$\underline{\mathsf{Dec}(\mathsf{pp_d}, c, w)}$:
1. parse $\mathsf{pp_d} = \widetilde{C}$
2. return $\widetilde{C}(c, w)$

Fig. 3. Construction of OWEs with optimal ciphertexts where $\mathcal{O}$ is either $i\mathcal{O}$ for normal OWE or $e\mathcal{O}$ for extractable OWE (EOWE)

when encrypting a λ-bit message. The $i\mathcal{O}$ and SSS-NIZK based construction of Abusalah et al. [1] delivers a ciphertext size of at least 64λ-bit (assuming a group element is of size 2λ-bit [1]). Both the OWE constructions of Pal et al. [24] and Chvojka et al. [12] achieve a ciphertext of size at least 10λ-bit. The encryption process of [12] uses a puncturable public-key encryption scheme to produce a ciphertext corresponding to the pair (x, m). We shift the computation power in the setup phase as much as possible to accomplish a more compact ciphertext size for our OWE than any other OWEs. This reduces the communication cost in practical applications. All existing OWEs utilize $i\mathcal{O}$ during the setup phase. This implies either $\mathsf{pp_e}$ or $\mathsf{pp_d}$ (or both) contains an obfuscated circuit the size of which depends on the simplicity of the circuit. The size of the public parameter for encryption ek (or $\mathsf{pp_e}$) is proportional to the size of the relation R'. We observe that the relation R' is as simple as checking a PRG computation, which means the evaluation key ek is independent of the relation R, and hence our OWE encryptions are more efficient than the reusable WE of Zhandry [26]. Furthermore, the notion of functional WE cannot be directly achieved from reusable WE whereas we extend our OWE to OFWE.

Theorem 1. *The* OWE = (Setup, Enc, Dec) *described in Fig. 3 with $\mathcal{O} = i\mathcal{O}$ is a semi-adaptively secure offline witness encryption if* PRG *is a secure pseudorandom generator,* pWPRF *is a selectively secure puncturable witness pseudorandom function, $i\mathcal{O}$ is an indistinguishability obfuscator for the circuit class $\mathcal{C}_\lambda$ and* SKE *is a* CIND *secure symmetric key encryption. More specifically, for any PPT adversary $\mathcal{A}$, there exist PPT adversaries $\mathcal{B}_1$, $\mathcal{B}_2$, $\mathcal{B}_3$ and a PPT distinguisher $\mathcal{D}$ such that:*

$$\mathsf{Adv}_{\mathcal{A}}^{\mathsf{OWE},R}(\lambda) \leq \mathsf{Adv}_{\mathcal{B}_1}^{\mathsf{PRG}}(\lambda) + \mathsf{Adv}_{\mathcal{B}_2}^{\mathsf{pWPRF},R'}(\lambda) + \mathsf{Adv}_{\mathcal{B}_3}^{\mathsf{SKE}}(\lambda) + \mathsf{Adv}_{\mathcal{D}}^{i\mathcal{O}}(\lambda)$$

Proof. We prove the theorem using the following sequence of games. We start with Game 0 which is the standard security experiment $\mathsf{Expt}_{\mathcal{A}}^{\mathsf{OWE},R}(1^\lambda)$ as defined in Fig. 2. For Game i, we denote by G_i the event $b = b'$. In each game, we assume that $\mathcal{A}$ submits two messages of equal length and that $x^* \notin L$ as otherwise the challenger always returns 0. The circuits used in the proof are assumed to be padded to a maximum size.

Game 0 $\Rightarrow$ Game 1: In Game 0, we compute the encryption key as $\mathsf{K} \leftarrow \mathsf{SKE.Gen}(1^\lambda; y)$ where $y \leftarrow \mathsf{pWPRF.Eval}(\mathsf{ek}, (x^*, v), u)$. But, Game 1 (Fig. 4) sets $y \leftarrow \mathsf{pWPRF.F}(\mathsf{fk}, (x^*, v))$ without using the witness u. By the correctness Eval:

$$\mathsf{pWPRF.Eval}(\mathsf{ek}, (x^*, v), u) = \mathsf{pWPRF.F}(\mathsf{fk}, (x^*, v)) \text{ as } R'((x^*, v), u) = 1.$$

Therefore, the distribution of ciphertexts in both the games are identical and hence they are indistinguishable from $\mathcal{A}$'s view. We have $\Pr[\mathsf{G}_0] = \Pr[\mathsf{G}_1]$.

Game 1 $\Rightarrow$ Game 2: In Game 2, described in Fig. 5, we pick v uniformly at random from $\{0,1\}^{2\lambda}$ instead of setting it as $v \leftarrow \mathsf{PRG}(x^* \oplus u)$. Note that, given x^*, the distribution of $x^* \oplus u$ is uniform over $\{0,1\}^\lambda$ for $u \leftarrow \{0,1\}^\lambda$. Let, $\mathcal{B}_1$ is a PRG-adversary. Then, by the security of PRG (Definition 1), the distinguishing advantage of $\mathcal{A}$ between Game 1 and Game 2 can be written as

$$|\Pr[\mathsf{G}_1] - \Pr[\mathsf{G}_2]| = \mathsf{Adv}_{\mathcal{B}_1}^{\mathsf{PRG}}(\lambda).$$

$x^* \leftarrow \mathcal{A}(1^\lambda)$
$(\mathsf{fk}, \mathsf{ek}) \leftarrow \mathsf{pWPRF.Gen}(1^\lambda, R')$
$\widetilde{C} \leftarrow i\mathcal{O}(1^\lambda, C[\mathsf{fk}])$
set $\mathsf{pp_e} = \mathsf{ek}, \mathsf{pp_d} = \widetilde{C}$
$(m_0, m_1) \leftarrow \mathcal{A}(\mathsf{pp_e}, \mathsf{pp_d})$
$u \leftarrow \{0,1\}^\lambda, v \leftarrow \mathsf{PRG}(x^* \oplus u)$
$y \leftarrow \mathsf{pWPRF.F}(\mathsf{fk}, (x^*, v))$
$\mathsf{K} \leftarrow \mathsf{SKE.Gen}(1^\lambda; y)$
$b \leftarrow \{0,1\}$
$c_s \leftarrow \mathsf{SKE.Enc}(\mathsf{K}, m_b)$
set $c = (c_s, x^*, v)$
$b' \leftarrow \mathcal{A}(c)$
return 1 if $(b = b')$

Fig. 4. Game 1

$x^* \leftarrow \mathcal{A}(1^\lambda)$
$(\mathsf{fk}, \mathsf{ek}) \leftarrow \mathsf{pWPRF.Gen}(1^\lambda, R')$
$\widetilde{C} \leftarrow i\mathcal{O}(1^\lambda, C[\mathsf{fk}])$
set $\mathsf{pp_e} = \mathsf{ek}, \mathsf{pp_d} = \widetilde{C}$
$(m_0, m_1) \leftarrow \mathcal{A}(\mathsf{pp_e}, \mathsf{pp_d})$
$v \leftarrow \{0,1\}^{2\lambda}$
$y \leftarrow \mathsf{pWPRF.F}(\mathsf{fk}, (x^*, v))$
$\mathsf{K} \leftarrow \mathsf{SKE.Gen}(1^\lambda; y)$
$b \leftarrow \{0,1\}$
$c_s \leftarrow \mathsf{SKE.Enc}(\mathsf{K}, m_b)$
set $c = (c_s, x^*, v)$
$b' \leftarrow \mathcal{A}(c)$
return 1 if $(b = b')$

Fig. 5. Game 2

Game 2 $\Rightarrow$ Game 3: In Game 3, described in Fig. 6, we replace the circuit $C[\mathsf{fk}]$ by a new circuit $C[\mathsf{fk}_{z^*}, x^*]$ and set the public parameter for decryption $\mathsf{pp_d} \leftarrow i\mathcal{O}(1^\lambda, C[\mathsf{fk}_{z^*}, x^*])$. The new circuit $C[\mathsf{fk}_{z^*}, x^*]$ is defined as follows:

$C[\mathsf{fk}_{z^*}, x^*](c, w)$

1. parse $c = (c_s, x, v)$
2. if $x = x^*$
3. return $\perp$
4. else if $R(x, w) = 1$
5. $y \leftarrow \mathsf{pWPRF.PuncF}(\mathsf{fk}_{z^*}, (x, v))$
6. $\mathsf{K} \leftarrow \mathsf{SKE.Gen}(1^\lambda; y)$
7. return $\mathsf{SKE.Dec}(\mathsf{K}, c_s)$
8. else
9. return $\perp$

Note that, the two circuits $C[\mathsf{fk}]$ and $C[\mathsf{fk}_{z^*}, x^*]$ are functionally equivalent. Let $(\bar{c}, \bar{w})$ be any arbitrary input where $\bar{c} = (\bar{c}_s, \bar{x}, \bar{v})$. If $\bar{x} = x^*$, then $C[\mathsf{fk}](\bar{c}, \bar{w})$ outputs $\perp$ since $x^* \notin L$ implies that $R(x^*, \bar{w}) = 0$ for any $\bar{w} \in \mathcal{W}$, and $C[\mathsf{fk}_{z^*}, x^*](\bar{c}, \bar{w})$ outputs $\perp$ because of the check in line 2 of the circuit. If $\bar{x} \neq x^*$, then $z^* \neq (\bar{x}, \bar{v})$ and by the correctness of PuncF we have

$$\mathsf{pWPRF.F}(\mathsf{fk}, (\bar{x}, \bar{v})) = \mathsf{pWPRF.PuncF}(\mathsf{fk}_{z^*}, (\bar{x}, \bar{v}))$$

and hence $C[\mathsf{fk}](\bar{c}, \bar{w}) = C[\mathsf{fk}_{z^*}, x^*](\bar{c}, \bar{w})$. Considering $\mathcal{D}$ as a PPT distinguisher for $i\mathcal{O}$, the indistinguishability property of $i\mathcal{O}$ (Definition 12) implies that

$$|\Pr[\mathsf{G}_2] - \Pr[\mathsf{G}_3]| = \mathsf{Adv}_{\mathcal{D}}^{i\mathcal{O}}(\lambda)$$

- $x^* \leftarrow \mathcal{A}(1^\lambda)$
- $(\mathsf{fk}, \mathsf{ek}) \leftarrow \mathsf{pWPRF.Gen}(1^\lambda, R')$
- $v \leftarrow \{0,1\}^{2\lambda}$, set $z^* = (x^*, v)$
- $\mathsf{fk}_{z^*} \leftarrow \mathsf{pWPRF.PuncKey}(\mathsf{fk}, z^*)$
- $\boxed{\widetilde{C} \leftarrow i\mathcal{O}(1^\lambda, C[\mathsf{fk}_{z^*}, x^*])}$
- set $\mathsf{pp_e} = \mathsf{ek}$, $\mathsf{pp_d} = \widetilde{C}$
- $(m_0, m_1) \leftarrow \mathcal{A}(\mathsf{pp_e}, \mathsf{pp_d})$
- $y \leftarrow \mathsf{pWPRF.F}(\mathsf{fk}, (x^*, v))$
- $\mathsf{K} \leftarrow \mathsf{SKE.Gen}(1^\lambda; y)$
- $b \leftarrow \{0,1\}$
- $c_s \leftarrow \mathsf{SKE.Enc}(\mathsf{K}, m_b)$
- set $c = (c_s, x^*, v)$
- $b' \leftarrow \mathcal{A}(c)$
- return 1 if $(b = b')$

Fig. 6. Game 3

- $x^* \leftarrow \mathcal{A}(1^\lambda)$
- $(\mathsf{fk}, \mathsf{ek}) \leftarrow \mathsf{pWPRF.Gen}(1^\lambda, R')$
- $v \leftarrow \{0,1\}^{2\lambda}$, set $z^* = (x^*, v)$
- $\mathsf{fk}_{z^*} \leftarrow \mathsf{pWPRF.PuncKey}(\mathsf{fk}, z^*)$
- $\widetilde{C} \leftarrow i\mathcal{O}(1^\lambda, C[\mathsf{fk}_{z^*}, x^*])$
- set $\mathsf{pp_e} = \mathsf{ek}$, $\mathsf{pp_d} = \widetilde{C}$
- $(m_0, m_1) \leftarrow \mathcal{A}(\mathsf{pp_e}, \mathsf{pp_d})$
- $\boxed{y \leftarrow \mathcal{Y}}$
- $\mathsf{K} \leftarrow \mathsf{SKE.Gen}(1^\lambda; y)$
- $b \leftarrow \{0,1\}$
- $c_s \leftarrow \mathsf{SKE.Enc}(\mathsf{K}, m_b)$
- set $c = (c_s, x^*, v)$
- $b' \leftarrow \mathcal{A}(c)$
- return 1 if $(b = b')$

Fig. 7. Game 4

Game 3 ⇒ Game 4: In Game 4, described in Fig. 7, we pick y uniformly at random from $\mathcal{Y}$ which is the co-domain of $\mathsf{pWPRF.F}(\mathsf{fk}, \cdot)$. We show that if $\mathcal{A}$ can distinguish between these two games, then there is an adversary $\mathcal{B}_2$ which will break the selective security of pWPRF (defined in Fig. 1). Let $z^* = (x^*, v)$ be the challenge statement of $\mathcal{B}_2$ for a random $v \leftarrow \{0,1\}^{2\lambda}$.

$\underline{\mathcal{B}_2(1^\lambda, z^*)}$:

1. send z^* to its challenger
2. The pWPRF-challenger does the following:
   (a) generate $(\mathsf{fk}, \mathsf{ek}) \leftarrow \mathsf{pWPRF.Gen}(1^\lambda, R')$
   (b) compute a punctured key $\mathsf{fk}_{z^*} \leftarrow \mathsf{pWPRF.PuncKey}(\mathsf{fk}, z^*)$
   (c) set $y_0 \leftarrow \mathsf{pWPRF.F}(\mathsf{fk}, z^*)$ and $y_1 \leftarrow \mathcal{Y}$
   (d) pick $\tilde{b} \leftarrow \{0,1\}$
   (e) return $(\mathsf{ek}, \mathsf{fk}_{z^*}, y_{\tilde{b}})$ to $\mathcal{B}_2$
3. compute $\widetilde{C} \leftarrow i\mathcal{O}(1^\lambda, C[\mathsf{fk}_{z^*}, x^*])$ and set $\mathsf{pp_e} = \mathsf{ek}, \mathsf{pp_d} = \widetilde{C}$
4. receive $(m_0, m_1) \leftarrow \mathcal{A}(\mathsf{pp_e}, \mathsf{pp_d})$
5. compute the encryption key as $\mathsf{K} \leftarrow \mathsf{SKE.Gen}(1^\lambda; y_{\tilde{b}})$
6. pick $b \leftarrow \{0,1\}$
7. compute the ciphertext as $c_s \leftarrow \mathsf{SKE.Enc}(\mathsf{K}, m_b)$
8. set $c = (c_s, x^*, v)$
9. get $b' \leftarrow \mathcal{A}(c)$
10. return 1 if $(b = b')$

First, we note that $z^* = (x^*, v) \notin L'$ with overwhelming probability. Since $v \leftarrow \{0,1\}^{2\lambda}$, the probability that $\mathsf{PRG}(x^* \oplus u) = v$ for some $u \in \{0,1\}^\lambda$ is at most $2^{-\lambda}$ which is negligible in λ. So, $\mathcal{B}_2$ is a legitimate pWPRF-adversary. If the pWPRF-challenger picks $\tilde{b} = 0$ then $\mathcal{B}_2$ simulates Game 3, and if it chooses $\tilde{b} = 1$ then $\mathcal{B}_2$ simulates Game 4. Therefore, the advantage of $\mathcal{A}$ in distinguishing between Game 3 and Game 4 is the same as the advantage of $\mathcal{B}_2$ in breaking the selective security of pWPRF. Hence the following holds:

$$|\Pr[\mathsf{G}_3] - \Pr[\mathsf{G}_4]| = \mathsf{Adv}_{\mathcal{B}_2}^{\mathsf{pWPRF}, R'}(\lambda)$$

Next, we note that in Game 4, the encryption key is computed as $\mathsf{K} \leftarrow \mathsf{SKE.Gen}(1^\lambda; y)$ with a fresh randomness y which is independent of the challenge statement x^*. Therefore, by the CIND security of SKE (Definition 5) we have

$$|\Pr[\mathsf{G}_4] - \frac{1}{2}| = \mathsf{Adv}_{\mathcal{B}_3}^{\mathsf{SKE}}(\lambda)$$

where $\mathcal{B}_3$ is an adversary of CIND security game. Finally, we conclude the proof by combining all the probabilities.

In the next theorem, we proof the security of EOWE (Fig. 3 with $\mathcal{O} = e\mathcal{O}$) utilizing the extractor of $e\mathcal{O}$.

Theorem 2. *The* EOWE = (Setup, Enc, Dec) *described in Fig. 3 with $\mathcal{O} = e\mathcal{O}$ is a semi-adaptively secure extractable offline witness encryption if* PRG *is a secure pseudorandom generator,* pWPRF *is a selectively secure puncturable witness pseudorandom function, $e\mathcal{O}$ is an extractability obfuscator for the circuit class $\mathcal{C}_\lambda$ and* SKE *is a* CIND *secure symmetric key encryption.*

Proof. We start with the standard EOWE experiment $\mathsf{Expt}_{\mathcal{A}}^{\mathsf{EOWE}, R}(1^\lambda)$ (Definition 11). We call it as EGame 0. Here, we denote the security games by EGame i and for each EGame i, let $\mathsf{EG_i}$ be the event $b = b'$. We assume that

$\mathcal{A}$ submits two messages of equal length in each game and all the circuits used in the proof are padded to a maximum size.

<u>EGame 0 ⇒ EGame 1</u>: EGame 1 is exactly the same as EGame 0 except we replace the circuit $C[\mathsf{fk}]$ with a new circuit $C[\mathsf{fk}, x^*]$ defined in Fig. 8. Suppose, the adversary $\mathcal{A}$ can distinguish between EGame 0 and EGame 1 with an advantage

$$\mathsf{Adv}_{\mathcal{A}}^{\mathsf{EG}\ 0\text{-}1}(\lambda) = |\Pr[\mathsf{EG}_0] - \Pr[\mathsf{EG}_1]| \geq \frac{1}{\mathsf{p}_{\mathcal{A}}(\lambda)}$$

for some polynomial $\mathsf{p}_{\mathcal{A}}(\lambda)$. Then, we show that there is a PPT extractor $\mathcal{E}$ and a polynomial $\mathsf{p}_{\mathcal{E}}$ such that $\mathcal{E}(1^\lambda, x^*)$ outputs a witness w^* satisfying $R(x^*, w^*) = 1$ with probability at least $\frac{1}{\mathsf{p}_{\mathcal{E}}(\lambda)}$.

We note that two games differ only in the obfuscated circuits. So, we consider a PPT distinguisher $\mathcal{D}$ of $e\mathcal{O}$ as defined in Definition 13. In particular, $\mathcal{D}$ collects two circuits from a circuit sampler $\mathsf{S}(1^\lambda, \cdot)$ and an obfuscated circuit (from it's challenger), then it simulates the security game for $\mathcal{A}$ as follows:

<u>$\mathcal{D}(1^\lambda, \widetilde{C}, C[\mathsf{fk}], C[\mathsf{fk}, x^*], \mathsf{aux})$:</u>

1. parse $\mathsf{aux} = (\mathsf{ek}, x^*)$
2. set $\mathsf{pp_e} = \mathsf{ek}, \mathsf{pp_d} = \widetilde{C}$
3. $(m_0, m_1) \leftarrow \mathcal{A}(\mathsf{pp_e}, \mathsf{pp_d})$
4. follow steps 6-10 as in EGame 1
5. set $c = (c_s, x^*, v)$
6. $b' \leftarrow \mathcal{A}(c)$
7. return 1 if $b = b'$

<u>$\mathsf{S}(1^\lambda, x^*)$</u>

1. $(\mathsf{fk}, \mathsf{ek}) \leftarrow \mathsf{pWPRF.Gen}(1^\lambda, R')$
2. construct $C[\mathsf{fk}], C[\mathsf{fk}, x^*]$
3. set $\mathsf{aux} = (\mathsf{ek}, x^*)$
4. return $(C[\mathsf{fk}], C[\mathsf{fk}, x^*], \mathsf{aux})$

1. $x^* \leftarrow \mathcal{A}(1^\lambda)$
2. $(\mathsf{fk}, \mathsf{ek}) \leftarrow \mathsf{pWPRF.Gen}(1^\lambda, R')$
3. $\boxed{\widetilde{C} \leftarrow e\mathcal{O}(1^\lambda, C[\mathsf{fk}, x^*])}$
4. set $\mathsf{pp_e} = \mathsf{ek}, \mathsf{pp_d} = \widetilde{C}$
5. $(m_0, m_1) \leftarrow \mathcal{A}(\mathsf{pp_e}, \mathsf{pp_d})$
6. $u \leftarrow \{0,1\}^\lambda, v \leftarrow \mathsf{PRG}(x^* \oplus u)$
7. $y \leftarrow \mathsf{pWPRF.Eval}(\mathsf{ek}, (x^*, v), u)$
8. $\mathsf{K} \leftarrow \mathsf{SKE.Gen}(1^\lambda; y)$
9. $b \leftarrow \{0,1\}$
10. $c_s \leftarrow \mathsf{SKE.Enc}(\mathsf{K}, m_b)$
11. set $c = (c_s, x^*, v)$
12. $b' \leftarrow \mathcal{A}(c)$
13. return 1 if $b = b'$

<u>$C[\mathsf{fk}, x^*](c, w)$</u>

```
1. parse c = (c_s, x, v)
2. if R(x, w) = 1
3.     if x = x*
4.        return ⊥
5.     else
6.        y ← pWPRF.F(fk, (x, v))
7.        K ← SKE.Gen(1^λ; y)
8.        return SKE.Dec(K, c_s)
9. else
10.    return ⊥
```

Fig. 8. EGame 1

If $\widetilde{C} \leftarrow e\mathcal{O}(1^\lambda, C[\mathsf{fk}])$ then $\mathcal{D}$ simulates EGame 0 and if $\widetilde{C} \leftarrow e\mathcal{O}(1^\lambda, C[\mathsf{fk}, x^*])$ then $\mathcal{D}$ simulates EGame 1. Therefore, $\mathcal{D}$ can distinguish between the obfuscated circuits with the same advantage of $\mathcal{A}$ in distinguishing EGame 0 and EGame 1.

By the extractability property of $e\mathcal{O}$ (Definition 13), there exists a PPT extractor $\mathcal{E}'$ and a polynomial $\mathsf{p}_{\mathcal{E}'}$ such that $\mathcal{E}'(1^\lambda, C[\mathsf{fk}], C[\mathsf{fk}, x^*], \mathsf{aux})$ outputs $(\bar{c}, \bar{w})$ at which the two circuits differ with probability at least $\frac{1}{\mathsf{p}_{\mathcal{E}'}(\lambda)}$. Note that, the two circuits differ only when $\bar{c} = (\bar{c}_s, x^*, \bar{v})$ is well formed and $R(x^*, \bar{w}) = 1$.

Now, the extractor $\mathcal{E}(1^\lambda, x^*)$ of EOWE simply runs $\mathsf{S}(1^\lambda, x^*)$ to obtain $(C[\mathsf{fk}], C[\mathsf{fk}, x^*], \mathsf{aux})$ and then executes $\mathcal{E}'(1^\lambda, C[\mathsf{fk}], C[\mathsf{fk}, x^*], \mathsf{aux})$ to get a witness w^* satisfying $R(x^*, w^*) = 1$ with probability $\geq \frac{1}{\mathsf{p}_{\mathcal{E}'}(\lambda)}$. Thus we can set $\mathsf{p}_{\mathcal{E}} = \mathsf{p}_{\mathcal{E}'}$ and more importantly we note that $\mathcal{E}$ is a PPT extractor since $\mathsf{S}(\cdot)$ runs in poly(λ) time and $\mathcal{E}'$ is a PPT extractor.

<u>EGame 1 $\Rightarrow$ EGame 2</u>: EGame 2 is exactly the same as EGame 1 except in line 7 of Fig. 8 where we compute $y \leftarrow \mathsf{pWPRF.F}(\mathsf{fk}, (x^*, v))$. By the correctness Eval (using the same argument as in the transition from Game 0 to Game 1 of Theorem 1), we have $\Pr[\mathsf{EG}_1] = \Pr[\mathsf{EG}_2]$.

<u>EGame 2 $\Rightarrow$ EGame 3</u>: In EGame 3, we choose $v \leftarrow \{0,1\}^{2\lambda}$ instead of computing $v \leftarrow \mathsf{PRG}(x^* \oplus u)$ as in EGame 2. By the security of PRG (Definition 1), we have

$$|\Pr[\mathsf{EG}_2] - \Pr[\mathsf{EG}_3]| = \mathsf{Adv}^{\mathsf{PRG}}_{\mathcal{B}_1}(\lambda)$$

where $\mathcal{B}_1$ is a PRG-adversary.

<u>EGame 3 $\Rightarrow$ EGame 4</u>: In EGame 4, we set $\mathsf{pp_d} \leftarrow e\mathcal{O}(1^\lambda, C[\mathsf{fk}_{z^*}, x^*])$ where $\mathsf{fk}_{z^*} \leftarrow \mathsf{pWPRF.PuncKey}(\mathsf{fk}, z^*)$ and $z^* = (x^*, v)$ for some $v \leftarrow \{0,1\}^{2\lambda}$. The circuit $C[\mathsf{fk}_{z^*}, x^*]$ is the same circuit defined in Fig. 8 except we replace fk by fk_{z^*} and use $\mathsf{pWPRF.PuncF}(\mathsf{fk}_{z^*}, (x, v))$ to compute y in line 6. It is easy to follow that the circuits $C[\mathsf{fk}, x^*], C[\mathsf{fk}_{z^*}, x^*]$ compute the same function by the correctness of PuncF. Suppose, $(\bar{c} = (\bar{c}_s, \bar{x}, \bar{v}), \bar{w})$ is any arbitrary input to the circuits. If $\bar{x} \neq x^*$, then $z^* \neq (\bar{x}, \bar{v})$ and hence $\mathsf{pWPRF.F}(\mathsf{fk}, (\bar{x}, \bar{v})) = \mathsf{pWPRF.PuncF}(\mathsf{fk}_{z^*}, (\bar{x}, \bar{v}))$. If $\bar{x} = x^*$, then both the circuits return $\perp$ because of the check in line 2 or 3. By the extractability property of $e\mathcal{O}$ (Definition 13), we have

$$|\Pr[\mathsf{EG}_3] - \Pr[\mathsf{EG}_4]| = \mathsf{Adv}^{e\mathcal{O}}_{\mathcal{D}}(\lambda) = \mu(\lambda)$$

where μ is a negligible function of λ. If the advantage is not bounded by a negligible function of λ, then there exists an extractor $\mathcal{E}'$ which would produce an input where the two circuits differ, leading towards a contradiction as the circuits are equivalent.

<u>EGame 4 $\Rightarrow$ EGame 5</u>: EGame 5 samples y uniformly at random from $\mathcal{Y}$ instead of computing $y \leftarrow \mathsf{pWPRF.F}(\mathsf{fk}, (x^*, v))$ as in EGame 4, where $\mathcal{Y}$ is the co-domain of $\mathsf{pWPRF.F}(\mathsf{fk}, \cdot)$. Note that the probability of $z^* = (x^*, v) \in L'$ for a random $v \leftarrow \{0,1\}^{2\lambda}$ is negligible in λ. By the selective security of pWPRF, we have

$$|\Pr[\mathsf{EG}_4] - \Pr[\mathsf{EG}_5]| = \mathsf{Adv}^{\mathsf{pWPRF}, R'}_{\mathcal{B}_2}(\lambda)$$

where $\mathcal{B}_2$ is a pWPRF-adversary. We skip the reduction as it is similar to the reduction described in the transition from Game 3 to Game 4 of Theorem 1.

Finally, the encryption key in EGame 5 is computed as $\mathsf{K} \leftarrow \mathsf{SKE.Gen}(1^\lambda; y)$ where y is a fresh randomness which is independent of the challenge statement x^*. The CIND security of SKE (Definition 5) guarantees that

$$|\Pr[\mathsf{EG}_5] - \frac{1}{2}| = \mathsf{Adv}_{\mathcal{B}_3}^{\mathsf{SKE}}(\lambda).$$

where $\mathcal{B}_3$ is an adversary of CIND game. Finally, we have

$$\begin{aligned}\mathsf{Adv}_{\mathcal{A}}^{\mathsf{EOWE},R}(\lambda) = |\Pr[\mathsf{EG}_0] - \frac{1}{2}| &\leq \sum_{i=0}^{4} |\Pr[\mathsf{EG}_i] - \Pr[\mathsf{EG}_{i+1}]| + |\Pr[\mathsf{EG}_5] - \frac{1}{2}| \\ &= \mathsf{Adv}_{\mathcal{A}}^{\mathsf{EG}\ 0\text{-}1}(\lambda) + \mathsf{Adv}_{\mathcal{B}_1}^{\mathsf{PRG}}(\lambda) + \mu(\lambda) + \mathsf{Adv}_{\mathcal{B}_2}^{\mathsf{pWPRF},R'}(\lambda) + \mathsf{Adv}_{\mathcal{B}_3}^{\mathsf{SKE}}(\lambda) \\ &< \mathsf{Adv}_{\mathcal{A}}^{\mathsf{EG}\ 0\text{-}1}(\lambda) + \mathsf{negl}(\lambda) \quad \text{(by the assumptions in the theorem)}\end{aligned}$$

Thus, $|\mathsf{Adv}_{\mathcal{A}}^{\mathsf{EOWE},R}(\lambda) - \mathsf{Adv}_{\mathcal{A}}^{\mathsf{EG}\ 0\text{-}1}(\lambda)| < \mathsf{negl}(\lambda)$ implies that $\mathsf{Adv}_{\mathcal{A}}^{\mathsf{EG}\ 0\text{-}1}(\lambda) = \mathsf{Adv}_{\mathcal{A}}^{\mathsf{EOWE},R}(\lambda)$ excluding the negligible term. Hence, by the similar arguments as in the transition from EGame 0 to EGame 1, we conclude that if $\mathsf{Adv}_{\mathcal{A}}^{\mathsf{EOWE},R}(\lambda) \geq \frac{1}{\mathsf{p}_{\mathcal{A}}(\lambda)}$ for some polynomial $\mathsf{p}_{\mathcal{A}}(\lambda)$, then there is a PPT extractor $\mathcal{E}$ and a polynomial $\mathsf{p}_{\mathcal{E}}$ such that $\Pr[w^* \leftarrow \mathcal{E}(1^\lambda, x^*) : R(x^*, w^*) = 1] \geq \frac{1}{\mathsf{p}_{\mathcal{E}}(\lambda)}$.

4 Informal Description: (Extractable) Offline Functional Witness Encryption

Apart from an NP language L with a witness relation R, *Offline functional witness encryption* (OFWE) is associated with a function class $\{\mathcal{F}_\lambda\}$. It encrypts a pair of function and message $(f, m) \in \mathcal{F}_\lambda \times \mathcal{M}$ with respect to a statement x. Instead of getting the whole message, a valid witness w for the statement x can only get a user to learn $f(m, w)$. The OWE described in Fig. 3 can be modified to achieve OFWE. While encryption, we use the key K (computed utilizing $\mathsf{pWPRF.Eval}$ for the statement (x, v)) to encrypt (f, m) via SKE encryption. The ciphertext becomes $c = (c_s, x, v)$ with $|c_s| = |f| + |m|$ where $|f|, |m|$ denote the sizes of f, m respectively. In Setup, we modify $C[\mathsf{fk}]$ in line 5 so that the circuit computes $(f, m) \leftarrow \mathsf{SKE.Dec}(\mathsf{K}, c_s)$ and then returns $f(m, w)$ if $R(x, w) = 1$ holds. The rest of the construction remains the same. Note that the size of ciphertext is optimal and the encryption maintains similar efficiency akin to our OWE. For security, we consider semi-adaptive model where the adversary $\mathcal{A}$ commits on the challenge statement x^* before the setup and adaptively selects two pairs (f_0, m_0), (f_1, m_1) such that $f_0(m_0, w) = f_1(m_1, w)$ for all w satisfying $R(x^*, w) = 1$. Detail construction with security analysis is available in the full version.

Replacing $i\mathcal{O}$ with an $e\mathcal{O}$ leads us to an *extractable* OFWE which is selectively secure means that $\mathcal{A}$ submits a challenge tuple (x^*, f, m_0, m_1) before setup. Depending on the wining advantage of $\mathcal{A}$ in guessing the bit b hidden inside a ciphertext corresponding to (x^*, f, m_b), there exists an extractor $\mathcal{E}$ which on input the challenge tuple outputs a witness w satisfying $f(m_0, w) \neq f(m_1, w)$ and $R(x^*, w) = 1$ with high probability. We prove the security in the full version of this paper.

5 Construction: Puncturable Witness(-Extractable) Pseudorandom Function

In this section, we show that WPRF construction of [24] satisfies our definition of pWPRF. In addition, we observe that if the indistinguishability obfuscator is replaced with an extractability obfuscator then the pWPRF becomes extractable. We now describe the pWPRF = (Gen, F, PuncKey, PuncF, Eval) for any NP language L with a relation $R : \mathcal{X} \times \mathcal{W} \rightarrow \{0, 1\}$.

The following primitives are required for the construction.

- A pPRF = (Gen, PuncKey, Eval, PuncEval) with domain $\mathcal{X}$ and co-domain $\mathcal{Y}$.
- An obfuscator $\mathcal{O}$ for the class of circuits $\mathcal{C}_\lambda$ required in the constructions. The only difference between the constructions of pWPRF and pWEPRF is that: $\mathcal{O}$ is an indistinguishability obfuscator ($i\mathcal{O}$) for pWPRF whereas $\mathcal{O}$ is an extractability obfuscator ($e\mathcal{O}$) for pWEPRF.

The constructions of pWPRFs are shown in Fig. 9. The correctness directly follows from the correctness of the underlying pPRF and functionality of $\mathcal{O}$.

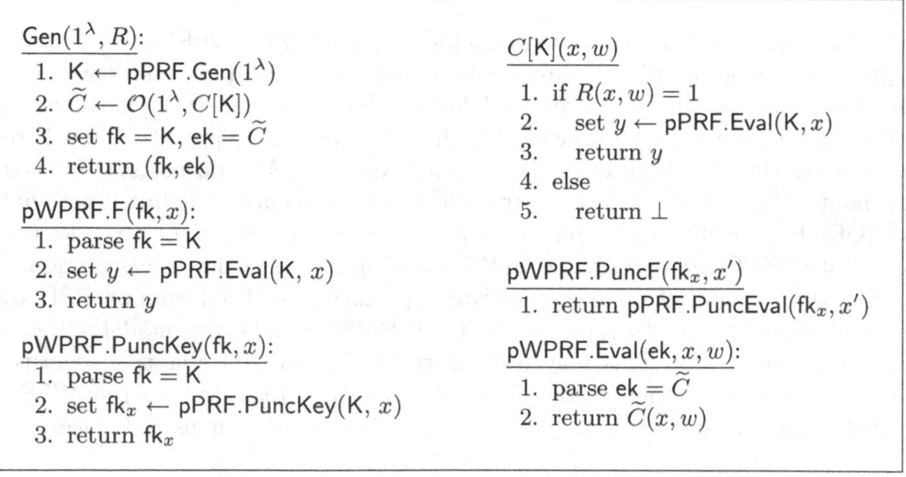

Gen(1^λ, R):
1. K ← pPRF.Gen(1^λ)
2. $\widetilde{C} \leftarrow \mathcal{O}(1^\lambda, C[\mathsf{K}])$
3. set fk = K, ek = $\widetilde{C}$
4. return (fk, ek)
pWPRF.F(fk, x):
1. parse fk = K
2. set y ← pPRF.Eval(K, x)
3. return y
pWPRF.PuncKey(fk, x):
1. parse fk = K
2. set fk_x ← pPRF.PuncKey(K, x)
3. return fk_x
$C[\mathsf{K}](x, w)$
1. if $R(x, w) = 1$
2. set y ← pPRF.Eval(K, x)
3. return y
4. else
5. return ⊥
pWPRF.PuncF(fk_x, x')
1. return pPRF.PuncEval(fk_x, x')
pWPRF.Eval(ek, x, w):
1. parse ek = $\widetilde{C}$
2. return $\widetilde{C}(x, w)$

Fig. 9. Construction of pWPRFs where $\mathcal{O}$ is either $i\mathcal{O}$ for normal pWPRF or $e\mathcal{O}$ for extractable pWPRF (pWEPRF)

Theorem 3. *The* $\mathsf{pWEPRF} = (\mathsf{Gen}, \mathsf{F}, \mathsf{PuncKey}, \mathsf{PuncF}, \mathsf{Eval})$ *described in Fig. 5 with $\mathcal{O} = i\mathcal{O}$ is a selectively secure puncturable witness pseudorandom function if* pPRF *is a secure puncturable pseudorandom function and $i\mathcal{O}$ is an indistinguishability obfuscator for the circuit class $\mathcal{C}_\lambda$. More specifically, for any PPT adversary $\mathcal{A}$, there exist a PPT adversary $\mathcal{B}$ and a PPT distinguisher $\mathcal{D}$ such that:*

$$\mathsf{Adv}_{\mathcal{A}}^{pWPRF,R}(\lambda) \leq \mathsf{Adv}_{\mathcal{B}}^{pPRF}(\lambda) + \mathsf{Adv}_{\mathcal{D}}^{i\mathcal{O}}(\lambda)$$

Proof Sketch. As usual, we start with game 0 which is the standard security experiment $\mathsf{Expt}_{\mathcal{A}}^{\mathsf{pWPRF},R}(1^\lambda)$ as defined in Fig. 1. Next, in game 1, we replace the circuit $C[\mathsf{K}]$ with a new circuit $C[\mathsf{fk}_{x^*}, x^*]$ where $\mathsf{fk}_{x^*} \leftarrow \mathsf{pPRF.PuncKey}(\mathsf{K}, x^*)$. For any arbitrary input (x, w), the new circuit returns the pseudorandom value as $\mathsf{pPRF.PuncEval}(\mathsf{fk}_{x^*}, x)$ if $x \neq x^*$ and $R(x, w) = 1$ hold, otherwise it returns $\perp$. It is easy to verify that the two circuits are functionally equivalent and hence by the security of $i\mathcal{O}$, game 0 and game 1 are indistinguishable. Now, the adversary knowing fk_{x^*} cannot distinguish $\mathsf{pWPRF.F}(\mathsf{fk}, x^*)$ from a random element due to the security of underlying pPRF (Definition 3). A formal proof is given in Appendix A.

We discuss the security of pWEPRF in the full version where the extractibility property of obfuscation (Definition 13) is utilized.

6 Conclusion

In this paper, we initiate the study of puncturable WPRF(pWPRF). We demonstrate that this puncturing technique enhances the applicability of WPRF. We construct semi-adaptively secure OWE that produces optimal size ciphertexts, in particular a ciphertext c for a message m has the size of only $|m| + 2\lambda$ bits where $|m|$ denotes the bit-length of m. Note that, existing OWEs do not satisfy such optimality. We further show that our OWE can be extended to offline functional WE (OFWE) providing more control over data. Moreover, using $e\mathcal{O}$ we construct extractable OWE and extractable OFWE with similar efficiency of encryption.

In future, we expect more cryptographic primitives realized from pWPRF. In terms of security, it is desirable to construct WPRF in adaptive model without multilinear maps [26]. This may lead us to OWE with full adaptive security. Finally, we note that a significant open problem in this area is to construct WPRF or OWE based on standard assumptions related to bilinear maps or lattices.

A Formal Proof of Theorem 3

Proof. We prove the security using two games. We start with Game 0 which is the standard selective security experiment as in Definition 6. Let $\mathsf{G_i}$ be the event $b = b'$ in each Game i.

Game 0 $\Rightarrow$ Game 1: Game 1 is exactly same as the Game 0 except we replace the circuit $C[\mathsf{K}]$ with a new circuit $C[\mathsf{fk}_{x^*}, x^*]$ defined in Fig. 10, where $\mathsf{fk}_{x^*} \leftarrow$ $\mathsf{pPRF.PuncKey}(\mathsf{K}, x^*)$. We show that the two circuits $C[\mathsf{K}]$ and $C[\mathsf{fk}_{x^*}, x^*]$ are functionally equivalent. For any arbitrary input $(\bar{x}, \bar{w})$ to the circuits, we see that if $\bar{x} \neq x^*$, then both the circuits return the same value as $\mathsf{pPRF.Eval}(\mathsf{K}, \bar{x}) =$ $\mathsf{pPRF.PuncEval}(\mathsf{fk}_{x^*}, \bar{x})$. Otherwise, if $\bar{x} = x^*$ then the circuit $C[\mathsf{K}]$ returns $\perp$, because $x^* \notin L$ implies that $R(\bar{x}, \bar{w}) = 0$ for all $\bar{w} \in \mathcal{W}$, and the circuit $C[\mathsf{fk}_{x^*}, x^*]$ returns $\perp$ because of the check in line 2 (Fig. 10). Thus, the indistinguishability property of $i\mathcal{O}$ (Definition 12) guarantees that

$$|\Pr[\mathsf{G}_0] - \Pr[\mathsf{G}_1]| = \mathsf{Adv}_{\mathcal{D}}^{i\mathcal{O}}(\lambda)$$

where $\mathcal{D}$ is a PPT distinguisher for $i\mathcal{O}$.

1. $x^* \leftarrow \mathcal{A}(1^\lambda)$
2. $\mathsf{K} \leftarrow \mathsf{pPRF.Gen}(1^\lambda)$
3. $\boxed{\widetilde{C} \leftarrow i\mathcal{O}(1^\lambda, C[\mathsf{fk}_{x^*}, x^*])}$
4. set $\mathsf{ek} = \widetilde{C}$
5. $\mathsf{fk}_{x^*} \leftarrow \mathsf{pPRF.PuncKey}(\mathsf{K}, x^*)$
6. $y_0 \leftarrow \mathsf{pPRF.Eval}(\mathsf{K}, x^*), y_1 \leftarrow \mathcal{Y}$
7. $b \leftarrow \{0, 1\}$
8. $b' \leftarrow \mathcal{A}(\mathsf{ek}, \mathsf{fk}_{x^*}, y_b)$
9. return 1 if $b = b'$

$C[\mathsf{fk}_{x^*}, x^*](x, w)$

```
1. if R(x, w) = 1
2.     if x = x*
3.         return ⊥
4.     else
5.         y ← pPRF.PuncEval(fk_{x*}, x)
6.         return y
7. else
8.     return ⊥
```

Fig. 10. Game 1

Suppose, the advantage of $\mathcal{A}$ in Game 1 is non-negligible. Then we construct an adversary $\mathcal{B}$ against the security of pPRF (Definition 2) with the same advantage as follow.

$\underline{\mathcal{B}(1^\lambda, x^*)}$:

1. send x^* to its challenger
2. The pPRF-challenger does the following:
   (a) generate $\mathsf{K} \leftarrow \mathsf{pPRF.Gen}(1^\lambda)$
   (b) compute $\mathsf{fk}_{x^*} \leftarrow \mathsf{pPRF.PuncKey}(\mathsf{K}, x^*)$
   (c) set $y_0 \leftarrow \mathsf{pPRF.Eval}(\mathsf{K}, x^*)$ and $y_1 \leftarrow \mathcal{Y}$
   (d) pick $b \leftarrow \{0, 1\}$
   (e) return (fk_{x^*}, y_b) to $\mathcal{B}$
3. compute $\widetilde{C} \leftarrow i\mathcal{O}(1^\lambda, C[\mathsf{fk}_{x^*}, x^*])$ and set $\mathsf{ek} = \widetilde{C}$
4. get $b' \leftarrow \mathcal{A}(\mathsf{ek}, \mathsf{fk}_{x^*}, y_b)$
5. return 1 if $b = b'$

Note that $\mathcal{B}$ perfectly simulates Game 1 for $\mathcal{A}$. If $\mathcal{A}$ can guess the bit b in Game 1 with a non-negligible advantage, then $\mathcal{B}$ breaks the security of pPRF with the same advantage. From the security of pPRF, we have

$$|\Pr[\mathsf{G}_1] - \frac{1}{2}| = \mathsf{Adv}_{\mathcal{B}}^{\mathsf{pPRF}}(\lambda)$$

Finally, combining all the probabilities we conclude the proof.

References

1. Abusalah, H., Fuchsbauer, G., Pietrzak, K.: Offline witness encryption. In: Manulis, M., Sadeghi, A.-R., Schneider, S. (eds.) ACNS 2016. LNCS, vol. 9696, pp. 285–303. Springer, Cham (2016). https://doi.org/10.1007/978-3-319-39555-5_16
2. Agrawal, S.: Indistinguishability obfuscation without multilinear maps: new methods for bootstrapping and instantiation. In: Ishai, Y., Rijmen, V. (eds.) EUROCRYPT 2019. LNCS, vol. 11476, pp. 191–225. Springer, Cham (2019). https://doi.org/10.1007/978-3-030-17653-2_7
3. Ananth, P., Jain, A.: Indistinguishability obfuscation from compact functional encryption. In: Gennaro, R., Robshaw, M. (eds.) CRYPTO 2015. LNCS, vol. 9215, pp. 308–326. Springer, Heidelberg (2015). https://doi.org/10.1007/978-3-662-47989-6_15
4. Ananth, P., Jain, A., Lin, H., Matt, C., Sahai, A.: Indistinguishability obfuscation without multilinear maps: new paradigms via low degree weak pseudorandomness and security amplification. In: Boldyreva, A., Micciancio, D. (eds.) CRYPTO 2019. LNCS, vol. 11694, pp. 284–332. Springer, Cham (2019). https://doi.org/10.1007/978-3-030-26954-8_10
5. Ananth, P., Sahai, A.: Projective arithmetic functional encryption and indistinguishability obfuscation from degree-5 multilinear maps. In: Coron, J.-S., Nielsen, J.B. (eds.) EUROCRYPT 2017. LNCS, vol. 10210, pp. 152–181. Springer, Cham (2017). https://doi.org/10.1007/978-3-319-56620-7_6
6. Barbosa, M., Portela, B., Scerri, G., Warinschi, B.: Foundations of hardware-based attested computation and application to SGX. In: 2016 IEEE European Symposium on Security and Privacy (EuroS&P), pp. 245–260. IEEE (2016)
7. Bitansky, N., Vaikuntanathan, V.: Indistinguishability obfuscation from functional encryption. J. ACM (JACM) **65**(6), 1–37 (2018)
8. Boyle, E., Chung, K.-M., Pass, R.: On extractability (aka differing-inputs) obfuscation. In: TCC (2014)
9. Boyle, E., Pass, R.: Limits of extractability assumptions with distributional auxiliary input. In: Iwata, T., Cheon, J.H. (eds.) ASIACRYPT 2015. LNCS, vol. 9453, pp. 236–261. Springer, Heidelberg (2015). https://doi.org/10.1007/978-3-662-48800-3_10
10. Brakerski, Z., Döttling, N., Garg, S., Malavolta, G.: Candidate iO from homomorphic encryption schemes. In: Canteaut, A., Ishai, Y. (eds.) EUROCRYPT 2020. LNCS, vol. 12105, pp. 79–109. Springer, Cham (2020). https://doi.org/10.1007/978-3-030-45721-1_4
11. Cheon, J.H., Cho, W., Hhan, M., Kim, J., Lee, C.: Statistical zeroizing attack: cryptanalysis of candidates of BP obfuscation over GGH15 multilinear map. Cryptology ePrint Archive, Report 2018/1081 (2018). https://eprint.iacr.org/2018/1081
12. Chvojka, P., Jager, T., Kakvi, S.A.: Offline witness encryption with semi-adaptive security. Cryptology ePrint Archive, Report 2019/1337 (2019). https://eprint.iacr.org/2019/1337
13. Coron, J.-S., Notarnicola, L.: Cryptanalysis of CLT13 multilinear maps with independent slots. IACR Cryptology ePrint Archive, 2019:309 (2019)
14. Damgard, I., Jurik, M.: A generalisation, a simplification and some applications of Paillier's probabilistic public-key system, pp. 13–15 (2001)
15. Fisch, B., Vinayagamurthy, D., Boneh, D., Gorbunov, S.: Iron: functional encryption using intel SGX. In: Proceedings of the 2017 ACM SIGSAC Conference on Computer and Communications Security, pp. 765–782. ACM (2017)

16. Garg, S., Gentry, C., Halevi, S., Raykova, M., Sahai, A., Waters, B.: Candidate indistinguishability obfuscation and functional encryption for all circuits. SIAM J. Comput. **45**(3), 882–929 (2016)
17. Garg, S., Gentry, C., Halevi, S., Wichs, D.: On the implausibility of differing-inputs obfuscation and extractable witness encryption with auxiliary input. Algorithmica **79**(4), 1353–1373 (2017)
18. Garg, S., Gentry, C., Sahai, A., Waters, B.: Witness encryption and its applications. In: Proceedings of the Forty-Fifth Annual ACM Symposium on Theory of Computing, pp. 467–476. ACM (2013)
19. Gentry, C.: Fully homomorphic encryption using ideal lattices. In: Proceedings of the Forty-First Annual ACM Symposium on Theory of Computing, pp. 169–178 (2009)
20. Gentry, C., Sahai, A., Waters, B.: Homomorphic encryption from learning with errors: conceptually-simpler, asymptotically-faster, attribute-based. In: Canetti, R., Garay, J.A. (eds.) CRYPTO 2013. LNCS, vol. 8042, pp. 75–92. Springer, Heidelberg (2013). https://doi.org/10.1007/978-3-642-40041-4_5
21. Goldwasser, S., Kalai, Y.T., Popa, R.A., Vaikuntanathan, V., Zeldovich, N.: How to run turing machines on encrypted data. In: Canetti, R., Garay, J.A. (eds.) CRYPTO 2013. LNCS, vol. 8043, pp. 536–553. Springer, Heidelberg (2013). https://doi.org/10.1007/978-3-642-40084-1_30
22. Lin, H.: Indistinguishability obfuscation from SXDH on 5-linear maps and locality-5 PRGs. In: Katz, J., Shacham, H. (eds.) CRYPTO 2017. LNCS, vol. 10401, pp. 599–629. Springer, Cham (2017). https://doi.org/10.1007/978-3-319-63688-7_20
23. Lin, H., Tessaro, S.: Indistinguishability obfuscation from trilinear maps and block-wise local PRGs. In: Katz, J., Shacham, H. (eds.) CRYPTO 2017. LNCS, vol. 10401, pp. 630–660. Springer, Cham (2017). https://doi.org/10.1007/978-3-319-63688-7_21
24. Pal, T., Dutta, R.: Offline witness encryption from witness PRF and randomized encoding in CRS model. In: Jang-Jaccard, J., Guo, F. (eds.) ACISP 2019. LNCS, vol. 11547, pp. 78–96. Springer, Cham (2019). https://doi.org/10.1007/978-3-030-21548-4_5
25. Sahai, A., Waters, B.: How to use indistinguishability obfuscation: deniable encryption, and more. In: Proceedings of the Forty-Sixth Annual ACM Symposium on Theory of Computing, pp. 475–484. ACM (2014)
26. Zhandry, M.: How to avoid obfuscation using witness PRFs. In: Kushilevitz, E., Malkin, T. (eds.) TCC 2016. LNCS, vol. 9563, pp. 421–448. Springer, Heidelberg (2016). https://doi.org/10.1007/978-3-662-49099-0_16

Improved Indistinguishability for Searchable Symmetric Encryption

Moesfa Soeheila Mohamad[1,2](✉) and Ji-Jian Chin[1,3]

[1] MIMOS Berhad, Kuala Lumpur, Malaysia
soeheila.mohamad@mimos.my
[2] Faculty of Computing and Informatics, Multimedia University, Cyberjaya, Malaysia
[3] Faculty of Engineering, Multimedia University, Cyberjaya, Malaysia

Abstract. This work presents a new experiment defining indistinguishability for searchable symmetric encryption to include security against published practical attacks. The proposed experiment allows the adversaries to use their prior knowledge about the stored documents to win. We solve the problem of modelling the adversaries with prior knowledge using the interacting split adversary technique. This new indistinguishability definition is aligned with the security goals and adversary capabilities listed in [4]. The correctness of the indistinguishability experiment is demonstrated by presenting proofs of strength and vulnerabilities of $\Sigma o\phi o\varsigma$-B and one of its variant. We write the security proofs based on the indistinguishability experiment with an adversary without any prior knowledge and adversary with full knowledge of the document set. We show how to win the indistinguishability experiment using the count attack by an adversary who knows the document distribution, and the file injection attack by an adversary without prior knowledge.

Keywords: Searchable symmetric encryption · Indistinguishability · Adversary model

1 Introduction

Searchable symmetric encryption (SSE) is a type of encryption scheme where the ciphertexts may be searched by keywords. SSE schemes are designed to work on a set of documents instead of a single document at each execution. Deploying SSE schemes for storing documents should protect the document secrecy and user's search privacy. However, to add the search functionality, a compromise has to be made on the encryption security. Information other than document length is disclosed to the storage server. This is where SSE security departs from encryption security definitions. Encryption security is defined as document secrecy with the ciphertext known to the adversary, and possibly encryption and decryption functions too. For SSE, the documents secrecy and user's search privacy are to be protected despite the ciphertexts, metadata and input-output pairs of query sequence being available to the adversary, along with search and update functions.

K. Nguyen et al. (Eds.): ProvSec 2020, LNCS 12505, pp. 190–212, 2020.
https://doi.org/10.1007/978-3-030-62576-4_10

SSE security specifically, indistinguishability and semantic security, currently holds the definition by Curtmola et al. [9], with some improvement for semantic security definition by Chase and Kamara [7]. In addition, under adaptive chosen keyword attack, SSE semantic security implies SSE indistinguishability [9]. Following that, SSE schemes publications including [5,12,13,16,19,22,26] present proof of the schemes achieving $\mathcal{L}$-security under adaptive chosen keyword attack. Other SSE security definitions use Universal Composibility [1,16,21] and Information Theoretic [25,28] models.

Nevertheless, attacks were designed, and the empirical evidence shows they are feasible and can recover query keywords from SSE schemes whose access pattern in search leakage reveals the actual keyword distribution [4,11,29]. The attacks are labelled Leakage Abuse Attack (LAA) and are applicable to the schemes proven secure using current SSE security models. The first published attack is [11], later named IKK after the authors. This attack recovers query keywords with 100% accuracy after observing 250 queries with the attacker knowing the whole document set. The count attack [4] exploits knowledge on keywords with unique frequencies. Combining this attack to the IKK attack, 100% accuracy in query recovery can be achieved even on obfuscated distribution in search results. Using the file injection attack, an attacker who knows only 1% of the documents can recover 30% of queried keywords. More attacks based on exploiting a scheme's leakage were published after these initial ideas [18,24]. Analysis of the attacks [4] provides the attack profile as shown in Table 1.

Table 1. Adversary model proposed by [4].

Attack mode	Adversary knowledge	Attack objectives
Passive[a]	Query distribution	Query recovery
Chosen query attack	Known queries	Plaintext recovery[b]
Chosen document attack	Document distribution	
	Known document	

[a]Passive adversary includes honest-but-curious server.
[b]The plaintext recovery goal includes partial plaintext recovery.

As a result of LAA, proposals are put forward including LAA-resistant scheme designs [28], vulnerability detection framework [27], scheme-strengthening [15] and data transformation methods [3,15,17,23]. These measures would result in SSE schemes strong against LAA and the results were proven by empirical evidence. However, their strengths cannot be expressed in their security proofs based on current SSE security definitions.

The successful practical attacks indicate some misfits between the SSE security definition and the practical attacks. SSE semantic security was defined in [6,7,9] and renamed as $\mathcal{L}$-security with $\mathcal{L}$ denoting the scheme's leakage function. The experiment means that by knowing only $\mathcal{L}$, an adversary cannot deduce the document content because the leakage may be produced by some other document set. SSE indistinguishability has been defined in [9,10] and the accepted definition currently is [9, Definition 5]. An SSE scheme is secure under the definition if the adversary cannot distinguish two independent document sets and query sequence (history), which implies the scheme conceals the content of the documents sets even with the revealed information. However, the experiment requires the input histories to produce equal leakage. This excludes queries specifically for differentiating the contents, such as keywords which are known to have unique frequencies. On the other hand, an attack on a scheme with respect to the semantic security experiment is the existence of one or more document sets and query sequences for which no simulator can produce indistinguishable replies. Similarly, for the indistinguishability experiment, an attack is when there exist two distinguishable histories which produce the same leakage. In both cases, an attack indicates that there is information revealed beyond $\mathcal{L}$. This is in accord to the SSE design intention. The metadata and search algorithm is designed so that the leakage is minimal, hence, the designer only has to prove the leakage is as declared.

From the discussion above, we understand that the SSE security is defined to be the secrecy of the document set despite the scheme's leakage. The misfit is that the experiments make the adversary generates the entire document set and hence has all knowledge about the document set. Curiously, the adversary is unable to use its knowledge to win as expected based on the analysis in [4]. The analysis shows that an adversary who knows the whole document set can breach document secrecy in many SSE schemes. In effect, the experiments restrict the definitions to security against adversaries who have access to the scheme's leakage only. In realisation of this [14,23] coined the name Leakage Only Attack(LOA) in which the $\mathcal{L}$-security game have the document set given in the environment, instead of being generated by the adversary. This change rectifies the current adversary model by excluding practical attackers. In other words, the adversary model now does not consider adversaries with prior knowledge. It remains to model adversary with prior knowledge.

Bost and Fouque formalised the adversary's knowledge and included it in the security definition by introducing the notion of constrained histories in [3] for Curtmola's indistinguishability game [9, Definition 4.10]. The adversary's prior knowledge is set as the constraint and the two histories to be chosen by the adversary must fulfil the constraints. The modified definition is named *constrained adaptive indistinguishability.* To model the LAA, constraint includes a fixed document set so that the known part of the document set is equal in the two histories. Hence, the two histories differ only in the query keywords sequence. With that, the constrained adaptive indistinguishability security definition includes the LAA setting. For a constraint C to be included in the security definition of a scheme with leakage $\mathcal{L}$, it has to be proven that C is $\mathcal{L}$-acceptable [3, Definition 3.3]. Having a constraint being acceptable for a leakage profile means schemes with that leakage profile is safe against an adversary with such prior knowledge. If it is not acceptable, it implies that schemes with that leakage profile are vulnerable against an adversary with such prior knowledge.

Cash et al. defined four leakage profiles in [4] by which SSE schemes may be categorised to indicate their security levels. Leveraging on those leakage profiles, the analysis in [3] is reduced to defining a constraint and proving that its acceptability towards a leakage profile. Nevertheless, the task of proving a constraint being acceptable for a leakage function is separated from proving that a scheme achieves the constrained adaptive indistinguishability.

Another misfit is the security goal. The SSE semantic security and indistinguishability are currently defined on the secrecy of the document set but LAA recovers query keywords. The strength against such attack goal is query keyword privacy and can be modelled by query indistinguishability. This model is formalised in [8,20] by a security game in which the adversary is required to distinguish the trapdoors of two query keywords. In [20] the definition for query indistinguishability was proven to imply $\mathcal{L}$-security and SSE indistinguishability. In [8] the security of a proposed database encryption scheme is proven to achieve query indistinguishability under chosen query attack against an adversary with the power to generate the database. Although this security goal models the published attacks accurately, SSE security should also include the secrecy of the stored documents.

Our Contributions. We propose here a new indistinguishability experiment for SSE security and a model for adversaries with prior-knowledge.

In the new indistinguishability experiment, only one set of documents are in play. For the security game, the adversary chooses two documents from the document set. The challenger then selects a keyword that only appears in one of the documents and generates the word's search token as the challenge. The adversary wins if it guesses the originating document of the search token correctly.

By defining the SSE security to be the indistinguishability of individual documents in one set, instead of document sets as in the current definition, the adversary will be able to exploit a scheme's leakage to win. That means the scheme's leakage can be proven to be safe-to-disclose to particular types of adversaries.

As a complement to the indistinguishability experiment, we propose a new SSE adversary model to describe adversaries with various type and amount of prior knowledge about the document set. This is the first proposal to directly use the adversary's knowledge in a scheme's analysis.

The variation of adversary models in an experiment to distinguish documents within a set provides the readers with clear assumptions and the security level of an SSE scheme. Application of additional measures to strengthen against attacks can also be seen in the adversary's advantage statement, hence removing the need for empirical evidence of security improvement.

We use $\Sigma o\phi o\varsigma$-B to illustrate the use of the indistinguishability experiment. We prove that the scheme achieves indistinguishability against a passive adversary without any prior knowledge and then provide an instance of the count attack by an adversary who knows the document distribution. For result-hiding $\Sigma o\phi o\varsigma$-B with cluster padding, we present the security proof against a passive adversary with full knowledge of the document set and an instance of the file injection attack by an adversary without prior knowledge.

2 Preliminaries

An SSE scheme is usually specified with two or three functions, namely Setup, Search, and Update for dynamic schemes. The functions are in fact protocols because they involve interaction between the SSE client and storage server.

Setup is when secret keys $\mathbf{K}$ are generated using KeyGen and a document set $\mathbf{D}$ is prepared for storing. The document set is preprocessed to generate the set of keywords $\mathbf{W}$ and then to build the mapping of every keyword to the identifiers of documents containing the keyword, $\mathsf{DB} = \{(w, \mathbf{D}(w))|w \in \mathbf{W}\}$ for input to BuildIndex. The documents are encrypted using a symmetric key encryption Encrypt with the generated secret key. This function concludes as the initial ciphertexts $\mathbf{c}$ and index $\mathbf{I}$ are sent to the storage server.

Search is when the user wants to extract some of the stored documents. The user will search the storage by keyword $w \in \mathbf{W}$ which invokes the Trapdoor on the client to obtain the search token τ_w. The search token is sent to the server for input to the server-side Search algorithm. The search result is a list of document identifiers. For result-hiding schemes, this algorithm returns the masked results to the client. For result-revealing schemes, the server unmasks the identifiers before returning them to the client.

Update is called when documents are to be added to the storage or removed from storage after Setup. The protocol to add a document uses Trapdoor and similar steps as BuildIndex to create the new index entries. There may be additional steps to obfuscate the new document's keyword list. Removing a document from storage would also modify the index.

An SSE scheme is correct when the search for a keyword w in the scheme returns identifiers of all documents containing keyword w. In notation, the scheme is correct if $\mathsf{Search}(\mathsf{Trapdoor}(w)) = \mathbf{D}(w)$.

2.1 Leakage Function

The metadata which enables the search will inevitably disclose information to the storage server. The disclosure makes SSE weak if considered as a conventional symmetric encryption scheme. So, in SSE security analysis the information learned by the server from viewing the index and ciphertexts after Setup, and all input-output pairs of the Search and Update functions must be considered.

The design of a scheme may produce different information or amount of leakage. Hence, [7] formalised leakage and makes it a parameter in SSE security. For every SSE scheme SSE, the leakage function should be declared $\mathcal{L} = (\mathcal{L}^{\mathsf{Setup}}, \mathcal{L}^{\mathsf{Search}}, \mathcal{L}^{\mathsf{Update}})$.

Setup Leakage. $\mathcal{L}^{\mathsf{Setup}}(DB, \mathbf{I}, \mathbf{c})$ specifies the information directly obtained from index $\mathbf{I}$ and ciphertexts $\mathbf{c}$. Minimally the leakage includes the number of documents and document sizes. Depending on the design of the index, the number of keywords or number of documents associated with every keyword may be leaked too.

Search Leakage. $\mathcal{L}^{\mathsf{Search}}(\mathbf{I}, \tau_w, w)$ specifies the information obtained from search results. For most SSE schemes, the search token τ_w is deterministic and therefore discloses search pattern which indicates whether the search token τ_w has been submitted previously. For static SSE scheme, the search pattern is also called the query pattern. The access pattern shows which ciphertext location or identifiers accessed during particular keyword search and hence, contains at least the length of search results. For result-hiding schemes, the access pattern contains masked identifiers. For result-revealing schemes, the access pattern contains the plain identifiers from which adversary may infer intersection pattern. Intersection pattern records the document identifiers which occur in the search results for distinct search tokens. In essence, from the intersection pattern, the server learns which search tokens are associated with one document, hence the keyword co-occurrence distribution. For dynamic schemes, the combination of search pattern and access pattern reveals new or omitted document identifiers in search results. Such accumulated information for a keyword w is denoted by $Hist(w)$.

Update Leakage. $\mathcal{L}^{\mathsf{Update}}(\mathsf{op}, D)$ specifies information disclosed during operation op (addition or deletion) of document D. A document addition or deletion may disclose the number of keywords contained in the document. Schemes that are not forward-secure would disclose whether D contains any of the searched keywords [26]. If a scheme is backward-secure, a keyword search would not disclose the identifiers of deleted documents which contain the keyword [26].

2.2 SSE Security Model

Security goals of SSE are to protect the document secrecy and the search keyword privacy. Extending the security definition of conventional symmetric encryption, SSE security is defined as semantic security or indistinguishability of the ciphertexts in the existence of metadata and leakage.

For SSE security analysis the adversary is an honest-but-curious server. That means the server performs its part in the protocol correctly but tries to learn contents of the stored documents. The server is modelled by giving the adversary all data and leakage in the defining game. Also, the attack being considered by most SSE schemes is chosen keyword attack. For this, the adversary has access to Search and Update oracles.

Semantic security for SSE is defined as $\mathcal{L}$-security to acknowledge the leakage. The defining game in [9] is a Real-Ideal game where the adversary is challenged to identify which environment it is playing. The experiment is presented in Appendix A. In the Real environment, the challenger runs the SSE scheme to reply to the adversary's queries. In the Ideal world, the adversary's queries are replied by a simulator based on the leakage of the scheme. Proving security of a scheme involves designing a simulator whose replies to the adversary is computationally indistinguishable from the real scheme's replies.

For the indistinguishability game proposed in [9], the challenge is to distinguish two document sets which produce equal leakage in the SSE scheme. The game is specified in Appendix B. The game begins with the challenger choosing randomly $b \in \{0,1\}$. Then the adversary submits two document sets, $\mathbf{D}_0, \mathbf{D}_1$ to the challenger. The challenger runs the SSE scheme Setup on $\mathbf{D}_b$. After receiving the index and ciphertexts, the adversary makes adaptive queries (w_0, w_1), where w_0 is a keyword from $\mathbf{D}_0$ and w_1 from $\mathbf{D}_1$, to the Search oracle. The oracle replies with the search token for w_b. After polynomially many queries, the adversary must guess which document set is being played by the challenger.

These two security games are adopted by almost all published SSE schemes.

2.3 Practical Attacks

The common factor for all attacks is that the attacker has some knowledge about the stored documents, as listed in Table 1. The adversary knowledge is also referred to as *prior knowledge* to mean information the adversary has before initiating the attacks.

The Count Attack. [4] is an improvement on the IKK attack [11]. This attack applies to SSE schemes whose $\mathcal{L}^{\mathsf{Search}}$ includes access pattern with actual result length and intersection pattern. The attacker's prior knowledge includes the whole or a large part of the document set, and a few pairs of trapdoor-keyword pairs.

In preparation, the attacker identifies from the known documents keywords with unique document counts. The documents are also processed to obtain the co-occurrence matrix. This matrix rows and columns are labelled with keywords symmetrically, and the element in location (i, j) are document identifiers which contain both keywords w_i and w_j.

During the attack, by observing the access pattern in $\mathcal{L}^{\mathsf{Search}}(w_q)$ of every search query w_q the attacker will capture those result lengths which match a unique document count, hence matches the keyword to the search token. Next, the observed intersection pattern is accumulated and at a time, the observed co-occurrence is matched to the co-occurrence matrix through simulated annealing to identify the closest match of co-occurrence. Combining the result to the known and recovered trapdoor-keyword pairs, more searched keywords are recovered.

File Injection Attack. [29] does not require any prior knowledge besides the set of keywords of the stored documents. However, the attacker needs to find a way to get their documents into the storage through the scheme and a way to recognise the injected document identifiers in the search results.

The attacker crafts documents containing keywords such that each keyword is a unique element in the content intersection for a set of the crafted documents. After injecting all of the crafted documents into the scheme, the attacker needs to observe access pattern in $\mathcal{L}^{\mathsf{Search}}$ of each search. By identifying which injected files are included in the access pattern, the attacker determines the keyword being represented by the search token.

There are variations in crafting the injected documents to reduce the size of documents or number of required injected files. If the attacker has some known documents, the attack becomes easier.

LZWT Attack. [18] is an attack where the attacker observes the search queries traffic to derive the queried keyword distribution from the search pattern in $\mathcal{L}^{\mathsf{Search}}$. This attack applies to SSE schemes whose search tokens are generated deterministically from the keywords. Similar to the IKK attack, the observed distribution is compared to a query distribution estimation to make good guesses of the queried keywords.

3 Redefining SSE Indistinguishability

Here we redefine SSE indistinguishability by considering the secrecy of individual documents within the protected document set instead of the secrecy of the document set as a whole. In one perspective, we are reviving SSE indistinguishability as defined by Goh in [10] by adopting it for SSE schemes with one index in the system. Also, we model the adversary whose prior knowledge may be less than the whole document set using the technique from [22].

3.1 Security Goals

The security goal here is the secrecy of every document in the storage, which also covers search privacy. We define this by an indistinguishability (IND) experiment under a chosen keyword attack (CKA) by an adversary $\mathcal{A}^{\text{prior}}$ with some prior knowledge as specified below. Table 2 shows the difference in the experiment for other attack modes.

In this experiment specification, for sets X and Y, $X \triangledown Y = (X \setminus Y) \cup (Y \setminus X)$ and $\widetilde{\mathbf{W}}(D_i)$ denotes the set of keywords in document D_i which has not been submitted to the Search oracle.

Definition 1 (IND-CKA by $\mathcal{A}^{\text{prior}}$). *Let* SSE *be an index-based SSE scheme consisting of (*Setup*,* Search*,* Update*), a positive integer* k *be the security parameter and* $\mathcal{A} = (\mathcal{A}_0, \mathcal{A}_1)$ *be a pair of adversaries who communicates by writing into the status* $st_{\mathcal{A}}$*. The indistinguishability experiment for chosen keyword attack by an adversary with prior knowledge,* $\mathbf{Ind}^{\text{CKA}}_{\mathsf{SSE},\mathcal{A}^{\text{prior}}}$*, is defined as follows:*

Initiation

1. *Given the security parameter* 1^k*, the adversary* $\mathcal{A}_0$ *chooses the document set* $\mathbf{D}$ *and submits* $\mathbf{D}$ *to the challenger* $\mathcal{C}$*.*

2. *Then* $\mathcal{A}_0$ *prepares the prior-knowledge as specified in Table 3 writes it into* $st_{\mathcal{A}}$.
3. *The challenger* $\mathcal{C}$ *calls* $\mathsf{Setup}(1^k, \mathbf{D})$ *to obtain the keys* $\mathbf{K} = \mathsf{KeyGen}(1^k)$, *index* $I = \mathsf{BuildIndex}(DB)$ *and ciphertexts* $\mathbf{c} = \mathsf{Encrypt}(\mathbf{K}, \mathbf{D})$.
4. *The outputs* $(I, \mathbf{c})$ *and the set of all keywords* $\mathbf{W}$ *are given to* $\mathcal{A}_1$.

Queries $\mathcal{A}_1$ *takes* $(I, \mathbf{c})$, $\mathbf{W}$ *and* $st_{\mathcal{A}}$ *as input and makes polynomially many queries to the* Search *oracle. The queried keywords and the corresponding replies are written into* $st_{\mathcal{A}}$.

Challenge

1. *On inputs* $\mathbf{D}$ *and* $st_{\mathcal{A}}$, $\mathcal{A}_0$ *chooses two documents* $D_0, D_1 \in \mathbf{D}$ *such that* $\widetilde{\mathbf{W}}(D_0) \triangledown \widetilde{\mathbf{W}}(D_1) \neq \emptyset$. *The documents are submitted to* $\mathcal{C}$ *and written into* $st_{\mathcal{A}}$.
2. $\mathcal{C}$ *randomly chooses* $b \in \{0,1\}$ *and choose* $w_b \in \widetilde{\mathbf{W}}(D_b) \setminus \widetilde{\mathbf{W}}(D_{1-b})$. *The challenge search token* $\tau_b = \mathsf{Trapdoor}(w_b)$ *is sent to* $\mathcal{A}_1$.
3. *After receiving the challenge,* $\mathcal{A}_1$ *may make more* Search *oracle queries except for the keywords in* D_0 *and* D_1.

Response

1. *Finally,* $\mathcal{A}_1$ *outputs* b' *as a guess of* b.
2. *The experiment outputs* 1 *if* $b' = b$, *otherwise output* 0.

We say $\mathcal{A}$ *wins the game if the experiment outputs* 1. *The advantage of* $\mathcal{A}$ *is defined as the probability of winning this game beyond guessing,*

$$\mathrm{Adv}^{\mathrm{IND-CKA}}_{\mathsf{SSE},\mathcal{A}^{\mathrm{prior}}}(k) = \left|\Pr\left[\mathbf{Ind}^{\mathrm{CKA}}_{\mathsf{SSE},\mathcal{A}^{\mathrm{prior}}}(k) = 1\right] - \frac{1}{2}\right|$$

where the probability is over $\mathcal{A}$ *and* $\mathcal{C}$*'s coin tosses. The* SSE *scheme is said to achieve indistinguishability under chosen keyword attack by an adversary with prior-knowledge if for any* $\mathcal{A} = (\mathcal{A}_0, \mathcal{A}_1)$,

$$\mathrm{Adv}^{\mathrm{IND-CKA}}_{\mathsf{SSE},\mathcal{A}^{\mathrm{prior}}}(k) \leq \mathsf{negl}(k).$$

Table 2. Attack mode determines the oracle access at the Query stage.

Attack Mode	$\mathcal{A}_0$	$\mathcal{A}_1$
Passive	May invoke Search and Update	Gets output of Search and Update
Chosen keyword attack	May invoke Update	Access to Search oracle and gets outputs from Update
Chosen document attack	No oracle access	Access to Search and Update oracles

3.2 Adversary Models

The adversary's prior knowledge has been listed in [4]. In order to allow the adversary set up the ideal document set for its attack but controls the knowledge it may use in the attack, the adversary is split into two adversaries which may communicate with each other, following the model in [22]. The first adversary, $\mathcal{A}_0$, prepares prior knowledge for the second adversary, $\mathcal{A}_1$, in the experiment initiation. After that $\mathcal{A}_1$ updates its status $st_{\mathcal{A}}$ based on which $\mathcal{A}_0$ may make Search or Update calls during query stage. The attack is executed by $\mathcal{A}_1$ using its prior knowledge, observed outputs and oracle access. Table 3 shows how our adversary model represents the adversaries with prior knowledge. Figure 1 shows the adversary's knowledge strength rank.

Table 3. Adversary's prior knowledge is modelled by what is generated by $\mathcal{A}_0$ and given to $\mathcal{A}_1$ at the experiment Initiation stage.

Prior Knowledge	Abbr.	Preparation by $\mathcal{A}_0$	Information for $\mathcal{A}_1$
No prior knowledge	LOA	Generates document set, **D**	None
Query distribution	KQDA	Generates the document set **D**, generates a search query sequence $w_1, w_2, \ldots, w_q$ for some $q < \lvert\mathbf{W}\rvert$	Searched keywords frequency table $\{(w_i, freq(w_i)) \mid 1 \leq i \leq q\}$
Query keywords	KQA	Generates document set **D**, use Search oracle to generate t searched keyword-token pairs for some $t < \lvert\mathbf{W}\rvert$	Keyword-token pairs $\{(w_i, \mathsf{Trapdoor}(w_i)) \mid 1 \leq i \leq t\}$
Document distribution	KDDA	Generates document set **D** and the keyword-documents mapping DB	Keywords frequency table $\{(w, \lvert\mathbf{D}(w)\rvert) \mid \text{all } w \in \mathbf{W}\}$
Partial document set	KDA	Generates document set **D**	A subset of the document set $\mathbf{S} \subset \mathbf{D}$
Full document set	KFDA	Generates document set **D**	The whole document set **D**

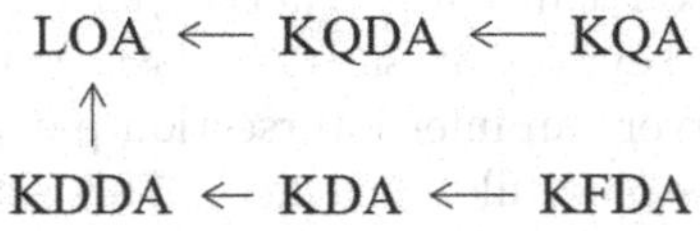

$$\begin{array}{ccccc} \text{LOA} & \longleftarrow & \text{KQDA} & \longleftarrow & \text{KQA} \\ \uparrow & & & & \\ \text{KDDA} & \longleftarrow & \text{KDA} & \longleftarrow & \text{KFDA} \end{array}$$

Fig. 1. A map showing the relation of adversary's strengths with the arrows pointing from the stronger to the weaker adversaries.

3.3 Relation to Current Security Definitions

The new indistinguishability experiment, $\mathbf{Ind}^{\text{CKA}}_{\mathsf{SSE},\mathcal{A}^{\text{prior}}}$, is nearer to practical security especially in considering the benefit of an SSE scheme's leakage to an adversary with prior knowledge. In Sect. 4.2 and 5.2, the practical attacks are used to win in the experiment. The same could not be done in the current indistinguishability (Appendix B) and $\mathcal{L}$-security (Appendix A) experiments.

Furthermore, Theorems 1 and 2 show how $\mathbf{Ind}^{\mathrm{CKA}}_{\mathsf{SSE},\mathcal{A}^{\mathrm{prior}}}$ allows security improvement to be proven. In the examples, the improvement materialises as the strength against a more powerful adversary. Besides that, the derived adversary's advantage over an SSE scheme contains statistics of the keyword distribution. This is aligned to the finding in [4] which identified the keyword distribution as a factor of an attack success rate.

Clearly, $\mathbf{Ind}^{\mathrm{CKA}}_{\mathsf{SSE},\mathcal{A}^{\mathrm{prior}}}$ is a document distinguishing experiment. In that perspective, document indistinguishability implies query indistinguishability as defined in [8,20]. We do not prove this statement in this work but this is apparent from the attack examples. The attack in Sect. 4.2 shows that a document distinguisher can be built from a query recovery adversary. On the other hand, Sect. 5.2 concludes that the attack to distinguish documents is easier than a query recovery attack. Finally, since [20] has proven that query indistinguishability implies both SSE indistinguishability and $\mathcal{L}$-security, $\mathbf{Ind}^{\mathrm{CKA}}_{\mathsf{SSE},\mathcal{A}^{\mathrm{prior}}}$ implies both security notions too.

4 $\Sigma o\phi o\varsigma$-B

An SSE scheme $\Sigma o\phi o\varsigma$-B was proposed in [2, §5]. The scheme was proven to achieve SSE indistinguishability as defined in [9]. The scheme is presented in Appendix C.

The leakage function of $\Sigma o\phi o\varsigma$-B is $\mathcal{L}_{\Sigma} = (\mathcal{L}_{\Sigma}^{\mathsf{Search}}, \mathcal{L}_{\Sigma}^{\mathsf{Update}})$ where

$$\mathcal{L}_{\Sigma}^{\mathsf{Search}}(w) = (SearchPattern(w), Hist(w))$$
$$\mathcal{L}_{\Sigma}^{\mathsf{Update}}(\mathsf{add}, w, ind) = \bot\ .$$

$\mathcal{L}_{\Sigma}^{\mathsf{Setup}}$ is not included because at that stage the server only obtains an empty index table. In the Search algorithm, the document identifiers are unmasked by the server. Thus, the server can learn whether there have been additions to the list of documents for keyword w since its last search, $Hist(w)$. Note also that from $Hist(w)$ the server can infer intersection pattern of all queried search tokens because it contains plain file identifiers. This scheme claims to have no leakage caused by Update because the algorithm is defined for one keyword in one document resulting on one entry in $\mathbf{I}$ of unique index key and masked file identifier.

Considering the $\Sigma o\phi o\varsigma$-B leakage functions, the scheme falls in the SSE schemes category vulnerable to the count attack. It is in the category of schemes defined in [4] as L1 where schemes leak access pattern in search results. The plain file identifiers in $\Sigma o\phi o\varsigma$-B search results directly reveal access pattern to the server. In the rest of this section, we prove using $\mathbf{Ind}^{\mathrm{CKA}}_{\mathsf{SSE},\mathcal{A}^{\mathrm{prior}}}$ that $\Sigma o\phi o\varsigma$-B is secure under leakage only attack but is vulnerable to the count attack under known documents attack.

4.1 IND-CKA by $\mathcal{A}^{\mathrm{LOA}}$

Here, we prove $\Sigma o\phi o\varsigma$-B achieves indistinguishability under Chosen Keyword Attack by an adversary without prior knowledge (LOA) using the experiment in Definition 1. This result agrees with the scheme's security proven in [2].

The adversary with no prior knowledge is modelled by having $\mathcal{A}_0$ preparing the document set but does not give any information about it to $\mathcal{A}_1$ at the initiation stage. Also, at the query stage, $\mathcal{A}_1$ is given access to Search oracle only, for the chosen keyword attack. The Update algorithm may be triggered by $\mathcal{A}_0$ by submitting a document to the challenger. The challenger gives $\mathcal{A}_1$ the update token only. $\mathcal{A}_0$ cannot give any information about the added document or keywords to $\mathcal{A}_1$. This experiment ensures that $\mathcal{A}_1$ can only use $\mathcal{L}^{\mathsf{Search}}$ of its choice of keywords and $\mathcal{L}^{\mathsf{Update}}$ observed to make its guess.

Theorem 1. *Suppose the trapdoor permutation π is one-way, the PRF F is pseudorandom and the hash functions H_1, H_2 modelled as random oracles. Then, $\Sigma o\phi o\varsigma$-B, denoted by Σ, achieves indistinguishability under chosen keyword attack by an adversary without prior knowledge.*

Proof. This proof is using the game hopping method. The main part of the proof is at the last hop, from game G_2 to G_3, where the scheme security is reduced to security of the PRF.
Game G_0 is the $\mathbf{Ind}^{\mathrm{CKA}}_{\Sigma,\mathcal{A}^{\mathrm{LOA}}}$ on the $\Sigma o\phi o\varsigma$-B scheme. So,

$$P\left[\mathbf{Ind}^{\mathrm{CKA}}_{\Sigma,\mathcal{A}^{\mathrm{LOA}}}(k) = 1\right] = P\left[G_0 = 1\right].$$

Game G_1 is the game G_0 on the scheme with hash functions H_1 and H_2 in Search and Update of the scheme being replaced by programmable random oracles which output binary strings of the same length of the hash outputs. So,

$$P\left[G_0 = 1\right] - P\left[G_1 = 1\right] \leq \mathbf{Adv}^{rand}_{H_1,\mathcal{B}_1}(k) + \mathbf{Adv}^{rand}_{H_2,\mathcal{B}_2}(k).$$

Next, game G_2 is the game G_1 on the scheme with the trapdoor π in Search and π^{-1} in Update replaced by a random permutation and its inversion mapping.

$$P\left[G_1 = 1\right] - P\left[G_2 = 1\right] \leq \mathbf{Adv}^{OW}_{\pi,\mathcal{B}_3}(k).$$

Lastly, Game G_3 is the game G_2 with the function F replaced with a random function. The reduction of winning probability depends on the advantage provided by exploiting the PRF to distinguish D_0 and D_1 by the challenge search token τ_b.

$$P\left[G_2 = 1\right] - P\left[G_3 = 1\right] \leq P\left[\text{Identify } b \text{ by exploiting } F\right].$$

Also, in the game G_3, the adversary only has the scheme leakage to determine b beyond simple guessing because all the primitives have been replaced by their respective ideals.

$$P\left[G_3 = 1\right] = P\left[\mathcal{A} \text{ identify } b \text{ from } \mathcal{L}\right].$$

Note that $\mathcal{L}^{\mathsf{Search}}(\tau_b) = (SearchPattern(w_b) = \perp, Hist(w_b) = \text{plain search results})$ because w_b has not been queried before. Since $\mathcal{A}^{\mathrm{LOA}}$ does not have any information regarding the documents or the keyword distribution, $Hist(w_b)$ does not provide any information to determine b, hence $P[G3 = 1] = \frac{1}{2}$.

Now, we find the probability of winning game G_2 by exploiting the PRF. To do this we reduce the scheme's security directly to the PRF. In other words, we show that the existence of adversary $\mathcal{A}^{\mathrm{LOA}}$ as distinguisher in the IND-CKA experiment on $\Sigma 2$ (the scheme in G_2) implies the existence of a PRF adversary.

Let $\mathcal{A} = (\mathcal{A}_0, \mathcal{A}_1)$ be an adversary without prior knowledge of document set of $\Sigma o\phi o\varsigma$-B. Consider an adversary $\mathcal{B}_4$ of the randomness of the PRF F. For security parameter k, the PRF indistinguishability game challenger, $\mathcal{C}'$ would select to play a random function $f(\cdot)$ or the PRF $F_K(\cdot)$, where K is a uniformly chosen key of length k. The task of $\mathcal{B}_4$ is to guess the challenger's choice of function. Here, $\mathcal{B}_4$ uses $\mathcal{A}$ in trying to win the PRF game.

The adversary $\mathcal{B}_4$ is going to perform the SSE indistinguishability experiment for $\mathcal{A}$, and submit every w_i in $\mathcal{A}$'s queries to $\mathcal{C}'$. The replies from $\mathcal{C}'$ will be the value used as K_{w_i}. When $\mathcal{A}_0$ submits file D_i to be added, $\mathcal{B}_4$ invokes the Update algorithm on (add, w_j, d_i) for all $w_j \in D_i$. In that, $\mathcal{B}_4$ submits w_j to $\mathcal{C}'$ and obtain value for K_{w_j} and then perform all other steps in the Update algorithm to return $(UT_{i,j}, c_j)$ to $\mathcal{A}_1$. When $\mathcal{A}_1$ queries w_i to the Search oracle, $\mathcal{B}_4$ submits w_i to $\mathcal{C}'$ for K_{w_i} value and then use it in the Search algorithm to return (K_{w_i}, ST_{c_i}, c_i).

At the challenge stage, $\mathcal{A}_0$ submits two files D_0 and D_1 as prescribed. For the challenge, $\mathcal{B}_4$ chooses keywords w_0 from D_0 and w_1 from D_1 such that $c_0 = c_1$ from $\mathbf{\Delta}[w_i] = (ST_i, c_i)$, if possible. Otherwise, $\mathcal{B}$ chooses any w_0 and w_1 from the set. Finally, $\mathcal{B}$ makes a random choice of $b \in \{0,1\}$ and gives to $\mathcal{A}_1$ (K_{w_b}, ST_{c_b}, c_b) as the challenge search token.

In the case that $c_0 = c_1$, if $\mathcal{A}_1$ guesses b correctly, $\mathcal{B}$ answers that $\mathcal{C}'$ plays the PRF $F_K(\cdot)$. If $\mathcal{A}_1$ guessed wrong, then $\mathcal{B}$ answers that $\mathcal{C}'$ plays the random function f. Otherwise, $\mathcal{B}$ guesses randomly, independent of $\mathcal{A}_1$'s guess.

If $\mathcal{C}'$ plays a random function against $\mathcal{B}$, then $\mathcal{A}_1$ would not have the advantage to distinguish the files by utilising the weakness of F_K. Hence,

$$\begin{aligned} P(\mathcal{B}\text{ wins}) &= P[E]\Big(P[\mathcal{A}\text{ wins}|F_K]P[F_K] + P[\mathcal{A}\text{ loses}|f]P[f]\Big) + \frac{1}{2} \\ &\geq P[E]\big(\mathbf{Adv}^{\mathrm{IND-CKA}}_{\Sigma 2,\mathcal{A}^{\mathrm{LOA}}}(k)\frac{1}{2}\big) + \frac{1}{2} \\ P(\mathcal{B}\text{ wins}) - \frac{1}{2} &\geq P[E]\big(\mathbf{Adv}^{\mathrm{IND-CKA}}_{\Sigma 2,\mathcal{A}^{\mathrm{LOA}}}(k)\frac{1}{2}\big). \end{aligned}$$

where E denotes the event that $c_0 = c_1$ and, F_K and f denote the event that $\mathcal{C}'$ plays the PRF and the random function, respectively. The inequality is brought about by the unknown probability that $\mathcal{A}$ loses$|f$ but it is at least 0. Consequently, by definition of an adversary's advantage in PRF experiment, and substituting $P[E]$ with the expected probability of E occuring, ε,

$$\mathbf{Adv}^{\mathrm{IND-CKA}}_{\Sigma 2,\mathcal{A}^{\mathrm{LOA}}}(k) \leq \frac{2}{\varepsilon}\mathbf{Adv}^{\mathrm{PRF}}_{F,\mathcal{B}}(k).$$

Finally, the sum of all inequalities from the games G_0 to G_3 gives

$$\begin{aligned}\mathbf{Adv}^{\mathrm{IND-CKA}}_{\Sigma,\mathcal{A}^{\mathrm{LOA}}}(k) &= P\left[\mathbf{Ind}^{\mathrm{CKA}}_{\Sigma,\mathcal{A}^{\mathrm{LOA}}}=1\right]-\frac{1}{2}\\ &\leq \mathbf{Adv}^{rand}_{H_1,\mathcal{A}}(k)+\mathbf{Adv}^{rand}_{H_2,\mathcal{A}}(k)+\mathbf{Adv}^{OW}_{\pi,\mathcal{A}}(k)+\frac{2}{\varepsilon}\mathbf{Adv}^{\mathrm{PRF}}_{F,\mathcal{B}}(k).\end{aligned}$$

The advantage statement implies if F, π, H_1 and H_2 are secure, then for document sets with large enough ε, $\Sigma o\phi o\varsigma$-B achieves indistinguishability under chosen keyword attack by an adversary without prior knowledge of the documents.

From the advantage statement, the tightness of $\mathcal{A}$'s advantage does depend on ε. In the extreme case where the distribution of documents over keyword is uniform, $\varepsilon = 1$, then $\mathcal{A}$'s advantage is tightly bound to the security of the PRF. On the other hand, if ε is very small, for example when each keyword is contained in a distinct number of documents, then $\mathcal{A}$'s advantage increases rapidly. This is aligned with the empirical evidence regarding the effect of data padding on the count attack complexity [3, §6.2].

4.2 Count Attack by $\mathcal{A}^{\mathrm{KDDA}}$

As a consequence of the result-revealing feature of $\Sigma o\phi o\varsigma$-B, $Hist(\cdot)$ in $\mathcal{L}^{\mathsf{Search}}_{\Sigma}$ contains the search token access pattern and intersection pattern. This puts $\Sigma o\phi o\varsigma$-B in leakage profile L1 [4] and makes it vulnerable to the count attack by adversaries stronger than $\mathcal{A}^{\mathrm{LOA}}$. We show here that an adversary with knowledge of the keyword distribution $\mathcal{A}^{\mathrm{KDDA}}$ can win the indistinguishability game on $\Sigma o\phi o\varsigma$-B by executing the count attack.

Initiation

1. The adversary $\mathcal{A}_0$ generates a document set $\mathbf{D}$ such that every keyword in the set is contained by a distinct number of documents. The set $\mathbf{D}$ is given to the challenger.
2. $\mathcal{A}_0$ generates the complete keyword distribution information and the set of all keywords $\mathbf{W}$ and gives it to $\mathcal{A}_1$.

Challenge

1. $\mathcal{A}_0$ chooses any two documents $D_0, D_1 \in \mathbf{D}$ and submit to the challenger and $\mathcal{A}_1$.
2. When $\mathcal{A}_1$ uses the challenge search token (ST_w, c_w) to search the index I, $\mathcal{A}_1$ gets the number of documents associated with w_b from $\mathcal{L}^{\mathsf{Search}}_{\Sigma}$.
3. Referring to the keyword frequency table, $\mathcal{A}_1$ can recover correctly the corresponding keyword, say w^*.

Response. By the design of the challenge search token, only one of D_0 and D_1 contains w^*. Hence, by searching for w^* in the documents, $\mathcal{A}_1$ can always identify the correct document and hence the correct value of b.

5 $\Sigma o\phi o\varsigma$-B with Cluster Padding

In this section, we analyse the security of $\Sigma o\phi o\varsigma$-B in the result-hiding scenario with frequency-based cluster padding parameterized by α [3, §5.4] applied on the data. The padding is added during preparation of the database DB before being input to the scheme. The padding algorithm clusters keywords with equal frequencies. Fake keyword-document pairs are added to the DB to make each cluster to contain at least α keywords.

For the result-hiding $\Sigma o\phi o\varsigma$-B, the server is prevented from unmasking the file identifiers. For completeness, the description of the slightly modified scheme is presented in Appendix D. The leakage function for the result-hiding $\Sigma o\phi o\varsigma$-B denoted by $\mathcal{L}_{\Sigma'} = (\mathcal{L}_{\Sigma'}^{\mathsf{Search}}, \mathcal{L}_{\Sigma'}^{\mathsf{Update}})$ is

$$\mathcal{L}_{\Sigma'}^{\mathsf{Search}}(w) = (SearchPattern(w), Hist'(w))$$
$$\mathcal{L}_{\Sigma'}^{\mathsf{Update}}(add, w, ind) = \perp$$

where $Hist'(w)$ is the history of keyword w search results. They are lists of masked file identifiers. Due to this, the intersection pattern cannot be derived because masked identifiers of the same file cannot be matched. The leakage is the number of file identifiers in the search result and whether there have been new files containing the keyword since it was last searched.

In the following sections, we present how result-hiding $\Sigma o\phi o\varsigma$-B in with frequency-based cluster padding achieves indistinguishability against a passive adversary who knows all of the plaintext documents, but vulnerable to file injection attack.

5.1 IND-CKA by $\mathcal{A}^{\text{KFDA}}$

Comparing this version to the original $\Sigma o\phi o\varsigma$-B, two protections has been added. The padding renders the observed keyword frequency less useful to identify keywords, and masked file identifiers in search results conceal intersection pattern. Therefore, this version of the scheme is expected to be strong against a more powerful adversary than in Theorem 1. It has been shown [3, Corollary 8] that result-hiding $\Sigma o\phi o\varsigma$-B with cluster padding achieves constrained adaptive indistinguishability against adversary with full knowledge of the document set. Here we show that we can use the proposed indistinguishability experiment and the model of an adversary with the full knowledge of document set to prove the same security statement.

For the indistinguishability experiment in Definition 1 the adversary with full knowledge of the document, $\mathcal{A}^{\text{KFDA}}$, is modelled by having $\mathcal{A}_0$ generates and gives the whole document set $\mathbf{D}$ to $\mathcal{A}_1$. Besides that, $\mathcal{A}_1$ has only the Search oracle access. Due to the padding scheme, when the challenger of the experiment receives the document set $\mathbf{D}$ from $\mathcal{A}_0$, it would execute the cluster padding scheme, to produce the padded data $\bar{\mathsf{DB}}$ before invoking the Update algorithm accordingly. Thus, $\mathcal{A}_1$ receives update tokens of the padded data.

Theorem 2. *Denote by Σ' the variation of $\Sigma o\phi o\varsigma$-B as defined in Appendix D. Suppose the trapdoor permutation π is one-way, the PRF F is pseudorandom and the hash functions H_1, H_2 modelled as random oracles. Then Σ' achieves indistinguishability under adaptive chosen keyword attack against an adversary with full knowledge of the document set.*

Proof. This proof is using the game hopping method in which at the last hop, from game G_2 to G_3, the scheme security is reduced to the security of the PRF. Since the changes to the scheme in the four games are identical to those in the proof of Theorem 1 and to adhere to the space limit, we begin with the sum of the inequalities from the games G_0, G_1, G_2 and G_3:

$$P\left[\mathbf{Ind}^{\mathrm{CKA}}_{\Sigma',\mathcal{A}^{\mathrm{KFDA}}}(k)=1\right] - P\left[G_3 = 1\right] \tag{1}$$
$$\leq \mathbf{Adv}^{rand}_{H_1,\mathcal{A}}(k) + \mathbf{Adv}^{rand}_{H_2,\mathcal{A}}(k) + \mathbf{Adv}^{OW}_{\pi,\mathcal{A}}(k) + P\left[\text{Identify } b \text{ by exploiting } F\right].$$

First, we calculate $P[G_3 = 1]$. In the game, the adversary has $\mathcal{L}^{\mathsf{Search}}_{\Sigma'}(w_b)$ and its full knowledge of the document set to determine b. $Hist(w_b)$ provides the length of results list which can be compared to $Hist(\tilde{w})$ for all $\tilde{w} \in \widetilde{\mathbf{W}}(D_i)$ for $i = 0, 1$. Let G^* denotes the event that w_0, w_1 belongs to the same cluster. There are two cases:
Case 1: G^* occurs which means the adversary could not determine b and thus the probability of winning is $\frac{1}{2}$.
Case 2: G^* does not occur which means there is no $\tilde{w} \in \widetilde{\mathbf{W}}(D_{1-b})$ that matches the length of search result. So, the adversary has probability 1 to win.
Thus, $P[G_3 = 1] = \frac{1}{2}P[G^*] + (1 - P[G^*]) = 1 - \frac{1}{2}P[G^*]$.

Secondly, we find the probability of winning game G_2 by exploiting the PRF. To do this we reduce the scheme's security directly to the PRF. In other words, we show that the existence of adversary $\mathcal{A}^{\mathrm{KFDA}}$ as distinguisher in the IND-CKA experiment on the scheme in G_2, $\Sigma 2$, implies the existence of a PRF adversary.

Let $\mathcal{A}$ be an adversary who knows the document set and wins the indistinguishability game with advantage $\mathbf{Adv}^{\mathrm{IND-CKA}}_{\Sigma 2,\mathcal{A}^{\mathrm{KFDA}}}(k)$. Consider the following adversary $\mathcal{B}$ of the randomness of PRF F. To answer the PRF game, $\mathcal{B}$ simulates the challenger in the indistinguishability game against $\mathcal{A}$. For the PRF, $\mathcal{B}$ queries $\mathcal{C}'$ in the PRF game. So, When $\mathcal{A}$ queries the Search oracle, $\mathcal{B}$ also query the $\mathcal{C}'$ on w to get K_w and produces (K_w, ST_c, c) as in the scheme $\Sigma 2$. When $\mathcal{A}_0$ triggers $\mathsf{Update}(d, w)$, $\mathcal{B}$ obtains K_w by querying $\mathcal{C}'$ on w and obtains K'_w by querying on $w||i$ for each counter i.

When given D_0 and D_1 at the challenge stage, $\mathcal{B}$ selects w_0 from D_0 and w_1 from D_1 such that w_0 and w_1 are from the same keyword cluster, say G^*, if possible. Then, $\mathcal{B}$ chooses b and proceeds to produce the challenge search token. If such keywords are not found then $\mathcal{B}$ just choose any keyword w_b from D_b.

If $\mathcal{B}$ use keywords from the same cluster and $\mathcal{A}$ guesses b correctly, then $\mathcal{B}$ outputs that it is playing the PRF. Otherwise, $\mathcal{B}$ outputs that it is playing a random function. In the case where $\mathcal{B}$ use an arbitrary keyword for the challenge, $\mathcal{B}$ makes a random guess in the PRF game.

Let G^* denotes the event that $\mathcal{B}$ found w_0, w_1 which belongs to the same cluster, F_K the event that $\mathcal{C}'$ plays the PRF and f denotes $\mathcal{C}'$ plays a random function.

$$\begin{aligned} P[\mathcal{B}\text{ wins}] &= P[G^*]\big(P[\mathcal{A}\text{ wins}|F_K]\cdot P[F_K] + P[\mathcal{A}\text{ loses}|f]\cdot P[f]\big) + \frac{1}{2} \\ &\geq P[G^*]\big(\frac{1}{2}\mathbf{Adv}^{\mathrm{IND-CKA}}_{\Sigma 2,\mathcal{A}^{\mathrm{KFDA}}}(k)\big) + \frac{1}{2} \\ P[\mathcal{B}\text{ wins}] - \frac{1}{2} &\geq P[G^*]\big(\frac{1}{2}\mathbf{Adv}^{\mathrm{IND-CKA}}_{\Sigma 2,\mathcal{A}^{\mathrm{KFDA}}}(k)\big). \end{aligned}$$

The equation becomes an inequality when we omit the term for the unknown probability for $\mathcal{A}$ loses$|f$ which is at least 0.

Let ε' be the expected probability of keywords to be in the same cluster in the cluster padding scheme. By the definition of an adversary's advantage in the PRF experiment, we have

$$\mathbf{Adv}^{\mathrm{IND-CKA}}_{\Sigma 2,\mathcal{A}^{\mathrm{KFDA}}}(k) \leq \frac{2}{\varepsilon'}\mathbf{Adv}_{\mathrm{PRF},\mathcal{B}}(k).$$

Finally, from Eq. 1,

$$\begin{aligned} &P\left[\mathbf{Ind}^{\mathrm{CKA}}_{\Sigma',\mathcal{A}^{\mathrm{KFDA}}}(k){=}1\right] - \big(1 - \frac{1}{2}P\left[G^*\right]\big) \\ &\leq \mathbf{Adv}^{rand}_{H_1,\mathcal{A}}(k) + \mathbf{Adv}^{rand}_{H_2,\mathcal{A}}(k) + \mathbf{Adv}^{OW}_{\pi,\mathcal{A}}(k) + \frac{2}{\varepsilon'}\mathbf{Adv}^{\mathrm{PRF}}_{F,\mathcal{B}}(k). \end{aligned}$$

which gives the upper bound for $\mathbf{Adv}^{\mathrm{IND-CKA}}_{\Sigma',\mathcal{A}^{\mathrm{KFDA}}}(k)$ to be

$$\mathbf{Adv}^{OW}_{\pi,\mathcal{A}}(k) + \mathbf{Adv}^{rand}_{H_1,\mathcal{A}}(k) + \mathbf{Adv}^{rand}_{H_2,\mathcal{A}}(k) + \frac{2}{\varepsilon'}\mathbf{Adv}^{\mathrm{PRF}}_{F,\mathcal{B}}(k) + \frac{1-\varepsilon'}{2}.$$

So, given that π, H_1, H_2 and F are secure, for a large enough ε', result-hiding $\Sigma o\phi o\varsigma$-B with cluster padding achieves indistinguishability under chosen keyword attack by an adversary with full knowledge of the document set.

5.2 File Injection Attack by $\mathcal{A}^{\mathrm{LOA}}$

We describe here the file injection attack [29], which is a chosen document attack, by an adversary with no prior knowledge on the result-hiding $\Sigma o\phi o\varsigma$-B with cluster padding. We assume the attacker knows details of the padding scheme during Update which processes and upload files by batch. Although the scheme does not leak access pattern, the attack uses the new index entries resulting from adding files to the storage.

Initiation

1. The adversary $\mathcal{A}_0$ generates a document set $\mathbf{D}$ and submit to $\mathcal{C}$.
2. $\mathcal{C}$ runs Setup and outputs to $\mathcal{A}_1$ the empty index I and public key PK.

3. $\mathcal{C}$ performs $\mathsf{Update}(D_i, w_j)$ for all $D_i \in \mathbf{D}$ and all keywords w_i, and $\mathcal{A}_1$ gets all update tokens $(UT_{i,j}, e_{i,j})$ and set of all keywords $\mathbf{W}$.

Queries

1. $\mathcal{A}_1$ generates documents containing subsets of keywords and organise them in sets $\mathbf{F}_1, \dots, \mathbf{F}_m$ such that keywords contained in each file set do not intersect. The set sizes match the batch size for Update.
2. The document set $\mathbf{F}_1$ is submitted to Update oracle and $\mathcal{A}_1$ records the update tokens $(UT_{w,d}, e_{w,d})$ for the set of injected files, name the set $\mathbf{U}_1$. From this, $\mathcal{A}_1$ knows the masked file identifiers for all of their keywords but cannot work out individual keyword-identifier pairs and group of identifiers of one file by one-wayness of H_1.
3. $\mathcal{A}_1$ performs the same for $\mathbf{F}_2, \dots, \mathbf{F}_m$ and record $\mathbf{U}_2, \dots, \mathbf{U}_m$.

Challenge. $\mathcal{A}_0$ considers $st_\mathcal{A}$ and chooses documents $D_0, D_1 \in \mathbf{D}$ such that $\widetilde{\mathbf{W}}(D_0) \setminus \widetilde{\mathbf{W}}(D_1)$ and $\widetilde{\mathbf{W}}(D_1) \setminus \widetilde{\mathbf{W}}(D_0)$ are contained in different batches of injected files. Let (ST_b, c_b) be the challenge search token from $\mathcal{C}$.

Response

1. $\mathcal{A}_1$ extract the keywords of D_0 and D_1 and matches them to the plain injected files to identify the injected file batch, say batch $\mathbf{F}_0$ for D_0 and $\mathbf{F}_1$ for D_1.
2. $\mathcal{A}_1$ uses (ST_b, c_b) to search I and gets the list of masked identifiers $\mathbf{e}_{w_b}$.
3. Compare the identifiers from $\mathbf{e}_{w_b}$ to set of $\mathbf{U}_0$ of $\mathbf{F}_0$ and $\mathbf{U}_1$ of $\mathbf{F}_1$.
4. By choice of D_0 and D_1, only one of $\mathbf{U}_0$ and $\mathbf{U}_1$ contains all identifiers from $\mathbf{e}_{w_b}$. Thus, $\mathcal{A}_1$ gets the correct value of b.

Notice that in the attack although the challenge keyword is not identified uniquely, it is enough to distinguish the two files. In addition, this attack requires fewer injected files because the target keyword subsets intersection is a list of keywords rather than unique keywords.

6 Conclusion

The proposed indistinguishability experiment for SSE is an adoption of conventional encryption indistinguishability definition similar to [10]. By taking $\Sigma o\phi o\varsigma$-B as an example SSE scheme, we have shown how the adversary with prior knowledge is modelled in the indistinguishability experiment. In the attacks, it is straightforward for the adversaries to use their prior knowledge on the scheme's leakage to win the experiment. Besides, the proposed indistinguishability experiment has forced the document distribution statistics into the adversary's advantage statement. With that, we have shown that the proposed experiment enables better security analysis on SSE schemes.

Acknowledgement. This work is part of a project under The 11th Malaysia Plan. The authors would like to thank the Ministry of Education of Malaysia for providing part of the financial support for this work through the Fundamental Research Grant Scheme (Project number: FRGS/1/2019/ICT04/MMU/02/5). Ji-Jian Chin would also like to thank the Information Security Lab at MIMOS Berhad for hosting his industrial attachment during which this paper was completed. Finally, we thank the anonymous reviewers and in particular our shepherd, Dr Benjamin Tan, for their help in improving this paper.

A $\mathcal{L}$-security by [7]

Let SSE$=$(Setup, Search, Update, Decrypt) be an SSE scheme with a leakage profile $\mathcal{L}_{\mathsf{SSE}} = (\mathcal{L}^{\mathsf{Setup}}_{\mathsf{SSE}}, \mathcal{L}^{\mathsf{Search}}_{\mathsf{SSE}}, \mathcal{L}^{\mathsf{Update}}_{\mathsf{SSE}})$. Then, SSE is $\mathcal{L}$-secure against adaptive chosen keyword attacks if for all PPT adversary $\mathcal{A}$, there exists a PPT simulator $\mathcal{S}$ such that

$$\mathbf{Adv}_{\mathsf{SSE},\mathcal{A},\mathcal{S}}(k) = |\Pr[\mathbf{Real}_{\mathsf{SSE},\mathcal{A}}(k) = 1] - \Pr[\mathbf{Ideal}_{\mathsf{SSE},\mathcal{A},\mathcal{S}}(k) = 1| \leq \mathtt{negl}(k)$$

where the games are as follows:

$\mathbf{Real}_{\mathsf{SSE},\mathcal{A}}(1^k)$

1. $\mathcal{A}$ generates DB and $\mathbf{D}$ and gives to the challenger, $\mathcal{C}$.
2. $\mathcal{C}$ executes Setup, where the resulting I and $\mathbf{c}$ are given to $\mathcal{A}$.
3. $\mathcal{A}$ then makes a polynomial number of Search and Update queries, and receives the search token and update results.
4. Finally, $\mathcal{A}$ returns a bit b as the output of the experiment.

$\mathbf{Ideal}_{\mathsf{SSE},\mathcal{A},\mathcal{S}}(1^k)$

1. $\mathcal{A}$ outputs DB and $\mathbf{D}$ to $\mathcal{C}$.
2. The simulator $\mathcal{S}$ simulates I and $\mathbf{c}$ based on the leakage information from $\mathcal{L}^{\mathsf{Setup}}_{\mathsf{SSE}}$, and gives I and $\mathbf{c}$ to $\mathcal{A}$.
3. $\mathcal{A}$ makes a polynomial number of Search and Update queries.
4. The simulator $\mathcal{S}$ returns the search tokens based on $\mathcal{L}^{\mathsf{Search}}_{\mathsf{SSE}}$ and update results based on $\mathcal{L}^{\mathsf{Update}}_{\mathsf{SSE}}$.
5. Finally, $\mathcal{A}$ returns a bit b as the output of the experiment.

B SSE Indistinguishability by [9]

Let SSE=(KeyGen, Encrypt, Trapdoor, Search, Decrypt) be an index-based SSE, $k \in \mathbb{N}$ be a security parameter, $\mathcal{A} = (\mathcal{A}_0, \ldots, \mathcal{A}_{q+1})$ be such that $q \in \mathbb{N}$ and consider the following probabilistic experiment $\mathbf{Ind}^*_{\mathcal{A},\mathsf{SSE}}(k)$

Initiation

1. Given the security parameter 1^k, challenger $\mathcal{C}$ generates the secret key K.
2. Then $\mathcal{C}$ randomly chooses a value $b \in \{0, 1\}$.
3. $\mathcal{A}_0$ generates two document sets, $\mathbf{D}_0$ and $\mathbf{D}_0$, such that $\mathcal{L}^{\mathsf{Setup}}(\mathbf{D}_0) = \mathcal{L}^{\mathsf{Setup}}(\mathbf{D}_1)$, and submits them to $\mathcal{C}$. Let $\mathbf{W}_0$ and $\mathbf{W}_1$ be the set of all keywords in $\mathbf{D}_0$ and $\mathbf{D}_1$ respectively.
4. $\mathcal{C}$ runs Setup on $\mathbf{D}_b$ and gives $\mathcal{A}$ the index I_b and ciphertexts $\mathbf{c}_b$.

Query

1. The adversary $\mathcal{A}$ makes q search queries by having $\mathcal{A}_i$ choosing $w_{0,i} \in \mathbf{W}_0$ and $w_{1,i} \in \mathbf{W}_1$ such that $\mathcal{L}^{\mathsf{Search}}(w_{0,i}) = \mathcal{L}^{\mathsf{Search}}(w_{1,i})$.

2. For each i, the Search oracle replies with the search token τ_i for keyword $w_{b,i}$.

Response

1. Finally, $\mathcal{A}_{q+1}$ makes a guess b'.
2. The experiment outputs 1 if $b' = b$. Otherwise, outputs 0.

We say that SSE is secure in the sense of adaptive indistinguishability if for all PPT adversaries $\mathcal{A} = (\mathcal{A}_0, \ldots, \mathcal{A}_{q+1})$ such that q=poly(k),

$$\Pr\left[\mathbf{Ind}^*_{\mathsf{SSE},\mathcal{A}}(k) = 1\right] \leq \frac{1}{2} + \mathsf{negl}(k),$$

where the probability is over the choice of b, and the coins of KeyGen and Encrypt.

C $\Sigma o\phi o\varsigma$-B

Here is the SSE scheme $\Sigma o\phi o\varsigma$-B as specified in [2, §5]. In this scheme F is a pseudorandom function, π is a trapdoor permutation, and H_1 and H_2 are keyed hash functions.

Setup. Given a security parameter 1^k, the algorithm generates a symmetric key $\mathbf{K_S} \in \{0,1\}^k$, an asymmetric key pair (SK, PK) and prepare two empty mappings $\mathbf{\Delta}$ and I. Output to the client $(\mathbf{\Delta}$, $(\mathbf{K_S}$, $SK))$ and to server $(\mathbf{I}$, $PK)$.

Search. To search for keyword w, the client prepares $K_w = F_{\mathbf{K_S}}(w)$ and extract $(ST_c, c) = \mathbf{\Delta}[w]$, and then sends (K_w, ST_c, c) to the server. If $(ST_c, c) = \perp$, directly output $\emptyset$. The server goes though counter $i = c, c-1, \ldots, 0$ to compute $UT_i = H_1(K_w, ST_i)$ and extract $e_i = \mathbf{I}[UT_i]$. The output is unmasked $d_i \leftarrow e_i \oplus H_2(K_w, ST_i)$. For the next counter, server computes $ST_{i-1} = \pi_{PK}(ST_i)$. Finally, The server returns a list of document identifiers $(d_i)_{i=0,1,\ldots,c}$.

Update. This algorithm is invoked to update the index for one keyword w from one document D. Let d denotes the identifier for document D. First the client recalculate the keyword key $K_w = F_{\mathbf{K_S}}(w)$ and extract $(ST_c, c) = \mathbf{\Delta}[w]$. If $\mathbf{\Delta}[w] = \perp$ this means the keyword is new, hence the client set the first token ST_0 for w to a random string and create new entry $\mathbf{\Delta}[w] = (ST_0, 0)$. Otherwise, calculate the next token, $ST_{c+1} = \pi^{-1}_{SK}(ST_c)$ and renew entry $\mathbf{\Delta}[w] = (ST_{c+1}, c+1)$. Next, compute index key $UT_{c+1} = H_1(K_w, ST_{c+1})$ and mask the identifier $e = d \oplus H_2(K_w, ST_{c+1})$. Finally, the client sends (UT_{c+1}, e) to the server which sets $\mathbf{I}[UT_{c+1}] = e$.

D Result-Hiding $\Sigma o\phi o\varsigma$-B

Here is a variation of $\Sigma o\phi o\varsigma$-B where the storage server returns masked file identifiers to the client during Search.

Setup. Given a security parameter 1^k, the algorithm generates a symmetric key $\mathbf{K_S} \in \{0,1\}^k$, an asymmetric key pair (SK, PK) and prepare two empty mappings $\mathbf{\Delta}$ and I. Output to the client ($\mathbf{\Delta}$, ($\mathbf{K_S}$, SK)) and to server ($\mathbf{I}$, PK).

Search. To search for keyword w, the client prepares $K_w = F_{\mathbf{K_S}}(w)$ and extract $(ST_c, c) = \mathbf{\Delta}[w]$, and then sends (K_w, ST_c, c) to the server. If $(ST_c, c) = \perp$, directly output $\emptyset$. The server goes though counter $i = c, c-1, \ldots, 0$ to compute $UT_i = H_1(K_w, ST_i)$ and then extract $e_i = \mathbf{I}[UT_i]$. For the next counter, server computes $ST_{i-1} = \pi_{PK}(ST_i)$. The server returns a list of masked document identifiers $(e_i)_{i=0,1,\ldots,c}$. Finally, the client unmasks the document identifiers $d_i = e_i \oplus H_2(K'_w, ST_i)$ where $K'_w = F_{\mathbf{K_S}}(w||i^{bin})$ for $i = 0, 1, \ldots, c$.

Update. This algorithm is invoked to update the index for one keyword w from one document D. Let d denotes the identifier for document D. First the client recalculate the keyword key $K_w = F_{\mathbf{K_S}}(w)$ and extract $(ST_c, c) = \mathbf{\Delta}[w]$. If $\mathbf{\Delta}[w] = \perp$ this means the keyword is new, hence set the first token ST_0 to a random string and set $\mathbf{\Delta}[w] = (ST_0, 0)$. Otherwise, calculate the next token, $ST_{c+1} = \pi_{SK}^{-1}(ST_c)$ and set $\mathbf{\Delta}[w] = (ST_{c+1}, c+1)$. Next, compute index key $UT_{c+1} = H_1(K_w, ST_{c+1})$ and mask the identifier $e = d \oplus H_2(K'_w, ST_{c+1})$ where $K'_w = F_{\mathbf{K_S}}(w||(c+1)^{bin})$. Finally, the client sends (UT_{c+1}, e) to the server which sets $\mathbf{I}[UT_{c+1}] = e$.

References

1. Bosch, C., et al.: Distributed searchable symmetric encryption. In: Proceedings of the Twelfth Annual Conference on Privacy, Security and Trust (PST 2014). IEEE (2014)
2. Bost, R.: $\sigma o \phi o \varsigma$-forward secure searchable encryption. In: Proceedings of the 23rd ACM SIGSAC Conference on Computer and Communications Security (CCS 2016), pp. 1143–1154. ACM (2016)
3. Bost, R., Fouque, P.A.: Thwarting leakage abuse attacks against searchable encryption a formal approach and applications to database padding. Cryptology ePrint Archive, Report 2017/1060 (2017). http://eprint.iacr.org/2017/1060/
4. Cash, D., Grubbs, P., Perry, J., Ristenpart, T.: Leakage-abuse attacks against searchable encryption. In: Proceedings of the 22nd ACM SIGSAC Conference on Computer and Communications Security, pp. 668–679. ACM (2015)
5. Cash, D., et al.: Dynamic Searchable Encryption in Very Large Databases: Data Structures and Implementation. Cryptology ePrint Archive, Report 2014/853 (2014). http://eprint.iacr.org/2014/853
6. Chang, Y.-C., Mitzenmacher, M.: Privacy preserving keyword searches on remote encrypted data. In: Ioannidis, J., Keromytis, A., Yung, M. (eds.) ACNS 2005. LNCS, vol. 3531, pp. 442–455. Springer, Heidelberg (2005). https://doi.org/10.1007/11496137_30
7. Chase, M., Kamara, S.: Structured encryption and controlled disclosure. In: Abe, M. (ed.) ASIACRYPT 2010. LNCS, vol. 6477, pp. 577–594. Springer, Heidelberg (2010). https://doi.org/10.1007/978-3-642-17373-8_33

8. Cui, S., Asghar, M.R., Galbraith, S.D., Russello, G.: ObliviousDB: practical and efficient searchable encryption with controllable leakage. In: Imine, A., Fernandez, J.M., Marion, J.-Y., Logrippo, L., Garcia-Alfaro, J. (eds.) FPS 2017. LNCS, vol. 10723, pp. 189–205. Springer, Cham (2018). https://doi.org/10.1007/978-3-319-75650-9_13
9. Curtmola, R., Garay, J.A., Kamara, S., Ostrovsky, R.: Searchable symmetric encryption: improved definitions and efficient constructions. In: Juels, A., Wright, R.N., di Vimercati, S.D.C. (eds.) ACM Conference on Computer and Communications Security, CCS 2006, pp. 79–88. ACM (2006)
10. Goh, E.J.: Secure indexes. Cryptology ePrint Archive, Report 2003/216 (2003). http://eprint.iacr.org/2003/216/
11. Islam, M.S., Kuzu, M., Kantarcioglu, M.: Access pattern disclosure on searchable encryption: ramification, attack and mitigation. In: 19th Annual Network and Distributed System Security Symposium, NDSS 2012. The Internet Society (2012)
12. Kamara, S., Papamanthou, C.: Parallel and dynamic searchable symmetric encryption. In: Sadeghi, A.-R. (ed.) FC 2013. LNCS, vol. 7859, pp. 258–274. Springer, Heidelberg (2013). https://doi.org/10.1007/978-3-642-39884-1_22
13. Kamara, S., Papamanthou, C., Roeder, T.: Dynamic searchable symmetric encryption. In: Yu, T., Danezis, G., Gligor, V.D. (eds.) ACM Conference on Computer and Communications Security - CCS 2012, pp. 965–976. ACM (2012)
14. Kamara, S., Moataz, T.: Boolean searchable symmetric encryption with worst-case sub-linear complexity. Cryptology ePrint Archive, Report 2017/126 (2017). http://eprint.iacr.org/2017/126/
15. Kamara, S., Moataz, T., Ohrimenko, O.: Structured encryption and leakage suppression. Cryptology ePrint Archive, Report 2018/551 (2018). http://eprint.iacr.org/2018/551/
16. Kurosawa, K., Ohtaki, Y.: UC-secure searchable symmetric encryption. In: Keromytis, A.D. (ed.) FC 2012. LNCS, vol. 7397, pp. 285–298. Springer, Heidelberg (2012). https://doi.org/10.1007/978-3-642-32946-3_21
17. Lacharité, M.S., Patterson, K.G.: Frequency-smoothing encryption: preventing snapshot attacks on deterministically-encrypted data. Cryptology ePrint Archive, Report 2017/1068 (2017). http://eprint.iacr.org/2017/1068/
18. Liu, C., Zhu, L., Wang, M., Tan, Y.: Search pattern leakage in searchable encryption: attacks and new construction. Inf. Sci. **265**, 176–188 (2014)
19. Moataz, T., Shikfa, A.: Boolean symmetric searchable encryption. In: Chen, K., Xie, Q., Qiu, W., Li, N., Tzeng, W.G. (eds.) 8th ACM Symposium on Information, Computer and Communications Security - ASIACCS 2013, pp. 265–276. ACM (2013)
20. Mohamad, M.S., Tan, S.Y., Chin, J.J.: Searchable symmetric encryption: defining strength against query recovery attacks. In: Proceedings of the 6th International Cryptology and Information Security Conference 2018, pp. 85–93 (2018)
21. Naveed, M., Prabhakaran, M., Gunter, C.A.: Dynamic searchable encryption via blind storage. In: 2014 IEEE Symposium on Security and Privacy, SP 2014, pp. 639–654. IEEE Computer Society (2014)
22. Ogata, W., Kurosawa, K.: No-dictionary searchable symmetric encryption. IEICE Trans. Fundam. **E102A**(1), 114–124 (2019)
23. Pouliot, D., Griffy, S., Wright, C.V.: The strength of weak randomization: efficiently searchable encryption with minimal leakage. Cryptology ePrint Archive, Report 2017/1098 (2017). http://eprint.iacr.org/2017/1098/

24. Pouliot, D., Wright, C.V.: Shadow nemesis: inference attacks on efficiently deployable, efficiently searchable encryption. In: 2016 ACM SIGSAC Conference on Computer and Communications Security, pp. 1341–1352. ACM (2016)
25. Sedghi, S., Doumen, J., Hartel, P., Jonker, W.: Towards an information theoretic analysis of searchable encryption. In: Chen, L., Ryan, M.D., Wang, G. (eds.) ICICS 2008. LNCS, vol. 5308, pp. 345–360. Springer, Heidelberg (2008). https://doi.org/10.1007/978-3-540-88625-9_23
26. Stefanov, E., Papamanthou, C., Shi, E.: Practical dynamic searchable encryption with small leakage. In: Network and Distributed System Security Symposium - NDSS 2014. Internet Society (2014). https://www.ndss-symposium.org/ndss2014/programme/practical-dynamic-searchable-encryption-small-leakage/
27. Wright, C.V., Pouliot, D.: Early detection and analysis of leakage abuse vulnerabilities. Cryptology ePrint Archive, Report 2017/1052 (2017). http://eprint.iacr.org/2017/1052/
28. Yoshizawa, T., Watanabe, Y., Shikata, J.: Unconditionally secure searchable encryption. In: 2017 51st Annual Conference on Information Sciences and Systems (CISS), pp. 1–6, March 2017
29. Zhang, Y., Katz, J., Papamanthou, C.: All Your Queries Are Belong To Us: The Power of File-Injection Attacks on Searchable Encryption. Cryptology ePrint Archive, Report 2016/172 (2016). http://eprint.iacr.org/2016/172/

Receiver Selective Opening CCA Secure Public Key Encryption from Various Assumptions

Yi Lu[1,2(✉)], Keisuke Hara[1,2], and Keisuke Tanaka[1]

[1] Tokyo Institute of Technology, Tokyo, Japan
{lu.y.ai,hara.k.am}@m.titech.ac.jp, keisuke@is.titech.ac.jp
[2] National Institute of Advanced Industrial Science and Technology (AIST), Tokyo, Japan

Abstract. Receiver selective opening (RSO) attacks for public key encryption (PKE) capture a situation where one sender sends messages to multiple receivers, and an adversary can corrupt a set of receivers and get their messages and secret keys. Security against RSO attack for a PKE scheme ensures confidentiality of other uncorrupted receivers' ciphertexts. Among all of the RSO security notions, simulation-based RSO security against chosen ciphertext attack (SIM-RSO-CCA security) is the strongest notion. In this paper, we explore constructions of SIM-RSO-CCA secure PKE from various computational assumptions. Toward this goal, we show that a SIM-RSO-CCA secure PKE scheme can be constructed based on an IND-CPA secure PKE scheme and a designated-verifier non-interactive zero-knowledge (DV-NIZK) argument satisfying one-time simulation soundness. Moreover, we give the first construction of DV-NIZK argument satisfying one-time simulation soundness. Consequently, through our generic construction, we obtain the first SIM-RSO-CCA secure PKE scheme under the computational Diffie-Hellman (CDH) or learning parity with noise (LPN) assumption.

Keywords: Public-key encryption · Receiver selective opening security · Chosen ciphertext attacks

1 Introduction

1.1 Background and Motivation

In the context of security notions of public key encryption (PKE), there are a lot of formulations considering different attack scenarios, such as chosen plaintext attacks (CPA) and chosen ciphertext attacks (CCA), and different attacker goals, such as one-wayness, indistinguishability (IND), and non-malleability. However, Bellare, Hofheinz, and Yilek [3] claimed that IND−CPA or IND−CCA security [7,9], which are the most accepted security notions for PKE, can not provide adequate security in a multi-user scenario. Concretely, they showed that

K. Nguyen et al. (Eds.): ProvSec 2020, LNCS 12505, pp. 213–233, 2020.
https://doi.org/10.1007/978-3-030-62576-4_11

when some of users has been corrupted, there are situations where we cannot preserve the other users' confidentiality of ciphertexts by using only IND−CPA or IND−CCA secure PKE schemes. Then, they proposed *selective opening (SO)* security for PKE which can ensure that the uncorrupted users' ciphertexts leak no information about their secrets.

Depending on different attack scenarios, SO security is divided into two settings: *sender selective opening (SSO)* security [3,4] and *receiver selective opening (RSO)* security [2,14]. In this paper, we focus on RSO security. In RSO security, we consider a situation where there are one sender and multiple receivers. An adversary can corrupt some receivers, which means he gets their secret keys and plaintexts. RSO security ensures the confidentiality of uncorrupted receivers' ciphertexts. Here, if we also consider an active adversary who can execute CCA, we can also consider RSO−CCA security for PKE.

From another point of view, there are two flavors of definitions for SO security: indistinguishability-based SO security and simulation-based SO security. As mentioned in some previous works [2,14], simulation-based SO security is more desirable than indistinguishability-based SO security, because the definition of indistinguishability-based SO security can support only a plaintext space which satisfies a notion called *efficient resamplability* [3]. Roughly, efficient resamplability refers to when a part of plaintexts are fixed, the remaining plaintexts can be resampled efficiently. This requirement is somewhat artificial and limits real-world applications because a plaintext distribution in practice scenarios do not necessarily satisfy this requirement.

From the above arguments, simulation-based RSO−CCA (SIM−RSO−CCA) security is the most favorable notion among all of the RSO security. Recently, some works [10–12] proposed constructions of SIM−RSO−CCA secure PKE under standard computational assumptions, such as the decisional Diffie-Hellman (DDH) assumption and the decisional composite residuosity (DCR) assumption. One of the important research area for cryptography is making a cryptographic primitive under the various assumptions. More specifically, we have two main problems in this area: Can we construct a cryptographic primitive under a *weaker computational assumption* or a *post-quantum computational assumption ?* In particular, National Institute of Standards and Technology (NIST) launched the Post-Quantum Cryptography Standardization in 2016, and thus post-quantum cryptography has been attracting more attention. Hence, in this paper, we tackle the following question:

> Is it possible to construct a SIM-RSO-CCA secure PKE scheme from weaker or post-quantum computational assumptions ?

1.2 Our Contribution

Based on the above motivation, we give affirmative answers to the question. More precisely, we show that SIM−RSO−CCA secure PKE can be constructed under the computational Diffie-Hellman (CDH) assumption (weaker computational assumption) or the learning parity with noise (LPN) assumption (new post-quantum computational assumption). In the following, we explain the details of our contribution.

Hara et al.'s Approach and Its Limitation. Toward our goal, we focus on the Hara et al.'s work [10,11]. In [10,11], they introduced the *receiver non-committing CCA (*RNC−CCA*)* security for receiver non-committing encryption (RNCE), which is a variant of PKE with a special non-committing property, then showed that RNC−CCA secure RNCE implies SIM−RSO−CCA secure PKE. Moreover, they proposed a construction of RNC−CCA secure RNCE by using an IND−CPA secure PKE scheme and a non-interactive zero-knowledge (NIZK) proof system satisfying one-time simulation soundness.[1] In a nutshell, their construction is obtained by combining the classical Naor-Yung paradigm [21] and a trick for a non-committing property that the decryption key used in a decryption algorithm of their RNCE scheme is chosen at random from two decryption keys of an underlying IND−CPA secure PKE scheme.

In order to obtain a SIM−RSO−CCA secure PKE scheme under the CDH or LPN assumption through their generic construction, all of the components of their construction should be realized under the CDH or LPN assumption. Actually, we can construct an IND−CPA secure PKE scheme based on the CDH assumption [13] or the LPN assumption [1,25]. However, NIZK proof system has not been proposed under these assumptions so far, and thus we cannot obtain a CDH or LPN based SIM−RSO−CCA secure PKE scheme through this generic construction.

Our Approach. In order to circumvent the above problem, we show that an NIZK proof system is not needed, but a *designated-verifier* NIZK (DV-NIZK) argument is sufficient for our goal. More specifically, we show that RNC−CCA secure RNCE can be obtained from IND−CPA secure PKE and DV-NIZK argument satisfying one-time simulation soundness. Roughly, a DV-NIZK argument is a relaxation of an NIZK proof system to the designated-verifier model, in other words, the model which only a user who has a secret verification key can verify a proof correctly. Although it is known that IND−CCA secure PKE scheme can be constructed from these two primitives [8], we have the following nebulous point for proving the RNC−CCA security for RNCE.

In contrast to IND−CCA security for PKE, when showing RNC−CCA security for RNCE, we have to consider a situation where an adversary can get a decryption key in a security game. For checking the validity of a ciphertext, we need to include a secret verification key of DV-NIZK argument into a decryption key of our RNCE scheme. Furthermore, as well as the original Naor-Yung

[1] Due to the previous works [22,24], it is known that both of an IND−CPA secure PKE scheme and an NIZK proof system can be constructed based on the learning with errors (LWE) assumption, which is one of the post-quantum computational assumption. Thus, by combining with the result [10], we can obtain a SIM−RSO−CCA secure PKE scheme based on the LWE assumption.

paradigm [21], we need to use zero-knowledge and (one-time simulation) soundness of a DV-NIZK argument in our security proof. However, in DV-NIZK setting, we cannot ensure soundness if a secret verification key is revealed to an adversary, while zero-knowledge still holds. Thus, it seems that our strategy does not make sense at first glance. However, by focusing on the details of a security proof, we have seen through that there is no problem. The main reason is that soundness is only used to prevent an adversary from making "unfavorable" decryption queries in a security proof, and thus soundness need to be held only while it makes decryption queries. Here, in RNC-CCA security, we consider decryption queries only before a decryption key (including a secret verification key) is revealed. Therefore, it is possible to prevent unfavorable decryption queries without a secret verification key, that is, soundness of DV-NIZK argument is sufficient for proving RNC−CCA security of RNCE. See Sect. 4.2 for more details.

Construction of One-time Simulation Sound DV-NIZK. Recently, a lot of works [6,17,18,20,23] showed that a DV-NIZK argument can be constructed under the CDH and LPN assumption. The notion of a one-time simulation sound DV-NIZK argument was considered in the Elkind et al.'s work [8]. However, a concrete construction of one-time simulation sound DV-NIZK argument has not been proposed so far. Then, in order to complete our RNC−CCA secure RNCE scheme, we propose a construction of one-time simulation sound DV-NIZK argument by combining (ordinary) DV-NIZK argument, strong one-time signature, and commitment based on the Lindell's approach [19]. See Sect. 3 for more details. (Note that we can construct strong one-time signature and commitment based on the one-way function, which is obtained under the CDH or LPN assumption.)

By combining the above results, we can obtain a SIM−RSO−CCA secure PKE scheme based on the CDH or LPN assumption.

1.3 Related Work

Jia et al. [15] proposed the first construction of SIM−RSO−CCA secure PKE using indistinguishability obfuscation. Moreover, Jia et al. [16] proposed indistinguishability-based RSO-CCA (IND-RSO-CCA) secure PKE schemes based on standard computational assumptions. Concretely, they showed two generic constructions of IND−RSO−CCA secure PKE. First, they gave a generic construction based on an IND−RSO−CPA secure PKE scheme, an IND−CCA secure PKE scheme, an NIZK proof system, and a strong one-time signature scheme. Second, they gave a generic construction based on a universal hash proof system. Recently, Huang et al. [12] showed that a SIM−RSO−CCA secure PKE scheme can be constructed under the DDH or DCR assumption. Moreover, they showed that a SIM−RSO−CCA secure PKE scheme can be constructed from an identity-based encryption scheme satisfying RSO security for a master secret key in the ideal cipher model.

2 Preliminaries

In this section, we define notations and recall the definitions for some cryptographic primitives.

2.1 Notations

In this paper, $x \leftarrow X$ denotes sampling an element x from a finite set X uniformly at random. $y \leftarrow \mathcal{A}(x; r)$ denotes that a probabilistic algorithm $\mathcal{A}$ outputs y for an input x using a randomness r, and we simply denote $y \leftarrow \mathcal{A}(x)$ when we do not need to write an internal randomness explicitly. For strings x and y, $x \| y$ denotes the concatenation of x and y. Also, $x := y$ denotes that x is defined by y. λ denotes a security parameter. A function $f(\lambda)$ is a negligible function in λ, if $f(\lambda)$ tends to 0 faster than $\frac{1}{\lambda^c}$ for every constant $c > 0$. $\mathsf{negl}(\lambda)$ denotes an unspecified negligible function. PPT stands for probabilistic polynomial time. If n is a natural number, $[n]$ denotes a set of integers $\{1, \cdots, n\}$. Also, if a and b are integers such that $a \leq b$, $[a, b]$ denotes a set of integers $\{a, \cdots, b\}$. If $\mathbf{m} = (m_1, \cdots, m_n)$ is an n-dimensional vector, $\mathbf{m}_J$ denotes a subset $\{m_j\}_{j \in J}$ where $J \subseteq [n]$. If $\mathcal{O}$ is a function or an algorithm and $\mathcal{A}$ is an algorithm, $\mathcal{A}^{\mathcal{O}}$ denotes that $\mathcal{A}$ has an oracle access to $\mathcal{O}$.

2.2 Public Key Encryption

Here, we review the definition of public key encryption (PKE).

Definition 1 (Public key encryption). *A PKE scheme with a plaintext space $\mathcal{M}$ consists of a tuple of the following three PPT algorithms $\Pi = (\mathbf{KG}, \mathbf{Enc}, \mathbf{Dec})$.*

KG: *The key generation algorithm, given a security parameter 1^λ, outputs a public key pk and a secret key sk.*

Enc: *The encryption algorithm, given a public key pk and a plaintext $m \in \mathcal{M}$, outputs a ciphertext c.*

Dec: *The (deterministic) decryption algorithm, given a public key pk, a secret key sk, and a ciphertext c, outputs a plaintext $m \in \{\perp\} \cup \mathcal{M}$.*

As the correctness for Π, we require that $\mathbf{Dec}(pk, sk, \mathbf{Enc}(pk, m)) = m$ holds for all $\lambda \in \mathbb{N}$, $m \in \mathcal{M}$, and $(pk, sk) \leftarrow \mathbf{KG}(1^\lambda)$.

Then, we recall IND−CPA security and SIM−RSO−CCA security for PKE.[2]

Definition 2 (IND-CPA security). *We say that $\Pi = (\mathbf{KG}, \mathbf{Enc}, \mathbf{Dec})$ is* IND−CPA *secure if for any PPT adversary $\mathcal{A} = (\mathcal{A}_1, \mathcal{A}_2)$,*

$$\mathsf{Adv}^{\mathsf{ind-cpa}}_{\Pi,\mathcal{A}}(\lambda) := 2 \cdot \Big| \Pr[b \leftarrow \{0,1\}; (pk, sk) \leftarrow \mathbf{KG}(1^\lambda); (m_0^*, m_1^*, \mathsf{st}_1) \leftarrow \mathcal{A}_1(pk); \\ c^* \leftarrow \mathbf{Enc}(pk, m_b^*); b' \leftarrow \mathcal{A}_2(c^*, \mathsf{st}_1) : b = b'] - \frac{1}{2} \Big| = \mathsf{negl}(\lambda),$$

[2] In this paper, as mentioned in Sect. 1.2, we focus on RNC−CCA secure RNCE to obtain a new SIM−RSO−CCA secure PKE scheme. Although we do not use a SIM−RSO−CCA security for PKE, we recall the definition here for completeness.

Definition 3 (SIM-RSO-CCA security). *Let n be the number of users. For a PKE scheme $\Pi = (\mathbf{KG}, \mathbf{Enc}, \mathbf{Dec})$, an adversary $\mathcal{A} = (\mathcal{A}_1, \mathcal{A}_2, \mathcal{A}_3)$, and a simulator $\mathcal{S} = (\mathcal{S}_1, \mathcal{S}_2, \mathcal{S}_3)$, we define the following pair of experiments.*

$\mathsf{Exp}^{\mathsf{rso-cca-real}}_{n,\Pi,\mathcal{A}}(\lambda)$:
- $(\mathbf{pk}, \mathbf{sk}) := (pk_j, sk_j)_{j\in[n]} \leftarrow (\mathbf{KG}(1^\lambda))_{j\in[n]}$
- $(\mathsf{Dist}, \mathsf{st}_1) \leftarrow \mathcal{A}_1^{\mathcal{O}_{\mathsf{Dec}}(\cdot,\cdot)}(\mathbf{pk})$
- $\mathbf{m}^* := (m_j^*)_{j\in[n]} \leftarrow \mathsf{Dist}$
- $\mathbf{c}^* := (c_j^*)_{j\in[n]} \leftarrow (\mathbf{Enc}(pk_j, m_j^*))_{j\in[n]}$
- $(J, \mathsf{st}_2) \leftarrow \mathcal{A}_2^{\mathcal{O}_{\mathsf{Dec}}(\cdot,\cdot)}(\mathbf{c}^*, \mathsf{st}_1)$
- $\mathsf{out} \leftarrow \mathcal{A}_3^{\mathcal{O}_{\mathsf{Dec}}(\cdot,\cdot)}(\mathbf{sk}_J, \mathbf{m}_J^*, \mathsf{st}_2)$
- Return $(\mathbf{m}^*, \mathsf{Dist}, J, \mathsf{out})$

$\mathsf{Exp}^{\mathsf{rso-cca-sim}}_{n,\Pi,\mathcal{S}}(\lambda)$:
- $(\mathsf{Dist}, \mathsf{st}_1) \leftarrow \mathcal{S}_1(1^\lambda)$
- $\mathbf{m}^* := (m_j^*)_{j\in[n]} \leftarrow \mathsf{Dist}$
- $(J, \mathsf{st}_2) \leftarrow \mathcal{S}_2(\mathsf{st}_1)$
- $\mathsf{out} \leftarrow \mathcal{S}_3(\mathbf{m}_J^*, \mathsf{st}_2)$
- Return $(\mathbf{m}^*, \mathsf{Dist}, J, \mathsf{out})$

In both of the experiments, we require that the distributions Dist *output by $\mathcal{A}$ and $\mathcal{S}$ be efficiently samplable. In $\mathsf{Exp}^{\mathsf{rso-cca-real}}_{n,\Pi,\mathcal{A}}(\lambda)$, a decryption query (c, j) is answered by $\mathbf{Dec}(pk_j, sk_j, c)$. $\mathcal{A}_2$ and $\mathcal{A}_3$ are not allowed to make a decryption query (c_j^*, j) for any $j \in [n]$. Furthermore, $\mathcal{A}_3$ is not allowed to make a decryption query (c, j) satisfying $j \in J$. (This is without losing generality, since $\mathcal{A}_3$ can decrypt any ciphertext using the given secret keys.)*

We say that Π is SIM−RSO−CCA *secure if for any PPT adversary $\mathcal{A}$ and any positive integer $n = n(\lambda)$, there exists a PPT simulator $\mathcal{S}$ such that for any PPT distinguisher $\mathcal{D}$,*

$$\begin{aligned}\mathsf{Adv}^{\mathsf{rso-cca}}_{n,\Pi,\mathcal{A},\mathcal{S},\mathcal{D}}(\lambda) := |\Pr[\mathcal{D}(\mathsf{Exp}^{\mathsf{rso-cca-real}}_{n,\Pi,\mathcal{A}}(\lambda)) = 1] - \Pr[\mathcal{D}(\mathsf{Exp}^{\mathsf{rso-cca-sim}}_{n,\Pi,\mathcal{S}}(\lambda)) = 1]| \\ = \mathsf{negl}(\lambda).\end{aligned}$$

2.3 Receiver Non-committing Encryption

Here, we review receiver non-committing encryption (RNCE) [5]. Informally, RNCE is public key encryption (PKE) having the property that it can generate a fake ciphertext which can be later opened to any plaintext (by showing an appropriate secret key). In the following, we give a syntax of RNCE and RNC−CCA security for it [10].

Definition 4 (Receiver non-committing encryption). *An RNCE scheme Π with a plaintext space $\mathcal{M}$ consists of the following seven PPT algorithms* $(\mathbf{KG}, \mathbf{Enc}, \mathbf{Dec}, \mathbf{FKG}, \mathbf{Fake}, \mathbf{Open}, \mathbf{FDec})$. $(\mathbf{KG}, \mathbf{Enc}, \mathbf{Dec})$ *are the same algorithms as those of a PKE scheme.* $(\mathbf{FKG}, \mathbf{Fake}, \mathbf{Open}, \mathbf{FDec})$ *are defined as follows.*

FKG*: The fake key generation algorithm, given a security parameter 1^λ, outputs a public key pk and a trapdoor td.*

Fake*: The fake encryption algorithm, given a public key pk and a trapdoor td, outputs a fake ciphertext $\widetilde{c}$.*

Open*: The opening algorithm, given a public key pk, a trapdoor td, a fake ciphertext $\widetilde{c}$, and a plaintext m, outputs a fake secret key $\widetilde{sk}$.*

FDec: *The fake decryption algorithm, given a public key pk, a trapdoor td, and a ciphertext c, outputs* $m \in \{\perp\} \cup \mathcal{M}$.

Definition 5 (RNC-CCA security). *For an RNCE scheme* $\Pi = (\mathbf{KG}, \mathbf{Enc}, \mathbf{Dec}, \mathbf{FKG}, \mathbf{Fake}, \mathbf{Open}, \mathbf{FDec})$ *and an adversary* $\mathcal{A} = (\mathcal{A}_1, \mathcal{A}_2, \mathcal{A}_3)$, *we consider the following pair of experiments.*

$\mathsf{Exp}^{\mathsf{rnc-real}}_{\Pi,\mathcal{A}}(\lambda)$:	$\mathsf{Exp}^{\mathsf{rnc-sim}}_{\Pi,\mathcal{A}}(\lambda)$:
$(pk, sk) \leftarrow \mathbf{KG}(1^\lambda)$	$(pk, td) \leftarrow \mathbf{FKG}(1^\lambda)$
$(m^*, \mathsf{st}_1) \leftarrow \mathcal{A}_1^{\mathcal{O}_{\mathbf{Dec}}(\cdot)}(pk)$	$(m^*, \mathsf{st}_1) \leftarrow \mathcal{A}_1^{\mathcal{O}_{\mathbf{Dec}}(\cdot)}(pk)$
$c^* \leftarrow \mathbf{Enc}(pk, m^*)$	$c^* \leftarrow \mathbf{Fake}(pk, td)$
$\mathsf{st}_2 \leftarrow \mathcal{A}_2^{\mathcal{O}_{\mathbf{Dec}}(\cdot)}(c^*, \mathsf{st}_1)$	$\mathsf{st}_2 \leftarrow \mathcal{A}_2^{\mathcal{O}_{\mathbf{Dec}}(\cdot)}(c^*, \mathsf{st}_1)$
$sk^* := sk$	$sk^* \leftarrow \mathbf{Open}(pk, td, c^*, m^*)$
Return $b' \leftarrow \mathcal{A}_3(sk^*, \mathsf{st}_2)$	Return $b' \leftarrow \mathcal{A}_3(sk^*, \mathsf{st}_2)$

In $\mathsf{Exp}^{\mathsf{rnc-real}}_{\Pi,\mathcal{A}}(\lambda)$, *a decryption query c is answered by* $\mathbf{Dec}(pk, sk, c)$. *On the other hand, in* $\mathsf{Exp}^{\mathsf{rnc-sim}}_{\Pi,\mathcal{A}}(\lambda)$, *a decryption query c is answered by* $\mathbf{FDec}(pk, td, c)$. *In both of the experiments,* $\mathcal{A}_2$ *is not allowed to make a decryption query* $c = c^*$ *and* $\mathcal{A}_3$ *is not allowed to make any decryption query. We say that Π is* RNC−CCA *secure if for any PPT adversary* $\mathcal{A}$, $\mathsf{Adv}^{\mathsf{rnc-cca}}_{\Pi,\mathcal{A}}(\lambda) := |\Pr[\mathsf{Exp}^{\mathsf{rnc-real}}_{\Pi,\mathcal{A}}(\lambda) = 1] - \Pr[\mathsf{Exp}^{\mathsf{rnc-sim}}_{\Pi,\mathcal{A}}(\lambda) = 1]| = \mathsf{negl}(\lambda)$ *holds.*

In the previous work [10], the following theorem was shown.

Theorem 1 ([10]). *If an RNCE scheme* $\Pi = (\mathbf{KG}, \mathbf{Enc}, \mathbf{Dec}, \mathbf{FKG}, \mathbf{Fake}, \mathbf{Open}, \mathbf{FDec})$ *is* RNC−CCA *secure, then a PKE scheme* $\Pi_{\mathsf{rso}} := (\mathbf{KG}, \mathbf{Enc}, \mathbf{Dec})$ *is* SIM−RSO−CCA *secure.*

2.4 Signature

Here, we review the definition of a signature scheme.

Definition 6 (Signature). *A signature scheme* Σ *with a message space* $\mathcal{M}$ *consists of the following three PPT algorithms.*

SKG: *The key generation algorithm, given a security parameter* 1^λ, *outputs a verification key vk and a signing key sigk.*

Sign: *The signing algorithm, given a signing key sigk and a message m, and outputs a signature* σ.

SVer: *The verification algorithm, given a verification key vk, a message m, and a signature* σ, *outputs either* 1 *(meaning "accept") or* 0 *(meaning "reject").*

As the correctness for Σ, *we require that for all* $\lambda \in \mathbb{N}$, $(vk, sigk) \leftarrow \mathbf{SKG}(1^\lambda)$, *and messages* $m \in \mathcal{M}$, *it holds that* $\mathbf{SVer}(vk, m, \mathbf{Sign}(sigk, m)) = 1$.

Next, we define strong one-time unforgeability under chosen message attacks for a signature scheme.

Definition 7 (Strong one-time unforgeability). *We say that a signature scheme* $\Sigma = (\mathbf{SKG}, \mathbf{Sign}, \mathbf{SVer})$ *satisfies strong one-time unforgeability if for any PPT adversary* $\mathcal{A} = (\mathcal{A}_1, \mathcal{A}_2)$*,*

$$\mathsf{Adv}^{\mathsf{unf}}_{\Omega,\mathcal{A}}(\lambda) := \Pr[(vk, sigk) \leftarrow \mathbf{SKG}(1^\lambda); (m, \mathsf{st}_1) \leftarrow \mathcal{A}_1(vk); \sigma \leftarrow \mathbf{Sign}(sigk, m); (m', \sigma') \leftarrow \mathcal{A}_2(\sigma, \mathsf{st}_1) : ((m', \sigma') \neq (m, \sigma)) \wedge (\mathbf{SVer}(vk, m', \sigma') = 1)] = \mathsf{negl}(\lambda)$$

holds.

2.5 Commitment

Here, we review the definition of a commitment scheme.

Definition 8 (Commitment). *A Commitment scheme* Ω *with a plaintext space* $\mathcal{M}$ *consists of the following two PPT algorithms.*

CKG*: The key generation algorithm, given a security parameter* 1^λ*, outputs a public commitment key* ck*.*

Commit*: The commit algorithm, given a public commitment key* ck *and a plaintext* m*, outputs a commitment* c*.*

Next, we define the following two security properties for commitment: *statistical binding* and *computationally hiding.*

Definition 9 (Statistical binding). *Let* $\Omega = (\mathbf{CKG}, \mathbf{Commit})$ *be a commitment scheme. We say that* Ω *satisfies statistical binding if for any computationally unbounded adversary* $\mathcal{A}$*,*

$$\mathsf{Adv}^{\mathsf{bind}}_{\Omega,\mathcal{A}}(\lambda) := \Pr[ck \leftarrow \mathbf{CKG}(1^\lambda); (m_0, m_1, r_0, r_1) \leftarrow \mathcal{A}(ck) : \mathbf{Commit}(ck, m_0; r_0) = \mathbf{Commit}(ck, m_1; r_1)] = \mathsf{negl}(\lambda)$$

holds.

Definition 10 (Computational hiding). *We say that a commitment scheme* $\Omega = (\mathbf{CKG}, \mathbf{Commit})$ *satisfies computationally hiding if for any PPT adversary* $\mathcal{A} = (\mathcal{A}_1, \mathcal{A}_2)$*,*

$$\mathsf{Adv}^{\mathsf{hide}}_{\Omega,\mathcal{A}}(\lambda) := \left| \Pr[b \leftarrow \{0,1\}; ck \leftarrow \mathbf{CKG}(1^\lambda); (m_0, m_1, \mathsf{st}_1) \leftarrow \mathcal{A}_1(ck); c \leftarrow \mathbf{Commit}(ck, m_b); b' \leftarrow \mathcal{A}_2(c, \mathsf{st}_1) : b = b'] - \frac{1}{2} \right| = \mathsf{negl}(\lambda)$$

holds.

2.6 Designated-Verifier Non-interactive Zero-Knowledge Arguments

Here, we review the definition of a designated-verifier non-interactive zero-knowledge (DV-NIZK) argument [6,17,18,20,23].

Definition 11 (DV-NIZK argument). *Let $\mathcal{R}$ be an efficiently computable binary relation and $\mathcal{L} := \{x \mid \exists w \text{ s.t.} (x, w) \in \mathcal{R}\}$. A DV-NIZK argument for $\mathcal{L}$ consists of a tuple of the following five PPT algorithms $\Phi = (\mathbf{CRSGen}, \mathbf{Prove}, \mathbf{Verify}, \mathbf{SimCRS}, \mathbf{SimPrv})$.*

CRSGen: *The common reference string (CRS) generation algorithm takes a security parameter 1^λ as input, and outputs a CRS crs and a secret verification key vsk.*

Prove: *The proving algorithm takes a CRS crs, a statement x, and a witness w as input, and outputs a proof π.*

Verify: *The (deterministic) verification algorithm takes a CRS crs, a secret verification key vsk, a statement x, and a proof π as input, outputs a bit $v \in \{0, 1\}$, which is either 1 (meaning "accept") or 0 (meaning "reject").*

SimCRS: *The simulator's CRS generation algorithm takes a security parameter 1^λ as input, outputs a simulated CRS crs, a simulated secret verification key vsk, and a trapdoor key tk.*

SimPrv: *The simulator's proving algorithm takes a trapdoor key tk and a statement x as input, and outputs a simulated proof π.*

We say that a DV-NIZK argument Φ is correct if we have $\mathbf{Verify}(crs, vsk, x, \mathbf{Prove}(crs, x, w)) = 1$ for all $\lambda \in \mathbb{N}$, $(crs, vsk) \leftarrow \mathbf{CRSGen}(1^\lambda)$, and valid statement / witness pairs $(x, w) \in \mathcal{R}$.

Next, we define (standard) soundness and one-time simulation soundness for a DV-NIZK argument. We adopt a definition of soundness which was considered in recent works [6,17,18,20,23]. Moreover, we adopt a definition of one-time simulation soundness proposed in [8]. We note that in both of security definitions, an adversary can make multiple verification queries.

Definition 12 (Soundness). *We say that a DV-NIZK argument $\Phi = (\mathbf{CRSGen}, \mathbf{Prove}, \mathbf{Verify}, \mathbf{SimCRS}, \mathbf{SimPrv})$ satisfies soundness if for any PPT adversary $\mathcal{A}$,*

$$\begin{aligned}\mathsf{Adv}^{\mathsf{sound}}_{\Phi,\mathcal{A}}(\lambda) := \Pr[&(crs, vsk) \leftarrow \mathbf{CRSGen}(1^\lambda); (x, \pi) \leftarrow \mathcal{A}^{\mathcal{O}(\cdot,\cdot)}(crs) \\ &: (x \notin \mathcal{L}) \wedge (\mathbf{Verify}(crs, vsk, x, \pi) = 1)] = \mathsf{negl}(\lambda)\end{aligned}$$

holds, where $\mathcal{O}(\cdot, \cdot)$ is a verification oracle which receives a query (x, π) and returns $v \leftarrow \mathbf{Verify}(vsk, x, \pi)$.

Definition 13 (One-time simulation soundness). *We say that a DV-NIZK argument* $\Phi = (\mathbf{CRSGen}, \mathbf{Prove}, \mathbf{Verify}, \mathbf{SimCRS}, \mathbf{SimPrv})$ *satisfies one-time simulation soundness if for any PPT adversary* $\mathcal{A} = (\mathcal{A}_1, \mathcal{A}_2)$,

$$\begin{aligned}\mathsf{Adv}^{\mathsf{ot-ss}}_{\Phi,\mathcal{A}}(\lambda) := \Pr[&(crs, tk, vsk) \leftarrow \mathbf{SimCRS}(1^\lambda); (x', st_1) \leftarrow \mathcal{A}_1^{\mathcal{O}(\cdot,\cdot)}(crs);\\ &\pi' \leftarrow \mathbf{SimPrv}(tk, x'); (x, \pi) \leftarrow \mathcal{A}_2^{\mathcal{O}(\cdot,\cdot)}(\pi', st_1)\\ &: ((x,\pi) \neq (x', \pi')) \wedge (x \notin \mathcal{L}) \wedge (\mathbf{Verify}(crs, vsk, x, \pi) = 1)] = \mathsf{negl}(\lambda)\end{aligned}$$

holds, where $\mathcal{O}(\cdot,\cdot)$ *is a verification oracle which receives a query* (x, π) *and returns* $v \leftarrow \mathbf{Verify}(vsk, x, \pi)$.

Then, we give the definitions of zero-knowledge and witness indistinguishability for a DV-NIZK argument. We adopt a definition of zero-knowledge which was considered in [8]. Our definition of witness indistinguishability is a natural extension from one of a (standard) NIZK proof system. It is easy to see that our witness indistinguishability is implied by zero-knowledge.

Definition 14 (Zero-knowledge). *For a DV-NIZK argument* $\Phi = (\mathbf{CRSGen}, \mathbf{Prove}, \mathbf{Verify}, \mathbf{SimCRS}, \mathbf{SimPrv})$ *and a PPT adversary* $\mathcal{A} = (\mathcal{A}_1, \mathcal{A}_2)$, *we consider the following two experiments.*

$\mathsf{Exp}^{\mathsf{zk-real}}_{\Phi,\mathcal{A}}(\lambda)$:	$\mathsf{Exp}^{\mathsf{zk-sim}}_{\Phi,\mathcal{A}}(\lambda)$:
$(crs, vsk) \leftarrow \mathbf{CRSGen}(1^\lambda)$	$(crs, vsk, tk) \leftarrow \mathbf{SimCRS}(1^\lambda)$
$(x, w, \mathsf{st}_1) \leftarrow \mathcal{A}_1(crs, vsk)$	$(x, w, \mathsf{st}_1) \leftarrow \mathcal{A}_1(crs, vsk)$
$\pi \leftarrow \mathbf{Prove}(crs, x, w)$	$\pi \leftarrow \mathbf{SimPrv}(tk, x)$
$b' \leftarrow \mathcal{A}_2(\pi, \mathsf{st}_1)$	$b' \leftarrow \mathcal{A}_2(\pi, \mathsf{st}_1)$
Return b'	Return b'

In both of the experiments, it is required that $x \in \mathcal{L}$ *and* w *be a witness for* $x \in \mathcal{L}$. *We say that* Φ *is zero-knowledge if for any PPT adversary* $\mathcal{A}$, $\mathsf{Adv}^{\mathsf{zk}}_{\Phi,\mathcal{A}}(\lambda) := |\Pr[\mathsf{Exp}^{\mathsf{zk-real}}_{\Phi,\mathcal{A}}(\lambda) = 1] - \Pr[\mathsf{Exp}^{\mathsf{zk-sim}}_{\Phi,\mathcal{A}}(\lambda) = 1]| = \mathsf{negl}(\lambda)$ *holds.*

Definition 15 (Witness indistinguishability). *We say that a DV-NIZK argument* $\Phi = (\mathbf{CRSGen}, \mathbf{Prove}, \mathbf{Verify}, \mathbf{SimCRS}, \mathbf{SimPrv})$ *satisfies witness indistinguishability if for any PPT adversary* $\mathcal{A} = (\mathcal{A}_1, \mathcal{A}_2)$,

$$\begin{aligned}\mathsf{Adv}^{\mathsf{wi}}_{\Phi,\mathcal{A}}(\lambda) := 2 \cdot \Big|\Pr[&(crs, vsk) \leftarrow \mathbf{CRSGen}(1^\lambda);\\ &(x, w_0, w_1, \mathsf{st}_1) \leftarrow \mathcal{A}_1(crs, vsk); b \leftarrow \{0,1\};\\ &\pi \leftarrow \mathbf{Prove}(crs, x, w_b); b' \leftarrow \mathcal{A}_2(\pi, \mathsf{st}_1) : b = b'] - \frac{1}{2}\Big| = \mathsf{negl}(\lambda),\end{aligned}$$

where $(x, w_0), (x, w_1) \in \mathcal{R}$ *holds.*

3 Construction of One-Time Simulation Sound DV-NIZK

In this section, we provide a construction of one-time simulation sound DV-NIZK. First, in Sect. 3.1, we describe our construction. Then, in Sect. 3.2, we give a security proof for our construction.

3.1 Description

In this section, we formally describe our construction of one-time simulation sound DV-NIZK argument for an NP language $\mathcal{L}'$. Let $\Sigma = (\mathbf{SKG}, \mathbf{Sign}, \mathbf{SVer})$ be a signature scheme, $\Omega = (\mathbf{CKG}, \mathbf{Commit})$ a commitment scheme, and $\Pi = (\mathbf{CRSGen}, \mathbf{Prove}, \mathbf{Verify}, \mathbf{SimCRS}, \mathbf{SimPrv})$ a (standard) DV-NIZK argument for $\mathcal{L}$, where

$$\mathcal{L} := \Big\{(x', ck, vk, c) \,|\, \exists\, (w', r)\, \text{s.t.}\, ((x', w') \in \mathcal{R}') \vee (c = \mathbf{Commit}(ck, vk; r))\Big\}.$$

Then, we construct our one-time simulation sound DV-NIZK argument $\Phi' = (\mathbf{CRSGen}', \mathbf{Prove}', \mathbf{Verify}', \mathbf{SimCRS}', \mathbf{SimPrv}')$ for $\mathcal{L}'$ as described in Fig.1.

3.2 Security Proof

In this section, we show that our scheme Φ' satisfies one-time simulation soundness (Theorem 2) and zero-knowledge (Theorem 3).

Theorem 2. *If Φ satisfies (standard) soundness, Ω satisfies statistical binding, and Σ satisfies strong one-time unforgeability, then Φ' satisfies one-time simulation soundness.*

Proof of Theorem 2. Let $\mathcal{A} = (\mathcal{A}_1, \mathcal{A}_2)$ be a PPT adversary that attacks the one-time simulation soundness of Φ'. The detailed description of one-time simulation soundness for Φ' is as follows.

1. The challenger generates $ck \leftarrow \mathbf{CKG}(1^\lambda)$, $(crs, vsk) \leftarrow \mathbf{CRSGen}(1^\lambda)$, and $(sigk^*, vk^*) \leftarrow \mathbf{SKG}(1^\lambda)$. Then, it samples $r \leftarrow \mathcal{R}_\Pi$ and computes $c^* \leftarrow \mathbf{Commit}(ck, vk^*; r)$. Finally, it sets $crs' := (crs, ck, c^*)$ and $tk := (vk^*, sigk^*, r)$, and runs $\mathcal{A}_1(crs')$. When $\mathcal{A}_1$ makes a verification query $(\widetilde{x}, \widetilde{\pi})$, the challenger returns $v \leftarrow \mathbf{Verify}(crs, vsk, \widetilde{x}, \widetilde{\pi})$ to $\mathcal{A}_1$.
2. When $\mathcal{A}_1$ outputs $(\hat{x}', \mathsf{st}_1)$ and terminates, the challenger sets $\hat{x} := (\hat{x}', ck, vk^*, c^*)$ and $\hat{w} := (\perp, r)$, and computes $\hat{\pi} \leftarrow \mathbf{Prove}(crs, \hat{x}, \hat{w})$ and $\hat{\sigma} \leftarrow \mathbf{Sign}(sigk^*, (\hat{x}', \hat{\pi}))$. Then, it sets $\hat{\pi}' := (vk^*, \hat{\pi}, \hat{\sigma})$ and runs $\mathcal{A}_2(\hat{\pi}', \mathsf{st}_1)$. When $\mathcal{A}_2$ makes a verification query $(\widetilde{x}, \widetilde{\pi})$, the challenger returns $v \leftarrow \mathbf{Verify}(crs, vsk, \widetilde{x}, \widetilde{\pi})$ to $\mathcal{A}_2$.
3. $\mathcal{A}_2$ outputs a pair of a statement and a proof $(x', \pi' = (vk, \pi, \sigma))$ and terminates.

Here, in the above experiment, we let **Win** be the event that $((x', \pi') \neq (\hat{x}', \hat{\pi}')) \wedge (x' \notin \mathcal{L}') \wedge (\mathbf{Verify}(crs', vsk, x', \pi') = 1)$ holds. We have the inequality $\mathsf{Adv}^{\mathsf{ot-ss}}_{\Phi', \mathcal{A}}(\lambda) = \Pr[\mathbf{Win}] = \Pr[\mathbf{Win} \wedge vk \neq vk^*] + \Pr[\mathbf{Win} \wedge vk = vk^*]$.

In the following, we show that there exist a PPT adversary $\mathcal{B}$ against the soundness of Φ such that $\mathsf{Adv}^{\mathsf{sound}}_{\Phi, \mathcal{B}}(\lambda) = \Pr[\mathbf{Win} \wedge vk \neq vk^*]$ (Lemma 1) and a PPT adversary $\mathcal{C} = (\mathcal{C}_1, \mathcal{C}_2)$ against the strong one-time unforgeability of Σ such that $\mathsf{Adv}^{\mathsf{unf}}_{\Sigma, \mathcal{C}}(\lambda) = \Pr[\mathbf{Win} \wedge vk = vk^*]$ (Lemma 2).

$\mathbf{CRSGen}'(1^\lambda)$: $ck \leftarrow \mathbf{CKG}(1^\lambda)$ $(crs, vsk) \leftarrow \mathbf{CRSGen}(1^\lambda)$ $r \leftarrow \mathcal{R}_\Omega$ $c \leftarrow \mathbf{Commit}(ck, 0^{\lvert vk \rvert}; r)$ $crs' := (crs, ck, c)$ Return (crs', vsk)	$\mathbf{Prove}'(crs', x', w')$: $(vk, sigk) \leftarrow \mathbf{SKG}(1^\lambda)$ $x := (x', ck, vk, c)$ $w := (w', \bot)$ $\pi \leftarrow \mathbf{Prove}(crs, x, w)$ $\sigma \leftarrow \mathbf{Sign}(sigk, (x', \pi))$ Return $\pi' := (vk, \pi, \sigma)$
	$\mathbf{Verify}'(crs', vsk, x', \pi')$: If $\mathbf{SVer}(vk, (x', \pi), \sigma) = 1$ $\wedge \mathbf{Verify}(crs, vsk, (x', ck, vk, c), \pi) = 1$ then Return 1 else Return 0
$\mathbf{SimCRS}'(1^\lambda)$: $ck \leftarrow \mathbf{CKG}(1^\lambda)$ $(crs, vsk) \leftarrow \mathbf{CRSGen}(1^\lambda)$ $(sigk^*, vk^*) \leftarrow \mathbf{SKG}(1^\lambda)$ $r \leftarrow \mathcal{R}_\Pi$ $c^* \leftarrow \mathbf{Commit}(ck, vk^*; r)$ $crs' := (crs, ck, c^*)$ $tk := (vk^*, sigk^*, r)$ Return (crs', tk, vsk)	$\mathbf{SimPrv}'(crs', tk, x')$: $x := (x', ck, vk^*, c^*)$ $w := (\bot, r)$ $\pi^* \leftarrow \mathbf{Prove}(crs, x, w)$ $\sigma^* \leftarrow \mathbf{Sign}(sigk^*, (x', \pi^*))$ Return $\pi' := (vk^*, \pi^*, \sigma^*)$

Fig. 1. Construction of one-time simulation sound DV-NIZK argument Φ'.

Lemma 1. *There exists a PPT adversary* $\mathcal{B}$ *such that* $\mathsf{Adv}^{\mathsf{sound}}_{\Phi,\mathcal{B}}(\lambda) = \Pr[\mathbf{Win} \wedge vk \neq vk^*]$.

Proof of Lemma 1. We construct a PPT adversary $\mathcal{B}$ that attacks the soundness of Φ so that $\mathsf{Adv}^{\mathsf{sound}}_{\Phi,\mathcal{B}}(\lambda) = \Pr[\mathbf{Win} \wedge vk \neq vk^*]$, using the adversary $\mathcal{A}$ as follows.

$\mathcal{B}(crs)$ **:** First, $\mathcal{B}$ generates $ck \leftarrow \mathbf{CKG}(1^\lambda)$, $(crs, vsk) \leftarrow \mathbf{CRSGen}(1^\lambda)$, and $(sigk^*, vk^*) \leftarrow \mathbf{SKG}(1^\lambda)$. Then, it samples $r \leftarrow \mathcal{R}_\Pi$ and computes $c^* \leftarrow \mathbf{Commit}(ck, vk^*; r)$. Next, it sets $crs' := (crs, ck, c)$ and $tk' := (vk^*, sigk^*, r)$, and runs $\mathcal{A}_1(crs')$. When $\mathcal{A}_1$ makes a verification query $(\widetilde{x}', (\widetilde{vk}, \widetilde{\pi}, \widetilde{\sigma}))$, $\mathcal{B}$ computes $s \leftarrow \mathbf{SVer}(\widetilde{vk}, (\widetilde{x}', \widetilde{\pi}), \widetilde{\sigma})$, makes a verification query $((\widetilde{x}', ck, \widetilde{vk}, c), \widetilde{\pi})$, and gets the result v. If $s = v = 1$ holds, $\mathcal{B}$ returns 1 to $\mathcal{A}_1$. Otherwise, $\mathcal{B}$ returns 0 to $\mathcal{A}_1$.
When $\mathcal{A}_1$ outputs a pair of a statement and state information $(\hat{x}', \mathsf{st}_1)$ and terminates, $\mathcal{B}$ sets $\hat{x} := (\hat{x}', vk, c)$ and $\hat{w} := (\bot, r)$. Next, $\mathcal{B}$ computes $\hat{\pi} \leftarrow \mathbf{Prove}(crs, \hat{x}, \hat{w})$ and $\hat{\sigma} \leftarrow \mathbf{Sign}(sigk^*, (\hat{\pi}, \hat{x}'))$. Then, $\mathcal{B}$ sets $\hat{\pi}' := (vk, \hat{\pi}, \hat{\sigma})$ and runs $\mathcal{A}_2(\hat{\pi}', \mathsf{st}_1)$. When $\mathcal{A}_2$ makes a verification query $((\widetilde{x}', ck, \widetilde{vk}, c), \widetilde{\pi})$, $\mathcal{B}$ answers in the same way as above. When $\mathcal{A}_2$ outputs a pair of a statement and a proof $(x', (vk, \pi, \sigma))$ and terminates, $\mathcal{B}$ sets $x := (x', ck, vk, c)$, returns (x, π) to its experiment, and terminates.

We can see that $\mathcal{B}$ perfectly simulates an experiment of one-time simulation soundness for $\mathcal{A}$. Here, we assume that $vk \neq vk^*$ holds. Firstly, if the event **Win** occurs, $\mathbf{Verify}'(crs', vsk, x', \pi') = 1$ holds, which means that $\mathbf{Verify}(crs, vsk, (x', ck, vk, c), \pi) = 1$ holds.

Secondly, $x' \notin L'$ holds now. Moreover, due to the fact that $vk \neq vk^*$ and the statistical binding of Ω hold, we can see $\mathbf{Commit}(ck, vk; r) \neq c$. Hence, we have $x \notin L$.

From the above argument, if **Win** occurs and $vk \neq vk^*$ holds, we can see that $\mathcal{B}$ can make a pair of a statement and a proof (x, π) breaking the soundness of Φ. Thus, $\mathsf{Adv}^{\mathsf{sound}}_{\Phi,\mathcal{B}}(\lambda) = \Pr[\mathbf{Win} \wedge vk \neq vk^*]$ holds. □ **(Lemma** 1)

Lemma 2. *There exists a PPT adversary* $\mathcal{C} = (\mathcal{C}_1, \mathcal{C}_2)$ *such that* $\mathsf{Adv}^{\mathsf{unf}}_{\Sigma,\mathcal{C}}(\lambda) = \Pr[\mathbf{Win} \wedge vk = vk^*]$.

Proof of Lemma 2. We construct a PPT adversary $\mathcal{C} = (\mathcal{C}_1, \mathcal{C}_2)$ that attacks the strong one-time unforgeability of Σ so that $\mathsf{Adv}^{\mathsf{unf}}_{\Sigma,\mathcal{C}}(\lambda) = \Pr[\mathbf{Win} \wedge vk = vk^*]$, using the adversary $\mathcal{A}$ as follows.

$\mathcal{C}_1(vk^*)$**:** First, $\mathcal{C}_1$ generates $ck \leftarrow \mathbf{CKG}(1^\lambda)$ and $(crs, vsk) \leftarrow \mathbf{CRSGen}(1^\lambda)$. Next, $\mathcal{C}_1$ samples $r \leftarrow \mathcal{R}_\Pi$ and computes $c \leftarrow \mathbf{Commit}(ck, vk^*; r)$. Then, $\mathcal{C}_1$ sets $crs' := (crs, ck, c)$ and runs $\mathcal{A}_1(crs')$. When $\mathcal{A}_1$ makes a verification query of $(\widetilde{x}', \widetilde{\pi}')$, $\mathcal{C}_1$ returns $v \leftarrow \mathbf{Verify}'(crs', vsk, \widetilde{x}', \widetilde{\pi}')$ to $\mathcal{A}_1$.
When $\mathcal{A}_1$ outputs a pair of a statement and state information $(\hat{x}', \mathsf{st}_1)$ and terminates, $\mathcal{C}_1$ sets $\hat{x} := (\hat{x}', ck, vk^*, c)$ and $\hat{w} := (\perp, r)$, and computes $\hat{\pi} \leftarrow \mathbf{Prove}(crs, \hat{x}, \hat{w})$. Then, $\mathcal{C}_1$ sets $\hat{m} := (\hat{x}', \hat{\pi})$ and st'_1 as all the information known to $\mathcal{C}_1$, returns $(\hat{m}, \mathsf{st}_1)$ to its experiment, and terminates.

$\mathcal{C}_2(\hat{\sigma}, \mathsf{st}_1)$**:** First, $\mathcal{C}_2$ sets $\hat{\pi}' := (vk^*, \hat{\sigma}, \hat{\pi})$ and runs $\mathcal{A}_2(\hat{\pi}', \mathsf{st}_1)$. When $\mathcal{A}_2$ outputs a pair of a challenge statement and a proof $(x', (vk, \pi, \sigma))$, and terminates, $\mathcal{C}_2$ sets $m' := (x', \pi)$, returns (σ, m') to its experiment, and terminates.

We can see that $\mathcal{C}$ perfectly simulates an experiment of one-time simulation soundness for $\mathcal{A}$. Here, we assume that $vk = vk^*$ holds. If the event **Win** occurs, $\mathbf{Verify}(crs', vsk, x', \pi') = 1$ holds, which means that $\mathbf{SVer}(vk^*, m', \sigma) = 1$ holds. Moreover, $(x', \pi') \neq (\hat{x}', \hat{\pi}')$ holds now, which implies $(m', \sigma) \neq (\hat{m}, \hat{\sigma})$. From the above argument, if **Win** occurs and $vk = vk^*$ holds, we can see that $\mathcal{C}$ can make a pair of a statement and a proof (x', π) breaking the strong one-time unforgeability of Σ. Thus, $\mathsf{Adv}^{\mathsf{unf}}_{\Sigma,\mathcal{C}}(\lambda) = \Pr[\mathbf{Win} \wedge vk = vk^*]$ holds. □ **(Lemma** 2)

Putting everything together, we obtain $\mathsf{Adv}^{\mathsf{ot-ss}}_{\Phi',\mathcal{A}}(\lambda) \leq \mathsf{Adv}^{\mathsf{sound}}_{\Phi,\mathcal{B}}(\lambda) + \mathsf{Adv}^{\mathsf{unf}}_{\Sigma,\mathcal{C}}(\lambda)$. Since Φ satisfies (standard) soundness and Σ satisfies strong one-time unforgeability, for any PPT adversary $\mathcal{A}$, $\mathsf{Adv}^{\mathsf{ot-ss}}_{\Phi',\mathcal{A}}(\lambda) = \mathsf{negl}(\lambda)$ holds. Therefore, Φ' satisfies one-time simulation soundness. □ **(Theorem** 2)

Theorem 3. *If* Φ *satisfies witness indistinguishability and* Ω *satisfies computationally hiding, then* Φ' *satisfies zero-knowledge.*

Proof of Theorem 3. Let $\mathcal{A} = (\mathcal{A}_1, \mathcal{A}_2)$ be a PPT adversary that attacks the zero-knowledge of Φ'. We introduce the following experiments $\{\mathsf{Exp}_i\}_{i=0}^2$.

Exp_0: Exp_0 is exactly the same as $\mathsf{Exp}^{\mathsf{zk-real}}_{\Phi',\mathcal{A}}(\lambda)$. The detailed description is as follows.

1. Exp_0 generates $ck \leftarrow \mathbf{CKG}(1^\lambda)$ and $(crs, vsk) \leftarrow \mathbf{CRSGen}(1^\lambda)$. Then, Exp_0 samples $r \leftarrow \mathcal{R}_\Omega$ and computes $c \leftarrow \mathbf{Commit}(0^{|vk|}; r)$. Next, Exp_0 sets $crs' := (crs, ck, c)$ and runs $\mathcal{A}_1(crs', vsk)$.
2. When $\mathcal{A}_1$ outputs a tuple (x', w', st_1) and terminates, Exp_0 generates $(vk, sigk) \leftarrow \mathbf{SKG}(1^\lambda)$ and sets $x := (x', ck, vk, c)$ and $w := (w', \perp)$. Then, Exp_0 computes $\pi \leftarrow \mathbf{Prove}(crs, x, w)$ and $\sigma \leftarrow \mathbf{Sign}(sigk, (x', \pi))$, and returns $\pi' := (vk, \pi, \sigma)$ to $\mathcal{A}_2$.
3. When $\mathcal{A}_2$ outputs a bit $b' \in \{0, 1\}$ and terminates, Exp_0 outputs b'.

Exp_1 : Exp_1 is identical to Exp_0 except that Exp_1 generates another $(sigk^*, vk^*) \leftarrow \mathbf{SKG}(1^\lambda)$ and computes $c \leftarrow \mathbf{Commit}(vk^*; r)$ instead of $c \leftarrow \mathbf{Commit}(0^{|vk|}; r)$.

Exp_2 : Exp_2 is identical to Exp_1 except that Exp_2 sets $w := (\perp, r)$ and uses this w to make a proof π. Note that Exp_2 is exactly the same as $\mathsf{Exp}^{\mathsf{zk-sim}}_{\Phi',\mathcal{A}}(\lambda)$.

We let $p_i := \Pr[\mathsf{Exp}_i(\lambda) = 1]$ for all $i \in [0, 2]$. Then, we have

$$\begin{aligned}\mathsf{Adv}^{\mathsf{zk}}_{\Phi',\mathcal{A}}(\lambda) &= |\Pr[\mathsf{Exp}^{\mathsf{zk-real}}_{\Phi',\mathcal{A}}(\lambda) = 1] - \Pr[\mathsf{Exp}^{\mathsf{zk-sim}}_{\Phi',\mathcal{A}}(\lambda) = 1]| \\ &= |p_0 - p_2| \le \sum_{i=0}^{1} |p_i - p_{i+1}|.\end{aligned}$$

It remains to show how each $|p_i - p_{i+1}|$ is upper-bounded. To this end, in the following, we show that there exist an adversary $\mathcal{D} = (\mathcal{D}_1, \mathcal{D}_2)$ against the computationally hiding of Ω such that $|p_0 - p_1| = \mathsf{Adv}^{\mathsf{hide}}_{\Omega,\mathcal{D}}(\lambda)$ (Lemma 3) and an adversary $\mathcal{E} = (\mathcal{E}_1, \mathcal{E}_2)$ against the witness indistinguishability of Φ such that $|p_1 - p_2| = \mathsf{Adv}^{\mathsf{wi}}_{\Phi,\mathcal{E}}(\lambda)$ (Lemma 4).

Lemma 3. *There exists a PPT adversary $\mathcal{D} = (\mathcal{D}_1, \mathcal{D}_2)$ such that $|p_0 - p_1| = \mathsf{Adv}^{\mathsf{hide}}_{\Omega,\mathcal{D}}(\lambda)$.*

Proof of Lemma 3. We construct a PPT adversary $\mathcal{D} = (\mathcal{D}_1, \mathcal{D}_2)$ that attacks the hiding property of Ω so that $|p_0 - p_1| = \mathsf{Adv}^{\mathsf{hide}}_{\Omega,\mathcal{D}}(\lambda)$, using the adversary $\mathcal{A} = (\mathcal{A}_1, \mathcal{A}_2)$ as follows.

$\mathcal{D}_1(ck)$: First, $\mathcal{D}_1$ generates $(crs, vsk) \leftarrow \mathbf{CRSGen}(1^\lambda)$ and $(sigk^*, vk^*) \leftarrow \mathbf{SKG}(1^\lambda)$. Then, $\mathcal{D}_1$ sets $m_0 := 0^{|vk^*|}$, $m_1 := vk^*$, and st_1 as all of the information known to $\mathcal{D}_1$, returns $(m_0, m_1, \mathsf{st}_1)$ to its experiment, and terminates.

$\mathcal{D}_2(c)$: First, $\mathcal{D}_2$ sets $crs' := (crs, c)$ and runs $\mathcal{A}_1(crs')$. When $\mathcal{A}_1$ outputs a tuple (x', w', st'_1), $\mathcal{D}_2$ sets $x := (x', ck, vk^*, c)$ and $w := (w', \perp)$. Then, $\mathcal{D}_2$ computes $\pi \leftarrow \mathbf{Prove}(crs, x, w)$ and $\sigma \leftarrow \mathbf{Sign}(sigk^*, (x', \pi))$, sets $\pi' := (vk^*, \pi, \sigma)$, and runs $\mathcal{A}_2(\pi', \mathsf{st}_1)$. When $\mathcal{A}_2$ outputs a bit $b' \in \{0, 1\}$ and terminates, $\mathcal{D}_2$ returns b' to its experiment and terminates.

We let b be the challenge bit for $\mathcal{D}$ in its experiment. When $b = 0$, we can see that $\mathcal{D}$ perfectly simulates Exp_0 for $\mathcal{A}$. This ensures that when $b = 0$, the probability that $\mathcal{D}$ outputs 1 is exactly the same as the probability that $\mathcal{A}$ outputs $b' = 1$ in Exp_0. On the other hand, when $b = 1$, we can see that $\mathcal{D}$ perfectly simulates Exp_1 for $\mathcal{A}$. This ensures that when $b = 1$, the probability that $\mathcal{D}$ outputs 1 holds is exactly the same as the probability that $\mathcal{A}$ outputs $b' = 1$ in Exp_1. Therefore, we have $\mathsf{Adv}^{\mathsf{hide}}_{\Omega,\mathcal{D}}(\lambda) = |\Pr[b' = 1|b = 0] - \Pr[b' = 1|b = 1]| = |p_0 - p_1|$. □ **(Lemma 3)**

Lemma 4. *There exists a PPT adversary* $\mathcal{E} = (\mathcal{E}_1, \mathcal{E}_2)$ *such that* $|p_1 - p_2| = \mathsf{Adv}^{\mathsf{wi}}_{\Phi,\mathcal{E}}(\lambda)$.

Proof of Lemma 4. We construct a PPT adversary $\mathcal{E} = (\mathcal{E}_1, \mathcal{E}_2)$ that attacks the witness indistinguishability of Φ so that $|p_1 - p_2| = \mathsf{Adv}^{\mathsf{wi}}_{\Phi,\mathcal{E}}(\lambda)$, using the adversary $\mathcal{A} = (\mathcal{A}_1, \mathcal{A}_2)$ as follows.

$\mathcal{E}_1(crs)$: First, $\mathcal{E}_1$ generates $ck \leftarrow \mathbf{CKG}(1^\lambda)$ and $(sigk^*, vk^*) \leftarrow \mathbf{SKG}(1^\lambda)$. Then, $\mathcal{E}_1$ samples $r \leftarrow \mathcal{R}_\Omega$ and computes $c \leftarrow \mathbf{Commit}(ck, vk^*; r)$. Next, $\mathcal{E}_1$ sets $crs' := (crs, c)$ and runs $\mathcal{A}_1(crs')$. When $\mathcal{A}_1$ outputs (x', w', st_1) and terminates, $\mathcal{E}_1$ sets $x := (x', ck, vk^*, c)$, $w_0 := (w', \bot)$, and $w_1 := (\bot, r)$. Then, $\mathcal{E}_1$ returns (x, w_0, w_1) and st'_1 including all of the information known to $\mathcal{E}_1$ to its experiment, and terminates.

$\mathcal{E}_2(\pi, \mathsf{st}'_1)$: First, $\mathcal{E}_2$ computes $\sigma \leftarrow \mathbf{Sign}(sigk, (x', \pi))$. Then, $\mathcal{E}_2$ sets $\pi' := (\pi, \sigma, vk^*)$ and runs $\mathcal{A}_2(\pi', \mathsf{st}_1)$. When $\mathcal{A}_2$ outputs a bit $b' \in \{0, 1\}$ and terminates, $\mathcal{E}_2$ returns b' to its experiment and terminates.

We let b be the challenge bit for $\mathcal{E}$ in its experiment. When $b = 0$, we can see that $\mathcal{E}$ perfectly simulates Exp_1 for $\mathcal{A}$. This ensures that when $b = 0$, the probability that $\mathcal{E}$ outputs 1 holds is exactly the same as the probability that $\mathcal{A}$ outputs 1 in Exp_1. On the other hand, when $b = 1$, $\mathcal{E}$ perfectly simulates Exp_2 for $\mathcal{A}$. This ensures that when $b = 0$, the probability that $\mathcal{E}$ outputs 1 is exactly the same as the probability that $\mathcal{A}$ outputs 1 in Exp_2. Therefore, we have $\mathsf{Adv}^{\mathsf{wi}}_{\Phi,\mathcal{E}}(\lambda) = |\Pr[b' = 1|b = 0] - \Pr[b' = 1|b = 1]| = |p_1 - p_2|$. □ **(Lemma 4)**

Putting everything together, we obtain $\mathsf{Adv}^{\mathsf{zk}}_{\Phi',\mathcal{A}}(\lambda) \leq \mathsf{Adv}^{\mathsf{hide}}_{\Omega,\mathcal{D}}(\lambda) + \mathsf{Adv}^{\mathsf{wi}}_{\Phi,\mathcal{E}}(\lambda)$. Since Ω satisfies computationally hiding and Φ satisfies witness indistinguishability, for any PPT adversary $\mathcal{A}$, $\mathsf{Adv}^{\mathsf{zk}}_{\Phi',\mathcal{A}}(\lambda) = \mathsf{negl}(\lambda)$ holds. Therefore, Φ' satisfies zero-knowledge. □ **(Theorem 3)**

4 Construction of RNC−CCA Secure RNCE

In this section, we show that our generic construction of RNC−CCA secure RNCE with the plaintext space $\{0, 1\}$. Firstly, in Sect. 4.1, we describe our generic construction. Then, in Sect. 4.2, we give a security proof for it.

$\mathbf{KG}'(1^\lambda)$:	$\mathbf{Enc}'(pk, m)$:	$\mathbf{Dec}'(pk, sk, c)$:
$\alpha \leftarrow \{0,1\}$ $(pk_0, sk_0) \leftarrow \mathbf{KG}(1^\lambda)$ $(pk_1, sk_1) \leftarrow \mathbf{KG}(1^\lambda)$ $(crs, vsk) \leftarrow \mathbf{CRSGen}(1^\lambda)$ $pk := (pk_0, pk_1, crs)$ $sk := (\alpha, sk_\alpha, vsk)$ Return (pk, sk)	$(r_0, r_1) \leftarrow (\mathcal{R}_\Pi)^2$ $c_0 \leftarrow \mathbf{Enc}(pk_0, m; r_0)$ $c_1 \leftarrow \mathbf{Enc}(pk_1, m; r_1)$ $x := (pk_0, pk_1, c_0, c_1)$ $w := (m, r_0, r_1)$ $\pi \leftarrow \mathbf{Prove}(crs, x, w)$ Return $c := (c_0, c_1, \pi)$	$x := (pk_0, pk_1, c_0, c_1)$ If $\mathbf{Verify}(crs, vsk, x, \pi) = 1$ then $m \leftarrow \mathbf{Dec}(pk_\alpha, sk_\alpha, c_\alpha)$ Return m else Return $\perp$
$\mathbf{FKG}'(1^\lambda)$: $\alpha \leftarrow \{0,1\}$ $(pk_0, sk_0) \leftarrow \mathbf{KG}(1^\lambda)$ $(pk_1, sk_1) \leftarrow \mathbf{KG}(1^\lambda)$ (crs, vsk, tk) $\leftarrow \mathbf{SimCRS}(1^\lambda)$ $pk := (pk_0, pk_1, crs)$ $td := (\alpha, sk_0, sk_1, vsk, tk)$ Return (pk, td)	$\mathbf{Fake}'(pk, td)$: $c_\alpha \leftarrow \mathbf{Enc}(pk_\alpha, 0)$ $c_{1\oplus\alpha} \leftarrow \mathbf{Enc}(pk_{1\oplus\alpha}, 1)$ $x := (pk_0, pk_1, c_0, c_1)$ $\pi \leftarrow \mathbf{SimPrv}(tk, x)$ Return $\widetilde{c} := (c_0, c_1, \pi)$ $\mathbf{Open}'(pk, td, \widetilde{c}, m)$: $\widetilde{sk} := (\alpha \oplus m,$ $sk_{\alpha\oplus m}, vsk)$ Return $\widetilde{sk}$	$\mathbf{FDec}'(pk, td, c)$: $x := (pk_0, pk_1, c_0, c_1)$ If $\mathbf{Verify}(crs, vsk, x, \pi) = 1$ then $m \leftarrow \mathbf{Dec}(pk_0, sk_0, c_0)$ Return m else Return $\perp$

Fig. 2. Construction of RNC−CCA secure RNCE Π'.

4.1 Description

In this section, we formally describe our generic construction of RNC-CCA secure RNCE with the plaintext space $\{0,1\}$. Let $\Pi = (\mathbf{KG}, \mathbf{Enc}, \mathbf{Dec})$ be a PKE scheme with the plaintext space $\{0,1\}$ and $\mathcal{R}_\pi$ a randomness space for the encryption algorithm **Enc**. Let $\Phi = (\mathbf{CRSGen}, \mathbf{Prove}, \mathbf{Verify}, \mathbf{SimCRS}, \mathbf{SimPrv})$ be a DV-NIZK argument for

$$\mathcal{L}_{eq} := \Big\{(pk_0, pk_1, c_0, c_1) \mid \exists (m, r_0, r_1) \in \{0,1\} \times (\mathcal{R}_\Pi)^2 \text{ s.t. } (c_0 = \mathbf{Enc}(pk_0, m; r_0)) \wedge (c_1 = \mathbf{Enc}(pk_1, m; r_1))\Big\}.$$

Then, we use them to construct our RNCE scheme $\Pi' = (\mathbf{KG}', \mathbf{Enc}', \mathbf{Dec}', \mathbf{FKG}', \mathbf{Fake}', \mathbf{Open}', \mathbf{FDec}')$ with the plaintext space $\{0,1\}$ as described in Fig. 2. We note that the correctness of our RNCE scheme holds due to the correctness of Π and Φ.

How to expand the plaintext space of our generic construction. In the above, we only give the construction whose plaintext space is $\{0,1\}$. However, we can expand the plaintext space by using our single-bit construction in a parallel way except for the generation of a proof of a DV-NIZK argument. More concretely, if we encrypt an ℓ-bit plaintext $m = m_1 \| \cdots \| m_\ell$, the procedure is as follows.

Firstly, we generate a public key $pk = ((pk_0^i, pk_1^i)_{i\in[\ell]}, crs)$ and a secret key $sk = (\alpha_i, sk_{\alpha_i}^i, vsk)_{i\in[\ell]}$, where $\alpha_1, \cdots, \alpha_\ell \leftarrow \{0,1\}$, $(pk_v^i, sk_v^i) \leftarrow \mathbf{KG}(1^\lambda)$ for all $(i, v) \in [\ell] \times \{0,1\}$, and crs (resp., vsk) denotes a CRS (resp., a secret verification key) of a DV-NIZK argument. Next, we compute a ciphertext $c = ((c_0^i)_{i\in[\ell]}, (c_1^i)_{i\in[\ell]}, \pi)$, where $c_v^i \leftarrow \mathbf{Enc}(pk_v^i, m_i)$ for all $(i, v) \in [\ell] \times \{0,1\}$ and π is a proof proving that, for each $i \in [\ell]$, the ciphertexts c_0^i and c_1^i encrypt the same plaintext $m_i \in \{0,1\}$. Similarly, for the other procedures, we execute one-bit version algorithms in a parallel way for all $i \in [\ell]$ except for the procedure of a DV-NIZK argument. See the full version of the paper for the details.

4.2 Security Proof

In this section, we show the following theorem.

Theorem 4. *If Π is an* IND−CPA *secure PKE scheme and Φ satisfies one-time simulation soundness and zero-knowledge, then Π' is* RNC−CCA *secure.*

Proof of Theorem 4. Let $\mathcal{A} = (\mathcal{A}_1, \mathcal{A}_2, \mathcal{A}_3)$ be a PPT adversary that attacks the RNC−CCA security of Π'. We introduce the following experiments $\{\mathsf{Exp}_i\}_{i=0}^5$.

Exp_0 : Exp_0 is exactly the same as $\mathsf{Exp}_{\Pi',\mathcal{A}}^{\mathsf{rnc-real}}(\lambda)$. The detailed description is as follows.

1. First, Exp_0 samples $\alpha \leftarrow \{0,1\}$ and computes $(pk_0, sk_0) \leftarrow \mathbf{KG}(1^\lambda)$, $(pk_1, sk_1) \leftarrow \mathbf{KG}(1^\lambda)$, and $(crs, vsk) \leftarrow \mathbf{CRSGen}(1^\lambda)$. Next, Exp_0 sets $pk := (pk_0, pk_1, crs)$ and $sk := (\alpha, sk_\alpha, vsk)$, and runs $\mathcal{A}_1(pk)$. When $\mathcal{A}_1$ makes a decryption query $c = (c_0, c_1, \pi)$, Exp_0 checks whether $\mathbf{Verify}(crs, vsk, (pk_0, pk_1, c_0, c_1), \pi) = 1$ or not. If this condition holds, Exp_0 computes $m \leftarrow \mathbf{Dec}(pk_\alpha, sk_\alpha, c_\alpha)$ and returns m to $\mathcal{A}_1$. Otherwise, Exp_0 returns $\perp$ to $\mathcal{A}_1$.
2. When $\mathcal{A}_1$ outputs (m^*, st_1) and terminates, Exp_0 computes the challenge ciphertext c^* as follows. First, Exp_0 samples $(r_0^*, r_1^*) \leftarrow (\mathcal{R}_\Pi)^2$ and computes $c_0^* \leftarrow \mathbf{Enc}(pk_0, m^*; r_0^*)$, $c_1^* \leftarrow \mathbf{Enc}(pk_1, m^*; r_1^*)$, and $\pi^* \leftarrow \mathbf{Prove}(crs, (pk_0, pk_1, c_0^*, c_1^*), (m^*, r_0^*, r_1^*))$. Next, Exp_0 sets $c^* = (c_0^*, c_1^*, \pi^*)$ and runs $\mathcal{A}_2(c^*, \mathsf{st}_1)$. When $\mathcal{A}_2$ makes a decryption query c, Exp_0 answers in the same way as above.
3. When $\mathcal{A}_2$ outputs state information st_2 and terminates, Exp_0 runs $\mathcal{A}_3(sk, \mathsf{st}_2)$.
4. When $\mathcal{A}_3$ outputs a bit b' and terminates, Exp_0 outputs b'.

Exp_1 : Exp_1 is identical to Exp_0 except for the following change. When computing the challenge ciphertext c^*, the common reference string crs is generated by executing $(crs, vsk, tk) \leftarrow \mathbf{SimCRS}(1^\lambda)$ instead of $(crs, vsk) \leftarrow \mathbf{CRSGen}(1^\lambda)$. Moreover, Exp_1 generates a simulated proof $\pi^* \leftarrow \mathbf{SimPrv}(tk, (pk_0, pk_1, c_0^*, c_1^*))$ instead of $\pi^* \leftarrow \mathbf{Prove}(crs, (pk_0, pk_1, c_0^*, c_1^*), (m^*, r_0^*, r_1^*))$.

Exp_2 : Exp_2 is identical to Exp_1 except that when computing the challenge ciphertext c^*, Exp_2 computes $c_{1\oplus\alpha}^* \leftarrow \mathbf{Enc}(pk_{1\oplus\alpha}, 1 \oplus m^*; r_{1\oplus\alpha}^*)$ instead of $c_{1\oplus\alpha}^* \leftarrow \mathbf{Enc}(pk_{1\oplus\alpha}, m^*; r_{1\oplus\alpha}^*)$.

Exp_3 : Exp_3 is identical to Exp_2 except that when responding to a decryption query $c = (c_0, c_1, \pi)$, if $\mathbf{Verify}(crs, vsk, (pk_0, pk_1, c_0, c_1), \pi) = 1$, Exp_3 answers $m \leftarrow \mathbf{Dec}(pk_0, sk_0, c_0)$ instead of $m \leftarrow \mathbf{Dec}(pk_\alpha, sk_\alpha, c_\alpha)$. Note that the decryption procedure in Exp_3 is exactly the same as $\mathbf{FDec}'(pk, td, c)$.

Exp_4 : Exp_4 is identical to Exp_3 except that $\alpha \oplus m^*$ is used instead of α. That is, when computing the challenge ciphertext c^*, Exp_4 computes c_0^* and c_1^* by $c^*_{\alpha\oplus m^*} \leftarrow \mathbf{Enc}(pk_{\alpha\oplus m^*}, m^*)$ and $c^*_{\alpha\oplus(1\oplus m^*)} \leftarrow \mathbf{Enc}(pk_{\alpha\oplus(1\oplus m^*)}, 1 \oplus m^*)$. Moreover, Exp_4 gives the secret key $sk = (\alpha \oplus m^*, sk_{\alpha\oplus m^*}, vsk)$ to $\mathcal{A}_3$ instead of $sk = (\alpha, sk_\alpha)$.

Exp_5 : Exp_5 is exactly the same as $\mathsf{Exp}^{\mathsf{rnc-sim}}_{\Pi',\mathcal{A}}(\lambda)$.

We let $p_i := \Pr[\mathsf{Exp}_i(\lambda) = 1]$ for all $i \in [0, 5]$. Then, we have $\mathsf{Adv}^{\mathsf{rnc-cca}}_{\Pi',\mathcal{A}}(\lambda) = |\Pr[\mathsf{Exp}^{\mathsf{rnc-real}}_{\Pi',\mathcal{A}}(\lambda) = 1] - \Pr[\mathsf{Exp}^{\mathsf{rnc-sim}}_{\Pi',\mathcal{A}}(\lambda) = 1]| = |p_0 - p_5| \le \sum_{i=0}^{4} |p_i - p_{i+1}|$. It remains to show how each $|p_i - p_{i+1}|$ is upper-bounded. To this end, we will show the following lemmata.

Lemma 5. *There exists a PPT adversary $\mathcal{E} = (\mathcal{E}_1, \mathcal{E}_2)$ against the zero-knowledge of Φ such that $|p_0 - p_1| = \mathsf{Adv}^{\mathsf{zk}}_{\Phi,\mathcal{E}}(\lambda)$.*

Lemma 6. *There exists a PPT adversary $\mathcal{F} = (\mathcal{F}_1, \mathcal{F}_2)$ against the* IND−CPA *security of Π such that $|p_1 - p_2| = \mathsf{Adv}^{\mathsf{ind-cpa}}_{\Pi,\mathcal{F}}(\lambda)$.*

Lemma 7. *There exists a PPT adversary $\mathcal{G} = (\mathcal{G}_1, \mathcal{G}_2)$ against the one-time simulation soundness of Φ such that $|p_2 - p_3| \le \mathsf{Adv}^{\mathsf{ot-ss}}_{\Phi,\mathcal{G}}(\lambda)$.*

Lemma 8. *$|p_3 - p_4| = 0$ holds.*

Lemma 9. *$|p_4 - p_5| = 0$ holds.*

As mentioned in Sect. 1.2, compared to the previous work [10], the most technically obscure part is Lemma 7 using the one-time simulation soundness of a DV-NIZK argument, and thus we show only it here due to the space limitation. We will show the rest lemmata formally in the full version of the paper.

Proof of Lemma 7. For $i \in \{2, 3\}$, we let $\mathbf{Bad}_i$ be the event that $\mathcal{A}_2$ makes a decryption query $c = (c_0, c_1, \pi)$ satisfying $(\mathbf{Dec}(pk_0, sk_0, c_0) \neq \mathbf{Dec}(pk_1, sk_1, c_1)) \wedge (\mathbf{Verify}(crs, vsk, (pk_0, pk_1, c_0, c_1), \pi) = 1)$ in Exp_i. (We call such a decryption query a *bad decryption query.*) Exp_2 proceeds identically to Exp_3 unless $\mathbf{Bad}_2$ happens. Therefore, the inequality $|p_2 - p_3| \le \Pr[\mathbf{Bad}_2] = \Pr[\mathbf{Bad}_3]$ holds. In the following, we show that one can construct a PPT adversary $\mathcal{G} = (\mathcal{G}_1, \mathcal{G}_2)$ that attacks the one-time simulation soundness of Φ so that $\Pr[\mathbf{Bad}_2] = \mathsf{Adv}^{\mathsf{ot-ss}}_{\Phi,\mathcal{G}}(\lambda)$, using the adversary $\mathcal{A} = (\mathcal{A}_1, \mathcal{A}_2, \mathcal{A}_3)$.

$\mathcal{G}_1(crs)$ **:** First, $\mathcal{G}_1$ samples $\alpha \leftarrow \{0, 1\}$ and computes $(pk_0, sk_0) \leftarrow \mathbf{KG}(1^\lambda)$ and $(pk_1, sk_1) \leftarrow \mathbf{KG}(1^\lambda)$. Next, $\mathcal{G}_1$ sets $pk := (pk_0, pk_1, crs)$ and runs $\mathcal{A}_1(pk)$. When $\mathcal{A}_1$ makes a decryption query $c = (c_0, c_1, \pi)$, $\mathcal{G}_1$ makes a verification query $((pk_0, pk_1, c_0, c_1), \pi)$ to its experiment. Upon receiving a verification

result $v \in \{0,1\}$, $\mathcal{G}_1$ checks whether $v = 1$ or not. If this is the case, then $\mathcal{G}_1$ computes $m \leftarrow \mathbf{Dec}(pk_\alpha, sk_\alpha, c_\alpha)$ and returns m to $\mathcal{A}_1$. Otherwise, $\mathcal{G}_1$ returns $\perp$ to $\mathcal{A}_1$.
When $\mathcal{A}_1$ outputs the challenge plaintext m^* and state information st_1, and terminates, $\mathcal{G}_1$ computes $c_\alpha^* \leftarrow \mathbf{Enc}(pk_\alpha, m^*)$ and $c_{1\oplus\alpha}^* \leftarrow \mathbf{Enc}(pk_{1\oplus\alpha}, 1 \oplus m^*)$. Finally, $\mathcal{G}_1$ sets st_1' as all the information known to it, returns $((pk_0, pk_1, c_0^*, c_1^*), \mathsf{st}_1')$ to its experiment, and terminates.

$\mathcal{G}_2(\pi^*, \mathsf{st}_1')$ **:** First, $\mathcal{G}_2$ sets $c^* := (c_0^*, c_1^*, \pi^*)$ and runs $\mathcal{A}_2(c^*, \mathsf{st}_1)$. When $\mathcal{A}_2$ makes a decryption query c, $\mathcal{G}_2$ parses $c := (c_0, c_1, \pi)$. Then, $\mathcal{G}_2$ makes a verification query $((pk_0, pk_1, c_0, c_1), \pi)$ to its experiment. If the verification result is 0, then $\mathcal{G}_2$ returns $\perp$ to $\mathcal{A}_2$. If the verification result is 1, then $\mathcal{G}_2$ checks whether $\mathbf{Dec}(pk_0, sk_0, c_0) \neq \mathbf{Dec}(pk_1, sk_1, c_1)$ or not. If this is the case, $\mathcal{G}_2$ returns $((pk_0, pk_1, c_0, c_1), \pi)$ to its experiment and terminates. Otherwise, $\mathcal{G}_2$ computes $m \leftarrow \mathbf{Dec}(pk_\alpha, sk_\alpha, c_\alpha)$ and returns m to $\mathcal{A}_2$. When $\mathcal{A}_2$ outputs state information st_2 and terminates, $\mathcal{G}_2$ gives up and terminates.

From the above construction of $\mathcal{G}$, it is easy to see that $\mathcal{G}$ perfectly simulates the experiment Exp_2 for $\mathcal{A}$. Here, the success condition of $\mathcal{G}$ is to output a pair of a statement and a proof (x, π) satisfying $((x^*, \pi^*) \neq (x, \pi)) \wedge (\mathbf{Verify}(crs, vsk, x, \pi) = 1) \wedge (x \notin \mathcal{L}_{eq})$, where $x^* = (pk_0, pk_1, c_0^*, c_1^*)$ and $x = (pk_0, pk_1, c_0, c_1)$. If $\mathcal{A}_2$ makes a bad decryption query $c = (c_0, c_1, \pi)$, then $\mathbf{Dec}(pk_0, sk_0, c_0) \neq \mathbf{Dec}(pk_1, sk_1, c_1)$ and $\mathbf{Verify}(crs, vsk, x, \pi) = 1$. Thus, we can see that $x \notin \mathcal{L}_{eq}$ holds now due to the correctness of Π.

Moreover, due to the condition of decryption queries by $\mathcal{A}_2$, we have $(c_0^*, c_1^*, \pi^*) = c^* \neq c = (c_0, c_1, \pi)$. That is, we have $(x^*, \pi^*) \neq (x, \pi)$. Thus, when $\mathcal{A}_2$ makes a bad decryption query c, $\mathcal{G}$ achieves its success condition by returning (x, π) to its experiment. We note that $\mathcal{G}$ can detect that the event $\mathbf{Bad}_2$ occurs because $\mathcal{G}$ has both of the secret keys sk_0 and sk_1, and can make a verification query (x, π) to its experiment. From the above arguments, the probability that $\mathcal{A}_2$ makes a bad decryption query is exactly the same as the probability that $\mathcal{G}$ breaks the one-time simulation soundness of Φ. Therefore, we have $\Pr[\mathbf{Bad}_2] = \mathsf{Adv}_{\Phi,\mathcal{G}}^{\mathsf{ot-ss}}(\lambda)$, which in turn implies $|p_2 - p_3| \leq \mathsf{Adv}_{\Phi,\mathcal{G}}^{\mathsf{ot-ss}}(\lambda)$. □ **(Lemma** 7**)**

Putting everything together, we obtain $\mathsf{Adv}_{\Pi',\mathcal{A}}^{\mathsf{rnc-cca}}(\lambda) \leq \mathsf{Adv}_{\Phi,\mathcal{E}}^{\mathsf{zk}}(\lambda) + \mathsf{Adv}_{\Pi,\mathcal{F}}^{\mathsf{ind-cpa}}(\lambda) + \mathsf{Adv}_{\Phi,\mathcal{G}}^{\mathsf{ot-ss}}(\lambda)$. Since Π is IND−CPA secure and Φ satisfies one-time simulation soundness and zero-knowledge, for any PPT adversary $\mathcal{A}$, $\mathsf{Adv}_{\Pi',\mathcal{A}}^{\mathsf{rnc-cca}}(\lambda) = \mathsf{negl}(\lambda)$ holds. Therefore, Π' satisfies RNC−CCA security. □ **(Theorem** 4**)**

Acknowledgement. A part of this work was supported by NTT Secure Platform Laboratories, JST OPERA JPMJOP1612, JST CREST JPMJCR14D6, JSPS KAKENHI JP16H01705, JP17H01695, JP20J14338.

References

1. Alekhnovich, M.: More on average case vs approximation complexity. In: 44th FOCS, pp. 298–307 (2003)

2. Bellare, M., Dowsley, R., Waters, B., Yilek, S.: Standard security does not imply security against selective-opening. In: Pointcheval, D., Johansson, T. (eds.) EUROCRYPT 2012. LNCS, vol. 7237, pp. 645–662. Springer, Heidelberg (2012). https://doi.org/10.1007/978-3-642-29011-4_38
3. Bellare, M., Hofheinz, D., Yilek, S.: Possibility and impossibility results for encryption and commitment secure under selective opening. In: Joux, A. (ed.) EUROCRYPT 2009. LNCS, vol. 5479, pp. 1–35. Springer, Heidelberg (2009). https://doi.org/10.1007/978-3-642-01001-9_1
4. Bellare, M., Yilek, S.: Encryption schemes secure under selective opening attack. Cryptology ePrint Archive, Report 2009/101 (2009)
5. Canetti, R., Halevi, S., Katz, J.: Adaptively-secure, non-interactive public-key encryption. In: Kilian, J. (ed.) TCC 2005. LNCS, vol. 3378, pp. 150–168. Springer, Heidelberg (2005). https://doi.org/10.1007/978-3-540-30576-7_9
6. Couteau, G., Hofheinz, D.: Designated-verifier pseudorandom generators, and their applications. In: Ishai, Y., Rijmen, V. (eds.) EUROCRYPT 2019. LNCS, vol. 11477, pp. 562–592. Springer, Cham (2019). https://doi.org/10.1007/978-3-030-17656-3_20
7. Dolev, D., Dwork, C., Naor, M.: Non-malleable cryptography (extended abstract). In: 23rd ACM STOC, pp. 542–552 (2020)
8. Elkind, E., Sahai, A.: A unified methodology for constructing public-key encryption schemes secure against adaptive chosen-ciphertext attack. Cryptology ePrint Archive, Report 2002/042 (2002)
9. Goldwasser, S., Micali, S.: Probabilistic encryption. J. Comput. Syst. Sci. **28**(2), 270–299 (1984)
10. Hara, K., Kitagawa, F., Matsuda, T., Hanaoka, G., Tanaka, K.: Simulation-based receiver selective opening CCA secure PKE from standard computational assumptions. In: Catalano, D., De Prisco, R. (eds.) SCN 2018. LNCS, vol. 11035, pp. 140–159. Springer, Cham (2018). https://doi.org/10.1007/978-3-319-98113-0_8
11. Hara, K., Kitagawa, F., Matsuda, T., Hanaoka, G., Tanaka, K.: Simulation-based receiver selective opening CCA secure PKE from standard computational assumptions. Theor. Comput. Sci. **795**, 570–597 (2019)
12. Huang, Z., Lai, J., Chen, W., Au, M.H., Peng, Z., Li, J.: Simulation-based selective opening security for receivers under chosen-ciphertext attacks. Des. Codes Cryptogr. **87**(6), 1345–1371 (2019)
13. Haralambiev, K., Jager, T., Kiltz, E., Shoup, V.: Simple and efficient public-key encryption from computational Diffie-Hellman in the standard model. In: Nguyen, P.Q., Pointcheval, D. (eds.) PKC 2010. LNCS, vol. 6056, pp. 1–18. Springer, Heidelberg (2010). https://doi.org/10.1007/978-3-642-13013-7_1
14. Hazay, C., Patra, A., Warinschi, B.: Selective opening security for receivers. In: Iwata, T., Cheon, J.H. (eds.) ASIACRYPT 2015. LNCS, vol. 9452, pp. 443–469. Springer, Heidelberg (2015). https://doi.org/10.1007/978-3-662-48797-6_19
15. Jia, D., Lu, X., Li, B.: Receiver selective opening security from indistinguishability obfuscation. In: Dunkelman, O., Sanadhya, S.K. (eds.) INDOCRYPT 2016. LNCS, vol. 10095, pp. 393–410. Springer, Cham (2016). https://doi.org/10.1007/978-3-319-49890-4_22
16. Jia, D., Lu, X., Li, B.: Constructions secure against receiver selective opening and chosen ciphertext attacks. In: Handschuh, H. (ed.) CT-RSA 2017. LNCS, vol. 10159, pp. 417–431. Springer, Cham (2017). https://doi.org/10.1007/978-3-319-52153-4_24

17. Katsumata, S., Nishimaki, R., Yamada, S., Yamakawa, T.: Designated verifier/prover and preprocessing NIZKs from Diffie-Hellman assumptions. In: Ishai, Y., Rijmen, V. (eds.) EUROCRYPT 2019. LNCS, vol. 11477, pp. 622–651. Springer, Cham (2019). https://doi.org/10.1007/978-3-030-17656-3_22
18. Kitagawa, F., Matsuda, T.: CPA-to-CCA transformation for KDM security. In: Hofheinz, D., Rosen, A. (eds.) TCC 2019. LNCS, vol. 11892, pp. 118–148. Springer, Cham (2019). https://doi.org/10.1007/978-3-030-36033-7_5
19. Lindell, Y.: A simpler construction of CCA2-secure public-key encryption under general assumptions. In: Biham, E. (ed.) EUROCRYPT 2003. LNCS, vol. 2656, pp. 241–254. Springer, Heidelberg (2003). https://doi.org/10.1007/3-540-39200-9_15
20. Lombardi, A., Quach, W., Rothblum, R.D., Wichs, D., Wu, D.J.: New constructions of reusable designated-verifier NIZKs. In: Boldyreva, A., Micciancio, D. (eds.) CRYPTO 2019. LNCS, vol. 11694, pp. 670–700. Springer, Cham (2019). https://doi.org/10.1007/978-3-030-26954-8_22
21. Naor, M., Yung, M.: Public-key cryptosystems provably secure against chosen ciphertext attacks. In: 22nd ACM STOC, pp. 427–437 (1990)
22. Peikert, C., Shiehian, S.: Noninteractive zero knowledge for NP from (Plain) learning with errors. In: Boldyreva, A., Micciancio, D. (eds.) CRYPTO 2019. LNCS, vol. 11692, pp. 89–114. Springer, Cham (2019). https://doi.org/10.1007/978-3-030-26948-7_4
23. Quach, W., Rothblum, R.D., Wichs, D.: Reusable designated-verifier NIZKs for all NP from CDH. In: Ishai, Y., Rijmen, V. (eds.) EUROCRYPT 2019. LNCS, vol. 11477, pp. 593–621. Springer, Cham (2019). https://doi.org/10.1007/978-3-030-17656-3_21
24. Regev, O.: On lattices, learning with errors, random linear codes, and cryptography. In: 37th ACM STOC, pp. 84–93 (2009)
25. Yu, Yu., Zhang, J.: Cryptography with auxiliary input and trapdoor from constant-noise LPN. In: Robshaw, M., Katz, J. (eds.) CRYPTO 2016. LNCS, vol. 9814, pp. 214–243. Springer, Heidelberg (2016). https://doi.org/10.1007/978-3-662-53018-4_9

A Practical NIZK Argument for Confidential Transactions over Account-Model Blockchain

Shunli Ma[1,2], Yi Deng[1,2(✉)], Mengqiu Bai[1,2], Debiao He[3], Jiang Zhang[4], and Xiang Xie[5]

[1] State Key Laboratory of Information Security, Institute of Information Engineering, Chinese Academy of Sciences, Beijing, China
{mashunli,deng,baimengqiu}@iie.ac.cn

[2] School of Cyber Security, University of Chinese Academy of Sciences, Beijing, China

[3] Key Laboratory of Aerospace Information Security and Trusted Computing, Ministry of Education, School of Cyber Science and Engineering, Wuhan University, Wuhan, China
hedebiao@163.com

[4] State Key Laboratory of Cryptology, Beijing, China
jiangzhang09@gmail.com

[5] PlatON, Hong Kong, China
xiexiangiscas@gmail.com

Abstract. We propose a novel non-interactive zero-knowledge (NIZK) argument for confidential transactions. Our NIZK argument provides a highly practical prover against other existing works, in which proof generation and verification times are at the same level. Our NIZK argument is *perfect* zero-knowledge in the common reference string model, with its soundness holds in the random oracle model. Based on the NIZK argument, we construct a *confidential transaction smart contract* (CTSC) scheme which enables transferring coins between users confidentially and automatically over the account-model blockchain. Furthermore, We provide a formal security definitions of such a primitive: *confidentiality* and *transaction soundness*, along with a security proof of the construction.

Keywords: Non-interactive zero knowledge · Smart contract · Account-model blockchain

1 Introduction

Blockchain systems enable peer-to-peer digital asset transfer in a decentralized paradigm by maintaining a global tamper-proof digital ledger of transactions arranged in a chronological order. In traditional blockchain systems such as Bitcoin [19] and Ethereum [24], all the nodes could verify the validity of the transactions in a plaintext manner. Therefore, the details of the all the transactions

K. Nguyen et al. (Eds.): ProvSec 2020, LNCS 12505, pp. 234–253, 2020.
https://doi.org/10.1007/978-3-030-62576-4_12

are known by all the participants of the system. In some application scenarios, this is prohibitive. A lot of sensitive information of the users is expected not put on chain in plaintext. Although most blockchains provide weak anonymity by using pseudonyms, they lack confidentiality of transactions (e.g. hiding amount transferred and balance).

Maxwell [18] startups the study of confidential transaction (CT). They employed Pedersen commitment to hide transfer amount and using range proofs to ensure correctness of transactions. The homomorphism of Pedersen commitment enables users to directly add up the inputs and outputs of a transaction respectively without revealing the real values.

Monero [20] used another variant CT approach (named as Ring Confidential Transaction, RingCT) to achieve confidentiality by using similar approaches as Maxwell's scheme, as well as anonymity by employing linkable ring signature which is modified from [16].

Zcash [1,5] protects the confidentiality of transactions using a more sophisticated zero-knowledge proof called zk-SNARK [6]. zkSNARKs generate short proofs with constantant group elements, and have very fast verification time. The downsides of using zk-SNARKs that is based on a *unfalsifiable assumption* are the prohibitive proof generation and the intensive memory usage. Although a subsequent works on zero knowledge such as Bulletproofs [11], zk-STARK [4], Hyrax [23], and Libra [25] improve the efficiency on different aspects, these general-purpose zero knowledge proofs do not exploit the characteristics of the statements that need to be proven but always convert them into large arithmetic circuits, which is very time consuming.

By observing that, Ma et al. [17] first focused on concealing the transferred details to protect the confidentiality of transactions in the account-based model.

The authors design an additive-homomorphic enryption to hide the balance and transfer amount, and construct an efficient NIZK to ensure the validity of transactions. Based on the NIZK scheme, they also proposed a decentralized smart contract (DSC) system to automatically and securely transfer coins. Taking use of ElGamal encryption and Bulletproofs, Bünz et al. [10] proposed Zether, a confidential payment system, which is compatible with Ethereum-like smart contract platforms. Although their proposal can achieve more practical hiding and timely updating operations, the homomorphic encryption schemes used in [10,17] only support small message space in one decryption. For a value that comes from a large message space, they must divide it into several shorter blocks, and then encrypt and prove each block separately.

Besides, the verification process in [17] is built under the expensive pairing operations. Furthermore, DSC presented in [17], as a secure protocol, lacks a formal security definition and suffers from replay attacks (any user can download a transaction from the public ledger and send it repeatedly to the designated recipient of that transaction without being blocked). All of these will greatly be limitations for many lightweight but widespread used applications such as mobile phones.

1.1 Our Contributions

In this paper, we address the aforementioned issues via three main contributions.

(1) We abstract the framework of [17] and give a definition of *confidential transaction smart contract* (CTSC) scheme over account-based model blockchain, along with a formal definition of its security goals: *confidentiality* and *transaction soundness*. Confidentiality captures the requirement that no one can learn the account balance and transfer amount except the parties in the transaction. Transaction soundness requires that no one is able to convince verification nodes of an invalid transaction, even if he has the secret key of sender.
(2) To instantiate CTSC, we use the additive-homomorphic encryption, Paillier cryptosystem that supports large message space, to hide the account balance and transfer amount. As a core building block, we construct an efficient NIZK argument to ensure the validity of confidential transactions, and such a NIZK is sound in the common reference string (CRS) model and perfect zero-knowledge in the random oracle (RO) model. We also prove the security of the CTSC instantiation under well-studied complexity assumptions.
(3) We propose a C++ implementation of our NIZK protocol. Compared to other related work, the results show that our scheme is more practicable and maneuverable in the mentioned actual applications from the analysis of the performance from both asymptotic and practical views. Indeed, while our scheme has a more efficient verifier algorithm, a prover algorithm with similar efficiency and a slightly larger proof size in the case of small message space $[0, 2^{30})$, we are actually better in the communication and computation complexity for large message space $[0, 2^{40})$.

1.2 Technical Overview

As an essential building block of CTSC scheme, we use a NIZK argument to ensure the validity of confidential transactions. We call a transaction *valid* if it is well-formed as stated. In our construction of the CTSC scheme based on account-based model, a user creates an account by initializing a Paillier keypair $(\mathsf{pk}, \mathsf{sk})$ and an encrypted balance $\tilde{C}$, where the public key serves the account address and the secret key is used to show ownership of the account.

To prevent replay attacks discussed above, for any transaction the user needs to append a unique serial number sn and generates a signature on this transaction. Such a serial number can be created from current timestamp and its own public key (e.g., using a secure hash function SHA256).

Let us now consider a scenario where a sender with address pk_s wants to transfer amount t to a receiver with address pk_r. Denote $\tilde{C}_s$ and $\tilde{C}_r$ the encrypted balance of the involving parties. The sender first encrypts t under both public keys and get C_s and C_r, respectively. Then the sender generates a NIZK proof π for a statement $x = (\mathsf{pk}_s, \mathsf{pk}_r, \tilde{C}_s, C_s, C_r)$ to ensure: (i) C_s and C_r are well-formed and encrypt the same value t; (ii) the transfer amount t and the remaining balance of the sender encrypted in $\tilde{C}_s/C_s$ are in a valid range. The transaction now is (x, π). After a successful verification of this transaction, the miners would update the encrypted balance of both parties to be $(\tilde{C}_s/C_s, \tilde{C}_r \cdot C_r)$ and post the transaction to the blockchain.

A Σ-protocol for plaintext-equality of Paillier ciphertexts can be used to prove that C_s and C_r encrypt the same value, and a range proof is very suitable to prove that t and the remaining balance are in a valid range. Though state-of-the-art range proof is Bulletproofs, it is not very compatible with our construction due to the following two points: (i) the recursive execution of the protocol gains the overhead of prover and verifier; (ii) the usage of Pedersen (vector) commitments to hide the secret enforces us to introduce this primitive and prove the plaintext-equality between Paillier ciphertexts and Pedersen (vector) commitments. Thus we follow the work of [17] to use the Boneh-Boyen signature-based range proof [12]. Suppose that the maximum value allowed in the CTSC scheme is $u^\ell - 1$. The main idea of proving $t \in [0, u^\ell)$ is representing t in u-ary as $t = \prod_{i=0}^{\ell-1} t_i \cdot u^i$ and showing that each t_i lies in $[0, u)$. First the receiver sets up a basic Boneh-Boyen signature keypair (sk, vk) and generates a set of signatures $S_\sigma = \{\sigma_j = g_1^{1/(sk+j)}\}$ on $j \in \{0, \ldots, u-1\}$. Then the sender runs a Σ-protocol to ensure the signatures $\sigma_{t_i} \in S_\sigma$. This range proof can be converted to a NIZK argument by applying Fiat-Shamir heuristic and putting the verification key and the set of signatures S_σ into the common reference string as public parameters. While in the design process of our NIZK augment, we encounter some specific technical challenges.

Obstacle of Handling Different Moduli. Due to the usage of Paillier cryptosystem, the encrypted transfer amount is presented in the form of $C_s = (1+N_s)^t \cdot r_1^{N_s} \bmod N_s^2$ and $C_r = (1+N_r)^t \cdot r_2^{N_r} \bmod N_r^2$. While in the employed range proof, the secret transfer amount $t = \prod_{i=0}^{\ell-1} t_i \cdot u^i$ is encoded into a group of prime order p. In order to prove the relations between the messages such as equality and being in the valid range, as a witness, we should blind t with the same randomness r. However, it doesn't work to choose r either from the Paillier moduli N_s, N_r or the prime modulus p. Such a randomness r should be large enough to completely cover the value space of t, otherwise there is a risk of leakage of t. To overcome this obstacle, we sample r from a modulus represented by the product $N_s \cdot N_r \cdot p$.

Obstacle of Removing Pairing. In the range proof that ensures the secret value $t \in [0, u^\ell)$, t is expressed as $t = \prod_{i=0}^{\ell-1} t_i \cdot u^i$, and each t_i is encoded as $\sigma_{t_i} = g_1^{1/(sk+t_i)}$ by using Boneh-Boyen signature which works on a bilinear group $\mathsf{gk} = (p, \mathbb{G}_1, \mathbb{G}_2, \mathbb{G}_T, e, g_1, g_2)$. As discussed above, we need to show $\sigma_{t_i} \in S_\sigma$ without revealing its value, otherwise t_i will be exposed to the receiver. A natural idea is to randomize σ_{t_i} to get $V_i = \sigma_{t_i}^{v_i}$, and then prove the statement $e(V_i, vk) = e(V_i, g_2)^{-t_i} \cdot e(g, g)^{v_i}$ using a Σ-protocol. In trying to remove the time-consuming pairing operations used above, we begin with the work of Arfaoui et al. [3]. Instead of directly proving $V_i = g_1^{v_i/(sk+t_i)}$ using pairing, we turn to prove $V_i^{sk} = V_i^{-t_i} \cdot g_1^{v_i}$. This form is similar to the Perdersen commitment by considering t_i and v_i as committed value and randomness, respectively. However, Note that the secret key sk of the signature scheme is choosed in the CRS, not by the verifier, which makes the verification algorithm in [3,12] fails to work. In order to get around the obstacle, we pre-compute all σ_i^{sk} and put them into the CRS.

2 Preliminaries

Notation. We denote the security parameter by n, and abbreviate probabilistic polynomial-time as PPT. For a set S, $x \leftarrow_\$ S$ means sampling uniformly at random an element x from the set S. For a distribution D over a finite set S_D, $x \leftarrow_\$ D$ means sampling $x \in S_D$ according to the distribution D. We write $y = A(x;r)$ to denote that an probabilistic algorithm A takes input x and randomness r, outputs y. The formula $y \leftarrow A(x)$ means picking randomness r uniformly at random and setting $y = A(x;r)$. A function $\epsilon(n)$ is negligible in n if $\epsilon(n) = o(1/n^c)$ for all $c \in \mathbb{N}$. $\epsilon(n) = \mathsf{negl}(n)$ denotes that $\epsilon(n)$ is a negligible function in n, and $\epsilon(n) = \mathsf{poly}(n)$ denotes that $\epsilon(n)$ is a polynomial function in n.

2.1 Cryptographic Primitives

In this section, we introduce some cryptographic primitives, including the necessary complexity assumptions and background tools used in our NIZK scheme.

Pairing. We call $\mathcal{G}_{bp}(1^n)$ the pairing generator which takes a security parameter as input and outputs a description of a bilinear group $\mathsf{gk} = (p, \mathbb{G}_1, \mathbb{G}_2, \mathbb{G}_T, e, g_1, g_2)$ where p is a n-bit prime. We follow the notations of [9]:

- $\mathbb{G}_1, \mathbb{G}_2, \mathbb{G}_T$ are multiplicative cyclic groups of order p. The elements g_1, g_2 generates $\mathbb{G}_1, \mathbb{G}_2$ respectively.
- e: $\mathbb{G}_1 \times \mathbb{G}_2 \to \mathbb{G}_T$ is a nondegenerate bilinear map, and $e(g_1, g_2)$ generates $\mathbb{G}_T$.
- $\forall a, b \in \mathbb{Z}, e(g_1^a, g_2^b) = e(g_1, g_2)^{ab}$.
- It is efficient to compute group operations, compute the bilinear map, and decide the membership in $\mathbb{G}_1, \mathbb{G}_2$ and $\mathbb{G}_T$.

Definition 1 (DCR assumption [21]**).** *Set $N = pq$ where p and q are two large prime numbers. Given two numbers z_0 and z_1 s.t. $\exists y_0 \in \mathbb{Z}_{n^2}^*, z_0 = y_0^n \bmod N^2$ and $\forall y_1 \in \mathbb{Z}_{n^2}^*, z_1 \neq y_1^n \bmod N^2$. We say the decisional composite residiosity (DCR) assumption holds if for any* PPT *distinguisher $\mathcal{D}$,*

$$\Big| \Pr[\mathcal{D}(z_0) = 1] - \Pr[\mathcal{D}(z_1)] \Big| \leq \mathsf{negl}(n).$$

Definition 2 (q-SDH assumption [8]**).** *The q-Strong Diffie-Hellman (q-SDH) assumption associated to* gk *holds if for all non-uniform* PPT *adversary $\mathcal{A}$, we have*

$$\Pr\left[\begin{array}{c} \mathsf{gk} \leftarrow \mathcal{G}_{bp}(1^n), x \leftarrow_\$ \mathbb{Z}_p : \\ (c, g_1^{1/(x+c)}) \leftarrow \mathcal{A}(\mathsf{gk}, g_1, g_1^x, \ldots, g_1^{x^q}, g_2, g_2^x) \end{array}\right] \leq \mathsf{negl}(n), \quad \textit{where } c \in \mathbb{Z}_p.$$

Paillier Encryption. Paillier encryption scheme [13,21] is a homomorphic public key encryption that is secure under the DCR assumption. It consists of three PPT algorithms $(\mathsf{KGen}, \mathsf{Enc}, \mathsf{Dec})$. The algorithm $\mathsf{KGen}(1^n)$ first chooses an admissible RSA modulus $N = pq$ and sets $\lambda = lcm(p-1, q-1)$, then outputs $(\mathsf{pk}, \mathsf{sk}) = (N, \lambda)$. Given a message $m \in \mathbb{Z}_N$ and public key N, Enc computes and outputs the ciphertext $c = (1+N)^m r^N \bmod N^2$, where $r \leftarrow_{\$} \mathbb{Z}_N^*$. The algorithm Dec takes as input the private key λ and a ciphertext c, and outputs $m = L(c^\lambda \bmod N^2) \cdot \lambda^{-1} \bmod N$, where $L(x) = \frac{x-1}{N}$.

Digital Signatures. A signature scheme consists of three polynomial-time algorithms $(\mathsf{KeyGen}, \mathsf{Sign}, \mathsf{Verify})$, where KeyGen outputs a secret signing key sk and a corresponding public verification key vk, Sign generates a signature on an input message, and Verify checks the validity of the signature w.r.t. the message. The correctness of a signature scheme states that any valid signature will be verified successfully. A signature scheme is said to be existentially unforgeable under a weak chosen message attack (EUF-WCMA) if no computationally bounded adversary can create a valid signature on a *new* message, even after seeing signatures on other messages.

The basic Boneh-Boyen signature [8] based on a bilinear group gk consists of a tuple of polynomial-time algorithms $(\mathsf{BB.KeyGen}, \mathsf{BB.Sign}, \mathsf{BB.Verify})$. The secret signing key is $(sk = \chi) \leftarrow_{\$} \mathbb{Z}_p$, and the corresponding public verification key is $vk = g_2^\chi$. The signature on an input message m is $\sigma = g_1^{1/(\chi+m)}$. The verification is done by checking that $e(\sigma, vk \cdot g_2^m) = e(g_1, g_2)$.

Lemma 1 ([8], Lemma 3.2). *Under the q-SDH assumption associated to a bilinear group* gk*, then Boneh-Boyen signature scheme is EUF-WCMA.*

2.2 Zero Knowledge Proof

Let $\mathcal{L}$ be an NP language and $\mathcal{R}$ the associated binary relation. We say an instance x lies in $\mathcal{L}$ if and only if there exists a witness w such that $(x, w) \in \mathcal{R}$.

We consider a 3-round public-coin protocol with the following form between two polynomial time parties, where P takes (x, w) as input and V takes x as input: (1) P sends a message a; (2) V sends a uniformly random challenge e; (3) P responses with a message z, and V decides to accept or reject based on the data (x, a, e, z).

Definition 3 (Σ-protocol [14]). *A protocol with the above form is a Σ-protocol if the following conditions hold:*

Completeness. *If* P *and* V *behave honestly, then* V *always accepts.*

Special Soundness. *There exists a* PPT *algorithm* Ext*, given any instance* $x \in \mathcal{L}$ *and two accepting transcripts* (a, e, z) *and* (a, e', z') *with* $e \neq e'$*, always computes a witness* w *s.t.* $(x, w) \in \mathcal{R}$.

Special Honest-Verifier Zero-Knowledge. *There exists a* PPT *algorithm* $\mathcal{S}$ *upon input* x *and a random* e *outputs an accepting transcript* (a, e, z)*, whose distribution is statistically indistinguishable from that of the real transcript between the honest* P, V *on input* x.

Non-interactive zero knowledge (NIZK) allows the user to convince anyone in only one round without leaking any other information.

Definition 4 (NIZK [7]**).** *A triple of* PPT *algorithms* $(\mathsf{K}, \mathsf{P}, \mathsf{V})$ *is called a NIZK argument system for language* $\mathcal{L}$ *if the following conditions hold:*

Completeness: *For each* $crs \leftarrow \mathsf{K}(1^n)$ *and* $(x, w) \in \mathcal{R}$*, we have:*

$$\Pr[\pi \leftarrow \mathsf{P}(crs, x, w) : \mathsf{V}(crs, x, \pi) = 1] \geq 1 - \mathsf{negl}(n) .$$

(Adaptive) Soundness: *For any non-uniform* PPT *prover* P^**, we have*

$$\Pr\left[\begin{array}{c} crs \leftarrow \mathsf{K}(1^n), (x, \pi) \leftarrow \mathsf{P}^*(crs) : \\ x \notin \mathcal{L} \wedge \mathsf{V}(crs, x, \pi) = 1 \end{array}\right] \leq \mathsf{negl}(n) .$$

(Adaptive) Zero-Knowledge: *There exists a* PPT *simulator* $\mathcal{S} = (\mathcal{S}_1, \mathcal{S}_2)$*, such that for all stateful non-uniform* PPT *adversaries* $\mathcal{A} = (\mathcal{A}_1, \mathcal{A}_2)$*, we have*

$$\left| \Pr\left[\begin{array}{c} crs \leftarrow \mathsf{K}(1^n); (x, w, state) \leftarrow \mathcal{A}_1(crs); \pi \leftarrow \mathsf{P}(crs, x, w) : \\ (x, w) \in R \wedge \mathcal{A}_2(crs, \pi, state) = 1 \end{array}\right] \right.$$
$$\left. - \Pr\left[\begin{array}{c} (crs, td) \leftarrow \mathcal{S}_1(1^n); (x, w, state) \leftarrow \mathcal{A}_1(crs); \pi \leftarrow \mathcal{S}_2(crs, x, td) : \\ (x, w) \in R \wedge \mathcal{A}_2(crs, \pi, state) = 1 \end{array}\right] \right| \leq \mathsf{negl}(n) .$$

We call it statistical zero-knowledge if the above holds even for unbounded $\mathcal{A}$.

Applying Fiat-Shamir heuristic [15], A Σ-protocol can be transformed into a NIZK under the RO model, via obtaining the challenge e from a random oracle which takes a as input.

2.3 Smart Contracts for Payment over Blockchains

Assume in a payment system deployed in a account-model blockchain, user A wants to transfer t coins to B. Following is a smart contract that automatically transfers coins between users.

User A posts a transaction to the blockchain address where the payment smart contract is deployed that basically says

Transfer t *of my coins to* B*, and* σ *is a signature of this transaction.*

Being triggered by this message, the smart contract executed by the miners first checks the validity of the signature, and ensures that A has more than t coins then does the transfer action and publishes the transaction on the blockchain if all the checks pass, otherwise it ignores the transaction.

Obviously, anyone can learn the balance and transaction amount of A during the process.

3 NIZK Argument and Its Application to CTSC

In this section, we follow the framework presented in [17], and introduce a confidential transaction smart contract (CTSC) scheme which enables transferring coins confidentially and automatically over the account-based model. As a main building block of CTSC, we also construct a new NIZK argument to ensure the validity of confidential transactions.

3.1 Definition of CTSC Scheme

A CTSC scheme consists of a tuple of polynomial-time algorithms described as below:

- Setup. This algorithm produces a list of system public parameters:
  - input: security parameter n;
  - output: system public parameters pp including the maximum amount allowed in the system MAX and other necessary information.
- CreateAccount. This algorithm generates a user's information by using a homomorphic encryption scheme:
  - input: public parameters pp, user id id, and an initial balance t_{id};
  - output: a keypair (pk_{id}, sk_{id}), and an encrypted balance $\tilde{C}_{id}$.

  The public key pk_{id} also links to the user account address. Only the ciphertext $\tilde{C}_{id}$ of the user balance t_{id} is stored in the account book.
- Transfer. This algorithm is invoked by a sender when he transfers t coins to a receiver.
  - input: pp, a keypair (sk_s, pk_s) of sender account, a receiver address pk_r, a sender encrypted balance $\tilde{C}_s$, a transfer amount t;
  - output: a confidential transaction tx. To prevent replay attacks, a unique serial number sn_s will be generated and put into tx.
- Update. This algorithm deployed in the blockchain for automatically transferring will be invoked by the miners.
  - input: pp, tx;
  - If the transaction tx is valid, the miners update the encrypted balance of involved parties; otherwise, ignore this transaction.
- CheckBalance. This algorithm is invoked by a user when he checks his balance:
  - input: a user secret key sk_{id}, and an encrypted balance $\tilde{C}_{id}$;
  - output: a balance t_{id} in plaintext.

Correctness. For a CTSC scheme described above, correctness captures the basic functionality that an honest-generated transaction should be accepted and appended to the blockchain. This property also requires, if a transaction is verified, the encrypted balance of involving parties will be updated correctly.

Security Requirements. We define two security requirements for a CTSC scheme $\Pi =$ (Setup, CreateAccount, Transfer, Update, CheckBalance): *confidentiality* and *transaction soundness*. Confidentiality ensures that any computationally bounded adversary cannot learn the value (i.e., the balance of both parties and the transfer amount) hidden in a confidential transaction except the sender and receiver. Soundness requires that any computationally bounded adversary cannot convince verification nodes with an invalid transaction (i.e., a transaction which is not well-formed as stated), even if he knows the secret key of sender.

More formally, a CTSC scheme is said to be secure (i.e., holding confidentiality and transaction soundness) if for any PPT adversary $\mathcal{A} = (\mathcal{A}_1, \mathcal{A}_2)$, it holds that

$$\left|\Pr[\mathsf{CONF}_{\Pi,\mathcal{A}}(n) = 1] - \frac{1}{2}\right| \leq \mathsf{negl}(n), \Pr[\mathsf{SOUND}_{\Pi,\mathcal{A}}(n) = 1] \leq \mathsf{negl}(n),$$

where the probability is over the coin tosses of $\mathcal{A}$, as well as the romdomness used in the experiments.

$\underline{\mathsf{CONF}_{\Pi,\mathcal{A}}(n)}$:

1. $\mathsf{pp} \leftarrow \mathsf{Setup}(1^n)$;
2. $((t_s^{(0)}, t^{(0)}, t_r^{(0)}), (t_s^{(1)}, t^{(1)}, t_r^{(1)}), state) \leftarrow \mathcal{A}_1(\mathsf{pp})$;
3. Return 0 if any of the following conditions holds:
   (a) For $i \in \{0, 1\}$, any of $t_s^{(i)}, t_r^{(i)}, t^{(i)}$ is not in the range $[0, \mathsf{MAX}]$;
   (b) $t_s^{(0)} < t^{(0)}$ or $t_s^{(1)} < t^{(1)}$.
4. $b \leftarrow_{\$} \{0, 1\}$;
5. $(pk_s, sk_s, \tilde{C}_s^{(b)}) \leftarrow \mathsf{CreateAccount}(\mathsf{pp}, id_s, t_s^{(b)})$;
6. $(pk_r, sk_r, \tilde{C}_r^{(b)}) \leftarrow \mathsf{CreateAccount}(\mathsf{pp}, id_r, t_r^{(b)})$;
7. $\mathsf{tx}^{(b)} \leftarrow \mathsf{Transfer}(\mathsf{pp}, sk_s, pk_s, pk_r, \tilde{C}_s^{(b)}, t^{(b)})$;
8. $b' \leftarrow \mathcal{A}_2(\mathsf{tx}^{(b)}, state)$;
9. Return 1 if $b = b'$.

$\underline{\mathsf{SOUND}_{\Pi,\mathcal{A}}(n)}$:

1. $\mathsf{pp} \leftarrow \mathsf{Setup}(1^n)$;
2. $(pk_s, sk_s, \tilde{C}_s, state) \leftarrow \mathcal{A}_1^{\mathcal{O}_{\mathsf{CreateAccount}}}(\mathsf{pp})$[1];
3. $\mathsf{tx}^* \leftarrow \mathcal{A}_2(\mathsf{pp}, pk_s, sk_s, \tilde{C}_s, state)$;
4. Return 1 iff.
   (a) tx^* is an invalid transactions that contains pk_s;
   (b) tx^* is accepted by verification nodes;

3.2 Non-interactive Zero-Knowledge Argument

Since we use Paillier cryptosystem to hide the balance and transfer amount, each transaction contains a zero-knowledge proof which ensures the validity of the transaction without revealing the reasons why it is valid.

[1] Adversary $\mathcal{A}$ queries the oracle $\mathcal{O}_{\mathsf{CreateAccount}}$ with a random choosed id and a random balance t_{id}, and obtains a reply containing $(pk_{id}, sk_{id}, \tilde{C}_{id})$.

Let us now consider a transaction where a user with balance t_s and a Paillier public key $\mathsf{pk}_s = N_s$ wants to transfer an amount t to a receiver with a public key $\mathsf{pk}_r = N_r$. Denote $\tilde{C}_s$ the encrypted balance of the sender. In order to hide the transfer amount t, the sender encrypts t under both public keys to obtain C_s, C_r, respectively. Now, the sender should provide a NIZK proof to show that:

- The ciphertexts C_s and C_r are well-formed and encrypt the same value t.
- The transfer amount t and the remaining balance of the sender whose ciphertext is $\tilde{C}_s/C_s$, say t', are in the valid range $[0, \mathsf{MAX}]$.

We set the value $\mathsf{MAX} = u^\ell - 1$ to make it compatible with the employed primitives.

The sender now should prove $(x = (\tilde{C}_s, C_s, C_r, \mathsf{pk}_s, \mathsf{pk}_r, vk, g_2)) \in \mathcal{L}$ in zero-knowledge, where the NP language $\mathcal{L}$ is defined as:

$$\mathcal{L} = \left\{ (\tilde{C}_s, C_s, C_r, \mathsf{pk}_s, \mathsf{pk}_r, vk, g_2) : \begin{array}{l} \exists w = (t_s, t, r, r_1, r_2) \text{ s.t.} \\ C_s = (1+N_s)^t \cdot r_1^{N_s} \bmod N_s^2 \wedge \\ C_r = (1+N_r)^t \cdot r_2^{N_r} \bmod N_r^2 \wedge \\ \tilde{C}_s/C_s = (1+N_s)^{(t_s-t)} \cdot (r/r_1)^{N_s} \bmod N_s^2 \wedge \\ t \in [0, u^\ell) \wedge t' = t_s - t \in [0, u^\ell) \textbf{ OR} \\ \exists \chi \text{ s.t.} \\ vk = g_2^\chi \end{array} \right\};$$

the associated binary relation is $\mathcal{R} = \{(x, w)\}$.

Remark 1. The introduction of values vk and g_2 allows the simulator to prove $vk = g_2^\chi$ with a trapdoor χ to obtain the zero-knowledge property under the CRS model. Since (vk, g_2) are public as shown in our NIZK construction (see Fig. 1), and the encrypted balance $\tilde{C}_s$ can be found in the public ledger according to its account address pk_s, the sender only needs to send $(C_s, C_r, \mathsf{pk}_s, \mathsf{pk}_r)$ to the receiver.

Note that in the verification algorithm of our NIZK, H represents a random oracle which can be instantiated by a secure hash function mapping any string into a k-bit one, where $k = \mathsf{poly}(n)$ such that 2^k is smaller than the smallest prime factor of N_s, N_r.

Theorem 1. *Under the q-SDH assumption associated to a bilinear group, the protocol described in Fig. 1 is a NIZK argument with soundness in the RO model and perfect (adaptive) zero-knowledge in the CRS model.*

The proof of Theorem 1 is in the Appendix A.

A true statement x implies $\tilde{C}_s = (1+N_s)^{t_s} \cdot r^{N_s} \bmod N_s^2$, but the sender probably does not know r since the ciphertexts on the ledger may be timely updated many times by the verification nodes. A question arises that how we can prove $\tilde{C}_s/C_s = (1+N_s)^{(t_s-t)} \cdot (r/r_1)^{N_s} \bmod N_s^2$ without the knowledge of r. Instead of using the randomness, the works of [10,17] take the private key

$\underline{crs \leftarrow \mathsf{K}(1^n):}$

1. $(p, \mathbb{G}_1, \mathbb{G}_2, \mathbb{G}_T, e, g_1, g_2) \leftarrow \mathbb{G}_{bp}(1^n)$;
2. $(sk = \chi, vk = g_2^{\chi}) \leftarrow \mathsf{BB.KeyGen}(1^n)$;
3. For $j = 0$ to $u-1$, compute $\sigma_j = \mathsf{BB.Sign}(sk, j) = g_1^{1/(\chi+j)}$, and $T_j = \sigma_j^{\chi}$;
4. $\sigma \leftarrow (\sigma_0, \dots, \sigma_{u-1}), T \leftarrow (T_0, \dots, T_{u-1})$;
5. Return $crs = (p, \mathbb{G}_1, \mathbb{G}_2, \mathbb{G}_T, e, g_1, g_2, vk, \sigma, T)$.

$\underline{\pi \leftarrow \mathsf{P}(crs, x, w):}$

1. Set $N = N_s \cdot N_r \cdot p$;
2. For $i = 0$ to $\ell - 1$, choose $\rho_i, \mu_i \leftarrow_{\$} \mathbb{Z}_N$ and compute $\rho = \sum_{i=0}^{\ell-1} \rho_i u^i$ and $\mu = \sum_{i=0}^{\ell-1} \mu_i u^i$;
3. $\gamma_1, \gamma_3 \leftarrow_{\$} \mathbb{Z}_{N_s}^*, \gamma_2 \leftarrow_{\$} \mathbb{Z}_{N_r}^*$;
4. $a_s = (1+N_s)^{\rho} \cdot \gamma_1^{N_s} \bmod N_s^2, a_r = (1+N_r)^{\rho} \cdot \gamma_2^{N_r} \bmod N_r^2$, and $a_s' = (1+N_s)^{\mu} \cdot \gamma_3^{N_s} \bmod N_s^2$;
5. For $i = 0$ to $\ell - 1$, choose $v_i, v_i', \eta_i, \tau_i \leftarrow_{\$} \mathbb{Z}_N$, and compute
   $V_i = \sigma_{t_i}^{v_i}, a_i = V_i^{-\rho_i} \cdot g_1^{\eta_i}, W_i = T_{t_i}^{v_i}, V_i' = \sigma_{t_i'}^{v_i'}, a_i' = V_i'^{-\mu_i} \cdot g_1^{\tau_i}, W_i' = T_{t_i}^{v_i'}$;
6. Select $\hat{c} \leftarrow_{\$} \{0,1\}^k, \hat{z} \leftarrow_{\$} \mathbb{Z}_p$, and compute $\alpha = g_2^{\hat{z}} / vk^{\hat{c}}$;
7. $\tilde{c} = \mathsf{H}(a_s, a_r, a_s', \{V_i, V_i', a_i, a_i', W_i, W_i'\}_{i=0}^{\ell-1}, \alpha)$;
8. $c = \tilde{c} + \hat{c} \bmod 2^k$;
9. For $i = 0$ to $\ell - 1$, compute (all modulo N)
   $z_{v_i} = \eta_i - c \cdot v_i,\ z_{v_i'} = \tau_i - c \cdot v_i'\ z_{t_i} = \rho_i - c \cdot t_i,\ z_{t_i'} = \mu_i - c \cdot t_i'$
10. Compute $z_1 = \gamma_1 / r_1^c \bmod N_s$, $z_2 = \gamma_2 / r_2^c \bmod N_r$, $z_3 = \gamma_3 / (r/r_1)^c \bmod N_s$
11. Return the proof π:
    $(a_s, a_r, a_s', \{V_i, V_i', a_i, a_i', W_i, W_i'\}_{i=0}^{\ell-1}, \alpha, c, z_1, z_2,\ z_3, \{z_{v_i}, z_{v_i'}, z_{t_i}, z_{t_i'}\}_{i=0}^{\ell-1}, \hat{z})$.

$\underline{0/1 \leftarrow \mathsf{V}(crs, x, \pi):}$

1. Parse the proof π into the form:
   $(a_s, a_r, a_s', \{V_i, V_i', a_i, a_i', W_i, W_i'\}_{i=0}^{\ell-1}, \alpha, c, z_1, z_2,\ z_3, \{z_{v_i}, z_{v_i'}, z_{t_i}, z_{t_i'}\}_{i=0}^{\ell-1}, \hat{z})$;
2. Compute $\tilde{c} = \mathsf{H}(a_s, a_r, a_s', \{V_i, V_i', a_i, a_i', W_i, W_i'\}_{i=0}^{\ell-1}, \alpha)$;
3. Compute $\hat{c} = c - \tilde{c} \bmod 2^k$;
4. Set $z_t = \sum_{i=0}^{\ell-1} u^i \cdot z_{t_i}$ and $z_{t'} = \sum_{i=0}^{\ell-1} u^i \cdot z_{t_i'}$;
5. Return 0 if any of the following conditions fails to pass:
   - $a_i = W_i^c \cdot V_i^{-z_{t_i}} \cdot g_1^{z_{v_i}}$ for $i \in [0, \ell-1]$,
   - $a_i' = (W_i')^c \cdot (V_i')^{-z_{t_i'}} \cdot g_1^{z_{v_i'}}$ for $i \in [0, \ell-1]$,
   - $a_s = (1+N_s)^{z_t} \cdot C_s^c \cdot z_1^{N_s} \bmod N_s^2$,
   - $a_r = (1+N_r)^{z_t} \cdot C_r^c \cdot z_2^{N_r} \bmod N_r^2$,
   - $a_s' = (1+N_s)^{z_{t'}} \cdot (\frac{\tilde{C}_s}{C_s})^c \cdot z_3^{N_s} \bmod N_s^2$,
   - $g_2^{\hat{z}} = \alpha \cdot vk^{\hat{c}}$;
6. Return 1.

Fig. 1. NIZK argument for validity of transactions

sk as a witness to prove that the ciphertext can be decrypted into the message $t' = t_s - t$. However using this approach for Paillier ciphertexts cannot induce an efficient Σ-protocol. To get around this obstacle, we follow the fact that the Paillier encryption is an isomorphism $\psi : \mathbb{Z}_{N_s} \times \mathbb{Z}^*_{N_s} \rightarrow \mathbb{Z}^*_{N_s^2}$ which can be inverted given Paillier private key λ_s, and the sender can use an extractor described below to compute the randomness r. We refer readers to [13,22] for background about this algorithm.

$\underline{\mathsf{Ext}(\tilde{C}_s, N_s, \lambda_s)}$:

1. Decrypt the ciphertext to get $t_s \leftarrow \mathsf{Dec}(\lambda_s, \tilde{C}_s)$;
2. Compute $\tilde{r} = \tilde{C}_s \cdot (1 + N_s)^{-t_s} \bmod N_s^2$;
3. Compute a such that $a\lambda_s + 1 = 0 \bmod N_s$, this is possible since $\gcd(\lambda_s, N_s) = 1$;
4. Compute $r = \tilde{r}^{(a\lambda_s+1)/N_s} \bmod N_s$;
5. Return (t_s, r).

3.3 Construction of CTSC Scheme

In a nutshell, we use Paillier encryption to hide the transfer amount and the account balance, and use NIZK to enforce senders to build confidential transactions honestly and make correctness publicly verifiable. We also use digital signature to authenticate transactions. Let $(\mathsf{KGen}, \mathsf{Enc}, \mathsf{Dec})$ be Paillier encryption scheme. Let $(\mathsf{K}, \mathsf{P}, \mathsf{V})$ be the NIZK protocol described in Fig. 1. Let $(\mathsf{KeyGen}, \mathsf{Sign}, \mathsf{Verify})$ be a signature which is EUF-WCMA. The construction is described as follows.

- Setup.
  - Input: security parameter n (in unary);
  - Output: $\mathsf{pp} = (crs, \mathsf{aux})$.
  1. $crs \leftarrow \mathsf{K}(1^n)$;
  2. Initialize aux that contains:
     * The maximum value $\mathsf{MAX} = u^\ell - 1$ allowed by CTSC scheme;
     * Public parameters required by Paillier encryption and the signature.
- CreateAccount.
  - Input: pp, user id id, and an initial balance $t_{id} \in [0, \mathsf{MAX}]$;
  - Output: public key$(\mathsf{pk}_{id}, vk_{id})$, secret key $(\mathsf{sk}_{id}, sk_{id})$, and an encrypted balance $\tilde{C}_{id}$.
  1. $(\mathsf{pk}_{id}, \mathsf{sk}_{id}) \leftarrow \mathsf{KGen}(1^n)$;
  2. $\tilde{C}_{id} \leftarrow \mathsf{Enc}(\mathsf{pk}_{id}, t_{id})$.
  3. $(sk_{id}, vk_{id}) \leftarrow \mathsf{KeyGen}(1^n)$.

- Transfer.
  - Input: pp, sender public key pk_s, receiver public key pk_r, sender secret key (sk_s, sk_s), sender encrypted balance $\tilde{C}_s$, transfer amount t;
  - Output: $\mathsf{tx} = (\mathsf{pk}_s, \mathsf{pk}_r, C_s, C_r, \pi, \sigma_{\mathsf{tx}}, \mathsf{sn}_s)$.
  1. Choose $r_1 \leftarrow_\$ \mathbb{Z}_{N_s}^*$, and compute $C_s = \mathsf{Enc}(\mathsf{pk}_s, t; r_1)$;
  2. Choose $r_2 \leftarrow_\$ \mathbb{Z}_{N_r}^*$, and compute $C_r = \mathsf{Enc}(\mathsf{pk}_r, t; r_2)$;
  3. $(t_s, r) \leftarrow \mathsf{Ext}(\tilde{C}_s, \mathsf{pk}_s, \mathsf{sk}_s)$;
  4. Set $x = (\tilde{C}_s, C_s, C_r, \mathsf{pk}_s, \mathsf{pk}_r, vk, g_2)$;
  5. Set $w = (t_s, t, r, r_1, r_2)$;
  6. $\pi \leftarrow \mathsf{P}(crs, x, w)$;
  7. Generate a unique serial number sn_s from current timestamp and pk_s.
  8. $\sigma_{\mathsf{tx}} \leftarrow \mathsf{Sign}(sk_s, (\mathsf{pk}_s, \mathsf{pk}_r, C_s, C_r, \pi, \mathsf{sn}_s))$.

- Update.
  - Input: pp, a transaction tx;
  1. Parse tx into the form $(\mathsf{pk}_s, \mathsf{pk}_r, C_s, C_r, \pi, \sigma_{\mathsf{tx}}, \mathsf{sn}_s)$;
  2. Ignore the transaction and abort if sn_s is not a fresh number;
  3. Seek the encrypted balance $\tilde{C}_s, \tilde{C}_r$ of both parties from the public ledger;
  4. Set $x = (\tilde{C}_s, C_s, C_r, \mathsf{pk}_s, \mathsf{pk}_r, vk, g_2)$;
  5. Abort if any of the following checks fails to pass:
     * $1 \leftarrow \mathsf{V}(crs, x, \pi)$;
     * $1 \leftarrow \mathsf{Verify}(vk_s, (\mathsf{pk}_s, \mathsf{pk}_r, C_s, C_r, \mathsf{sn}_s), \sigma_{\mathsf{tx}})$;
  6. Set $\tilde{C}_s = \tilde{C}_s / C_s$ and $\tilde{C}_r = \tilde{C}_r \cdot C_r$.

- CheckBalance.
  - Input: private key sk_{id}, encrypted balance $\tilde{C}_{id}$;
  - Output: balance t_{id}.
  1. $t_{id} \leftarrow \mathsf{Dec}(\mathsf{sk}_{id}, \tilde{C}_{id})$.

Correctness of the above CTSC construction immediately follows the correctness of Paillier encryption, the correctness of the underlying signature, and the completeness of our NIZK argument.

Theorem 2. *Assuming the security of Paillier encryption, NIZK scheme and the signature scheme, the above construction is a secure CTSC scheme.*

Proof. To prove the confidentiality, we now describe a sequence of hybrid experiments $\mathsf{CONF}^0_{\Pi,\mathcal{A}}(n), \mathsf{CONF}^1_{\Pi,\mathcal{A}}(n), \mathsf{CONF}^2_{\Pi,\mathcal{A}}(n)$.

Experiment $\mathsf{CONF}^0_{\Pi,\mathcal{A}}(n)$: This experiment is the same as $\mathsf{CONF}_{\Pi,\mathcal{A}}(n)$ defined in Sect. 3.1, thus

$$\left| \Pr[\mathsf{CONF}_{\Pi,\mathcal{A}}(n) = 1] - \Pr[\mathsf{CONF}^0_{\Pi,\mathcal{A}}(n) = 1] \right| = 0. \tag{1}$$

Experiment $\mathsf{CONF}^1_{\Pi,\mathcal{A}}(\mathsf{n})$. This experiment is the same as $\mathsf{CONF}^0_{\Pi,\mathcal{A}}(\mathsf{n})$ except the following point. Instead of using t_s^b and t_r^b from the adversary where

$b \leftarrow_{\$} \{0,1\}$, the challenger creates two accounts by choosing two random values t_s, t_r from the set $[0, \mathsf{MAX}]$ such that $t_s \geq t^b$:

$$(\mathsf{pk}_s, vk_s, \mathsf{sk}_s, sk_s, \tilde{C}_s) \leftarrow \mathsf{CreateAccount}(\mathsf{pp}, id_s, t_s),$$
$$(\mathsf{pk}_r, vk_r, \mathsf{sk}_r, sk_r, \tilde{C}_r) \leftarrow \mathsf{CreateAccount}(\mathsf{pp}, id_r, t_r).$$

Since Paillier encryption is IND-CPA, we have:

$$\left|\Pr[\mathsf{CONF}^0_{\Pi,\mathcal{A}}(n) = 1] - \Pr[\mathsf{CONF}^1_{\Pi,\mathcal{A}}(n) = 1]\right| \leq \mathsf{negl}(n). \tag{2}$$

Experiment $\mathsf{CONF}^2_{\Pi,\mathcal{A}}(n)$. This experiment is the same as $\mathsf{CONF}^1_{\Pi,\mathcal{A}}(n)$ except the challenger runs $(\mathsf{pp}, \chi) \leftarrow \mathsf{SimSetup}(1^n)$ and $\mathsf{tx} \leftarrow \mathsf{SimTransfer}(\mathsf{pp}, \mathsf{pk}_s, \mathsf{pk}_r, \tilde{C}_s, t, \chi)$, where t is selected randomly from $[0, \mathsf{MAX}]$ and $t \leq t_s$. SimSetup uses the simulator $\mathcal{S}_1$ to fulfill pp, along with a trapdoor χ, and SimTransfer uses the simulator $\mathcal{S}_2$ to simulate the proof using the trapdoor χ and outputs the simulated transaction. The simulator $\mathcal{S} = (\mathcal{S}_1, \mathcal{S}_2)$ can be found in Fig. 2. Due to the adaptively zero-knowledge of our NIZK argument, we have:

$$\left|\Pr[\mathsf{CONF}^1_{\Pi,\mathcal{A}}(n) = 1] - \Pr[\mathsf{CONF}^2_{\Pi,\mathcal{A}}(n) = 1]\right| \leq \mathsf{negl}(n). \tag{3}$$

Note that tx, the output of experiment $\mathsf{CONF}^2_{\Pi,\mathcal{A}}(n)$, has nothing to do with b. Thus,

$$\Pr[\mathsf{CONF}^2_{\Pi,\mathcal{A}}(n) = 1] = \frac{1}{2}. \tag{4}$$

From the above formula (1), (2), (3) and (4), we have:

$$\left|\Pr[\mathsf{CONF}_{\Pi,\mathcal{A}}(n) = 1] - \frac{1}{2}\right| \leq \mathsf{negl}(n).$$

The transaction soundness directly follows the soundness of NIZK and the unforgeability of underlying signature scheme, and we just sketch its proof here. Suppose there exists an efficient adversary $\mathcal{A}$ that can break such a property with a non-negligible probability $\epsilon(n)$. That is, the probability that $\mathcal{A}$ finally outputs a *new* accepted but invalid transaction tx^* is $\epsilon(n)$:

$$\Pr[\mathsf{SOUND}_{\Pi,\mathcal{A}}(n) = 1] = \epsilon(n).$$

Parse the transaction tx^* into the form $(x^*_{\mathsf{tx}} = (\mathsf{pk}_s, \mathsf{pk}^*_r, C^*_s, C^*_r), \pi^*, \sigma^*_{\mathsf{tx}}, \mathsf{sn}^*_s)$. Since tx^* is accepted, we have

$$1 \leftarrow \mathsf{Verify}(vk_s, (x^*_{\mathsf{tx}}, \mathsf{sn}^*_s), \sigma^*_{\mathsf{tx}}), 1 \leftarrow \mathsf{V}(crs, (\tilde{C}_s, x^*_{\mathsf{tx}}, vk, g_2), \pi^*).$$

There exist two cases to be considered. In the first case, x^*_{tx} is well-formed (i.e., C^*_s and C^*_r are ciphertext of $t \in [0, \mathsf{MAX}]$ under pk_s and pk^*_r, respectively.) and π^* is generated honestly, but σ^*_{tx} is an incorrect signature of $(x^*_{\mathsf{tx}}, \pi^*, \mathsf{sn}^*_s)$ but can be validated, which immediately breaks the unforgeability of underlying signature scheme with probability $\mathsf{poly}_1(\epsilon(n))$. In the second case, σ^*_{tx} is indeed a valid signature, but x^*_{tx} is not well-formed which means $(x = (\tilde{C}_s, x^*_{\mathsf{tx}}, vk, g_2)) \notin \mathcal{L}$. An accepted proof π^* directly breaks the soundness of NIZK with probability $\mathsf{poly}_2(\epsilon(n))$. All of the above shows that $\epsilon(n)$ must be negligible.

4 Optimization and Evaluation

In this section, we optimize the proof size of our NIZK scheme shown in Fig. 1 and briefly prove its security, then evaluate its performance.

4.1 Optimization

The main idea is that prover P uses H on the values $(a_s, a_r, a'_s, \alpha, \{a_i, a'_i\}_{i=0}^{\ell-1})$ and gets $(c_s, c_r, c'_s, c_\alpha, \{c_i, c'_i\}_{i=0}^{\ell-1})$, respectively. Then compute $\tilde{c} = \mathsf{H}(c_s, c_r, c'_a, \{V_i, V'_i, c_i, c'_i, W_i, W'_i\}_{i=0}^{\ell-1}, c_\alpha)$. The new proof now is:

$$\pi = \big(a = (c_s, c_r, c'_s, \{V_i, V'_i, c_i, c'_i, W_i, W'_i\}_{i=0}^{\ell-1}, c_\alpha), c, \\ z = (z_1, z_2, z_3, \{z_{v_i}, z_{v'_i}, z_{t_i}, z_{t'_i}\}_{i=0}^{\ell-1}, \hat{z})\big).$$

In the verification procedure, we need to check the following conditions:

- $c_i = \mathsf{H}(W_i^c \cdot V_i^{-z_{t_i}} \cdot g_1^{z_{v_i}})$;
- $c'_i = \mathsf{H}((W'_i)^c \cdot (V'_i)^{-z_{t'_i}} \cdot g_1^{z_{v'_i}})$;
- $c_s = \mathsf{H}((1+N_s)^{z_t} \cdot C_s^c \cdot z_1^{N_s} \bmod N_s^2)$;
- $c_r = \mathsf{H}((1+N_r)^{z_t} \cdot C_r^c \cdot z_2^{N_r} \bmod N_r^2)$;
- $c'_s = \mathsf{H}((1+N_s)^{z_{t'}} \cdot (\tilde{C}_s/C_s)^c \cdot z_3^{N_s} \bmod N_s^2)$;
- $c_\alpha = \mathsf{H}(g_2^{\hat{z}} \cdot vk^{-\hat{c}})$.

Lemma 2. *Assume the NIZK argument in Fig. 1 is secure, the new protocol is a NIZK argument.*

Proof (Sketch). Completeness is obvious. To show soundness, suppose a PPT prover P^* generates an accepted proof $\pi = (a, c, z)$ for a false statement with a non-negligible probability. Fix his random tape, there exists an extractor output another valid proof $\pi' = (a, c', z')$ by rewinding P^* to a different oracle reply $\tilde{c}'$ in an expected polynomial time. We have $\mathsf{H}((1+N_s)^{z_t} \cdot C_s^c \cdot z_1^{N_s} \bmod N_s^2) = \mathsf{H}((1+N_s)^{z'_t} \cdot C_s^{c'} \cdot {z'_1}^{N_s} \bmod N_s^2)$. Since H is a random oracle, $(1+N_s)^{z_t} \cdot C_s^c \cdot z_1^{N_s} = (1+N_s)^{z'_t} \cdot C_s^{c'} \cdot {z'_1}^{N_s} \bmod N_s^2$, we can extract partial witness (t, r_1) by following the steps as shown in Appendix A. Similarly, we can continue to extract the remaining witness (t_s, r, r_2). If $t \notin [0, u^\ell)$ or $t_s - t \notin [0, u^\ell)$, we can break the EUF-WCMA of Boneh-Boyen signature with a non-negligible probability by using P^* as a subroutine as shown in Appendix A. To argue its zero-knowledge, we construct a simulator same as the one described in Fig. 2 except computing H on the values $(a_s, a_r, a'_s, \alpha, \{a_i, a'_i\}_{i=0}^{\ell-1})$ and putting the respective output $(c_s, c_r, c'_s, c_\alpha, \{c_i, c'_i\}_{i=0}^{\ell-1})$ in the proof. It can be seen that the simulated proof is distributed as the real protocol.

4.2 Evaluation

We first analyze the efficiency theoretically and then conduct experiments to verify the analysis result. To evaluate the communication and storage complexity of schemes, we count the size of system parameter pp and the proof in every scheme. In the construction of NIZK scheme, the public parameter size is $|\mathbb{G}_2| + 2u|\mathbb{G}_1|$ ($|\mathbb{G}_1|$ and $|\mathbb{G}_2|$ denote the element size in groups $\mathbb{G}_1$ and $\mathbb{G}_2$, respectively), which is $\mathcal{O}(2u)$ as shown in Table 1. The proof size in our scheme is $(4\ell+1)|\mathbb{G}_1| + |\mathbb{G}_2| + 2|\mathbb{Z}_{N_s}| + |\mathbb{Z}_{N_r}| + 4\ell|\mathbb{Z}_N| + (2\ell+5)|\mathbb{Z}_{2^k}|$. It is worth nothing that we omit the basic parameters of ECC including (e, p, g_1, g_2, g_t) which only account for a small proportion.

Table 1. Comparison results of computation and communication complexity.

		NIZK[17]		This paper	
Theory	Public parameter size	$\lvert G_2\rvert + u(\lvert G_1\rvert + \lvert G_T\rvert)$		$\lvert\mathbb{G}_2\rvert + 2u\lvert\mathbb{G}_1\rvert$	
	Proof size	$(2\ell+5)\cdot\lvert G_1\rvert+2\ell\cdot\lvert G_T\rvert +(4\ell+6)\cdot\lvert\mathbb{Z}_p\rvert$		$(4\ell+1)\lvert\mathbb{G}_1\rvert + \lvert\mathbb{G}_2\rvert + 2\lvert\mathbb{Z}_{N_s}\rvert + \lvert\mathbb{Z}_{N_r}\rvert + 4\ell\lvert\mathbb{Z}_N\rvert + (2\ell+5)\lvert\mathbb{Z}_{2^k}\rvert$	
Practice	Choice of MAX	2^{30}	2^{40}	2^{30}	2^{40}
	Setup (ms)	8700	8700	873	873
	Proof (ms)	64.97	130	62	64
	Verify (ms)	48.96	98	37.25	40.29
	Public parameter size (KB)	451	451	133	133
	Proof size (Bytes)	3680	7360	4608	5952

We conduct an experimental evaluation for our NIZK scheme. The SHA256 secure hash function is selected to instantiate our argument. We choose two different message spaces to compare the efficiency of our scheme with related work [17]: $[0, 2^{30})$ and $[0, 2^{40})$. We also follow their work to set $u = 2^{10}$. We set the bit of Paillier modulus and the bit of the order of bilinear group to be 1024. We run the experiments using the miracle library [2] (a popular cryptographic library, version 7.0). The system configuration is the Windows system (Windows 10, 64 bits) with an Intel(R) Core(TM) i7 4770 at 3.40 GHz and 16 GB RAM. The setup phase need only 873 ms to complete and the public parameter size is only 133 KB, all of which dramatically improves the performance compared with related work. From the experiment result, in the case that the message space is $[0, 2^{30})$, our NIZK scheme has a more efficient verifier and a similar efficient prover, at the cost of a slightly longer proof size than the scheme in work [17]. Unfortunately, their scheme fails to support large message space, which leads to doubled efficiency lose in computation and communication when turning to the message space $[0, 2^{40})$. To avoid this problem, we use the Paillier encryption which supports the large message space. In the case of MAX $= 2^{40} - 1$, our scheme actually performs better than that in [17] in prover time, verifier time and proof size.

Acknowledgements. We thank the anonymous reviewers for their invaluable comments. This work is supported by the National Key Research and Development Program of China (Grant No. 2017YFB0802500), PlatON, the National Natural Science Foundation of China (Grant Nos. 61932019, 61772521, 61772522 and 61972294), the Key Research Program of Frontier Sciences, CAS (Grant No. QYZDB-SSW-SYS035), the Natural Science Foundation of Hubei Province (Grant No. 2020CFA052), the Wuhan Municipal Science and Technology Project(Grant No. 202001060101 2187).

A Missing Proof of Theorem 1

(Perfect) Completeness. The completeness is trivial, we omit the details here.

(Adaptive) Soundness. Suppose that the soundness does not hold. Then there must exist a PPT prover P^* with random tape r_{P^*} that generates an accepted proof π for a false statement with probability at least $\epsilon(n) > \frac{1}{2^k}$, where

$$\pi = \big(a = (a_s, a_r, a'_s, \{V_i, V'_i, a_i, a'_i, W_i, W'_i\}_{i=0}^{\ell-1}, \alpha), \\ c, z = (z_1, z_2, z_3, \{z_{v_i}, z_{v'_i}, z_{t_i}, z_{t'_i}\}_{i=0}^{\ell-1}, \hat{z})\big).$$

Fix such a random tape, the probability that P^* answers different challenges c correctly is at least $\epsilon(n)$. Then, we construct such an extractor: Upon seeing an accepted proof π, $\mathcal{E}$ rewinds P^* to the oracle query $\mathsf{H}(a)$ that returned $\tilde{c}$. It then reprogram the random oracle such that $\tilde{c}' = \mathsf{H}(a)$ with $\tilde{c} \neq \tilde{c}'$ and continue the execution of P^* with the modified random oracle. In expected polynomial time $\mathcal{O}(\frac{1}{\epsilon(n)})$, another valid proof is obtained: $\pi' = (a, c' = \tilde{c}' + \hat{c}, z'_1, z'_2, z'_3, \{z'_{v_i}, z'_{v'_i}, z'_{t_i}, z'_{t'_i}\}_{i=0}^{\ell-1}, \hat{z})$.

From the validity of the two transcripts, we have

$$\begin{aligned}
a_s &= (1+N_s)^{z_t} \cdot C_s^c \cdot z_1^{N_s} \bmod N_s^2, & a_s &= (1+N_s)^{z'_t} \cdot C_s^{c'} \cdot {z'_1}^{N_s} \bmod N_s^2;\\
a_r &= (1+N_r)^{z_t} \cdot C_r^c \cdot z_2^{N_r} \bmod N_r^2, & a_r &= (1+N_r)^{z'_t} \cdot C_r^{c'} \cdot {z'_2}^{N_r} \bmod N_r^2;\\
a'_s &= (1+N_s)^{z_{t'}} \cdot (\frac{\tilde{C}_s}{C_s})^c \cdot z_3^{N_s} \bmod N_s^2, & a'_s &= (1+N_s)^{z'_{t'}} \cdot (\frac{\tilde{C}_s}{C_s})^{c'} \cdot {z'_3}^{N_s} \bmod N_s^2;\\
a_i &= W_i^c \cdot V_i^{-z_{t_i}} \cdot g_1^{z_{v_i}}, & a_i &= W_i^{c'} \cdot V_i^{-z'_{t_i}} \cdot g_1^{z'_{v_i}};\\
a'_i &= (W'_i)^c \cdot (V'_i)^{-z_{t'_i}} \cdot g_1^{z_{v'_i}}, & a'_i &= (W'_i)^{c'} \cdot (V'_i)^{-z'_{t'_i}} \cdot g_1^{z'_{v'_i}}.
\end{aligned}$$

Since $c \in \{0,1\}^k$ and 2^k is smaller than the smallest prime factor of N_s and N_r, $(c - c')$ is invertible in $\mathbb{Z}_{N_s}$ and $\mathbb{Z}_{N_r}$. Hence we get

$$C_s = (1+N_s)^{(z'_t - z_t)/(c-c')} \cdot ((z'_1/z_1)^{(c-c')^{-1}})^{N_s} \bmod N_s^2;$$

$$C_r = (1+N_r)^{(z'_t - z_t)/(c-c')} \cdot ((z'_2/z_2)^{(c-c')^{-1}})^{N_r} \bmod N_r^2;$$

$$\frac{\tilde{C}_s}{C_s} = (1+N_s)^{(z'_{t'} - z_{t'})/(c-c')} \cdot ((z'_3/z_3)^{(c-c')^{-1}})^{N_s} \bmod N_s^2;$$

$$W_i = V_i^{(z_{t_i} - z'_{t_i})/(c-c')} \cdot g_1^{(z'_{v_i} - z_{v_i})/(c-c')}; W'_i = (V'_i)^{(z_{t'_i} - z'_{t'_i})/(c-c')} \cdot g_1^{(z'_{v'_i} - z_{v'_i})/(c-c')}.$$

Thus, $t_i = (z'_{t_i} - z_{t_i})/(c - c'), v_i = (z'_{v_i} - z_{v_i})/(c - c')$, $t'_i = (z'_{t'_i} - z_{t'_i})/(c - c')$, and $v'_i = (z'_{v'_i} - z_{v'_i})/(c - c')$ for all $i \in [0, \ell)$. From the fact that Paillier encryption algorithm is an isomorphism from the message and the randomness to the ciphertext, the witness can be obtained by computing modulo N_s:

$$t = (z'_t - z_t)/(c - c'), t' = (z'_{t'} - z_{t'})/(c - c'),$$
$$r_1 = (z'_1/z_1)^{(c-c')^{-1}}, r_2 = (z'_2/z_2)^{(c-c')^{-1}}, r = r_1(z'_3/z_3)^{(c-c')^{-1}}.$$

Thus if an argument π is accepted by the verifier, one can extract a valid witness $w = (t_s = t + t', t, r, r_1, r_2)$.

If $t \notin [0, u^\ell)$ or $t' \notin [0, u^\ell)$, then there must be some t_i or t'_i not in $[0, u)$. That is, P^* generates a valid signature $V_i^{v_i^{-1}}$ on t_i or $(V'_i)^{v_i'^{-1}}$ on t'_i with probability $\mathsf{poly}(\epsilon(n))$. This contradicts to the EUF-WCMA of Boneh-Boyen signature scheme. Thus $\epsilon(n)$ must be negligible.

$\underline{\mathcal{S}(1^n)}$:

1. $(crs = (p, \mathbb{G}_1, \mathbb{G}_2, \mathbb{G}_T, e, g_1, g_2, vk, \sigma, T), \chi) \leftarrow \mathcal{S}_1(1^n)$;
2. Given $x = (\tilde{C}_s, C_s, C_r, \mathsf{pk}_s = N_s, \mathsf{pk}_r = N_r)$, compute $N = N_s \cdot N_r \cdot p$;
3. Choose $t, t' \leftarrow\!\!\$ [0, u^\ell)$ and $c \leftarrow\!\!\$ \{0,1\}^k$;
4. For $i = 0$ to $\ell - 1$, select $v_i, v'_i \leftarrow\!\!\$ \mathbb{Z}_N$, and compute $V_i = \sigma_{t_i}^{v_i}, V'_i = \sigma_{t'_i}^{v'_i}$, $W_i = T_i^{v_i}, W'_i = T_i^{v'_i}$.
5. Choose $z_{v_i}, z_{v'_i}, z_{t_i}, z_{t'_i} \leftarrow\!\!\$ \mathbb{Z}_N$ and compute $a_i = W_i^c \cdot V_i^{-z_{t_i}} \cdot g_1^{z_{v_i}}, a'_i = (W'_i)^c \cdot (V'_i)^{-z_{t'_i}} \cdot g_1^{z_{v'_i}}$;
6. Set $z_t = \sum_{i=0}^{\ell-1} u^i \cdot z_{t_i}$ and $z_{t'} = \sum_{i=0}^{\ell-1} u^i \cdot z_{t'_i}$;
7. Choose $z_1, z_3 \leftarrow\!\!\$ \mathbb{Z}_{N_s}^*, z_2 \leftarrow\!\!\$ \mathbb{Z}_{N_r}^*, \beta \leftarrow\!\!\$ \mathbb{Z}_p$, and compute
   (i) $a_s = (1 + N_s)^{z_t} C_s^c z_1^{N_s} \bmod N_s^2, a_r = (1 + N_r)^{z_t} C_r^c z_2^{N_r} \bmod N_r^2$,
   (ii) $a'_s = (1 + N_s)^{z_{t'}} (\tilde{C}_s/C_s)^c z_3^{N_s} \bmod N_s^2, \alpha = g_2^\beta$;
8. Set $a = (a_s, a_r, a'_s, \{V_i, V'_i, a_i, a'_i, W_i, W'_i\}_{i=0}^{\ell-1}, \alpha)$, and compute $\tilde{c} = \mathsf{H}(a)$;
9. Compute $\hat{c} = c - \tilde{c}, \hat{z} = \beta + \hat{c}\chi \bmod p$;
10. Return the proof $\pi = \left(a, c, z_1, z_2, z_3, \{z_{v_i}, z_{v'_i}, z_{t_i}, z_{t'_i}\}_{i=0}^{\ell-1}, \hat{z}\right)$

Fig. 2. Simulator for our NIZK argument

Perfect (Adaptive) Zero-Knowledge. To argue zero-knowledge we construct a simulator $\mathcal{S} = (\mathcal{S}_1, \mathcal{S}_2)$ in Fig. 2. We prove the property of zero-knowledge via a hybrid experiment where we use $\mathcal{S}_1$ to generate crs, but follow the real prover strategy to produce a NIZK proof. Since $\mathcal{S}_1$ proceeds as K except outputting an additional trapdoor χ s.t. $vk = g_2^\chi$, for all $\mathcal{A} = (\mathcal{A}_1, \mathcal{A}_2)$ we have

$$\Big| \Pr\Big[\begin{array}{c} crs \leftarrow \mathsf{K}(1^n); (x, w, state) \leftarrow \mathcal{A}_1(crs); \pi \leftarrow \mathsf{P}(crs, x, w): \\ (x, w) \in R \wedge \mathcal{A}_2(crs, \pi, state) = 1 \end{array}\Big]$$
$$- \Pr\Big[\begin{array}{c} (crs, \chi) \leftarrow \mathcal{S}_1(1^n); (x, w, state) \leftarrow \mathcal{A}_1(crs); \pi \leftarrow \mathsf{P}(crs, x, w): \\ (x, w) \in R \wedge \mathcal{A}_2(crs, \pi, state) = 1 \end{array}\Big]\Big| = 0.$$

Next, instead of generating the proof from $\mathsf{P}(x, w)$, we use the trapdoor χ produced by $\mathcal{S}_1$ to simulate the NIZK proof. In the simulated proofs, $(\alpha, c, z_1, z_2, z_3, \{z_{v_i}, z_{v'_i}, z_{t_i}, z_{t'_i}\}_{i=0}^{\ell-1}, \hat{z})$ are uniformly randomly distributed in their different distributions, So do a_s, a_r, a'_s which are determined by these above values. $\{V_i, V'_i, a_i, a'_i, W_i, W'_i\}_{i=0}^{\ell-1}$ are obvious uniformly distributed at random. While in the real proofs, the values $a_s, a_r, a'_s, \{V_i, V'_i, a_i, a'_i, W_i, W'_i\}_{i=0}^{\ell-1}$, $c, \alpha, \hat{z}$ are distributed uniformly and randomly due to the usage of uniform randomness. Thus, the distribution of the remaining values z_1, z_2, z_3, $\{z_{v_i}, z_{v'_i}, z_{t_i}, z_{t'_i}\}_{i=0}^{\ell-1}$ is uniformly distributed at random. Thus, for all PPT $\mathcal{A} = (\mathcal{A}_1, \mathcal{A}_2)$ we have

$$\Big| \Pr\Big[\begin{array}{c} (crs, \chi) \leftarrow \mathcal{S}_1(1^n); (x, w, state) \leftarrow \mathcal{A}_1(crs); \pi \leftarrow \mathsf{P}(crs, x, w): \\ (x, w) \in R \wedge \mathcal{A}_2(crs, \pi, state) = 1 \end{array}\Big]$$
$$- \Pr\Big[\begin{array}{c} (crs, \chi) \leftarrow \mathcal{S}_1(1^n); (x, w, state) \leftarrow \mathcal{A}_1(crs); \pi \leftarrow \mathcal{S}_2(crs, x, \chi): \\ (x, w) \in R \wedge \mathcal{A}_2(crs, \pi, state) = 1 \end{array}\Big]\Big| = 0.$$

Hence, the perfect zero-knowledge property holds in the standard CRS model.

References

1. Zcash: Privacy-protecting digital currency. https://z.cash/
2. miracl (2012). https://github.com/miracl/MIRACL
3. Arfaoui, G., Lalande, J.-F., Traoré, J., Desmoulins, N., Berthomé, P., Gharout, S.: A practical set-membership proof for privacy-preserving NFC mobile ticketing. Proc. Priv. Enhanc. Technol. **2015**(2), 25–45 (2015)
4. Ben-Sasson, E., Bentov, I., Horesh, Y., Riabzev, M.: Scalable, transparent, and post-quantum secure computational integrity. Cryptology ePrint Archive, Report 2018/046 (2018). https://eprint.iacr.org/2018/046
5. Ben-Sasson, E., et al.: Decentralized anonymous payments from bitcoin. In: 2014 IEEE Symposium on Security and Privacy, SP 2014, Berkeley, CA, USA, 18–21 May 2014, pp. 459–474. IEEE Computer Society (2014)
6. Ben-Sasson, E., Chiesa, A., Genkin, D., Tromer, E., Virza, M.: SNARKs for C: verifying program executions succinctly and in zero knowledge. In: Canetti, R., Garay, J.A. (eds.) CRYPTO 2013. LNCS, vol. 8043, pp. 90–108. Springer, Heidelberg (2013). https://doi.org/10.1007/978-3-642-40084-1_6
7. Blum, M., Feldman, P., Micali, S.: Non-interactive zero-knowledge and its applications. In Proceedings of the 20rd Annual ACM Symposium Theory of Computing-STOC 1988, pp. 103–112. ACM Press (1988)
8. Boneh, D., Boyen, X.: Short signatures without random oracles. In: Cachin, C., Camenisch, J.L. (eds.) EUROCRYPT 2004. LNCS, vol. 3027, pp. 56–73. Springer, Heidelberg (2004). https://doi.org/10.1007/978-3-540-24676-3_4

9. Boneh, D., Lynn, B., Shacham, H.: Short signatures from the Weil pairing. In: Boyd, C. (ed.) ASIACRYPT 2001. LNCS, vol. 2248, pp. 514–532. Springer, Heidelberg (2001). https://doi.org/10.1007/3-540-45682-1_30
10. Bünz, B., Agrawal, S., Zamani, M., Boneh, D.: Zether: towards privacy in a smart contract world. In: Financial Cryptography and Data Security (2020). https://eprint.iacr.org/2019/191
11. Bünz, B., Bootle, J., Boneh, D., Poelstra, A., Wuille, P., Maxwell, G.: Bulletproofs: short proofs for confidential transactions and more. In: 2018 IEEE Symposium on Security and Privacy, pp. 315–334. IEEE (2018)
12. Camenisch, J., Chaabouni, R., shelat: Efficient protocols for set membership and range proofs. In: Pieprzyk, J. (ed.) ASIACRYPT 2008. LNCS, vol. 5350, pp. 234–252. Springer, Heidelberg (2008). https://doi.org/10.1007/978-3-540-89255-7_15
13. Damgård, I., Jurik, M., Nielsen, J.B.: A generalization of Paillier's public-key system with applications to electronic voting. Int. J. Inf. Secur. **9**(6), 371–385 (2010)
14. Damgård, I.: On sigma protocols (2010). http://www.cs.au.dk/~ivan/Sigma.pdf
15. Fiat, A., Shamir, A.: How To prove yourself: practical solutions to identification and signature problems. In: Odlyzko, A.M. (ed.) CRYPTO 1986. LNCS, vol. 263, pp. 186–194. Springer, Heidelberg (1987). https://doi.org/10.1007/3-540-47721-7_12
16. Liu, J.K., Wei, V.K., Wong, D.S.: Linkable spontaneous anonymous group signature for ad hoc groups. In: Wang, H., Pieprzyk, J., Varadharajan, V. (eds.) ACISP 2004. LNCS, vol. 3108, pp. 325–335. Springer, Heidelberg (2004). https://doi.org/10.1007/978-3-540-27800-9_28
17. Ma, S., Deng, Y., He, D., Zhang, J., Xie, S.: An efficient Nizk scheme for privacy-preserving transactions over account-model blockchain. IEEE Trans. Depend. Secure Comput. (2020, early access). https://doi.org/10.1109/TDSC.2020.2969418
18. Maxwell, G.: Confidential transactions
19. Nakamoto, S..: Bitcoin: A peer-to-peer electronic cash system (2008, Consulted)
20. Noether, S., Mackenzie, A., et al.: Ring confidential transactions. Ledger **1**, 1–18 (2016)
21. Paillier, P.: Public-key cryptosystems based on composite degree residuosity classes. In: Stern, J. (ed.) EUROCRYPT 1999. LNCS, vol. 1592, pp. 223–238. Springer, Heidelberg (1999). https://doi.org/10.1007/3-540-48910-X_16
22. Volkhausen, T.: Paillier cryptosystem: A mathematical introduction. In: Seminar Public-Key Kryptographie (WS 05/06) bei Prof. Dr. J. Blömer (2006)
23. Wahby, R.S., Tzialla, I., Shelat, A., Thaler, J., Walfish, M.: Doubly-efficient zksnarks without trusted setup. In: 2018 IEEE Symposium on Security and Privacy (SP), pp. 926–943 (2018)
24. Wood, G.: Ethereum: A secure decentralised generalised transaction ledger. Ethereum Project Yellow Paper 151 (2014)
25. Xie, T., Zhang, J., Zhang, Y., Papamanthou, C., Song, D.: Libra: succinct zero-knowledge proofs with optimal prover computation. In: Boldyreva, A., Micciancio, D. (eds.) CRYPTO 2019. LNCS, vol. 11694, pp. 733–764. Springer, Cham (2019). https://doi.org/10.1007/978-3-030-26954-8_24

Secure Machine Learning and Multiparty Computation

Secure Cumulative Reward Maximization in Linear Stochastic Bandits

Radu Ciucanu[1(✉)], Anatole Delabrouille[2], Pascal Lafourcade[3], and Marta Soare[4]

[1] INSA Centre Val de Loire, Univ. Orléans, LIFO EA 4022, Orléans, France
radu.ciucanu@insa-cvl.fr

[2] Univ. Bordeaux, LIMOS/LIFO, Clermont-Ferrand, France
anatole.delabrouille@etu.u-bordeaux.fr

[3] Univ. Clermont Auvergne, LIMOS CNRS UMR 6158, Clermont-Ferrand, France
pascal.lafourcade@uca.fr

[4] Univ. Orléans, INSA Centre Val de Loire, LIFO EA 4022, Orléans, France
marta.soare@univ-orleans.fr

Abstract. The linear stochastic multi-armed bandit is a sequential learning setting, where, at each round, a learner chooses an arm and receives a stochastic reward based on an unknown linear function of the chosen arm. The goal is to collect as much reward as possible. Linear bandits have popular applications such as online recommendation based on user preferences, where obtaining a high reward means recommending an item with high expected rating. We address the security concerns that occur when outsourcing the data and the cumulative reward maximization algorithm to an honest-but-curious cloud. We propose LinUCB-DS, a distributed and secure protocol that achieves the same cumulative reward as the standard LinUCB algorithm, without disclosing to the cloud the linear function used to draw arm rewards. We formally prove the complexity and security properties of LinUCB-DS. We also show that LinUCB-DS can be easily adapted to secure the SpectralUCB algorithm, which improves LinUCB for a class of linear bandits. We show the feasibility of our protocols via a proof-of-concept experimental study using the MovieLens movie recommendation dataset.

1 Introduction

The *stochastic multi-armed bandit* game is a sequential learning framework, which consists of a repeated interaction between a learner and the environment. The learner is given a set of choices (arms) with unknown associated rewards and a limited number of allowed interactions with the environment (budget). With the goal of maximizing the sum of the observed rewards, the learner sequentially chooses an arm at each time step and the environment responds with a stochastic reward corresponding to the chosen arm. In the *linear stochastic bandit* setting, the input set of arms is a fixed subset of $\mathbb{R}^d$, revealed to the learner at the beginning of the game. When pulling an arm, the learner observes a noisy

K. Nguyen et al. (Eds.): ProvSec 2020, LNCS 12505, pp. 257–277, 2020.
https://doi.org/10.1007/978-3-030-62576-4_13

reward whose expected value is the inner product between the chosen arm and an unknown parameter characterizing the underlying linear function (common to all arms).

Stochastic linear bandits can be used to model online recommendation: the arms are the objects that might be recommended and a reward is the user's response to a recommendation e.g., the click through rate or the score associated to the recommendation. The recommender wants to maximize the sum of rewards, thus the recommender needs to predict which object is more likely to be of interest for a certain user. Also, while discovering such object, the recommender must not disappoint the user with too much bad recommendations. The unknown parameter of the reward function is the user preference, more precisely the weights that the user gives to each of the d features in assessing an item.

Fig. 1. Outsourcing data and computations.

In this paper, we consider a scenario inspired from the *machine learning as a service* cloud computing model, where the machine learning data and algorithms are outsourced to the cloud, which yields inherent data security concerns [5]. We depict this scenario in Fig. 1 and we illustrate it next with an example. Let the *data owner* be a large company owning multiple surveys on many types of items and users. Then, let the *data client* be a small recommendation company that is willing to pay a budget to acquire a part of a survey i.e., to find out the cumulative reward obtainable for a subset of types of items and users. This is a classical scenario, where small companies benefit of large scale data without having to perform the survey themselves, and where large companies monetize their data. The accuracy of the result returned to the data client is correlated to the invested budget.

The machine learning as a service cloud computing model is useful when neither the data owner nor the data client want to perform the computations. They rather choose to entrust the computation to a third-party, for example to a public cloud such as Google Cloud Platform, Amazon Web Services, or Microsoft Azure. However, cloud providers do not usually address the fundamental problem of protecting data security. The outsourced data can be communicated over some network and processed on some machines where malicious cloud admins could learn and leak sensitive user data. The data owner wishes to remain the only one that has the complete knowledge of her data, and only the data client should be able to gain knowledge of the cumulative reward for which she paid.

We address the data security issues that occur when outsourcing the linear bandit data and cumulative reward maximization algorithm to a public cloud.

We propose LinUCB-DS, a secure and distributed protocol based on the standard LinUCB algorithm [1], which yields the same cumulative reward as LinUCB while satisfying desirable security properties that we formally prove. The key ingredients of LinUCB-DS are (i) *Paillier cryptographic scheme* that is additive homomorphic i.e., it allows to compute the encrypted value of the sum of two numbers, given only their ciphertexts, without revealing the numbers in plain, and (ii) *secure multi-party computation* i.e., the computation is split among two cloud participants, which can jointly compute the algorithm output, without revealing their partial input to each other.

Related Work. Algorithms based on computing *upper confidence bounds (UCB)* on arm values are commonly used for cumulative reward maximization strategies. The classical UCB algorithm [3] for multi-armed bandits has been applied to linear bandits in various works (for instance [1,2,12]) and is referred to as LinUCB, OFUL (Optimism in the Face of Uncertainty for Linear bandits), or LinRel (Linear Reinforcement Learning). Following [11, Chapter 19], we use LinUCB as a generic name for UCB applied to stochastic linear bandits and we specifically rely on the algorithm in [1], in the case where the set of arms is fixed.

There is a recent line of research on adding privacy-preserving guarantees to UCB-like algorithms, mostly using differential privacy techniques [7,13,16] including for linear bandits [15]. The use of differential privacy has a low impact on execution time compared to non-secured algorithms, but outputs different cumulative rewards. This is a consequence of the noise added to the input or the output of differentially-private algorithms. This difference propagates in the regret analysis, which suffers an additive or multiplicative factor compared to the regret of standard non-secured algorithms.

In contrast, our approach based on cryptographic schemes and secure multi-party computation implies heavier computations, but outputs exactly the same cumulative reward as standard non-secured algorithms. Hence, both approaches (differential privacy vs cryptography) have advantages and disadvantages. Secure bandit algorithms using cryptographic techniques have been already proposed for a different problem: best arm identification in multi-armed bandits [6].

To the best of our knowledge, our work is the first one that adds security guarantees to linear bandit algorithms using cryptographic techniques.

Summary of Contributions and Paper Organization. In Sect. 2 we introduce LinUCB algorithm and some cryptographic tools. Section 3 is the main contribution of the paper: we formalize the expected security properties, and we propose LinUCB-DS, a secure and distributed protocol based on LinUCB. We show its correctness and we analyze its theoretical complexity by characterizing the number of cryptographic operations. In Sect. 4, we show the security properties of LinUCB-DS. In Sect. 5, we present our experimental study based on the MovieLens dataset, which confirms the feasibility of LinUCB-DS. In Sect. 6, we show how our protocol can be easily adapted to secure SpectralUCB [17] that is another algorithm that relies on UCB in the linear setting.

2 Preliminaries

We introduce LinUCB algorithm, Paillier encryption, and IND-CPA security.

LinUCB. In cumulative reward maximization algorithms, the learner faces the so-called *exploration-exploitation dilemma*: at each round, she has to decide whether to *explore* arms with more uncertain associated values, or to *exploit* the information already acquired by selecting the arm with the seemingly largest value. UCB-like algorithms guide the exploration-exploitation trade-off by updating, after each new observed reward, a *score* for each arm, given by the upper-confidence bound of the estimated arm value. In LinUCB, the arm scores are based on a regularized least-squares estimate of the unknown parameter of the linear reward function. At the next round, the arm with the largest updated score is pulled. Following [1], we present the LinUCB algorithm in Fig. 2.

Input: Budget N and K arms $x_1, x_2, \ldots, x_K$ in $\mathbb{R}^d$
Constants: Regularizer $\gamma > 0$; confidence parameter $\delta > 0$; noise parameter $R > 0$; $S > 0$ such that $||\theta||_2 \leq S$; $L > 0$ such that $\forall\, i \in [\![K]\!], ||x_i||_2 \leq L$
Unknown environment: Expected arm values; the learner has access only to the output of reward function $pull(x_i)$
Output: Sum of observed rewards for all arms

/ Initialization: Pull an arm and initialize variables /
Let $r = pull(x_i)$ */ Random reward (scalar) for a randomly selected arm x_i /*
Let $s = r$ */ Sum of rewards of all arms (scalar) /*
Let $A = \gamma I_d + x_i x_i^\top$ */ $(d \times d)$ matrix /*
Let $b = r x_i$ */ $(d \times 1)$ vector /*

/ Exploration-Exploitation: At each round, pull an arm and update variables /
For $1 \leq t < N$
  Let $\widehat{\theta} = A^{-1} b$ */ Compute the regularized least-squares estimate of θ /*
  Let $\omega = R\sqrt{d \cdot \log(\frac{1+tL^2/\gamma}{\delta})} + \gamma^{\frac{1}{2}} \cdot S$ */ Exploration parameter /*
  / Compute the UCB arm score B_i (scalar) for each arm based on current $\widehat{\theta}$. First term for exploitation, second term for exploration /
  For $1 \leq i \leq K$
    Let $B_i = \langle x_i, \widehat{\theta} \rangle + \omega ||x_i||_{A^{-1}}$ */ With probability $\geq 1-\delta$, B_i is an UCB of $\langle x_i, \theta \rangle$ /*
  Let $x_m = \arg\max_{i \in [\![K]\!]} B_i$ */ Randomly choose among arms maximizing B_i /*
  Let $r = pull(x_m)$ */ Pull arm x_m and update the corresponding variables /*
  Let $s = s + r$
  Let $A = A + x_m x_m^\top$
  Let $b = b + r x_m$
Return s */ Return sum of observed rewards for all arms /*

Fig. 2. LinUCB Algorithm [1].

We rely on the following notations:

- $[\![z]\!]$ is the set $\{1, 2, \ldots, z\}$.
- K is the number of arms.
- N is the client's budget = the number of allowed arm pulls = the number of observed rewards.
- d is the space dimension = the size of each arm vector = the number of features of the unknown parameter θ.
- x_i (for $i \in [\![K]\!]$) is an arm = a $(d \times 1)$ vector; we assume that all arms are pairwise distinct.
- $||v||_2$ is the 2-norm of a $\mathbb{R}^d$ vector v.
- $||v||_A = \sqrt{v^\top Av}$ is the weighted 2-norm of a $\mathbb{R}^d$ vector v, where A is a $(d \times d)$ positive definite matrix.
- θ is a $(d \times 1)$ vector (unknown to the learner) that is the parameter of the linear reward function.
- $\langle x_i, \theta \rangle$ (for $i \in [\![K]\!]$) is a scalar (unknown to the learner) defining the expected reward value of arm x_i, computed as the dot product of vectors x_i and θ.
- $pull(x_i)$ is a function that returns a noisy reward $\langle x_i, \theta \rangle + \eta$, where the noise η is an R-sub-Gaussian random variable, where $R \geq 0$ is a fixed constant.
- $v(j)$ is the jth element of a vector v and $M(j)$ is the jth row of a matrix M.

Paillier Asymmetric Encryption. Paillier [14] is an asymmetric partial homomorphic encryption scheme defined by a triple of polynomial-time algorithms $(\mathcal{G}, \mathcal{E}, \mathcal{D})$ and a security parameter λ. By 1^λ we denote the unary representation of λ, which is a standard notation in cryptography.

- $\mathcal{G}(1^\lambda)$ generates two prime numbers p and q according to λ, sets $n = p \cdot q$ and $\Lambda = \text{lcm}(p-1, q-1)$ (i.e., the least common multiple), generates the group $(\mathbb{Z}^*_{n^2}, \cdot)$, randomly picks $g \in \mathbb{Z}^*_{n^2}$ such that $M = (L(g^\Lambda \mod n^2))^{-1} \mod n$ exists, with $L(x) = (x-1)/n$. It sets $\mathsf{sk} = (\Lambda, M)$, $\mathsf{pk} = (n, g)$, it returns $(\mathsf{sk}, \mathsf{pk})$.
- $\mathcal{E}(m)$ randomly picks $r \in \mathbb{Z}^*_n$, computes $c = g^m \cdot r^n \mod n^2$ using pk, and outputs c.
- $\mathcal{D}(c)$ computes $m = L(c^\Lambda \mod n^2) \cdot M \mod n$ using sk, and outputs m.

Paillier's cryptosystem is *additive homomorphic.* Let m_1 and m_2 be two plaintexts in $\mathbb{Z}_n$. The product of the two associated ciphertexts with the public key $\mathsf{pk} = (n, g)$, denoted $c_1 = \mathcal{E}(m_1) = g^{m_1} \cdot r_1^n \mod n^2$ and $c_2 = \mathcal{E}(m_2) = g^{m_2} \cdot r_2^n \mod n^2$, is the encryption of the sum of m_1 and m_2. Indeed, we have: $\mathcal{E}(m_1) \cdot \mathcal{E}(m_2) = c_1 \cdot c_2 \mod n^2 = (g^{m_1} \cdot r_1^n) \cdot (g^{m_2} \cdot r_2^n) \mod n^2 = (g^{m_1+m_2} \cdot (r_1 \cdot r_2)^n) \mod n^2 = \mathcal{E}(m_1 + m_2)$.

It is also possible to compute the encryption of the product of a ciphertext and a plaintext: $\mathcal{E}(m_1)^{m_2} = c_1^{m_2} \mod n^2 = (g^{m_1} \cdot r^n)^{m_2} \mod n^2 = g^{m_1 \cdot m_2} \cdot r^{n \cdot m_2} \mod n^2 = g^{m_1 \cdot m_2} \cdot (r')^n \mod n^2 = \mathcal{E}(m_1 \cdot m_2)$.

Encryption and decryption with the public and private key of entity E are noted $\mathcal{E}_{\mathsf{E}}(.)$ and $\mathcal{D}_{\mathsf{E}}(.)$ respectively.

IND-CPA (INDistinguishability under Chosen-Plaintext Attack)

Let $\Pi = (\mathsf{KeyGen}, \mathsf{Encrypt}, \mathsf{Decrypt})$ be a cryptographic scheme. The *probabilistic polynomial-time (PPT) adversary* $\mathcal{A}$ tries to break the security of Π. The IND-CPA game, denoted by $\text{EXP}(\mathcal{A})$, works as follows: the adversary $\mathcal{A}$ chooses two messages (m_0, m_1) and receives a challenge $c = \mathsf{Encrypt}(LR_b(m_0, m_1))$ from the *challenger* who selects a bit $b \in \{0,1\}$ uniformly at random, and where $LR_b(m_0, m_1)$ is equal to m_0 if $b = 0$, and m_1 otherwise. The adversary, knowing m_0, m_1 and c, is allowed to perform any number of polynomial computations or encryptions of any messages, using the encryption oracle, in order to output a guess b' of the encrypted message in c chosen by the challenger. Intuitively, Π is IND-CPA if there is no PPT adversary that can guess b with a probability significantly better than $\frac{1}{2}$. By $\alpha = \Pr[b' \leftarrow \text{EXP}(\mathcal{A}); b = b']$, we denote the probability that $\mathcal{A}$ correctly outputs her guessed bit b' when the bit chosen by the challenger in the experiment is b. A scheme is IND-CPA secure if $\alpha - \frac{1}{2}$ is negligible function in λ, where a function φ is negligible in λ, denoted $\text{negl}(\lambda)$, if for every positive polynomial $p(\cdot)$ and sufficiently large λ, $\varphi(\lambda) < 1/p(\lambda)$. Paillier is IND-CPA secure under the decisional composite residuosity assumption [14].

3 LinUCB-DS

We propose LinUCB-DS, a secure and distributed algorithm based on LinUCB cf. Figure 2 in the setting from Fig. 1. We first list the desired security properties and the security hypothesis. We next outline the challenges of our problem setting and the ideas behind our solution. Then, we present the participants of LinUCB-DS and their pseudo-code. We end this section by arguing the correctness of LinUCB-DS and analyzing its cryptographic overhead.

Security Properties. We expect the following properties, which should hold until the end of the protocol:

1. No cloud node knows θ.
2. No cloud node knows the cumulative reward, nor any individual reward.
3. An external observer having captured all messages exchanged over the network does not know θ, the rewards, nor which arms have been pulled.

Security Hypothesis. We assume that the cloud is *honest-but-curious* i.e., it executes tasks dutifully, but tries to extract as much information as possible from the data that it sees. Our model follows a classical formulation [9] (Ch. 7.5, where *honest-but-curious* is denoted *semi-honest*), in particular (i) each cloud node is trusted: it correctly does the required computations, it does not sniff the network and it does not collude with other nodes, and (ii) an external observer has access to all messages exchanged over the network. The aforementioned security model is of practical interest in a real-world cloud environment. In particular, to satisfy all our theoretical security properties while achieving the no-collusion hypothesis, it suffices to host each cloud node of our protocol by a different cloud provider. This should be feasible as our protocol requires only two cloud nodes.

Challenges. Our problem could be theoretically solved by using a fully homomorphic encryption scheme [8], which allows to compute any function directly in the encrypted domain. However, it remains an open question how to make such a scheme work fast and be accurate in practice when working with real numbers. Indeed, by using state-of-the-art fully homomorphic systems (e.g., Microsoft SEAL[1] or HElib[2]), it is not currently possible to obtain exactly the same output as the standard, non-encrypted version when securing LinUCB.

Paillier additive-homomorphic encryption and secure multi-party computation (where some party does computations on reals in clear) allow us to develop a protocol satisfying the expected security properties while being feasible in practice. Indeed, if the data owner outsources $\mathcal{E}(\theta(1)), \ldots, \mathcal{E}(\theta(d))$, the cloud can generate an encrypted reward of arm x_i as $\mathcal{E}(\theta(1))^{x_i(1)} \cdots \mathcal{E}(\theta(d))^{x_i(d)} \mathcal{E}(\eta)$. Then, variables s, b, and B_i can be also updated in the encrypted domain. Since the B_i are encrypted, the cloud cannot compare them and we need to find a secure way to decrypt and compare the B_i. The idea (already known in the literature e.g., in the context of private outsourced sort [4]) is that the data owner does not use the data client's public key to outsource θ, but instead uses the key of a second cloud node whose only task is to compare the B_i. At the end, the cloud nodes perform a key switching without revealing s to the cloud.

Participants of LinUCB-DS (2 of them in the cloud).

- DO (data owner) outsources data to the cloud.
- DC (data client) sends the budget to the cloud. At the end, she receives the result of the algorithm.
- P is the principal node of the cloud, which receives the arms, budget, and encrypted θ. This node pulls the arms and updates the variables.
- Comp is a cloud node whose Paillier public key is used to outsource θ. Comp is the only node that can decrypt and compare the B_i.

Next, we present the three phases of LinUCB-DS: *Initialization*, *Exploration-Exploitation*, and *Key Switching*. The numbers of the steps refer to those from Fig. 3 and 4. We rely on the following additional notation:

- z^* is $\mathcal{E}_{\mathsf{E}}(z)$, where E is clear from the context.
- $\mathit{EDP}_{\mathsf{pk}}(v^*, w) = \prod_{j=1}^{d} (v(j)^*)^{w(j)}$ is the *E*ncrypted *D*ot *P*roduct of v^* (vector of size d of data encrypted with pk) and w (vector of size d of data in clear).
- $\mathit{pull}^*(x_i) = \mathit{EDP}_{\mathsf{Comp}}(\theta^*, x_i)\mathcal{E}_{\mathsf{Comp}}(\eta)$ is the encrypted reward drawn for an arm x_i using the encrypted unknown parameter θ^* and a scalar noise η cf. Sect. 2. This computation is the encrypted version of the scalar product defined by the *pull*(.) function and the homomorphic addition of η.

[1] https://github.com/Microsoft/SEAL.
[2] http://homenc.github.io/HElib/.

Initialization.

- Step (1): DC sends to P the budget N. Furthermore, DO sends to P the arms $x_1, \ldots, x_K$, the encrypted unknown parameter $\theta^* = (\theta(1)^*, \ldots, \theta(d)^*) = (\mathcal{E}_{\mathsf{Comp}}(\theta(1)), \ldots, \mathcal{E}_{\mathsf{Comp}}(\theta(d)))$, as well as all algorithm constants cf. Figure 2.

- Step (2): P randomly chooses an arm x_i, generates an encrypted reward $r^* = pull^*(x_i)$, and initializes variables:

$$s^* = r^*.$$
$$A = \gamma I_d + x_i x_i^\top.$$
$$b^* = (b^*(1), \ldots, b^*(d)) = ((r^*)^{x_i(1)}, \ldots, (r^*)^{x_i(d)}).$$

Exploration-Exploitation. At each round, an interaction between P and Comp occurs to decide the next arm to pull. More precisely, for $1 \leq t < N$, we repeat:

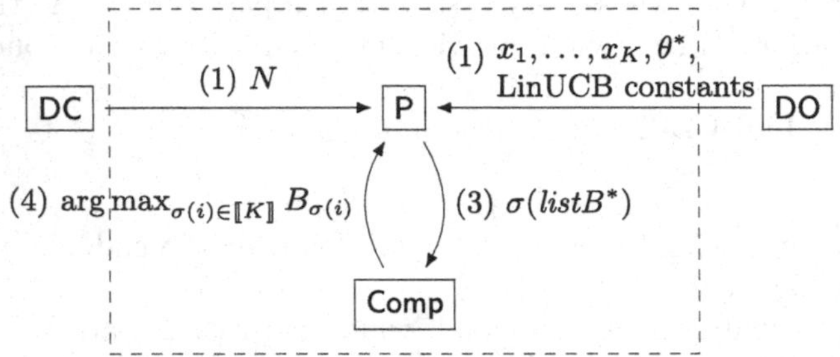

(a) Initialization and Exploration-Exploitation Phases.

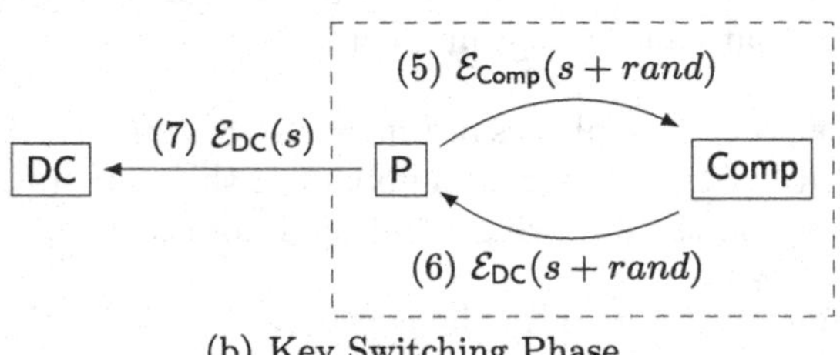

(b) Key Switching Phase.

Fig. 3. Messages exchanged between LinUCB-DS participants. Steps 3 and 4 are done $N-1$ times. The dashed rectangle is the cloud. Details on each step are given in Sect. 3.

- Step (3):

(i) P computes $\widehat{\theta}^*$ as the product between matrix A^{-1} and vector b^*:
$\widehat{\theta}^* = (\widehat{\theta}(1)^*, \ldots, \widehat{\theta}(d)^*) = (EDP_{\mathsf{Comp}}(b^*, A^{-1}(1)), \ldots, EDP_{\mathsf{Comp}}(b^*, A^{-1}(d)))$.

(ii) P computes $listB^*$ that is the list of $B_1^*, \ldots, B_K^*$ such that, for each arm x_i, $B_i^* = EDP_{\mathsf{Comp}}(\widehat{\theta}^*, x_i)\mathcal{E}_{\mathsf{Comp}}(\omega||x_i||_{A^{-1}})$, where ω is the exploration parameter cf. Fig. 2. Then, P generates a random permutation $\sigma : [\![K]\!] \rightarrow [\![K]\!]$ and sends $\sigma(listB^*)$ to Comp.

- Step (4):

(i) Comp decrypts each element of the permuted list of encrypted B_i values. Then, Comp sends $\arg\max_{\sigma(i)\in[\![K]\!]} B_{\sigma(i)}$ to P.
(ii) P retrieves x_m that is an arm maximizing B_i. Then, P computes $r^* = pull^*(x_m)$ and updates the variables:

$$s^* = s^* r^*.$$
$$A = A + x_m x_m^\top.$$
$$b^* = (b^*(1), \ldots, b^*(d)) = (b^*(1)(r^*)^{x_m(1)}, \ldots, b^*(d)(r^*)^{x_m(d)}).$$

Key Switching. The sum of rewards is re-encrypted using the DC's public key.

- Step (5): P chooses a random number $rand$ and sends to Comp the following $\mathcal{E}_{\mathsf{Comp}}(rand)s^* = \mathcal{E}_{\mathsf{Comp}}(rand + s)$.
- Step (6): Comp decrypts $\mathcal{E}_{\mathsf{Comp}}(rand+s)$, encrypts the result using DC's public key, and sends it back to P. Note that Comp sees in clear $rand + s$ but cannot infer s because it does not know $rand$.
- Step (7): P sends $\mathcal{E}_{\mathsf{DC}}(s) = \mathcal{E}_{\mathsf{DC}}(rand + s)\mathcal{E}_{\mathsf{DC}}(-rand)$ to DC, which decrypts $\mathcal{E}_{\mathsf{DC}}(s)$ and learns s.

This concludes the presentation of the steps of LinUCB-DS. Before ending this section, we analyze the correctness and complexity of LinUCB-DS.

Correctness. LinUCB-DS outputs exactly the same cumulative reward as LinUCB and it computes the same reward for the same arm at each round. The reason is that the Paillier scheme does not change the value of any element, hence throughout the exact computations on encrypted numbers we conserve the correctness. In fact, Paillier scheme operates in $\mathbb{N}$, but the values of the arms and θ are defined in $\mathbb{R}$. Furthermore, $\widehat{\theta}$ and the B_i are computed using matrix inverse, square root and division (all these operations are done in plain, but the results are added or multiplied to ciphered values). Consequently, we need to use Paillier with real numbers, or the other way around, use real numbers as integers. Transforming a value in order to use it with an encryption scheme is called *encoding*. The encoding[3] we perform on a decimal number is simply to multiply it by a power of 16 to make it an integer. When we decrypt it, we divide the result by the same power of 16. This implies storing that power alongside the ciphertext, in plain. In order not to leak any information on the ciphertexts, we can use the same power for every encryption. Moreover, we can reduce the choice of the random permutation σ that P generates at each step to the randomness

[3] https://python-paillier.readthedocs.io/en/stable/_modules/phe/encoding.html.

```
/ Initialization: Pull an arm and initialize variables /
Receive N from DC                                                    / Step 1 /
Receive x_1, ..., x_K, θ*, and algorithm constants from DO
Randomly choose i ∈ ⟦K⟧                                             / Step 2 /
Let r* = pull*(x_i)
Let s* = r*
Let A = γI_d + x_i x_i^⊤
Let b* = ((r*)^{x_i(1)}, ..., (r*)^{x_i(d)})
/ Exploration-Exploitation: At each round, pull an arm and update variables /
For 1 ≤ t < N
    Let θ̂* = (EDP_Comp(b*, A^{-1}(1)), ..., EDP_Comp(b*, A^{-1}(d)))   / Step 3 /
    For 1 ≤ i ≤ K
        Let B_i* = listB*(i) = EDP_Comp(θ̂*, x_i) ℰ_Comp(ω||x_i||_{A^{-1}})
    Randomly choose permutation σ : ⟦K⟧ → ⟦K⟧
    Send σ(listB*) to Comp
    Receive σ(m) from Comp                                           / Step 4 /
    Let m = σ^{-1}(σ(m))
    Let r* = pull*(x_m)
    Let s* = s* r*
    Let A = A + x_m x_m^⊤
    Let b* = (b*(1)(r*)^{x_m(1)}, ..., b*(d)(r*)^{x_m(d)})
/ Key Switching /
Randomly choose rand ∈ ℝ                                             / Step 5 /
Send ℰ_Comp(rand)s* to Comp
Receive ℰ_DC(rand + s) from Comp                                     / Step 6 /
Send ℰ_DC(s) = ℰ_DC(rand + s)ℰ_DC(−rand) to DC                       / Step 7 /
```

(a) Pseudo-code of P.

```
/ Exploration-Exploitation /
For 1 ≤ t < N                                                        / Step 4 /
    Receive σ(listB*) from P
    For 1 ≤ i ≤ K       / Decrypt all elements of the permuted list of B_i values /
        Let B_σ(i) = 𝒟_Comp(σ(listB*)(i))
    Send arg max_{σ(i)∈⟦K⟧} B_σ(i) to P
/ Key Switching /
Receive ℰ_Comp(rand)s* from P                                        / Step 5 /
Let rand + s = 𝒟_Comp(ℰ_Comp(rand)s*)                                / Step 6 /
Send ℰ_DC(rand + s) to P
```

(b) Pseudo-code of Comp.

Fig. 4. Pseudo-code of cloud nodes.

in the arg max function of standard LinUCB when several B_i are equal. Thus, the task distribution does not change the choice of the next arm to pull. We also confirmed experimentally that there is no difference between the arm-selection strategy and the outputs of LinUCB vs LinUCB-DS.

Complexity. In Fig. 5, we show the number of Paillier encryptions, decryptions, and operations on encrypted numbers. We have $O(N+d)$ encryptions, $O(NK)$ decryptions, $O(N(d^2+Kd))$ additions and $O(N(d^2+Kd))$ multiplications.

Phase	*Encryptions*	*Decryptions*	*Additions*	*Multiplications*
Initialization	$d+1$		d	$2d$
Exploration - Exploitation	$N-1$	$(N-1)K$	$(N-1)(d^2+Kd+2d)$	$(N-1)(d^2+Kd+2d)$
Key Switching	1	2	2	

Fig. 5. Number of Paillier cryptographic operations.

4 Security Analysis

In this section, we take a close look at what each participant knows and does not know, and we formally show the security properties of LinUCB-DS.

- DC knows, at the end of LinUCB-DS, the cumulative reward for which she paid. DC does not take part in the cumulative reward maximization algorithm.
- P knows which arm is pulled at each round, this is why it can update A in plain. Since P sees θ and the rewards encrypted, it cannot see in plain the value of any among s, b, $\widehat{\theta}$, B_i, hence it cannot learn θ nor the sum of rewards.
- Comp decrypts all B_i, but sees these values in a permuted order hence it cannot associate an arm x_i with its value B_i. Since Comp does not know θ, then every arm could have possibly produced every B_i with some θ, hence Comp cannot compute the exploration term of a B_i, hopping to retrieve the rewards generated by some arm.
- An *external network observer* has access to the exchanged data shown in Fig. 3. It sees in plain N and the arms, and at each round $\sigma(listB^*)$ as well as $\sigma(m)$ the index of the maximal element in the list. As σ is changed every round, it cannot deduce the arm that is really pulled. Moreover, it cannot retrieve s or θ because $\sigma(listB^*)$ and s are encrypted.

In the rest of this section, we formally state the security properties of P, of an external observer, and of Comp. We formally prove all these properties in Appendix A. Recall that we have presented the security hypothesis in Sect. 3. In particular, we assume that the cloud nodes Comp and P do not collude. For a participant E, we denote by $data_{\mathsf{E}}$ the data to which E has access. By $\mathcal{A}^{pb}(d)$ we denote the answer of a Probabilistic Polynomial-Time (PPT) adversary $\mathcal{A}$ that knows data d and tries to solve problem pb. We recall that by $[\![K]\!]$ we denote the set $\{1,2,\ldots,K\}$. By $\text{negl}(\lambda)$ we denote any negligible function in λ.

Security of P. The data to which P has access is θ^*, then at each round t: the arm pulled, r^*, b^*, $\widehat{\theta}^*$, the matrix A, and s^*. At the end, P also knows $\mathcal{E}_{\mathsf{DC}}(s)$.

Theorem 1. *An honest-but-curious* P *cannot infer any coordinate* $\theta(i)$ *of the secret* θ *with probability better than random. More precisely, for all PPT adversary* $\mathcal{A}$, $|P\left[(i,\theta(i)') \leftarrow \mathcal{A}^{\theta}(data_{\mathsf{P}}); \theta(i)' = \theta(i)\right] - \frac{1}{|\theta(i)|}| \leq negl(\lambda)$, *with* $\theta(i)'$ *the guess of* $\mathcal{A}$ *of* $\theta(i)$, *and* $|\theta(i)|$ *the cardinality of the set of possible values of a coordinate.*

Theorem 2. *An honest-but-curious* P *cannot infer any reward generated during the protocol with better probability than random. More precisely, for any PPT adversary* $\mathcal{A}$, $|P\left[(t,r') \leftarrow \mathcal{A}^{r}(data_{\mathsf{P}}); r' = r\right] - \frac{1}{|r|}| = negl(\lambda)$, *with* (t,r') *the guess of* $\mathcal{A}$ *of the reward generated at round* t, *and* $|r|$ *the cardinality of the set of possible rewards for the arm chosen at round* t.

Theorem 3. *An honest-but-curious* P *cannot infer cumulative reward* s.

Security of an External Observer. An external observer has access to the following data: at the beginning θ^*, the arms and the budget N; at each round, $\sigma(listB^*)$ and the argmax of the list; at the end, $\mathcal{E}_{\mathsf{Comp}}(rand + s)$, $\mathcal{E}_{\mathsf{DC}}(rand + s)$, and then $\mathcal{E}_{\mathsf{DC}}(s)$.

Theorem 4. *An external observer having access to the set* $\mathcal{M}$ *of all the messages exchanged during the protocol cannot infer the value of any coordinate of* θ *with better probability than random. More precisely, for any PPT adversary* $\mathcal{A}$, $|P\left[(i,\theta(i)') \leftarrow \mathcal{A}^{\theta}(M); \theta(i)' = \theta(i)\right] - \frac{1}{|\theta(i)|}| \leq negl(\lambda)$, *with* $\theta(i)'$ *the guess of* $\mathcal{A}$ *of* $\theta(i)$, *and* $|\theta(i)|$ *the cardinality of the set of possible values of a coordinate.*

Theorem 5. *An external observer having access to the set* $\mathcal{M}$ *of all messages exchanged during the protocol cannot infer the value of the sum of rewards with better probability than random. More precisely, for any PPT adversary* $\mathcal{A}$, $|P\left[s' \leftarrow \mathcal{A}^{s}(\mathcal{M}); s' = s\right] - \frac{1}{|s|}| \leq negl(\lambda)$, *with* s' *the guess of* $\mathcal{A}$ *of the sum of rewards, and* $|s|$ *the cardinality of the set of possible sums at the end of the protocol.*

Lemma 1. *Consider a list* $l = [l_1, \ldots, l_n]$, *a random permutation* σ *and the permuted list* $\sigma(l) = [l_{\sigma(1)}, \ldots, l_{\sigma(n)}]$. *Knowing* $\sigma(l)$, *a PPT adversary* $\mathcal{A}$ *cannot guess one element of* l *with probability better than random. More specifically,* $P\left[(i, g(i)) \leftarrow \mathcal{A}^{\sigma^{-1}}(\sigma(l)) \in \{i, \sigma^{-1}(i)\}_{i \in [\![K]\!]}\right] = \frac{1}{K} + negl(\lambda)$, *where* $g(i)$ *is* $\mathcal{A}$*'s guess for the preimage of the element in position* i.

Theorem 6. *An external observer having access to the set* $\mathcal{M}$ *of all messages exchanged during the protocol cannot infer the arm pulled at any round. More precisely for any PPT adversary* $\mathcal{A}$, $P\left[(t, x_t') \leftarrow \mathcal{A}^{x}(\mathcal{M}); x_t' = x_t\right] = \frac{1}{K} + negl(\lambda)$, *with* x_t' *being* $\mathcal{A}$*'s guess of the arm pulled at round* t.

Security of Comp. Comp can decrypt the elements received from P, hence the data to which it has access is: at each round, a permuted list $\sigma(listB)$ of all B_i, and at the end the value $rand + s$.

Theorem 7. *An honest-but-curious* Comp *cannot associate an element of* $\sigma(listB)$ *to the arm to which it belongs. More precisely, for any PPT adversary* $\mathcal{A}$, $P\left[(i, B_i') \leftarrow \mathcal{A}^{\sigma^{-1}}(data_{\mathsf{Comp}}); B_i' = B_i\right] = \frac{1}{K} + negl(\lambda)$.

Theorem 8. *An honest-but-curious* Comp *cannot infer cumulative reward* s.

5 Experiments

We present a proof-of-concept experimental study that confirms the theoretical analysis, and shows the scalability and feasibility of LinUCB-DS. For reproducibility reasons, we make our code available on a public Git repository[4].

Experimental Setup. We implemented LinUCB-DS in Python 3 and did our experiments on a laptop with CPU Intel Core i5-8350U @ 1.70 GHz and 16 GB RAM, running Ubuntu 18.04.5. For Paillier we used the *phe* library[5].

MovieLens Dataset. All our experiments are done on real data using the 100 K MovieLens dataset [10]. This dataset is a collection of 100 K movie ratings on a scale of 1 to 5, given by 943 users of the MovieLens website on 1682 movies. The collection of ratings is represented by a matrix F (943×1682), whose element (i, j) is the rating of user i on movie j if the rating exists, otherwise the element is 0. Since the user-movie matrix F is very sparse, we factored it using low-rank matrix factorization. To this purpose, we used the Google Colab matrix factorization code[6] and we obtained: a user embedding matrix U $(943 \times d)$, where row i is the embedding for user i, and a movie embedding matrix M $(1682 \times d)$, where row j is the embedding for movie j. The embeddings are learned such that the product $UM^\top$ is a good approximation of the ratings matrix F. Note that the (i, j) entry of $UM^\top$ is the dot product of the embeddings of user i and movie j, computed such that it should be close to the (i, j) entry of F. Then, for every user i in matrix U, we were able to use linear bandit algorithms to recommend movies j from matrix M. In the presentation of the experimental results, the reported d values correspond to choices of d in the aforementioned matrix factorization approach, whereas the reported K arms correspond to choosing the first K movies in the dataset. We set algorithm constants as in a standard related work setting [17]: $\gamma = 0.01, \delta = 0.001, R = 0.01$, and $S = \log t$.

Before discussing our experimental results, we would like to stress that for each run of LinUCB-DS we use exactly the same arm-selection strategy and obtain the same cumulative reward as LinUCB. The focus of our experiments is on the study of the feasibility and scalability of LinUCB-DS.

---

[4] https://github.com/anatole33/LinUCB-secure.

[5] https://python-paillier.readthedocs.io/en/develop/.

[6] https://github.com/google/eng-edu/blob/master/ml/recommendation-systems/recommendation-systems.ipynb.

Experimental Results. As outlined in the theoretical complexity analysis at the end of Sect. 3, LinUCB-DS has an inherent overhead due to the use of cryptographic operations w.r.t. standard LinUCB. Our first implementation naturally showed this overhead. For example, for $d = 3$, $K = 15$, $N = 1000$, and Paillier keys of 1024 bits, LinUCB-DS takes 115 s, whereas LinUCB takes less than a second. Seen this overhead, we zoomed on the time taken by the different steps of LinUCB-DS to understand how we can optimize our implementation. We observed that three steps of LinUCB-DS take the lion's share of the computation time. We refer to these steps using the numbers listed in Sect. 3:

- Step (3).i (done by P): compute $\widehat{\theta}^*$ as the product of a matrix of dimension $(d \times d)$ and a vector of size $(d \times 1)$. This involves d^2 multiplications and d^2 additions on cyphertexts.
- Step (3).ii (done by P): compute B_i^* in the encrypted domain as the scalar product of two vectors of size d, which is done K times as there is a B_i^*-value for each arm.
- Step (4).i (done by Comp): decrypt the list of B_i^*, which takes K decryptions. The time of a decryption is higher than the time of an addition or a multiplication.

Each of the aforementioned three steps is done $N - 1$ times. Fortunately, these steps are parallelizable. For instance, (3).ii and (4).i can be equivalently computed by splitting the list and parallelizing the computations. In (3).i, a coordinate of $\widehat{\theta}^*$ is obtained as the scalar product of a row of matrix A^{-1} and the vector b^*. We can divide the matrix and compute the coordinates of $\widehat{\theta}^*$ in parallel. We used the *multiprocessing*[7] library to implement a parallel version of LinUCB-DS that takes advantage of these ideas for parallelizing our code.

In Fig. 6(a) and 6(b), we present the *speedup of parallelization* on LinUCB-DS computation time, while zooming on the three aforementioned costliest steps (the other steps take negligible time), using two distinct input configurations. We used Paillier keys of 2048 bits. We believe that these figures are sufficient to show that our implementation correctly follows the theoretical expectations. Indeed, the computation of $\widehat{\theta}^*$ depends only on d, the decryption of the list of B_i^* only on K, and the construction of the list of B_i^* on both. Moreover, the computation time decreases when increasing the number of cores, which is a desirable feature as our implementation is able to take advantage of modern multi-core architectures in order to reduce the practical overhead due to cryptographic primitives.

In Fig. 6(c), we *stress test the scalability* of LinUCB-DS, in a scenario where K is 10 times larger than d. Indeed, in stochastic linear bandits the goal is to exploit the linear structure and reduce the number of needed estimations, from the estimation of K arm values to the estimation of the d features of the common unknown parameter θ. The observed computation time confirms our theoretical analysis. Moreover, we showed that the parallelization leads to a significant reduction in the computation time of LinUCB-DS.

[7] https://docs.python.org/3/library/multiprocessing.html.

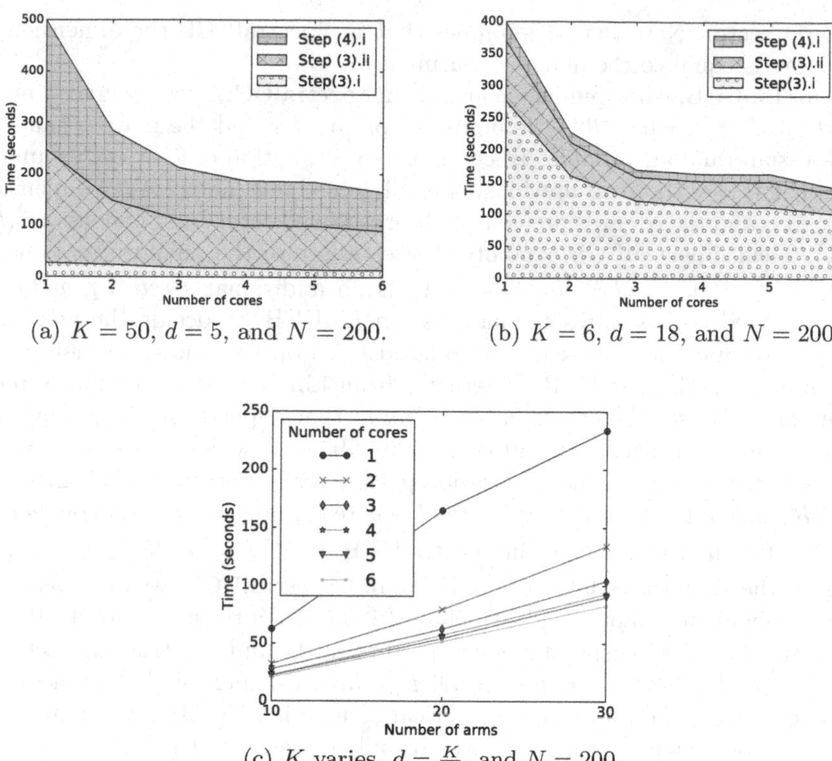

(a) $K = 50$, $d = 5$, and $N = 200$. (b) $K = 6$, $d = 18$, and $N = 200$.

(c) K varies, $d = \frac{K}{10}$, and $N = 200$.

Fig. 6. Computation time of LinUCB-DS split on the three costliest steps, with different parameters, when increasing the number of cores (6(a) and 6(b)), and the scalability of LinUCB-DS when increasing K and d (6(c)).

6 Adaptability of LinUCB-DS

We show that LinUCB-DS can be easily adapted to secure SpectralUCB [17], an algorithm that models with linear bandits the problem of cumulative reward maximization on a graph. The arms are the graph nodes and the reward of an arm is a smooth function on the graph. A smooth graph function returns similar values for close nodes. When the graph models a social network, such a setting is useful for recommendation systems, since we expect that people close on the graph have similar tastes and probably like the same recommended items.

To give the right input to SpectralUCB, some preprocessing is necessary. A matrix of similarities (edge weights) of the graph is used to construct a graph Laplacian $\mathcal{L}$ that is a $(K \times K)$ matrix. Then, SpectralUCB computes the eigendecomposition of $\mathcal{L}$ as $\mathcal{Q}\Lambda_{\mathcal{L}}\mathcal{Q}^\top$, with $\mathcal{Q}$ a $(K \times K)$ orthogonal matrix whose columns are the eigenvectors and $\Lambda_{\mathcal{L}}$ is a diagonal matrix whose elements are the corresponding eigenvalues. An arm is a row of $\mathcal{Q}$, and the expected reward value of arm q_i is given by $\langle q_i, \theta \rangle$, with θ the parameter of the smooth function, a $(K \times 1)$ vector. Note that this implies that in SpectralUCB the dimension of the vectors is equal to the number of arms ($K = d$).

As for LinUCB, when pulling an arm q_i, in SpectralUCB, one observes a noisy reward $\langle q_i, \theta \rangle + \eta$, where θ is the unknown parameter and the noise η is an R-sub-Gaussian random variable. To compute an estimation of θ, at each round t, SpectralUCB uses the arms previously pulled, joined in a matrix A_S of dimension $(K \times (t-1))$ and the rewards previously observed in a vector b_S of dimension $((t-1) \times 1)$. Then, SpectralUCB computes the estimate of the unknown parameter as $\widehat{\theta}_S = (A_S + \Lambda_{\mathcal{L}} + \gamma I_d)^{-1} b_S$, where $\Lambda_{\mathcal{L}}$ is an additional *spectral penalty* for the regularized least-squares estimate. As in LinUCB, to decide the next arm to be pulled, SpectralUCB relies on updated UCB on the arm-values and picks the arm with the largest UCB. Differently from LinUCB, the exploration term in SpectralUCB uses the *effective dimension* d' that depends on the eigenvalues and is small when eigenvalues grow rapidly above t, which is the case when $d = K >> t$. Specifically, the exploration parameter of SpectralUCB is given by $\omega_S = 2R\sqrt{d' \log(1 + t/\gamma) + 2\log(1/\delta)} + C$, where C is an upper-bound on $||\theta||_{\Lambda_{\mathcal{L}}}$. The UCB for an arm q_i is given in SpectralUCB by $B_{i,S} = \langle q_i, \widehat{\theta}_S \rangle + \omega_S ||q_i||_{A_S^{-1}}$.

Given the similarities between LinUCB and SpectralUCB, we observed that it is not difficult to adapt the ideas behind LinUCB-DS to secure SpectralUCB. Encrypting θ results in generating encrypted rewards, and constructing vector b_s with encrypted values. Then, $\widehat{\theta}_S$ and all $B_{i,S}$ are also encrypted. The messages exchanged during the protocol are identical as for LinUCB-DS (cf. Figure 3), in particular Comp chooses the next arm to pull. By SpectralUCB-DS we denote the secure and distributed version of SpectralUCB.

In SpectralUCB, the dimension of the vectors is equal to the number of arms: $K = d$ and for our proof-of-concept experiment (reported in Fig. 7), we fixed $K = N = d$. Following the setting in [17], we used a similarity graph over movies from the MovieLens dataset: the graph contains an edge between movies i and j if the movie j is among the 10 nearest neighbors of the movie i in the latent space M. As in [17], the weight on all edges is 1 and parameters' values are: $\gamma = 0.01, \delta = 0.001, R = 0.01, C = \log t$. As expected, SpectralUCB-DS is slightly faster than LinUCB-DS because it manipulates a $\widehat{\theta}$ computed with a matrix of size depending on t, and $t \leq K$. We have also zoomed on the time taken by each step of SpectralUCB-DS to observe that the three costliest steps are the same as for LinUCB-DS, and we have also observed that the parallelization technique described for LinUCB-DS has a similar positive impact on SpectralUCB-DS.

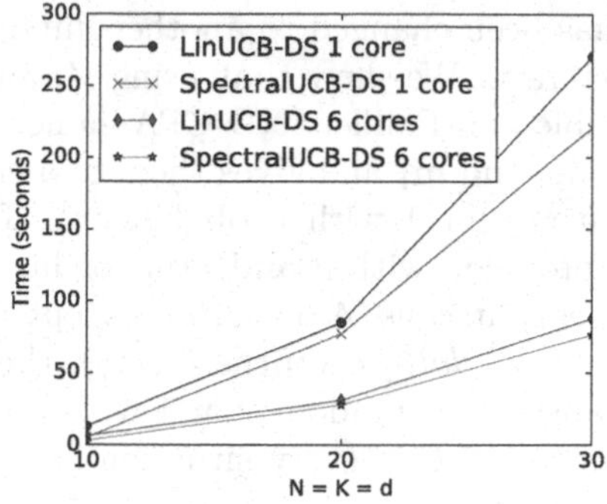

Fig. 7. Time of LinUCB-DS vs SpectralUCB-DS.

7 Conclusions

We tackled the problem of *secure cumulative reward maximization in linear stochastic bandits.* This problem has applications in recommendation systems and Web-targeted advertisements, where sensitive user data and preferences are used for personalized recommendations. We considered a *machine learning as a service* scenario, where data and computations are outsourced to some honest-but-curious cloud, which yields inherent security concerns. We proposed LinUCB-DS, a distributed and secure protocol that outputs exactly the same cumulative reward as standard LinUCB, while enjoying desirable security properties. Towards this goal, we relied on Paillier encryption scheme and secure multi-party computation. We characterized the overhead of cryptography from both theoretical and empirical points of view. Our experiments on the MovieLens movie recommendation dataset showed the scalability and feasibility of LinUCB-DS. Moreover, we showed that LinUCB-DS can be easily adapted to secure other UCB-like linear bandit algorithms. This happens because the security properties of our protocol hold true irrespective of the arm-selection strategy, which differs from an algorithm to another. To show this, we adapted LinUCB-DS to secure SpectralUCB.

Providing security guarantees for machine learning algorithms is a growing research topic. The use of distribution of tasks and cryptography is still an under-explored research direction for this task. We plan to rely on such techniques to develop further security protocols for other types of bandit algorithms and for different machine learning settings.

A Appendix: Security Proofs for Sect. 4

Proof of Theorem 1. Assume a PPT adversary $\mathcal{A}$ who, given $data_{\mathsf{P}}$ has a probability of $\frac{1}{|\theta(i)|} + x + \text{negl}(\lambda)$ of guessing one coordinate of θ. In the worst case, it makes a guess on each coordinate with the same probability $\frac{1}{d}$. We also assume that if $data_{\mathsf{P}}$ is different from the data P has really collected during the protocol (for instance if a value has been changed to another unrelated to the protocol), then $\mathcal{A}$ has not any advantage. We show that using $\mathcal{A}$, an adversary $\mathcal{B}$ obtains an advantage non-negligible in a Paillier IND-CPA game.

$\mathcal{B}$ chooses two values m_0 and m_1 and gives them to a challenger who returns $m_b^* = \mathcal{E}_{\mathsf{Comp}}(m_b)$, with $b = 0$ or 1 with probability $\frac{1}{2}$. Then $\mathcal{B}$ constructs an execution of the secure protocol, with θ and arms of his choice. In particular, it sets $\theta_1 = m_1$. At the end, it calls $\mathcal{A}$ on $data_{\mathsf{P}}$ except that it replaces θ_1' by m_b^*. Let us call it $data_{\mathsf{P}}'$. If $\mathcal{A}^\theta(data_{\mathsf{P}}')$ returns $(1, m_1)$, then $\mathcal{B}$ answers 1 to the challenger, otherwise it answers at random 0 or 1 with probability $\frac{1}{2}$.

The probability of success of $\mathcal{B}$ in every situation is:

- In $\mathcal{A}$'s guess, if $i \neq 1$ (with probability $1 - \frac{1}{d}$), then $\mathcal{B}$ answers at random and his probability of success is $\frac{1}{2}$.
- If $i = 1$ (with probability $\frac{1}{d}$):
  - If $b = 0$ (with probability $\frac{1}{2}$) then $data_{\mathsf{P}}'$ is not valid and $\mathcal{A}$ has not any advantage.
    - ∗ It answers $(1, m_1)$ with probability $\frac{1}{|\theta_1|}$, where $\mathcal{B}$ answers 1 to the IND-CPA game and is wrong.
    - ∗ It gives an other value for θ_1' with probability $1 - \frac{1}{|\theta_1|}$, then $\mathcal{B}$ answers at random and has a probability of success of $\frac{1}{2}$.
  - If $b = 1$ (with probability $\frac{1}{2}$) then $\mathcal{A}$ benefits of its advantage.
    - ∗ By hypothesis, $\mathcal{A}$ returns $(1, m_1)$ with probability $\frac{1}{|\theta_1|} + x + \text{negl}(\lambda)$. Then $\mathcal{B}$ trusts him and is right.
    - ∗ By hypothesis, $\mathcal{A}$ returns another value for θ_1' with probability $1 - (\frac{1}{|\theta_1|} + x + \text{negl}(\lambda))$. $\mathcal{B}$ answers randomly and is correct with probability $\frac{1}{2}$.

Summing it up, the probability of success of $\mathcal{B}$ in his IND-CPA game is: $P(\mathcal{B}) = (1 - \frac{1}{d})\frac{1}{2} + \frac{1}{d}\frac{1}{2}(1 - \frac{1}{|\theta_1|})\frac{1}{2} + \frac{1}{d}\frac{1}{2}(\frac{1}{|\theta_1|} + x + \text{negl}(\lambda)) + \frac{1}{d}\frac{1}{2}(1 - \frac{1}{|\theta_1|} - x - \text{negl}(\lambda))\frac{1}{2}\frac{1}{2} - \frac{1}{2d} + \frac{1}{4d} - \frac{1}{4d|\theta_1|} + \frac{1}{2d|\theta_1|} + \frac{1}{2d}x + \frac{1}{4d} - \frac{1}{4d|\theta_1|} - \frac{1}{4d}x + \text{negl}(\lambda) = \frac{1}{2} + \frac{1}{4d}x + \text{negl}(\lambda)$. It gives him a non-negligible advantage in a classical IND-CPA game on Paillier scheme, which contradicts the fact that Paillier is IND-CPA secure. Then our assumption was wrong and an adversary who has an advantage in retrieving a coordinate of θ with $data_{\mathsf{P}}$ cannot exist.

Proof of Theorem 2. The same proof as above can be applied, with $\mathcal{B}$ changing one of the rewards with m_1^* after the execution of the protocol. It yields to $\mathcal{B}$ an advantage of $\frac{1}{2} + \frac{1}{4N}x + \text{negl}(\lambda)$ to an IND-CPA game (with N the budget and the number of pulls) which is impossible if Paillier is IND-CPA secure.

Proof of Theorem 3. Let $\mathcal{A}$ be a PPT adversary trying to retrieve the cumulative sum of rewards and $\mathcal{B}$ an adversary trying to retrieve any of the N rewards generated. $\mathcal{A}^s(data)$ has a non-negligible advantage $\Leftrightarrow$ $\mathcal{B}^r(data)$ has a non-negligible advantage.

$\Leftarrow$ $\mathcal{A}$ can call $\mathcal{B}$ and obtains the correct value of one reward with probability non-negligible. It gives him a lower bound on the sum of all rewards, and consequently reduces the possibilities of s. It now has a better probability than random to guess s.

$\Rightarrow \mathcal{B}$ calls $\mathcal{A}$ and obtains the correct value of s with a non-negligible probability. It is an upper bound on the value of one reward, and reduces the possibilities of all r_t.

The bounds do not reduce significantly the space of possibilities if N is big but N can very well be small, even 1. In any case, the advantage one benefits from the other is non-negligible.

This ensures that P cannot retrieve s, because it would give him an advantage in retrieving one of the rewards, and it has been proven impossible.

Proof of Theorem 4. Same proof as for Theorem 1 applies.

Proof of Theorem 5. Assume a PPT adversary $\mathcal{A}$ who, given $\mathcal{M}$, has a probability of guessing the correct s with probability $\frac{1}{|s|} + x + \text{negl}(\lambda)$. Then we show how an adversary $\mathcal{B}$ can use $\mathcal{A}$ to gain a non-negligible advantage in a Paillier IND-CPA game. Again, we assume that if $\mathcal{M}$ is changed with a value unrelated to the protocol, then $\mathcal{A}$ does not conserve its advantage. $\mathcal{B}$ simulates the execution of the protocol with θ and arms of his choice. It knows the value of s at the end. He then chooses s as m_1 for the IND-CPA challenge, and a value out of the set of possible s for m_0. It gives m_0 and m_1 to the challenger who returns $\mathcal{E}_{\mathsf{DC}}(m_b)$ with $b = 0$ or 1 with probability $\frac{1}{2}$. $\mathcal{B}$ takes the set $\mathcal{M}$ of all messages exchanged by the nodes for the protocol, and replaces $\mathcal{E}_{\mathsf{DC}}(s)$ with $\mathcal{E}_{\mathsf{DC}}(m_b)$. It calls $\mathcal{A}^s(\mathcal{M}')$ and observes the output. If it is s, it answers 1 to the decisional challenge. Else, it answers at random 0 or 1 with probability $\frac{1}{2}$.

- $b = 0$ (with probability $\frac{1}{2}$)
  - $\mathcal{A}$ returns s with probability $\frac{1}{|s|}$ and $\mathcal{B}$ is wrong.
  - $\mathcal{A}$ returns something else with probability $1 - \frac{1}{|s|}$, $\mathcal{B}$ answers at random and is right with probability $\frac{1}{2}$.
- $b = 1$ (with probability $\frac{1}{2}$)
  - $\mathcal{A}$ returns s with probability $\frac{1}{|s|} + x + \text{negl}(\lambda)$, and $\mathcal{B}$ answers 1 and is right.
  - $\mathcal{A}$ returns something else with probability $1-(\frac{1}{|s|}+x+\text{negl}(\lambda))$, $\mathcal{B}$ answers at random and is right with probability $\frac{1}{2}$.

In total, $\mathcal{B}$ answers correctly the challenge with probability $P(\mathcal{B}) = \frac{1}{2}(1 - \frac{1}{|s|})\frac{1}{2} + \frac{1}{2}(\frac{1}{|s|} + x + \text{negl}(\lambda)) + \frac{1}{2}(1 - \frac{1}{|s|} - x - \text{negl}(\lambda))\frac{1}{2} = \frac{1}{4} - \frac{1}{4|s|} + \frac{1}{2|s|} + \frac{1}{2}x + \frac{1}{4} - \frac{1}{4|s|} - \frac{1}{4}x + \text{negl}(\lambda) = \frac{1}{2} + \frac{1}{4}x + \text{negl}(\lambda)$. He has gain a non-negligible advantage in the Paillier IND-CPA game, which is impossible. Thus, such an adversary $\mathcal{A}$ cannot exist.

Proof of Lemma 1. This is immediate, as all images/preimages are equally likely if σ is uniformly selected.

Proof of Theorem 6. Assume an adversary $\mathcal{A}^x(\mathcal{M})$ who has a probability $\frac{1}{K} + x + \text{negl}(\lambda)$ of guessing the correct arm pulled at round t. It also knows the index of the maximal element in the permuted list of B_i that P and Comp exchange at round t. That index is the permuted index of the arm who is really pulled, x_t. It means that $\mathcal{A}$ can make a guess on an element of the permutation σ_t and is right with the same probability as it is right at guessing the arm pulled at round t, and it benefits of the same non-negligible advantage. But $\mathcal{A}$ does not know σ and should only have a probability of $\frac{1}{K}$ of guessing an element of σ according to Lemma 1. This is a contradiction, so $\mathcal{A}$ cannot exist.

Proof of Theorem 7. Assume a PPT adversary $\mathcal{A}$ who, given $data_{\mathsf{Comp}}$ is able to retrieve the value B_i of arm i with probability $\frac{1}{K} + x + \text{negl}(\lambda)$. After making his guess B'_i, he can look in $\sigma(listB)$ the position of B'_i and make a guess on the value of $\sigma(i)$. It benefits of the same non-negligible advantage in guessing an element of the permutation σ on which it has no information. This contradicts Lemma 1, thus such an adversary cannot exist.

Proof of Theorem 8. For a fixed s, if the random number $rand$ is uniformly chosen, then $rand + s$ can take all possible values with the same probability. Hence when Comp sees $rand + s$, it gains no information on s.

References

1. Abbasi-Yadkori, Y., Pál, D., Szepesvári, C.: Improved algorithms for linear stochastic bandits. In: NIPS, pp. 2312–2320 (2011)
2. Auer, P.: Using confidence bounds for exploitation-exploration trade-offs. JMLR **3**, 397–422 (2002)
3. Auer, P., Cesa-Bianchi, N., Fischer, P.: Finite-Time analysis of the multiarmed Bandit problem. Mach. Learn. **47**(2–3), 235–256 (2002)
4. Baldimtsi, F., Ohrimenko, O.: Sorting and searching behind the curtain. In: Böhme, R., Okamoto, T. (eds.) FC 2015. LNCS, vol. 8975, pp. 127–146. Springer, Heidelberg (2015). https://doi.org/10.1007/978-3-662-47854-7_8
5. Bourse, F., Minelli, M., Minihold, M., Paillier, P.: Fast homomorphic evaluation of deep discretized neural networks. In: Shacham, H., Boldyreva, A. (eds.) CRYPTO 2018. LNCS, vol. 10993, pp. 483–512. Springer, Cham (2018). https://doi.org/10.1007/978-3-319-96878-0_17
6. Ciucanu, R., Lafourcade, P., Lombard-Platet, M., Soare, M.: Secure best ARM identification in multi-armed bandits. In: Heng, S.-H., Lopez, J. (eds.) ISPEC 2019. LNCS, vol. 11879, pp. 152–171. Springer, Cham (2019). https://doi.org/10.1007/978-3-030-34339-2_9
7. Gajane, P., Urvoy, T., Kaufmann, E.: Corrupt Bandits for preserving local privacy. In: ALT, pp. 387–412 (2018)
8. Gentry, C.: Fully homomorphic encryption using ideal lattices. In: STOC, pp. 169–178 (2009)
9. Goldreich, O.: The Foundations of Cryptography - Volume 2: Basic Applications. Cambridge University Press, Cambridge (2004)
10. Harper, F.M., Konstan, J.A.: The movielens datasets: history and context. ACM Trans. Interact. Intell. Syst. (tiis) **5**(4), 1–19 (2016)

11. Lattimore, T., Szepesvári, C.: Bandit Algorithms. Cambridge University Press (2020). https://tor-lattimore.com/downloads/book/book.pdf
12. Li, L., Chu, W., Langford, J., Schapire, R.E.: A contextual-bandit approach to personalized news article recommendation. In: WWW, pp. 661–670 (2010)
13. Mishra, N., Thakurta, A.: (Nearly) optimal differentially private stochastic multi-arm bandits. In: UAI, pp. 592–601 (2015)
14. Paillier, P.: Public-key cryptosystems based on composite degree residuosity classes. In: Stern, J. (ed.) EUROCRYPT 1999. LNCS, vol. 1592, pp. 223–238. Springer, Heidelberg (1999). https://doi.org/10.1007/3-540-48910-X_16
15. Shariff, R., Sheffet, O.: Differentially private contextual linear bandits. In: NeurIPS, pp. 4301–4311 (2018)
16. Tossou, A.C.Y., Dimitrakakis, C.: Algorithms for differentially private multi-armed bandits. In: AAAI,pp. 2087–2093 (2016)
17. Valko, M., Munos, R., Kveton, B., Kocák, T.: Spectral bandits for smooth graph functions. In: ICML, pp. 46–54 (2014)

Secure Transfer Learning for Machine Fault Diagnosis Under Different Operating Conditions

Chao Jin[1](✉), Mohamed Ragab[2], and Khin Mi Mi Aung[1]

[1] Institute for Infocomm Research, A*STAR, Singapore, Singapore
{jin_chao,mi_mi_aung}@i2r.a-star.edu.sg

[2] School of Computer Science and Engineering, Nanyang Technological University, Singapore, Singapore
mohamedr002@e.ntu.edu.sg

Abstract. The success of deep learning is largely due to the availability of big training data nowadays. However, data privacy could be a big concern, especially when the training or inference is done on untrusted third-party servers. Fully Homomorphic Encryption (FHE) is a powerful cryptography technique that enables computation on encrypted data in the absence of decryption key, thus could protect data privacy in an outsourced computation environment. However, due to its large performance and resource overheads, current applications of FHE to deep learning are still limited to very simple tasks. In this paper, we first propose a neural network training framework on FHE encrypted data, namely PrivGD. PrivGD leverages the Single-Instruction Multiple-Data (SIMD) packing feature of FHE to efficiently implement the Gradient Descent algorithm in the encrypted domain. In particular, PrivGD is the first to support training a multi-class classification network with double-precision float-point weights through approximated Softmax function in FHE, which has never been done before to the best of our knowledge. Then, we show how to apply FHE with transfer learning for more complicated real-world applications. We consider outsourced diagnosis services, as with the Machine-Learning-as-a-Service paradigm, for multi-class machine faults on machine sensor datasets under different operating conditions. As directly applying the source model trained on the source dataset (collected from source operating condition) to the target dataset (collect from the target operating condition) will lead to degraded diagnosis accuracy, we propose to transfer the source model to the target domain by retraining (fine-tuning) the classifier of the source model with data from the target domain. The target domain data is encrypted with FHE so that its privacy is preserved during the transfer learning process. We implement the secure transfer learning process with our PrivGD framework. Experiments results show that by fine-tuning a source model for fewer than 10 epochs with encrypted target domain data, the model can converge to an increased diagnosis accuracy by up to 20%, while the

This research/project is supported by A*STAR under its RIE2020 Advanced Manufacturing and Engineering (AME) Programmatic Programme (Award A19E3b0099).

K. Nguyen et al. (Eds.): ProvSec 2020, LNCS 12505, pp. 278–297, 2020.
https://doi.org/10.1007/978-3-030-62576-4_14

whole fine-tuning process takes approximate 3.85 h on our commodity server.

Keywords: Homomorphic encryption · Data privacy · Transfer learning · Fault diagnosis

1 Introduction

Machine Learning as a Service (MLaaS) is becoming an increasingly hot topic in recent years. In this paradigm, large organisations with large amounts of data can train high quality models, and share their models with other users who do not own enough data or cannot afford to train complete models of their own. This is extremely useful when the data of interest is hard to acquire. For instance, in the healthcare domain, to train a deep learning model that can predict a rare disease from a patient's X-Ray image, we need enough amount of positive samples, i.e., patents' X-Ray images with that particular disease. While a large hospital may possess enough data to train a good model, individual clinics may not have the data and resources to do so. It is therefore beneficial for the hospital to put its model on the cloud and provide inference services for the clinics. Another example is the machine fault diagnosis in the advanced manufacturing domain. It usually requires time and efforts to collect enough sensor data under machine faulty conditions to train an accurate fault diagnosis model, especially when there are multiple different failure types and different operating environments. Take the training of a simple logistic regression model as an example, it is suggested that at least $N = 10 \cdot k/p$ training samples are required, where k is the number of covariates (independent variables), and p is the smallest of the proportions of negative or positive cases in the dataset [1].

Although MLaaS enables model owners to share the usage of their models without transferring them to the users, it poses data privacy risks on the users' side, as the users need to upload their private data to the outsourced inference servers. In order to solve the data privacy issue, researchers have proposed numbers of privacy-preserving neural network inference solutions, based on cryptography technologies like Fully Homomorphic Encryption (FHE) [2–9], Multi-Party Computation (MPC) [10,11], or hybrid of FHE and MPC [12,13]. In particular, FHE [14] provides strong crypto primitives that enable computation directly on encrypted data. To apply FHE in the MLaaS scenario, a model is pre-trained on the clear data and deployed on an inference server, a user encrypts his data using a FHE scheme before sending the data to the inference server, and then the encrypted user data is evaluated homomorphically with the model on the inference server, and finally the inference result which is also in encrypted form is sent back to the user for decryption. FHE based solutions are considered as non-interactive, in which the server can independently evaluate the whole model and generate the predicted result. On the other hand, MPC based solutions, built on top of techniques like Garbled Circuits [15] and Secrete Sharing [16], require interactive communications between the user and the server, and considerable amount of computational load at the user side, which may not be the optimal case in many application scenarios.

Despite of its strong crypto primitives, FHE in its current state cannot be directly applied to large and deep neural network models, due to its large computational and memory resource overhead, as well as the noise growth along with computational depth. Therefore, current FHE-based solutions are only targeting for simple inference tasks like MNIST [2–5] and CIFAR10 [3,4,8], and even simpler training tasks like logistic regression [17].

In this paper, we apply FHE to the MLaaS scenario with a real-world application, machine fault diagnosis on the vibration sensor data. Furthermore, the sensor data may be collected under different machine operating conditions. We first assume that a model owner who possesses enough data trains a complete fault diagnosis model (including a feature extractor and a classifier) for a certain operating condition. Then the model owner deploys his model on a server and provides inference services for other users. On the other hand, the users who could not afford to train their own models can encrypt their own sensor data using FHE and send to the server for inference. However, multiple challenges may be faced here. First, the model may be too big and cannot be evaluated efficiently as a whole in the FHE domain. Second, the user data may be collected in a different machine operating conditions which may results in lower inference accuracy if directly apply the model on it. To address these challenges, we propose to use a transfer learning approach: 1) the model owner shares the feature extractor of his model among the users for them to extract the common features from their time-series sensor data; and 2) the user extracts and encrypts the features from his own data and send to the inference server to fine-tune the classifier; and finally 3) the fine-tuned classifier can be used for fault diagnosis for the user's new incoming data. Noted that we leverage transfer learning in two ways here. First, it enables sharing the common part (i.e., feature extractor) and protecting only the task-specific part (i.e., classifier) of the model, thus can significantly reduce the network size in the FHE domain. Second, the fine-tuning process with user's private data leverages on the prior knowledge (weights and biases) of the source model's classifier, thus can converge to an increased accuracy with less data and fewer number of training iterations (compared to training from scratch).

The fine-tuning process of the fault diagnosis model involves training of a multi-class classifier in the FHE domain. While training a binary classifier (logistic regression) with FHE may be an easier task, training a multi-class classifier is a much harder problem as it requires implementation of Softmax activation function in the FHE domain. To enable efficient neural network training on FHE encrypted data, we design and implement the PrivGD framework. PrivGD supports the multi-class classifier training through approximating an estimated Softmax function in the FHE domain. Moreover, PrivGD offers a more parallelized Mini-Batch Gradient Descent training procedure, by designing more efficient matrix multiplications on the encrypted data based on the powerful SIMD packing features [18] of modern FHE schemes.

The major contributions of our paper are summarized as follows.

- We design and implement PrivGD, a secure neural network training framework on FHE encrypted data. PrivGD offers optimized Mini-Batch Gradient Descent training with FHE, and is the first to support secure training of double-precision float-point networks for multi-class classification tasks, to the best of our knowledge.
- We propose a new paradigm of privacy-preserving MLaaS based on transfer learning, where a user can use his private data to fine-tune the classifier model for personalized inference services with improved accuracy.
- We demonstrate the efficiency of our secure transfer learning paradigm on a real-world application, machine fault diagnosis through sensor data under different operating conditions. By using PrivGD, one diagnosis model for a source condition can be fine-tuned with encrypted data from a target condition, to achieve improved accuracy by up to 20% on the target condition through fewer than 10 training epochs.

The rest of the paper is organized as follows. The next section introduces preliminaries and background knowledge. In Sect. 3 we describe PrivGD, our neural network training framework on FHE encrypted data. In Sect. 4 we describe our secure transfer learning paradigm with the real-world application of machine fault diagnosis, and the experiment results are discussed in Sect. 5. In Sect. 6 we discuss about related work and finally we conclude the paper in Sect. 7.

2 Preliminaries

2.1 Fully Homomorphic Encryption

Since its first introduction by Rivest et al. [19], FHE has always been an intriguing technology due to its ability of computing on encrypted data in the absence of the decryption key. In 2009, Gentry proposed the first construction of a FHE scheme [14]. Since then, this field has been seen great advancements and a number of new FHE schemes have been proposed [20–22]. Generally, the FHE plaintext and ciphertext spaces are polynomial rings. FHE is instantiated to preserve the algebraic structure between plaintext and ciphertext, and provides the user with two main computational operations: homomorphic addition and homomorphic multiplication. These operations can manipulate ciphertexts and produce encrypted results that are equivalent to the corresponding plaintext results after decryption.

Modern FHE schemes conceal plaintext messages with noise that can be identified and removed with the secret key [23]. As we compute on encrypted data, the noise magnitude accumulated in a ciphertext increases at a certain rate (high rate for multiplication and low rate for addition). As long as the noise is below a certain threshold, that depends on the encryption parameters, decryption can filter out the noise and retrieve the plaintext message successfully. Although FHE schemes include a primitive (known as *bootstrapping*) to refresh the noise [14] inside ciphertexts, it is extremely computationally expensive. Instead, one can use a *levelled* FHE scheme [20] that allows evaluating circuits of multiplicative depth below a certain threshold, which can be controlled by the encryption parameters. In this way, one can avoid the expensive bootstrapping operations by selecting the appropriate encryption parameters that can accommodate the computational needs of the applications.

Next we briefly introduce a levelled FHE scheme we use in this paper, the CKKS scheme [22]. The plaintext and ciphertext are ring elements of a polynomial ring $R_q = Z_q[X]/(X^N + 1)$, where $X^N + 1$ is the polynomial modulus with degree N and $Z_q[x]$ is the polynomial with integer coefficients based on modulus q. In particular, q is the product of a group of prime factors, where the number of primes is called the "*level*" of the ciphertext. When the input data is first encrypted, its ciphertext is at the highest level, say level L. Then along with the computations, the ciphertext may gradually move down to lower levels, by removing one prime factor from q at a time. In General, L determines the largest multiplication depth a single ciphertext can have.

CKKS supports standard FHE primitives like *encode* and *decode*, *encrypt* and *decrypt*, *addition* and *multiplication* (with both ciphertexts and plaintexts). Besides that, a unique feature of CKKS is that it supports fixed-point arithmetic for approximate computing on encrypted numbers. To implement this, the input real numbers are first scaled with a large scaling factor and rounded to the nearest integer (quantization). Then they are encoded into plaintexts and subsequently encrypted into ciphertexts. To maintain a constant scaling factor in the ciphertext after multiplication, CKKS offers an efficient *rescaling* procedure which moves down the ciphertext to the next lower level by removing a prime factor from coefficient modulus q, at the same time scales down the amplified scaling factor in the ciphertext by the prime that removed from q. As mentioned before, one can drastically improve FHE performance via Single-Instruction Multiple-Data (SIMD) packing methods. In CKKS, a vector of up to $N/2$ complex numbers can be encoded in a single plaintext element. This allows one to perform parallelized SIMD homomorphic operations on packed ciphertexts efficiently. Packing can be viewed as if the ciphertext has independent slots, each concealing one data item. To manipulate the slots within a ciphertext, CKKS offers the *rotate* primitive that can circularly shift the data locations across the slots.

2.2 Neural Network Inference and Training

A feed-forward neural network composes of a stack of processing layers, where each layer performs certain computation on its input data according to the layer type, and outputs the processed data to the next layer for further computation. The common types of a nerual network layer are as follows.

- Convolution layer. This layer computes weighted sum of the input data. Each convolution operation is computing the dot product between a weight vector (i.e., filter map) and a data vector, and then adding a bias to it. The locations of the filter maps are shifted so as to compute with different data vectors from the whole input data.

- Fully connected layer. This layer can be viewed as a special kind of convolution layer, where the weighted sum (dot product) is always done between a weight vector and the whole input data.
- Activation layer. This layer applies an activation function to each of the input data. The activation functions are usually non-linear functions like Sigmoid, ReLU, etc.
- Pooling layers. This layer is usually used to down sample the input data to a smaller size, by returning the maximum (max-pooling) or average (average-pooling) of input vectors from the whole input data.

Neural networks are used for inference tasks like classification and regression. The inference phase only involves forward-propagation, where the input data is feed into the network, processed layer by layer, and the last layer gives the final output of the network. Before a neural network can be used for inference tasks, it must be trained. The training phase involves both forward-propagation and backward-propagation, whereas the backward-propagation is used to compute the derivatives (gradients) of a loss function with regard to the network weights and biases. An optimization algorithm (e.g., Gradient Descent) is then used to update the weights and biases according to the gradients, to minimize the value of the loss function.

A straightforward implementation of the Gradient Descent (GD) algorithm would be to update the weights and biases after each training sample, which is called Stochastic Gradient Descent (SGD). However, in practice people often adopt a more optimized form called Mini-Batch based GD, which accumulates the gradients from a batch of training samples, and then update the weights and biases at one time. Specifically, if the batch size equals the whole training set, the method is also called Batch Gradient Descent. In our secure training framework, we adopt Mini-Batch (Batch) Gradient Descent with HE packed data, to take full advantage of the performance benefit from SIMD-styled computations.

2.3 Transfer Learning

Deep learning (DL) is one of the most successful paradigms in data-driven approaches that has wide acclaimed performance in many practical applications. Yet, it works only under the assumption that training data and testing data are sampled from the same distribution, which may not hold at many practical scenarios. Naive approach is to train new model independently for each new data distribution. Training a new model from scratch for each new data distribution not only adds additional computational burdens but it also requires large amount of labeled data. Transfer Learning, which aims to transfer knowledge among different domains, can be a promising candidate to address the aforementioned challenges [24]. Different from DL, transfer learning leverages the knowledge from one or more source domains to maximize the performance in the target domain. Recently, transfer learning has been shown great capability with reducing the deep learning requirements for both computational requirements and the amount of labeled data [25]. Wide range of deep learning applications has benefited from transfer learning including Natural Language Processing (NLP), Computer Vision, and Robotics [26–28]. In our approach, we leverage transfer learning to realize efficient machine fault diagnosis across different operating conditions.

3 PrivGD: Secure Neural Network Training with FHE

In this section, we introduce our design and implementation of PrivGD, a FHE-based secure neural network training framework. We describe the components and considerations for a generate framework for different network architectures.

3.1 Matrix Multiplications with Packed FHE Ciphertexts

Matrix multiplication is a core operation in neural networks. To enable efficient matrix multiplications with encrypted data, we leverage the HE packing feature to pack multiple matrix elements into slots of a single ciphertext. This gives the dual benefits of reduced ciphertext amount and SIMD-styled parallel computation. Specifically, we adopt the following formats in PrivGD to pack a matrix into ciphertexts:

- Row-majored Packing (RP). A m-row n-column matrix $X^{m \times n}$ is packed into m ciphertexts, with Row $\boldsymbol{r}_i$ encrypted in ciphertext C_i $(1 \leq i \leq m)$.
- Column-majored Packing (CP). A Matrix $X^{m \times n}$ is packed into n ciphertexts, with Column $\boldsymbol{c}_j$ in Ciphertext C_j $(1 \leq j \leq n)$.
- Replicated Packing (REP). A Matrix $X^{m \times n}$ is packed into $m \times n$ ciphertexts, with each element $e_{i,j}$ is replicated in all the slots in Ciphertext $C_{i,j}$.

Subsequently, we define the following matrix multiplication operations.

- A REP matrix $X^{m \times k}$ multiplies a RP matrix $Y^{k \times n}$, the result $Z^{m \times n}$ is a RP matrix. In particular, we have the equation: $[C_i]_Z = \sum_{j=1}^{k}([C_{i,j}]_X \times [C_j]_Y)$, where $[C_i]_Z$ is the ciphertext for row $\boldsymbol{r}_i$ of Z, $[C_{i,j}]_X$ is the ciphertext for element $e_{i,j}$ of X, and $[C_j]_Y$ is the ciphertext for row $\boldsymbol{r}_j$ of Y.
- A CP matrix $X^{m \times k}$ multiplies a REP matrix $Y^{k \times n}$, the result $Z^{m \times n}$ is a CP matrix. Similarly, we have the equation: $[C_j]_Z = \sum_{i=1}^{k}([C_i]_X \times [C_{i,j}]_Y)$.
- A RP matrix $X^{m \times k}$ multiplies a CP matrix $Y^{k \times n}$, the result $Z^{m \times n}$ is a REP matrix. The ciphertext $[C_{i,j}]_Z$ for element $e_{i,j}$ of Z is produced by $[C_i]_X \times [C_j]_Y$, followed by applying the *AllSum* [29] algorithm to the multiplied ciphertext. Note that *AllSum* adds all the slots in a ciphertexts, and the sum is replicated in all the slots in that ciphertext. The algorithm uses $\log_2 N$ rotations and additions on the ciphertext, where N is the number of slots.

It should be noted that different matrix formats can be converted between each other by masking and rotation operations. For example, a REP matrix can be converted into a RP matrix, and the j-th slot of RP Matrix's i-th row $[C_i]_{RP}$ is produced by masking out (i.e., multiplying with a one-hot vector where only the masking location is one) the j-th slot of $[C_{i,j}]_{REP}$ in REP matrix and add into $[C_i]_{RP}$. However, matrix format conversions are generally expensive operations which cost additional multiplication depths and noise budgets, and should be avoided wherever possible.

In the next subsection, we will show how to utilize these matrix formats and multiplication functions to efficiently implement the neural network training processes.

3.2 Neural Network Training with FHE

Training a neural network generally involves multiple steps. For each iteration of training, first is to run the forward pass that takes in input and computes final output of the network, and second is to compute the loss function and its gradients with regard to the network output, and last is to run the backward pass that reversely computes the gradients for each layer using chain rule, and updates the weights and biases accordingly. To enable training with FHE, we target to solve the challenges in all these steps in PrivGD.

Forward Propagation. The linear computation layers, such as convolution and fully-connected layers, constitute the major computations in the forward pass. These layers are generally computing the weighted sum of layer inputs with regard to weights and biases, which can further be converted into matrix multiplications. As we adopt mini-batch based gradient descent algorithm in PrivGD, we target to compute the entire mini-batch in one shot through packed matrix multiplications described above. In particular, we adopt REP matrix format for weights and biases, and RP matrix format for batched inputs, where each column is an input vector and each row ciphertext pack a single element from each vector. The result of the matrix multiplication is another RP matrix that holds the output vectors, which is ready to be feed into the next layer for processing.

On the other hand, the non-linear activation layers, such as ReLU and Sigmoid, cannot be directly computed with FHE, and they need to be approximated by polynomials [2,17], or implemented through private table lookups for a quantized version [30]. Max-pooling layers can be replaced with average-pooling or sum-pooling [2], which are actually special kinds of convolution layers with constant weights.

Loss and Gradient Computation. After getting the last linear-layer's output vector $\boldsymbol{z}$ from forward pass, we need to compute a loss function and its gradient with regard to $\boldsymbol{z}$. For classification tasks, $\boldsymbol{z}$ usually needs to go through another activation layer (Sigmoid or Softmax) before loss computation, and for regression tasks, it is usually directly used for loss computation. Table 1 summarizes the common loss functions and their gradients with regard to $\boldsymbol{z}$ for various tasks. For regression tasks, the gradients can be computed by the weighted difference between z and the ground truth label t, which can be computed in HE directly. For classification tasks, the gradients can be computed by the difference between the last activation function outputs and the ground truth labels. While the Sigmoid activation function is easier to be approximated with polynomials and computed in FHE, the polynomial approximation for Softmax, however, is a harder problem and little work has been done on it to the best of our knowledge. In Subsect. 3.3, we introduce a new and efficient way to train multi-class classifier in FHE with approximated Softmax.

Table 1. Common Loss functions and their Gradients.

Task	Activation function on z	Loss function	Loss Gradient w.r.t z
Binary classification	Sigmoid	Binary Cross-Entropy	Sigmoid(z) - t
Multi-class classification	Softmax	Multi-class Cross-Entropy	Softmax(z) - t
Regression	–	Mean Squared Error	$\frac{2}{N}(z - t)$

Backward Propagation. After getting the gradients for the last linear-layer's outputs, we can start the backward pass and reversely compute the gradients for the weights and biases in all the layers. For each linear layer, two major types of computations are performed in the backward pass: one is to compute gradients for the layer weights and biases, and the other is to compute the gradients for the layer inputs (previous layers' outputs). Recall that the inputs X and outputs Y of each layer, as well as their gradients dX and dY, are stored as RP-formatted matrices, and the layer weights and biases are stored as REP-formatted matrices. According to chain rule, the gradient of each weight is the multiplication of the layer input and the gradient of the layer output it associates. Therefore, we have the following equation for gradient computation of layer weights.

$$[dW]_{REP} = [dY]_{RP} \times [X^T]_{CP} \tag{1}$$

In Eq. 1, dY is the RP matrix holding layer output's gradients, and X^T is the transpose of layer inputs, which is in CP format. Their multiplication produces a REP matrix dW, in which each element is exactly the corresponding weight's gradient summed on the entire minibatch. For biases, their gradients db simply equals the gradients of the associated layer outputs, therefore can directly do a sum up for the minibatch using *AllSum* on the Ciphertexts. The summed gradients can be directly used to update the weights and biases in a later step. Pay attention that we do not take the additional step of computing the average gradients for the minibatch, as this can be combined with adjusting of the learning rate.

On the other hand, computing the gradients for the layer inputs, as shown in Eq. 2, is very similar like the forward propagation process.

$$[dX]_{RP} = [W^T]_{REP} \times [dY]_{RP} \tag{2}$$

Back propagating through an activation function layer is different from a linear layer in two ways. First, there is no weights in the activation function layer, thus no weight gradients computation; second, the derivative of the activation function needs to be computed in order to compute the gradients of the layer input. As we use polynomials to approximate the activation functions (e.g., ReLU), we can take the derivative of the polynomial, which is also an polynomial, as the derivative of the activation function. On the other hand, for some activation functions the derivatives can also be computed in FHE in their native forms. For example, the derivative of Sigmoid layer $Y = Sigmoid(X)$ can be simply computed as $Y(1 - Y)$, and the derivative of Tanh layer $Y = Tanh(X)$ is $1 - Y^2$.

After the gradients of weights and biases in all the linear layers are computed, the next step is to update the weights and biases based on some optimization method. The original version of SGD optimizer, $W = W - \eta \cdot dW$ where η is the learning rate, can be directly computed in FHE. One can also add a weight decay term or momentum term into the optimizer, but at the cost of some additional computational complexity.

3.3 Multi-class Classifier Training in FHE with Approximated Softmax

Training a multi-class classifier in FHE requires approximating the Softmax function with polynomials, which is very challenging due to the fact that Softmax is a multi-variate function. In PrivGD, we do not target to directly approximate Softmax with polynomials. Instead, we approximate an estimated version of Softmax [31], which is proved to be able to achieve very close parameter estimations with original Softmax in multi-class classifier training. The output probability for each of the classes computed by the Estimated Softmax is described in Eq. 3.

$$P_c = \prod_{m \neq c} Sigmoid(z_c - z_m) \tag{3}$$

Then, we can further compute the Negative Log Likelihood loss function and its gradients with regard to the last linear layer outputs, which can be expressed in Eq. 4. We assume each training sample is encrypted and its class label is known to the training server, and thus it is straightforward to compute the gradients in Eq. 4. In case the class labels are also encrypted, we just need some additional masking and addition operations for the gradient computation.

$$\begin{cases} dz_t = \sum_{m \neq t} (Sigmoid(z_t - z_m) - 1) & \text{for class t matches sample label} \\ dz_m = 1 - Sigmoid(z_t - z_m) & \text{for all the rest classes} \end{cases} \tag{4}$$

To compute the gradients in Eq. 4 with FHE, we only need to approximate the Sigmoid function with polynomials, which is a simpler task as Sigmoid approximation has been widely studied in prior arts [32–34] and used in logistic regression training with FHE [17]. What's more, it should be noted that the multiplication depth for gradient computation in Eq. 4 equals only a single Sigmoid approximation, which is the same as in logistic regression training.

3.4 Current Challenges and Our Approach

It should be noted that neural network training with FHE, although possible, still faces multiple challenges especially for larger networks: 1) deeper networks consume more multiplication depths as ciphertexts are computed throughout the layers, and 2) the multiplication depths are doubled in the training phase as it involves both forward and backward propagation; 3) the training losses usually need a large number of training iterations to converge, which further amplifies the multiplication depths; and 4) non-linear functions in the network may need to be approximated with high-degree polynomials in order to be evaluated accurately in FHE. Therefore, in order to avoid the expensive bootstrapping operations, one needs very large encryption parameters to accommodate the large multiplication depths, which are deemed to be impractical due to high resource overhead and low performance.

Due to the above reasons, we are not targeting to train complete new models from scratch with FHE, instead, our approach is to use private data to refine existing models to make them adapt to new tasks, with a transfer learning approach. In later section, we will demonstrate the efficiency of our framework with a practical application to fine-tune machine fault diagnosis models with encrypted user data.

4 Secure Transfer Learning for Personalized Machine Fault Diagnosis

In this section, we demonstrate our new paradigm of private and personalized MLaaS through secure transfer learning, with the real-world application of machine fault diagnosis under different operating conditions.

4.1 The Machine Vibration Sensor Datasets

Our application scenario is to utilize deep learning models for diagnosing motor bearing faults from vibration sensor data attached to the machines. The datasets are downloaded from the Case Western Reserve University Bearing Data Center Website [35]. The CWRU bearing dataset is time-series data that collected at 12k sampling rate. It composes 4 different subsets which corresponds to different loading torques (i.e., operating conditions), where the torque values ranges from 0 to 3. In each subset, the data instances fall into 4 different categories, one normal category and three faulty categories including inner-race faults (IF), outer-race faults (OF), and bearing-race faults (BF). Each faulty category could have 3 fault sizes, i.e., 0.007 in., 0.014 in., and 0.021 in., which leads to 10 total classes (1 normal class, and 9 faulty classes), as shown in Table 2.

4.2 Network Model for Machine Fault Diagnosis

Our model for the fault diagnosis is composed of two components, a feature extractor and a classifier. In particularly, the feature extractor is a 5-layer convolutional neural network with 1-dimensional kernels (1D-CNN). It aims to find a latent representation of the time-series data that could be class discriminative. On the other

Table 2. CWRU bearing dataset description [36]

Class label	Fault type	Fault size (inches)	Load (hp)
1	Normal	0	0, 1, 2, 3
2	IF	0.007	0, 1, 2, 3
3	IF	0.014	0, 1, 2, 3
4	IF	0.021	0, 1, 2, 3
5	OF	0.007	0, 1, 2, 3
6	OF	0.014	0, 1, 2, 3
7	OF	0.021	0, 1, 2, 3
8	BF	0.007	0, 1, 2, 3
9	BF	0.014	0, 1, 2, 3
10	BF	0.021	0, 1, 2, 3

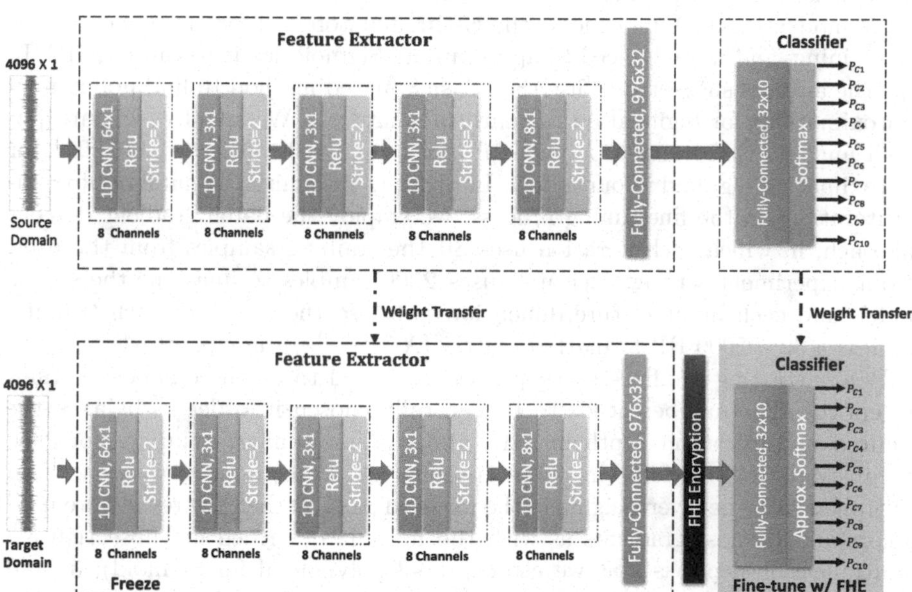

Fig. 1. Fault diagnosis model and the secure transfer learning approach.

hand, the classifier which is composed of a fully connected layer followed by a Softmax activation layer, takes the extracted features from the 1D-CNN network as inputs, and outputs the probabilities the input sample belongs to each of the 10 classes. The detailed structure of our model is shown in Fig. 1.

4.3 Secure Model Fine-Tuning Across Different Operating Conditions

In the MLaaS paradigm, the model owner deploys his model (i.e., source model) on a cloud server to provide inference services for other users. In our application scenario, we assume each user's machine is operating at a different condition, and directly applying the source model to the target conditions may lead to degraded diagnosis accuracy. To solve the problem, we propose a secure transfer learning approach, where a user can fine-tune the source model with encrypted data samples from his own machine and the corresponding working condition. Specifically, the model owner first distributes the source model's feature extractor to all the users, and then the users use the feature extractor to extract features from their own data samples, encrypt the features with FHE, and send them to the cloud server to fine tune the classifier of the source model. It must be noted that, when the classifier is fine-tuned by a particular user, its weights and biases are becoming encrypted, and it can only be used to provide diagnosis services for that user after fine-tuning.

4.4 Implementation of Secure Fine-Tuning Process

We use PrivGD to implement the fine-tuning process. As shown in Fig. 1, the user utilizes the encrypted features as input to fine-tune the classifier part of the source model. PrivGD implements the Estimated Softmax for multi-class classifier training, and we only need to approximate Sigmoid for it to run in FHE. In [17], the authors suggested to use the Least Squared method to find polynomial approximations for Sigmoid on certain input interval. We adopt a similar approach and use the degree-3 polynomial $g(x) = 0.5 + 0.15012x - 0.00159x^3$ for approximating Sigmoid in our model. In order to minimize the number of training iterations in the fine-tuning process, we employ the batch gradient descent approach, in which each iteration uses all the training samples from the user. In our experiment setting, each user uses 2000 samples to fine-tune the source model, and each input feature dimension is 32, so the input for each training batch is a 32×2000 RP-formatted matrix $[X^{32\times 2000}]_{RP}$ in ciphertexts.

Before starting the fine-tuning process, we need to fix the number of training epochs. The number needs to be carefully chosen in order to balance the required multiplication depth in FHE and the fine-tuning accuracy. For each training iteration, the following steps are involved: 1) the input features are first multiplied with the layer weights in the forward pass; 2) then the results are used to compute the loss gradients as with the formula described in Subsection 3.3 (multiplication-depth is 2 as we use degree-3 polynomial for Sigmoid); 3) and then the computed gradients are multiplied with the input features to get the gradients for the weights; 4) at last the weights are updated by subtracting the gradients multiplied with the learning rate. The total multiplication depth in one round of training iteration is 5. In our experiments, we will show that after fine-tuning the source model by 10 epochs, it already converges to optimal accuracy on the target data, therefore the total number of multiplicative depths in the whole fine-tuning process can be set to 50.

4.5 FHE Parameters Selection

We choose CKKS to be the underlying FHE scheme as it natively supports double-precision float-point numbers in neural network training. The CKKS scheme is governed by three major parameters, the ring dimension (polynomial modulus degree) N, the scaling factor Δ that controls the precision of the plaintext value, and the ciphertext coefficient modulus q that determines the largest multiplication depth D of a ciphertext. As with previous analysis, the whole fine-tuning process needs a multiplication depth of 50, and this requires q to have at least 52 prime factors[1]. We select the first and the last factors to be 50-bit primes, and all the intermediate factors to be 30-bit primes. As a result, the ciphertext coefficient modulus q is to be 1600 bits in total. On the other hand, we select the scaling factor Δ to be 2^{30}, and the rescaling operation after each multiplication can maintain the same scaling factor for the plaintext value in the ciphertext. The last step is to choose an appropriate ring dimension N for the encryption scheme. On the one hand, we need a large enough N to meet the required security level, and on the other hand, we need to keep N as small as possible for more efficient FHE computation. Following the recommendation of NIST [37], we set the security level to be at least 80 bits, and according to the parameter estimation equation given in [17], we need N to be 2^{16}.

5 Experiment Evaluation

5.1 Experiment Server Setup

We carry out the experiments on a server with an Intel Xeon Platinum 8170 CPU @ 2.10 GHz with 26 cores, and 188 GB RAM. The operating system is Arch Linux. The fault diagnosis model training and fine-tuning on clear (i.e., unencrypted) data is done using Pytorch at version 1.3.1, and for the secure fine-tuning process we use our PrivGD framework implemented on Microsoft SEAL FHE library version 3.4.5.

[1] For CKKS implementation in the SEAL library, the first prime is consumed in the encryption process, the last prime is used to accommodate the scaled plaintext value, and all the other primes in between are consumed one by one after each multiplication.

5.2 Experiment Results

We have 4000 data samples in each of the four vibration sensor datasets as described in Sect. 4.1, denoted as 0hp, 1hp, 2hp, and 3hp according to the machine operating conditions. For each of the datasets, we first train a complete model (including feature extractor and classifier) with Pytorch and the original Softmax using all the 4000 samples on the clear data, in which 3000 randomly chosen samples are used as training set and the rest are used as test set. In each training, we vary the Mini-Batch size and learning rate to maximize the classification accuracy on the test set. The best test accuracy we can get are 97.6%, 97.75%, 98.15%, 98.65% on the four datasets respectively. Pay attention to the fact that these are the *same-domain* accuracy where the trained models are applied to the data from the same operating condition. In the following transfer learning experiments, the models will be in turn set as the source model, and be applied to the data from the other operating conditions, the test accuracy will be *cross-domain* accuracy.

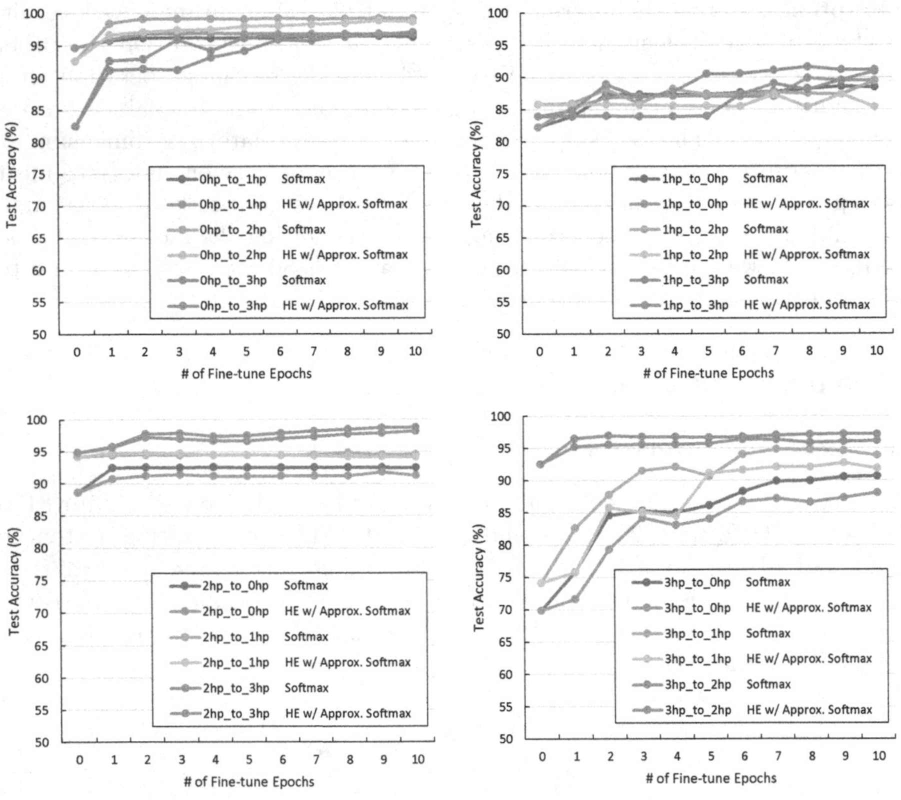

Fig. 2. Fine-tuned accuracy of transferred models on the target datasets.

For each transfer learning experiment, we select one operating condition as source domain, and the rest operating conditions as target domains. We separately fine-tune the source model on each of the target domains. For each fine-tuning process, we randomly choose 2000 samples from the target dataset and use Batch Gradient Descent to fine-tune the classifier of the source model, and another 1000 samples to test the accuracy of the fine-tuned model. Specifically, we implement two versions of the fine-tuning processes, one is the unencrypted version with Pytorch and the original Softmax function, and the other is the encrypted version with PrivGD and approximated Softmax. We also log down the test accuracy after 1 to 10 fine-tuning epochs respectively, as shown in Fig. 2.

We can see that, before fine-tuning (i.e., at fine-tune epoch #0), the model accuracy generally drops quite significantly on the target data, compared with the *same-domain* accuracy. The fine-tuning process can efficiently improve the accuracy of the source model on the target data, especially in the first few epochs. The fine-tuning accuracy converges to the optimal after around 8 epochs, and after that, the improvement becomes marginal. The fine-tuning improvements are not the same for different experiments, with the maximal improvement of 20% across all the experiments (70% to 90% in the 3hp_to_0hp case). On the other hand, the secure encrypted version achieves quite close accuracy to the unencrypted version, at most of the time the difference is within 3%.

5.3 Running Performances of Fine-Tuning with FHE

Memory Usage. A CKKS ciphertext is composed of two degree-N polynomials, with q to be the polynomial coefficient modulus. As with the parameters chosen in our experiments, we can estimate that each ciphertext is 25MB. We can further compute that the total number of ciphertexts for the inputs, weights and biases, and outputs of the classifier as shown in Fig. 1 is 372. Therefore, the total memory resource usage is about 9.1 GB.

Latency Performance. The total run time for the 10 epochs of fine-tuning is 3.85 h on our experiment server. Pay attention to the fact that the run time for each epoch gradually decreases with the number of epochs, where the first epoch takes the longest run time of 42.9 min, and the last epoch takes the shortest of 3.3 min. This is because the level of the ciphertexts is reduced by the *rescaling* operations along with the multiplication operations, which results in smaller coefficient modulus parameters and more efficient ciphertext operations.

6 Related Work

The major effort of our work is to apply transfer learning to the secure MLaaS scenario. In the convention of transfer learning, the feature extractor is usually considered as public and shared across different domains, while the domain-specific part of the model is trained or fine-tunned on domain-specific data. Several previous arts have demonstrated the applicability and efficiency of transfer learning with FHE-based secure MLaaS [3,6]. For example, In [3], the authors proposed the workflow that the user used a public feature extractor to extract features from medical images, and then encrypted the features with FHE and sent to cloud for private inference. Similar like [3] and [6], in our approach, we assume the MLaaS service provider makes the feature extractor public to all the users, and puts the classifier on the cloud for private inference. However, our work further demonstrates that, if the classifier of the service provider was previously trained with data in a different domain (ie, working condition) from the user data, it may not work well on the user data. Therefore, what our approach is different from [3] and [6] is that, we propose to use a small amount of encrypted user data to fine-tune the original classifier of the service provider, and the fine-tuned classifier can provide higher inference accuracy on the user data. Our approach not only applies to the machine fault diagnosis task in our paper, but in fact provides a general paradigm that can be applied to other MLaaS tasks in similar use scenarios.

Our work belongs to the category of secure neural network training on encrypted data with FHE. Due to the large performance gap compared with the clear data counterpart, there are very limited prior arts in this category and most of them focus on the simple task of logistic regression training [17,38]. In [17], the authors tried to train a binary classifier on the encrypted medical images. They targeted to train a complete model from scratch, which needs many training iterations and subsequently very larger encryption parameters. On the contrast, we demonstrate a more practical way of applying secure training with transfer learning for the real world applications. We show that by fine-tuning on existing models, it requires much fewer training epochs and smaller encryption parameters, although for more complicated multi-class classification tasks.

Another category of related work is the secure inference of neural networks. CryptoNets [2] was the first to implement a inference network with FHE, but limited to the MNIST dataset. FasterCryptoNets [3] was among the first to try deeper networks and larger datasets with FHE, but suffered from high resources overhead. E2DM [5] and LoLa [6] tried to employ the SIMD packing feature to optimize the performance and resource overhead of inference network with FHE. These work commonly used polynomials to approximate the ReLU activation function inside the networks. As they didn't handle the training phase, there was no need to approximate the last Sigmoid or Softmax layers for the classification models. On the other hand, MPC-based solutions, such as Gazelle [13] and XONN [10], were free from approximation of non-linear functions in networks, but required both server and client to be constantly online and suffered from high communication overhead between them.

7 Conclusion

In this paper, we propose a new secure MLaaS paradigm, in which the user uses his private data to fine-tune the model on the cloud for higher inference accuracy. We build up PrivGD, a secure neural network training framework with FHE, and implement the fine-tuning process with it. In particular, PrivGD is the first to support the approximation of Softmax to train multi-class classifiers in FHE. We have demonstrated the efficiency of our secure transfer learning approach on the machine fault diagnosis tasks and datasets. In the future, we plan to apply our framework and approach to more real-world tasks and datasets.

References

1. Peduzzi, P., Concato, J., Kemper, E., Holford, T.R., Feinstein, A.R.: A simulation study of the number of events per variable in logistic regression analysis. J. Clin. Epidemiol. **49**(12), 1373–1379 (1996)
2. Gilad-Bachrach, R., Dowlin, N., Laine, K., Lauter, K., Naehrig, M., Wernsing, J.: CryptoNets: applying neural networks to encrypted data with high throughput and accuracy. In: International Conference on Machine Learning, pp. 201–210 (2016)
3. Chou, E., Beal, J., Levy, D., Yeung, S., Haque, A., Fei-Fei, L.: Faster cryptonets: leveraging sparsity for real-world encrypted inference. arXiv preprint arXiv:1811.09953 (2018)
4. Al Badawi, A., et al.: The AlexNet moment for homomorphic encryption: HCNN, the first homomorphic CNN on encrypted data with GPUs. arXiv preprint arXiv:1811.00778 (2018)
5. Jiang, X., Kim, M., Lauter, K., Song, Y.: Secure outsourced matrix computation and application to neural networks. In: Proceedings of the 2018 ACM SIGSAC Conference on Computer and Communications Security, pp. 1209–1222 (2018)
6. Brutzkus, A., Elisha, O., Gilad-Bachrach, R.: Low latency privacy preserving inference. arXiv preprint arXiv:1812.10659 (2018)
7. Bourse, F., Minelli, M., Minihold, M., Paillier, P.: Fast homomorphic evaluation of deep discretized neural networks. In: Shacham, H., Boldyreva, A. (eds.) CRYPTO 2018. LNCS, vol. 10993, pp. 483–512. Springer, Cham (2018). https://doi.org/10.1007/978-3-319-96878-0_17
8. Hesamifard, E., Takabi, H., Ghasemi, M.: CryptoDL: deep neural networks over encrypted data. arXiv preprint arXiv:1711.05189 (2017)
9. Jin, C., et al.: CareNets: compact and resource-efficient CNN for homomorphic inference on encrypted medical images. arXiv preprint arXiv:1901.10074 (2019)
10. Sadegh Riazi, M., Samragh, M., Chen, H., Laine, K., Lauter, K., Koushanfar, F.: XONN: Xnor-based oblivious deep neural network inference. In: 28th USENIX Security Symposium (USENIX Security 2019), pp. 1501–1518 (2019)
11. Mishra, P., Lehmkuhl, R., Srinivasan, A., Zheng, W., Popa, R.A.: Delphi: a cryptographic inference service for neural networks. In: 29th USENIX Security Symposium (USENIX Security 20) (2020)
12. Liu, J., Juuti, M., Lu, Y., Asokan, N.: Oblivious neural network predictions via minionn transformations. In: Proceedings of the 2017 ACM SIGSAC Conference on Computer and Communications Security, pp. 619–631 (2017)
13. Juvekar, C., Vaikuntanathan, V., Chandrakasan, A.: GAZELLE: a low latency framework for secure neural network inference. In: 27th USENIX Security Symposium (USENIX Security 2018), pp. 1651–1669 (2018)
14. Gentry, C.: Fully homomorphic encryption using ideal lattices. In: Proceedings of the Forty-first Annual ACM Symposium on Theory of Computing, pp. 169–178 (2009)

15. Yao, A.C.-C.: How to generate and exchange secrets. In: 27th Annual Symposium on Foundations of Computer Science (SFCs 1986), pp. 162–167. IEEE (1986)
16. Goldreich, O., Micali, S., Wigderson, A.: How to play any mental game, or a completeness theorem for protocols with honest majority. In Proceedings of the Nineteenth ACM Symposium on Theory of Computing, STOC, pp. 218–229 (1987)
17. Kim, M., Song, Y., Wang, S., Xia, Y., Jiang, X.: Secure logistic regression based on homomorphic encryption: design and evaluation. JMIR Med. Inf. **6**(2), e19 (2018)
18. Smart, N.P., Vercauteren, F.: Fully homomorphic SIMD operations. Des. Codes Cryptogr. **71**(1), 57–81 (2014)
19. Rivest, R.L., Adleman, L., Dertouzos, M.L., et al.: On data banks and privacy homomorphisms. Found. Secure Comput. **4**(11), 169–180 (1978)
20. Brakerski, Z., Gentry, C., Vaikuntanathan, V.: (leveled) fully homomorphic encryption without bootstrapping. ACM Trans. Comput. Theory (TOCT) **6**(3), 1–36 (2014)
21. Fan, J., Vercauteren, F.: Somewhat practical fully homomorphic encryption. IACR Cryptology ePrint Archive 2012, 144 (2012)
22. Cheon, J.H., Kim, A., Kim, M., Song, Y.: Homomorphic encryption for arithmetic of approximate numbers. In: Takagi, T., Peyrin, T. (eds.) ASIACRYPT 2017. LNCS, vol. 10624, pp. 409–437. Springer, Cham (2017). https://doi.org/10.1007/978-3-319-70694-8_15
23. Brakerski, Z., Vaikuntanathan, V.: Fully homomorphic encryption from ring-LWE and security for key dependent messages. In: Rogaway, P. (ed.) CRYPTO 2011. LNCS, vol. 6841, pp. 505–524. Springer, Heidelberg (2011). https://doi.org/10.1007/978-3-642-22792-9_29
24. Pan, S.J., Yang, Q.: A survey on transfer learning. IEEE Trans. Knowl. Data Eng. **22**(10), 1345–1359 (2009)
25. Yosinski, J., Clune, J., Bengio, Y., Lipson, H.: How transferable are features in deep neural networks? In: Advances in Neural Information Processing Systems, pp. 3320–3328 (2014)
26. Yu, J., Jiang, J.: Learning sentence embeddings with auxiliary tasks for cross-domain sentiment classification. In: Proceedings of the 2016 Conference on Empirical Methods in Natural Language Processing, pp. 236–246 (2016)
27. Zhang, C., Bengio, S., Hardt, M., Recht, B., Vinyals, O.: Understanding deep learning requires rethinking generalization. arXiv preprint arXiv:1611.03530 (2016)
28. Rusu, A.A., Večerík, M., Rothörl, T., Heess, N., Pascanu, R., Hadsell, R.: Sim-to-real robot learning from pixels with progressive nets. In: Conference on Robot Learning, pp. 262–270 (2017)
29. Halevi, S., Shoup, V.: Algorithms in HElib. In: Garay, J.A., Gennaro, R. (eds.) CRYPTO 2014. LNCS, vol. 8616, pp. 554–571. Springer, Heidelberg (2014). https://doi.org/10.1007/978-3-662-44371-2_31
30. Thaine, P., Gorbunov, S., Penn, G.: Efficient evaluation of activation functions over encrypted data. In: 2019 IEEE Security and Privacy Workshops (SPW), pp. 57–63. IEEE (2019)
31. Titsias, M.: RC AUEB. One-vs-each approximation to softmax for scalable estimation of probabilities. In: Advances in Neural Information Processing Systems, pp. 4161–4169 (2016)
32. Basterretxea, K., Tarela, J.M., Del Campo, I.: Approximation of sigmoid function and the derivative for hardware implementation of artificial neurons. IEE Proc. Circuits, Devices Syst. **151**(1), 18–24 (2004)
33. Vlcek, M.: Chebyshev polynomial approximation for activation sigmoid function. Neural Netw. World **4**(12), 387–393 (2012)

34. Mohassel, P., Zhang, Y.: SecureML: a system for scalable privacy-preserving machine learning. In: 2017 IEEE Symposium on Security and Privacy (SP), pp. 19–38. IEEE (2017)
35. Case Western Reserve University Bearing Data Center. Motor bearing fault datasets. https://csegroups.case.edu/bearingdatacenter/home
36. Jiang, G.-Q., Xie, P., Wang, X., Chen, M., He, Q.: Intelligent fault diagnosis of rotary machinery based on unsupervised multiscale representation learning. Chin. J. Mech. Eng. **30**(6), 1314–1324 (2017)
37. Barker, E., Barker, W., Burr, W., Polk, W., Smid, M., et al.: Recommendation for key management: Part 1: General. National Institute of Standards and Technology, Technology Administration (2006)
38. Kim, A., Song, Y., Kim, M., Lee, K., Cheon, J.H.: Logistic regression model training based on the approximate homomorphic encryption. BMC Med. Genom. **11**(4), 83, (2018)

Private Decision Tree Evaluation with Constant Rounds via (Only) SS-3PC over Ring

Hikaru Tsuchida[1,2(✉)], Takashi Nishide[1], and Yusaku Maeda[3]

[1] University of Tsukuba, Tsukuba, Japan
s2030119@s.tsukuba.ac.jp, nishide@risk.tsukuba.ac.jp
[2] NEC Corporation, Tokyo, Japan
[3] The University of Tokyo, Tokyo, Japan
yusaku-maeda@g.ecc.u-tokyo.ac.jp

Abstract. Secure computation is the technology that computes an arbitrary function represented as a circuit without revealing input values. Typical technologies related to secure computation are secure multiparty computation (MPC) that uses secret sharing (SS) schemes, for example, SS-MPC, garbled circuit (GC), and homomorphic encryption (HE). These cryptographic technologies have a trade-off relationship with respect to the computation cost, communication cost, and type of computable circuit. Hence, the optimal choice depends on the computing resources, communication environment, and function related to applications. The private decision tree evaluation (PDTE) is one of important applications of secure computation. There exist several PDTE protocols with constant communication rounds that use GC, HE, and SS-MPC over the field. However, to the best of our knowledge, PDTE protocols with constant communication rounds that use SS-MPC over the ring (requiring only lower computation costs and communication complexity) is non-trivial and still missing. In this paper, we propose a PDTE protocol that uses a secure three-party computation (3PC) protocol over the ring with one corruption.

Keywords: Private decision tree evaluation · Secure multiparty computation · Constant-round protocol

1 Introduction

1.1 Backgrounds

Secure multiparty computation (MPC) [6,23,46] is the cryptographic technology that enables multiple parties to compute an arbitrary joint function represented as a circuit securely. MPC does not reveal each party's inputs during its execution even if an adversary corrupts a certain rate of parties. There are two types of adversaries in MPC protocols: *semi-honest adversary* and *malicious adversary*. The former follows the specifications of the protocol. However, it attempts to

K. Nguyen et al. (Eds.): ProvSec 2020, LNCS 12505, pp. 298–317, 2020.
https://doi.org/10.1007/978-3-030-62576-4_15

obtain as much information as possible. The latter does not follow the specifications, and also attempts to obtain as much information as possible about other parties' inputs. Therefore, the malicious adversary is stronger than the semi-honest one.

There are two types of typical MPC: *garbled circuit* (*GC*) [5,46] and *secret sharing based MPC* (*SS-MPC*) [6,23]. Most GC protocols compute an arbitrary function represented as a binary circuit among two parties by using encrypted truth tables (garbled tables) and oblivious transfer (OT) [1,35] that is a public key primitive. A GC protocol requires many communication bits and small and constant communication rounds.

In SS-MPC, each party distributes its inputs, and the computation proceeds with secret shares that look like random numbers among a number of parties. In the SS-MPC protocol, each party computes a function, which is represented as a binary, arithmetic, or mixed circuit (composed of binary and arithmetic circuits) by using shares locally and communicating among parties. The SS-MPC protocol requires small communication bits and many communication rounds. There are two types of SS-MPC: *SS-MPC over the field* and *SS-MPC over the ring*. The two schemes differ in the mathematical structure they use.

The former [6,11] uses a finite field. SS-MPC over the field can compute an arbitrary function represented as an arithmetic circuit. It can construct constant-round protocols by using the multiplicative inverse. However, it requires modulo operations with a large prime number. Therefore, the computational cost of SS-MPC over the field is heavier than SS-MPC over the ring.

The latter uses a residue ring (e.g., power-of-two ring). In particular, the secure three-party computation protocol (3PC) over the ring [3] and four-party computation protocol over the ring [9,38] have gained attention in recent years because they can perform high throughput even when they compute a complex function represented as mixed circuits. SS-MPC on the power-of-two ring benefits from not only a small communication complexity but also a small computation cost because there is no need to perform a modulo operation explicitly if it uses a power-of-two ring that equals the size of the data type. However, SS-MPC over the ring cannot easily construct the constant-round protocol due to a lack of the multiplicative inverse.

In addition, *homomorphic encryption* (*HE*) [16,21,22,24,37,39] computes the function represented as an arithmetic circuit without revealing input values, which is different from MPC. Although HE does not require communications during computation, it requires a large computation cost.

As mentioned above, GC, SS-MPC, and HE have a trade-off relationship with respect to the computation cost, communication cost, and type of computable circuit. Hence, the optimal choice depends on the computing resources, communication environment, and function related to applications. To mitigate this problem, a hybrid scheme of GC and SS-MPC [17,34,38] and that of GC and HE [25] were proposed and studied. In particular, to mitigate the communication cost problem, the offline-online paradigm is also widely known. It divides the MPC protocol into an offline phase (where the protocol processes part of computation that can be computed independently of parties' inputs) and online phase (where the protocol processes the rest of computation with parties' inputs). The offline-online paradigm can reduce the communication cost of the online phase even if it increases the communication cost of the offline phase and the whole computation. Therefore, the offline-online paradigm is useful for MPC applications that focus on the response time of queries.

One typical applications of secure computation (e.g., GC, SS-MPC, and HE) that has gained attention in recent years is the private decision tree evaluation (PDTE). A decision tree is a commonly-used tool of decision support and widely studied in machine learning. The PDTE protocol outputs the (encrypted) class label assigned to the leaf node as the correct classification result without revealing confidential (or sensitive) information about the tree (e.g., decision threshold values assigned to the internal node, comparison operations assigned to the internal node, or class label assigned to the leaf node) and the input feature vector. For example, there are several applications of the PDTE: electrocardiogram classification [4,8], and remote diagnosis [8]. Araki et al. [2] conducted an experiment about the private evaluation of a decision tree for credit decisions using 3PC over the ring.

Kiss et al. [29] published a systematization of knowledge paper about the PDTE. In [29], the PDTE is divided into three phases: *feature selection*, *comparison*, and *path evaluation*. In the feature selection phase, a feature is selected from the input feature vector without revealing the values of the input feature vector, value of the selected feature, or index. In the comparison phase, the selected feature is compared with the threshold value without revealing the selected feature, threshold value, or comparison result. In the path evaluation phase, the classification result is outputted without revealing the comparison results. In [29], Kiss et al. focused on a constant-round protocol by using GC, HE, and a hybrid scheme of GC and SS-MPC, but did not mention the constant-round protocol using only the SS-MPC.

SS-MPC over the field can provide constant-round equality-testing, less-than, and k-ary OR[1] (AND) protocols [11]. Thus, we can easily obtain a constant-round (but somewhat less efficient) protocol for the PDTE. However, it is non-trivial to construct the PDTE protocol with constant rounds using only SS-MPC over the ring. For example, Cock et al. proposed a PDTE protocol using only the SS-MPC over the ring in [13]. However, the round complexity of their protocol is proportional to the height of the tree and the bit length of the ring.

If we use GC, HE, or SS-MPC over the field, it is trivial to construct a constant-round PDTE protocol. However, these techniques are less efficient regarding the communication complexity and computation cost than SS-MPC over the ring. On the other hand, it is non-trivial to construct the PDTE protocol with constant rounds using only SS-MPC over the ring. Therefore, the PDTE protocol with SS-MPC over the ring has a larger round complexity. Thus, we ask the following: Could we construct the constant-round PDTE protocol with constant rounds using only SS-MPC over the ring (e.g., the 3PC that is based on the secret sharing scheme over the ring)?

[1] This computes $\bigvee_{i=1}^{k} x_i$ where $x_i \in \{0, 1\}$.

1.2 Our Results

We propose a PDTE protocol with constant rounds using the semi-honest 3PC with single corruption. We propose an efficient constant-round protocol over the ring in each phase as follows.

1. We propose a more efficient most significant bit (MSB) extraction protocol with constant rounds than SecureNN [42]. Our scheme is used to construct the constant-round less-than protocol and the constant-round equality-testing protocol. Hence, our scheme can compute the process in the comparison phase with constant rounds efficiently.
2. We propose a more efficient oblivious array read (OAR) protocol over the ring than existing ones [7]. Our scheme can compute the process in the feature selection phase with constant rounds efficiently.
3. We propose a path evaluation protocol with constant rounds. To the best of our knowledge, this is the first constant-round path evaluation protocol over the ring.
4. We propose a PDTE protocol with constant rounds over the ring using the above contributions. To the best of our knowledge, this is the first PDTE protocol proposed with constant rounds over the ring without GC, HE, or OT (i.e., without public key primitives). Our scheme is based on a 3PC over the ring that has efficient communication complexity and computation cost. Therefore, our scheme can be performed efficiently even if the communication environment has a large latency and limited communication bandwidth.

Table 1 shows the theoretical performance comparison of MSB extraction protocol between SecureNN [42] and our scheme. Let L be an even number. The MSB extraction protocol in SecureNN [42] takes the shares over the odd ring $\mathbb{Z}_{L-1}$ as inputs and outputs the shares over the even ring $\mathbb{Z}_L$. However, SS-MPC over the ring often uses the power-of-two ring (i.e., the even ring) for computational efficiency. Hence, we should compare the performance of our scheme with the combination of a share conversion protocol that converts the shares on $\mathbb{Z}_L$ to the shares on $\mathbb{Z}_{L-1}$ and the MSB extraction protocol. The protocol combining the share conversion and MSB extraction protocols in SecureNN [42] requires 9 rounds through the overall computation. On the other hand, our scheme (that takes the shares on $\mathbb{Z}_{2^k}$ as inputs and outputs the shares on $\mathbb{Z}_2$) requires 7 rounds in the online phase and 8 rounds in the online + offline phase. If we use the bit conversion protocol [34] and convert the output the shares of our scheme to the shares on $\mathbb{Z}_{2^k}$, the number of rounds in the online phase is fewer than those of SecureNN. Therefore, our scheme is superior to SecureNN with respect to round complexity.

Table 2 shows the theoretical performance comparison of the OAR protocol between our schemes and the existing schemes [7]. The OAR protocol takes the shared array elements and shared index value as inputs and outputs the shared array element corresponding to the index value. Existing schemes [7] take the shares of the index value on $\mathbb{Z}_m$ (where m is the length of the array) or shares of Shamir's secret sharing as input. However, we note that the share of the index value may not always be on $\mathbb{Z}_m$ as it depends on the preceding and subsequent processes of the computation. In the context of the PDTE, both shares of the index value and array elements may be over the same residue ring if the secure computing methods (GC, HE, or SS-MPC) are used for not only evaluation but also constructing the decision tree. Hence, the OAR protocol is required to be a constant-round protocol even if both shares of the index value and array elements are over the same residue ring. However, it is not clear whether the existing schemes [7] are constant-round protocols or not even if both shares of the index value and array elements are on the same residue ring because most share conversion methods over the ring require many rounds. On the other hand, our scheme over the ring (Protocol 3) is a constant-round protocol even if both shares of the index value and array elements are over the same residue ring $\mathbb{Z}_{2^k}$.

Tables 3 and 4 show the theoretical performance comparison of the PDTE protocol between our schemes and naive constructions. The naive construction over the ring (Protocol 9) and [13] are not a constant-round protocol, but our scheme over the ring (Protocol 8) is.

Table 1. Comparison of communication complexity of secure three-party MSB extraction protocol between existing protocol and ours (k: bit length of ring, $L(=2^k)$: modulus of ring, p': smallest prime number greater than k, $(2,2)$-ASS: 2-out-of-2 additive secret sharing scheme, $(2,3)$-RSS: 2-out-of-3 replicated secret sharing scheme)

	Input Share	Output Share	Offline		Online	
			Rounds	Comm. [bits/all parties]	Rounds	Comm. [bits/all parties]
Naive MSB Extraction (using bit-decomposition protocol of ABY3 [34])	(2,3)-RSS on $\mathbb{Z}_{2^k}$	(2,3)-RSS on $\mathbb{Z}_2$	-	-	$1+\log_2(k)$	$3k$
SecureNN [42] (MSB Extraction)	(2,2)-ASS on $\mathbb{Z}_{L-1}$	(2,2)-ASS on $\mathbb{Z}_L$	-	-	5	$4k\log_2(p')+13k$
SecureNN [42] (Share Convert + MSB Extraction)	(2,2)-ASS on $\mathbb{Z}_L$	(2,2)-ASS on $\mathbb{Z}_L$	-	-	9	$8k\log_2(p')+19k$
This Work (Protocol 1)	(2,3)-RSS on $\mathbb{Z}_{2^k}$	(2,3)-RSS on $\mathbb{Z}_2$	1	$6k(k-1)$	7	$11k+3(k-1)\log_2(p')+4$
This Work (Protocol 1) + Bit Conversion of ABY3 [34]	(2,3)-RSS on $\mathbb{Z}_{2^k}$	(2,3)-RSS on $\mathbb{Z}_{2^k}$	1	$6k(k-1)$	8	$17k+3(k-1)\log_2(p')+4$

Table 2. Comparison of communication complexity of oblivious array read protocol between existing protocols and ours (m: length of array, k: bit length of ring, p: prime number, p': smallest prime number greater than k, n: number of parties, $t(< n/2)$: number of corrupted parties, $(t+1,n)$-ASS: $(t+1)$-out-of-n additive secret sharing scheme, $(t+1,n)$-SSS: $(t+1)$-out-of-n Shamir's secret sharing scheme, $(t+1,n)$-RSS: $(t+1)$-out-of-n replicated secret sharing scheme)

	Share of Input and Output Array Element	Share of Input Index	Rounds	Comm. [bits/all parties]
[30]	(t + 1,n)-SSS on $\mathbb{F}_p$	(t + 1,n)-SSS on $\mathbb{F}_p$	$m+3$	$(m+3)n(n+1)\log_2(p)$
Custom Three-party Construction over ring [7]	(2,2)-ASS on $\mathbb{Z}_{2^k}$	(3,3)-ASS on $\mathbb{Z}_m$	2	$4mk$
Custom Three-party Construction over field [7]	(2,2)-ASS on $\mathbb{F}_p$	(2,3)-SSS on $\mathbb{F}_p$	12	$(7m+5\log(m)+6)\log(p)$
General Construction (with Constant Rounds) [7]	$(t+1,n)$-SSS on $\mathbb{F}_p$	$(t+1,n)$-SSS on $\mathbb{F}_p$	5	$(4m\log_2(\log_2(m))+\log_2(m)+2)n(n-1)\log_2(p)$
This Work over Ring (Protocol 3)	(2,3)-RSS on $\mathbb{Z}_{2^k}$	(2,3)-RSS on $\mathbb{Z}_{2^k}$	13	$\log_2(m)(6k^2+9k+(3k-3)\log_2(p')+6m+4)+4mk+2m+3k$

1.3 Related Work

Feature Selection Protocol (Oblivious Array Read Protocol). There are two types of OAR protocol: *circuit-based approach using general MPC* [28,30–32] and *oblivious random access machine* (*ORAM*) [18,20,27,43,44,47]. Blanton et al. [7] proposed the OAR (and write) protocol with constant rounds. They demonstrated through their experiments that their scheme is superior to state-of-the-art schemes of the former [31] and the latter [18]. Therefore, to the best of our knowledge, the OAR protocols in [7] are the latest and most efficient protocol with constant rounds.

Table 3. Comparison of total communication complexity between naive PDTE protocols and ours (m: number of features, k: bit length of ring, p': smallest prime number greater than k, h: height of tree)

	Total	
	Rounds	Comm. [bits/all parties]
Naive Construction over ring (Protocol 9)	$\log_2(m) + 2\log_2(k) + \log_2(h) + 9$	$(2^h - 1) \cdot (3\log_2(m)\log_2(k) + 6k\log_2(k) + 6m\log_2(m) + 4mk$ $+5m + 17k + 3) + 2^h \cdot (3h + 6k - 3) + 3k$
[13]	$h + \log_2(k) + 5$	$(2^h - 1) \cdot (10m\log_2(m) + 30k - 10\log_2(k) - 20) + 2^h \cdot 10hk$
This Work over Ring (Protocol 8)	28	$(2^h - 1) \cdot (\log_2(m)(6k^2 + 9k + (3k - 3)\log_2(p') + 4)$ $+6m\log_2(m) + 4mk + 2m + 18k^2 + 35k + (9k - 9)\log_2(p') + 22)$

Table 4. Comparison of communication complexity between naive PDTE protocols and ours (m: number of features, k: bit length of ring, p': smallest prime number greater than k, h: height of tree)

	Feature Selection		Comparison		Path Evaluation	
	Rounds	Comm. [bits/all parties]	Rounds	Comm. [bits/all parties]	Rounds	Comm. [bits/all parties]
Naive Construction over Ring (Protocol 9)	$\log_2(m) + 5$	$(2^h - 1) \cdot (3\log_2(m)\log_2(k)$ $+6m\log_2(m) + 4mk + 5m + 8k)$	$2\log_2(k) + 2$	$(2^h - 1) \cdot (6k\log_2(k) + 9k + 3)$	$\log_2(h) + 2$	$2^h \cdot (3(h - 1) + 6k) + 3k$
[13]	2	$(2^h - 1) \cdot 10m\log_2(m)$	$\log_2(k) + 2$	$(2^h - 1) \cdot (30k - 10\log_2(k) - 220$	$h + 1$	$2^h \cdot 10hk$
This Work over Ring (Protocol 8)	13	$(2^h - 1) \cdot (\log_2(m)(6k^2 + 9k$ $+(3k - 3)\log_2(p') + 4)$ $+6m\log_2(m) + 4mk + 2m + 8k)$	11	$(2^h - 1) \cdot (18k^2 + 27k$ $+(9k - 9)\log_2(p') + 22)$	4	$2^h \cdot (6k + 9h)$

Comparison Protocol. In [14,15,19,36], efficient comparison protocols are proposed. However, these schemes compute the less-than circuit and are not constant-rounds protocols. ABY [17] and ABY3 [34] can construct a constant-round comparison protocol over the ring by using GC. However, the constant-round comparison protocol using *only* SS-MPC over the ring is not proposed in [17,34]. To the best of our knowledge, the SecureNN [42] is the only 3PC based on the secret sharing scheme (SS-3PC) including the MSB extraction protocol with constant rounds over the ring[2]. We note that SecureNN [42] did not propose a constant-round equality testing protocol.

[2] In the conference version of FLASH [9], Byali et al. proposed a constant-round MSB extraction protocol over the ring. However, the flaw was found and fixed in the preprint version uploaded to the ePrint server. The MSB extraction protocol of Trident [38] used the same approach as FLASH and had the same flaw. As a result, the MSB extraction protocols of FLASH and Trident are not constant-round protocols.

Path Evaluation Protocol (k-ary AND/OR Protocol). The path evaluation protocol outputs the shares of class labels assigned to the leaf node where the comparison result bits regarding the internal nodes included in its path are all 1. That is, it is easy to construct the path evaluation protocol if the k-ary AND/OR protocol exists.

Catrina and Hoogh [11] proposed a constant-round k-ary OR protocol over the field. Ohata and Nuida [36] proposed an efficient k-ary AND protocol (i.e., multi-fan-in multiplication/AND protocol) over the ring. However, their protocol is not a constant-round protocol. To the best of our knowledge, there is no constant-round k-ary AND protocol over the ring. Therefore, it is still non-trivial to construct a constant-round path evaluation protocol over the ring.

Private Decision Tree Evaluation Protocol. There are many constructions of the PDTE protocol including those based on HE [40,45] and GC+HE [4,8]. Kiss et al. published [29] a systematization of knowledge paper that mainly focused on the constant-round constructions based on GC or HE. On the other hand, constructions of the PDTE protocol based on ORAM are proposed in [26,41]. However, these constructions are not constant-round protocols.

Cock et al. [13] proposed an efficient PDTE protocol over the ring in commodity-based two-party computation. However, in their protocol, each party must clearly know the features and threshold values or has the shares of the binary representation of these values. The protocol of Cock et al. uses only the greater-than-equal protocol in comparison phase, not equality-testing protocol. In their protocol, the outputs must be clear plain values or the shares of the binary representation of the class label. Furthermore, their private decision tree protocol in [13] is not a constant-round protocol. Hence, to the best of our knowledge, there is no PDTE protocol with constant rounds over the ring using only SS-MPC.

2 Preliminaries

2.1 Notations

Let $\mathbb{Z}_2$, $\mathbb{Z}_{2^k}$, $\mathbb{Z}_p(=\mathbb{F}_p$, where p is prime) and $\mathbb{Z}_{p'}(=\mathbb{F}_{p'}$, where p' is the smallest prime larger than k) be the residue rings modulo 2, 2^k, p or p'. We denote the exclusive OR (XOR) operator and AND operator by $\oplus$ and $\cdot$, respectively. We also use $\cdot$ as the multiplication operator on $\mathbb{Z}_L$ where $L = 2,\ 2^k, p$ or p'. Let P_i be the i-th party ($i = 0,\ 1,\ 2$). The security parameter is denoted by λ. The λ-bit string is $\{0,1\}^\lambda$. We use the (cryptographically secure) pseudo-random functions $F_L : \{0,1\}^\lambda \times \{0,1\}^\lambda \rightarrow \mathbb{Z}_L$ where $L = 2,\ 2^k, p$ or p'.

Let $a|_j \in \mathbb{Z}_2$ be j-th bit of $a \in \mathbb{Z}_{2^k}$. We also denote by $a|_{j,\ldots,i} \in \mathbb{Z}_{2^k}$ the part of bit strings of $a \in \mathbb{Z}_{2^k}$ from $j(\geq i)$-th bit to i-th bit. Let $\mathsf{msb}(a)$ be the MSB of a. For example, if $a = 100_{(2)} = 4 \in \mathbb{Z}_{2^3}$, we have that $a|_0 = 0$, $a|_1 = 0$, $a|_2 = \mathsf{msb}(a) = 1$ and $a|_{1,\ldots,0} = 00_{(2)} = 0$.

2.2 2-Out-of-3 Replicated Secret Sharing Scheme ((2,3)-RSS) and 2-Out-of-2 Additive Secret Sharing Scheme ((2,2)-ASS)

We denote the (2,3)-RSS shares of x on $\mathbb{Z}_L$ ($L = 2,\ 2^k,\ p,\ p'$) by $[x]_L = ([x]_{L,0},\ [x]_{L,1},\ [x]_{L,2})$ where $x \in \mathbb{Z}_L$. P_i has the share of x, $[x]_{L,i} = (x_i,\ x_{i+1})$ where $x = x_0 + x_1 + x_2 \mod L$ ($x_i \in \mathbb{Z}_L,\ i = 0, 1, 2$) and $x_{2+1} = x_0$. We also denote the (2,2)-ASS shares of x on $\mathbb{Z}_L$ by $\langle x\rangle_{L,(i,j)} = (\langle x\rangle_{L,i}, \langle x\rangle_{L,j})$. P_i and P_j have the share of x, $\langle x\rangle_{L,i} = x_i$ and $\langle x\rangle_{L,j} = x_j$ where $x = x_i + x_j \mod L$ ($x_i \in \mathbb{Z}_L,\ i, j \in \{0, 1, 2\}$ $(i \neq j)$), respectively. In particular, we assume $0 \leq x \leq 2^{k-1} - 1$ if we use $[x]_{2^k}$ or $\langle x\rangle_{2^k}$.

2.3 Secure Three-Party Computation with One Corruption over Ring

We use the same addition and multiplication of shares as [3] denoted as $[x]_L + [y]_L$ and $[x]_L \cdot [y]_L$, respectively. We also use the same scalar addition and multiplication of shares as [3] denoted as $c + [x]_L$ and $c \cdot [x]_L$ where $c \in \mathbb{Z}_L$, respectively. We use the same notation for operations of scalars and one of the shares to keep the description simple.

We also note that P_i has the pair of shared keys $(\mathsf{k}_i, \mathsf{k}_{i+1})$ where $\mathsf{k}_i \in \{0,1\}^\lambda$ and $\mathsf{k}_{2+1} = \mathsf{k}_0$.

2.4 Structure of Decision Tree

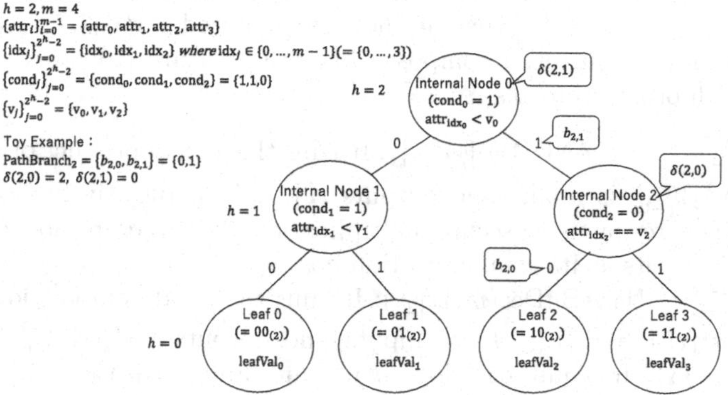

Fig. 1. Toy example of decision tree structure

Let $\{\mathsf{attr}_i\}_{i=0}^{m-1}$ ($\mathsf{attr}_i \in \mathbb{Z}_{2^k}$) be an input array as the feature vector. Its length is m. We assume that attr_i is the i-th attribute.

The tree is assumed to be a complete binary tree. We set $\mathcal{T} = (h, \delta, \{\mathsf{idx}_j\}_{j=0}^{2^h-2}, \{\mathsf{v}_j\}_{j=0}^{2^h-2}, \{\mathsf{cond}_j\}_{j=0}^{2^h-2}, \{\mathsf{leafVal}_{j'}\}_{j'=0}^{2^h-1})$ as a complete binary tree. Let h be the height of the tree. We denote the set of the index value idx_j by

$\{\mathsf{idx}_j\}_{j=0}^{2^h-2}$. The $j(=0,\ldots,2^h-2)$-th index value $\mathsf{idx}_j \in \mathbb{Z}_m$ is used to select the idx_j-th attribute for comparison at the j-th internal node. Let $\{\mathsf{v}_j\}_{j=0}^{2^h-2}$ be the set of the decision threshold value. We assume $\mathsf{v}_j \in \mathbb{Z}_{2^k}$ to be the threshold value assigned to the j-th internal node. Let $\{\mathsf{cond}_j\}_{j=0}^{2^h-2}$ be the set of the conditional bits to select which comparison operations (less-than ($<$) or equality-testing ($==$)) to perform. If $\mathsf{cond}_j = 0$, it checks whether $\mathsf{attr}_{\mathsf{idx}_j} < \mathsf{v}_j$. If $\mathsf{cond}_j = 1$, it checks whether $\mathsf{attr}_{\mathsf{idx}_j} == \mathsf{v}_j$.

If the comparison result is true (i.e., 1), the next step is to judge the right child node. If the comparison result is false (i.e., 0), the next step is to judge the left child node. That is, 1 or 0 is assigned to each branch.

Each $j'(\in \{0,1,\ldots,2^h-1\})$-th leaf node has the class label value $\mathsf{leafVal}_{j'} \in \mathbb{Z}_{2^k}$. Let $\{\mathsf{leafVal}_{j'}\}_{j'=0}^{2^h-1}$ be a set of class label values assigned to leaf nodes. Also, let $\mathsf{PathBranch}_{j'} = \{b_{j',\ell}\}_{\ell=0}^{h-1}$ (where $b_{j',\ell} \in \{0,1\}$) be a set of paths to the leaf nodes. We denote the bit assigned to the branch at the height ℓ in the path to the j'-th leaf node by $b_{j',\ell}$. Let $\delta : \{0,\ldots,2^h-1\} \times \{0,\ldots,h-1\} \to \{0,\ldots,2^h-2\}$ be the map function that takes j' (i.e., the position of the leaf node) and the height ℓ as inputs and outputs the position of the corresponding internal node. Figure 1 shows the toy example of the complete binary tree where $h = 2$ and $m = 4$.

2.5 Building Blocks of Three-Party Computation Protocol over Ring

The following building blocks have perfect security with computational indistinguishability in the presence of one semi-honest corrupted party [3,7,12,33,34,42]. These protocols are universal composability (UC) secure [10], so they can be combined with other protocols.

- $[\bigwedge_{j=0}^{h-1} b_j]_2 \leftarrow \mathsf{rArrayAND}(\{[b_j]_2\}_{j=0}^{h-1})$: It runs the logical product of h bits and takes $\{[b_j]_2\}_{j=0}^{h-1}$ as inputs and outputs $[\prod_{j=0}^{h-1} b_j]_2$. Intuitively, it computes $h-1$ AND gates by using secure multiplication [3]. It requires $\log_2(h)$ rounds and $3(h-1)$ bits as its communication cost.
- $\{[x|_j]_2\}_{j=0}^{m-1} \leftarrow \mathsf{NaiveBitDec}(m, [x]_{2^k})$: It runs the bit-decomposition protocol and takes $[x]_{2^k}$ and $m(\leq k)$ as inputs and outputs $\{[x|_j]_2\}_{j=0}^{m-1}$. For more details, see [34]. It requires $1+\log_2(m)$ rounds and $3m + 3\log_2(m)$ bits as its communication cost.
- $[x]_{2^k} \leftarrow \mathsf{BitConversion}([x]_2)$: It runs the bit conversion protocol and takes $[x]_2$ (where $x \in \mathbb{Z}_2$) as input and outputs $[x]_{2^k}$. For more details, see [34]. It requires 1 round and $6k$ bits as its communication cost.
- $[b]_2 \leftarrow \mathsf{NaiveRingLT}([x]_{2^k}, [y]_{2^k})$: It runs the less-than protocol and takes $[x]_{2^k}$ and $[y]_{2^k}$ as inputs and outputs $[b]_2$ (where $b = 1$ iff $x < y$ and $b = 0$ otherwise). Intuitively, it runs $\{[(x-y)|_j]_2\}_{j=0}^{k-1} \leftarrow \mathsf{NaiveBitDec}(k, [x-y]_{2^k}$ internally. Then, it outputs $[b]_2 = [\mathsf{msb}(x-y)]_2$. It requires $1+\log_2(k)$ rounds and $3k + 3\log_2(k)$ bits as its communication cost.

- $[b]_2 \leftarrow \mathsf{NaiveRingEQ}([x]_{2^k}, [y]_{2^k})$: It runs the equality testing protocol and takes $[x]_{2^k}$ and $[y]_{2^k}$ as inputs and outputs $[b]_2$ (where $b = 1$ iff $x = y$ and $b = 0$ otherwise). Intuitively, it runs $\{[(x-y)|_j]_2\}_{j=0}^{k-1} \leftarrow \mathsf{NaiveBitDec}(k, [x - y]_{2^k})$ internally. Then, it runs $[b]_2 \leftarrow \mathsf{rArrayAND}(\{[(x-y)|_j]_2 \oplus 1\}_{j=0}^{k-1})$ and outputs $[b]_2$. It requires $1 + 2\log_2(k)$ rounds and $6k + 3k\log_2(k) - 3$ bits as its communication cost.
- $[\sum_{j=0}^{h-1} x_j \cdot y_j]_{2^k} \leftarrow \mathsf{rInnerProduct}(\{[x_j]_{2^k}\}_{j=0}^{h-1}, \{[y_j]_{2^k}\}_{j=0}^{h-1})$: It runs the inner-product protocol and takes $\{[x_j]_{2^k}\}_{j=0}^{h-1}$ and $\{[y_j]_{2^k}\}_{j=0}^{h-1}$ as inputs and outputs $[\sum_{j=0}^{h-1} x_j \cdot y_j]_{2^k}$. For more details, see [3]. It requires 1 round and $3k$ bits as its communication cost.
- $[r]_{L,i} \leftarrow \mathsf{RndGen}(L, \mathsf{k}_i, \mathsf{k}_{i+1})$: It generates the share of a random value on $\mathbb{Z}_L$. It is called by each P_i using pseudo-random function F_L and the pair of shared keys $(\mathsf{k}_i, \mathsf{k}_{i+1})$. For more details, see [3]. It requires no communication cost.
- $[x]_L \leftarrow \mathsf{rShare}(L, P_i, x)$: It runs the input sharing protocol and takes the modulus L, the input dealer P_i and the input value x as inputs and outputs $[x]_L$. For more details, see [3]. It requires 1 round and $4\log_2(L)$ bits as its communication cost.
- $x \leftarrow \mathsf{rOpen}(P_i, [x]_{2^k})$: It runs the opening protocol and takes the receiver P_i and the share $[x]_{2^k}$ as inputs and outputs x. For more details, see [3]. It requires 1 round and $\log_2(L)$ bits as its communication cost.
- $\langle x\rangle_{L,(i,i+1)} \leftarrow \mathsf{aShare}(P_{i+2}, L, x, P_i, P_{i+1})$: It runs the input sharing protocol and takes the input dealer P_{i+2}, the modulus L, the input value x and the receivers P_i and P_{i+1} as inputs and outputs $\langle x\rangle_{L,(i,i+1)}$. It requires 1 round and $2\log_2(L)$ bits as its communication cost.
- $[x_a]_{2^k} \leftarrow \mathsf{rArrayRead}(\{[x_j]_{2^k}\}_{j=0}^{m-1}, [a]_m)$: It runs the OAR protocol and takes the shared array $\{[x_j]_{2^k}\}_{j=0}^{m-1}$ and the shared index $[a]_m$ as inputs and outputs $[x_a]_{2^k}$. First, P_0 and P_1 generate $\{\langle x_j\rangle_{2^k,(0,1)}\}_{j=0}^{m-1}$ from $\{[x_j]_{2^k}\}_{j=0}^{m-1}$ by setting $\langle x_j\rangle_{2^k,0} = x_{j,0} + x_{j,1} \mod 2^k$ for P_0 and $\langle x_j\rangle_{2^k,1} = x_{j,2}$ for P_1 where $[x_j]_{2^k,0} = (x_{j,0}, x_{j,1})$ and $[x_j]_{2^k,1} = (x_{j,1}, x_{j,2})$. Each party generates the (2, 2)-ASS share of an index from $[a]_m$. Then, each party runs the OAR protocol of the custom three-party construction [7] and obtains $\langle x_a\rangle_{2^k,(0,2)}$. Next, P_0 and P_2 run $[\langle x_a\rangle_{2^k,0}]_{2^k} \leftarrow \mathsf{rShare}(2^k, P_0, \langle x_a\rangle_{2^k,0})$ and $[\langle x_a\rangle_{2^k,2}]_{2^k} \leftarrow \mathsf{rShare}(2^k, P_2, \langle x_a\rangle_{2^k,2})$, respectively. Finally, it outputs $[x_a]_{2^k} = [\langle x_a\rangle_{2^k,0}]_{2^k} + [\langle x_a\rangle_{2^k,2}]_{2^k}$. It requires 3 rounds and $4mk + 2m + 8k$ bits as its communication cost.
- $b \leftarrow \mathsf{PrivateCompare}(x, \{\langle a|_j\rangle_{p',(0,1)}\}_{j=0}^{k-1}, \beta, \{s_j\}_{j=0}^{k-1}, \{u_j\}_{j=0}^{k-1}, P_2)$: This is the private compare protocol [42] and takes the value $x (\in \mathbb{Z}_{2^k})$ known to P_0 and P_1, the shares of binary values $\{\langle a|_j\rangle_{p',(0,1)}\}_{j=0}^{k-1}$ ($a|_j \in \mathbb{Z}_2$), the random bit (known to P_0 and P_1) β, the random values (known to P_0 and P_1) $\{s_j\}_{j=0}^{k-1}$ and $\{u_j\}_{j=0}^{k-1}$ (where $s_j, u_j \in \mathbb{F}_{p'}^*$) and the receiver P_2 as inputs and outputs the masked comparison result bit $b = \beta \oplus (a > x)$ to P_2. It takes 1 round and $2k\log_2(p')$ bits as its communication cost.

- $\{\mathcal{R}_{\sigma(j)}\}_{j=0}^{m-1} \leftarrow \mathsf{rSetShuffle}(\{\mathcal{R}_j\}_{j=0}^{m-1})$: It runs the oblivious shuffle protocol for the multidimensional shared array. Let $\mathcal{R}_j = \{[v_j]_{2^k}, [c_{j,0}]_2, \ldots, [c_{j,h-1}]_2\}$ be the set of shares and S_m be the set of all permutation $\sigma : \{0, \ldots, m-1\} \rightarrow \{0, \ldots, m-1\}$. It takes the set of shares $\{\mathcal{R}_j\}_{j=0}^{m-1}$ as inputs and outputs $\{\mathcal{R}_{\sigma(j)}\}_{j=0}^{m-1} = \{[v_{\sigma(j)}]_{2^k}, [c_{\sigma(j),0}]_2, \ldots, [c_{\sigma(j),h-1}]_2\}$ while no one knows σ. Intuitively, it runs the oblivious shuffle protocol for (single) shared array [12,33] in parallel. It requires 3 rounds and $6m(k+h)$ bits as its communication cost.

3 Proposed Protocol in Feature Selection Phase

In the feature selection phase, our protocol takes the share of the index $[\mathsf{idx}]_{2^k}$ (where $0 \leq \mathsf{idx} \leq m-1$) and the set of shared attributes $\{[\mathsf{attr}_j]_{2^k}\}_{j=0}^{m-1}$ as inputs and outputs $[\mathsf{attr}_{\mathsf{idx}}]_{2^k}$. To construct our feature selection protocol (Protocol 3), we propose a subprotocol, the bit-decomposition protocol (Protocol 2) that takes the bit length m and the shares $[x]_{2^k}$ as inputs and outputs the binary shares $\{[x|_j]\}_{j=0}^{m-1}$ of m bits. To construct the subprotocol, we also propose the MSB extraction protocol (Protocol 1). Therefore, we will explain, Protocols 1, 2 and 3.

Protocol 1. $[\mathsf{msb}(a)]_2 \leftarrow \pi_{\mathsf{msbExt}}([a]_{2^k})$

Input: $[a]_{2^k}$ s.t. $a \in \mathbb{Z}_{2^k}, a = \sum_{j=0}^{k-1} 2^j \cdot a|_j$
Output: $[\mathsf{msb}(a)]_2 (= [a|_{k-1}]_2)$

(Offline phase)
for $j = 0, \ldots, k-1$ **do in parallel**
  Each P_i runs $[r|_j]_{2,i} \leftarrow \mathsf{RndGen}(2, \mathsf{k}_i, \mathsf{k}_{i+1})$ where $r = \sum_{j=0}^{k-1} 2^j \cdot r|_j$. (for $i = 0, 1, 2$)
  $[r|_j]_{2^k} \leftarrow \mathsf{BitConversion}([r|_j]_2)$ `// 1 round & 6k bits`
end for
$[r|_{k-2,\ldots,0}]_{2^k} = \sum_{j=0}^{k-2} 2^j \cdot [r|_j]_{2^k}$
$[2^{k-1} \cdot \mathsf{msb}(r)]_{2^k} = 2^{k-1} \cdot [r|_{k-1}]_{2^k}$
(Online phase)
$[a + (r|_{k-2,\ldots,0})]_{2^k} = [a]_{2^k} + [r|_{k-2,\ldots,0}]_{2^k}$
$[2 \cdot ((a+r)|_{k-2,\ldots,0})]_{2^k} = 2 \cdot [a + (r|_{k-2,\ldots,0})]_{2^k}$
for $i = 0, 1$ **do in parallel**
  $2 \cdot ((a+r)|_{k-2,\ldots,0}) \leftarrow \mathsf{rOpen}(P_i, [2 \cdot ((a+r)|_{k-2,\ldots,0})]_{2^k})$ `// 1 round & k bits`
end for
$r|_{k-2,\ldots,0} \leftarrow \mathsf{rOpen}(P_2, [r|_{k-2,\ldots,0}]_{2^k})$ `// 1 round & k bits`
for $j = 0, \ldots, k-2$ **do in parallel**
  $\langle r|_j \rangle_{p',(0,1)} \leftarrow \mathsf{aShare}(P_2, p', r|_j, P_0, P_1)$ `// 1 round & log2(p') bits`
end for
P_0 and P_1 generate $\beta \in \{0,1\}$, s_j, $u_j \in \mathbb{Z}_p^*$ by using F_p and k_1 for $j = 0, \ldots, k-2$.

$\beta \oplus (r|_{k-2,\ldots,0} > (a+r)|_{k-2,\ldots,0}) \leftarrow \mathsf{PrivateCompare}((a+r)|_{k-2,\ldots,0}, \{\langle r|_j\rangle_{p',(0,1)}\}_{j=0}^{k-2}, \beta, \{s_j\}_{j=0}^{k-2}, \{u_j\}_{j=0}^{k-2}, P_2)$ `// 1 round & ` $2(k-1)\log_2(p')$ `bits`

P_0, P_1 and P_2 set $[\beta]_{2^k} = ((0,\beta),\ (\beta,0),\ (0,0))$

P_0, P_1 and P_2 set $[(a+r)|_{k-2,\ldots,0}]_{2^k} = ((0,(a+r)|_{k-2,\ldots,0}), ((a+r)|_{k-2,\ldots,0}, 0), (0,0))$.

$[r|_{k-2,\ldots,0}]_{2^k} \leftarrow \mathsf{rShare}(2^k, P_2, r|_{k-2,\ldots,0})$ `// 1 round & ` $4k$ `bits`

$[u]_{2^k} = [\beta \oplus (r|_{k-2,\ldots,0} > (a+r)|_{k-2,\ldots,0})]_{2^k} \leftarrow \mathsf{rShare}(2^k, P_2, \beta \oplus (r|_{k-2,\ldots,0} > (a+r)|_{k-2,\ldots,0}))$ `// 1 round and ` $4k$ `bits`

$[r|_{k-2,\ldots,0} > (a+r)|_{k-2,\ldots,0}]_{2^k} = ([u]_{2^k} - [\beta]_{2^k})^2$ `// 1 round & ` $3k$ `bits`

$[a|_{k-2,\ldots,0}]_{2^k} = [(a+r)|_{k-2,\ldots,0}]_{2^k} - [r|_{k-2,\ldots,0}]_{2^k} + 2^{k-1} \cdot [r|_{k-2,\ldots,0} > (a+r)|_{k-2,\ldots,0}]_{2^k}$

$[2^{k-1} \cdot \mathsf{msb}(a)]_{2^k} = [2^{k-1} \cdot a|_{k-1}] = [a]_{2^k} - [a|_{k-2,\ldots,0}]_{2^k}$

$[2^{k-1} \cdot (\mathsf{msb}(a) \oplus \mathsf{msb}(r))]_{2^k} = [2^{k-1} \cdot \mathsf{msb}(a)]_{2^k} + [2^{k-1} \cdot \mathsf{msb}(r)]_{2^k} = 2^{k-1} \cdot [a|_{k-1}]_{2^k} + 2^{k-1} \cdot [r|_{k-1}]_{2^k}$

$2^{k-1} \cdot (\mathsf{msb}(a) \oplus \mathsf{msb}(r)) \leftarrow \mathsf{rOpen}(P_0, [2^{k-1} \cdot (\mathsf{msb}(a) \oplus \mathsf{msb}(r))]_{2^k})$ `// 1 round & ` k `bits`

$[\mathsf{msb}(a) \oplus \mathsf{msb}(r)]_2 \leftarrow \mathsf{rShare}(2,\ P_0,\ \mathsf{msb}(a) \oplus \mathsf{msb}(r))$ `// 1 round & 4 bits`

$[\mathsf{msb}(a)]_2 = [\mathsf{msb}(a) \oplus \mathsf{msb}(r)]_2 \oplus [r|_{k-1}]_2$

return $[\mathsf{msb}(a)]_2$

Protocol 2. $\{[x|_j]_2\}_{j=0}^{m-1} \leftarrow \pi_{\mathsf{rBitDec}}(m, [x]_{2^k})$

Input: $m(\leq k)$, $[x]_{2^k}$ (s.t. $x \in \mathbb{Z}_{2^k}$, $x = \sum_{j=0}^{k-1} 2^j \cdot x|_j$, $x|_j \in \mathbb{Z}_2$ for $j = 0, \ldots, k-1$).

Output: $\{[x|_j]_2\}_{j=0}^{m-1}$

for $j = 0, \ldots, m-1$ **do in parallel**

  $[2^{k-1-j} \cdot x|_{j,\ldots,0}]_{2^k} = 2^{k-1-j} \cdot [x]_{2^k}$

  $[x|_j]_2 = [\mathsf{msb}(2^{k-1-j} \cdot x|_{j,\ldots,0})]_2 \leftarrow \pi_{\mathsf{msbExt}}([2^{k-1-j} \cdot x|_{j,\ldots,0}]_{2^k})$ `// 9 rounds & ` $6k^2 + 9k + (3k-3)\log_2(p) + 4$ `bits`

end for

return $\{[x|_j]_2\}_{j=0}^{m-1}$

Protocol 3. $[\mathsf{attr}_{\mathsf{idx}}]_{2^k} \leftarrow \pi_{\mathsf{rFSelection}}([\mathsf{idx}]_{2^k},\ \{[\mathsf{attr}_j]_{2^k}\}_{j=0}^{m-1})$

Input: $[\mathsf{idx}]_{2^k}$, $\{[\mathsf{attr}_j]_{2^k}\}_{j=0}^{m-1}$ (s.t. $0 \leq \mathsf{idx} < m \leq 2^k$).

Output: $[\mathsf{attr}_{\mathsf{idx}}]_{2^k}$

$\{[\mathsf{idx}|_i]_2\}_{i=0}^{\log_2(m)-1} \leftarrow \pi_{\mathsf{rBitDec}}(\log_2(m), [\mathsf{idx}]_{2^k})$ `// 9 rounds & ` $\log_2(m)(6k^2 + 9k + (3k-3)\log_2(p) + 4)$ `bits`

for $i = 0, \ldots, \log_2(m) - 1$ **do in parallel**

  $[\mathsf{idx}|_i]_m \leftarrow \mathsf{BitConversion}(m, [\mathsf{idx}|_i]_2)$ `// 1 round & ` $6m$ `bits`

end for

return $[\mathsf{attr}_{\mathsf{idx}}]_{2^k} \leftarrow \mathsf{rArrayRead}(\{[\mathsf{attr}_i]_{2^k}\}_{i=0}^{m-1}, \sum_{i=0}^{\log_2(m)-1} 2^i \cdot [\mathsf{idx}|_i]_m)$ `// 3 rounds & ` $4mk + 2m + 8k$ `bits`

Intuition behind Protocol 1. In the offline phase, each party prepares three types of the shares of random numbers $[r|_{k-2,\ldots,0}]_{2^k}, [2^{k-1} \cdot \mathsf{msb}(r)]_{2^k}, [r|_{k-1}]_2$ $(r = \sum_{j=0}^{k-1} 2^k \cdot r|_j, r|_j \in \mathbb{Z}_2)$ (from Step 1 to 7).

In the online phase, our first goal is to compute $[a|_{k-2,\ldots,0}]_{2^k} (= [a \bmod 2^{k-1}]_{2^k})$. First, each party uses $[r|_{k-2,\ldots,0}]_{2^k} (= [r \bmod 2^{k-1}]_{2^k})$ to mask the input share $[a]_{2^k}$, then computes the masked share $[a + (r|_{k-2,\ldots,0})]_{2^k}$ (at Step 9). Next, each party computes $[2 \cdot ((a + r)|_{k-2,\ldots,0})]_{2^k} (= 2 \cdot [a + (r|_{k-2,\ldots,0})]_{2^k})$ (at Step 10). Then, P_0 and P_1 reveal $[2 \cdot ((a+r)|_{k-2,\ldots,0})]_{2^k}$ and obtain $2 \cdot ((a + r)|_{k-2,\ldots,0}) \bmod 2^k$, from which they can obtain $(a+r)|_{k-2,\ldots,0}$ (from Step 11 to 13). We note that P_0 and P_1 cannot know the plain MSB bit, $\mathsf{msb}(a)$. In parallel, P_2 obtain $r|_{k-2,\ldots,0}$ (at Step 14). Next, each party runs $\mathsf{PrivateCompare}$ [42] and P_2 obtains the masked comparison result bit $\beta \oplus (r|_{k-2,\ldots,0} > (a + r)|_{k-2,\ldots,0})$ (from Step 15 to 19). Then, each party removes the mask β by performing arithmetic XOR operation over the ring (i.e., $([u]_{2^k} - [\beta]_{2^k})^2$ at Step 24), and obtains the share of comparison bit $[r|_{k-2,\ldots,0} > (a + r)|_{k-2,\ldots,0}]_{2^k}$ (from Step 20 to 24). Finally, each party computes $[a|_{k-2,\ldots,0}]_{2^k} = [(a + r)|_{k-2,\ldots,0}]_{2^k} - [r|_{k-2,\ldots,0}]_{2^k} + 2^{k-1} \cdot [r|_{k-2,\ldots,0} > (a + r)|_{k-2,\ldots,0}]_{2^k} (= [(a + r) \bmod 2^{k-1}]_{2^k} - [r \bmod 2^{k-1}]_{2^k} + 2^{k-1} \cdot [(r \bmod 2^{k-1}) > ((a + r) \bmod 2^{k-1})]_{2^k})$.

We note that $[a|_{k-2,\ldots,0}]_{2^k} = [(a+r)|_{k-2,\ldots,0}]_{2^k} - [r|_{k-2,\ldots,0}]_{2^k}$ does not hold in general. The reason that the equation does not work is because the wrap-around phenomenon may occur. The wrap-around phenomenon means that the modulo operation may make $(a+r)|_{k-2,\ldots,0} \bmod 2^k$ less than $r|_{k-2,\ldots,0} \bmod 2^k$. To deal with a case where wrap-around phenomenon occurs, we must compute $[(a+r)|_{k-2,\ldots,0}]_{2^k} - [r|_{k-2,\ldots,0}]_{2^k} + 2^{k-1} \cdot [r|_{k-2,\ldots,0} > (a+r)|_{k-2,\ldots,0}]_{2^k}$ similarly to [14,15,19] to ignore the effect of the wrap-around phenomenon.

Next, each party computes $[2^{k-1} \cdot \mathsf{msb}(a)]_{2^k} = [2^{k-1} \cdot a|_{k-1}]_{2^k} = [a]_{2^k} - [a|_{k-2,\ldots,0}]_{2^k} = [a]_{2^k} - [a \bmod 2^{k-1}]_{2^k}$ (at Step 26). Then, P_0 obtains $2^{k-1} \cdot (\mathsf{msb}(a) \oplus \mathsf{msb}(r))$, from which P_0 can obtain $\mathsf{msb}(a) \oplus \mathsf{msb}(r)$ (from Step 27 and 28). P_0 distributes $[\mathsf{msb}(a) \oplus \mathsf{msb}(r)]_2$ (at Step 29). Finally, each party computes $[\mathsf{msb}(a)]_2 = [\mathsf{msb}(a) \oplus \mathsf{msb}(r)]_2 \oplus [r|_{k-1}]_2$.

Intuitions Behind Protocols 2 and 3. In Protocol 2, each party computes the right shift (at Step 2) and invokes π_{msbExt} (at Step 3), repeatedly. Then, each party gets the shares of each bit over $\mathbb{Z}_2$.

In Protocol 3, to convert $[\mathsf{idx}]_{2^k}$ to $[\mathsf{idx}]_m$, each party invokes π_{rBitDec} and runs $\mathsf{BitConversion}$ (from Step 1 to Step 4). Then, each party uses the OAR protocol [7], $\mathsf{rArrayRead}$ and obtains $[\mathsf{attr}_{\mathsf{idx}}]_{2^k}$ (at Step 5).

We emphasize that it is non-trivial to convert $[\mathsf{idx}]_{2^k}$ to $[\mathsf{idx}]_m$ with constant rounds. For example, if we use the (naive) circuit-based bit-decomposition protocol, BitDec, and $\mathsf{BitConversion}$, the conversion of the shared index is not a constant-round protocol. Hence, the whole of the feature selection protocol is also not a constant-round protocol if the conversion of the shared index is not a constant-round protocol.

4 Proposed Protocol in Comparison Phase

In comparison phase, it is required to compare the attribute value and the decision threshold value without revealing these values, the comparison operators, and comparison results. Hence, we construct the less-than protocol (Protocol 4) and the equality-testing protocol (Protocol 5) as subprotocols. Then, we also construct the comparison protocol (Protocol 6) by using these subprotocols, i.e., oblivious selection protocol for the comparison result.

Protocol 4. $[a < b]_2 \leftarrow \pi_{\mathsf{rLT}}([a]_{2^k},\ [b]_{2^k})$

Input: $[a]_{2^k},\ [b]_{2^k}$ (s.t. $a, b \in \mathbb{Z}_{2^k}$)
Output: $[a < b]_2$

1: $[c]_{2^k} = [a]_{2^k} - [b]_{2^k}$
2: $[\mathsf{msb}(c)]_2 \leftarrow \pi_{\mathsf{msbExt}}([c]_{2^k})$ `// 9 rounds &` $6k^2+9k+(3k-3)\log_2(p)+4$ `bits`
3: return $[\mathsf{msb}(c)]_2$

Protocol 5 . $[a == b]_2 \leftarrow \pi_{\mathsf{rEQ}}([a]_{2^k},\ [b]_{2^k})$

Input: $[a]_{2^k},\ [b]_{2^k}$ (s.t. $a, b \in \mathbb{Z}_{2^k}$)
Output: $[a == b]_2$

1: $[a < b]_2 \leftarrow \pi_{\mathsf{rLT}}([a]_{2^k},\ [b]_{2^k})$ `// 9 rounds &` $6k^2+9k+(3k-3)\log_2(p)+4$ `bits`
2: $[b < a]_2 \leftarrow \pi_{\mathsf{rLT}}([b]_{2^k},\ [a]_{2^k})$ `// 9 rounds &` $6k^2+9k+(3k-3)\log_2(p)+4$ `bits`
3: $[\mathsf{res}]_2 = ([a < b]_2 \oplus 1) \cdot ([b < a]_2 \oplus 1)$ `// 1 round & 3 bits`
4: return $[\mathsf{res}]_2$

Protocol 6. $\{[\mathsf{comp}_j]_2\}_{j=0}^{2^h-2} \leftarrow \pi_{\mathsf{rComp}}(\{[\mathsf{attr}_{\mathsf{idx}_j}]_{2^k}\}_{j=0}^{2^h-2}, \{[\mathsf{v}_j]_{2^k}\}_{j=0}^{2^h-2}, \{[\mathsf{cond}_j]_2\}_{j=0}^{2^h-2})$

Input: Attribute set $\{[\mathsf{attr}_{\mathsf{idx}_j}]_{2^k}\}_{j=0}^{2^h-2}$, threshold values $\{[\mathsf{v}_j]_{2^k}\}_{j=0}^{2^h-2}$, conditional values $[\mathsf{cond}_j]_2\}_{j=0}^{2^h-2}$
Output: $\{[\mathsf{comp}_j]_2\}_{j=0}^{2^h-2}$

1: **for** $j = 0, \ldots, 2^h-2$ **do in parallel**
2: $[\mathsf{v}_j < \mathsf{attr}_{\mathsf{idx}_j}]_2 \leftarrow \pi_{\mathsf{rLT}}([\mathsf{v}_j]_{2^k}, [\mathsf{attr}_{\mathsf{idx}_j}]_{2^k})$ `// 9 rounds &` $6k^2+9k+(3k-3)\log_2(p)+4$ `bits`
3: $[\mathsf{v}_j == \mathsf{attr}_{\mathsf{idx}_j}]_2 \leftarrow \pi_{\mathsf{rEQ}}([\mathsf{v}_j]_{2^k}, [\mathsf{attr}_{\mathsf{idx}_j}]_{2^k})$ `// 10 rounds &` $12k^2+18k+2\cdot(3k-3)\log_2(p)+12$ `bits`
4: $[\mathsf{comp}_j]_2 = [\mathsf{cond}_j]_2 \cdot [\mathsf{v}_j < \mathsf{attr}_{\mathsf{idx}_j}]_2 \oplus (1 \oplus [\mathsf{cond}_j]_2) \cdot [\mathsf{v}_j == \mathsf{attr}_{\mathsf{idx}_j}]_2$ `// 1 round & 6 bits`
5: **end for**
6: return $\{[\mathsf{comp}_j]_2\}_{j=0}^{2^h-2}$

In Protocol 4, to run the less-than protocol, each party computes $[a-b]_{2^k} = [a]_{2^k} - [b]_{2^k}$ where we assume $0 \leq a, b \leq 2^{k-1}-1$ and invokes π_{msbExt}. If a is smaller than b, $\mathsf{msb}(a-b)$ equals 1 and can be outputted as the result of the less-than protocol. If not, $\mathsf{msb}(a-b)$ equals 0 and can be outputted. In Protocol 5, to run the equality-testing protocol, each party invokes $\pi_{\mathsf{rLT}}([a]_{2^k}, [b]_{2^k})$ and $\pi_{\mathsf{rLT}}([b]_{2^k}, [a]_{2^k})$ in parallel. $a = b$ holds if $(a < b) \oplus 1 = 1$ and $(b < a) \oplus 1 = 1$. Therefore, each party outputs $([a < b]_2 \oplus 1) \cdot ([b < a]_2 \oplus 1)$ as the result of the equality-testing protocol.

Protocol 6 takes the shares of the conditional values $\{[\mathsf{cond}_j]_2\}_{j=0}^{2^h-2}$ as inputs and outputs the oblivious comparison results for each internal node. It either outputs the results of π_{rLT} (if $c_j = 1$) or π_{rEQ} (if $c_j = 0$). Hence, each party invokes π_{rLT} and π_{rEQ} (at Steps 2 and 3). Then, each party selects one result or the other as the shared comparison result bit $[\mathsf{comp}_j]_2$, obliviously (at Step 4).

Protocol 7. $[\mathsf{leafVal}_{j'}]_{2^k} \leftarrow \pi_{\mathsf{rPathEval}}(\{[\mathsf{comp}_j]_2\}_{j=0}^{2^h-2}, \{[\mathsf{leafVal}_{j'}]_{2^k}\}_{j'=0}^{2^h-1}, \delta)$

Input: Comparison result of intermediate nodes $\{[\mathsf{comp}_j]_2\}_{j=0}^{2^h-2}$, set of shared values assigned to leaf nodes $\{[\mathsf{leafVal}_{j'}]_{2^k}\}_{j'=0}^{2^h-1}$, mapping function δ

Output: shared values assigned to leaf node of correct path $[\mathsf{leafVal}_{j'}]_{2^k}$ where j' s.t. $\bigwedge_{\ell=0}^{h-1}(j'|_\ell \oplus \mathsf{comp}_{\delta(j',\ell)} \oplus 1) = 1$.

for $j' = 0, \ldots, 2^h - 1$ **do in parallel**
  Initialize $\mathsf{Path}_{j'} = \{[\mathsf{comp}_{\delta(j',0)}]_2, [\mathsf{comp}_{\delta(j',1)}]_2, \ldots, [\mathsf{comp}_{\delta(j',h-1)}]_2\}$.
  for $\ell = 0, \ldots, h-1$ **do in parallel**
    Compute $[c_{j',\ell}]_2 = j'|_\ell \oplus [\mathsf{comp}_{\delta(j',\ell)}]_2 \oplus 1$ by picking up $[\mathsf{comp}_{\delta(j',\ell)}]_2$ from $\mathsf{Path}_{j'}$.
  end for
  Set $\mathcal{R}_{j'} = \{[\mathsf{leafVal}_{j'}]_{2^k}, [c_{j',0}]_2, \ldots, [c_{j',h-1}]_2\}$
end for
$\{\mathcal{R}_{\sigma(j')}\}_{j'=0}^{2^h-1} \leftarrow \mathsf{rSetShuffle}(\{\mathcal{R}_{j'}\}_{j'=0}^{2^h-1})$ `// 3 rounds &` $6 \cdot 2^h \cdot (k+h)$ `bits`
Initialize $\mathsf{count}_{\sigma(j')} = 0$ for $j' = 0, \ldots, 2^h - 1$.
for $j' = 0, \ldots, 2^h - 1; \ell = 0, \ldots, h-1$ **do in parallel**
  Pick up $[c_{\sigma(j'),\ell}]_2$ from $\mathcal{R}_{\sigma(j')}$. Then, $c_{\sigma(j'),\ell} \leftarrow \mathsf{Open}(P_i, [c_{\sigma(j'),\ell}]_2)$ for $i = 0, 1, 2$. `// 1 round & 3 bits`
  $\mathsf{count}_{\sigma(j')} = \mathsf{count}_{\sigma(j')} + 1$ if $c_{\sigma(j'),\ell} = 1$.
end for
return $[\mathsf{leafVal}_{\sigma(j')}]_{2^k}$ where $\mathsf{count}_{\sigma(j')} = h$.

Protocol 8. $[\mathsf{leafVal}]_{2^k} \leftarrow \pi_{\mathsf{rDTEval}}(\{[\mathsf{idx}_j]_{2^k}\}_{j=0}^{2^h-2}, \{[\mathsf{attr}_i]_{2^k}\}_{i=0}^{m-1}, \{[\mathsf{v}_j]_{2^k}\}_{j=0}^{2^h-2}, \{[\mathsf{cond}_j]_{2^k}\}_{j=0}^{2^h-2}, \{[\mathsf{leafVal}_{j'}]_{2^k}\}_{j'=0}^{2^h-1}, \delta)$

Input: Set of shared index number $\{[\mathsf{idx}_j]_{2^k}\}_{j=0}^{2^h-2}$, shared feature array $\{[\mathsf{attr}_i]_{2^k}\}_{i=0}^{m-1}$, threshold values $\{[\mathsf{v}_j]_{2^k}\}_{j=0}^{2^h-2}$, conditional values $\{[\mathsf{cond}_j]_{2^k}\}_{j=0}^{2^h-2}$, set of shared values assigned to leaf nodes $\{[\mathsf{leafVal}_{j'}]_{2^k}\}_{j'=0}^{2^h-1}$, mapping function δ

Output: shared values assigned to leaf node of correct path $[\mathsf{leafVal}_{j'}]_{2^k}$ where j' s.t. $\bigwedge_{\ell=0}^{h-1}(j'|_\ell \oplus \mathsf{comp}_{\delta(j',\ell)} \oplus 1) = 1$. Let $\mathsf{comp}_{\delta(j',\ell)}$ be $\mathsf{cond}_{\delta(j',\ell)} \cdot (\mathsf{v}_{\delta(j',\ell)} < \mathsf{attr}_{\mathsf{idx}_{\delta(j',\ell)}}) \oplus (\mathsf{cond}_{\delta(j',\ell)} \oplus 1)(\mathsf{v}_{\delta(j',\ell)} == \mathsf{attr}_{\mathsf{idx}_{\delta(j',\ell)}})$.

Initialize $\mathcal{A}$.
for $j = 0, \ldots, 2^h - 2$ **do in parallel**
  $[\mathsf{attr}_{\mathsf{idx}_j}]_{2^k} \leftarrow \pi_{\mathsf{rFSelection}}([\mathsf{idx}_j]_{2^k}, \{[\mathsf{attr}_i]_{2^k}\}_{i=0}^{m-1})$. `// 13 rounds &` $\log_2(m)(6k^2 + 9k + (3k-3)\log_2(p) + 4) + 6m^2 + 4mk + 2m)$ `bits`
  Set $[\mathsf{attr}_{\mathsf{idx}_j}]_{2^k}$ into $\mathcal{A}$.
end for
$\{[\mathsf{comp}_j]_2\}_{j=0}^{2^h-2} \leftarrow \pi_{\mathsf{Comp}}(\mathcal{A} = \{[\mathsf{attr}_{\mathsf{idx}_j}]_{2^k}\}_{j=0}^{2^h-2}, \{[\mathsf{v}_j]_{2^k}\}_{j=0}^{2^h-2}, \{[\mathsf{cond}_j]_{2^k}\}_{j=0}^{2^h-2})$ `// 11 rounds &` $(2^h - 1) \cdot (18k^2 + 27k + (9k-9)\log_2(p) + 22)$ `bits`
$[\mathsf{leafVal}]_{2^k} \leftarrow \pi_{\mathsf{PathEval}}(\{[\mathsf{comp}_j]_2\}_{j=0}^{2^h-2}, \{[\mathsf{leafVal}_{j'}]_{2^k}\}_{j'=0}^{2^h-1}, \delta)$ `// 4 rounds &` $2^h(6k + 9h)$ `bits`
return $[\mathsf{leafVal}]_{2^k}$

5 Proposed Protocol in Path Evaluation Phase

In path evaluation phase, it is required to choose the correct path (and leaf node) by using the shared comparison result of each node and the shared class labels assigned to leaf nodes without revealing the information about paths, comparison results, and class labels. We construct the path evaluation protocol (Protocol 7) and explain the intuition behind it. Each party initializes $\mathsf{Path}_{j'} = \{[\mathsf{comp}_{\delta(j',\ell)}]_2\}_{\ell=0}^{h-1}$ for each j'-th leaf node (at Step 2). δ is the mapping function defined in Sect. 2.4. Next, let $[\mathsf{leafVal}_{j'}]_{2^k}$ be the shares of each class label value and $c_{j',\ell}$ be the result of the equality-testing between the bit assigned to the branch that has the ℓ-th height on the path to the j'-th leaf node, $j'|_\ell$ and the comparison result $\mathsf{comp}_{\delta(j',\ell)}$. Each party computes $\mathcal{R}_{j'} = \{[\mathsf{leafVal}_{j'}]_{2^k}, [c_{j',0}]_2, \ldots, [c_{j',h-1}]_2\}$ (from Step 1 to 6).

Next, each party computes $\{\mathcal{R}_{\sigma(j')}\}_{j'=0}^{2^h-1}$ by shuffling $\{\mathcal{R}_{j'}\}_{j'=0}^{2^h-1}$ obliviously by using the random permutation σ (at Step 8). After initializing $\mathsf{count}_{\sigma(j')} = 0$ (at Step 9). Then, each party obtains $c_{\sigma(j'),\ell}$ by choosing $[c_{\sigma(j'),\ell}]_2$ from $\mathcal{R}_{\sigma(j')}$ and revealing it. If $c_{\sigma(j'),\ell} = 1$, each party increases $\mathsf{count}_{\sigma(j')}$ by 1 (from Step 10 to Step 13). We note that $c_{\sigma(j'),\ell}$ does not leak the positional information j'. In addition, an adversary can obtain no information about $\{\mathsf{comp}_{\delta(j',\ell)}\}_{\ell=0}^{2^h-2}$ and $\mathsf{leafVal}_{j'}$ from $c_{\sigma(j'),\ell}$ because the tree is a complete binary tree. For example, we assume that $h = 2$. If the correct output leaf node is the leaf node $2(= 10_{(2)})$, it holds that $c_{\sigma(0),0} = 1$, $c_{\sigma(0),1} = 0$, $c_{\sigma(1),0} = 0$, $c_{\sigma(1),1} = 0$, $c_{\sigma(2),0} = 1$, $c_{\sigma(2),1} = 1$, $c_{\sigma(3),0} = 0$, and $c_{\sigma(3),1} = 1$. That is, the adversary gets all the 2-bit sequences, $00_{(2)}$, $01_{(2)}$, $10_{(2)}$, and $11_{(2)}$. As another example, if the correct output leaf node is the leaf node $3(= 11_{(2)})$, it holds that $c_{\sigma(0),0} = 0$, $c_{\sigma(0),1} = 0$, $c_{\sigma(1),0} = 1$, $c_{\sigma(1),1} = 0$, $c_{\sigma(2),0} = 0$, $c_{\sigma(2),1} = 1$, $c_{\sigma(3),0} = 1$, and $c_{\sigma(3),1} = 1$. In this case, the adversary also obtains all 2-bit sequences, $00_{(2)}$, $01_{(2)}$, $10_{(2)}$, and $11_{(2)}$. We note that the random permutation σ is different for each execution of $\mathsf{rSetShuffle}$. Therefore, the adversary can get no information from $c_{\sigma(j'),\ell}$.

If $\mathsf{count}_{\sigma(j')} = h$, $\bigwedge_{\ell=0}^{h-1}(\sigma(j')|_\ell \oplus \mathsf{comp}_{\delta(\sigma(j'),\ell)} \oplus 1) = 1$ holds. Therefore, each party outputs $[\mathsf{leafVal}_{\sigma(j')}]_{2^k}$ (at Step 14).

6 Proposed Protocol of Private Decision Tree Evaluation

Protocol 8 is our construction of PDTE over the ring. It employs Protocol 3 in the feature selection phase, Protocol 6 in the comparison phase, and Protocol 7 in the path evaluation phase.

7 Security Proof

We follow the formal security definition of perfect security in the presence of one semi-honest corrupted party [3]. Loosely speaking, our schemes are composed of the UC secure building blocks and a number of operations without communications. Therefore, our scheme is secure as long as the building blocks are secure.

8 Conclusion

In this paper, we proposed the PDTE protocol with constant rounds using (only) the 3PC over the ring for the first time. Our scheme provides the PDTE efficiently even where the communication environment has a large latency and limited communication bandwidth. The generalization of the proposed protocol to the N-party protocol and improvement of its security (e.g., malicious security or information-theoretic security) are open problems to be addressed in the future.

Acknowledgement. This work was supported in part by JSPS KAKENHI Grant Number 20K11807.

A Naive Construction of PDTE

To the best of our knowledge, Protocol 9 is the naive construction, i.e., the best combination of the existing protocols based only on SS-3PC over the ring.

Protocol 9. Naive Construction of PDTE via 3PC over Ring

Input: Set of shared index number $\{[\mathsf{idx}_j]_{2^k}\}_{j=0}^{2^h-2}$, shared feature array $\{[\mathsf{attr}_i]_{2^k}\}_{i=0}^{m-1}$, threshold values $\{[\mathsf{v}_j]_{2^k}\}_{j=0}^{2^h-2}$, conditional values $\{[\mathsf{cond}_j]_{2^k}\}_{j=0}^{2^h-2}$, set of shared values assigned to leaf nodes $\{[\mathsf{leafVal}_{j'}]_{2^k}\}_{j'=0}^{2^h-1}$, mapping function δ

Output: shared values assigned to leaf node of correct path $[\mathsf{leafVal}_{j'}]_{2^k}$ where j' s.t. $\bigwedge_{\ell=0}^{h-1}(j'|_\ell \oplus \mathsf{comp}_{\delta(j',\ell)} \oplus 1) = 1$. Let $\mathsf{comp}_{\delta(j',\ell)}$ be $\mathsf{cond}_{\delta(j',\ell)} \cdot (\mathsf{v}_{\delta(j',\ell)} < \mathsf{attr}_{\mathsf{idx}_{\delta(j',\ell)}}) \oplus (\mathsf{cond}_{\delta(j',\ell)} \oplus 1)(\mathsf{v}_{\delta(j',\ell)} == \mathsf{attr}_{\mathsf{idx}_{\delta(j',\ell)}})$.

for $j = 0, \dots, 2^h - 2$ **do in parallel**
  (Feature Selection Phase)
  $\{[\mathsf{idx}_j|_{i'}]_2\}_{i'=0}^{\log_2(m)-1} \leftarrow \mathsf{NaiveBitDec}(\log_2(m), [\mathsf{idx}_j]_{2^k})$ `// 1 +` $\log_2(m)$ `rounds &` $3\log_2(m) + 3\log_2(m) \cdot \log_2(\log_2(m))$ `bits`
  for $i' = 0, \dots, \log_2(m) - 1$ **do in parallel**
    $[\mathsf{idx}_j|_{i'}]_m \leftarrow \mathsf{BitConversion}(m, [\mathsf{idx}_j|_{i'}]_2)$ `// 1 round &` $6m$ `bits`
  end for
  $[\mathsf{idx}_j]_m = \sum_{i'=0}^{\log_2(m)} 2^{i'} \cdot [\mathsf{idx}_j|_{i'}]_m$
  $[\mathsf{attr}_{\mathsf{idx}_j}]_{2^k} \leftarrow \mathsf{rArrayRead}(\{[\mathsf{attr}_i]_{2^k}\}_{i=0}^{m-1}, [\mathsf{idx}_j]_m)$ `// 3 rounds &` $4mk + 2m + 8k$ `bits`
  (Comparison Phase)
  $[\mathsf{v}_j < \mathsf{attr}_{\mathsf{idx}_j}]_2 \leftarrow \mathsf{NaiveRingLT}([\mathsf{v}_j]_{2^k}, [\mathsf{attr}_{\mathsf{idx}_j}]_{2^k})$ `//` $1 + \log_2(k)$ `rounds &` $3k + 3k \cdot \log_2(k)$ `bits`
  $[\mathsf{v}_j == \mathsf{attr}_{\mathsf{idx}_j}]_2 \leftarrow \mathsf{NaiveRingEQ}([\mathsf{v}_j]_{2^k}, [\mathsf{attr}_{\mathsf{idx}_j}]_{2^k})$ `//` $1 + 2\log_2(k)$ `rounds &` $6k + 3k\log_2(k) - 3$ `bits`
  $[\mathsf{comp}_j]_2 = [\mathsf{cond}_j]_2 \cdot [\mathsf{v}_j < \mathsf{attr}_{\mathsf{idx}_j}]_2 \oplus (1 \oplus [\mathsf{cond}_j]_2) \cdot [\mathsf{v}_j == \mathsf{attr}_{\mathsf{idx}_j}]_2$ `// 1 round & 6 bits`
end for

(Path Evaluation Phase)
Initialize $\mathsf{Path}_{j'} = \{[\mathsf{comp}_{\delta(j',0)}]_2, [\mathsf{comp}_{\delta(j',1)}]_2, \ldots, [\mathsf{comp}_{\delta(j',h-1)}]_2\}$ by picking up $[\mathsf{comp}_{\delta(j',\ell)}]_2$ corresponding to the intermediate value which has $(\ell+1)$-th height in the path to the j'-th leaf node from $\{[\mathsf{comp}_j]_2\}_{j=0}^{2^h-2}$.
for $j' = 0, \ldots, 2^h - 1$ **do in parallel**
  $[\mathsf{pathBit}_{j'}]_2 \leftarrow \mathsf{rArrayAND}(\mathsf{Path}_{j'})$ `//` $\log_2(h)$ `rounds &` $3(h-1)$ `bits`
  $[\mathsf{pathBit}_{j'}]_{2^k} \leftarrow \mathsf{BitConversion}([\mathsf{pathBit}_{j'}]_2)$ `// 1 round &` $6k$ `bits`
end for
return $[\mathsf{leafVal}]_{2^k} \leftarrow \mathsf{rInnerProduct}(\{[\mathsf{pathBit}_{j'}]_{2^k}\}_{j'=0}^{2^h-1}, \{[\mathsf{leafVal}_{j'}]_{2^k}\}_{j'=0}^{2^h-1})$. `// 1 round &` $3k$ `bits`

References

1. Aiello, W., Ishai, Y., Reingold, O.: Priced oblivious transfer: how to sell digital goods. In: Pfitzmann, B. (ed.) EUROCRYPT 2001. LNCS, vol. 2045, pp. 119–135. Springer, Heidelberg (2001). https://doi.org/10.1007/3-540-44987-6_8
2. Araki, T., Barak, A., Furukawa, J., Keller, M., Ohara, K., Tsuchida, H.: How to choose suitable secure multiparty computation using generalized SPDZ. In: ACM Conference on Computer and Communications Security, pp. 2198–2200. ACM (2018)
3. Araki, T., Furukawa, J., Lindell, Y., Nof, A., Ohara, K.: High-throughput semi-honest secure three-party computation with an honest majority. In: ACM Conference on Computer and Communications Security, pp. 805–817. ACM (2016)
4. Barni, M., Failla, P., Kolesnikov, V., Lazzeretti, R., Sadeghi, A.-R., Schneider, T.: Secure evaluation of private linear branching programs with medical applications. In: Backes, M., Ning, P. (eds.) ESORICS 2009. LNCS, vol. 5789, pp. 424–439. Springer, Heidelberg (2009). https://doi.org/10.1007/978-3-642-04444-1_26
5. Beaver, D., Micali, S., Rogaway, P.: The round complexity of secure protocols (extended abstract). In: STOC, pp. 503–513. ACM (1990)
6. Ben-Or, M., Goldwasser, S., Wigderson, A.: Completeness theorems for non-cryptographic fault-tolerant distributed computation (extended abstract). In: STOC, pp. 1–10. ACM (1988)
7. Blanton, M., Kang, A., Yuan, C.: Improved building blocks for secure multi-party computation based on secret sharing with honest majority. Cryptology ePrint Archive, Report 2019/718 (2019). https://eprint.iacr.org/2019/718 (Accepted in ACNS 2020)
8. Brickell, J., Porter, D.E., Shmatikov, V., Witchel, E.: Privacy-preserving remote diagnostics. In ACM Conference on Computer and Communications Security, pp. 498–507. ACM (2007)
9. Byali, M., Chaudhari, H., Patra, A., Suresh, A.: FLASH: fast and robust framework for privacy-preserving machine learning. IACR Cryptology ePrint Archive, vol. 2019, p. 1365 (2019). (accepted in PETS 2020)
10. Canetti, R.: Universally composable security: a new paradigm for cryptographic protocols. In FOCS, pp. 136–145. IEEE Computer Society (2001)
11. Catrina, O., de Hoogh, S.: Improved primitives for secure multiparty integer computation. In: Garay, J.A., De Prisco, R. (eds.) SCN 2010. LNCS, vol. 6280, pp. 182–199. Springer, Heidelberg (2010). https://doi.org/10.1007/978-3-642-15317-4_13

12. Chida, K., et al.: An efficient secure three-party sorting protocol with an honest majority. Cryptology ePrint Archive, Report 2019/695 (2019). https://eprint.iacr.org/2019/695
13. De Cock, M., et al.: Efficient and private scoring of decision trees, support vector machines and logistic regression models based on pre-computation. IEEE Trans. Dependable Secur. Comput. **16**(2), 217–230 (2019)
14. Dalskov, A., Escudero, D., Keller, M.: Secure evaluation of quantized neural networks. Cryptology ePrint Archive, Report 2019/131 (2019). https://eprint.iacr.org/2019/131 (Accepted in PETS 2020)
15. Damgård, I., Escudero, D., Frederiksen, T.K., Keller, M., Scholl, P., Volgushev, N.: New primitives for actively-secure MPC over rings with applications to private machine learning. In IEEE Symposium on Security and Privacy, pp. 1102–1120. IEEE (2019)
16. Damgård, I., Jurik, M.: A generalisation, a simplification and some applications of Paillier's probabilistic public-key system. In: Kim, K. (ed.) PKC 2001. LNCS, vol. 1992, pp. 119–136. Springer, Heidelberg (2001). https://doi.org/10.1007/3-540-44586-2_9
17. Demmler, D., Schneider, T., Zohner, M.: ABY-A framework for efficient mixed-protocol secure two-party computation. In: NDSS, The Internet Society (2015)
18. Doerner, J., Shelat, A.: Scaling ORAM for secure computation. In: ACM Conference on Computer and Communications Security, pp. 523–535. ACM (2017)
19. Escudero, D., Ghosh, S., Keller, M., Rachuri, R., Scholl, P.: Improved primitives for MPC over mixed arithmetic-binary circuits. In: Micciancio, D., Ristenpart, T. (eds.) CRYPTO 2020. LNCS, vol. 12171, pp. 823–852. Springer, Cham (2020). https://doi.org/10.1007/978-3-030-56880-1_29
20. Faber, S., Jarecki, S., Kentros, S., Wei, B.: Three-party ORAM for secure computation. In: Iwata, T., Cheon, J.H. (eds.) ASIACRYPT 2015. LNCS, vol. 9452, pp. 360–385. Springer, Heidelberg (2015). https://doi.org/10.1007/978-3-662-48797-6_16
21. El Gamal, T.: A public key cryptosystem and a signature scheme based on discrete logarithms. IEEE Trans. Inf. Theory **31**(4), 469–472 (1985)
22. Gentry, C.: A fully homomorphic encryption scheme. PhD thesis, Stanford University (2009). https://crypto.stanford.edu/craig
23. Goldreich, O., Micali, S., Wigderson, A.: How to play any mental game or a completeness theorem for protocols with honest majority. In: STOC, pp. 218–229. ACM (1987)
24. Goldwasser, S., Micali, S.: Probabilistic encryption and how to play mental poker keeping secret all partial information. In: STOC, pp. 365–377. ACM (1982)
25. Henecka, W., Kögl, S., Sadeghi, A.-R., Schneider, T., Wehrenberg, I.: TASTY: tool for automating secure two-party computations. In: ACM Conference on Computer and Communications Security, pp. 451–462. ACM (2010)
26. Ichikawa, A., Ogata, W., Hamada, K., Kikuchi, R.: Efficient secure multi-party protocols for decision tree classification. In: Jang-Jaccard, J., Guo, F. (eds.) ACISP 2019. LNCS, vol. 11547, pp. 362–380. Springer, Cham (2019). https://doi.org/10.1007/978-3-030-21548-4_20
27. Jarecki, S., Wei, B.: 3PC ORAM with low latency, low bandwidth, and fast batch retrieval. In: Preneel, B., Vercauteren, F. (eds.) ACNS 2018. LNCS, vol. 10892, pp. 360–378. Springer, Cham (2018). https://doi.org/10.1007/978-3-319-93387-0_19
28. Keller, M., Scholl, P.: Efficient, oblivious data structures for MPC. In: Sarkar, P., Iwata, T. (eds.) ASIACRYPT 2014. LNCS, vol. 8874, pp. 506–525. Springer, Heidelberg (2014). https://doi.org/10.1007/978-3-662-45608-8_27

29. Kiss, Á., Naderpour, M., Liu, J., Asokan, N., Schneider, T.: SoK: modular and efficient private decision tree evaluation. PoPETs **2019**(2), 187–208 (2019)
30. Laud, P.: A private lookup protocol with low online complexity for secure multiparty computation. In: Hui, L.C.K., Qing, S.H., Shi, E., Yiu, S.M. (eds.) ICICS 2014. LNCS, vol. 8958, pp. 143–157. Springer, Cham (2015). https://doi.org/10.1007/978-3-319-21966-0_11
31. Laud, P.: Parallel oblivious array access for secure multiparty computation and privacy-preserving minimum spanning trees. PoPETs **2015**(2), 188–205 (2015)
32. Launchbury, J., Diatchki, I.S., DuBuisson, T., Adams-Moran, A.: Efficient lookup-table protocol in secure multiparty computation. In: ICFP, pp. 189–200. ACM (2012)
33. Laur, S., Willemson, J., Zhang, B.: Round-efficient oblivious database manipulation. In: Lai, X., Zhou, J., Li, H. (eds.) ISC 2011. LNCS, vol. 7001, pp. 262–277. Springer, Heidelberg (2011). https://doi.org/10.1007/978-3-642-24861-0_18
34. Mohassel, P., Rindal, P.: Aby^3: A mixed protocol framework for machine learning. In: ACM Conference on Computer and Communications Security, pp. 35–52. ACM (2018)
35. Naor, M., Pinkas, B.: Efficient oblivious transfer protocols. In: SODA, pp. 448–457. ACM/SIAM (2001)
36. Ohata, S., Nuida, K.: Towards high-throughput secure MPC over the internet: Communication-efficient two-party protocols and its application. CoRR, abs/1907.03415 (2019). (Accepted in FC 2020)
37. Paillier, P.: Public-key cryptosystems based on composite degree residuosity classes. In: Stern, J. (ed.) EUROCRYPT 1999. LNCS, vol. 1592, pp. 223–238. Springer, Heidelberg (1999). https://doi.org/10.1007/3-540-48910-X_16
38. Rachuri, R., Suresh, A.: Trident: efficient 4PC framework for privacy preserving machine learning. Cryptology ePrint Archive, Report 2019/1315 (2019). https://eprint.iacr.org/2019/1315
39. Rivest, R.L., Shamir, A., Adleman, L.M.: A method for obtaining digital signatures and public-key cryptosystems (reprint). Commun. ACM **26**(1), 96–99 (1983)
40. Tai, R.K.H., Ma, J.P.K., Zhao, Y., Chow, S.S.M.: Privacy-preserving decision trees evaluation via linear functions. In: Foley, S.N., Gollmann, D., Snekkenes, E. (eds.) ESORICS 2017. LNCS, vol. 10493, pp. 494–512. Springer, Cham (2017). https://doi.org/10.1007/978-3-319-66399-9_27
41. Tueno, A., Kerschbaum, F., Katzenbeisser, S.: Private evaluation of decision trees using sublinear cost. PoPETs **2019**(1), 266–286 (2019)
42. Wagh, S., Gupta, D., Chandran, N.: Securenn: 3-party secure computation for neural network training. PoPETs **2019**(3), 26–49 (2019)
43. Wang, X., Hubert Chan, T.-H., Shi, E.: Circuit ORAM: on tightness of the goldreich-ostrovsky lower bound. IACR Cryptology ePrint Archieve, vol. 2014, p. 672 (2014)
44. Wang, X.S., Huang, Y., Hubert Chan, T.-H., Shelat, A., Shi, E.: SCORAM: oblivious RAM for secure computation. In: ACM Conference on Computer and Communications Security, pp. 191–202. ACM (2014)
45. Wu, D.J., Feng, T., Naehrig, M., Lauter, K.E.: Privately evaluating decision trees and random forests. PoPETs **2016**(4), 335–355 (2016)
46. Yao, A.C.-C.: How to generate and exchange secrets (extended abstract). In: FOCS, pp. 162–167. IEEE Computer Society (1986)
47. Zahur, S., et al.: Revisiting square-root ORAM: efficient random access in multiparty computation. In: IEEE Symposium on Security and Privacy, pp. 218–234. IEEE Computer Society (2016)

Dispelling Myths on Superposition Attacks: Formal Security Model and Attack Analyses

Luka Music[1(✉)], Céline Chevalier[2], and Elham Kashefi[1,3]

[1] Département Informatique et Réseaux, CNRS, Sorbonne Université, Paris, France
luka.music@lip6.fr

[2] CRED, Université Panthéon-Assas Paris 2, Paris, France

[3] School of Informatics, University of Edinburgh, Edinburgh, Scotland

Abstract. With the emergence of quantum communication, it is of folkloric belief that the security of classical cryptographic protocols is automatically broken if the Adversary is allowed to perform superposition queries and the honest players forced to perform actions coherently on quantum states. Another widely held intuition is that enforcing measurements on the exchanged messages is enough to protect protocols from these attacks.

However, the reality is much more complex. Security models dealing with superposition attacks only consider unconditional security. Conversely, security models considering computational security assume that all supposedly classical messages are measured, which forbids by construction the analysis of superposition attacks. To fill in the gap between those models, Boneh and Zhandry have started to study the quantum computational security for classical primitives in their seminal work at Crypto'13, but only in the single-party setting. To the best of our knowledge, an equivalent model in the multiparty setting is still missing.

In this work, we propose the first computational security model considering superposition attacks for multiparty protocols. We show that our new security model is satisfiable by proving the security of the well-known One-Time-Pad protocol and give an attack on a variant of the equally reputable Yao Protocol for Secure Two-Party Computations. The post-mortem of this attack reveals the precise points of failure, yielding highly counter-intuitive results: Adding extra classical communication, which is harmless for classical security, can make the protocol become subject to superposition attacks. We use this newly imparted knowledge to construct the first concrete protocol for Secure Two-Party Computation that is resistant to superposition attacks. Our results show that there is no straightforward answer to provide for either the vulnerabilities of classical protocols to superposition attacks or the adapted countermeasures.

Keywords: Cryptographic protocols · Superposition attack · Post quantum security · Security model · Yao's protocol

See [16] for the full version.

K. Nguyen et al. (Eds.): ProvSec 2020, LNCS 12505, pp. 318–337, 2020.
https://doi.org/10.1007/978-3-030-62576-4_16

1 Introduction

Recent advances in quantum technologies threaten the security of many widely-deployed cryptographic primitives if we assume that the Adversary has classical access to the primitive but can locally perform quantum computations. This scenario has led to the emergence of *post-quantum cryptography.* But the situation is even worse in the *fully quantum* scenario, if we assume the Adversary further has quantum access to the primitive and can query the oracle with quantum states in superposition. Such access can arise in the case where the Adversary has direct access to the primitive that is being implemented (eg. symmetric encryption, hash functions), or if a protocol is used as a sub-routine where the Adversary plays all roles (as in the Fiat-Shamir transform based on Sigma Protocols) and can therefore implement them all quantumly. In the future, various primitives might natively be implemented on quantum machines and networks, either to benefit from speed-ups or because the rest of the protocol is inherently quantum. In this case, more information could be leaked, leading to new non-trivial attacks, as presented in a series of work initiated in [1,4,9]. A possible countermeasure against such *superposition attacks* is to forbid any kind of quantum access to the oracle through measurements. However, the security would then rely on the physical implementation of the measurement tool, which itself could be potentially exploited by a quantum Adversary. Thus, providing security guarantees in the fully quantum model is crucial. We focus here on the multiparty (interactive) setting.

Analysis of Existing Security Models. Modelling the security of classical protocols in a quantum world (especially multiparty protocols) is tricky, since various arbitrages need to be made concerning the (quantum or classical) access to channels and primitives.

A first possibility is to consider classical protocols embedded as quantum protocols, thus allowing the existence of superposition attacks. However, in such a setting, previous results only consider *perfect security,* meaning that the messages received by each player do not contain more information than its input and output. The seminal papers starting this line of work are those proving the impossibility of bit commitment [13,14]. The perfect security of the protocol implies that no additional information is stored in the auxiliary quantum registers of both parties at the end of the protocol and can therefore be traced out, so that an Adversary can easily produce a superposition of inputs and outputs.

This is for example the approach of [4,18], where the perfect correctness requirement is in fact a perfect (unconditional) security requirement (the protocol implements the functionality and *only* the functionality). In [4], they consider an even more powerful adversarial scenario where not only the honest player's actions are described as unitaries (their inputs are also in superposition) but the Adversary can corrupt parties in superposition (the corruption is modelled as an oracle call whose input is a subset of parties and which outputs the view of the corresponding parties). Both papers show that protocols are insecure in such a setting: In [4], they show that in the case of a multi-party protocol implementing a general functionality (capable of computing any function), no Simulator can perfectly replicate the superposition of views of the parties returned by the corruption oracle by using only an oracle call to an Ideal Functionality. In the case of a deterministic functionality, they give a necessary and sufficient condition for such a Simulator to exist, but which cannot be efficiently verified and is not constructive. In [18], they prove that any non-trivial Ideal Functionalities that accept superposition queries (or, equivalently, perfectly-secure protocols emulating them) must leak information to the Adversary beyond what the classical functionality does (meaning that the Adversary can do better than simply measure in the computational basis the state that it receives from the superposition oracle). In both cases, they heavily rely on the assumption of unconditional security to prove strong impossibility results and their proof techniques cannot be applied to the computational setting.

The second possibility to model the security of classical protocols in a quantum world is to define purely classical security models, in the sense that all supposedly classical messages are measured (Stand-Alone Model of [8] or the Quantum UC Model of [20]). Some (computationally) secure protocols exist in this setting, as shown by a series of articles in the literature (eg. [12]). However, these models forbid by construction the analysis of superposition attacks, precisely since all classical communications are modelled as measurements.

The Missing Link. The results of [4,18] in the unconditional security setting are not directly applicable to a *Computationally-Bounded Adversary.* The premiss to their analyses is that since the perfect execution of non-trivial functionalities is insecure, any real protocol implementing these functionalities is also insecure against Adversaries with quantum access (even more since they are simply computationally secure). However it turns out that, precisely because the protocol is only computationally-secure, the working registers of the parties cannot be devoid of information as is the case in the perfectly-secure setting (the messages contain exactly the same information as the secret inputs of the parties, but it is hidden to computationally-bounded Adversaries) and the techniques used for proving the insecurity of protocols in the perfect scenario no longer work.

This issue has been partially solved for single-party protocols with oracle queries in the line of work from [1], but never extended fully to the multi-party setting. The difficulty arises by the interactive property of such protocols. Indeed, in a real protocol, more care needs to be taken in considering all the registers that both parties deal with during the execution (auxiliary qubits that can be entangled due to the interactive nature of the protocols). Furthermore, care must also be taken in how the various classical operations are modelled quantumly, as choosing standard or minimal oracle representations may influence the applicability of some attacks [10]. The naive implementation of superposition attacks, applied to a real-world protocol, often leads to a joint state of the form $\sum_{x,m_1,m_2} |x\rangle |m_1\rangle |m_2\rangle |f(x,y)\rangle$ for a given value y of the honest player's input, and with the second register (containing the set of messages m_1 sent by the Adversary) being in the hands of the honest player (m_2 is the set of messages sent by the honest player and $f(x, y)$ is the result for input x). This global state does not allow the known attacks (such as [9]) to go through as the message registers cannot simply be discarded. This shows that the simple analysis of basic ideal primitives in the superposition attack setting is not sufficient to conclude on the security of the overall computationally-secure protocol and motivates the search for a framework for proving security of protocols against such attacks.

Our Contributions. The main purpose of this paper is thus to bridge a gap between two settings: one considers the security analysis of superposition attacks, but either for perfect security [4,18] (both works preclude the existence of secure protocols by being too restrictive) or only for single-party primitives with oracle access [1], while the other explicitly forbids such attacks by measuring classical messages [8,20].

To our knowledge, our result is the first attempt to formalize a security notion capturing security of two-party protocols against superposition attacks with computationally-bounded Adversaries as a simulation-based definition. We consider a more realistic scenario where a computational Adversary corrupts a fixed set of players at the beginning of the protocol and the input of the honest players are fixed classical values. We suppose that the ideal world trusted third party always measures its queries (it acts similarly to a classical participant), while the honest player always performs actions in superposition unless specifically instructed by the quantum embedding of the protocol (the Adversary and the Simulator can do whatever they want). Security is then defined by considering that an attack is successful if an Adversary is able to distinguish between the real and ideal executions with non-vanishing probability. The reason for adding a measurement to the functionality is to enforce that the (supposedly classical) protocol behaves indeed as a classical functionality. This is further motivated by the results of previous papers proving that functionalities with quantum behavior are inherently broken.

Case Studies. We present an attack on a slight variant of the Honest-but-Curious version of the classical Yao's protocol [19] for Secure Two-Party Computation. On the other hand, it is secure against Adversaries that have a quantum computer internally but send classical messages, therefore showing a separation. The variant is presented to demonstrate unusual and counter-intuitive reasons for which protocols may be insecure against superposition attacks.

Proof Technique. During the superposition attack, the Adversary essentially makes the honest player implement the oracle call in Deutsch-Jozsa's (DJ) algorithm [5] through its actions on a superposition provided by the Adversary. The binary function for which this oracle query is performed is linked to two possible outputs of the protocol. The Adversary can then apply the rest of the DJ algorithm to decide the nature of the function,[1] which allows it to extract the XOR of the two outputs. Similarly to the DJ algorithm where the state containing the output of the oracle remains in the $|-\rangle$ state during the rest of the algorithm

[1] The DJ algorithm decides whether a binary function is balanced or constant.

(it is not acted upon by the gates applied after the oracle call), the Adversary's actions during the rest of the attack do not affect the output register. Interestingly, this means that the attack can thus also be performed on the same protocol but where the Adversary has no output.

Superposition-Secure Two-Party Computation. Counter-intuitively, it is therefore not the output that makes the attack possible, but in this case the attack vector is a message consisting of information that, classically, the Adversary should already have, along with a partial measurement on the part of the honest player (which is even stranger considering that it is usually thought that the easiest way to prevent superposition attack is to measure the state). This shows that adding extra communication, even an exchange of classical information which seems meaningless for classical security, can make the protocol become subject to superposition attacks. Removing the point of failure by never sending back this information to the Adversary (as is the case in the original Yao Protocol) restores the protocol's security and therefore we show that Yao's protocol is secure against superposition attacks if the (honest) Evaluator recovers the output and does not divulge whether or not it has aborted. The proof relies on the no-signalling principle of quantum mechanics since in this case the honest player has no communication with the Adversary after receiving the state in superposition.

Contribution Summary and Outline. After basic notations in Sect. 2:

- Section 3 gives a new security model for superposition attacks;
- Section 4 describes a variant of Yao's protocol and proves its security against adversaries exchanging classical messages;
- Section 5.1 presents a superposition attack against this modified protocol;
- Section 5.2 builds a superposition-resistant version of Yao's protocol by leveraging the knowledge acquired through the attack;
- All proofs are postponed to the full version [16].

2 Preliminaries

All protocols will be two-party protocols (between parties P_1 and P_2). P_1 will be considered as the Adversary (written P_1^* when corrupted), while P_2 is honest.

Although we consider purely classical protocol, in order to be able to execute superposition attacks, both parties will have access to multiple quantum registers. All communications are considered as quantum unless specified (see Sect. 3 for a definition of the network models) and we call quantum operations any completely positive and trace non-decreasing superoperator acting on quantum registers (see [17] and the full version [16] for more details).

The principle of superposition attacks is to consider that a player, otherwise honestly behaving, performs all of its operations on quantum states rather than on classical states. In fact, any classical operation defined as a binary circuit with bit-strings as inputs can be transformed into a unitary operation that has the same effect on each bit-string (now considered a basis state in the computational basis) as the original operation by using Toffoli gates. Although any quantum computation can be turned into a unitary operation (using a large enough ancillary quantum register to purify it), it may be that the honest player may have to take a decision based on the value of its internal computations. This is more naturally defined as a measurement, and therefore such operations will be allowed but only when required by the protocol (in particular, when the protocol branches out depending on the result of some computation being correct). The rest of the protocol (in the honest case) will be modelled as unitary operations on the quantum registers of the players.

There are two ways to represent a classical function $f : \{0,1\}^n \leftarrow \{0,1\}^m$ as a unitary operation. The most general way (called *standard oracle* of f) is defined on basis state $|x\rangle |y\rangle$ (where $x \in \{0,1\}^n$ and $y \in \{0,1\}^m$) by $U_f |x\rangle |y\rangle = |x\rangle |y \oplus f(x)\rangle$, where $\oplus$ corresponds to the bit-wise XOR operation. On the other hand, if $n = m$ and f is a permutation over $\{0,1\}^n$, then it is possible (although in general inefficient) to represent f as a *minimal oracle* by $M_f |x\rangle = |f(x)\rangle$. Note that this is in general more powerful than the standard orale representation (see [10] for more information).

The security parameter will be noted η throughout the paper (it is passed implicitly as 1^η to all participants in the protocol and we omit when unambiguous). A function μ is *negligible in* η if, for every polynomial p, for η sufficiently large it holds that $\mu(\eta) < \frac{1}{p(\eta)}$. For any positive integer $N \in \mathbb{N}$, let $[N] := \{1, \ldots, N\}$. For any element X, $\#X$ corresponds to the number of parts in X (eg. size of a string, number of qubits in a register). The special symbol Abort will be used to indicate that a party in a protocol has aborted.

3 New Security Model for Superposition Attacks

General Protocol Model. All parties considered in this paper are modelled as BQP machines, which are also called polynomial quantum Turing machines and recognise languages in the BQP class of complexity [3,17]. They can perform any polynomial-sized family of quantum circuits and interact quantumly with other participants (by sending quantum states which may or may not be in superposition).

We assume that the input of the honest player is classical, meaning it is a pure state in the computational basis, unentangled from the rest of the input state (which corresponds to the Adversary's input). This is in stark contrast with other papers considering superposition attacks [4,18] where the input of the honest players is always a uniform superposition over all possible inputs. We also consider that the corrupted party is chosen and fixed from the beginning of the protocol. We will often abuse notation and consider the corrupted party and the Adversary as one entity.

The security of protocols will be defined using the *real/ideal simulation paradigm*, adapted from the Stand-Alone Model of [8]. The parties involved are: an Environment $\mathcal{Z}$, the parties participating in the protocol, a Real-World

Adversary $\mathcal{A}$ and an Ideal-World Adversary also called Simulator $\mathcal{S}$ that runs $\mathcal{A}$ internally and interacts with an Ideal Functionality (that the protocol strives to emulates). An execution of the protocol (in the real or ideal case) works as follows:

1. The Environment $\mathcal{Z}$ produces the input y of P_2, the auxiliary input state $\rho_{\mathcal{A}}$ of the Adversary (containing an input for corrupted party P_1^*, possibly in superposition).
2. The Adversary interacts with either the honest player performing the protocol or a Simulator with single-query access to an Ideal Functionality.
3. Based on its internal state, it outputs a bit corresponding to its guess about whether the execution was real or ideal. If secure, no Adversary should be able to distinguish with high probability the two scenarios.
4. The Adversary sends a state to the Environment $\mathcal{Z}$.
5. The Environment $\mathcal{Z}$ takes as input this final state and outputs a bit corresponding to its guess of whether the execution was real or ideal.

Network Model. To capture both the security against Adversaries with and without superposition (so that we may compare both securities for a given protocol), we parametrize the security Definition 1 below with a network model $\mathfrak{N}$. The quantum network $\mathfrak{Q}$ is modelled by having both players interact not only with their internal quantum registers but also with a shared quantum communication register $\mathcal{Q}$. These actions are defined as unitaries. On the other hand, the classical network $\mathfrak{C}$ is modelled as both players having access to a shared classical tape $\mathcal{C}$ which is read the beginning of each activation of a player and a quantum register initialised using the computational basis vector corresponding to the message contained within (or equivalently, the shared quantum register $\mathcal{Q}$ from the quantum network is measured in the computational basis). The outgoing messages are written to the tape at the end of each player's activation. The case where the network is classical is called *classical-style* security (as it is simply a weaker variant of Stand-Alone Security in the usual sense of [8]), while a protocol that remains secure when the network is quantum is said to be *superposition-resistant.* This allows us to demonstrate a separation between Adversaries with and without superposition access. Conversely, since the classical network can be seen as a restricted quantum channel, security with superposition access automatically implies classical-style security.

Ideal Functionality Behaviour and Formal Security Definition. This section differs crucially from previous models of security. The Two-Party Computation Ideal Functionality implementing a binary function f, formally defined in the full version [16], takes as input a quantum state from each party, measures it in the computational basis to get $x \in \{0,1\}^{n_X}$ and $y \in \{0,1\}^{n_Y}$, applies the function f to the classical measurement results and returns the classical inputs to each party while one of them also receives the single bit of output z.

While it can seem highly counter-intuitive to consider an ideal scenario where a measurement is performed (since it is not present in the real scenario), this measurement by the Ideal Functionality is necessary in order to have a meaningful definition of security. It is only if the protocol with superposition access behaves similarly to a classical protocol that it can be considered as resistant to superposition attacks. It is therefore precisely because we wish to capture the security against superposition attack, that we define the Ideal Functionality as purely classical (hence the measurement). If the Ideal Adversary (a Simulator interacting classically with the Ideal Functionality) and the Real Adversary (which can interact in superposition with the honest player) are indistinguishable to the Environment, only then is the protocol superposition-secure.

Furthermore, as argued briefly in the Introduction, Ideal Functionalities which do not measure the inputs of both parties when they receive them as they always allow superposition attacks, which then extract more information than the classical case (as proven in [18]). A superposition attack against a protocol implementing such a functionality is therefore not considered an attack since it is by definition a tolerated behaviour in the ideal scenario.

We can now give our security Definition 1. A protocol between parties P_1 and P_2 is said to securely compute two-party functions of a given set $\mathfrak{F}$ against corrupted party P_1^* if, for all functions $f : \{0,1\}^{n_X} \times \{0,1\}^{n_Y} \longrightarrow \{0,1\}^{n_Z}$ with $f \in \mathfrak{F}$, no Environment $\mathcal{Z}$ can distinguish between the real and ideal executions with high probability.

Definition 1 (Computational Security in Network Class $\mathfrak{N}$). *Let $\epsilon(\eta) = o(1)$ be a function of the security parameter η. Let $f \in \mathfrak{F}$ be the function to be computed by protocol Π between parties P_1 and P_2. We say that a protocol Π $\epsilon(\eta)$-securely emulates Ideal Functionality $\mathcal{F}$ computing functions from set $\mathfrak{F}$ against adversarial P_1^* in network $\mathfrak{N}$ (with $\mathfrak{N} \in \{\mathfrak{C}, \mathfrak{Q}\}$) if for all quantum polynomial-time Adversaries $\mathcal{A}$ controlling the corrupted party P_1^* and Environments $\mathcal{Z}$ producing y and $\rho_{\mathcal{A}}$, there exists a Simulator $S_{P_1^*}$ such that, in network $\mathfrak{N}$*

$$\left|\mathbb{P}\Big[b = 0 \mid b \leftarrow \mathcal{Z}\Big(v_{\mathcal{A}}(S_{P_1^*}, \rho_{\mathcal{A}})\Big)\Big] - \mathbb{P}\Big[b = 0 \mid b \leftarrow \mathcal{Z}\Big(v_{\mathcal{A}}(P_2(y), \rho_{\mathcal{A}})\Big)\Big]\right| \leq \epsilon(\eta) \tag{1}$$

In the equation above, the variable $v_{\mathcal{A}}(S_{P_1^*}, \rho_{\mathcal{A}})$ corresponds to the final state (or view) of the Adversary in the ideal execution when interacting with Simulator $S_{P_1^*}$ with Ideal Functionality $\mathcal{F}$ and $v_{\mathcal{A}}(P_2(y), \rho_{\mathcal{A}})$ corresponds to the final state of the Adversary when interacting with honest party P_2 in the real protocol Π. The probability is taken over all executions of protocol Π.

We define input-indistinguishability in Definition 2. In the case where the adversarial player has no input, the two security notions are equivalent (the Simulator simply performs the protocol with a random input). This is formally proven in the full version [16].

Definition 2 (Input-Indistinguishability in Network Class $\mathfrak{N}$). *Let Π be protocol between parties P_1 and P_2 with input space $\{0,1\}^{n_Y}$ for P_2. We say that the execution of Π is ϵ-*input-indistinguishable *for P_1^* in network $\mathfrak{N}$ if* *there exists an* $\epsilon(\eta) = o(1)$ *such that, for all computationally-bounded quantum Distinguishers* $\mathcal{D}$ *and any two inputs* $y_1, y_2 \in \{0,1\}^{n_Y}$*:*

$$\left|\mathbb{P}\Big[b=0 \mid b \leftarrow \mathcal{D}\Big(v_{\mathcal{A}}(P_2(y_1), \rho_{\mathcal{A}})\Big)\Big] - \mathbb{P}\Big[b=0 \mid b \leftarrow \mathcal{D}\Big(v_{\mathcal{A}}(P_2(y_2), \rho_{\mathcal{A}})\Big)\Big]\right| \leq \epsilon(\eta) \tag{2}$$

In the equation above, the variable $v_{\mathcal{A}}(P_2(y_i), \rho_{\mathcal{A}})$ *corresponds to the final state of the Adversary when interacting with honest party* P_2 *(with input* y_i*) in the real protocol* Π*. The probability is taken over all executions of protocol* Π*.*

Adversarial Classes. Quantifying Definition 1 or 2 over a subset of Adversaries in each class yields flavours such as Honest-but-Curious or Malicious. The behaviour of an Honest-but-Curious Adversary in a classical network $\mathfrak{C}$ is the same as a classical Honest-but-Curious Adversary during the protocol but it may use its quantum capabilities in the post-processing phase of its attack. We define an extension of these Adversaries in Definition 3: they are almost Honest-but-Curious in that there is an Honest-but-Curious Adversary whose Simulator also satisfies the security definition for the initial Adversary. This is required as the adversarial behaviour of our attack is not strictly Honest-but-Curious when translated to classical messages, but it does follow this new definition.

Definition 3 (Extended Honest-but-Curious Adversaries). *Let* Π *be a protocol that is secure according to Definition 1 against Honest-but-Curious Adversaries in a classical network* $\mathfrak{C}$*. We say that an Adversary* $\mathcal{A}$ *is Extended Honest-but-Curious if there exists an Honest-but-Curious Adversary* $\mathcal{A}'$ *such that the associated Simulator* $\mathcal{S}'$ *satisfies Definition 1 for* $\mathcal{A}$ *if we allow it to output* Abort *when the honest party would abort as well.*

Comments on the Security Model. The superposition-security of the Classical One-Time Pad is proven in the full version [16]. In our security model, both the Adversary and Simulator can have superpositions of states as input. However, if the Simulator chooses to send a state to the Ideal Functionality, it knows that this third party will perform on it a measurement in the computational basis. Note that in any security proof, the Simulator may choose not to perform the call to the Ideal Functionality. This is because the security definition does not force the Simulator to reproduce faithfully the output of the honest Client, as the distinguishing done by the Environment takes only the Adversary's output into account. This also means that sequential composability explicitly does not hold with such a definition, even with the most basic functionalities (whereas the Stand-Alone Framework of [8] guarantees it). An interesting research direction would be to find a composable framework for proving security against superposition attacks and we leave this as an open question. The subtlety of our attack vector presented below tends to suggest a negative answer.

4 The Modified Honest-but-Curious Yao Protocol

In order to demonstrate the capabilities of our new model in the case of more complex two-party scenarios, we will analyse the security of the well-known Yao

Protocol, pioneer of Secure Two-Party Computation, in classical and quantum networks.

Its purpose is to allow two Parties, the Garbler and the Evaluator, to compute a joint function on their two classical inputs. The Garbler starts by preparing an encrypted version of the function and then the Evaluator decrypts it using keys that correspond to the two players' inputs, the resulting decrypted value being the final output.

The Original Yao Protocol secure against Honest-but-Curious classical Adversaries has first been described by Yao in the oral presentation for [19], but a rigorous formal proof was only presented in [11]. It has been proven secure against quantum Adversaries with no superposition access to the honest player in [2] (for a quantum version of IND-CPA that only allows random oracle queries to be in superposition).

We start by presenting informal definitions for symmetric encryption schemes in Sect. 4.1. We then present in Sect. 4.2 the garbled table construction which is the main building block of Yao's Protocol and give an informal description of the Original Yao Protocol. Then in Sect. 4.3 we give a description of a slight variant of the original protocol, resulting in the Modified Yao Protocol. The modifications do not make the protocol less secure in classical networks, but will make superposition attacks possible as presented in Sect. 5.

4.1 Definitions for Symmetric Encryption Schemes

An encryption scheme consists of two classical efficiently computable deterministic functions $\mathsf{Enc} : \mathfrak{K}\times\mathfrak{A}\times\mathfrak{M} \to \mathfrak{K}\times\mathfrak{A}\times\mathfrak{C}$ and $\mathsf{Dec} : \mathfrak{K}\times\mathfrak{A}\times\mathfrak{C} \to \mathfrak{K}\times\mathfrak{A}\times\mathfrak{M}$ (where $\mathfrak{K} = \{0,1\}^{n_K}$ is the set of valid keys, $\mathfrak{A} = \{0,1\}^{n_A}$ the set of auxiliary inputs, $\mathfrak{M}$ the set of plaintext messages and $\mathfrak{C}$ the set of ciphertexts, which is supposed equal to $\mathfrak{M} = \{0,1\}^{n_M}$). We suppose that for all $(k, \text{aux}, m) \in \mathfrak{K} \times \mathfrak{A} \times \mathfrak{M}$, we have that $\mathsf{Dec}_k(\text{aux}, \mathsf{Enc}_k(\text{aux}, m)) = m$.

We will use a symmetric encryption scheme with slightly different properties compared to the original protocol of [19] or [11]. The purpose of these modifications is to make it possible to later represent the action of the honest player (the decryption of garbled values) using a minimal oracle representation when embedded as a quantum protocol. We give a concrete instantiation of a scheme satisfying the definitions below in the full version [16].

Definition 4 (Minimal Oracle Representation). *Let* $(\mathsf{Enc}, \mathsf{Dec})$ *be an encryption scheme defined as above, we say that it has a Minimal Oracle Representation if there exists efficiently computable unitaries* $\mathsf{M}_{\mathsf{Enc}}$ *and* $\mathsf{M}_{\mathsf{Dec}}$*, called minimal oracles, such that for all* $k \in \mathfrak{K}$, $\text{aux} \in \mathfrak{A}$ *and* $m \in \mathfrak{M}$, $\mathsf{M}_{\mathsf{Enc}} |k\rangle |\text{aux}\rangle |m\rangle = |e_K(k)\rangle |e_A(\text{aux})\rangle |\mathsf{Enc}_k(\text{aux}, m)\rangle$ *(in which case* $\mathsf{M}_{\mathsf{Enc}}^\dagger = \mathsf{M}_{\mathsf{Dec}}$*), where* e_K *and* e_A *are efficiently invertible permutations of the key and auxiliary value.*

We then define the quantum security of such a symmetric encryption scheme by imposing that sampling the key and giving a black-box access to an encryption quantum oracle is indistinguishable for a quantum Adversary from giving it superposition access to a random permutation. This is simply a quantum game-based version of the definition for pseudo-random permutations [7].

Definition 5 (Real-or-Permutation Security of Symmetric Encryption). *Let* $(\mathsf{Enc}, \mathsf{Dec})$ *be a symmetric encryption scheme with Minimal Oracle Representation. Let* $\mathcal{S}_{n_M}$ *be the set of permutations over* $\{0,1\}^{n_M}$*. Consider the following game* Γ *between a Challenger and the Adversary:*

1. *The Challenger chooses uniformly at random a bit* $b \in \{0,1\}$ *and:*
   - *If* $b = 0$*, it samples a key* $k \in \{0,1\}^{n_K}$ *uniformly at random, and sets the oracle* $\mathcal{O}$ *by defining it over the computational basis states* $|\mathrm{aux}\rangle |m\rangle$ *for* $m \in \{0,1\}^{n_M}$ *and* $\mathrm{aux} \in \{0,1\}^{n_A}$ *as* $\mathcal{O}|\mathrm{aux}\rangle|m\rangle = U_{\mathsf{Enc}}|k\rangle|\mathrm{aux}\rangle|m\rangle = |k\rangle|e_A(\mathrm{aux})\rangle|\mathsf{Enc}_k(\mathrm{aux}, m)\rangle$ *(the oracle first applies the minimal encryption oracle* $\mathsf{M}_{\mathsf{Enc}}$ *and then the inverse of* d_K *to the register containing the key).*
   - *If* $b = 1$*, it samples a permutation over* $\{0,1\}^{n_M}$ *uniformly at random* $\sigma \in \mathcal{S}_{n_M}$ *and sets the oracle* $\mathcal{O}$ *as* $\mathcal{O}|\mathrm{aux}\rangle|m\rangle = U_{\sigma,e_A}|\mathrm{aux}\rangle|m\rangle = |e_A(\mathrm{aux})\rangle|\sigma(m)\rangle$*.*
2. *For* $i \leq q$ *with* $q = \mathrm{poly}(\eta)$*, the Adversary sends a state* ρ_i *of its choice (composed of* n_M *qubits) to the Challenger. The Challenger responds by sampling an auxiliary value at random* $\mathrm{aux}_i \in \{0,1\}^{n_A}$*, applying the oracle to the state* $|\mathrm{aux}_i\rangle \otimes \rho_i$ *and sending the result back to the Adversary along with the modified auxiliary value (notice that the oracle has no effect on the key if there is one and so it remains unentangled from the Adversary's system).*
3. *The Adversary outputs a bit* $\tilde{b}$ *and stops.*

A symmetric encryption scheme is said to be secure against quantum Adversaries if there exists $\epsilon(\eta)$ *negligible in* η *such that, for any Adversary* $\mathcal{A}$ *with superposition access and initial auxiliary state* ρ_{aux}*:*

$$Adv_{\Gamma}(\mathcal{A}) := \left|\frac{1}{2} - \mathbb{P}\left[b = \tilde{b} \mid \tilde{b} \leftarrow \mathcal{A}(\rho_{aux}, \Gamma)\right]\right| \leq \epsilon(\eta) \tag{3}$$

4.2 The Original Yao Protocol

The protocol will be presented in a hybrid model where both players have access to a trusted third party implementing a 1-out-of-2 String Oblivious Transfer, in which one party (P_1 in our case) has two strings (k_0, k_1) and the other (P_2) has a bit $b \in \{0,1\}$. The output of P_2 is the string k_b (with no knowledge about $k_{\bar{b}}$), while on the other hand P_1 has no output and no knowledge about choice-bit b. The attack presented further below does not rely on an insecurity from the OT (the classical correctness of the Oblivious Transfer is sufficient), which will therefore be supposed to be perfectly implemented and, as all Ideal Functionalities in this model, without superposition access.

We focus on the case where the Garbler's output is a single bit. Suppose that the Garbler and Evaluator have agreed on the binary function to be evaluated

$f : \{0,1\}^{n_X} \times \{0,1\}^{n_Y} \longrightarrow \{0,1\}$, with the Garbler's input being $x \in \{0,1\}^{n_X}$ and the Evaluator's input being $y \in \{0,1\}^{n_Y}$.

The protocol can be summarised as follows. Let $(\mathsf{Enc}, \mathsf{Dec})$ be a symmetric encryption scheme. The Garbler G samples keys $\left\{k_0^{G,i}, k_1^{G,i}\right\}_{i\in[n_X]}$ and $\left\{k_0^{E,i}, k_1^{E,i}\right\}_{i\in[n_Y]}$ for the Garbler's and Evaluator's input respectively. To each bit of input correspond two keys, one (lower-indexed with 0) if the player chooses the value 0 for this bit-input and the other if it chooses the value 1. They invoke n_Y instances of a 1-out-of-2 String OT Ideal Functionality, the Evaluator's input (as Receiver of the OT) to these is y_i for $i \in [n_Y]$, while the Garbler inputs (as Sender) the keys $(k_0^{E,i}, k_1^{E,i})$ corresponding to input i of the Evaluator. The Evaluator therefore recovers $k_{y_i}^{E,i}$ at the end of each activation of the OT. The Garbler then sends the keys $\{k_{x_i}^{G,i}\}_{i\in[n_X]}$ corresponding to its own input along with the garbled circuit GC_f which is constructed as follows.

For a gate computing a two-bit function g, with inputs wires labelled a and b and output wire z, the Garbler first chooses keys $(k_0^a, k_1^a, k_0^b, k_1^b) \in \mathfrak{K}^4$ for the input wires and $k^z \in \{0,1\}$ for the output.[2] Let aux_a and aux_b be two auxiliary values for the encryption scheme. It then iterates over all possible values $\tilde{a}, \tilde{b} \in \{0,1\}$ to compute the garbled table values $E_{\tilde{a},\tilde{b}}^{k^z}$ defined as (with padding length $p = n_M - 1$, where n_M is the bit-length of the messages of the encryption scheme and $\|$ represents string concatenation):

$$E_{\tilde{a},\tilde{b}}^{k^z} := \mathsf{Enc}_{k_{\tilde{a}}^a}\left(\mathrm{aux}_a, \mathsf{Enc}_{k_{\tilde{b}}^b}(\mathrm{aux}_b, g(\tilde{a}, \tilde{b}) \oplus k^z \parallel 0^p)\right) \tag{4}$$

The ordered list thus obtained is called the *initial* garbled table. The Garbler then chooses a random permutation $\pi \in \mathcal{S}_4$ and applies it to this list, yielding the *final* garbled table $GT_g^{(a,b,z)}$. For gates with fan-in l, the only difference is that the number of keys used will be $2l$ (two for each input bit) and the number of values in the garbled table will be 2^l, the rest may be computed in a similar way (by iterating over all possible values of the function's inputs). The keys are always used in an fixed order which is known to both players at time of execution (we suppose for example that, during encryption, all the keys of the Evaluator are applied first, followed by the keys of the Garbler).

Finally, after receiving the keys (through the OT protocols for its own, and via direct communication for the Garbler's) and garbled table, the Evaluator uses them to decrypt sequentially each entry of the table and considers it a success if the last p bits are equal to 0 (except with probability negligible in p, the decryption of a ciphertext with the wrong keys will not yield p bits set to 0, see Lemma 1). It then returns the decrypted value to the Garbler.

[2] The value k^z One-Time-Pads the output, preserving security for the Garbler after decryption as only one value from the garbled table can be decrypted correctly.

4.3 Presentation of the Modified Yao Protocol

Differences with the Original Yao Protocol. There are four main differences between our Modified Yao Protocol 1 and the well-known protocol from [19] recalled above. The first two are trivially just as secure in the classical case (as they give no more power to either player): the Garbler sends one copy of its keys to the Evaluator for each entry in the garbled table and instructs it to use a "fresh" copy for each decryption; and the Evaluator returns to the Garbler the copy of the Garbler's keys that were used in the successful decryption. There is only one garbled table for the whole function instead of a series of garbled tables corresponding to gates in the function's decomposition. This means that the size of the garbled table is 2^l for inputs of size l (equivalently, this modified protocol can only be used for logarithmically-sized inputs). This is less efficient but no less secure than the original design in a classical network, as a player breaking the scheme for this configuration would only have more power if it has access to intermediate keys as well. The last difference is the use of a weaker security assumption for the symmetric encryption function (indistinguishability from a random permutation instead of the quantum equivalents of IND-CPA security from [1,6,15]). This lower security requirement is imposed in order to model the honest player's actions using the minimal oracle representation. This property influences the security against an adversarial Evaluator, but Theorem 2 shows that this assumption is sufficient here. The reasons for these modifications, related to our attack, are developed in Sect. 5.

The full protocol for a single bit of output is described formally in Protocol 1. Its correctness and security in classical networks are captured by Theorems 1 and 2, showing that the modifications above have no impact in this setting (against both quantum and classical Adversaries).

Theorem 1 (Correctness of the Modified Yao Protocol). *Let* $(\mathsf{Enc}, \mathsf{Dec})$ *be a symmetric encryption scheme with a Minimal Oracle Representation (Definition 4). Protocol 1 is correct with probability exponentially close to* 1 *in* η *for* $p = \eta$.

Theorem 2 (Classical-Style Security of the Modified Yao Protocol). *Consider a hybrid execution where the Oblivious Transfer is handled by a classical trusted third party. Let* $(\mathsf{Enc}, \mathsf{Dec})$ *be a symmetric encryption scheme that is* ϵ_{Sym}*-real-or-permutation-secure (Definition 5). Then, in classical network* $\mathfrak{C}$*, Protocol 1 is perfectly-secure against adversarial Garbler (with advantage* 0*) and* $(2^{n_X+n_Y}-1)\epsilon_{Sym}$*-secure against adversarial Evaluator.*

5 Analysis of Yao's Protocol with Superposition Access

Section 5.1 presents a superposition attack on the Modified Yao Protocol (Protocol 1). Section 5.2 then analyses it post-mortem to build a Superposition-Resistant Yao Protocol. The formal description of the attacks are given in the full version [16]. We also show in the full version how to slightly improve the

Protocol 1. Modified Yao Protocol for One Output Bit.

Input: The Garbler and Evaluator have inputs $x \in \{0,1\}^{n_X}$ and $y \in \{0,1\}^{n_Y}$ respectively, with $n_X + n_Y = \mathcal{O}(\log(\eta))$.
Output: The Garbler has one bit of output, the Evaluator has no output.
Public Information: The function f to be evaluated, the encryption scheme $(\mathsf{Enc}, \mathsf{Dec})$ and the size of the padding p.
The Protocol:

1. The Garbler chooses uniformly at random the values $\left\{k_0^{G,i}, k_1^{G,i}\right\}_{i\in[n_X]}$, $\left\{k_0^{E,j}, k_1^{E,j}\right\}_{j\in[n_Y]}$ from $\mathfrak{K}$ and $k^z \in \{0,1\}$. It uses those values to compute the garbled table $GT_f^{(X,Y,Z)}$, with X being the set of wires for the Garbler's input, Y the set of wires for the evaluators input, and Z the output wire.
2. The Garbler and Evaluator perform n_Y interactions with the trusted third party performing the OT Ideal Functionality. In interaction j:
   - The Garbler's inputs are the keys $(k_0^{E,j}, k_1^{E,j})$, the Evaluator's input is y_j.
   - The Evaluator's output is the key $k_{y_j}^{E,j}$.
3. The Garbler sends the garbled table $GT_f^{(X,Y,Z)}$ and $2^{n_X+n_Y}$ copies of the keys corresponding to its input $\{k_{x_i}^{G,i}\}_{i\in[n_X]}$. It also sends the auxiliary values $\{\mathrm{aux}_k\}_{k\in[n_X+n_Y]}$ that were used for the encryption of the garbled values.
4. For each entry in the garbled table:
   (a) The Evaluator uses the next "fresh" copy of the keys supplied by the Garbler along with the keys that it received from the OT Ideal Functionality to decrypt the entry in the garbled table.
   (b) It checks that the last p bits of the decrypted value are all equal to 0. If so it returns the register containing the output value and the ones containing the Garbler's keys to the Garbler.
   (c) Otherwise it discards this "used" copy of the keys and repeats the process with the next entry in the garbled table. If this was the last entry it outputs Abort and halts.
5. If the Evaluator did no output Abort, the Garbler applies the One-Time-Pad defined by the key associated with wire z to decrypt the output: if $k^z = 1$, it flips the corresponding output bit, otherwise it does nothing. It then sets the bit in the output register as its output.

bound on the attack by applying the free-XOR technique to an instance of the Yao Protocol computing the OT function.

Note that this attack does not simply distinguish between the ideal and real executions, but allows the Adversary to extract one bit of information from the honest player's input. It is therefore a concrete attack on the Modified Yao Protocol 1 (as opposed to a weaker statement about not being able to perform an indistinguishable simulation in our model).

5.1 Attacking the Modified Yao Protocol via Superpositions

In the following, the classical protocol is embedded in a quantum framework, all message are stored in quantum registers as quantum states that can be in superposition. The encryption and decryption procedures are performed using the Minimal Oracle Representation from Definition 4. The OT Ideal Functionality measures the inputs and outputs states in the computational basis. The checks of the Evaluator on the padding for successful decryption are modelled as a quantum measurement of the corresponding register.

We start by presenting the action of the adversarial Garbler during the execution of Protocol 1 (its later actions are described below). Its aim is to generate a state containing a superposition of its inputs and the corresponding outputs for a fixed value of the Evaluator's input. This State Generation Procedure on the Modified Yao Protocol 1 can be summarised as follows (it is generalized to more superpositions in the full version [16]):

1. The Adversary's choice of keys, garbled table generation (but for both values of k^z) and actions in the OT are performed honestly.
2. Instead of sending one set of keys as its input, it sends a superposition of keys for two different non-trivial values of the Garbler's input $(\widehat{x_0}, \widehat{x_1})$ (they do not uniquely determine the output).
3. For each value in the garbled table, it instead sends a uniform superposition over all calculated values (with a phase of -1 for states representing garbled values where $k^z = 1$).
4. It then waits for the Evaluator to perform the decryption procedure and, if the Evaluator succeeded in decrypting one of the garbled values and returns the output and register containing the Garbler's keys, the Adversary performs a clean-up procedure which translates each key for bit-input 0 (respectively 1) into a logical encoding of 0 (respectively 1). This procedure depends only on its own choice of keys.

Theorem 3 (State Generation Analysis). *The state contained in the Garbler's attack registers at the end of a successful Superposition Generation Procedure is negligibly close to* $\frac{1}{2}\sum_{x,k^z}(-1)^{k^z}\left|x^L\right\rangle|f(x,\hat{y})\oplus k^z\rangle$*, where* x^L *is a logical encoding of* x *and* $x \in \{\widehat{x_0}, \widehat{x_1}\}$*. Its success probability is lower bounded by* $1-e^{-1}$ *for all values of* n_X *and* n_Y*.*

Proof (Sketch).
The Evaluator's state after one decryption of a garbled table entry is (for $x \in \{\widehat{x_0}, \widehat{x_1}\}$, tracing out the unentangled values and with $g_{x,y}^{x',y',c}$ representing incorrectly decrypted values):

$$\left(\sum_{x,k^z}(-1)^{k^z}\left|k_x^G\right\rangle|f(x,\hat{y})\oplus k^z\rangle|0\rangle^{\otimes p}+\sum_{\substack{k^z,x,x',y'\\(x,y)\neq(x',\hat{y})}}(-1)^{k^z}\left|k_x^G\right\rangle\left|g_{x,\hat{y}}^{x',y',k^z}\right\rangle\right) \tag{5}$$

With overwhelming probability in η, $g_{x,\hat{y}}^{x',y',c} \neq r \parallel 0^p$ and the states in both sums are orthogonal. Checking the padding is modelled as a measurement with successful outcome $|0^p\rangle\langle 0^p|$. If successful, the projected state received by the Garbler is then:

$$\sum_{x,k^z}(-1)^c\left|k_x^G\right\rangle|f(x,\hat{y})\oplus k^z\rangle \tag{6}$$

The final result after the clean-up procedure is $\frac{1}{2}\sum_{x,k^z}(-1)^{k^z}|x^{L'}\rangle|f(x,\hat{y})\oplus k^z\rangle$ (where $x^{L'}$ is a logical encoding of x) .

If a given measurement fails, the Evaluator moves to the next garbled table value with fresh keys, essentially repeating the same procedure. The success probability of each attempt is simply given by the number of states correctly decrypted out of the total number of states $\frac{1}{2^{n_X+n_Y}}$. The probability that no measurement succeeds in $2^{n_X+n_Y}$ independent attempts is given by $\left(1-\frac{1}{2^{n_X+n_Y}}\right)^{2^{n_X+n_Y}} \leq e^{-1}$. The success probability is therefore lower-bounded by $1-e^{-1}$.

□

We can now analyse the actions of the Adversary after the protocol has terminated. The Full Attack breaking the security of the Modified Yao Protocol 1 (Theorem 4) can be summarised as follows:

1. The Environment provides the Adversary with the values of the Garbler's input $(\widehat{x_0},\widehat{x_1})$. The input of the honest Evaluator is $\hat{y}$.
2. The Adversary performs the State Generation Procedure with these inputs.
3. If it has terminated successfully, the Adversary performs an additional clean-up procedure (which only depends on the values of $(\widehat{x_0},\widehat{x_1})$) to change the logical encoding of $\widehat{x_b}$ into an encoding of b. The resulting state is $\frac{1}{\sqrt{2}}(|0\rangle + (-1)^{b_0\oplus b_1}|1\rangle)\otimes|-\rangle$ (omitting the logical encoding, with $b_i := f(\widehat{x_i},\hat{y})$).
4. The Adversary recover the XOR of the output values for the two inputs by applying a Hadamard gate to its first register and measuring it in the computational basis.[3]

Theorem 4 (Vulnerability to Superposition Attacks of the Modified Yao Protocol). *For any non-trivial two-party function $f:\{0,1\}^{n_X}\times\{0,1\}^{n_Y}\to\{0,1\}$, let $(\widehat{x_0},\widehat{x_1})$ be a pair of non-trivial values in $\{0,1\}^{n_X}$. For all inputs $\hat{y}$ of honest Evaluator in Protocol 1, let $\mathsf{P}_f^E(\hat{y}) = f(\widehat{x_0},\hat{y})\oplus f(\widehat{x_1},\hat{y})$. Then there exists a real-world Adversary $\mathcal{A}$ in quantum network $\mathfrak{Q}$ against Protocol 1 implementing f such that for any Simulator $\mathcal{S}$, the advantage of the Adversary over the Simulator in guessing the value of $\mathsf{P}_f^E(\hat{y})$ is lower-bounded by $\frac{1}{2}(1-e^{-1})$.*

Proof (Sketch). The Superposition Generation Procedure succeeds with probability $1-e^{-1}$. Then the Adversary applies the final steps of Deutsch's algorithm as follows and recover the value of the XOR with probability 1. The Adversary first applies the clean-up procedure on the registers containing $\widehat{x_i}^{L'}$ and obtains (for a different value L for the logical encoding):

$$\frac{1}{2}\left(|0\rangle^{\otimes L}|f(\widehat{x_0},\hat{y})\rangle - |0\rangle^{\otimes L}|f(\widehat{x_0},\hat{y})\oplus 1\rangle + |1\rangle^{\otimes L}|f(\widehat{x_1},\hat{y})\rangle - |1\rangle^{\otimes L}|f(\widehat{x_1},\hat{y})\oplus 1\rangle\right) \tag{7}$$

[3] This corresponds to the final steps of the DJ algorithm.

Let $b_i := f(\widehat{x_i}, \hat{y})$, the state is then $\frac{1}{\sqrt{2}}(-1)^{b_0}\left(|0\rangle^{\otimes L} + (-1)^{b_0 \oplus b_1}|1\rangle^{\otimes L}\right) \otimes |-\rangle$. The Adversary then applies the logical Hadamard gate, the resulting state is $|b_0 \oplus b_1\rangle^{\otimes L} \otimes |-\rangle$. The Adversary measures the first qubit in the computational basis to obtain $b_0 \oplus b_1 = f(\widehat{x_0}, \hat{y}) \oplus f(\widehat{x_1}, \hat{y})$.

If the state generation fails, Adversary resorts to guessing the value of the value of $\mathsf{P}_f^E(\hat{y})$, winning with a probability $\frac{1}{2}$. On the other hand, any Simulator is only able to guess the value of $\mathsf{P}_f^E(\hat{y})$. The advantage of the Adversary over any Simulator is lower-bounded by $\frac{1}{2}(1 - e^{-1})$.

□

Finally, the following lemma captures the fact that the previously described Adversary does not break the Honest-but-Curious security of the Modified Yao Protocol if it does not have superposition access (a fully-malicious one can trivially break it), thereby demonstrating the separation between Adversaries with and without superposition access. See full version [16] for a detailed explanation.

Lemma 1 (Adversarial Behaviour Analysis). *In a classical network* $\mathfrak{C}$, *the Adversary described in the Full Attack is an* Extended Honest-but-Curious Adversary *(Definition 3).*

Justifying the Differences in the Protocol Variant. The fact that the Garbler sends multiple copies of its keys is what allows the success probability to be constant and independent from the size of the inputs. Returning the Garbler's keys to the Adversary is an essential part of the attack, as described below. The specificities of the encryption scheme removes the need to add an ancillary register for encryption and decryption. For the same reason, we do not decompose the function into elementary gates, as the intermediate keys would add another entangled register as well.

5.2 Superposition-Resistant Yao Protocol

We can now analyse the crucial points where the security breaks down and propose counter-measures. We notice that all actions of the Adversary only act on the registers that contain its own keys (recall that the Evaluator sends back the Garbler's keys after a successful decryption) and have no effect on the output register, which stays in the $|-\rangle$ state the whole time. It is thus unentangled from the rest of the state and the attack on the protocol can therefore also be performed if the Garbler has no output. As the security in this case still holds for Adversaries in classical network $\mathfrak{C}$ via input-indistinguishability, this security property does not carry over from the classical to the quantum network case.

Therefore, counter-intuitively, the precise point that makes the attack possible is a seemingly innocuous message consisting of information that the Adversary should (classically) already have, along with a partial measurement on the part of the honest player (usually, measuring the state is thought to be the easiest way to prevent superposition attacks).

Not sending back this register to the Adversary (as in the Original Yao Protocol) yields the following protocol structure: one party sends everything to the other, who then simply applies local operations. If the Environment is able to guess whether it is in the real or ideal situation, this would violate the no-signalling condition of quantum mechanics. This technique can be used if the Evaluator has no further communication with the Adversary (by hiding the success or failure of the garbled table decryption).

We give now a sketch of the formal Superposition-Secure Yao Protocol 2, along with a statement of security against an adversarial Garbler with superposition access. It uses Yao's original construction for the garbled table, where the function is decomposed into elementary gates (of constant fan-in) and can therefore be applied to any binary function with inputs that are of polynomial size in the security parameter [11], as opposed to the Modified Yao Protocol 1.

Protocol 2. Superposition-Secure Yao Protocol (Sketch).

Input: The Garbler and Evaluator have inputs $x \in \{0,1\}^{n_X}$ and $y \in \{0,1\}^{n_Y}$ respectively, with $n_X + n_Y = poly(\eta)$.

Output: The Garbler has no output, the Evaluator has one bit of output.

Public Information: The function f to be evaluated, the encryption scheme $(\mathsf{Enc}, \mathsf{Dec})$ and the size of the padding p.

The Protocol:

1. The Garbler creates the keys and garbled table as in the original Yao's Protocol (with no k^z).
2. The Garbler and the Evaluator participate in the OT ideal executions, at the end of which the Evaluator receives its evaluation keys for its input of choice.
3. The Garbler sends the evaluation keys for its inputs and stops.
4. The Evaluator decrypts each entry in the garbled table sequentially. It stops if the padding is 0^p, the first bit is then set as its output.
5. Otherwise (if none of the values were decrypted correctly), it sets as its output Abort. This is not communicated to the Garbler.

Theorem 5 (Superposition-Resistant Two-Party Computation). *The Superposition-Resistant Yao Protocol 2 is perfectly-secure against an adversarial Garbler in quantum network $\mathfrak{Q}$ in an OT-hybrid execution (Definition 1).*

6 Conclusion

Our security model and the attack analysis performed in this paper lie completely outside of the existing models of security against superposition attacks. They either consider the computational security of basic primitives or, for more complex protocols with multiple interactions between distrustful parties, the protocols are all considered to be statistically-secure (and are therefore essentially extensions of [14]). This leads to many simplifications which have no equivalent in the computational setting. We develop a novel security framework, based on the simple premise that to be secure from superposition attacks means emulating a purely classical functionality. We show that, given slight modifications that preserves classical security, it is possible to show superposition attacks on computationally-secure protocols. The intuition gained from the attack allows us to build a computationally superposition-resistant protocol for Two-Party Secure Function Evaluation, a task never achieved before.

Our results demonstrate once again the counter-intuitive nature of quantum effects, regarding not only the vulnerability of real-world protocols to superposition attacks (most would require heavy modifications for known attacks to work), but also attack vectors and the optimal ways to counter them (as partial measurements can even lead to attacks).

Acknowledgments. This work was supported in part by the French ANR project CryptiQ (ANR-18-CE39-0015). We acknowledge support of the European Union's Horizon 2020 Research and Innovation Program under Grant Agreement No. 820445 (QIA). We would like to thank Michele Minelli, Marc Kaplan and Ehsan Ebrahimi for fruitful discussions.

References

1. Boneh, D., Zhandry, M.: Secure signatures and chosen ciphertext security in a quantum computing world. In: Canetti, R., Garay, J.A. (eds.) CRYPTO 2013. LNCS, vol. 8043, pp. 361–379. Springer, Heidelberg (2013). https://doi.org/10.1007/978-3-642-40084-1_21
2. Büscher, N., et al.: Secure two-party computation in a post-quantum world. In: 18th International Conference on Applied Cryptography and Network Security (ACNS'2020), October 2020. http://tubiblio.ulb.tu-darmstadt.de/119789/
3. Yao, A.C.-C: Quantum circuit complexity. In: Proceedings of 1993 IEEE 34th Annual Foundations of Computer Science, pp. 352–361, November 1993. https://doi.org/10.1109/SFCS.1993.366852
4. Damgård, I., Funder, J., Nielsen, J.B., Salvail, L.: Superposition attacks on cryptographic protocols. In: Padró, C. (ed.) ICITS 2013. LNCS, vol. 8317, pp. 142–161. Springer, Cham (2014). https://doi.org/10.1007/978-3-319-04268-8_9
5. Deutsch, D., Jozsa, R.: Rapid solution of problems by quantum computation. Proc. Royal Soc. Lond. Ser. A: Math. Phys. Sci. **439**(1907), 553–558 (1992). https://doi.org/10.1098/rspa.1992.0167
6. Gagliardoni, T., Hülsing, A., Schaffner, C.: Semantic security and indistinguishability in the quantum world. In: Robshaw, M., Katz, J. (eds.) CRYPTO 2016. LNCS, vol. 9816, pp. 60–89. Springer, Heidelberg (2016). https://doi.org/10.1007/978-3-662-53015-3_3
7. Goldreich, O.: Pseudorandom Permutations, vol. 1, pp. 164–169. Cambridge University Press, Cambridge (2004). https://doi.org/10.1017/CBO9780511721656
8. Hallgren, S., Smith, A., Song, F.: Classical cryptographic protocols in a quantum world. Int. J. Quantum Inf., **13**(04), p. 1550028 (2015). https://doi.org/10.1142/S0219749915500288, https://www.worldscientific.com/doi/abs/10.1142/S0219749915500288

9. Kaplan, M., Leurent, G., Leverrier, A., Naya-Plasencia, M.: Breaking symmetric cryptosystems using quantum period finding. In: Robshaw, M., Katz, J. (eds.) CRYPTO 2016. LNCS, vol. 9815, pp. 207–237. Springer, Heidelberg (2016). https://doi.org/10.1007/978-3-662-53008-5_8
10. Kashefi, E., Kent, A., Vedral, V., Banaszek, K.: Comparison of quantum oracles. Phys. Rev. A, **65**, p. 050304 (2002). https://doi.org/10.1103/PhysRevA.65.050304, https://link.aps.org/doi/10.1103/PhysRevA.65.050304
11. Lindell, Y., Pinkas, B.: A proof of security of Yao's protocol for two-party computation. J. Cryptol. **22**(2), 161–188 (2009). https://doi.org/10.1007/s00145-008-9036-8
12. Liu, M., Krämer, J., Hu, Y., Buchmann, J.A.: Quantum security analysis of a lattice-based oblivious transfer protocol. Front. Inf. Technol. Electron. Eng. **18**(9), 1348–1369 (2017). https://doi.org/10.1631/FITEE.1700039
13. Lo, H.K.: Insecurity of quantum secure computations. Phys. Rev. A **56**(2), 1154–1162 (1997). https://doi.org/10.1103/physreva.56.1154, http://dx.doi.org/10.1103/PhysRevA.56.1154
14. Mayers, D.: Unconditionally secure quantum bit commitment is impossible. Phys. Rev. Lett. **78**, 3414–3417 (1997). https://doi.org/10.1103/PhysRevLett.78.3414, http://link.aps.org/doi/10.1103/PhysRevLett.78.3414
15. Mossayebi, S., Schack, R.: Concrete Security Against Adversaries with Quantum Superposition Access to Encryption and Decryption Oracles, September 2016. arXiv e-prints arXiv:1609.03780
16. Music, L., Chevalier, C., Kashefi, E.: Dispelling Myths on Superposition Attacks: Formal Security Model and Attack Analyses, July 2020. arXiv e-prints arXiv:2007.00677
17. Nielsen, M.A., Chuang, I.L.: Quantum Computation and Quantum Information. Cambridge University Press, Cambridge (2000)
18. Salvail, L., Schaffner, C., Sotáková, M.: Quantifying the leakage of quantum protocols for classical two-party cryptography. Int. J. Quantum Inf. **13**(04), 14500441 (2015). https://doi.org/10.1142/S0219749914500415
19. Tarjan, R., Lipton, R.J.: Applications of a planar separator theorem. In: 2013 IEEE 54th Annual Symposium on Foundations of Computer Science, Los Alamitos, CA, USA, pp. 162–170. IEEE Computer Society, October 1977. https://doi.org/10.1109/SFCS.1977.6, https://doi.ieeecomputersociety.org/10.1109/SFCS.1977.6
20. Unruh, D.: Universally composable quantum multi-party computation. In: Gilbert, H. (ed.) EUROCRYPT 2010. LNCS, vol. 6110, pp. 486–505. Springer, Heidelberg (2010). https://doi.org/10.1007/978-3-642-13190-5_25

Secret Sharing Schemes

Fair and Sound Secret Sharing from Homomorphic Time-Lock Puzzles

Jodie Knapp(✉) and Elizabeth A. Quaglia(✉)

Information Security Group, Royal Holloway, University of London, London, UK
{jodie.knapp.2018,elizabeth.quaglia}@rhul.ac.uk

Abstract. Achieving fairness and soundness in non-simultaneous rational secret sharing schemes has proved to be challenging. On the one hand, soundness can be ensured by providing side information related to the secret as a check, but on the other, this can be used by deviant players to compromise fairness. To overcome this, the idea of incorporating a time delay was suggested in the literature: in particular, time-delay encryption based on memory-bound functions has been put forth as a solution. In this paper, we propose a different approach to achieve such delay, namely using homomorphic time-lock puzzles (HTLPs), introduced at CRYPTO 2019, and construct a fair and sound rational secret sharing scheme in the non-simultaneous setting from HTLPs.

HTLPs are used to embed sub-shares of the secret for a predetermined time. This allows to restore fairness of the secret reconstruction phase, despite players having access to information related to the secret which is required to ensure the soundness of the scheme. Key to our construction is the fact that the time-lock puzzles are homomorphic so that players can compactly evaluate sub-shares. Without this efficiency improvement, players would have to independently solve each puzzle sent from the other players to obtain a share of the secret, which would be computationally inefficient. We argue that achieving both fairness and soundness in a non-simultaneous scheme using a time delay based on CPU-bound functions rather than memory-bound functions is more cost-effective and realistic in relation to the implementation of the construction.

1 Introduction

Threshold secret sharing (SS) schemes provide a way to split a secret into shares such that the secret can be reconstructed by a threshold number of mutually distrustful parties. Knowledge of fewer than the threshold number of shares reveals nothing about the secret [5,37]. SS schemes are an important primitive used in a variety of settings from multiparty computation [7,9], to attribute-based encryption [20,41], and threshold cryptography [4,12].

In a SS scheme, a trusted dealer splits the secret into shares and distributes one to each authorised party. Parties then communicate and process their collective shares in a reconstruction phase. During the communication phase, parties broadcast their shares in one of two ways: *simultaneously* or *non-simultaneously*.

K. Nguyen et al. (Eds.): ProvSec 2020, LNCS 12505, pp. 341–360, 2020.
https://doi.org/10.1007/978-3-030-62576-4_17

That is, with or without synchronicity. Properties of SS schemes are better understood and easier to guarantee in the simultaneous setting [10], due to the fact that a non-simultaneous construction needs to ensure the final party to communicate is still incentivised to follow the protocol. However, simultaneous schemes are difficult to implement in practice, therefore attention has recently turned to non-simultaneous communication [2].

Typically, in the non-simultaneous setting [17,25,26], schemes consists of rounds, where one round of the reconstruction phase simply translates to a capped period of time in which parties have the opportunity to communicate their share. Parties learn the secret is reconstructed when they reconstruct some publicly known value (for example, an indicator), in what is known as a revelation round [22,29]. The previous round to the revelation round is assumed to be the one in which the secret can be reconstructed from, allowing parties to identify when they will reconstruct the correct secret.

There is abundant literature for cryptographic [3,4,8,18,22,27–29,34,38] and game-theoretical SS schemes [2,10,17,19,21,30], two somewhat independent research areas considering honest/malicious parties and rational players, respectively. We refer to Appendix G of [24] for a brief summary of past works. Rational secret sharing (RSS) was introduced by [21], where they consider the problem of secret sharing and multiparty computation assuming players prefer to learn the secret over not learning it, and secondly, prefer that as few as possible other players learn the secret. While for some applications the cryptographic setting is appropriate, for other applications of secret sharing it may be more suitable to view all parties as rational players. RSS is a good approach to capture more interesting scenarios, such as how to motivate or force players to participate honestly and even how a scheme can penalise players for deviant play. Furthermore, modelling players as rational is not limited to assuming players always want to learn the secret above all else. Indeed, as we will explore, an emerging scenario in RSS considers players that prefer to mislead others above learning the secret. For these reasons, our attention focuses on RSS schemes.

In RSS schemes, the outcome of the game influences the players' strategies, as they seek to maximise their payoff. Security of the game requires the strategies of players to be in some form of equilibrium which motivates them to honestly communicate[1]. Achieving an equilibrium between players' strategies is the most natural way to demonstrate a fundamental property of SS schemes, called *fairness* [14,23].

A fair scheme ensures that if a player deviates, the probability that they can recover the shared secret over honest players is negligible. That is, a player is at no advantage in learning the secret if they withhold or dishonestly send a share. In the simultaneous setting, [19,21] both achieve fairness using some form of publicly known indicator and by demonstrating that their protocol is in a form of Nash equilibrium [33]. In the non-simultaneous setting, however, a basic threat to fairness arises: in a (t, n) threshold RSS scheme, the last player out of

[1] See Appendices D.1, and D.2 for further discussion on payoff functions and equilibrium concepts.

t can decide not to communicate their share and use all the other players' shares to reconstruct the secret, leaving the $(t-1)$ honest players with an insufficient number of shares to do so. The rational behaviour of all parties would therefore be to withhold their share. In works such as [17,26,30], fairness can be achieved similarly to the simultaneous setting, whereby players can recognise the revelation round using (or reconstructing) some form of public indicator. However, this only works under the assumption that players prefer everyone to obtain the correct output over misleading others [2,10]. If this assumption does not hold, an alternative way of providing fairness needs to be used, as another property of SS schemes is no longer ensured, *soundness*.

In RSS schemes, *soundness* [2,10] ensures players never reconstruct an incorrect secret except with negligible probability. In other words, honest players are guaranteed to output a correct value, or a special abort symbol $\perp$ [2]. Soundness is becoming of emerging relevance in the non-simultaneous setting, assuming rational players obtain a greater payoff from misleading other players compared to learning the secret. Soundness has been achieved in prior work [10] focusing on non-simultaneous communication as follows: before reconstruction begins, all players are given protocol-induced side information alongside their list of shares. They must assume that when a player aborts communication, the previous round was the revelation round. Even if a deviant player has aborted early, using this side information, honest players can check that they have the correct value after reconstruction. If not, they terminate the reconstruction altogether.

However, achieving soundness this way compromises fairness, as a deviant player can use the side-information to check whether they can abort early and learn the secret before honest players. The authors of [30] were the first to propose a fair RSS scheme that can tolerate *arbitrary* side-information, by proposing the use of time-delay encryption (TDE) [6,32]. The basic idea of a TDE scheme is to encrypt a message such that it can only be decrypted after a specific amount of time has elapsed. The scheme in [30] employs a cryptographic memory-bound function[2] (CMBF) [1,16] as a way to achieve time-delay in the recovery of an encrypted sub-share of the secret. The fairness of their scheme is restored by setting the runtime of rounds of the secret sharing scheme to be less than the time it takes to decrypt the encrypted shares. Thus, there is no way for a deviant player to learn anything about the secret during a reconstruction round before they must decide whether to abort communication. In addition, a proof of the sender's work in computing their message is sent. The scheme proposed in [10] builds upon [30], by encrypting shares (shares are computed using Shamir's SS scheme) using the CMBF and further splits the encrypted shares into sub-shares, distributed to players. During processing, players independently evaluate the encrypted sub-shares to obtain the encrypted share, decrypt and then reconstruct the polynomial to obtain the secret. They use a *specific* form of side-information, called a checking share, which is an actual share of the secret

[2] A CMBF is a family of deterministic algorithms such that an efficiently generated key can decrypt the encrypted input, with a lower-bound on the number of memory-access steps to do so.

that players can use to confirm they have reconstructed the correct secret, thus achieving soundness.[3] We note that the memory-bound running times of employing the MBF in [16], a cryptographic version of which is used for time-delay in [10,30], endows a high cost on the players who have to verify the proof of work from messages received by other players. In addition, the players sending the message can potentially perform less work than what is stated in their accompanying proof [15,36]. These drawbacks suggest that a better time-delay mechanism should be explored to guarantee fairness, that reduces verification costs of the communicated messages and\or increases computational efficiency for honest players obtaining the secret shares after the delay.

1.1 Our Contributions

In this paper, we improve on [10] and propose a RSS scheme achieving fairness and soundness in the non-simultaneous communication setting from a CPU-bound function, as opposed to a CMBF, namely a *homomorphic time-lock puzzle.*

Informally, a time-lock puzzle (TLP) [35] embeds a secret into a puzzle such that it cannot be decrypted until a certain amount of time $\mathcal{T}$ has elapsed. Characteristics of a TLP include fast puzzle generation and security against parallel algorithms, assuming the sequentiality of the underlying mathematical problem [35]. A *homomorphic* time-lock puzzle (HTLP) scheme evaluates puzzles homomorphically using some operation, without the evaluator knowing the secret shares encapsulated within the corresponding puzzles. The resulting puzzle output contains the homomorphic evaluation of the input puzzles, enabling a more efficient way for decryptors to obtain the final output solution, as they can solve just one puzzle rather than solving all of the puzzles individually with standard TLPs, and then evaluating a final solution.

In our scheme, the dealer splits the secret into shares and creates an additional share which is broadcast to all players, i.e., the checking share. The rest of the shares are split into sub-shares, embedded into HTLPs and distributed to the corresponding players in such a way that the HTLP scheme can reconstruct the share from them. Intuitively, the checking share is used to verify the soundness of the secret that players reconstruct, and the delay provided by the HTLP scheme is used to guarantee fairness in the presence of a checking share for players communicating non-simultaneously. More specifically, the HTLP scheme embeds the sub-shares into puzzles that cannot be decrypted before a round of communication in the reconstruction phase has finished. Fairness is achieved by setting each round of communication to have an upper time bound of $\mathcal{T}$. Thus, a player wishing to deviate from their prescribed strategy and quit communication will not be able to derive the secret before the end of the round, in which case, the other players realise the deviant player has quit and output the result of the previous rounds reconstruction. We show that even if a player quits in a round

[3] Note that [30] works under the assumption that players prefer everyone to obtain the correct output over misleading others, therefore soundness is not an issue that needs to be addressed.

and manages to learn the secret, the only case in which they can do so results in the honest players also learning the secret. Therefore there is no advantage in a player deviating from their prescribed strategy.

From our generic construction, which we show satisfies soundness and fairness, we provide a concrete instantiation using the multiplicative variant of the HTLP scheme proposed in [31]. The result is a concrete, efficient scheme whose security relies on standard assumptions.

We argue that our improvement on prior work is threefold: we base the time delay of the construction on CPU-bound functions, as opposed to CMBFs; we provide an efficiency gain by using HTLPs instead of TLPs, and our solution has inherent flexibility.

Basing the time-delay primitive on CPU-bound functions as opposed to memory-bound functions captures a more realistic, inexpensive way to implement a SS scheme construction. Processors are faster than memory and scale better; even more so, fast memory is considerably more expensive. In practice, it is easier to raise the computational requirements of a player than it is memory accesses, up to a point, as adding more processors to a computer is more accessible than making memory accesses faster. A justification for using MBFs in [10,30] is that disparities in the computational power of players can cause unfairness when using standard TLPs for time-delay. However, with reasonable assumptions on the CPU-power of players, this disparity is not significant.

Furthermore, we use a HTLP for time-delay, which requires less computational work on behalf of the players decrypting puzzles compared to using standard TLPs. This efficiency improvement means that the consequence of disparities in CPU-power becomes less significant. To see this, evaluating several puzzles homomorphically, and then solving just *one* puzzle, requires fewer computational steps than solving individual puzzles and evaluating a function over the outputs, as in [10].

Finally, the instantiation of our generic scheme can use any correct SS scheme with a suitable HTLP, dependent on the application. The HTLPs that we use, from [31], are adaptable in the following ways: different operators (linear, multiplicative, and XOR) can be used, we can augment the setup with puzzles of different time hardness parameters $(\mathcal{T}_1, \ldots, \mathcal{T}_n)$ or have a reusable setup, in which the scheme remains efficiently computable.

We refer the reader to the full version of this paper [24] for the formal security analysis of our generic scheme and concrete instantiation using multiplicative-homomorphic TLPs and a multiplicative SS scheme. For the remainder of this paper, any reference to appendices is in relation to the full version of our paper.

2 Definitions and Modelling

2.1 Secret Sharing

Informally, a (t, n) secret sharing scheme (SS) involves a dealer D, some secret s, and a set $P = \{P_1, P_2, \ldots, P_n\}$ of n players. The dealer distributes shares of a secret s chosen according to an efficiently samplable distribution of the set of secrets, labelled $\mathcal{S} = \{\mathcal{S}_\lambda\}_{\lambda \in \mathbb{N}}$, with security parameter λ. The key idea behind threshold SS is that no subset $t' < t$ of players in P can learn the secret s, including an adversary controlling t' players. Conversely, every subset $t' \geq t$ of players in P is capable of reconstructing s.

A SS protocol is composed of two phases, share and reconstruction. During the share phase, the dealer samples a secret s from $\mathcal{S}_\lambda$ and generates n shares from the secret being distributed to each player in P. The dealer does this non-interactively, using a share algorithm to generate the set of shares to be distributed. The dealer digitally signs (typically using information-theoretically secure MACs) and encrypts the shares before distributing them to individual players over a broadcast channel [4].

The reconstruction phase itself is composed of two parts: communication and processing. The communication phase has players interact by sending their share over the broadcast channel to every other player in P (if a broadcast channel is not available to parties, then they have to send their share to each of the other players separately). Once players have communicated, they can move to the processing phase where they embark on reconstructing the secret s from the shares that they have received. This is under the assumption that a sufficient number of shares have been sent and received from other players, and that players followed the protocol (correctness). If an insufficient amount of shares have been received, the secret cannot be reconstructed, so players output $\bot$. Any player taking part in reconstruction proceeds to output their result.

Threshold secret sharing schemes have been explored extensively, and were introduced independently by Shamir [37] and Blakley [5]: Shamir's scheme is based on polynomial interpolation over a finite field of prime order, and Blakley's scheme is based on the uniqueness of hyperplane intersection. Extending the work of [37], [11,13,40] propose multiplicative homomorphic secret sharing schemes based on polynomial interpolation over finite groups with respect to multiplication, that need not be of prime order (See Appendix B [24]).

Next, we recall the formal definition of a threshold secret sharing scheme, with the implicit assumption that the dealer has digitally signed the shares before distributing:

Definition 1 (**(t, n) Secret Sharing**). *Given a dealer D, a secret $s \in \mathcal{S}_\lambda$ for security parameter λ, and a set of n authorised players $P = \{P_1, \ldots, P_n\}$, a (t, n) secret sharing scheme is a tuple of three PPT algorithms* (Setup, Share, Recon) *defined as follows:*

- **Share Phase**: D takes as input the secret s and performs the following steps non-interactively:
  1. $pp \leftarrow \mathsf{Setup}(1^\lambda)$ a probabilistic algorithm that takes as input security parameter 1^λ and outputs public parameters pp, which are broadcast to all players in P.

[4] Privacy and authentication of the distribution of shares is a standard cryptographic assumption in secret sharing schemes [34].

2. $\{s_1, \ldots, s_n\} \leftarrow \mathsf{Share}(pp, s)$ a probabilistic algorithm that takes as input the secret $s \in \mathcal{S}_\lambda$ and outputs n shares s_i, one for each player in P.
3. Distribute s_i to player P_i for every $i \in [n]$ over a secret, authenticated channel.

- **Reconstruction Phase**: Any player in $P = \{P_1, \ldots, P_n\}$ is able to take part in this phase.
  1. Communication:
     (a) Each player P_i sends their share s_i over a secure broadcast channel to all other players in P.
     (b) P_i checks that they have received $(t-1)$ or more shares. If so, they proceed to processing.[5]
  2. Processing:
     Once P_i has a set of t' shares labelled S', they independently do the following:
     (a) $\{s, \perp\} \leftarrow \mathsf{Recon}(pp, S')$ a deterministic algorithm that takes as input the set S' of t' shares and outputs the secret s if $t' \geq t$ or outputs abort $\perp$ otherwise.

A (t, n) threshold SS scheme needs to satisfy the properties of correctness and secrecy, whose definitions are provided in [24], Appendix A.3. Informally, correctness means that an honest execution of the scheme results in the true secret being output, except with negligible probability; and secrecy ensures that reconstruction with fewer shares than the threshold (t) results in abort $(\perp)$ being output, except with negligible probability.

2.2 Rational Secret Sharing

Using game-theory notions, players are considered to be rational if they have a preference in the outcome of the reconstruction phase. In a rational secret sharing (RSS) scheme, a players strategy is to maximise their payoff from the outcome of the game. The strategy σ_i taken by each player P_i must be determined by the dealer in order to achieve a fair outcome. Observe that depending on the scheme, the strategies of players in P may be the same or different.

In Definition 1, players only participate in the reconstruction phase. Therefore, we define a RSS scheme by providing a definition of the reconstruction phase only.

Definition 2 ((t, n) Rational Secret Reconstruction [10]). A reconstruction phase $\Gamma_{t,n}$ is defined by $\Gamma_{t,n} = (\Gamma, \overrightarrow{\sigma})$ where Γ is the game to be played by players during the reconstruction phase and $\overrightarrow{\sigma} = (\sigma_1, \cdots, \sigma_n)$ denotes the strategy profile of the players in P prescribed by the dealer D during the share phase for that scheme.

[5] Whilst not explicit in the definition, there is an upper bound on how long players can communicate their shares for. Therefore, at the end of their communication, if a player P_i has not obtained a sufficient number of shares, then they output $\perp$ at the end of the reconstruction phase.

The outcome of the phase for all players is defined by the n-dimensional vector

$$\overrightarrow{\omega}((\Gamma, \overrightarrow{\sigma})_{t,n}) = (\omega_1, \ldots, \omega_n)$$

where ω_i refers to the outcome of the phase for player P_i.

The outcome ω_i alludes to whether player P_i learns the entirety of s, nothing of s, is mislead into learning a fake secret s' or aborts the reconstruction phase altogether ($\perp$). It is important to note that the outcome of the phase depends on the strategy of the player.

One of the fundamental properties of secret sharing is *fairness* [39], which guarantees that no player has an advantage in the protocol over other players. The following defines fairness in the context of a RSS scheme. We use the following notation for a deviating strategy σ_i' for player P_i, to signify when a player behaves in a different way to how they are meant to. That is, they do not follow the protocol. In addition, P_{-i} represents all players in P excluding player P_i, and σ_{-i} signifies the honest strategies of this set of $(n-1)$ players, P_{-i}.

Definition 3 (Fairness [10]**).** *The reconstruction phase $\Gamma_{t,n}$ is* completely fair *if for every arbitrary alternative strategy σ_i' followed by player P_i for some $i \in [n]$, there exists a negligible function μ in the security parameter λ such that the following holds:*

$$\Pr[\omega_i(\Gamma, (\sigma_i', \sigma_{-i})) = s] \leq Pr[\omega_{-i}(\Gamma, (\sigma_i', \sigma_{-i})) = s] + \mu(\lambda).$$

That is, the probability of player P_i learning the secret when they deviate from their prescribed strategy in phase $\Gamma_{t,n}$ (but all other players follow their prescribed strategies) is only ever negligibly more than the probability of the other players learning the secret too. Consequently, such a player has no real advantage in deviating from their strategy.

How do we ensure that players (despite any preferences they may have) are motivated to follow a strategy in the non-simultaneous setting? This is typically done by assuming that the strategies of players are in a computationally strict Nash equilibrium (or some other variant of a Nash equilibrium) [14,23,33]. This concept makes certain that if every player $P_i \in P$ believes all other players in P are following their prescribed strategy in the phase, then they have nothing to gain in deviating from their own strategy and are penalised in some way by deviating. In our construction, we need to ensure players strategies are in a computationally strict Nash equilibrium when they additionally have access to side-information related to the secret. We discuss this further in Appendix D.2 of the full version of this paper [24].

Another fundamental property of RSS is soundness. Simply put, soundness of the reconstruction phase output means that the probability of players following the scheme outputting an incorrect secret when another player deviates from their own strategy is negligible.

Definition 4 (Soundness [10]**).** *Reconstruction phase $\Gamma_{t,n}$ is* sound *if for every arbitrary alternative strategy σ_i' followed by player P_i for $i \in [n]$, there* *exists a negligible function μ in the security parameter λ such that the following holds:*

$$\Pr[\omega_{-i}(\Gamma, (\sigma'_i, \sigma_{-i})) \notin \{s, \perp\}] \leq \mu(\lambda)$$

In our construction, as we shall see, we achieve this property by using a checking share, similarly to [10]. A checking share is an actual share of the secret, kept separate from the other shares and publicly broadcast to players. In order to formalise our scheme, discussed in Sect. 3, we recall the definition of a homomorphic time-lock puzzle (HTLP) [31], on which our construction relies.

2.3 Homomorphic TLPs

Informally, a time-lock puzzle (TLP) scheme embeds a secret into a puzzle such that it cannot be decrypted until a certain amount of time $\mathcal{T}$ has elapsed. The seminal work of [35] outlined the characteristics of a TLP:

- Fast puzzle generation: namely, the time t required to generate a puzzle $\mathcal{Z}$ must be $t << \mathcal{T}$, for a given (time) hardness parameter $\mathcal{T}$.
- Security against parallel algorithms: that is, the encapsulated secret s is disguised within the puzzle $\mathcal{Z}$ for circuits of depth $< \mathcal{T}$, regardless of the size of the circuit.

However, when the decryptor is faced with a significant number of puzzles to solve, a standard TLP scheme requires the decryptor to solve each individual puzzle, which could be very inefficient. Driven by this limitation [31] introduced the notion of a homomorphic TLP (HTLP), a scheme that compactly evaluates puzzles homomorphically.

Homomorphic time-lock puzzles are augmented TLPs allowing anyone to evaluate a circuit C over sets of puzzles $(\mathcal{Z}_1, \ldots, \mathcal{Z}_n)$ homomorphically using operation Ψ[6], without the evaluator necessarily knowing the secret values $(s_1, \ldots, s_n)$ encapsulated within the corresponding puzzles. The resulting output (a puzzle $\mathcal{Z}$) contains the circuit output $C(s_1, \ldots, s_n)$, and the hardness parameter $\mathcal{T}$ does not depend on the size of the circuit C that was evaluated (this is called compactness).

Definition 5 (HTLP [31]). *Let $C = \{\mathcal{C}_\lambda\}_{\lambda \in \mathbb{N}}$ be a class of circuits and let secret space $\mathcal{S}_\lambda$ be a finite domain for security parameter λ. A homomorphic time-lock puzzle (HTLP) with respect to C and $\mathcal{S}_\lambda$ is defined by a tuple of four PPT algorithms (HP.Setup, HP.Gen, HP.Solve, HP.Eval) as follows:*

- $pp \leftarrow \mathsf{HP.Setup}(1^\lambda, \mathcal{T})$ is a probabilistic algorithm that takes as input security parameter 1^λ and hardness parameter $\mathcal{T}$ and outputs public parameters pp.
- $\mathcal{Z} \leftarrow \mathsf{HP.Gen}(pp, s)$ a probabilistic algorithm that takes as input the public parameters pp and a secret $s \in \mathcal{S}_\lambda$ and outputs a puzzle $\mathcal{Z}$.

[6] What Ψ is depends on the application the HTLP is being used for. It could be addition, multiplication or XOR for example.

- $s \leftarrow \mathsf{HP.Solve}(pp, \mathcal{Z})$ is a deterministic algorithm that takes as input public parameters pp and puzzle $\mathcal{Z}$, and outputs a solution s.
- $\tilde{\mathcal{Z}} \leftarrow \mathsf{HP.Eval}(pp, C, \Psi, \mathcal{Z}_1, \ldots, \mathcal{Z}_n)$ is a probabilistic algorithm taking as input a circuit $C \in \mathcal{C}_\lambda$, parameters pp, homomorphic-operation Ψ, and a set of n puzzles $(\mathcal{Z}_1, \ldots, \mathcal{Z}_n)$, and outputs a master puzzle $\tilde{\mathcal{Z}}$.

A HTLP scheme should satisfy correctness, security, and compactness. Informally, correctness means that if a scheme is executed properly, then the probability of the output being anything other than the solution is negligible. Captured within the definition of the correctness of a HTLP scheme [31] is the time-delay in solving a HTLP puzzle. Informally, given a puzzle evaluated in the scheme, there exists a fixed polynomial over the security and time hardness parameters which bounds the runtime solving the puzzle in the HTLP scheme.

Intuitively, a scheme is considered secure if the output of execution is indistinguishable from random to an eavesdropping adversary. Compactness is a non-trivial property requiring that the complexity of decrypting an evaluated ciphertext does not depend on the function used to evaluate the ciphertext. Intuitively, it means that the ciphertext size should not grow through homomorphic operations and the output length of the homomorphically evaluated ciphertext only depends on the security parameter. In the context of a HTLP, compactness therefore requires the size of the evaluated puzzle ciphertexts to be independent of the size of the circuit, and for the runtime of the evaluation algorithm to be independent of the hardness parameter $\mathcal{T}$.

3 A Fair and Sound Non-simultaneous Rational Secret Sharing Scheme

We consider a RSS scheme with the reconstruction phase defined as in Definition 2. In our construction, the dealer runs the share phase, where they sample a value for the number of shares needed to reconstruct the secret, as well as splitting the secret into shares and further into sub-shares, similarly to the approach in [10]. Then, the dealer distributes a unique, ordered list of sub-shares to each player, alongside broadcasting public parameters.

The reconstruction phase works in rounds, with the n players in P performing the communication phase and processing phase in parallel. In the first round of the reconstruction phase, only the communication phase occurs. The processing phase does not start until the second round onwards. Each round (after the first) of the reconstruction phase works as follows. Players communicate (following the order of their given list) the sub-share corresponding to the round of Γ that they are in, one at a time. They must check at the end of the round that they have obtained sub-shares from all other players.

At the same time, players process the sub-shares received in the previous round, evaluating them over some function to obtain a share of the secret. After a certain number of rounds, as decided by the dealer, a sufficient number of shares will have been derived and players can use these shares to reconstruct the correct secret. The concept of rounds in RSS means that players gradually recover the secret, by reconstructing just one share per round, motivating all players to continue following the reconstruction phase.

More specifically, we let the dealer D be honest and non-interactive, only taking part in the share phase. Following [25], we assume that the dealer (information-theoretically) authenticates the shares distributed to players so that a player cannot send an incorrect share to another player, and the set of shares that a player sends to other players is unique. These assumptions translate to only one of two actions that a player can perform in each round: communicate (follow their strategy) or remain silent. We assume the players' strategies in the reconstruction phase are in a (computationally) strict Nash equilibrium in order to motivate them to follow the phase and not deviate.

In the share phase of our construction, D samples r, the revelation value. The revelation value signifies how many correctly run rounds, or equivalently, how many recovered shares are sufficient for a player to reconstruct the secret. D determines r by randomly sampling from an efficiently samplable discrete distribution $\mathcal{G}$, keeping the value secret from all players. Next, D obtains the first $(r+1)$ shares of the secret s; where the 0th share s_0 will be the checking share and is kept separate and broadcast to all players before the reconstruction phase. We note that the checking share is only used to verify the output of the reconstruction phase, and cannot be used to reconstruct the secret itself. This is necessary in order to ensure the soundness of the output.

Additionally, the dealer randomly samples a value d from an efficiently samplable discrete distribution $\mathcal{G}'$ and generates d fake shares, used to disguise the value r. Typically both $\mathcal{G}$ and $\mathcal{G}'$ are geometric distributions [10,18] (see Appendix C of [24]). Letting $m = r + d$, the dealer proceeds to create n sub-shares for each of the m shares, so that each player has a sub-share of every share, for a total of m sub-shares in each of the n lists, one for each player.

Similarly to [30], we need the sub-shares to be encrypted before being distributed to a player in a way that no player can decrypt their sub-shares before a round of communication is over. This is done so that players communicating non-simultaneously do not know until after they have broadcast their share for a given round, whether or not that was the revelation round. This is crucial to achieve fairness and ensure that players continue to be motivated to follow the scheme [21].

Our construction achieves this time delay using homomorphic time-lock puzzles (HTLPs), first introduced in [31] (see Definition 5). Using a HTLP scheme with hardness parameter $\mathcal{T}$, the dealer sets the time limit for each round of communication to be bounded above by time $\mathcal{T}$. Encrypting the sub-shares creates so-called sub-puzzles[7] of the sub-shares, which the dealer distributes as a list to individual players before reconstruction begins.

[7] We call the HTLP encryption of the sub-shares sub-puzzles for ease of understanding. They are simply time-lock puzzles that can be homomorphically evaluated to obtain a puzzle of the share which corresponds to the homomorphic evaluation of the given sub-shares.

Each round of the reconstruction phase $\Gamma_{r,r+1}$ has players communicate non-simultaneously the corresponding sub-puzzle from their list, whilst processing in parallel the sub-puzzles received from the previous round. In a round of the communication phase, players must send their sub-share before time $\mathcal{T}$. Once this time has elapsed, a player checks that they have received $(n-1)$ sub-puzzles from the other players. In this case, in the next round of the reconstruction phase, these n sub-puzzles will be processed.

In the processing phase, players work independently and evaluate the n sub-puzzles from the previous round. In doing so, they will obtain a puzzle of the share for the previous round. This is computationally correct given that the sub-shares were derived by the dealer such that over some function the sub-shares homomorphically compute this share. The puzzle of the share is decrypted using the solve algorithm in the HTLP scheme to obtain the corresponding share.

Players attempt to reconstruct the actual secret from the shares that they have reconstructed so far. They determine whether they have reached the revelation round by using the checking share s_0 to confirm whether their solution is the real secret. If so, players output the secret s. If the reconstructed value as determined by the checking share, is $s' \neq s$, the players do not output a result. Instead, they will start the subsequent reconstruction phase round. Players repeat this cycle of steps until they have reconstructed the correct secret s unless either of the following scenarios occurs:

1. A deviant player has quit communicating in a round of the phase. Even if they correctly guess the right round to quit (round r), the time delay of the encrypted sub-puzzles ensures that the deviant player cannot decrypt the evaluated puzzle of the share before the end of a round.
   The non-deviant players quit communicating if at the end of the round they have received fewer than $(n-1)$ sub-puzzles. As a consequence, they cannot reconstruct a puzzle share for that round and will have an insufficient number of reconstructed shares, so the outcome for reconstruction will be $\bot$. The act of aborting means that no player learns the secret including the deviant player, as they are identified as a cheater before they can reconstruct the secret, if at all.
2. Players have sent the final, mth sub-puzzle from their list and so have no more sub-puzzles to share after this round. Players quit communication and attempt to reconstruct the secret from the shares that were reconstructed in the previous rounds.

3.1 Our Construction

Given an honest, non-interactive dealer D and a set of n rational players $P = \{P_1, \ldots, P_n\}$ communicating non-simultaneously, we use a HTLP to build a fair RSS scheme with sound output. Assume that each round of the reconstruction phase is bounded by the time hardness parameter $\mathcal{T}$.

Definition 6 (Non-Simultaneous RSS Scheme).

Given security parameter λ, time hardness parameter $\mathcal{T}$, an efficiently samplable distribution of the set of secrets $\mathcal{S}_\lambda$ with operator Ψ, secret $s \in \mathcal{S}_\lambda$, efficiently samplable discrete distributions $\mathcal{G}, \mathcal{G}'$, we construct a RSS scheme with reconstruction phase in the non-simultaneous setting as a tuple of three PPT algorithms (Setup', Share', Recon') from a secret sharing scheme (Setup, Share, Recon) and a HTLP scheme
($\mathsf{HP.Setup}$, $\mathsf{HP.Gen}$, $\mathsf{HP.Solve}$, $\mathsf{HP.Eval}$) as follows:

- **Sharing Phase:** The honest dealer D takes as input the secret $s \in \mathcal{S}_\lambda$ and performs the following steps non-interactively:
  1. $pp' \leftarrow \mathsf{Setup}'(1^\lambda, \mathcal{T})$ a probabilistic algorithm on inputs $1^\lambda, \mathcal{T}$ in which the dealer runs:
     (a) $pp_1 \leftarrow \mathsf{HP.Setup}(1^\lambda, \mathcal{T})$ which outputs public parameters pp_1.
     (b) $pp_2 \leftarrow \mathsf{Setup}(1^\lambda, \mathcal{T})$ which outputs the public parameters pp_2. Additionally let for $r \leftarrow_\$ \mathcal{G}$ be the sampled revelation value and d be a random value $d \leftarrow_\$ \mathcal{G}'$.
     Outputs are sampled values r, d and public parameters $pp' := \{pp_1, pp_2\}$.
  2. $\{s_0, \{list_1, \dots, list_n\}\} \leftarrow \mathsf{Share}'(pp', s)$: a probabilistic algorithm that takes as input the secret $s \in \mathcal{S}_\lambda$ and public parameters pp'. The output consists of a checking share s_0 and lists labelled $list_j$ for $j \in [n]$, each composed of m sub-puzzles for $m = r + d$.
     (a) Run $\{s_0, \{s_1, \dots, s_r\}\} \leftarrow \mathsf{Share}(pp_2, s)$ a probabilistic algorithm with inputs the public parameters pp_2 and secret $s \in \mathcal{S}_\lambda$. The outputs are $(r+1)$ shares of the secret; the checking share s_0 and s_i for $i \in [r]$.
     (b) $\{s_{r+1}, \dots, s_m\} \leftarrow_\$ \mathcal{S}_\lambda$, randomly sample d fake shares from $\mathcal{S}_\lambda$.
     (c) For every $i \in [m]$, compute the list of sub-shares $\{s_{i,1}, \dots, s_{i,n}\}$ such that $s_i = \underset{j \in [n]}{\Psi} s_{i,j}$.
     (d) Run $\mathcal{Z}_{i,j} \leftarrow \mathsf{HP.Gen}(pp_1, s_{i,j})$ a probabilistic algorithm that takes as input sub-shares $s_{i,j}$ and public parameters pp_1, and outputs sub-puzzles $\mathcal{Z}_{i,j}$, $\forall i \in [m], \forall j \in [n]$.
     (e) D distributes $\text{list}_j = \{\mathcal{Z}_{1,j}, \cdots, \mathcal{Z}_{r,j}, \mathcal{Z}_{r+1,j}, \cdots, \mathcal{Z}_{m,j}\}$ to the corresponding player P_j, for every $j \in [n]$.
  3. The dealer distributes the following:
     (a) D broadcasts $\{pp', s_0\}$ to all P the public parameters pp' and checking share s_0.
     (b) D distributes list_j to P_j for every $j \in [n]$.

- **Reconstruction Phase:** All players in $P = \{P_1, \dots, P_n\}$ independently take part in this phase.

  1. Communication: We are in the kth round of the communication, for some $1 < k \le m$.
     (a) P_j sends to all of P the sub-puzzle $\mathcal{Z}_{k,j}$ for every $j \in [n]$ non-simultaneously.

(b) At the end of round k (after time $\mathcal{T}$ has elapsed), along with their own sub-puzzle, player P_j should have received $\{\mathcal{Z}_{k,1}, \ldots, \mathcal{Z}_{k,n}\}$ from all of P.

(c) Move to round $(k+1)$ of communication and round k of processing, unless fewer than $(n-1)$ sub-puzzles have been received. In this case, proceed to abort communication and move to 2c with reconstructed shares $\{s_1, \ldots, s_{k-1}\}$.

2. Processing: We are in round $(k-1)$ of processing, for some $1 < k \leq m$.[8] For any $j \in [n]$, P_j does the following:

(a) $\mathcal{Z}_{k-1} \leftarrow \mathsf{HP.Eval}(pp_1, \mathcal{T}, \Psi, \mathcal{Z}_{k-1,1}, \cdots, \mathcal{Z}_{k-1,n})$: Run the probabilistic algorithm HP.Eval with inputs the public parameters pp_1, hardness parameter $\mathcal{T}$, and the list of n sub-puzzles for the $(k-1)$th round, a player homomorphically evaluates sub-puzzles with operator Ψ to output share puzzle $\mathcal{Z}_{k-1}$.

(b) $s_{k-1} \leftarrow \mathsf{HP.Solve}(pp_1, \mathcal{T}, \mathcal{Z}_{k-1})$: Run the probabilistic algorithm HP.Solve that takes as input the public parameters pp_1; hardness parameter $\mathcal{T}$; and puzzle share $\mathcal{Z}_{k-1}$ and outputs secret share s_{k-1}. Output the round share s_{k-1} and move to reconstructing s.

(c) $\{s, \perp\} \leftarrow \mathsf{Recon}'(pp', s_0, \{s_1, \ldots, s_{k-1}\})$: where the players run $\{s, \perp\} \leftarrow \mathsf{Recon}(pp_2, \{s_1, \ldots, s_m\})$, a deterministic algorithm that inputs public parameters pp_2 and $(k-1)$ reconstructed shares of the secret $\{s_1, \ldots, s_{k-1}\}$. Player P_j uses checking share s_0 to confirm the soundness of their reconstructed value and outputs either the correct secret s or abort $\perp$.

(d) If P_j outputs $\perp$, but no player quit in round k of communication and every player $P_j \in P$ has $list_j \neq \emptyset$, then players go to $(k+1)$th round of reconstruction phase. If either case holds, output $\perp$.

We have the following result.

Theorem 1. *Our non-simultaneous rational secret scheme* (Setup', Share', Recon') *satisfies correctness, fairness and soundness in the presence of side information related to the secret, assuming the following properties:*

- *correctness, security, and compactness of the HTLP scheme,*
- *correctness and secrecy of the SS scheme,*
- *the checking share side information is correct, protocol-induced auxiliary information.*

We prove Theorem 1 in Appendix F of [24], demonstrating that our construction satisfies correctness, achieves soundness in the non-simultaneous setting using protocol-induced side information, and achieves fairness despite the presence of this side-information by using a HTLP to provide a time-delay to the scheme.

[8] At least one round of communication is required before players can start processing.

More specifically, in our security analysis, we summarise the scenarios in which a deviant player attempts to mislead. In particular, we demonstrate that if a player aborts in a round k with respect to revelation round r, regardless of the round that k is, the outcome for all players is the same. Analysing the scenarios in which a players quits communicating aids the proofs of fairness and correctness, by providing an intuition to the outcome of the reconstruction phase.

Fairness of the scheme is proven as follows: we show that Definition 3 is satisfied in our construction assuming the correctness and security of the HTLP scheme [31] (definitions of which are provided in [24], Appendix A.2), which is employed to implement a time-delay in the scheme. We use a reduction to break the correctness and security of the HTLP scheme, contradicting our assumptions, in order to show that there does not exist a deviant player with the ability to decrypt a puzzle in time less than $\mathcal{T}$. Furthermore, assuming the correctness and secrecy of the underlying SS scheme (see Appendix A.3 [24]), we show that the probability of a deviant player learning the secret, whilst other players do not, is negligible in the security parameter λ. Observe that we additionally show in [24] that the rational players strategies $\overrightarrow{\sigma}$ are in a computationally strict Nash equilibrium (Appendix D.2, Definition 16 [24]) following the proofs of [10,30].

In order to prove soundness, we provide an Appendix E preceding the analysis of Theorem 1 in the full version of our paper [24], to define the side information used to achieve soundness. We closely follow the proof of [10] by firstly defining a membership oracle. Informally, this is an oracle queried by players in reconstruction in order to check the soundness of their reconstructed value [30]. Following [10], we claim and prove that the checking share in our construction can be used in place of a sound membership oracle (see Definition 18, Appendix E [24]), as a specific form of protocol-induced side information to ensure soundness. Finally, we prove that our generic construction achieves soundness with a checking share (found in Appendix F, Theorem 2 of [24]).

We defer the reader to [24], Appendix F for the full details of our proofs.

Next, we highlight the efficiency improvements our construction achieves by using a HTLP over standard TLPs. We then discuss how our results improve upon the scheme of [10], the most relevant related work.

HTLPs vs. TLPs. The homomorphic property of a HTLP scheme means that solving a puzzle, the most computationally expensive step for the players, need only be run once rather than n times in the processing phase of our scheme. The computational cost of running HP.Solve is $\Omega(2^{\mathcal{T}})$-steps[9].

Indeed, if we were to use a standard TLP in the processing phase of our scheme, each player would independently have to solve each of the n sub-puzzles using P.Solve, and then evaluate the n sub-shares to obtain the share for that round. Conversely, by using a HTLP in our scheme, players must run HP.Eval

[9] In a standard TLP scheme, the computational complexity of the puzzle-solving algorithm P.Solve is the same as HP.Solve.

once over the n sub-puzzles, outputting a master puzzle, and proceed to run HP.Solve *once* on this master puzzle to obtain the corresponding share. Thus, HTLPs are more efficient by a linear factor of n, where n corresponds to the number of players participating in the reconstruction phase.

It is important that the homomorphic property of the HTLP scheme satisfies the definition of compactness in [31] (found in the full version of this paper [24], Appendix A.2, Definition 9). This means that the runtime of homomorphically evaluating puzzles, is bounded above by a fixed polynomial that only depends on the security parameter λ and not the time hardness parameter $\mathcal{T}$. Otherwise, the trivial solution would be indeed to use a standard TLP scheme.

Comparison with [10]**.** Our scheme closely follows the work of [10]. Their construction involves linearly evaluating sub-shares encrypted using memory-bound functions for the time-delay to ensure fairness of the scheme and reconstructing the secret using Shamir's SS scheme. In contrast, our generic construction uses CPU-bound HTLPs to ensure a time-delay in rounds of the scheme, which we have argued in the Introduction constitutes an improvement.

Furthermore, the construction of [10] requires players to independently decrypt each share before they proceed to the secret reconstruction using Shamir SS scheme. The advantage of using HTLPs is that they provide an efficiency improvement for the honest players evaluating puzzles in comparison to using standard TLPs. Therefore our contributions are the efficiency improvements for honest players in homomorphically evaluating puzzles.

Finally, we have generalised our construction so that it can be adapted for different applications. The HTLP schemes of [31] are flexible in using different homomorphic operations and can be extended to using puzzles with varying levels of hardness (different $\mathcal{T}$ values), with potential for public-coin setup schemes and reusable setup schemes. Unlike [10] who provide a concrete scheme, our construction is generic and adaptable to the application for which it is being used.

3.2 A Concrete Instantiation

Our final contribution is to provide a concrete fair and sound RSS scheme by instantiating our construction with a specific variant of Shamir's SS scheme and a multiplicative HTLP (MHTLP [31]). In more detail, we instantiate our construction as follows:

- A multiplicative homomorphic threshold secret sharing scheme (Setup, Share, Recon) (Appendix B of [24]), for a secret space $\mathcal{S}_\lambda$ over a finite group with respect to multiplication, defined as in [11,13,40],
- A MHTLP scheme (MHP.Setup, MHP.Gen, MHP.Eval, MHP.Solve) (in [24], Appendix B), which is multiplicatively homomorphic over a ring $(\mathbb{J}_N, \cdot)$.

The multiplicative operator $\otimes$ enables the dealer to split the ith share, for some $i \in [m]$, of the secret into n sub-shares in the following way,

$$s_{i,n} = s_i \cdot \left(\prod_{j=1}^{n-1} s_{i,j} \right)^{-1},$$

enabling players to homomorphically evaluate sub-puzzles by running MHP.Eval, and MHP.Solve on the master puzzle output from evaluation to obtain the correctly reconstructed share for the ith round. To ensure soundness of the concrete instantiation, the dealer distributes a checking share s_0 to all players. This is computed as $s_0 = f(y_0) \pmod{N}$, for some polynomial f determined in the setup phase of the scheme from a multiplicative homomorphic threshold SS scheme.

Whilst we have not implemented the concrete instantiation here, we note the following: firstly, the inclusion of a MHTLP scheme to a secret sharing scheme does increase the computational burden on the players participating in reconstruction, however it provides the important property of fairness in our scheme when soundness is additionally being provided by the means of side information. Secondly, we use a multiplicative-homomorphic TLP rather than a standard TLP in order to reduce the computational overhead for players by a linear factor. Indeed, in the instantiation, one run of MHP.Eval is necessary, which translates to n multiplications. This is followed by one run of MHP.Solve of complexity $\Omega(2^{\mathcal{T}})$. If we used a plain TLP in the instantiation instead, assuming the same parameters, we require n runs of HP.Solve of complexity $\Omega(2^{\mathcal{T}})$, followed by n runs of HP.Eval, which means n multiplications.

In addition to the assumptions used in the security analysis of our generic construction, the instantiation relies on standard cryptographic and number-theoretical assumptions, including the sequential squaring and decisional Diffie-Hellman assumptions for a MHTLP [31], found in Appendix A.2 of [24]. We defer to [24] (Appendix C) for a full description of the instantiation of our construction.

Final Remarks. In this paper we have proposed a construction for a fair and sound rational secret sharing scheme in the non-simultaneous setting of communication from homomorphic time-lock puzzles. We have argued the benefits of this novel approach, and we have suggested a concrete scheme, relying on standard assumptions.

References

1. Abadi, M., Burrows, M., Manasse, M., Wobber, T.: Moderately hard, memory-bound functions. ACM Trans. Internet Technol. **5**, 299–327 (2005)
2. Asharov, G., Lindell, Y.: Utility dependence in correct and fair rational secret sharing. In: Halevi, S. (ed.) CRYPTO 2009. LNCS, vol. 5677, pp. 559–576. Springer, Heidelberg (2009). https://doi.org/10.1007/978-3-642-03356-8_33

3. Beimel, A.: Secure Schemes for Secret Sharing and Key Distribution. PhD thesis, Technion-Israel Institute of technology, Faculty of computer science, Israel (1996)
4. Beimel, A.: Secret-sharing schemes: a survey. In: Chee, Y.M., et al. (eds.) IWCC 2011. LNCS, vol. 6639, pp. 11–46. Springer, Heidelberg (2011). https://doi.org/10.1007/978-3-642-20901-7_2
5. Blakley, G.R.: Safeguarding cryptographic keys. In: Proceedings of the AFIPS National Computer Conference, NCC 1979, vol. 48, pp. 313–318. International Workshop on Managing Requirements Knowledge (MARK). IEEE (1979)
6. Cathalo, J., Libert, B., Quisquater, J.-J.: Efficient and non-interactive timed-release encryption. In: Qing, S., Mao, W., López, J., Wang, G. (eds.) ICICS 2005. LNCS, vol. 3783, pp. 291–303. Springer, Heidelberg (2005). https://doi.org/10.1007/11602897_25
7. Chaum, D., Crépeau, C., Damgård, I.: Multiparty unconditionally secure protocols (abstract). In: Pomerance, C. (ed.) CRYPTO 1987. LNCS, vol. 293, pp. 11–19. Springer, Heidelberg (1988). https://doi.org/10.1007/3-540-48184-2_43
8. Cleve, R.: Limits on the security of coin flips when half the processors are faulty. In: Proceedings of the Eighteenth Annual ACM Symposium on Theory of Computing, STOC 1986, pp. 364–369. Association for Computing Machinery (1986)
9. Cramer, R., Damgård, I., Maurer, U.: General secure multi-party computation from any linear secret-sharing scheme. In: Preneel, B. (ed.) EUROCRYPT 2000. LNCS, vol. 1807, pp. 316–334. Springer, Heidelberg (2000). https://doi.org/10.1007/3-540-45539-6_22
10. De, S.J., Pal, A.K.: Achieving correctness in fair rational secret sharing. In: Abdalla, M., Nita-Rotaru, C., Dahab, R. (eds.) CANS 2013. LNCS, vol. 8257, pp. 139–161. Springer, Cham (2013). https://doi.org/10.1007/978-3-319-02937-5_8
11. Desmedt, Y., Di Crescenzo, G., Burmester, M.: Multiplicative non-abelian sharing schemes and their application to threshold cryptography. In: Pieprzyk, J., Safavi-Naini, R. (eds.) ASIACRYPT 1994. LNCS, vol. 917, pp. 19–32. Springer, Heidelberg (1995). https://doi.org/10.1007/BFb0000421
12. Desmedt, Y., Frankel, Y.: Shared generation of authenticators and signatures. In: Feigenbaum, J. (ed.) CRYPTO 1991. LNCS, vol. 576, pp. 457–469. Springer, Heidelberg (1992). https://doi.org/10.1007/3-540-46766-1_37
13. Desmedt, Y.G., Frankel, Y.: Homomorphic zero-knowledge threshold schemes over any finite abelian group. SIAM J. Dis. Math. **7**(4), 667–679 (1994)
14. Dodis, Y., Rabin, T.: Cryptography and game theory. Algorithmic Game Theor. 181–207 (2007)
15. Doshi, S., Monrose, F., Rubin, A.D.: Efficient memory bound puzzles using pattern databases. In: Zhou, J., Yung, M., Bao, F. (eds.) ACNS 2006. LNCS, vol. 3989, pp. 98–113. Springer, Heidelberg (2006). https://doi.org/10.1007/11767480_7
16. Dwork, C., Goldberg, A., Naor, M.: On memory-bound functions for fighting spam. In: Boneh, D. (ed.) CRYPTO 2003. LNCS, vol. 2729, pp. 426–444. Springer, Heidelberg (2003). https://doi.org/10.1007/978-3-540-45146-4_25
17. Fuchsbauer, G., Katz, J., Naccache, D.: Efficient rational secret sharing in standard communication networks. In: Micciancio, D. (ed.) TCC 2010. LNCS, vol. 5978, pp. 419–436. Springer, Heidelberg (2010). https://doi.org/10.1007/978-3-642-11799-2_25
18. Gordon, S.D., Hazay, C., Katz, J., Lindell, Y.: Complete fairness in secure two-party computation. J. ACM (JACM) **58**(6), 1–37 (2011)
19. Gordon, S.D., Katz, J.: Rational secret sharing, revisited. In: De Prisco, R., Yung, M. (eds.) SCN 2006. LNCS, vol. 4116, pp. 229–241. Springer, Heidelberg (2006). https://doi.org/10.1007/11832072_16

20. Goyal, V., Pandey, O., Sahai, B., Waters, A.: Attribute-based encryption for fine-grained access control of encrypted data. In: Proceedings of the 13th ACM Conference on Computer and Communications Security, CCS 2006, pp. 89–98. Association for Computing Machinery (2006)
21. Halpern, J., Teague, V.: Rational secret sharing and multiparty computation: extended abstract. In: Proceedings of the Thirty-Sixth Annual ACM Symposium on Theory of Computing, STOC 2004, pp. 623–632. Association for Computing Machinery (2004)
22. Harn, L., Lin, C., Li, Y.: Fair secret reconstruction in (t, n) secret sharing. J. Inf. Secur. Appl. **23**, 1–7 (2015)
23. Katz, J.: Bridging game theory and cryptography: recent results and future directions. In: Canetti, R. (ed.) TCC 2008. LNCS, vol. 4948, pp. 251–272. Springer, Heidelberg (2008). https://doi.org/10.1007/978-3-540-78524-8_15
24. Knapp, J., Quaglia, E.A.: Fair and sound secret sharing from homomorphic time-lock puzzles. Cryptology ePrint Archive, Report 2020/1078 (2020). https://eprint.iacr.org/2020/1078
25. Kol, G., Naor, M.: Cryptography and game theory: designing protocols for exchanging information. In: Canetti, R. (ed.) TCC 2008. LNCS, vol. 4948, pp. 320–339. Springer, Heidelberg (2008). https://doi.org/10.1007/978-3-540-78524-8_18
26. Kol, G., Naor, M.: Games for exchanging information. In: Proceedings of the Fortieth Annual ACM Symposium on Theory of Computing, STOC 2008, pp. 423–432. Association for Computing Machinery (2008)
27. Krawczyk, H.: Secret sharing made short. In: Stinson, D.R. (ed.) CRYPTO 1993. LNCS, vol. 773, pp. 136–146. Springer, Heidelberg (1994). https://doi.org/10.1007/3-540-48329-2_12
28. Laih, C.-S., Lee, Y.-C.: V-fairness (t, n) secret sharing scheme. IEE Proc. Comput. Digit. Tech. **144**(4), 245–248 (1997)
29. Lin, H.-Y., Harn, L.: Fair reconstruction of a secret. Inf. Process. Lett. **55**(1), 45–47 (1995)
30. Lysyanskaya, A., Segal, A.: Rational secret sharing with side information in point-to-point networks via time-delayed encryption. IACR Cryptology ePrint Archive **2010**, 540 (2010)
31. Malavolta, G., Thyagarajan, S.A.K.: Homomorphic time-lock puzzles and applications. In: Boldyreva, A., Micciancio, D. (eds.) CRYPTO 2019. LNCS, vol. 11692, pp. 620–649. Springer, Cham (2019). https://doi.org/10.1007/978-3-030-26948-7_22
32. May, T.C.: Time-release crypto. In: Manuscript (1993)
33. Nash, J.: Non-cooperative games. Ann. Math. 286–295 (1951)
34. Pedersen, T.P.: Non-interactive and information-theoretic secure verifiable secret sharing. In: Feigenbaum, J. (ed.) CRYPTO 1991. LNCS, vol. 576, pp. 129–140. Springer, Heidelberg (1992). https://doi.org/10.1007/3-540-46766-1_9
35. Rivest, R.L., Shamir, A., Wagner, D.A.: Time-lock puzzles and timed-release crypto. Technical Report MIT/LCS/TR-684 (1996)
36. Rosenthal, D.: On the cost distribution of a memory bound function. arXiv preprint cs/0311005 (2003)
37. Shamir, A.: How to share a secret. Commun. ACM **22**(11), 612–613 (1979)
38. Tian, Y., Ma, J., Peng, C., Zhu, J.: Secret sharing scheme with fairness. In: 10th International Conference on Trust, Security and Privacy in Computing and Communications, pp. 494–500. IEEE (2011)
39. Tompa, M., Woll, H.: How to share a secret with cheaters. J. Cryptol. **1**(3), 133–138 (1988). https://doi.org/10.1007/BF02252871

40. Wang, H., Lam, K.Y., Xiao, G.-Z., Zhao, H.: On multiplicative secret sharing schemes. In: Dawson, E.P., Clark, A., Boyd, C. (eds.) ACISP 2000. LNCS, vol. 1841, pp. 342–351. Springer, Heidelberg (2000). https://doi.org/10.1007/10718964_28
41. Waters, B.: Ciphertext-policy attribute-based encryption: an expressive, efficient, and provably secure realization. In: Catalano, D., Fazio, N., Gennaro, R., Nicolosi, A. (eds.) PKC 2011. LNCS, vol. 6571, pp. 53–70. Springer, Heidelberg (2011). https://doi.org/10.1007/978-3-642-19379-8_4

Optimal Threshold Changeable Secret Sharing with New Threshold Change Range

Jian Ding[1,2], Changlu Lin[1,2], and Fuchun Lin[3(✉)]

[1] College of Mathematics and Informatics, Fujian Normal University, Fujian, China
dingjian_happy@163.com, cllin@fjnu.edu.cn

[2] Fujian Provincial Key Lab of Network Security and Cryptology, Fujian Normal University, Fujian, China

[3] Department of Electrical and Electronic Engineering, Imperial College London, London, UK
flin@ic.ac.uk

Abstract. Motivated by the need of catering for changes of security policy during the deployment of distribution of trust, threshold changeable secret sharing studies the construction of secret sharing schemes that have a built-in mechanism that, when activated, transforms the scheme into one with different access structures. By combining the two main techniques frequently used in previous constructions: packing and folding, we construct optimal threshold changeable ramp schemes that cover the full threshold change range, while known constructions either achieve only reconstruction threshold change or change both privacy and reconstruction thresholds but require the two thresholds to change proportionally. We justify the claim that the full threshold change range for which optimal schemes are possible is completely covered by proving a completeness result information-theoretically. The share size of these threshold changeable ramp schemes are much bigger than the lower bounds for plain ramp schemes (without requiring threshold changeability). This suggests the natural open question of understanding the share size lower and upper bounds for ramp schemes with built-in structures.

Keywords: Threshold changeable secret sharing · Universal threshold changeable secret sharing · Communication efficient secret sharing · Admissible threshold change range

1 Introduction

Secret sharing, introduced independently by Blakley [3] and Shamir [18], plays fundamental roles in many cryptographic applications. The goal in secret sharing is to divide a secret $\mathbf{s}$ into a number of *shares* $s_1, \ldots, s_n$ that are distributed among n participants such that the shares in an *authorized subset* of the players can reconstruct the secret, while on the other hand, the shares in an *unauthorized* subset contains no information about the secret. A secret sharing is called

K. Nguyen et al. (Eds.): ProvSec 2020, LNCS 12505, pp. 361–378, 2020.
https://doi.org/10.1007/978-3-030-62576-4_18

perfect if all subsets of $[n]$ are either authorized or unauthorized. The set of authorized and unauthorized subsets define an access structure, of which the most widely used is the so-called *threshold* access structure. A threshold secret sharing scheme is defined with respect to an integer parameter r called reconstruction threshold and satisfies the following property: Any set $\mathcal{A} \subset [n]$ with $|\mathcal{A}| < r$ is an unauthorized set and any set $\mathcal{A} \subset [n]$ with $|\mathcal{A}| \geq r$ is an authorized set. A threshold secret sharing is then a perfect secret sharing. The Shamir scheme with threshold r represents a secret as a finite field element and divides it by first sampling a uniform random polynomial of degree at most $r-1$ that has the given secret as its constant term and then evaluating the random polynomial at n distinct non-zero elements in the same finite field to generate the shares. It is straightforward to verify that with r shares, the random polynomial (including its constant term, the secret) can be recovered through interpolation and any up to $r-1$ shares contain no information about the secret. The Shamir scheme is *optimal* in the sense that its secret (same size as each share) is the largest possible for a threshold scheme. Let log be the logarithm to the base 2, then the share size of Shamir scheme with n participants is at least $\log(n+1)$ bits, since we need n distinct non-zero evaluation points from the underlying finite field for generating the n shares. It turns out that this is also almost the best possible for a threshold scheme, even when we only share one bit secret [5].

The notion of threshold secret sharing can be relaxed to *ramp* secret sharing which allows some subset of participants to learn some partial information about the secret (no longer a perfect secret sharing). A ramp scheme is defined with respect to two threshold parameters, the privacy threshold t and the reconstruction threshold r. In a (t, r, n)-ramp scheme, the knowledge of any t shares or fewer does not reveal any information about the secret, any r shares can be used to reconstruct the secret and subsets of size in between $t+1$ and $r-1$ may reveal some partial information about the secret. We consider a threshold secret sharing scheme with threshold r as a special case of a (t, r, n)-ramp scheme with $t = r-1$. We denote it a (r, n)-threshold scheme. The largest size of secret that is possible for a (t, r, n)-ramp scheme is larger than the special case of threshold scheme (proportional to the threshold gap $g = r - t$). If a (t, r, n)-ramp scheme has minimum share size, then it is called an *optimal* (t, r, n)*-ramp scheme*, which can be constructed by extending Shamir's construction. The share size of this approach, however, is much larger than the share size lower bound for a (t, r, n)-ramp scheme, which is reversely proportional to the threshold gap $g = r - t$ [5]. The construction from algebraic geometric codes gives near optimal (t, r, n)-ramp schemes that also have share size almost matching the share size lower bound.

These secret sharing schemes with simple access structures (but can be constructed with rich algebraic structures) are particularly important building blocks in *threshold cryptography* [7], which is devoted to mitigate breakdowns that result from differences between ideal and real implementations of cryptographic algorithms by enabling distribution of trust across operators. In these applications, we usually do not consider complicated access structures in the underlying secret sharing scheme, but crucially need some homomorphic properties. A good example is the application of secret sharing in the constructions of secure multi-party computation [6]. Here we need the underlying secret sharing scheme to allow for each participant to locally compute on his/her shares of a set of secrets to generate a share of a function of the set of secrets. For example, each participant adds up his/her share for secret one and his/her share for secret two to obtain a share for the sum of the two secrets. Continuing on the motivation of bridging ideal and real implementations of cryptographic algorithms, in real life implementations the threshold is determined by a security policy based on an assessment of the running environment. But more than often we encounter a change of running environment during the life time of the system and need to adjust the threshold. A standard solution is to discard all the stored data and re-initiate the system use the new threshold, which demands huge computational and communicational resources. A much more economic solution would be to build some flexibility into the underlying secret sharing scheme such that during a change of running environment, each operator is prompt to (through broadcast or some form of public discussion) locally apply a share conversion function to transform a share of the secret sharing scheme corresponding to the initial threshold to a share of one corresponding to the new threshold, and the system seamlessly transits into one running with a different threshold.

The concept of *threshold changeable secret sharing* [1,4,8,15] was proposed for different models in particular, the model studied in [15] assumes no secure communication channels nor dealer intervention, hence allows for the local conversion. A threshold scheme with minimum share size that can be converted into such a ramp scheme with minimum share size and minimum combiner communication complexity is defined to be optimal. An explicit construction of such optimal *(r,n)-threshold scheme threshold changeable to r'* was also given in [15] using the geometric construction of Blakley [3]. There are follow up works on this model of threshold changeability that gave new constructions of optimal (or near optimal) threshold changeable secret sharing with various features [11,14,21,22]. For example, the packed Shamir scheme construction in [21] is essentially an optimal construction for threshold changeable secret sharing and [22] proposed a variant of the construction that reduces the share size. All these constructions consider the special case of changing the reconstruction threshold (the privacy threshold remains the same), which makes this model of threshold changeable secret sharing coincides with the study of *communication efficient* secret sharing [21], where the goal is to minimise the overall download bandwidth for reconstructing the secret through contacting a given number (bigger than the threshold of the threshold scheme) of shares and only download partial information from each share.

For the above applications in threshold cryptography sketched above, we would need a threshold changeable secret sharing that is capable of both privacy threshold and reconstruction threshold changes. The constructions of threshold changeable secret sharing in [19,20] not only allow both privacy threshold and reconstruction threshold to change at the same time, but also enjoy the freedom of choosing the new thresholds after the secret is shared by the dealer. The later property is termed *universal* in the line of works on communication efficient secret sharing [2,9,16]. Threshold changeable secret sharing with both privacy threshold and reconstruction threshold change was formerly defined for general threshold change range $(t, r, n) \to (t', r', n)$ and a new construction with universal property was proposed in [13]. Interestingly, the constructions in [19,20] and [13], though using totally different philosophy, yield schemes with the same threshold change pattern, more concretely, the initial thresholds (t, r) and the new thresholds (t', r') satisfy the relation

$$\frac{t'}{t} = \frac{r'}{r}.$$

This leaves open the question of whether (optimal) threshold changeable secret sharing can be constructed for thresholds not satisfying $\frac{t'}{t} = \frac{r'}{r}$ and moreover, what is the complete range of threshold change that admits (optimal) threshold changeable secret sharing.

Our Contributions. We propose a generic construction that takes a threshold changeable ramp scheme that only changes its reconstruction threshold (this is also known as a *communication efficient secret sharing*) and construct a $(t, r, n) \to (t', r', n)$ threshold changeable ramp scheme that is capable of changing both privacy and reconstruction thresholds for any $1 < \frac{t'}{t} < \frac{r'}{r}$. Threshold changeable ramp schemes with this type of threshold change range was not known before. We then show that when the input threshold changeable ramp scheme is optimal, the $(t, r, n) \to (t', r', n)$ threshold changeable ramp scheme constructed using the generic construction is also optimal. We then obtain optimal $(t, r, n) \to (t', r', n)$ threshold changeable ramp schemes for the new threshold change range $1 < \frac{t'}{t} < \frac{r'}{r}$. These new optimal threshold changeable ramp schemes together with the optimal threshold changeable ramp schemes that only change the reconstruction threshold $(t' = t)$ and those with proportional changes of both privacy and reconstruction thresholds $\frac{t'}{t} = \frac{r'}{r}$ cover the threshold change range $1 \leq \frac{t'}{t} \leq \frac{r'}{r}$. We take one step further and consider a (t, r, n)-ramp scheme which is capable of changing its thresholds to a set of new threshold pairs $\mathcal{T} = \{(t'_k, r'_k)\}$ universally, where $\mathcal{T}$ contains all the pair (t'_k, r'_k) that satisfies $1 \leq \frac{t'_k}{t} \leq \frac{r'_k}{r}$. With the above newly constructed optimal threshold changeable ramp schemes, we are now, for the first time, able to construct a universal threshold changeable ramp scheme such that for each new threshold pair (t'_k, r'_k) in the set $\mathcal{T}$, the scheme is an optimal $(t, r, n) \to (t'_k, r'_k, n)$ threshold changeable ramp scheme. We then call such universal threshold changeable ramp scheme universal optimal threshold changeable ramp scheme. We note here that our results are readily extended to near optimal cases that greatly reduce the share size, by plugging in the algebraic geometry codes based secret sharing constructions. We discuss these developments in the full version of this paper.

We also obtain results that argue to the effect that the threshold change range $t < r < r', t' < r' \le n, 1 \le \frac{t'}{t} \le \frac{r'}{r}$, namely,

$$t < r < r', t' < r' \le n, 1 \le \frac{t'}{t} \le \frac{r'}{r} \tag{1}$$

is complete range that admits constructions of optimal threshold changeable ramp schemes. For clarity, we write the proofs for ramp schemes with *full reconstruction*, which means that the reconstruction algorithm not only reconstructs the secret but also reconstructs the full share vector. We present two claims to describe the relationship about thresholds r, r', t, t' and the entropy of the shares between the initial (t, r, n)-ramp scheme and resulting (t', r', n)-ramp scheme. We then apply claims to an optimal $(t, r, n) \to (t', r', n)$ ramp scheme, and get the range (1) by using some bounds about share sizes which have been given in [10,13]. We further find that this range is covered by our constructions together with [2,13], which means the range (1) is complete range that admits constructions of optimal threshold changeable ramp schemes. In other words, we get a necessary and sufficient condition for the existence of an optimal $(t, r, n) \to (t', r', n)$ ramp scheme. Meanwhile, a range

$$t < r, t \le t' < r' \le n, r' - t' > r - t,$$

that presented in [13] is only a necessary condition.

Open Questions. Lower and upper bounds on share size for secret sharing (even sharing one bit secret) with a given access structure is a fundamental topic in secret sharing. For simple access structures such as (r, n)-threshold scheme and more generally (t, r, n)-ramp scheme, there are known tight bounds [5]. Our study of threshold changeable secret sharing suggests an interesting problem of bounding the share size of simple secret sharing schemes with threshold change properties. It can be observed that the share size of the constructed threshold changeable secret sharing schemes increases as the amount of flexibility in threshold change increases and there is a big gap between the lower bound of plain ramp secret sharing and the constructed threshold changeable secret sharing. It is interesting to see how much a particular threshold change requirement affects the share size lower bound of a ramp scheme.

Related Works. The works most related to this work are the lattice based construction [19,20] and the binary secret sharing based construction [13] of $(t, r, n) \to (t', r', n)$ ramp secret sharing. Firstly, in terms of the coverage of the threshold change range, all previous constructions only achieve the threshold change type $1 < \frac{t'}{t} = \frac{r'}{r}$ while the results presented in this work cover the full range of $1 \le \frac{t'}{t} \le \frac{r'}{r}$. Secondly, on one hand, the universal threshold changeable ramp secret sharing constructed in all previous works have small share size while the universal variants constructed in this work are huge. On the other hand, the universal threshold changeable ramp secret sharing constructed in all previous works have weaker forms of privacy/correctness definitions. Though the initial schemes are standard Shamir scheme and Chinese Remainder Theorem secret sharing, the privacy of the resulting ramp scheme after applying the share conversion functions in [19,20] is probabilistic over the randomness of some public parameters and the secrecy guarantee is to leak at most a $\eta \mathsf{H}(\mathbf{S})$ bits of entropy, where η can be made as small as one wishes when the secret is uniformly distributed. The binary secret sharing based construction of [13] gives statistical secret sharing, where the privacy is measured by statistical distance. There are evidence that standard secret sharing and secret sharing with weaker form of privacy/correctness definitions obey different share size bounds [12].

2 Preliminaries

Let $\mathbf{X}$ denote a random variable. The Shannon entropy of $\mathbf{X}$ is denoted by $\mathsf{H}(\mathbf{X})$. The mutual information between $\mathbf{X}$ and $\mathbf{Y}$ is given by

$$\mathsf{I}(\mathbf{X};\mathbf{Y}) = \mathsf{H}(\mathbf{X}) - \mathsf{H}(\mathbf{X}|\mathbf{Y}) = \mathsf{H}(\mathbf{Y}) - \mathsf{H}(\mathbf{Y}|\mathbf{X}),$$

where $\mathsf{H}(\mathbf{Y}|\mathbf{X})$ denotes the conditional Shannon entropy.

Definition 1. *Let $\mathcal{P} = \{P_1, \ldots, P_n\}$ be a group of n participants (a.k.a. shareholders). Let $\mathcal{S}$ be the set of secrets and a secret $\mathbf{s} \in \mathcal{S}$ is denoted in boldface. Let $\mathcal{S}_i$ be the share space of the participant P_i. A secret sharing scheme of n participants is a pair of algorithms: the dealer and the combiner. For a given secret from $\mathcal{S}$ and some random string from $\mathcal{R}$, the dealer algorithm applies the mapping*

$$\mathsf{D}\colon \mathcal{S} \times \mathcal{R} \rightarrow \mathcal{S}_1 \times \cdots \times \mathcal{S}_n$$

to assign shares to participants from $\mathcal{P}$. The shares of a subset $\mathcal{A} \subset [n]$ of participants can be input into the combiner algorithm

$$\mathsf{C}\colon \prod_{P_i \in \mathcal{A}} \mathcal{S}_i \rightarrow \mathcal{S}$$

to reconstruct the secret.

Definition 2. *A (t, r, n)-ramp scheme is a secret sharing scheme with n participants such that the combiner algorithm always reconstructs the correct secret for any $\mathcal{A} \subset [n]$ of size $|\mathcal{A}| \geq r$ and for any $\mathcal{A} \subset [n]$ of size $|\mathcal{A}| \leq t$, no information about the secret can be learned from pooling their shares together. Moreover if $t < r - 1$, for any $\mathcal{A} \subset [n]$ of size $t < |\mathcal{A}| < r$, neither the combiner algorithm can uniquely reconstruct a secret nor the secret can remain unknown. That is r is the smallest integer such that correct reconstruction is guaranteed and t is the biggest integer such that privacy is guaranteed. We associate a probability with each $\mathbf{s} \in \mathcal{S}$ and obtain a random secret $\mathbf{S} \leftarrow \mathcal{S}$. The share vector obtained from sharing the random secret $\mathbf{S}$ is denoted by*

$$\mathbf{V} \leftarrow \mathcal{S}_1 \times \cdots \times \mathcal{S}_n.$$

Let $\mathsf{H}(\mathbf{S}|\mathbf{V}_{\mathcal{A}})$ *denote the entropy of the random variable* $\mathbf{S}$ *conditioned on the knowledge of the shares held by the participants in* $\mathcal{A}$. *The above conditions defining a* (t, r, n)*-ramp scheme can be described information-theoretically as follows.*

- *Correctness:* $\mathsf{H}(\mathbf{S}|\mathbf{V}_{\mathcal{A}}) = 0$, *for any* $\mathcal{A} \subset [n]$ *of size* $|\mathcal{A}| \geq r$;
- *Privacy:* $\mathsf{H}(\mathbf{S}|\mathbf{V}_{\mathcal{A}}) = \mathsf{H}(\mathbf{S})$, *for any* $\mathcal{A} \subset [n]$ *of size* $|\mathcal{A}| \leq t$;
- *Ramp security:* $0 < \mathsf{H}(\mathbf{S}|\mathbf{V}_{\mathcal{A}}) < \mathsf{H}(\mathbf{S})$, *for any* $\mathcal{A} \subset [n]$ *of size* $t < |\mathcal{A}| < r$.

The parameter t is called the *privacy threshold* and the parameter r is called the *reconstruction threshold*. The difference of these two thresholds is called the gap and denoted by $g = r - t$. The last item *ramp security* in Definition 2 is void when $t = r - 1$, as there is no integer lying in between t and r. In this case when the gap $g = 1$, we call it a *(r,n)-threshold scheme* for short.

Definition 3 ([13]). *A* (t, r, n)*-ramp scheme threshold changeable to* (t', r', n)*, or a* $(t, r, n) \to (t', r', n)$ *ramp scheme for short, is a* (t, r, n)*-ramp scheme together with a set of publicly known share conversion functions*

$$h_i \colon \mathcal{S}_i \to \mathcal{S}'_i, i = 1, \ldots, n,$$

and a new combiner algorithm

$$\mathsf{C}' \colon \prod_{P_i \in \mathcal{A}} \mathcal{S}'_i \to \mathcal{S}$$

for a subset $\mathcal{A} \subset [n]$ *of participants such that the following properties are satisfied. The share conversion function* h_i *convert the share* $s_i \in \mathcal{S}_i$ *of the ith participant* P_i *into a new share* $s'_i = h_i(s_i) \in \mathcal{S}'_i$. *The new combiner algorithm* C' *always reconstructs the correct secret for any* $\mathcal{A} \subset [n]$ *of size* $|\mathcal{A}| \geq r'$ *and for any* $\mathcal{A} \subset [n]$ *of size* $|\mathcal{A}| \leq t'$, *no information about the secret can be learned from pooling their new shares together. Moreover for any* $\mathcal{A} \subset [n]$ *of size* $t' < |\mathcal{A}| < r'$, *neither the combiner algorithm can uniquely reconstruct a secret nor the secret can remain unknown. That is* r' *is the smallest integer such that correct reconstruction is guaranteed and* t' *is the biggest integer such that privacy is guaranteed. We associate a probability with each* $\mathbf{s} \in \mathcal{S}$ *and obtain a random secret* $\mathbf{S} \leftarrow \mathcal{S}$. *The share vector obtained from sharing the random secret* $\mathbf{S}$ *and then applying the share conversion functions is denoted by*

$$\mathbf{V}' \leftarrow \mathcal{S}'_1 \times \cdots \times \mathcal{S}'_n.$$

Let $\mathsf{H}(\mathbf{S}|\mathbf{V}'_{\mathcal{A}})$ *denote the entropy of the random variable* $\mathbf{S}$ *conditioned on the knowledge of the new shares held by the participants in* $\mathcal{A}$. *The above conditions can be described information-theoretically as follows.*

- *Correctness:* $\mathsf{H}(\mathbf{S}|\mathbf{V}'_{\mathcal{A}}) = 0$, *for any* $\mathcal{A} \subset [n]$ *of size* $|\mathcal{A}| \geq r'$;
- *Privacy:* $\mathsf{H}(\mathbf{S}|\mathbf{V}'_{\mathcal{A}}) = \mathsf{H}(\mathbf{S})$, *for any* $\mathcal{A} \subset [n]$ *of size* $|\mathcal{A}| \leq t'$;
- *Ramp security:* $0 < \mathsf{H}(\mathbf{S}|\mathbf{V}'_{\mathcal{A}}) < \mathsf{H}(\mathbf{S})$, *for any* $\mathcal{A} \subset [n]$ *of size* $t' < |\mathcal{A}| < r'$.

In Definition 3, the set of share conversion functions $\{h_i\}_{i\in[n]}$ together with the dealer algorithm D of the initial (t,r,n)-ramp scheme in fact define a new dealer algorithm D' through composition of functions.

$$\mathsf{D}': \mathcal{S} \times \mathcal{R} \to \mathcal{S}'_1 \times \cdots \times \mathcal{S}'_n. \tag{2}$$

This new dealer algorithm D' together with the new combiner algorithm C' define a new secret sharing scheme. In this interpretation, a $(t,r,n) \to (t',r',n)$ ramp scheme is a (t,r,n)-ramp scheme equipped with a set of share conversion functions that can transform it into a (t',r',n)-ramp scheme.

Theorem 1 ([13]). *Let Π be a $(t,r,n) \to (t',r',n)$ ramp scheme, where $r < r' \le n$ and $t \le t' < r' - (r-t)$. Let $h_i\colon \mathcal{S}_i \to \mathcal{S}'_i, i = 1,\dots,n$, be its share conversion functions. Then the following three bounds hold.*

1. *Bound on initial share size:* $\max_{1\le i\le n} \log|\mathcal{S}_i| \ge \frac{\mathsf{H}(\mathbf{S})}{r-t}$;
2. *Bound on new share size:* $\max_{1\le i\le n} \log|\mathcal{S}'_i| \ge \frac{\mathsf{H}(\mathbf{S})}{r'-t'}$;
3. *Bound on combiner communication complexity: for any $I \subset [n]$ of $|I| = r'$,*

$$\sum_{i\in I} \log|\mathcal{S}'_i| \ge \frac{r'\mathsf{H}(\mathbf{S})}{r'-t'}.$$

Definition 4 ([13]). *A $(t,r,n) \to (t',r',n)$ ramp scheme is called optimal if equality is achieved in all the bounds in Theorem 1.*

In other words, a $(t,r,n) \to (t',r',n)$ ramp scheme is optimal if and only if both its initial scheme with (D,C) and its new scheme with $(\mathsf{D}',\mathsf{C}')$ have minimum share size, where D' is the composition of the initial dealer algorithm D and the share conversion functions $\{h_i\}_{i\in[n]}$ as described in (2). Our focus in this work is the range of achievable new privacy threshold t' and new reconstruction threshold r' by optimal $(t,r,n) \to (t',r',n)$ ramp schemes.

3 Constructions with New Threshold Change Range

We begin with describing our generic construction, which can be understood as a compiler that takes a threshold changeable secret sharing that only changes reconstruction threshold to one that changes both privacy and reconstruction thresholds.

3.1 Generic Construction

Let t,t',u,v be positive integers such that $1 \le \frac{v}{u} = \frac{t'}{t}$. Let $\widetilde{\Pi}$ be a $(tv,rv,nv) \to (tv,r'u,nv)$ ramp scheme. Let $\widetilde{\Pi}'$ denote the resulting $(tv,r'u,nv)$ scheme after applying the share conversion functions of $\widetilde{\Pi}$. We aim to construct a $(t,r,n) \to$

(t', r', n) ramp scheme Π out of $\widetilde{\Pi}$. The idea of the construction is illustrated in Fig. 1. The scheme Π is simply the v-folding of $\widetilde{\Pi}$. We then define the share conversion functions of Π with respect to share conversion functions of $\widetilde{\Pi}$ such that resulting (t', r', n) scheme (call it Π') after applying share conversion functions of Π is the u-folding of the $\widetilde{\Pi}'$.

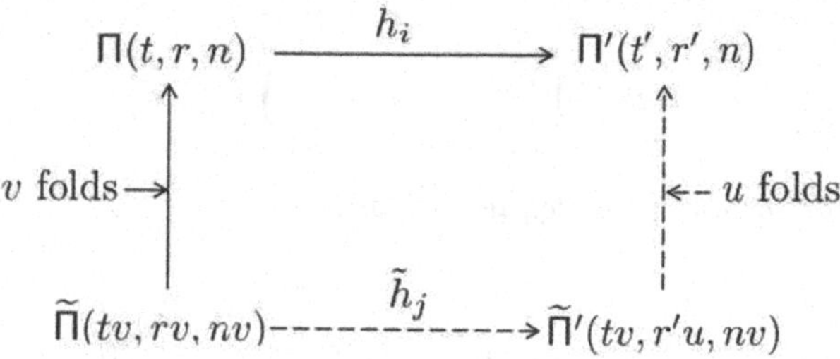

Fig. 1. Generic construction of a $(t, r, n) \to (t', r', n)$ ramp scheme with $1 \leq \frac{v}{u} = \frac{t'}{t}$.

Construction 1 : Generic construction

Let the dealer algorithm $\tilde{\mathsf{D}}$, combiner algorithm $\tilde{\mathsf{C}}$, share conversion functions $\{\tilde{h}_j\}$ and new combiner algorithm $\tilde{\mathsf{C}}'$ of $\widetilde{\Pi}$ be as follows.

$$\tilde{\mathsf{D}}\colon \mathcal{S} \times \mathcal{R} \to \tilde{\mathcal{S}}_1 \times \cdots \times \tilde{\mathcal{S}}_{nv};\ \tilde{\mathsf{C}}_{\tilde{\mathcal{A}}}\colon \prod_{\tilde{P}_j \in \tilde{\mathcal{A}}} \tilde{\mathcal{S}}_j \to \mathcal{S},$$

for $\tilde{\mathcal{A}} \subset [nv]$ and

$$\tilde{h}_j\colon \tilde{\mathcal{S}}_j \to \tilde{\mathcal{S}}'_j, j = 1, \ldots, nv;\ \tilde{\mathsf{C}}'_{\tilde{\mathcal{A}}}\colon \prod_{\tilde{P}_j \in \tilde{\mathcal{A}}} \tilde{\mathcal{S}}'_j \to \mathcal{S},$$

for $\tilde{\mathcal{A}} \subset [nv]$.

The dealer algorithm D, combiner algorithm C, share conversion functions $\{h_j\}$ and new combiner algorithm C' of Π are defined as follows.

1. Dealer algorithm D: *Given a secret s from $\mathcal{S}$, the dealer samples a random string from $\mathcal{R}$ and use the dealer algorithm $\tilde{\mathsf{D}}$ of $\widetilde{\Pi}$ to generate*

$$\{\tilde{s}_j \in \tilde{\mathcal{S}}_j | j = 1, 2, \ldots, nv\}.$$

The dealer prepares n shares by v-folding the above share vector of $\widetilde{\Pi}$.

$$\boldsymbol{s}_i \triangleq (\tilde{s}_{(i-1)v+1}, \tilde{s}_{(i-1)v+2}, \ldots, \tilde{s}_{iv}),\ i \in [n].$$

The dealer then distributes $\boldsymbol{s}_i$ to the ith participant P_i for $i \in [n]$.

2. Combiner algorithm C: *Given any $\mathcal{A} \subset [n]$ of size $|\mathcal{A}| \geq r$, for $\boldsymbol{s}_i, i \in \mathcal{A}$, the combiner parses*

$$\boldsymbol{s}_i = (\tilde{s}_{(i-1)v+1}, \tilde{s}_{(i-1)v+2}, \ldots, \tilde{s}_{iv}).$$

The combiner then recovers $\tilde{\mathcal{A}} \subset [nv]$ from $\mathcal{A} \subset [n]$ and invoke the combiner algorithm $\tilde{\mathsf{C}}$ of $\tilde{\Pi}$ with $\tilde{\mathcal{A}} \subset [nv]$ on the parsed $\boldsymbol{s}_i, i \in \mathcal{A}$.

3. Share conversion functions*: For any $i \in [n]$, the public known share conversion function*

$$h_i : \prod_{j=(i-1)v+1}^{iv} \tilde{\mathcal{S}}_j \longmapsto \prod_{j=(i-1)v+1}^{iv-(v-u)} \tilde{\mathcal{S}}'_j$$

for the ith participant P_i is defined as follows.

$$\begin{aligned} & h_i(\boldsymbol{s}_i) \\ & = h_i(\tilde{s}_{(i-1)v+1}, \tilde{s}_{(i-1)v+2}, \ldots, \tilde{s}_{(i-1)v+u}, \tilde{s}_{(i-1)v+u+1}, \tilde{s}_{(i-1)v+u+2}, \ldots, \tilde{s}_{iv}) \\ & = (\tilde{h}_{(i-1)v+1}(\tilde{s}_{(i-1)v+1}), \tilde{h}_{(i-1)v+2}(\tilde{s}_{(i-1)v+2}), \ldots, \tilde{h}_{(i-1)v+u}(\tilde{s}_{(i-1)v+u})) \\ & \triangleq \boldsymbol{s}'_i. \end{aligned}$$

4. New combiner algorithm C': *Given any $\mathcal{A} \subset [n]$ of size $|\mathcal{A}| \geq r'$, for $\boldsymbol{s}'_i, i \in \mathcal{A}$, the combiner parses*

$$\boldsymbol{s}'_i = (\tilde{s}'_{(i-1)v+1}, \tilde{s}'_{(i-1)v+2}, \ldots, \tilde{s}_{(i-1)v+u}).$$

The combiner then recovers $\tilde{\mathcal{A}} \subset [nv]$ from $\mathcal{A} \subset [n]$ and invoke the combiner algorithm $\tilde{\mathsf{C}}'$ of $\tilde{\Pi}'$ with $\tilde{\mathcal{A}} \subset [nv]$ on the parsed $\boldsymbol{s}'_i, i \in \mathcal{A}$.

Lemma 1. *Construction 1 gives a $(t, r, n) \to (t', r', n)$ threshold changeable secret sharing.*

Proof. Since each share $\mathbf{s}_i$ consists of v shares of $\tilde{\Pi}$, then it is easy to check that the dealer algorithm D and combiner algorithm C form a (t, r, n)-ramp scheme.

Next, we prove that Π is a $(t, r, n) \to (t', r', n)$ ramp scheme with share conversion functions $\{h_j\}$ and new combiner algorithm C'. According to our short-hand notation, $\tilde{h}_j(\tilde{s}_j)$ is a share of $\tilde{\Pi}'$ for $j = 1, \ldots, nv$. This means that each $\mathbf{s}'_i = h_i(\mathbf{s}_i)$ consists of u shares of $\tilde{\Pi}'$ for $i = 1, \ldots, n$. (In the process of share conversion of Π, $nv - nu$ shares of $\tilde{\Pi}'$ are dropped.) We now verify explicitly the three defining properties for the share conversion functions and new combiner algorithm.

- Correctness: Since $lu \geq r'u$ for any $l \geq r'$, then, from the combiner algorithm C' and correctness of $\tilde{\Pi}'$, we have $\mathsf{H}(\mathbf{S}|\mathbf{V}'_{\mathcal{A}}) = 0$, for any $\mathcal{A} \subset [n]$ of size $|\mathcal{A}| \geq r'$.

- Privacy: Since t, t', u, v are positive integers such that $1 \leq \frac{v}{u} = \frac{t'}{t}$, for any $l \leq t'$ we have

$$lu = \frac{l}{t'} tv \leq tv.$$

From the combiner algorithm C' and privacy of $\tilde{\Pi}'$, we get $\mathsf{H}(\mathbf{S}|\mathbf{V}'_{\mathcal{A}}) = \mathsf{H}(\mathbf{S})$, for any $\mathcal{A} \subset [n]$ of size $|\mathcal{A}| \leq t'$.

- Ramp security: Let $t' < l < r'$. Since $1 \leq \frac{v}{u} = \frac{t'}{t}$, then

$$tv < \frac{l}{t'} tv = lu < r'u = \frac{t}{t'} r'v \leq r'v.$$

From the combiner algorithm C' and ramp security of $\tilde{\Pi}'$, we derive $0 < \mathsf{H}(\mathbf{S}|\mathbf{V}'_{\mathcal{A}}) < \mathsf{H}(\mathbf{S})$, for any $\mathcal{A} \subset [n]$ of size $t' < |\mathcal{A}| < r'$.

According to Definition 3, the scheme Π obtained from Construction 1 is a $(t, r, n) \to (t', r', n)$ ramp scheme.

3.2 New Optimal Threshold Changeable Secret Sharing

Theorem 2. *For any positive integers t, t', r, r', n satisfying $t < r, t' < r' \leq n$ and $1 < \frac{t'}{t} < \frac{r'}{r}$, there is an optimal $(t, r, n) \to (t', r', n)$ threshold changeable secret sharing scheme with share size $\frac{tt'(r'-t')}{\gcd^2(t',t)} \log q$, where q is a prime power such that $q > \frac{nt'}{\gcd(t',t)}$.*

Proof. Since $1 < \frac{v}{u} = \frac{t'}{t} < \frac{r'}{r}$, then $r'u > rv$, and so we let $\tilde{\Pi}$ be an optimal $(tv, rv, nv) \to (tv, r'u, nv)$ ramp scheme that constructed in [2].

- Applying $\tilde{\Pi}$ and its share conversion functions to Construction 1, we can get an optimal $(t, r, n) \to (t', r', n)$ ramp scheme. Indeed, Π is a $(t, r, n) \to (t', r', n)$ ramp scheme from Lemma 1. Since $\tilde{\Pi}$ is an optimal $(tv, rv, nv) \to (tv, r'u, nv)$ ramp scheme, then, the share size of $\tilde{\Pi}$ and $\tilde{\Pi}'$ are

$$\log|\tilde{\mathcal{S}}_j| = \frac{\mathsf{H}(\mathbf{S})}{v(r-t)}, \log|\tilde{\mathcal{S}}'_j| = \frac{\mathsf{H}(\mathbf{S})}{r'u - tv},$$

respectively. From Construction 1 we know that the share size of Π and Π' are

$$\log|\mathcal{S}_i| = v \log|\tilde{\mathcal{S}}_j| = \frac{\mathsf{H}(\mathbf{S})}{r-t}$$

and

$$\log|\mathcal{S}'_i| = u \log|\tilde{\mathcal{S}}'_j| = \frac{\mathsf{H}(\mathbf{S})}{r' - \frac{tv}{u}} = \frac{\mathsf{H}(\mathbf{S})}{r' - t'}$$

respectively, which implies that Π is an optimal $(t, r, n) \to (t', r', n)$ ramp scheme from Theorem 1 and Definition 4.

- Let $v = \frac{t'}{\gcd(t',t)}$, then v is the smallest positive integer such that u is a positive integer and $\frac{v}{u} = \frac{t'}{t}$. On the other hand, from [2] we have

$$\mathsf{H}(\mathbf{S}) = v(r-t)(r'u - tv)\log q$$

with $q > nv$. Then the share size bound of Π is

$$\log|\mathcal{S}_i| = \frac{\mathsf{H}(\mathbf{S})}{r-t} = \frac{tt'(r'-t')}{\gcd^2(t',t)}\log q,$$

where q is a prime power such that $q > \frac{nt'}{\gcd(t',t)}$.

3.3 Extending the Results to Universal Threshold Change

Definition 5. *A universal threshold changeable (t,r,n)-ramp scheme with respect to a set $\mathcal{T} \subset [n] \times [n]$ of new thresholds is a (t,r,n)-ramp scheme together with publicly known share conversion functions*

$$h_i^{(t',r')} : \mathcal{S}_i \to \mathcal{S}_i^{(t',r')}, i = 1, \ldots, n, \ (t',r') \in \mathcal{T},$$

and combiner algorithms

$$\mathsf{C}^{(t',r')} : \prod_{P_i \in \mathcal{A}} \mathcal{S}_i^{(t',r')} \to \mathcal{S}, \ (t',r') \in \mathcal{T},$$

for a subset $\mathcal{A} \subset [n]$ of participants such that the following properties are satisfied. The share conversion function $h_i^{(t',r')}$ converts the share $s_i \in \mathcal{S}_i$ of the ith participant P_i into a new share $s_i^{(t',r')} = h_i^{(t',r')}(s_i) \in \mathcal{S}_i^{(t',r')}$. The new combiner algorithm $\mathsf{C}^{(t',r')}$ correctly reconstructs the secret for any $\mathcal{A} \subset [n]$ of size $|\mathcal{A}| \geq r'$ and for any $\mathcal{A} \subset [n]$ of size $|\mathcal{A}| \leq t'$, no information about the secret is contained in new shares specified by $\mathcal{A}$. Moreover for any $\mathcal{A} \subset [n]$ of size $t' < |\mathcal{A}| < r'$, neither the combiner algorithm can uniquely reconstruct a secret nor the secret can remain unknown. That is r' is the smallest integer such that correct reconstruction is guaranteed and t' is the biggest integer such that privacy is guaranteed. We associate a probability with each $\mathbf{s} \in \mathcal{S}$ and obtain a random secret $\mathbf{S} \leftarrow \mathcal{S}$. The share vector obtained from sharing the random secret $\mathbf{S}$ and then applying the share conversion functions is denoted by

$$\mathbf{V}^{(t',r')} \leftarrow \mathcal{S}_1^{(t',r')} \times \cdots \times \mathcal{S}_n^{(t',r')}.$$

Let $\mathsf{H}(\mathbf{S}|\mathbf{V}_{\mathcal{A}}^{(t',r')})$ denote the entropy of the random variable $\mathbf{S}$ conditioned on the knowledge of the new shares held by the participants in $\mathcal{A}$. The above conditions can be described information-theoretically as follows.

- *Correctness:* $\mathsf{H}(\mathbf{S}|\mathbf{V}_{\mathcal{A}}^{(t',r')}) = 0$, *for any $\mathcal{A} \subset [n]$ of size $|\mathcal{A}| \geq r'$;*
- *Privacy:* $\mathsf{H}(\mathbf{S}|\mathbf{V}_{\mathcal{A}}^{(t',r')}) = \mathsf{H}(\mathbf{S})$, *for any $\mathcal{A} \subset [n]$ of size $|\mathcal{A}| \leq t'$;*
- *Ramp security:* $0 < \mathsf{H}(\mathbf{S}|\mathbf{V}_{\mathcal{A}}^{(t',r')}) < \mathsf{H}(\mathbf{S})$, *for any $\mathcal{A} \subset [n]$ with $t' < |\mathcal{A}| < r'$.*

We say a $(t,r,n) \to \mathcal{T}$ ramp scheme is optimal if each $(t,r,n) \to (t',r',n)$ ramp scheme is optimal for any $(t',r') \in \mathcal{T}$.

Theorem 3. *For any set $\mathcal{T} = \{(t'_1,r'_1),(t'_2,r'_2),\ldots,(t'_m,r'_m)\}$ with positive integers r, r'_k, t, t'_k satisfying $t < r < r'_k, t'_k < r'_k \le n, 1 \le \frac{t'_k}{t} \le \frac{r'_k}{r}$ and $k = 1,\ldots,m$, there is an optimal $(t,r,n) \to \mathcal{T}$ threshold changeable secret sharing scheme with share size bound*

$$v \cdot \mathrm{lcm}\left(\frac{tv(r'_{k_1} - t'_{k_1})}{t'_{k_1}},\ldots,\frac{tv(r'_{k_{m^*}} - t'_{k_{m^*}})}{t'_{k_{m^*}}}\right)\log q,$$

where

$$v = \mathrm{lcm}\left(\frac{t'_1}{\gcd(t,t'_1)},\frac{t'_2}{\gcd(t,t'_2)},\ldots,\frac{t'_m}{\gcd(t,t'_m)}\right),$$

$$m^* = |\widetilde{\mathcal{T}}^*|, \widetilde{\mathcal{T}}^* = \left\{(tv,\frac{tvr'_k}{t'_k})|\frac{r'_k}{r} \ne \frac{t'_k}{t}, \text{for } k = 1,\ldots,m\right\},$$

$$\text{denote } \widetilde{\mathcal{T}}^* \text{ by } \left\{(tv,\frac{tvr'_{k_l}}{t'_{k_l}}) \in \widetilde{\mathcal{T}}^* \text{ for } l = 1,\ldots,m^*\right\},$$

and $q > nv$ is a prime power.

Proof. Since r, r'_k, t, t'_k are positive integers such that $1 \le \frac{t'_k}{t} \le \frac{r'_k}{r}$, then $\frac{r}{t} \le \frac{r'_k}{t'_k}$ for $k = 1,\ldots,m$. Without loss of generality, we let

$$\frac{r}{t} \le \frac{r'_m}{t'_m} \le \frac{r'_{m-1}}{t'_{m-1}} \le \cdots \le \frac{r'_2}{t'_2} \le \frac{r'_1}{t'_1}.$$

Let $\frac{v}{u_k} = \frac{t'_k}{t}$ for $k = 1,\ldots,m$, then $rv = \frac{r}{t}tv \le \frac{r'_m}{t'_m}tv = r'_m u_m$, and similarly we have

$$tv < rv \le r'_m u_m \le r'_{m-1}u_{m-1} \le \cdots \le r'_2 u_2 \le r'_1 u_1 = r'_1 v\frac{t}{t'_1} \le nv.$$

Clearly, $\mathcal{T}^* = \{(tv, r'_k u_k)|r'_k u_k \ne rv, \frac{v}{u_k} = \frac{t'_k}{t}, \text{for } k = 1,\ldots,m\}$. If $\mathcal{T}^* = \varnothing$, namely,

$$\frac{r}{t} = \frac{r'_m}{t'_m} = \frac{r'_{m-1}}{t'_{m-1}} = \cdots = \frac{r'_2}{t'_2} = \frac{r'_1}{t'_1},$$

then there is an optimal $(t,r,n) \to \mathcal{T}$ ramp scheme by using folding technique [13], where the share size bound is $v \log q$ and satisfies our statements. Next, we consider the case $\mathcal{T}^* \ne \varnothing$.

- Let $\tilde{\Pi}^{(tv,rv)}$ be an optimal $(tv,rv,nv) \to \mathcal{T}^*$ ramp scheme that is constructed in [2]. Let $(t',r') \in \mathcal{T}$.

- If $1 \le \frac{v}{u} = \frac{t'}{t} < \frac{r'}{r}$, then $(tv, r'u) \in \mathcal{T}^*$, which means $\tilde{\Pi}^{(tv,rv)}$ is an optimal $(tv, rv, nv) \to (tv, r'u, nv)$ ramp scheme. Moreover, Theorem 2 can be easily extended from $1 < \frac{v}{u} = \frac{t'}{t} < \frac{r'}{r}$ to $1 \le \frac{v}{u} = \frac{t'}{t} < \frac{r'}{r}$, and then we get an optimal $(t, r, n) \to (t', r', n)$ ramp scheme.
- If $1 < \frac{v}{u} = \frac{t'}{t} = \frac{r'}{r}$, then there is an optimal $(t, r, n) \to (t', r', n)$ ramp scheme by using folding technique [13].

In a word, there is an optimal $(t, r, n) \to \mathcal{T}$ ramp scheme if $\mathcal{T}^* \neq \varnothing$.

- Let $v = \text{lcm}(\frac{t_1}{\gcd(t,t_1)}, \frac{t_2}{\gcd(t,t_2)}, \dots, \frac{t_m}{\gcd(t,t_m)})$, then v is the smallest positive integer such that u is a positive integer and $\frac{v}{u} = \frac{t'}{t}$ for any $(t', r') \in \mathcal{T}$. On the other hand, from [2] we have that the share size of $\tilde{\Pi}^{(tv,rv)}$ is $\log |\tilde{\mathcal{S}}_j^{(tv,rv)}| = \frac{\mathsf{H}(\mathbf{S})}{v(r-t)}$, where

$$\mathsf{H}(\mathbf{S}) = v(r-t) \cdot \text{lcm}\left(\frac{tv(r'_{k_1} - t'_{k_1})}{t'_{k_1}}, \dots, \frac{tv(r'_{k_{m^*}} - t'_{k_{m^*}})}{t'_{k_{m^*}}}\right) \log q.$$

Then the share size of this optimal $(t, r, n) \to \mathcal{T}$ ramp scheme is

$$\begin{aligned} \log |\mathcal{S}_i^{(t,r)}| &= v \cdot \log |\tilde{\mathcal{S}}_j^{(tv,rv)}| \\ &= v \cdot \text{lcm}\left(\frac{tv(r'_{k_1} - t'_{k_1})}{t'_{k_1}}, \dots, \frac{tv(r'_{k_{m^*}} - t'_{k_{m^*}})}{t'_{k_{m^*}}}\right) \log q. \end{aligned} \tag{3}$$

In conclusion, there is is an optimal $(t, r, n) \to \mathcal{T}$ ramp scheme, and its share size is bounded by equation (3).

4 Completeness Results for Secret Sharing with Full Reconstruction

The definition of full reconstruction threshold is given by Nielsen and Simkin [17] recently. It defines how many shares are needed to reconstruct all shares of a secret sharing. We restrict to a special class of secret sharing whose full reconstruction thresholds are the same as their reconstruction thresholds, and then argue that the new optimal threshold changeable ramp schemes constructed in this work together with the constructions from [2,13] cover the full admissible threshold change range.

Definition 6. *For a (t, r, n)-ramp scheme with share vector*

$$\mathbf{V} \leftarrow \mathcal{S}_1 \times \cdots \times \mathcal{S}_n,$$

we say it has full reconstruction if $\mathsf{H}(\mathbf{V}|\mathbf{V}_{\mathcal{A}}) = 0$ *for any $\mathcal{A} \subset [n]$ of size $|\mathcal{A}| \ge r$.*

Many secret sharing schemes have full reconstruction such as Shamir's (r, n) secret sharing scheme. Any r participants can reconstruct the random polynomial $f(x)$ with Lagrange interpolating formula, and then all the shares can be computed with public known values x_i for $i \in [n]$. This is also true for the optimal threshold secret sharing schemes constructed in [2,9,13,16,22]. Clearly, this class of schemes have been used in many scenarios. We assume all the secret sharing schemes have full reconstruction in the following.

Theorem 4. *Let r, r', t, t', n be positive integers. Then there is an optimal $(t, r, n) \to (t', r', n)$ ramp scheme if and only if $t < r < r', t' < r' \leq n$ and $1 \leq \frac{t'}{t} \leq \frac{r'}{r}$.*

Proof. We begin by presenting two claims, which will make our proof more clearly.

Claim (1). If Π is a $(t, r, n) \to (t', r', n)$ ramp scheme, then

$$\mathsf{H}(\mathcal{S}_i) \geq \mathsf{H}(\mathcal{S}'_i), \mathsf{H}(\mathbf{V}'_{\mathcal{A}'}|\mathbf{V}_{\mathcal{A}'}) = 0, \mathsf{H}(\mathsf{V}_{\mathcal{A}}) \geq \mathsf{H}(\mathsf{V}'_{\mathcal{A}'}),$$

where $i \in [n]$, and $\mathcal{A}, \mathcal{A}' \subset [n]$ of size $|\mathcal{A}| = r$ and $|\mathcal{A}'| = r'$ respectively.

Proof of Claim (1): Let $\mathbf{s}_i \in \mathcal{S}_i$ and $\mathbf{s}'_i \in \mathcal{S}'_i$ be the shares of Π and Π' respectively, then $\mathbf{s}'_i = h_i(\mathbf{s}_i)$ with public known share functions h_i for $i \in [n]$. Consequently, $\mathsf{H}(\mathcal{S}'_i|\mathcal{S}_i) = 0$ and $\mathsf{H}(\mathcal{S}_i) \geq \mathsf{H}(\mathcal{S}'_i)$. This implies that for any $\mathcal{A}, \mathcal{A}' \subset [n]$ of size $|\mathcal{A}| = r$ and $|\mathcal{A}'| = r'$, we have $\mathsf{H}(\mathbf{V}'_{\mathcal{A}'}|\mathbf{V}_{\mathcal{A}'}) = 0$. From Definition 6 we know that $\mathsf{H}(\mathbf{V}|\mathbf{V}_{\mathcal{A}}) = 0$. Meanwhile, $\mathbf{V}_{\mathcal{A}'} \subset \mathbf{V}$, and so $\mathsf{H}(\mathbf{V}'_{\mathcal{A}'}|\mathbf{V}_{\mathcal{A}}) = 0$. By the chain rule of mutual information we have

$$\begin{aligned} \mathsf{I}(\mathbf{V}_{\mathcal{A}}, \mathbf{V}'_{\mathcal{A}'}) &= \mathsf{H}(\mathbf{V}'_{\mathcal{A}'}) - \mathsf{H}(\mathbf{V}'_{\mathcal{A}'}|\mathbf{V}_{\mathcal{A}}) \\ &= \mathsf{H}(\mathbf{V}_{\mathcal{A}}) - \mathsf{H}(\mathbf{V}_{\mathcal{A}}|\mathbf{V}'_{\mathcal{A}'}). \end{aligned}$$

Therefore

$$\begin{aligned} \mathsf{H}(\mathbf{V}_{\mathcal{A}}) &= \mathsf{H}(\mathbf{V}'_{\mathcal{A}'}) - \mathsf{H}(\mathbf{V}'_{\mathcal{A}'}|\mathbf{V}_{\mathcal{A}}) + \mathsf{H}(\mathbf{V}_{\mathcal{A}}|\mathbf{V}'_{\mathcal{A}'}) \\ &= \mathsf{H}(\mathbf{V}'_{\mathcal{A}'}) + \mathsf{H}(\mathbf{V}_{\mathcal{A}}|\mathbf{V}'_{\mathcal{A}'}) \\ &\geq \mathsf{H}(\mathbf{V}'_{\mathcal{A}'}). \end{aligned}$$

Claim (2). If Π is a $(t, r, n) \to (t', r', n)$ ramp scheme, then

$$t < r \leq r', t \leq t' < r' \leq n, (t, r) \neq (t', r').$$

Proof of Claim (2): It is straightforward that $t < r, t' < r' \leq n$ and $(t, r) \neq (t', r')$ from Definition 3. Next, we give the proof of $r \leq r'$. For any $\mathcal{A}' \subset [n]$ of size $|\mathcal{A}'| = r'$, we have $\mathsf{H}(\mathbf{S}|\mathbf{V}'_{\mathcal{A}'}) = 0$. Since $\mathsf{H}(\mathbf{V}'_{\mathcal{A}'}|\mathbf{V}_{\mathcal{A}'}) = 0$ from Claim 4, then $\mathsf{H}(\mathbf{S}|\mathbf{V}_{\mathcal{A}'}) = 0$, which implies that $r' = |\mathcal{A}'| \geq r$ from Definition 2. Finally, we prove $t \leq t'$ which has been given by Lin et al. [13]. From $\mathbf{s}'_i = h_i(\mathbf{s}_i)$ we know that no information can be generated other than those already contained in $\mathbf{s}_i$. Since t participants learn nothing about the secret with their initial shares $\mathbf{s}_i$, we then obtain that any set of t new shares $\mathbf{s}'_i$ does not contain information about the secret. This indicates that $t \leq t'$, and then complete the proof of this claim.

Next, we prove this theorem. Assume that Π is an optimal $(t,r,n) \to (t',r',n)$ ramp scheme, then $t < r \leq r', t \leq t' < r' \leq n$ and $(t,r) \neq (t',r')$ from Claim (2). Moreover, the share size of Π and Π' are minimum, namely,

$$\log|\mathbf{S}_i| = \mathsf{H}(\mathbf{S}_i) = \frac{\mathsf{H}(\mathbf{S})}{r-t}, \quad \log|\mathbf{S}'_i| = \mathsf{H}(\mathbf{S}'_i) = \frac{\mathsf{H}(\mathbf{S})}{r'-t'},$$

for any $i \in [n]$. Since $\mathsf{H}(\mathbf{S}_i) \geq \mathsf{H}(\mathbf{S}'_i)$ from Claim (1), then $r - t \leq r' - t'$, which shows that $r < r'$ for $r \leq r', t \leq t'$ and $(t,r) \neq (t',r')$. Let $\mathcal{A}, \mathcal{A}' \subset [n]$ of size $|\mathcal{A}| = r$ and $|\mathcal{A}'| = r'$ respectively, then, from Theorem 5 and Result 3 in [10] we have

$$\frac{r\mathsf{H}(\mathbf{S})}{r-t} \leq \mathsf{H}(\mathsf{V}_{\mathcal{A}}) \leq \sum_{i\in\mathcal{A}} \mathsf{H}(\mathbf{S}_i) = \frac{r\mathsf{H}(\mathbf{S})}{r-t}$$

and

$$\frac{r'\mathsf{H}(\mathbf{S})}{r'-t'} \leq \mathsf{H}(\mathsf{V}'_{\mathcal{A}'}) \leq \sum_{i\in\mathcal{A}'} \mathsf{H}(\mathbf{S}'_i) = \frac{r\mathsf{H}(\mathbf{S})}{r'-t'}.$$

This implies that $\mathsf{H}(\mathsf{V}_{\mathcal{A}}) = \dfrac{r\mathsf{H}(\mathbf{S})}{r-t}$ and $\mathsf{H}(\mathsf{V}'_{\mathcal{A}'}) = \dfrac{r'\mathsf{H}(\mathbf{S})}{r'-t'}$. Since $\mathsf{H}(\mathsf{V}_{\mathcal{A}}) \geq \mathsf{H}(\mathsf{V}'_{\mathcal{A}'})$ from Claim (1), then $\dfrac{r'}{r} \leq \dfrac{r'-t'}{r-t}$. From the above discussion, we have $t < r < r', t \leq t' < r' \leq n$ and $\dfrac{r'}{r} \leq \dfrac{r'-t'}{r-t}$, which are equivalent to $t < r < r', t' < r' \leq n$ and $1 \leq \frac{t'}{t} \leq \frac{r'}{r}$. This gives the proof of the necessary part of this theorem.

On the other hand, there is an optimal $(t,r,n) \to (t',r',n)$ ramp scheme under the following parameters range.

- Ours (Theorem 2): $t < r, t' < r' \leq n$ and $1 < \frac{t'}{t} < \frac{r'}{r}$.
- Bitar et al. [2]: $t = t' < r < r' \leq n$.
- Lin et al. [13]: $t' < r' \leq n, 1 < \frac{t'}{t} = \frac{r'}{r}$.

We can check that the union of these ranges are equivalent to $t < r < r', t' < r' \leq n$ and $1 \leq \frac{t'}{t} \leq \frac{r'}{r}$, and complete the proof of the sufficient part of this theorem.

A necessary condition for the existence of an optimal $(t,r,n) \to (t',r',n)$ ramp scheme is given in [13], which is $t < r, t \leq t' < r' \leq n$ and $r'-t' > r-t$. On the other hand, from the proof of Theorem 4, we know that the full admissible threshold change range can be also written by $t < r < r', t \leq t' < r' \leq n$ and $\dfrac{r'}{r} \leq \dfrac{r'-t'}{r-t}$, namely, $t < r, t \leq t' < r' \leq n$ and $1 < \dfrac{r'}{r} \leq \dfrac{r'-t'}{r-t}$. Our result is a necessary and sufficient condition for the existence of an optimal $(t,r,n) \to (t',r',n)$ ramp scheme.

Remark 1. In this work, we present a new threshold change range $1 < \frac{t'}{t} < \frac{r'}{r}$ in Theorem 2, while the previous range in [13] is $1 < \frac{t'}{t} = \frac{r'}{r}$. When we consider to transform the reconstruction threshold r to a given r', the privacy threshold can be changed from t to t'_1 in the new range and t'_2 in the previous range, respectively, such that $1 < \frac{t'_1}{t} < \frac{r'}{r}$ and $1 < \frac{t'_2}{t} = \frac{r'}{r}$. One may wonder why we need the new threshold change range that makes the privacy threshold t'_1 smaller than t'_2? Note that the gap $g_1 = r' - t'_1$ in this work is bigger than the previous gap $g_2 = r' - t'_2$. This shows that we can share more secrets in new threshold change range than in the previous range. In fact, this statement is also true for the scenarios that require to change privacy threshold t to a given t'.

5 Conclusion

We continued the study of threshold changeable ramp scheme with the goal of making it more practical. Previous constructions either enable only the reconstruction threshold change or require both thresholds to change proportionally. We constructed optimal threshold changeable secret sharing schemes with both thresholds changes and without the limitation of proportionality for privacy threshold and reconstruction threshold. We further investigate the full admissible threshold change range for optimal schemes and concluded that our new schemes together with previous schemes cover the complete range. We also extend these results to construct optimal schemes that can change both thresholds universally within the complete threshold change range. An open question of theoretical interest is how much a special threshold change requirement affects the lower bound of the share size for a ramp scheme.

Acknowledgements. The authors would like to thank the anonymous reviewers for their helpful and valuable suggestions. Especially, Remark 1 was inspired by a question from one of the reviewers. The work of Jian Ding and Changlu Lin was supported partly by National Natural Science Foundation of China (U1705264 and 61572132), Natural Science Foundation of Fujian Province (2019J01275), and Anhui Province Natural Science Research (KJ2018A0584). The work of Fuchun Lin was supported by EPSRC grant EP/S021043/1.

References

1. Barwick, S.G., Jackson, W.-A., Martin, K.M.: Updating the parameters of a threshold scheme by minimal broadcast. IEEE Trans. Inf. Theory **51**(2), 620–633 (2005)
2. Bitar, R., El Rouayheb, S.: Staircase codes for secret sharing with optimal communication and read overheads. IEEE Trans. Inf. Theory **64**(2), 933–943 (2017)
3. Blakley, G.R.: Safeguarding cryptographic keys. In: Proceedings of the National Computer Conference, vol. 48 (1979)
4. Blundo, C., Cresti, A., De Santis, A., Vaccaro, U.: Fully dynamic secret sharing schemes. In: Stinson, D.R. (ed.) CRYPTO 1993. LNCS, vol. 773, pp. 110–125. Springer, Heidelberg (1994). https://doi.org/10.1007/3-540-48329-2_10

5. Bogdanov, A., Guo, S., Komargodski, I.: Threshold secret sharing requires a linear size alphabet. In: Hirt, M., Smith, A. (eds.) TCC 2016. LNCS, vol. 9986, pp. 471–484. Springer, Heidelberg (2016). https://doi.org/10.1007/978-3-662-53644-5_18
6. Cramer, R., Damgård, I., Nielsen, J.B.: Secure Multiparty Computation and Secret Sharing. Cambridge University Press, Cambridge (2015)
7. Desmedt, Y.: Threshold Cryptography, pp. 1288–1293. Springer, Boston (2011)
8. Desmedty, Y., Jajodiay, S.: Redistributing secret shares to new access structures and its applications (1997)
9. Huang, W., Langberg, M., Kliewer, J., Bruck, J.: Communication efficient secret sharing. IEEE Trans. Inf. Theory **62**(12), 7195–7206 (2016)
10. Jackson, W.-A., Martin, K.M.: A combinatorial interpretation of ramp schemes. Australas. J. Comb. **14**, 51–60 (1996)
11. Jia, X., Wang, D., Nie, D., Luo, X., Sun, J.Z.: A new threshold changeable secret sharing scheme based on the chinese remainder theorem. Inf. Sci. **473**, 13–30 (2019)
12. Lin, F., Cheraghchi, M., Guruswami, V., Safavi-Naini, R., Wang, H.: Secret sharing with binary shares. In: 10th Innovations in Theoretical Computer Science Conference (ITCS 2019). Schloss Dagstuhl-Leibniz-Zentrum fuer Informatik (2018)
13. Lin, F., Ling, S., Wang, H., Zeng, N.: Threshold changeable ramp secret sharing. In: Mu, Y., Deng, R.H., Huang, X. (eds.) CANS 2019. LNCS, vol. 11829, pp. 308–327. Springer, Cham (2019). https://doi.org/10.1007/978-3-030-31578-8_17
14. Maeda, A., Miyaji, A., Tada, M.: Efficient and unconditionally secure verifiable threshold changeable scheme. In: Varadharajan, V., Mu, Y. (eds.) ACISP 2001. LNCS, vol. 2119, pp. 403–416. Springer, Heidelberg (2001). https://doi.org/10.1007/3-540-47719-5_32
15. Martin, K.M., Pieprzyk, J., Safavi-Naini, R., Wang, H.: Changing thresholds in the absence of secure channels. In: Pieprzyk, J., Safavi-Naini, R., Seberry, J. (eds.) ACISP 1999. LNCS, vol. 1587, pp. 177–191. Springer, Heidelberg (1999). https://doi.org/10.1007/3-540-48970-3_15
16. Martínez-Peñas, U.: Communication efficient and strongly secure secret sharing schemes based on algebraic geometry codes. IEEE Trans. Inf. Theory **64**(6), 4191–4206 (2018)
17. Nielsen, J.B., Simkin, M.: Lower bounds for leakage-resilient secret sharing. In: Canteaut, A., Ishai, Y. (eds.) EUROCRYPT 2020. LNCS, vol. 12105, pp. 556–577. Springer, Cham (2020). https://doi.org/10.1007/978-3-030-45721-1_20
18. Shamir, A.: How to share a secret. Commun. ACM **22**(11), 612–613 (1979)
19. Steinfeld, R., Pieprzyk, J., Wang, H.: Lattice-based threshold-changeability for standard CRT secret-sharing schemes. Finite Fields Appl. **12**(4), 653–680 (2006)
20. Steinfeld, R., Pieprzyk, J., Wang, H.: Lattice-based threshold changeability for standard shamir secret-sharing schemes. IEEE Trans. Inf. Theory **53**(7), 2542–2559 (2007)
21. Wang, H., Wong, D.S.: On secret reconstruction in secret sharing schemes. IEEE Trans. Inf. Theory **54**(1), 473–480 (2008)
22. Zhang, Z., Chee, Y.M., Ling, S., Liu, M., Wang, H.: Threshold changeable secret sharing schemes revisited. Theory Comput. Sci. **418**, 106–115 (2012)

Security Analyses

Key Recovery Under Plaintext Checking Attack on LAC

Ke Wang[1,2](✉), Zhenfeng Zhang[1,2], and Haodong Jiang[3]

[1] TCA Laboratory, State Key Laboratory of Computer Science, Institute of Software, Chinese Academy of Sciences, Beijing, China
{wangke,zfzhang}@tca.iscas.ac.cn

[2] University of Chinese Academy of Sciences, Beijing, China

[3] State Key Laboratory of Mathematical Engineering and Advanced Computing, Zhengzhou, Henan, China
hdjiang13@gmail.com

Abstract. The National Institute of Standards and Technology (NIST) is working on the standardization of post-quantum algorithms. In February 2019, NIST announced 26 candidate post-quantum cryptosystems had entered the Round 2. Prior work has shown how to mount key recovery attacks on several candidates like FrodoKEM, NewHope, and Kyber, but their methods do not work for LAC, which uses a different encoding scheme and rounding method. To address this gap, we describe a powerful new attack on LAC. In particular, we propose a simple and effective method to recover the reused secret key of LAC.CPA. Following the method we show that, using the recommended parameters, thousands of queries are sufficient to recover the full secret key with a 100% probability, which is verified by experiments. Since LAC.KE is based on LAC.CPA, our method can be used to assess the key-reuse resilience of LAC.KE. In particular, if Alice reuses a secret key, Bob can recover it by communicating with Alice thousands of times. Since LAC is a Round 2 candidate in the NIST PQ process, the presented result may well have a high impact on the understanding of this important cryptosystem.

Keywords: LAC · PKE · IND-CPA · NIST · Post quantum · Lattice based · Active attack · Key reuse

1 Introduction

In 1994, Shor [5] proposed a quantum algorithm, which can break most current public key cryptosystems based on integer factoring problem, discrete logarithm problem etc. Public key cryptosystems based on these hard problems are no longer secure when large quantum computers are implemented. There is an urgent need to replace them. For this purpose, the National Institute of Standards and Technology (NIST) initiated a standardization process for post-quantum algorithms, and in January 03, 2017, they called for proposals [27] for

K. Nguyen et al. (Eds.): ProvSec 2020, LNCS 12505, pp. 381–401, 2020.
https://doi.org/10.1007/978-3-030-62576-4_19

post-quantum cryptosystems [26,28], including Key Encapsulation Mechanism (KEM), Public Key Encryption (PKE) and signature.

By the end of 2017, many submissions were present. After the first round of evaluation, in February 2019, NIST announced 26 candidate post-quantum cryptosystems have entered the Round 2 [15]. Among these, only a very few types of algorithms are proposed, such as lattice-based, code-based, hash-based, multivariate-based or isogeny-based. One of the most promising algorithms is lattice-based [8,9]. Most lattice-based candidate algorithms, including Frodo, NewHope, Kyber [11,13,29] and LAC, are based on core IND-CPA PKEs. These PKEs are inspired by the Regev cryptosystem [23], such as the Lyubashevsky-Peikert-Regev cryptosystem [7]. Even for these candidate PKEs for which secret key reuse is considered as a misuse of the mechanism, having an accurate estimate of the complexity of the secret key recovery really helps to assess the possible danger [12]. In order to analyze how easy it is to run a key recovery under multiple key reuse, Băetu et al. [6] mounted a classical key recovery under plaintext checking attack (KR-PCA) (i.e., with a plaintext checking oracle (PCO) saying if a given ciphertext decrypts well to a given plaintext) on 12 IND-CPA PKEs entering the Round 1 [14].

KR-PCA attack is an adaptive key recovery attack and comes from the model of Fluhrer attacks [1] where an adversary encrypts a message by deviating a bit from the protocol. Then, he sends the ciphertext for decryption and checks if the decryption matches what he expected. After a few trials, the adversary recovers the secret key. The predecessor of KR-PCA attack is what is called a"reaction attack" in [32] or a "sloppy Alice attack" in [33]: adversary has a guess for the output of each decryption, and learns whether actual decryption output matches this guess. Adversary does not need any further information. KR-PCA attack does not need the full power of a CCA decryption oracle. Security against KR-PCA attack is implied by IND-CCA security. In particular, at PKC'19, D'Anvers et al. [31] explored decryption failure attacks on IND-CCA secure lattice-based schemes, which are CCA attacks. Recently, at ASIACRYPT'2019, the attack Guo et al. [16] have proposed also falls into this category. KR-PCA attack is not in the IND-CPA security framework. Hence, a PKE could be IND-CPA secure but still vulnerable to a KR-PCA attack. In particular, Băetu et al. [6] can recover the reused secret key of FrodoPKE with a 100% probability by querying oracle PCO thousands of times.[1] However, the method doesn't work for NewHope, Kyber and LAC which shorten ciphertexts by rounding off the low bits and enlarge them when decrypting.[2]

In order to assess the key-reuse resilience of NewHope [20], Bauer et al. [12] came up with a new method which can recover the reused secret key of

[1] Băetu et al. also recovered the reused secret keys of the other 8 IND-CPA PKEs, but these schemes did not advance to the second round.

[2] In implementation of LAC, in order to minimize the size of the ciphertext, the lower 4 bits for each coefficient in $\mathbf{v}$ are discarded, and each coefficient is enlarged by shifting 4 bits to the left when decrypting.

NewHope-CPA-PKE [20] with high probability.[3] Recently, Qin et al. [2] and Okada S et al. [38] improved this method and recovered the secret key with a higher probability and fewer queries. In addition, Qin et al. [18] also put forward a method to recover the reused secret key of Kyber.CPAPKE.[4] However, these methods can't be used directly to analyze LAC.CPA, which uses different encoding method and rounding method.

1.1 Our Contributions

In this paper, we fill a gap in the post-quantum literature. In particular, we assess the key-reuse resilience of LAC.CPA and propose a new method to recover the reused secret key of LAC.CPA by querying oracle PCO. The secret key is a polynomial of degree n, and recovering the full secret key requires recovering each coefficient. Using our method, each coefficient can be recovered with a 100% probability with at most 2.63 queries on average, which is verified by experiments. Since LAC.KE is directly obtained from LAC.CPA, our method can be used to recover the reused secret key in LAC.KE. In particular, if Alice reuses secret key, Bob can recover it by communicating with Alice several thousands of times.

1.2 Techniques

In Băetu's work [6], in order to recover the reused secret key sk, attacker adds disturbance x to ciphertext $\mathsf{ct} = (\mathbf{u}, \mathbf{v})$ and queries oracle PCO with the disturbed ciphertext $(\mathbf{u}, \mathbf{v}+x)$ and a given plaintext m. The oracle will return a bit saying if $(\mathbf{u}, \mathbf{v}+x)$ decrypts well to m. The returned bit will leak information about the noise δ to the attacker. By constantly changing the value of x and repeating the above operations, the attacker can recover δ. Based on the relationship between sk and δ, the attacker can build a system of equations. By solving the system, the attacker can get the secret key sk. The noise δ is so small that the attacker has to change the value of x carefully in this process.

Candidates NewHope-CPA-PKE, Kyber.CPAPKE and LAC.CPA shorten ciphertexts by rounding off the low bits, which is a common technique for reducing ciphertext size. In these schemes, ciphertext $(\mathbf{u}, \mathbf{v})$ falls into a small space and is enlarged back into the original space when decrypting. If attacker adds a disturbance x to $(\mathbf{u}, \mathbf{v})$, x will be amplified when decrypting. Unable to fine tune the value of x, the attacker can't recover the secret key sk according to Băetu's method.

Before introducing our method, we give two observations:

[3] In the paper, they recovered the reused secret key of NewHope-CPA-KEM by querying a key mismatch oracle, which can be regarded as an adaptive variant of the plaintext checking oracle in KEM or key exchange.

[4] In the paper, they proposed an efficient key mismatch attack on Kyber.CCAKEM. However, they replaced oracle $\mathcal{O}$ with oracle $\mathcal{O}_m$ in the attack, where these two oracles are not equivalent. In fact, they presented a new method to recover the reused secret key of Kyber.CPAPKE.

- When querying oracle PCO with ciphertext $(\mathbf{u}, \mathbf{v})$ and a given plaintext m, the oracle will return a bit saying if $m' = m$, where m' is the result of decrypting $(\mathbf{u}, \mathbf{v})$. In the decryption algorithm of LAC.CPA, $m' = \mathsf{ECCDec}(\widehat{m})$, then the returned bit indicates whether $\mathsf{ECCDec}(\widehat{m}) = m$.
- LAC.CPA adopts error correcting codes, which can correct at most l_v errors, that is to say, at most l_v differences between $\widehat{m}$ and $\mathsf{ECCEnc}(m)$ are allowed.

In LAC.CPA, the secret key $\mathbf{s} \in R_q$ is a polynomial of degree n. Therefore, recovering the complete $\mathbf{s}$ requires recovering n coefficients. In order to recover coefficient $\mathbf{s}_i, i = 0, ..., n-1$, we construct $(\mathbf{u}, \mathbf{v})$ skillfully based on the algebra and the encoding method of scheme so that whether (the 0-th positions of) $\widehat{m}$ and $\mathsf{ECCEnc}(m)$ are equal or not depends entirely on $\mathbf{s}_i$. Thus, when the attacker queries oracle PCO with $(\mathbf{u}, \mathbf{v})$, the returned bit will leak 1 bit information of $\mathbf{s}_i$. Since $\mathbf{s}_i$ has 3 possible values, -1,0 and 1, $\mathbf{s}_i$ can be completely recovered by a second query.

First, we assume that the error correcting code has no error ability, that is to say, no difference between $\widehat{m}$ and $\mathsf{ECCEnc}(m)$ is allowed. At this time, the attacker constructs $(\mathbf{u}, \mathbf{v})$ so that

$$\widehat{m}_0 \begin{cases} \neq \mathsf{ECCEnc}(m)_0, & \mathbf{s}_i = 1 \\ = \mathsf{ECCEnc}(m)_0, & \mathbf{s}_i \in \{-1, 0\}, \end{cases} \qquad \widehat{m}_j = \mathsf{ECCEnc}(m)_j, \quad j \in [1, l_v).$$

Thus, whether $\widehat{m}$ and $\mathsf{ECCEnc}(m)$ are equal or not depends entirely on $\mathbf{s}_i$. Then when the attacker queries oracle PCO with $(\mathbf{u}, \mathbf{v})$, the returned bit can determine $\mathbf{s}_i = 1$. In order to determine $\mathbf{s}_i$ completely, the attacker makes a second query where $(\mathbf{u}, \mathbf{v})$ satisfies

$$\widehat{m}_0 \begin{cases} \neq \mathsf{ECCEnc}(m)_0, & \mathbf{s}_i = -1 \\ = \mathsf{ECCEnc}(m)_0, & \mathbf{s}_i \in \{0, 1\}, \end{cases} \qquad \widehat{m}_j = \mathsf{ECCEnc}(m)_j, \quad j \in [1, l_v).$$

When the error correction code can correct up to l_t errors, the attacker first chooses l_t positions from $[1, l_v - 1]$ and record them in set I_{err}, then constructs $(\mathbf{u}, \mathbf{v})$ so that

$$\widehat{m}_0 \begin{cases} \neq \mathsf{ECCEnc}(m)_0, & \mathbf{s}_i = 1 \\ = \mathsf{ECCEnc}(m)_0, & \mathbf{s}_i \in \{-1, 0\}, \end{cases} \qquad \widehat{m}_j \begin{cases} \neq \mathsf{ECCEnc}(m)_j, & j \in I_{err} \\ = \mathsf{ECCEnc}(m)_j, & j \in ([1, l_v) - I_{err}). \end{cases}$$

Thus, whether $\widehat{m}$ and $\mathsf{ECCEnc}(m)$ are equal or not depends entirely on $\mathbf{s}_i$ except for these l_t positions. Since the error correcting code can correct these l_t errors, when querying oracle PCO with $(\mathbf{u}, \mathbf{v})$, the returned bit can determine $\mathbf{s}_i = 1$. In the second query, $(\mathbf{u}, \mathbf{v})$ satisfies

$$\widehat{m}_0 \begin{cases} \neq \mathsf{ECCEnc}(m)_j, & \mathbf{s}_i = -1 \\ = \mathsf{ECCEnc}(m)_j, & \mathbf{s}_i \in \{0, 1\}, \end{cases} \qquad \widehat{m}_j \begin{cases} \neq \mathsf{ECCEnc}(m)_j, & j \in I_{err} \\ = \mathsf{ECCEnc}(m)_j, & j \in ([1, l_v) - I_{err}). \end{cases}$$

In summary, in order to recover $\mathbf{s}_i$, the attacker needs to query the oracle PCO 2 times. Therefore, it takes $2n$ queries to recover complete secret key $\mathbf{s}$.

In fact, $2n$ is just an upper bound. Since $\frac{h}{2}$ coefficients can be determined by querying once, the actual total number of queries is $2n - \frac{h}{2}$.

Using the method, we successfully recover the secret keys of LAC-128 and LAC-192, not LAC-256, which adds one more step of D2 encoding to reduce decryption failure rate. In order to recover the secret key of LAC-256, we improve the method and recover $\mathbf{s}_i$ and $\mathbf{s}_{i+l_v}$ together. In particular, we describe how to recover $\mathbf{s}_0$ and $\mathbf{s}_{l_v}$. First, we construct $(\mathbf{u}, \mathbf{v})$ so that whether (the 0-th positions of) $\widehat{m}$ and $\mathsf{ECCEnc}(m)$ are equal or not depends entirely on $\mathbf{s}_0 + \mathbf{s}_{l_v}$. When querying oracle PCO with $(\mathbf{u}, \mathbf{v})$, the returned bit will leak information of $\mathbf{s}_0 + \mathbf{s}_{l_v}$. After at most 4 queries, we can determine the value of $\mathbf{s}_0 + \mathbf{s}_{l_v}$. Then we construct $(\mathbf{u}, \mathbf{v})$ so that whether (the 0-th positions of) $\widehat{m}$ and $\mathsf{ECCEnc}(m)$ are equal or not depends entirely on $\mathbf{s}_0 - \mathbf{s}_{l_v}$. And after at most 4 more queries, we can determine the values of $\mathbf{s}_0$ and $\mathbf{s}_{l_v}$ completely. Therefore, we can recover both coefficients $\mathbf{s}_0$ and $\mathbf{s}_{l_v}$ with a 100% probability after at most 8 queries. In this way, we can recover $2l_v$ coefficients of the secret key by querying at most $8l_v$ times. In LAC-256, $n = 1024$, $l_v = 400$, we can recover the first 800 coefficients using the method. When recovering the coefficient $\mathbf{s}_{800+i}, i \in [0, 224)$, at most 2 queries will suffice because $\mathbf{s}_{800+i+l_v} = \mathbf{s}_{800+i+l_v-n} = \mathbf{s}_{i+176}$ and we have found this coefficient. Therefore, the total number of queries to recover the complete $\mathbf{s}$ is at most $8l_v + 2(n - 2l_v)$. If we consider the distribution of the secret key, the actual total number should be $\frac{46}{8}l_v + \frac{7}{4}(n - 2l_v)$.

LAC.KE is constructed from LAC.CPA by using LAC.CPA to convey a secret message m. Our method can also be used to recover the reused secret key of LAC.KE, where Alice reuses key pair and Bob can communicate with Alice which responds honestly. In particular, according to the results above, Bob can recover the reused secret key of Alice by communicating with Alice several thousands of times.

1.3 Related Work

Key leakage in RLWE-based key exchange with reused keys was first pointed out in [17] but without any concrete description of an attack to exploit the leakage. In 2016, Fluhrer [1] showed how several RLWE-based key exchange protocols can be broken, under the assumption that the same public key is used for multiple exchanges. Following this idea, Ding et al. [3] described an attack on DING12's one pass case without relying on the signal function output but using only the information of whether the final key of both parties agree, and Bernstein et al. [24] developed a similar attack on HILA5 [19]. In 2017, Ding et al. [4] showed that the signal function used in RLWE-based key exchange could leak information to find the secret key of a reused public key. They gave an insight into how long-term public keys reuse in RLWE-based key exchange protocols can be exploited. They specifically focused on the attack on the key exchange protocol in [10]. In response to the attack, Ding Key Exchange, one of cryptosystems entering the Round 1 [14], includes a RLWE-based key exchange protocol with reusable keys, which can achieve secure key reuse. Gao et al. [21] constructed a new randomized RLWE-based key exchange protocol secure against the signal leakage attack. In particular, they incorporated an additional ephemeral public error term into key exchange materials. However, these two countermeasures only focused on the security of one party's reused key and ignored the other party, especially Wang et al. [30] improved the two countermeasures. Directly motivated by the work [4], Liu et al. [22] described a new key reuse attack against the NewHope key exchange protocol proposed by Alkim et al. [25] in 2016. In particular, Ding et al. [35] presented a simple key reuse attack on LWE and RLWE encryption schemes used directly as KEMes. This attack could work due to the fact that a key mismatch in a KEM is accessible to an adversary. At PQCrypto'19, D'Anvers et al. [34] pointed out that the higher-than-expected failure rate could lead to more efficient cryptanalysis of the schemes based on Ring/Module Learning with Errors/Rounding through decryption failure attacks. They provided a method to estimate the decryption failure probability, taking into account the bit failure dependency.

Concurrent and Independent Work. We have recently become aware of a concurrent and independent work by Greuet et al. [36]. In particular, they studied the security of LAC.KE in a misuse context: when the same secret key is reused for several key exchanges and an active adversary has access to a mismatch oracle. This oracle indicates information on the possible mismatch at the end of the KE protocol. In fact, the oracle is an adaptive variant of the plaintext checking oracle in key exchange, and the key to the success of the attack on LAC.KE is essentially that LAC.CPA is vulnerable to a KR-PCA attack.

Having grasped the key point, we focus on the analysis of LAC.CPA. We also include the analysis of LAC.KE, which is based on the results of LAC.CPA. In fact, Greuet's attack is easy to detect because m is always 0^{l_v} in many queries. For this reason, we consider the case of random choice of m. Further, when analyzing the number of queries required, we give a more accurate estimate based on the distribution of secret key. This result has been experimentally confirmed using the reference implementations of LAC.

Most recently, we have noticed another independent work [37] by Dumittan and Vaudenay, who also studied KR-PCA attack on LAC.CPA and recovered the reused secret key of LAC-128 successfully. However, they lacked analysis of LAC-192 and LAC-256, especially LAC-256 which adds one more step of D2 encoding. Similarly, they chose m to be 0^{l_v} in many queries, and the number of queries they theoretically analyzed can be further reduced and refined.

1.4 Organization

In Sect. 2, We introduce some preliminaries, including mathematical notations, centered binomial distribution, hard problem, PKE, KR-PCA attack and LAC.CPA algorithm. In Sect. 3, we use our method to recover the reused secret key of the LAC.CPA by querying the oracle PCO. The secret key $\mathbf{s}$ is a polynomial of degree n, and recovering $\mathbf{s}$ requires recovering each coefficient. When recovering $\mathbf{s}_i$, we first consider a simple case where the attacker chooses a special

m, then consider the general case where a random m is chosen. In each case, we start by assuming that the error correcting code has no error correcting ability, then consider that it can correct up to l_t errors. We also consider the case where the lower 4 bits of each coefficient in $\mathbf{v}$ are discarded. Using the method, we successfully recover the secret keys of LAC-128 and LAC-192, not LAC-256, which adds one more step of D2 encoding. In particular, we improve the method to recover the secret key. Based on the results in Sect. 3, we recover the reused secret key of LAC.KE in Sect. 4. Finally, we make a conclusion in Sect. 5.

2 Preliminaries

2.1 Mathematical Notations

For an integer $q \geq 1$, let $\mathbb{Z}_q$ be the residue class ring modulo q and $\mathbb{Z}_q = \{0, ..., q-1\}$. Define the ring of integer polynomials modulo $x^n + 1$ as $R = \mathbb{Z}[x]/(x^n + 1)$ for integer $n \geq 1$, and the ring $R_q = \mathbb{Z}_q[x]/(x^n + 1)$ denotes the polynomial ring modulo $x^n + 1$ where the coefficients are from $\mathbb{Z}_q$. The addition and multiplication of the elements in R_q are operated according to those of polynomials. Vectors are denoted by bold lower-case characters, such as $\mathbf{a}$. For a n-dimensional vector $\mathbf{a}$, where the $\mathbf{a}_i$'s are the components of $\mathbf{a}$ for $0 \leq i \leq n-1$. The elements in R_q can also be represented as vectors whose i-th coordinate is the coefficient related to x^i. In the sequel, we use either the polynomial notation or the vectorial one. In particular, for $\mathbf{a} \in R_q$, $\mathbf{a}_i$ denotes the i-th coefficient of $\mathbf{a}$, $0 \leq i \leq n-1$. $\mathbb{Z}_q^l$ denotes a set of vector of length l and vector components are taken from $\mathbb{Z}_q$. For $\mathbf{a} \in \mathbb{Z}_q^l$, $\mathbf{a}_i$ denotes the i-th component of $\mathbf{a}$, $1 \leq i \leq l$. $\{0,1\}^\ell$ denotes a set of strings of length ℓ. For $a \in \{0,1\}^\ell$, a_i denotes the i-th bit of a, $0 \leq i \leq \ell - 1$. In particular, 0^ℓ denotes an all 0 bit string of length ℓ. For a set S, $x \overset{\$}{\leftarrow} S$ denotes that an element x is chosen from S uniformly at random. For a distribution χ, $x \overset{\$}{\leftarrow} \chi$ denotes that an element x is sampled according to the distribution χ. A polynomial $f \in R_q$ is chosen from S (sampled from χ), we mean that each coefficient is chosen from S (sampled from χ).

Centered Binomial Distribution. We define centered binomial distribution B_η as follows:

$$(a_1, ..., a_\eta, b_1, ..., b_\eta) \overset{\$}{\leftarrow} \{0,1\}^{2\eta}$$

and output

$$\sum_{i=1}^{\eta}(a_i - b_i).$$

The samples are in the interval $[-\eta, \eta]$. When we write that a polynomial $f \in R_q$ is sampled from B_η, we mean that each coefficient is sampled from B_η.

See Appendix A for RLWE problems (A.1) and cryptographic definitions (A.2).

2.2 KR-PCA Attack

Definition 1 [6]. *The key recovery game with oracle PCO is shown in Fig. 1, where PCO(ct, m) is a plaintext checking oracle which receives ciphertext* ct *and plaintext m, runs the decryption and only returns one bit saying if it decrypts to m.*

Game $\mathsf{KR}^{\mathsf{PCO}}_{\mathcal{A}}()$:	**Oracle** $\mathsf{PCO}(\mathsf{ct}, m)$
$\mathsf{KeyGen}() \rightarrow (\mathsf{pk}, \mathsf{sk})$	$\mathsf{Dec}(\mathsf{ct}, \mathsf{sk}) \rightarrow m'$
$\mathcal{A}^{\mathsf{PCO}(\cdot)}(\mathsf{pk}) \rightarrow \mathsf{sk}'$	return $1_{m'=m}$
return $1_{\mathsf{sk}=\mathsf{sk}'}$	

Fig. 1. KR-PCA game

The KR-PCA model comes from the model of Fluhrer attack [1] and makes sense when an adversary can play with a server with a modified ciphertext and check if it still decrypts to the same plaintext as before. For instance, in the client-server protocol where the encryption is used to transport a symmetric key to start secure messaging, an adversary can try to encrypt a symmetric key by deviating from the protocol. He generates malformed ciphertexts which may decrypt to the chosen symmetric key or not. By sending the malformed ciphertext to the server, the adversary can easily see if secure messaging with the server is possible, hence simulate a PCO oracle. Clearly, it is devastating that such an attack would lead to a key recovery [6].

Security against KR-PCA attack is implied by IND-CCA security. KR-PCA attack is not in the IND-CPA security framework. Hence, a PKE could be IND-CPA secure but still vulnerable to a KR-PCA attack.

2.3 LAC.CPA

Algorithm 1. LAC.CPA.KeyGen():

Output: Secret key $\mathsf{sk} \in R_q$
Output: Public key $\mathsf{pk} \in R_q \times \{0,1\}^{l_s}$

$\mathsf{seed}_{\mathbf{a}} \xleftarrow{\$} \{0,1\}^{l_s}$
$\mathbf{a} \leftarrow \mathsf{Samp}(U(R_q), \mathsf{seed}_{\mathbf{a}}) \in R_q$
$\mathbf{s} \leftarrow \mathsf{Samp}(B^h_\eta, \epsilon) \in R_q$
$\mathbf{d} \leftarrow \mathsf{Samp}(B^h_\eta, \epsilon) \in R_q$
$\mathbf{b} = \mathbf{as} + \mathbf{d} \in R_q$
$\mathsf{sk} = \mathbf{s}$
$\mathsf{pk} = (\mathbf{b}, \mathsf{seed}_{\mathbf{a}})$
return(sk,pk)

Algorithm 2. LAC.CPA.Enc(m, pk, seed):

Output: Ciphertext $\mathsf{ct} \in R_q \times \mathbb{Z}_q^{l_v}$

$\mathbf{a} \leftarrow \mathsf{Samp}(U(R_q), \mathsf{seed}_{\mathbf{a}}) \in R_q$
$\mathbf{t} \leftarrow \mathsf{Samp}(B^h_\eta, \mathsf{seed}) \in R_q$
$\mathbf{e} \leftarrow \mathsf{Samp}(B^h_\eta, \mathsf{seed}) \in R_q$
$\mathbf{f} \leftarrow \mathsf{Samp}(B_\eta, \mathsf{seed}) \in \mathbb{Z}_q^{l_v}$
$\mathbf{u} = \mathbf{at} + \mathbf{e} \in R_q$
$\mathbf{v} = (\mathbf{bt})_{l_v} + \mathbf{f} + \lfloor \frac{q}{2} \rceil \cdot (\mathsf{ECCEnc}(m)) \in \mathbb{Z}_q^{l_v}$
return $\mathsf{ct} = (\mathbf{u}, \mathbf{v})$

Algorithm 3. LAC.CPA.Dec(ct,sk): decryption

Output: Message $m' \in \{0,1\}^{l_m}$
$\widetilde{m} = \mathbf{v} - (\mathbf{us})_{l_v}$
for $j = 0$ to l_v-1 **do**
  if $\frac{q}{4} \leq \widetilde{m}_j < \frac{3q}{4}$ **then**
    $\widehat{m}_j \leftarrow 1$
  else
    $\widehat{m}_j \leftarrow 0$
  end if
end for
$m' \leftarrow \mathsf{ECCDec}(\widehat{m})$
return m'

LAC [15] is a suit of public key cryptographic primitives based on Ring Learning With Errors. The foundation of LAC is LAC.CPA, an IND-CPA secure public key encryption scheme. LAC.CPA comprises three algorithms: the key generation algorithm LAC.CPA.KeyGen, the encryption algorithm LAC.CPA.Enc, the decryption algorithm LAC.CPA.Dec, as illustrated in Algorithms 1, 2 and 3, which are simplified descriptions of the algorithms and may partly deviate from the notations the original specification of these algorithms [15].

See Appendix A for the notations (A.3) and parameters (A.4).

3 KR-PCA Attack on LAC.CPA

In this section, we show how the attacker recover reused secret key $\mathbf{s}$ of LAC.CPA by querying the oracle PCO with ($\mathsf{ct} = (\mathbf{u}, \mathbf{v})$, m).

The secret key $\mathbf{s} \in R_q$ is a polynomial of degree n, and recovering the complete $\mathbf{s}$ requires recovering n coefficients. In our attack, the method of recovering each coefficient is the same. Generally, we consider recovering coefficient $\mathbf{s}_i, i = 0, ..., n-1$.

3.1 Choosing Special m

When recovering $\mathbf{s}_i$, the attacker needs to construct $\mathsf{ct} = (\mathbf{u}, \mathbf{v})$ skillfully based on $\mathsf{ECCEnc}(m)$. In particular, we first consider a simple case where the attacker chooses m such that $\mathsf{ECCEnc}(m) = 0^{l_v} \in \{0,1\}^{l_v}$.[5]

In LAC.CPA, the byte level modulus incurs a very high decryption error rate by design. In order to reduce the decryption error rate, LAC.CPA adopts error correcting codes, which can correct at most l_t errors. Next, we will take two steps to recover $\mathbf{s}_i$: the first step is to assume that the error correcting code has no error correcting ability, and the second step is to consider it can correct at most l_t errors.

[5] $\mathsf{ECCEnc}(m)$ is chosen to be 0^{l_v} for ease of explanation. In fact, it's ok to randomly choose m and generate $\mathsf{ECCEnc}(m)$, which will be explained further later.

The Error Correcting Code Has No Error Correcting Ability. Assuming the error correcting code has no error correcting ability, the attacker constructs ct such that $\widehat{m}$ and $\mathsf{ECCEnc}(m)$ are the same except for the 0-th position, and the 0-th position of $\widehat{m}$ depends on $\mathbf{s}_i$. Thus, whether $\mathsf{ECCDec}(\widehat{m})$ (or m') and m are equal depends on $\mathbf{s}_i$. Then, when querying the oracle PCO with (ct, m), the returned bit will leak the information about $\mathbf{s}_i$.

In particular, when recovering $\mathbf{s}_i$,

- the attacker first chooses m such that $\mathsf{ECCEnc}(m) = 0^{l_v}$.
- Then, the attacker chooses $\mathbf{u} = \frac{q}{8}x^{n-i}$ and constructs $\mathbf{v}^1$ and $\mathbf{v}^2$ as follows:

$$\mathbf{v}_j^1 = \begin{cases} \frac{3q}{16}, & j = 0 \\ 0, & j \in [1, l_v), \end{cases} \qquad \mathbf{v}_j^2 = \begin{cases} \frac{13q}{16}, & j = 0 \\ 0, & j \in [1, l_v). \end{cases}$$

- Next, the attacker queries the oracle PCO with $(\mathsf{ct} = (\frac{q}{8}x^{n-i}, \mathbf{v}^1), m)$, and the oracle will return a bit to indicate whether m' and m are equal.
- Finally, the attacker queries the oracle PCO with $(\mathsf{ct} = (\frac{q}{8}x^{n-i}, \mathbf{v}^2), m)$, and gets the returned bit.

After getting these two returned bits, the attacker can recover $\mathbf{s}_i \in \{-1, 0, 1\}$, and the explanation is as follows. Recall that in the decryption algorithm LAC.CPA.Dec,

$$\widetilde{m} = \mathbf{v} - (\mathbf{us})_{l_v}, \qquad \widehat{m}_j = \begin{cases} 1, & \widetilde{m}_j \in [\frac{q}{4}, \frac{3q}{4}) \\ 0, & \widetilde{m}_j \in ([0, \frac{q}{4}) \cup [\frac{3q}{4}, q)), \end{cases} \qquad m' = \mathsf{ECCDec}(\widehat{m}).$$

Given that $\mathbf{u} = \frac{q}{8}x^{n-i}$, $\mathbf{v} = \mathbf{v}^1$, we have

$$\widetilde{m}_j = \begin{cases} \frac{3q}{16} + \frac{q}{8}\mathbf{s}_i, & j = 0 \\ \pm\frac{q}{8}\mathbf{s}_{(i+j) \bmod n}, & j \in [1, l_v), \end{cases}$$

where

$$\frac{3q}{16} + \frac{q}{8}\mathbf{s}_i \in \begin{cases} [\frac{q}{4}, \frac{3q}{4}), & \mathbf{s}_i = 1 \\ ([0, \frac{q}{4}) \cup [\frac{3q}{4}, q)), & \mathbf{s}_i \in \{-1, 0\}, \end{cases} \qquad \pm\frac{q}{8}\mathbf{s}_{(i+j) \bmod n} \in ([0, \frac{q}{4}) \cup [\frac{3q}{4}, q)).$$

Therefore, we have

$$\widehat{m}_0 = \begin{cases} 1, & \mathbf{s}_i = 1 \\ 0, & \mathbf{s}_i \in \{-1, 0\}, \end{cases} \qquad \widehat{m}_j = 0, \quad j \in [1, l_v),$$

and

$$\widehat{m} \begin{cases} \neq \mathsf{ECCEnc}(m), & \mathbf{s}_i = 1 \\ = \mathsf{ECCEnc}(m), & \mathbf{s}_i \in \{-1, 0\}. \end{cases}$$

Assuming that the error correction code has no error correction capability, we have

$$m' \begin{cases} \neq m, & \mathbf{s}_i = 1 \\ = m, & \mathbf{s}_i \in \{-1, 0\}, \end{cases}$$

that is to say, when querying the oracle PCO with ($\mathsf{ct} = (\frac{q}{8}x^{n-i}, \mathbf{v}^1), m$), the returned bit 0 indicates that $\mathbf{s}_i = 1$, and the bit 1 indicates that $\mathbf{s}_i \in \{-1, 0\}$.[6]

In order to further determine whether $\mathbf{s}_i$ is equal to -1 or 0, the attacker queries the oracle PCO with ($\mathsf{ct} = (\frac{q}{8}x^{n-i}, \mathbf{v}^2), m$), and we have

$$\widetilde{m}_j = \begin{cases} \frac{13q}{16} + \frac{q}{8}\mathbf{s}_i, & j = 0 \\ \pm\frac{q}{8}\mathbf{s}_{(i+j) \bmod n}, & j \in [1, l_v), \end{cases}$$

where

$$\frac{13q}{16} + \frac{q}{8}\mathbf{s}_i \in \begin{cases} [\frac{q}{4}, \frac{3q}{4}), & \mathbf{s}_i = -1 \\ ([0, \frac{q}{4}) \cup [\frac{3q}{4}, q)), & \mathbf{s}_i \in \{0, 1\}. \end{cases}$$

Then

$$\widehat{m}_0 = \begin{cases} 1, & \mathbf{s}_i = -1 \\ 0, & \mathbf{s}_i \in \{0, 1\}, \end{cases} \qquad \widehat{m}_j = 0, \quad j \in [1, l_v),$$

and

$$\widehat{m} \begin{cases} \neq \mathsf{ECCEnc}(m), & \mathbf{s}_i = -1 \\ = \mathsf{ECCEnc}(m), & \mathbf{s}_i \in \{0, 1\}. \end{cases}$$

Therefore, we have

$$m' \begin{cases} \neq m, & \mathbf{s}_i = -1 \\ = m, & \mathbf{s}_i \in \{0, 1\}, \end{cases}$$

which means that when querying the oracle PCO with ($\mathsf{ct} = (\frac{q}{8}x^{n-i}, \mathbf{v}^2), m$), the bit 0 indicates that $\mathbf{s}_i = -1$, and the returned bit 1 indicates that $\mathbf{s}_i = 0$. Therefore, after these two queries, the attacker can recover $\mathbf{s}_i$ completely.

The Error Correcting Code can Correct Up to l_t Errors. When the error correcting code can correct up to l_t errors, the attacker constructs ct such that there are l_t differences between $\widehat{m}$ and $\mathsf{ECCEnc}(m)$ except for the 0-th position. In particular, he chooses the l_t positions from the 1-th to the l_v-th and constructs $\mathbf{v}^1$ and $\mathbf{v}^2$ as follows:

$$\mathbf{v}^1_j = \begin{cases} \frac{3q}{16}, & j = 0 \\ \frac{q}{2}, & j = [1, l_t] \\ 0, & j = (l_t, l_v), \end{cases} \qquad \mathbf{v}^2_j = \begin{cases} \frac{13q}{16}, & j = 0 \\ \frac{q}{2}, & j \in [1, l_t] \\ 0, & j \in (l_t, l_v). \end{cases}$$

Given that $\mathbf{u} = \frac{q}{8}x^{n-i}$, $\mathbf{v} = \mathbf{v}^1$, we have

$$\widetilde{m}_j = \begin{cases} \frac{3q}{16} + \frac{q}{8}\mathbf{s}_i, & j = 0 \\ \frac{q}{2} \pm \frac{q}{8}\mathbf{s}_{(i+j) \bmod n}, & j \in [1, l_t] \\ \pm\frac{q}{8}\mathbf{s}_{(i+j) \bmod n}, & j \in (l_t, l_v), \end{cases}$$

where

$$\frac{q}{2} \pm \frac{q}{8}\mathbf{s}_{(i+j) \bmod n} \in [\frac{q}{4}, \frac{3q}{4}).$$

[6] Recall that in KR-PCA game, when querying the oracle PCO, the oracle return $1_{m'=m}$ or $0_{m' \neq m}$.

Then

$$\widehat{m}_0 = \begin{cases} 1, & \mathbf{s}_i = 1 \\ 0, & \mathbf{s}_i \in \{-1, 0\}, \end{cases} \qquad \widehat{m}_j = \begin{cases} 1, & j \in [1, l_t] \\ 0, & j \in (l_t, l_v). \end{cases}$$

Since the error correction code ECCDec can correct at most l_t errors, we have

$$m' \begin{cases} \neq m, & \mathbf{s}_i = 1 \\ = m, & \mathbf{s}_i \in \{-1, 0\}. \end{cases}$$

Similarly, given that $\mathbf{u} = \frac{q}{8}x^{n-i}$, $\mathbf{v} = \mathbf{v}^2$, we have

$$\widetilde{m}_j = \begin{cases} \frac{13q}{16} + \frac{q}{8}\mathbf{s}_i, & j = 0 \\ \frac{q}{2} \pm \frac{q}{8}\mathbf{s}_{(i+j) \bmod n}, & j \in [1, l_t] \\ \pm\frac{q}{8}\mathbf{s}_{(i+j) \bmod n}, & j \in (l_t, l_v). \end{cases}$$

Then

$$\widehat{m}_0 = \begin{cases} 1, & \mathbf{s}_i = -1 \\ 0, & \mathbf{s}_i \in \{0, 1\}, \end{cases} \qquad \widehat{m}_j = \begin{cases} 1, & j \in [1, l_t] \\ 0, & j \in (l_t, l_v). \end{cases}$$

Therefore,

$$m' \begin{cases} \neq m, & \mathbf{s}_i = -1 \\ = m, & \mathbf{s}_i \in \{0, 1\}. \end{cases}$$

3.2 Choosing m Randomly

When the attacker randomly chooses m and generates $\mathsf{ECCEnc}(m)$, he will do the same except that he will query the oracle PCO with different $\mathbf{v}^1$ and $\mathbf{v}^2$. Similarly, we will take two steps and the first step is to assume that the error correcting code has no error correcting ability.

The Error Correcting Code Has No Error Correcting Ability. After choosing m and generating $\mathsf{ECCEnc}(m)$, the attacker records the positions of 1 and 0 in $\mathsf{ECCEnc}(m)$ except for 0-th position in sets I_1 and I_0 respectively, and constructs $\mathbf{v}^1$ and $\mathbf{v}^2$ as follows:

$$\mathbf{v}^1_j = \begin{cases} \frac{3q}{16}, & j = 0 \\ \frac{q}{2}, & j \in I_1 \\ 0, & j \in I_0, \end{cases} \qquad \mathbf{v}^2_j = \begin{cases} \frac{13q}{16}, & j = 0 \\ \frac{q}{2}, & j \in I_1 \\ 0, & j \in I_0. \end{cases}$$

The Error Correcting Code Can Correct up to l_t errors. When the error correcting code can correct up to l_t errors, the attacker chooses l_t positions from $I_1 \bigcup I_0$, records these positions in set I_{err}, and constructs $\mathbf{v}^1$ and $\mathbf{v}^2$ as follows:

$$\mathbf{v}^1_j = \begin{cases} \frac{3q}{16}, & j = 0 \\ \frac{q}{2}, & j \in I_1 - I_{err} \\ 0, & j \in I_1 \bigcap I_{err} \\ 0, & j \in I_0 - I_{err} \\ \frac{q}{2}, & j \in I_0 \bigcap I_{err}, \end{cases} \qquad \mathbf{v}^2_j = \begin{cases} \frac{13q}{16}, & j = 0 \\ \frac{q}{2}, & j \in I_1 - I_{err} \\ 0, & j \in I_1 \bigcap I_{err} \\ 0, & j \in I_0 - I_{err} \\ \frac{q}{2}, & j \in I_0 \bigcap I_{err}. \end{cases}$$

Discarding the Lower 4 Bits of Each Coefficient in v. In the implementation of LAC.CPA, in order to minimize the size of the ciphertext, the lower 4 bits for each coefficient in $\mathbf{v}$ are discarded in the algorithm of LAC.CPA.Enc. Therefore, $\mathbf{v}_j$ has 16 possible values and they are $k, k = 0, 1, ..., 15$.

In order to carry out the attack, when querying the oracle PCO, $\frac{3q}{16}$ will be replaced with such a k that $16k$ is closest to $\frac{3q}{16}$. It's the same for $\frac{q}{2}$ and $\frac{13q}{16}$. Since $\frac{3q}{16}, \frac{q}{2}$ and $\frac{13q}{16}$ are closest to 48, 128 and 208 respectively, they will be replaced with 3, 8 and 13. In general, when the error correcting code can correct up to l_t errors, the attacker chooses m randomly and queries the oracle PCO with

$$\mathbf{v}_j^1 = \begin{cases} 3, & j = 0 \\ 8, & j \in I_1 - I_{err} \\ 0, & j \in I_1 \bigcap I_{err} \\ 0, & j \in I_0 - I_{err} \\ 8, & j \in I_0 \bigcap I_{err}, \end{cases} \qquad \mathbf{v}_j^2 = \begin{cases} 13, & j = 0 \\ 8, & j \in I_1 - I_{err} \\ 0, & j \in I_1 \bigcap I_{err} \\ 0, & j \in I_0 - I_{err} \\ 8, & j \in I_0 \bigcap I_{err}. \end{cases}$$

Finally, we summarize the process of recovering secret key $\mathbf{s}$ into Algorithm 4.

Algorithm 4. Recovering secret key $\mathbf{s}$ of LAC.CPA

```
Input: parameters (n, q, η, l_m, l_v, l_t, h)
Output: s (All the coefficients in s)
choose m randomly
construct v^1 and v^2 as described in the previous section
for i = 0 to n − 1 do
    queries the oracle PCO with (ct = ((q/8)x^{n−i}, v^1), m);
    queries the oracle PCO with (ct = ((q/8)x^{n−i}, v^2), m);
    recover s_i according to these 2 returned bits;
end for
return s
```

3.3 Attack on LAC-256

According to the Algorithm 4, the attacker can recover the secret keys of LAC-128 and LAC-192, not LAC-256, where D2 encoding is used in the encryption procedure and the coordinates of $\mathbf{v}$ are duplicated: for all $0 \le j \le l_v - 1$, $\mathbf{v}_{j+l_v} = \mathbf{v}_j$. This redundancy in $\mathbf{v}$ allows to decrease the decoding error when decrypting. In the decryption procedure, the first step is to compute $\widetilde{m} = \mathbf{v} - (\mathbf{us})_{2l_v}$ and when computing $\widehat{m}_j$, the decryption algorithm considers two cases: if $\widetilde{m}_j$ and $\widetilde{m}_{j+l_v} < \frac{q}{2}$ or $\widetilde{m}_j$ and $\widetilde{m}_{j+l_v} \ge \frac{q}{2}$, the algorithm compares: $\frac{q}{4} < \frac{\widetilde{m}_j + \widetilde{m}_{j+l_v}}{2} < \frac{3q}{4}$; if $\widetilde{m}_j < \frac{q}{2}$ and $\widetilde{m}_{j+l_v} \ge \frac{q}{2}$ or $\widetilde{m}_j \ge \frac{q}{2}$ and $\widetilde{m}_{j+l_v} < \frac{q}{2}$, the algorithm compares: $0 < \frac{|\widetilde{m}_j - \widetilde{m}_{j+l_v}|}{2} < \frac{q}{4}$.

Next, we consider recovering $\mathbf{s}_0$ and $\mathbf{s}_{l_v}$ together. In particular, we denote $(I_0 - I_{err}) \bigcup ((I_0 - I_{err}) + l_v), (I_0 \bigcap I_{err}) \bigcup ((I_0 \bigcap I_{err}) + l_v), (I_1 - I_{err}) \bigcup ((I_1 - I_{err}) + l_v)$ and $(I_1 \bigcap I_{err}) \bigcup ((I_1 \bigcap I_{err}) + l_v)$ as $\bar{I_0}, \hat{I_0}, \bar{I_1}$ and $\hat{I_1}$, and construct $\mathbf{v}^3 \sim \mathbf{v}^8$ as follows:

$$\mathbf{v}_j^3 = \begin{cases} \frac{7q}{32}, & j = 0, l_v \\ \frac{q}{8}, & j \in \bar{I}_0 \\ \frac{5q}{8}, & j \in \hat{I}_0 \\ \frac{5q}{8}, & j \in \bar{I}_1 \\ \frac{q}{8}, & j \in \hat{I}_1, \end{cases} \quad \mathbf{v}_j^4 = \begin{cases} \frac{q}{4}, & j = 0, l_v \\ \frac{q}{8}, & j \in \bar{I}_0 \\ \frac{5q}{8}, & j \in \hat{I}_0 \\ \frac{5q}{8}, & j \in \bar{I}_1 \\ \frac{q}{8}, & j \in \hat{I}_1, \end{cases} \quad \mathbf{v}_j^5 = \begin{cases} \frac{25q}{32}, & j = 0, l_v \\ \frac{q}{8}, & j \in \bar{I}_0 \\ \frac{5q}{8}, & j \in \hat{I}_0 \\ \frac{5q}{8}, & j \in \bar{I}_1 \\ \frac{q}{8}, & j \in \hat{I}_1, \end{cases}$$

$$\mathbf{v}_j^6 = \begin{cases} \frac{3q}{4}, & j = 0, l_v \\ \frac{q}{8}, & j \in \bar{I}_0 \\ \frac{5q}{8}, & j \in \hat{I}_0 \\ \frac{5q}{8}, & j \in \bar{I}_1 \\ \frac{q}{8}, & j \in \hat{I}_1, \end{cases} \quad \mathbf{v}_j^7 = \begin{cases} \frac{3q}{4}, & j = 0 \\ \frac{q}{4}, & j = l_v \\ \frac{q}{8}, & j \in \bar{I}_0 \\ \frac{5q}{8}, & j \in \hat{I}_0 \\ \frac{5q}{8}, & j \in \bar{I}_1 \\ \frac{q}{8}, & j \in \hat{I}_1, \end{cases} \quad \mathbf{v}_j^8 = \begin{cases} \frac{3q}{4}, & j = 0 \\ \frac{3q}{8}, & j = l_v \\ \frac{q}{8}, & j \in \bar{I}_0 \\ \frac{5q}{8}, & j \in \hat{I}_0 \\ \frac{5q}{8}, & j \in \bar{I}_1 \\ \frac{q}{8}, & j \in \hat{I}_1. \end{cases}$$

Since $\mathbf{s}_0, \mathbf{s}_{l_v} \in \{-1, 0, 1\}$, we have $\mathbf{s}_0 + \mathbf{s}_{l_v} \in \{-2, -1, 0, 1, 2\}$. When the attacker queries the oracle PCO with $(\mathsf{ct} = (\frac{q}{16}, \mathbf{v}^3), m)$, the returned bit can reveal that $\mathbf{s}_0 + \mathbf{s}_{l_v} = -2$. When querying the oracle PCO with $(\mathsf{ct} = (\frac{q}{16}, \mathbf{v}^4), m)$, the returned bit can further reveal that $\mathbf{s}_0 + \mathbf{s}_{l_v} = -1$. When the attacker queries the oracle PCO with $(\mathsf{ct} = (\frac{q}{16}, \mathbf{v}^5), m)$, he can further determine that $\mathbf{s}_0 + \mathbf{s}_{l_v} = 2$. When he queries the oracle PCO with $(\mathsf{ct} = (\frac{q}{16}, \mathbf{v}^6), m)$, he can further determine that $\mathbf{s}_0 + \mathbf{s}_{l_v} = 1$. In summary, after 4 queries, the attacker can determine $\mathbf{s}_0 + \mathbf{s}_{l_v}$ completely.

In order to further determine $\mathbf{s}_0$ and $\mathbf{s}_{l_v}$, the attacker first queries the oracle PCO with $(\mathsf{ct} = (\frac{q}{16}, \mathbf{v}^7), m)$ to determine if $\mathbf{s}_0 - \mathbf{s}_{l_v} = 1$ or -1, and if $\mathbf{s}_0 - \mathbf{s}_{l_v} = 2$ or $-2(0)$. Then, the attacker queries the oracle PCO with $(\mathsf{ct} = (\frac{q}{16}, \mathbf{v}^8), m)$ to further determine if $\mathbf{s}_0 - \mathbf{s}_{l_v} = -2$ or 0. Therefore, the attacker can recover both coefficients $\mathbf{s}_0$ and $\mathbf{s}_{l_v}$ with a 100% probability after 8 queries. In particular, he can recover $2l_v$ coefficients of secret key $\mathbf{s}$ after $8l_v$ queries.

In LAC-256, $n = 1024$, $l_v = 400$, the attacker can recover the first 800 coefficients by querying 3200 times. When recovering the coefficient $\mathbf{s}_{800+i}, i \in [0, 224)$, 2 queries will suffice because $\mathbf{s}_{800+i+l_v} = \mathbf{s}_{800+i+l_v-n} = \mathbf{s}_{i+176}$ and he has already found this coefficient. Similarly, when the lower 4 bits for each coefficient in $\mathbf{v}$ are discarded, corresponding queries will change, as shown in Appendix A.5.

3.4 Number of Queries and Probability of Success

To sum up, in LAC-128 and LAC-192, we can recover the each coefficient $\mathbf{s}_i$ with a 100% probability after 2 queries, and the total number of queries to recover the complete $\mathbf{s}$ is $2n$. However, it is a rough estimate. In fact, when querying the oracle with $(\mathsf{ct} = (\frac{q}{8}x^{n-i}, \mathbf{v}^1), m)$, $\mathbf{s}_i = 1$ can be determined. Since $\mathbf{s}$ is sampled from B_η^h, the numbers of both 1's and -1's are $h/2$, the number of 0 is $n - h$. Therefore, the actual total number of queries to recover the complete $\mathbf{s}$ can be estimated as

$$\frac{h}{2} + (\frac{h}{2} + n - h) \times 2 = 2n - \frac{h}{2},$$

and it is $\frac{7}{4}n$ in LAC-128 and $\frac{15}{8}n$ in LAC-192.

Based on the results from the previous section, the total number of queries to recover the complete $\mathbf{s}$ of LAC-256 is $8l_v + 2(n - 2l_v)$. Similarly, it is a rough estimate, and the actual total number should be $\frac{46}{8}l_v + \frac{7}{4}(n - 2l_v)$, which is obtained based on the distribution of the secret key.

Experiments. We implement the attack on LAC.CPA's source code submitted to NIST, and then compile it with the same makefile in the source code. In particular, our attack is based on the source code of reference implementation. The platform of our experiments is Ubuntu 16.04.3 running on a 3.4 GHZ Intel Core i7 processor with 16 GB RAM. All experiments are in C and compiled with gcc version 5.4.0. LAC recommends 3 parameter sets for different security levels and they are LAC-128, LAC-192 and LAC-256. In each parameter set, we first generate a secret key, count the number of queries and time to recover the full secret key, then repeat 100 times and average. In particular, the time starts from the initial generation of the secret key to the recovery of the whole secret key by accessing the oracle multiple times.

Table 1. The number of queries and time in each parameter set

	LAC-128	LAC-192	LAC-256
Queries	896	1920	2692
Times(ms)	104.550	813.595	1153.519

4 Recovering Reused Key in LAC.KE

LAC.KE is a passively secure unauthenticated key exchange protocol and it is directly obtained from LAC.CPA, as described in Fig. 2. In particular, LAC.KE can be divided into three stages. In the first stage, Alice invokes LAC.CPA.KeyGen, generates public key pk and secret key sk, and sends pk to Bob. In the second stage, Bob picks secret m and encrypts it by invoking LAC.CPA.Enc, generates ciphertext ct and sends ct to Alice. In the third stage, Alice recovers secret m' by invoking LAC.CPA.Dec. The final shared secret K (K') is derived from the pk and m (m') by hashing.

According to the results in the previous section, if honest Alice reuses key pair $(\mathsf{pk}, \mathsf{sk})$ and malicious Bob can communicate with Alice who responds honestly, then Bob can recover the secret key sk of Alice. In particular, in order to recover the i-th coefficient of sk of LAC-128 and LAC-192,

- Bob first chooses m randomly.

$H : \{0,1\}^* \rightarrow \{0,1\}^{l_k}$		
Alice		Bob
$(\mathsf{pk}, \mathsf{sk}) \leftarrow$ LAC.CPA.KeyGen()	$\xrightarrow{\mathsf{pk}}$	
		$m \xleftarrow{\$} \{0,1\}^{l_m}$
	$\xleftarrow{\mathsf{ct}}$	$\mathsf{ct} \leftarrow$ LAC.CPA.Enc(m, pk)
$m' \leftarrow$ LAC.CPA.Dec$(\mathsf{ct}, \mathsf{sk})$		$K \leftarrow H(\mathsf{pk}, m) \in \{0,1\}^{l_k}$
$K' \leftarrow H(\mathsf{pk}, m') \in \{0,1\}^{l_k}$		

Fig. 2. LAC.KE

- Then, he sends $\mathsf{ct} = (\frac{q}{8}x^{n-i}, \mathbf{v}^1)$ to Alice and determines whether m' and m are equal.[7]
- Next, Bob sends $\mathsf{ct} = (\frac{q}{8}x^{n-i}, \mathbf{v}^2)$ and determines whether m' and m are equal.
- Finally, Bob recovers the i-th coefficient of sk based on the information obtained in these two communications.

After recovering each coefficient, Bob will get the full secret key sk, which requires Bob to communicate with Alice $2n - \frac{h}{2}$ times. Similarly, based on the results in previous section, in order to get the full secret key of LAC-256, Bob needs to communicate with Alice $\frac{46}{8}l_v + \frac{7}{4}(n - 2l_v)$ times.

5 Conclusion

In this paper, we propose a simple and effective method to recover the reused secret key of LAC.CPA by querying the plaintext checking oracle. The secret key $\mathbf{s} \in R_q$ is a polynomial of degree n. Therefore, recovering the complete $\mathbf{s}$ requires recovering n coefficients. When recovering coefficient $\mathbf{s}_i$, we first consider a very simple case where the attacker chooses m such that $\mathsf{ECCEnc}(m) = 0^{l_m}$, and then analyze the general case where a random m is chosen. In each case, we start by assuming that the error correcting code has no error correcting ability and then consider that it can correct at most l_t errors. We also consider the case where the lower 4 bits of each coefficient in $\mathbf{v}$ are discarded. Using the method, the secret keys of LAC-128 and LAC-192 can be recovered completely after $2n - \frac{h}{2}$ queries, and $\frac{46}{8}l_v + \frac{7}{4}(n - 2l_v)$ queries to recover the secret key of LAC-256.

Since LAC.CPA is used to construct LAC.KE, our method can be used to recover the reused secret key of Alice in LAC.KE. In particular, based on the

[7] In LAC.KE, shared secret is usually used to generate symmetric keys that Alice and Bob would use to communicate. Bob can generate his symmetric keys based on his shared secret K; if Alice is able to decrypt (and respond) based on those keys, then (with high probability) Bob's shared key K matches Alice's shared key K'; if Alice rejects, then Bob's shared key K mismatches Alice's shared key K', which is why the attack is called key mismatch attack [2,12,18].

above results, malicious Bob can recover the reused secret key of Alice by communicating with Alice thousands of times. Our future work is to investigate if it is possible to recover the reused secret keys of other NIST candidates.

Acknowledgements. This work is supported by the National Key Research and Development Program of China (No. 2017YFB0802000), the National Natural Science Foundation of China (No. U1536205, 61802376).

Appendix A

A.1 RLWE Problems

Decisional Ring Learning with Errors (RLWE) [7]. Let n, q be positive integers, and χ_s, χ_e be distributions over R. Distinguish the following two distributions: D_0: $(\mathbf{a}, \mathbf{b})$ and D_1: $(\mathbf{a}, \mathbf{u})$, where $\mathbf{b} = \mathbf{as} + \mathbf{e}$ for $\mathbf{a} \overset{\$}{\leftarrow} R_q$, $\mathbf{s} \overset{\$}{\leftarrow} \chi_s$ and $\mathbf{e} \overset{\$}{\leftarrow} \chi_e$, and $\mathbf{u} \overset{\$}{\leftarrow} R_q$.

A.2 Cryptographic Definitions

A public key encryption scheme PKE is a tuple of algorithms (KeyGen, Enc, Dec):

- KeyGen() $\rightarrow$ (pk, sk): A probabilistic key generation algorithm that outputs a public key pk and a secret key sk.
- Enc(m, pk) $\rightarrow$ ct: A probabilistic encryption algorithm that takes as input a message m and public key pk, and outputs a ciphertext ct. The deterministic form is denoted as Enc(m, pk, r) $\rightarrow$ ct, where the randomness r is passed as an explicit input.
- Dec(ct, sk) $\rightarrow m'$: A deterministic decryption algorithm that takes as input a ciphertext ct and secret key sk, and outputs a message m'.

We use the notion of indistinguishability under chosen plaintext attacks (IND-CPA) to define the advantage of an adversary A by:

$$Adv_{\text{PKE}}^{\text{ind-cpa}}(A) = \left| Pr\left[b' = b : \begin{array}{c} (\mathsf{pk}, \mathsf{sk}) \leftarrow \mathtt{KeyGen}(); \\ (m_0, m_1) \leftarrow A(\mathsf{pk}); \\ b \leftarrow \mathcal{U}(0,1); \mathsf{ct} \leftarrow \mathtt{Enc}(m_b, \mathsf{pk}); \\ b' \leftarrow A(\mathsf{pk}, \mathsf{ct}); \end{array} \right] - \frac{1}{2} \right|.$$

A.3 Notations

Samp is an abstract algorithm which samples a random variable according to a distribution with a given seed: $x \leftarrow \mathsf{Samp}(D, \mathsf{seed})$, where D is a distribution, and seed is the random seed used to sample x. For an empty seed ϵ, the process $x \leftarrow \mathsf{Samp}(D, \epsilon)$ is the same as $x \overset{\$}{\leftarrow} D$. B_η^h is a n-ary centered binomial distribution with fixed Hamming weight. For a random variable according to the distribution, its Hamming weight is fixed to the expectation h, and the numbers of both 1's and -1's are $h/2$, the number of 0 is $n - h$. ECCEnc and ECCDec are the encoding and decoding of the error correction codes, which switch between a message $m \in \{0,1\}^{l_m}$ and its encoding $\widehat{m} \in \{0,1\}^{l_v}$, where l_v is a positive integer denoting the length of the encoding. $(\cdot)_{l_v}$ is a function that inputs a polynomial and outputs the first l_v coefficients of the polynomial. For an element $x \in \mathbb{Q}$ we denote by $\lfloor x \rceil$ rounding of x to the closest integer with ties being rounded up.

A.4 Parameters

The main parameters of the LAC.CPA are integers $n, q, \eta, l_m, l_v, l_t, h$, where n, q are the parameters of the polynomial ring R_q, η is the parameter of the centered binomial distribution B_η, l_m and l_v are the length of the message and the encoding, respectively, l_t is the maximum number of errors that can be corrected by error correcting code, h is the hamming weight of the centered binomial distribution. LAC.CPA recommends 3 parameter sets: LAC-128, LAC-192, LAC-256. Throughout these parameter sets q is always 251, l_m is always 256. The values of n, η, l_v and h vary for different security levels. In particular,

- In LAC-128, $n = 512$, $\eta = 1$, $l_v = l_m + 18 \times 8$, $h = \frac{n}{2}$.
- In LAC-192, $n = 1024$, $\eta = \frac{1}{2}$, $l_v = l_m + 9 \times 8$, $h = \frac{n}{4}$.
- In LAC-256, $n = 1024$, $\eta = 1$, $l_v = l_m + 18 \times 8$, $h = \frac{n}{2}$.

The centered binomial distribution B_η with $\eta = \frac{1}{2}$ is defined as follows: sample $(a, b) \leftarrow (B_1, B_1)$ and output $a \times b$, and the samples are in the interval $[-1, 1]$.

A.5 Discarding the Lower 4 Bits of Each Coefficient of v in LAC-256. When the lower 4 bits for each coefficient in $\mathbf{v}$ are discarded in the algorithm of LAC.CPA.Enc, $\mathbf{v}_j$ has 16 possible values and they are $k, k = 0, 1, ..., 15$. In order to carry out the attack, the attacker constructs $\mathbf{v}_3 \sim \mathbf{v}_8$ as follows:

$$\mathbf{v}_j^3 = \begin{cases} 3, & j = 0, l_v \\ 2, & j \in \bar{I}_0 \\ 10, & j \in \hat{I}_0 \\ 10, & j \in \bar{I}_1 \\ 2, & j \in \hat{I}_1, \end{cases} \quad \mathbf{v}_j^4 = \begin{cases} 3, & j = 0, l_v \\ 2, & j \in \bar{I}_0 \\ 10, & j \in \hat{I}_0 \\ 10, & j \in \bar{I}_1 \\ 2, & j \in \hat{I}_1, \end{cases} \quad \mathbf{v}_j^5 = \begin{cases} 12, & j = 0, l_v \\ 2, & j \in \bar{I}_0 \\ 10, & j \in \hat{I}_0 \\ 10, & j \in \bar{I}_1 \\ 2, & j \in \hat{I}_1, \end{cases}$$

$$\mathbf{v}_j^6 = \begin{cases} 12, & j = 0, l_v \\ 2, & j \in \bar{I}_0 \\ 10, & j \in \hat{I}_0 \\ 10, & j \in \bar{I}_1 \\ 2, & j \in \hat{I}_1, \end{cases} \quad \mathbf{v}_j^7 = \begin{cases} 12, & j = 0 \\ 4, & j = l_v \\ 2, & j \in \bar{I}_0 \\ 10, & j \in \hat{I}_0 \\ 10, & j \in \bar{I}_1 \\ 2, & j \in \hat{I}_1, \end{cases} \quad \mathbf{v}_j^8 = \begin{cases} 11, & j = 0 \\ 4, & j = l_v \\ 2, & j \in \bar{I}_0 \\ 10, & j \in \hat{I}_0 \\ 10, & j \in \bar{I}_1 \\ 2, & j \in \hat{I}_1. \end{cases}$$

The attacker queries the oracle PCO with $(\mathsf{ct} = (\frac{q}{16}, \mathbf{v}^3), m)$ to determine that $\mathbf{s}_0 + \mathbf{s}_{l_v} = -2$, and queries the oracle PCO with $(\mathsf{ct} = (\frac{2q}{17}, \mathbf{v}^4), m)$ to further determine that $\mathbf{s}_0 + \mathbf{s}_{l_v} = -1$. When he queries the oracle PCO with $(\mathsf{ct} = (\frac{q}{34}, \mathbf{v}^5), m)$, he can further determine that $\mathbf{s}_0 + \mathbf{s}_{l_v} = 2$. When he queries the oracle PCO with $(\mathsf{ct} = (\frac{2q}{17}, \mathbf{v}^6), m)$, he can further determine that $\mathbf{s}_0 + \mathbf{s}_{l_v} = 1$.

When querying the oracle PCO with $(\mathsf{ct} = (\frac{q}{16}, \mathbf{v}^7), m)$, he can determine if $\mathbf{s}_0 - \mathbf{s}_{l_v} = 1$ or -1, and if $\mathbf{s}_0 - \mathbf{s}_{l_v} = 2$ or $-2(0)$. When querying the oracle PCO with $(\mathsf{ct} = (\frac{q}{16}, \mathbf{v}^8), m)$, he can determine if $\mathbf{s}_0 - \mathbf{s}_{l_v} = -2$ or 0.

References

1. Fluhrer, S.R.: Cryptanalysis of ring-LWE based key exchange with key share reuse. IACR Cryptol. ePrint Arch. **2016**, 85 (2016)
2. Qin, Y., Cheng, C., Ding, J.: A complete and optimized key mismatch attack on NIST candidate NewHope. In: Sako, K., Schneider, S., Ryan, P.Y.A. (eds.) ESORICS 2019. LNCS, vol. 11736, pp. 504–520. Springer, Cham (2019). https://doi.org/10.1007/978-3-030-29962-0_24
3. Ding, J., Fluhrer, S., Rv, S.: Complete attack on RLWE key exchange with reused keys, without signal leakage. In: Susilo, W., Yang, G. (eds.) ACISP 2018. LNCS, vol. 10946, pp. 467–486. Springer, Cham (2018). https://doi.org/10.1007/978-3-319-93638-3_27
4. Ding, J., Alsayigh, S., Saraswathy, R.V., et al.: Leakage of signal function with reused keys in RLWE key exchange. In: 2017 IEEE International Conference on Communications (ICC), pp. 1–6. IEEE (2017)
5. Shor, P.W.: Algorithms for quantum computation: Discrete logarithms and factoring. In: Proceedings 35th Annual Symposium on Foundations of Computer Science, pp. 124–134. IEEE (1994)
6. Băetu, C., Durak, F.B., Huguenin-Dumittan, L., Talayhan, A., Vaudenay, S.: Misuse attacks on post-quantum cryptosystems. In: Ishai, Y., Rijmen, V. (eds.) EUROCRYPT 2019. LNCS, vol. 11477, pp. 747–776. Springer, Cham (2019). https://doi.org/10.1007/978-3-030-17656-3_26
7. Lyubashevsky, V., Peikert, C., Regev, O.: On ideal lattices and learning with errors over rings. In: Gilbert, H. (ed.) EUROCRYPT 2010. LNCS, vol. 6110, pp. 1–23. Springer, Heidelberg (2010). https://doi.org/10.1007/978-3-642-13190-5_1
8. Micciancio, D.: Lattice-based cryptography. In: Tilborg, H.C.V., Jajodia, S. (eds.) Encyclopedia of Cryptography and Security, pp. 713–715. Springer, Boston (2011). https://doi.org/10.1007/978-3-540-88702-7_5
9. Regev, O.: Lattice-based cryptography. In: Dwork, C. (ed.) CRYPTO 2006. LNCS, vol. 4117, pp. 131–141. Springer, Heidelberg (2006). https://doi.org/10.1007/11818175_8
10. Ding, J., Xie, X., Lin, X.: A simple provably secure key exchange scheme based on the learning with errors problem. IACR Cryptol. EPrint Arch. **2012**, 688 (2012)
11. Bos, J., Ducas, L., Kiltz, E., et al.: CRYSTALS-Kyber: a CCA-secure module-lattice-based KEM. In: IEEE European Symposium on Security and Privacy (EuroS&P), pp. 353–367. IEEE (2018)
12. Bauer, A., Gilbert, H., Renault, G., Rossi, M.: Assessment of the Key-Reuse Resilience of NewHope. In: Matsui, M. (ed.) CT-RSA 2019. LNCS, vol. 11405, pp. 272–292. Springer, Cham (2019). https://doi.org/10.1007/978-3-030-12612-4_14
13. Langlois, A., Stehlé, D.: Worst-case to average-case reductions for module lattices. Des. Codes Crypt. **75**(3), 565–599 (2014). https://doi.org/10.1007/s10623-014-9938-4
14. National institute of standards and technology: post-quantum cryptography round 1 submissions (2018). https://csrc.nist.gov/projects/post-quantum-cryptography/round-1-submissions

15. National institute of standards and technology: post-quantum cryptography round 2 submissions (2018). https://csrc.nist.gov/Projects/post-quantum-cryptography/round-2-submissions
16. Guo, Q., Johansson, T., Yang, J.: A novel CCA attack using decryption errors against LAC. In: Galbraith, S.D., Moriai, S. (eds.) ASIACRYPT 2019. LNCS, vol. 11921, pp. 82–111. Springer, Cham (2019). https://doi.org/10.1007/978-3-030-34578-5_4
17. Kirkwood, D., Lackey, B.C., McVey, J., et al.: Failure is not an option: standardization issues for post-quantum key agreement. Talk at NIST workshop on cybersecurity in a post-quantum world (2015). http://www.nist.gov/itl/csd/ct/post-quantum-crypto-workshop-2015.cfm
18. Qin, Y., Cheng, C., Ding, J.: An efficient key mismatch attack on the NIST second round candidate Kyber. IACR Cryptol. ePrint Arch. **2019**, 1343 (2019)
19. Saarinen, M.-J.O.: HILA5: on reliability, reconciliation, and error correction for ring-LWE encryption. In: Adams, C., Camenisch, J. (eds.) SAC 2017. LNCS, vol. 10719, pp. 192–212. Springer, Cham (2018). https://doi.org/10.1007/978-3-319-72565-9_10
20. Alkim, E., et al.: NewHope: algorithm specifcations and supporting documentation (2017). https://newhopecrypto.org/data/NewHope2018_12_02.pdf
21. Gao, X., Ding, J., Li, L., et al.: Practical randomized RLWE-based key exchange against signal leakage attack. IEEE Trans. Comput. **1**, 1–1 (2018)
22. Liu, C., Zheng, Z., Zou, G.: Key reuse attack on NewHope key exchange protocol. In: Lee, K. (ed.) ICISC 2018. LNCS, vol. 11396, pp. 163–176. Springer, Cham (2019). https://doi.org/10.1007/978-3-030-12146-4_11
23. Regev, O.: On lattices, learning with errors, random linear codes, and cryptography. J. ACM (JACM) **56**(6), 34 (2009)
24. Bernstein, D.J., Groot Bruinderink, L., Lange, T., Panny, L.: HILA5 Pindakaas: on the CCA security of lattice-based encryption with error correction. In: Joux, A., Nitaj, A., Rachidi, T. (eds.) AFRICACRYPT 2018. LNCS, vol. 10831, pp. 203–216. Springer, Cham (2018). https://doi.org/10.1007/978-3-319-89339-6_12
25. Alkim, E., Ducas, L., Pöppelmann, T., et al.: Post-quantum key exchange-a new hope. In: USENIX Security Symposium (2016)
26. Bernstein, D.J.: Introduction to post-quantum cryptography. In: Bernstein, D.J., Buchmann, J., Dahmen, E. (eds.) Post-Quantum Cryptography, pp. 1–14. Springer, Heidelberg (2009). https://doi.org/10.1007/978-3-540-88702-7_1
27. National institute of standards and technology: announcing request for nominations for public-key post-quantum cryptographic algorithms (2016). https://csrc:nist:gov/news/2016/public-key-post-quantum-cryptographic-algorithms
28. Buchmann, J., Ding J.: PQCrypto, Post-quantum cryptography. In: Second International Workshop, pp. 17–19 (2008)
29. Banerjee, A., Peikert, C., Rosen, A.: Pseudorandom functions and lattices. In: Pointcheval, D., Johansson, T. (eds.) EUROCRYPT 2012. LNCS, vol. 7237, pp. 719–737. Springer, Heidelberg (2012). https://doi.org/10.1007/978-3-642-29011-4_42
30. Wang, K., Jiang, H.: Analysis of two countermeasures against the signal leakage attack. In: Buchmann, J., Nitaj, A., Rachidi, T. (eds.) AFRICACRYPT 2019. LNCS, vol. 11627, pp. 370–388. Springer, Cham (2019). https://doi.org/10.1007/978-3-030-23696-0_19

31. D'Anvers, J.-P., Guo, Q., Johansson, T., Nilsson, A., Vercauteren, F., Verbauwhede, I.: Decryption failure attacks on IND-CCA secure lattice-based schemes. In: Lin, D., Sako, K. (eds.) PKC 2019. LNCS, vol. 11443, pp. 565–598. Springer, Cham (2019). https://doi.org/10.1007/978-3-030-17259-6_19
32. Hall, C., Goldberg, I., Schneier, B.: Reaction attacks against several public-key cryptosystem. In: Varadharajan, V., Mu, Y. (eds.) ICICS 1999. LNCS, vol. 1726, pp. 2–12. Springer, Heidelberg (1999). https://doi.org/10.1007/978-3-540-47942-0_2
33. Verheul, E.R., Doumen, J.M., van Tilborg, H.C.A.: Sloppy Alice attacks! Adaptive chosen ciphertext attacks on the McEliece public-key cryptosystem. In: Blaum, M., Farrell, P.G., van Tilborg, H.C.A. (eds.) Information, Coding and Mathematics, pp. 99–119. Springer, Boston (2002). https://doi.org/10.1007/978-1-4757-3585-7_7
34. D'Anvers, J.-P., Vercauteren, F., Verbauwhede, I.: The impact of error dependencies on ring/Mod-LWE/LWR based schemes. In: Ding, J., Steinwandt, R. (eds.) PQCrypto 2019. LNCS, vol. 11505, pp. 103–115. Springer, Cham (2019). https://doi.org/10.1007/978-3-030-25510-7_6
35. Ding, J., Cheng, C., Qin, Y.: A simple key reuse attack on LWE and ring LWE encryption schemes as key encapsulation mechanisms (KEMs). IACR Cryptol. ePrint Arch. **2019**, 271 (2019)
36. Greuet, A., Montoya, S., Renault, G.: Attack on LAC key exchange in misuse situation. IACR Cryptol. ePrint Arch. **2020**, 063 (2020)
37. Dumittan, L.H., Vaudenay, S.: Classical misuse attacks on NIST round 2 PQC: the power of rank-based schemes. IACR Cryptol. ePrint Arch. **2020**, 409 (2020)
38. Okada, S., Wang, Y., Takagi, T.: Improving key mismatch attack on NewHope with fewer queries. IACR Cryptol. ePrint Arch. **2020**, 585 (2020)

Security of Two NIST Candidates in the Presence of Randomness Reuse

Ke Wang[1,2(✉)], Zhenfeng Zhang[1,2], and Haodong Jiang[3]

[1] TCA Laboratory, State Key Laboratory of Computer Science, Institute of Software, Chinese Academy of Sciences, Beijing, China
{wangke,zfzhang}@tca.iscas.ac.cn

[2] University of Chinese Academy of Sciences, Beijing, China

[3] State Key Laboratory of Mathematical Engineering and Advanced Computing, Zhengzhou, Henan, China
hdjiang13@gmail.com

Abstract. The National Institute of Standards and Technology (NIST) is working on the standardization of post-quantum algorithms. In February 2019, NIST announced 26 candidate post-quantum cryptosystems, including NewHope and LAC, had entered the second round. In order to investigate the resilience of various candidate algorithms in key reuse situations, a series of work has been carried out.

In fact, randomness also has the risk of reuse, and in the real word random number generators (RNGs) frequently fail and produce bad randomness. In this work, we assess the resilience of candidate NewHope-CPA-KEM and LAC.KE in randomness reuse situations. In particular, we propose a method, which can recover the reused randomness after several communications. NewHope-CPA-KEM and LAC.KE are based on NewHope-CPA-PKE and LAC.CPA, respectively. The key to our method is that they share a common feature: if public key satisfies certain conditions, the ciphertext will reveal information about the randomness of encryption. The recovered randomness can be used to attack another session where the same randomness is used.

Keywords: NewHope · LAC · KEM · PKE · IND-CPA · NIST · Post quantum · Lattice based · Active attack · Randomness reuse

1 Introduction

In 1994, Shor [34] proposed a quantum algorithm, which can break currently widely deployed public key cryptosystems based on integer factoring problem, discrete logarithm problem. Public key cryptosystems based on these hard problems are no longer secure when large-scale quantum computers are implemented. There is an urgent need to replace them. For this purpose, the National Institute of Standards and Technology (NIST) initiated a standardization process for post-quantum algorithms, and on January 03, 2017, they called for proposals

K. Nguyen et al. (Eds.): ProvSec 2020, LNCS 12505, pp. 402–421, 2020.
https://doi.org/10.1007/978-3-030-62576-4_20

[26] for post-quantum cryptosystems, including Key Encapsulation Mechanism (KEM), Public Key Encryption (PKE) and signature.

By the end of 2017, many algorithms had been submitted. After the first round of evaluation, in February 2019, NIST announced 26 candidate post-quantum cryptosystems had entered the second round. Among these, only a very few types of algorithms are proposed, such as lattice-based, code-based, hash-based, multivariate-based or isogeny-based. One of the most promising algorithms is lattice-based, and some lattice-based candidate cryptosystems, including NewHope [1] and LAC [24], contain a weaker scheme. In particular, NewHope and LAC contain NewHope-CPA-KEM and LAC.KE, respectively. Even for these candidate schemes for which secret key reuse is considered as a misuse of the mechanism, having an accurate estimate of the complexity of the secret key recovery really helps to assess the possible danger [6]. Aiming to analyze how easy it is to run a secret key recovery under multiple key reuse, a series of work [6,18,27,30] has been carried out.[1] In particular, after thousands of communications, the reused secret keys of most candidates can be recovered.

Usually, these candidates are used to implement a purely ephemeral key exchange protocol [26]. In this case, the randomness can be regarded as (Bob's) secret in the protocol, which also has the risk of reuse. In particular, Ding et al. [11] studied Bob's reuse of secrets in DING12 [14], and Liu et al. put forward an attack [23] on NewHope'16 [3] with static Bob. In fact, in the real word, random number generators (RNGs) are consistently a weak link in the secure use of cryptography [33], and RNGs used in practice frequently fail, causing spectacular attacks [36].

Determining how an incorrect use of randomness affects the security of a candidate can help to identify potential dangers, and also may well have a high impact on the understanding of the important cryptosystem.

1.1 Our Contributions

In this work, we assess the security of NewHope-CPA-KEM and LAC.KE in randomness reuse situations. Since they are constructed directly from NewHope-CPA-PKE and LAC.CPA respectively, we start with these underlying PKEs.

- first, we develop a meta-PKE construction and show both NewHope-CPA-PKE and LAC.CPA follow this construction.
- next, we observe a feature of meta-PKE: if the public key satisfies certain conditions, the ciphertext may reveal information about the randomness of encryption. The feature is true in NewHope-CPA-PKE and LAC.CPA.
- then, based on the features of NewHope-CPA-PKE and LAC.CPA, we recover the reused randomness in NewHope-CPA-KEM and LAC.KE after several communications (queries).[2] The results in each recommended parameter set are shown in Table 1.

[1] There is also some work to analyze other candidates, such as [4,7,13,21,31].

[2] In Sect. 5, we define a reused randomness recovery game and simulate communication by querying the game.

- finally, after recovering the reused randomness in LAC.KE, we demonstrate that these randomness can be used to recover the shared secret in another session where the same randomness is used.

Table 1. The results in each recommended parameter set

Algorithm	NewHope-CPA-KEM		LAC.KE		
Parameter set	NewHope512	NewHope1024	LAC-128	LAC-192	LAC-256
Number of queries	8	8	2	4	2

1.2 Techniques

NewHope-CPA-PKE consists of three algorithms.

- The key generation algorithm NewHope-CPA-PKE.KeyGen generates public key $\mathsf{pk} = (\mathbf{b}, \mathbf{a})$[3] and secret key $\mathsf{sk} = \mathbf{s}$, where $\mathbf{b} = \mathbf{as} + \mathbf{d}$.
- The encryption algorithm NewHope-CPA-PKE.Enc encrypts secret pt with public key pk and random coinB to produce ciphertext $\mathsf{ct} = (\mathbf{u}, \mathsf{Compress}(\mathbf{v}))$, where $\mathbf{u} = \mathbf{at} + \mathbf{e}$, $\mathbf{v} = \mathbf{bt} + \mathbf{f} + \mathsf{Encode}(\mathsf{pt})$, $\mathbf{t}, \mathbf{e}, \mathbf{f}$ are randomness with coinB as seed.
- The decryption algorithm NewHope-CPA-PKE.Dec recovers secret pt with secret key sk.

In NewHope-CPA-PKE, the randomness $\mathbf{t}$, $\mathbf{e}$, $\mathbf{f}$ are sampled from centered binomial distribution B_η and their coefficients are in set $\{-\eta, -\eta+1, ..., \eta-1, \eta\}$. The coefficients of $\mathsf{Encode}(\mathsf{pt})$ belong to set $\{0, \lfloor \frac{q}{2} \rfloor\}$. If public key $\mathbf{b}$ is an integer in $\mathbb{Z}_q$, there are at most $2(2\eta+1)^2$ possible values for the coefficients of $\mathbf{v}$. In particular, if $\mathbf{b}$ is chosen to make the coefficients of $\mathbf{v}$ have exactly $2(2\eta+1)^2$ possibilities, $\mathbf{v}$ will reveal the values of $\mathbf{t}$, $\mathbf{f}$, $\mathsf{Encode}(\mathsf{pt})$ (then pt) completely. However, in order to reduce bandwidth, NewHope-CPA-PKE compresses $\mathbf{v}$, causing the coefficients of close size in $\mathbf{v}$ are compressed into a same coefficient in $\mathsf{Compress}(\mathbf{v})$. As a result, $\mathsf{Compress}(\mathbf{v})$ can reveal the complete pt and part of the information about $\mathbf{t}$, not $\mathbf{f}$. In order to give the results above, we first develop a meta-PKE construction. Then, we give a feature of the meta-PKE (Theorem 1). Finally, we show NewHope-CPA-PKE follows the construction (Example 1) and also has the feature (Corollary 1 and Example 3).

NewHope-CPA-PKE is directly used to construct NewHope-CPA-KEM, which can be divided into three stages.

- First, the initiator Alice invokes NewHope-CPA-PKE.KeyGen to generates public key pk and secret key sk, sends pk to the responder Bob.
- After receiving public key pk, Bob produces secret pt and random coinB, encrypts pt by invoking NewHope-CPA-PKE.Enc to produce ciphertext ct, sends ct to Alice.

[3] In order to reduce the bandwidth, the public key pk usually contains only a seed $\mathsf{seed}_{\mathbf{a}}$, and then generates $\mathbf{a}$ through an expansion algorithm.

- After receiving ciphertext ct, Alice recovers secret pt by invoking NewHope-CPA-PKE.Dec. The final shared secret K is derived from the pt by hashing.

When honest responder Bob generates static randomness $\mathbf{t}$, and reuses it for multiple communications with malicious initiator Alice, based on the feature of NewHope-CPA-PKE, Alice can recover $\mathbf{t}$.

In LAC.CPA, $\mathbf{v} = (\mathbf{bt})_{l_v} + \mathbf{f} + \lfloor \frac{q}{2} \rfloor \cdot (\mathsf{ECCEnc}(\mathsf{pt}))$, where function $(\cdot)_{l_v}$ is used to take the first l_v coefficients of the polynomial $\mathbf{bt}$. Similarly, if $\mathbf{b}$ is chosen properly, $\mathbf{v}$ can reveal the complete $\mathbf{f}$, pt and part of the information about $\mathbf{t}$. However, in order to minimize the size of the ciphertext, in implementation the lower 4 bits for each coefficient in $\mathbf{v}$ are discarded, causing the coefficients of close size in $\mathbf{v}$ are converted into a same coefficient in $\overline{\mathbf{v}}$, where $\overline{\mathbf{v}}$ is the value after discarding the lower 4 bits of each coefficient in $\mathbf{v}$. As a result, $\overline{\mathbf{v}}$ can reveal the complete pt and part of the information about $\mathbf{t}$, not $\mathbf{f}$. In order to get the results, we show LAC.CPA follows the meta-PKE construction (Example 2) and also has the feature (Corollary 2 and Example 4). Based on the feature, in LAC.KE, when honest responder Bob generates static randomness $\mathbf{t}$, and reuses it for multiple communications with malicious initiator Alice, Alice can recover $\mathbf{t}$.

1.3 Related Work

Key leakage in RLWE-based key exchange with reused keys was first pointed out in [22] but without any concrete description of an attack to exploit the leakage. In 2016, Fluhrer [15] showed how several RLWE-based key exchange protocols can be broken, under the assumption that the same public key is used for multiple exchanges. Following this idea, Ding et al. [11] proposed a signal leakage attack on DING12 [14]. In order to resist the signal leakage attack, Ding Key Exchange, one of cryptosystems entering the first round [26], includes a RLWE-based key exchange protocol with reusable keys, which can achieve secure key reuse. Gao et al. [17] constructed a new randomized RLWE-based key exchange protocol secure against the signal leakage attack. However, these two countermeasures only focused on the security of one party's reused key and ignored the other party. Recently, Wang et al. [35] improved the two countermeasures. At PKC'19, D'Anvers et al. [8] explored decryption failure attacks on IND-CCA secure lattice-based schemes, which are CCA attacks. At ASIACRYPT'19, Guo et al. [19] proposed an CCA attack against LAC using decryption error. At PQCrypto'19, D'Anvers et al. [10] pointed out that the higher-than-expected failure rate could lead to more efficient cryptanalysis of the schemes based on Ring/Module Learning with Errors/Rounding through decryption failure attacks. They provided a method to estimate the decryption failure probability, taking into account the bit failure dependency. In addition, Ding et al. [12] presented a simple key reuse attack on LWE and RLWE encryption schemes used directly as KEMs. Recently, at EUROCRYPT'20, D'Anvers et al. [9] extended the "failure boosting" technique in PKC'19 and proposed an approach that we call "directional failure boosting" that uses previously found "failing ciphertexts" to accelerate the search for new ones.

Concurrent and Independent Work. In [6], Bauer et al. also assessed the security of NewHope-CPA-KEM in randomness reuse situation in Appendix A. In particular, they proposed a method to recover the reused randomness in NewHope-CPA-KEM. The method requires Alice to use a different **a** for each communication, which makes it does not apply to the situation where the public global parameter **a** is cached. In practice, if it turns out to be too expensive to generate **a** for every public key, it is possible to cache **a** [1].

Different from Bauer's method, our method does't requires Alice to change the public global parameter **a**, so it can apply to the situation where **a** is cached. Our method can also be used to analyze other candidate schemes, such as LAC.KE. Moreover, the analysis of NewHope-CPA-KEM with randomness reused is only part of our work.

1.4 Organization

In Sect. 2, We introduce some preliminaries including mathematical notations, RLWE problem, cryptographic definitions, NewHope-CPA-PKE and LAC.CPA. In Sect. 3, we develop a meta-PKE construction and show both NewHope-CPA-PKE and LAC.CPA follow this construction. In Sect. 4, we show a feature of meta-PKE, which is also true in NewHope-CPA-PKE and LAC.CPA. Based on the features of NewHope-CPA-PKE and LAC.CPA, in Sect. 5, we recover the reused randomness in LAC.KE and NewHope-CPA-KEM. After recovering the reused randomness, we also show that these recovered randomness is disastrous for another session where the same randomness is used. Finally, we make a conclusion in Sect. 6.

2 Preliminaries

2.1 Mathematical Notations

Let q be a prime number in $\mathbb{N}$ and let $\mathbb{Z}_q$ denote the ring elements $\mathbb{Z}/q\mathbb{Z}$. The elements in $\mathbb{Z}_q$ can be equivalently represented as integers in $\{0, ..., q-1\}$. Define the ring of integer polynomials modulo x^n+1 as $R = \mathbb{Z}[x]/(x^n+1)$ for integer $n \geq 1$, and the ring $R_q = \mathbb{Z}_q[x]/(x^n+1)$ refers to the polynomial ring modulo x^n+1 where the coefficients are from $\mathbb{Z}_q$. The addition and multiplication of the elements in R_q are operated according to those of polynomials. For $a \in R_q$, a_i denotes the ith coefficient of a, $1 \leq i \leq n$. $\mathbb{Z}_q^l$ denotes a set of vector of length l and vector components are taken from $\mathbb{Z}_q$. For $a \in \mathbb{Z}_q^l$, a_i denotes the ith component of a, $1 \leq i \leq l$. $\{0,1\}^l$ denotes a set of strings of length l. For $a \in \{0,1\}^l$, a_i denotes the ith bit of a, $1 \leq i \leq l$. For a set S, $x \xleftarrow{\$} S$ means that an element x is chosen from S uniformly at random. For a distribution χ, $x \xleftarrow{\$} \chi$ means that an element x is sampled according to the distribution χ. A polynomial $f \in R_q$ or a vector in $\mathbb{Z}_q^l$ is chosen from S (sampled from χ), we mean that each coefficient is chosen from S (sampled from χ).

Centered Binomial Distribution. We define centered binomial distribution B_η as follows:

$$(a_1, ..., a_\eta, b_1, ..., b_\eta) \xleftarrow{\$} \{0,1\}^{2\eta}$$

$$\text{and output} \sum_{i=1}^{\eta}(a_i - b_i).$$

The samples are in the interval $[-\eta, \eta]$.

2.2 RLWE Problem

Decisional Ring Learning with Errors (RLWE) [25]. Let n, q be positive integers, and χ_s, χ_e be distributions over R. Distinguish the following two distributions:

- D_0: (a, b), and
- D_1: (a, u)

where $b = as + e$ for $a \xleftarrow{\$} R_q$, $s \xleftarrow{\$} \chi_s$ and $e \xleftarrow{\$} \chi_e$, and $u \xleftarrow{\$} R_q$.

2.3 Cryptographic Definitions

Public Key Encryption (PKE). A public key encryption scheme PKE is a tuple of algorithms (KeyGen, Enc, Dec):

- KeyGen() $\rightarrow$ (pk, sk): A probabilistic key generation algorithm that outputs a public key pk and a secret key sk.
- Enc(pt, pk) $\rightarrow$ ct: A probabilistic encryption algorithm that takes as input a message pt and public key pk, and outputs a ciphertext ct. The deterministic form is denoted Enc(pt, pk, coin) $\rightarrow$ ct, where the random coin is passed as an explicit input.
- Dec(ct, sk) $\rightarrow$ pt': A deterministic decryption algorithm that takes as input a ciphertext ct and secret key sk, and outputs a message pt'.

We use the notion of indistinguishability under chosen plaintext attacks (IND-CPA) to define the advantage of an adversary A by:

$$Adv_{\text{PKE}}^{\text{ind-cpa}}(A) = \left| Pr\left[b' = b : \begin{array}{c} (\mathsf{pk}, \mathsf{sk}) \leftarrow \mathsf{KeyGen}(); \\ (\mathsf{pt}_0, \mathsf{pt}_1) \leftarrow A(\mathsf{pk}); \\ b \leftarrow \mathcal{U}(0,1); \mathsf{ct} \leftarrow \mathsf{Enc}(\mathsf{pt}_b, \mathsf{pk}); \\ b' \leftarrow A(\mathsf{pk}, \mathsf{ct}); \end{array} \right] - \frac{1}{2} \right|.$$

2.4 NewHope-CPA-PKE

NewHope [1] is a suit of cryptographic primitives that rely on the hardness of RLWE. Its core component is NewHope-CPA-PKE, an IND-CPA secure public key encryption. NewHope-CPA-PKE has first been described in [2] and it consists of three algorithms: NewHope-CPA-PKE.KeyGen, NewHope-CPA-PKE.Enc and NewHope-CPA-PKE.Dec, as shown in Algorithms 3, 4, 5, which can be abbreviated as NewHope.KeyGen/Enc/Dec, respectively. In these algorithms, we omit some details (e.g. the so-called NTT transform or the encoding of the messages) to simplify the presentation. These simplifications do not imply any loss of generality for our analysis. In order to keep the context consistent, the notations of the algorithms may be different from the original specification of these algorithms [1].

Notations and Parameters. H is a hash function. Gen_a is the generating function of global parameter. Samp is an abstract algorithm which samples a random variable according to a distribution with a given seed: $x \leftarrow \mathsf{Samp}(D, \mathsf{seed})$, where D is a distribution, and seed is the random seed used to sample x. NewHope-CPA-PKE uses three main parameters n, q, η, where n, q are the parameters of the polynomial ring R_q, η is the parameter of the centered binomial distribution B_η. NewHope-CPA-PKE recommends 2 parameter sets:

- NewHope512: $(n, q, \eta) = (512, 12289, 8)$.
- NewHope1024: $(n, q, \eta) = (1024, 12289, 8)$.

NewHope-CPA-PKE uses four specific functions: Encode, Decode, Compress and Decompress. The following paragraphs describe these functions.

Encode and Decode. The Encode function takes a 256-bit input ν and creates an element $K \in R_q$ which stores 2 (or 4) times the element ν. The redundancy is used by the function Decode to recover ν with a noisy K.

Compress and Decompress. NewHope-CPA-PKE shortens ciphertexts by rounding off the low bits as in LWR-based schemes [5], which is a common technique for reducing ciphertext size also in LWE-based schemes [28,29]. In particular, this technology is realized by function Compress, which takes as input a vector C in R_q and applies on each of its component a modulus switching to obtain an element c in $\mathbb{Z}_8[x]/(x^n + 1)$. For an element $x \in \mathbb{Q}$ we denote by $\lfloor x \rceil$ rounding of x to the closest integer with ties being rounded up. In particular,

$$\mathsf{Compress}(C_i) = \lfloor (8/q) \cdot C_i \rceil, \quad \mathsf{Decompress}(c_i) = \lfloor (q/8) \cdot c_i \rceil.$$

Algorithm 1. Encode: $\{0,1\}^{256} \rightarrow R_q$

Input: $\nu \in \{0,1\}^{256}$
Output: $K \in R_q$
$K \leftarrow 0$
for $i = 0$ to 255 **do**
  $K_i \leftarrow \nu_i \cdot \lfloor \frac{q}{2} \rfloor$
  $K_{i+256} \leftarrow \nu_i \cdot \lfloor \frac{q}{2} \rfloor$
  if $n = 1024$ **then**
    $K_{i+512} \leftarrow \nu_i \cdot \lfloor \frac{q}{2} \rfloor$
    $K_{i+768} \leftarrow \nu_i \cdot \lfloor \frac{q}{2} \rfloor$
  end if
end for
return K

Algorithm 2. Decode: $R_q \rightarrow \{0,1\}^{256}$

Input: $K \in R_q$
Output: $\nu \in \{0,1\}^{256}$
$\nu \leftarrow 0$
for $i = 0$ to 255 **do**
  $t \leftarrow \sum_{j=0}^{1} |K_{i+256j} - \lfloor \frac{q}{2} \rfloor|$
  if $n = 1024$ **then**
    $t \leftarrow \sum_{j=0}^{3} |K_{i+256j} - \lfloor \frac{q}{2} \rfloor|$
  end if
  if $t < q$ **then** $\nu_i \leftarrow 1$ **else** $\nu_i \leftarrow 0$
  end if
end for
return ν

Algorithm 3. NewHope.KeyGen()

Output: Secret key $\mathsf{sk} \in \{0,1\}^{14 \cdot n}$
Output: Public key $\mathsf{pk} \in \{0,1\}^{14 \cdot n + 256}$
$\mathsf{seed} \xleftarrow{\$} \{0,1\}^{256}$
$(\mathsf{seed}_{\mathbf{a}}, \mathsf{coinA}) = \mathsf{H}(\mathsf{seed})$
$\mathbf{a} \leftarrow \mathsf{Gen}_a(\mathsf{seed}_{\mathbf{a}}) \in R_q$
$\mathbf{s} \leftarrow \mathsf{Samp}(B_\eta, \mathsf{coinA}) \in R_q$
$\mathbf{d} \leftarrow \mathsf{Samp}(B_\eta, \mathsf{coinA}) \in R_q$
$\mathbf{b} = \mathbf{as} + \mathbf{d} \in R_q$
$\mathsf{sk} = \mathbf{s}$, $\mathsf{pk} = (\mathbf{b}, \mathsf{seed}_a)$
return (sk,pk)

Algorithm 4. NewHope.Enc(pt, pk, coinB)

Output: Ciphertext $\mathsf{ct} \in \{0,1\}^{14 \cdot n + 8 \cdot n}$
$\mathbf{a} \leftarrow \mathsf{Gen}_a(\mathsf{seed}_{\mathbf{a}}) \in R_q$
$\mathbf{t} \leftarrow \mathsf{Samp}(B_\eta, \mathsf{coinB}) \in R_q$
$\mathbf{e} \leftarrow \mathsf{Samp}(B_\eta, \mathsf{coinB}) \in R_q$
$\mathbf{f} \leftarrow \mathsf{Samp}(B_\eta, \mathsf{coinB}) \in R_q$
$\mathbf{u} = \mathbf{at} + \mathbf{e} \in R_q$
$\mathbf{v} = \mathbf{bt} + \mathbf{f} + \mathsf{Encode}(\mathsf{pt}) \in R_q$
$\mathsf{ct} = (\mathbf{u}, \mathsf{Compress}(\mathbf{v}))$
return ct

Algorithm 5. NewHope.Dec(ct,sk): decryption

Output: Message $\mathsf{pt'} \in \{0,1\}^{256}$
$\mathbf{v} = \mathsf{Decompress}(\mathsf{Compress}(\mathbf{v})) \in R_q$
$\mathsf{pt'} = \mathsf{Decode}(\mathbf{v} - \mathbf{us})$
return pt'

2.5 LAC.CPA

LAC [24] is a suit of public key cryptographic primitives based on RLWE. The foundation of LAC is LAC.CPA, an IND-CPA PKE. LAC.CPA comprises three algorithms: LAC.CPA.KeyGen, LAC.CPA.Enc, and LAC.CPA.Dec, as illustrated in Algorithm 6, 7, 8, which are simplified descriptions of the algorithms and may partly deviate from the notations the original specification of these algorithms [24].

Notations and Parameters. $\{0,1\}^{l_s}$ is the space of random seeds and $\{0,1\}^{l_m}$ is the message space, where l_s, l_m are positive integers. For an empty seed ϵ, the process $x \leftarrow \mathsf{Samp}(D, \epsilon)$ is the same as $x \xleftarrow{\$} D$. B_η^h is a n-ary centered binomial distribution with fixed Hamming weight, where $0 < h < n/2$ is even. For a random variable according to the distribution, the numbers of both 1's and -1's are $h/2$, the number of 0 is $n - h$. ECCEnc and ECCDec are the encoding and decoding of the error correction codes, which switch between a message $\mathsf{pt} \in \{0,1\}^{l_m}$ and its encoding $\widehat{\mathsf{pt}} \in \{0,1\}^{l_v}$, where l_v is a positive integer denoting the length of the encoding. $(\cdot)_{l_v}$ is a function that inputs a polynomial and outputs the first l_v coefficients of the polynomial. LAC.CPA recommends 3 parameter sets: LAC-128, LAC-192, LAC-256. Throughout these parameter sets q is always 251, l_m is always 256. The values of n, η and l_v vary for different security levels. In particular,

- In LAC-128, $n = 512$, $\eta = 1$, $l_v = l_m + 18 \times 8$.
- In LAC-192, $n = 1024$, $\eta = \frac{1}{2}$, $l_v = l_m + 9 \times 8$.
- In LAC-256, $n = 1024$, $\eta = 1$, $l_v = (l_m + 18 \times 8) \times 2$.

The centered binomial distribution B_η with $\eta = \frac{1}{2}$ is defined as follows: sample $(a, b) \leftarrow (B_1, B_1)$ and output $a \times b$, and the samples are in the interval $[-1, 1]$.

Algorithm 6. LAC.CPA.KeyGen()

Output: Secret key $\mathsf{sk} \in R_q$
Output: Public key $\mathsf{pk} \in R_q \times \{0,1\}^{l_s}$
$\mathsf{seed}_\mathbf{a} \xleftarrow{\$} \{0,1\}^{l_s}$
$\mathbf{a} \leftarrow \mathsf{Gen}_a(\mathsf{seed}_\mathbf{a}) \in R_q$
$\mathbf{s} \leftarrow \mathsf{Samp}(B_\eta^h, \epsilon) \in R_q$
$\mathbf{d} \leftarrow \mathsf{Samp}(B_\eta^h, \epsilon) \in R_q$
$\mathbf{b} = \mathbf{as} + \mathbf{d} \in R_q$
$\mathsf{sk} = \mathbf{s}$, $\mathsf{pk} = (\mathbf{b}, \mathsf{seed}_\mathbf{a})$
return (sk,pk)

Algorithm 7. LAC.CPA.Enc(pt, pk, coinB)

Output: Ciphertext $\mathsf{ct} \in R_q \times \mathbb{Z}_q^{l_v}$
$\mathbf{a} \leftarrow \mathsf{Gen}_a(\mathsf{seed}_\mathbf{a}) \in R_q$
$\mathbf{t} \leftarrow \mathsf{Samp}(B_\eta^h, \mathsf{coinB}) \in R_q$
$\mathbf{e} \leftarrow \mathsf{Samp}(B_\eta^h, \mathsf{coinB}) \in R_q$
$\mathbf{f} \leftarrow \mathsf{Samp}(B_\eta, \mathsf{coinB}) \in \mathbb{Z}_q^{l_v}$
$\mathbf{u} = \mathbf{at} + \mathbf{e} \in R_q$
$\mathbf{v} = (\mathbf{bt})_{l_v} + \mathbf{f} + \lfloor \frac{q}{2} \rceil \cdot (\mathsf{ECCEnc}(\mathsf{pt})) \in \mathbb{Z}_q^{l_v}$
$\mathsf{ct} = (\mathbf{u}, \mathbf{v})$
return ct

Algorithm 8. LAC.CPA.Dec(ct,sk)

Output: Message pt' $\in \{0,1\}^{l_m}$
$\widetilde{\mathsf{pt}} = \mathbf{v} - (\mathbf{us})_{l_v}$
for $i = 0$ to l_v-1 **do**
  if $\frac{q}{4} \le \widetilde{\mathsf{pt}}_i < \frac{3q}{4}$ **then**
    $\mathsf{pt}_i \leftarrow 1$
  else
    $\widehat{\mathsf{pt}}_i \leftarrow 0$
  end if
end for
pt' $\leftarrow \mathsf{ECCDec}(\widehat{\mathsf{pt}})$
return pt'

3 A Meta-PKE Construction

At Eurocrypt'19, Băetu et al. [4] proposed a meta-PKC construction and showed 9 IND-CPA PKEs [26] entering the first round all follow the construction. In fact, this construction is inspired by the Regev cryptosystem [32] such as the Lyubashevsky-Peikert-Regev cryptosystem [25]. In this section, we give a meta-PKE construction, which is a further refinement of meta-PKC construction. In particular, both NewHope-CPA-PKE and LAC.CPA follow this construction.

Algorithm $\mathsf{KeyGen}()$:
generate a random seed_A and coinA
generate $A \leftarrow \mathsf{GenA}(\mathsf{seed}_A) \in S_A$
sample secrets $\mathsf{sk} \in S_{\mathsf{sk}}, d \in S_B$ from distribution Ψ by using coinA
$B \leftarrow A \times \mathsf{sk} + d \in S_B$
$\mathsf{pk} \leftarrow (\mathsf{seed}_A, B)$
return $(\mathsf{sk}, \mathsf{pk})$

Algorithm $\mathsf{Enc}(\mathsf{pt}, \mathsf{pk}, \mathsf{coinB})$:
parse $\mathsf{pk} = (\mathsf{seed}_A, B)$
generate $A \leftarrow \mathsf{GenA}(\mathsf{seed}_A)$
sample randomness $t \in S_t, e \in S_U, f \in S_V$ from distribution Ψ by using coinB
$U \leftarrow t \times A + e \in S_U$
$V \leftarrow t \times B + f + \mathsf{encode}(\mathsf{pt}) \in S_V$
return $\mathsf{ct} = (U, V)$

Algorithm $\mathsf{Dec}(\mathsf{ct}, \mathsf{sk})$:
parse $\mathsf{ct} = (U, V)$
$W \leftarrow V - U \times \mathsf{sk} \in S_V$
$\mathsf{pt} \leftarrow \mathsf{decode}(W) \in M$
return pt

Fig. 1. The meta-PKE defined on the algebra

We consider six additive Abelian groups S_{sk}, S_A, S_B, S_t, S_U, and S_V and four bilinear mappings which are all denoted with $\times$. The relationships between the four bilinear mappings and the six additive Abelian groups are as follows: $S_A \times S_{\mathsf{sk}} \to S_B$, $S_U \times S_{\mathsf{sk}} \to S_V$, $S_t \times S_A \to S_U$, and $S_t \times S_B \to S_V$. In particular, there is an associativity in the sense that $(t \times A) \times \mathsf{sk} = t \times (A \times \mathsf{sk})$ for all $t \in S_t$, $A \in S_A$, and $\mathsf{sk} \in S_{\mathsf{sk}}$. We also define three functions $\mathsf{GenA} : S_{\mathsf{seed}_A} \to S_A$, $\mathsf{encode} : M \to S_V$ and $\mathsf{decode} : S_V \to M$.

Finally, we give meta-PKE construction in Fig. 1 where the choice of the algebra, bilinear mapping, $\mathsf{GenA}/\mathsf{encode}/\mathsf{decode}$, and the probability distribution Ψ are left free. Compared with meta-PKC in [4], meta-PKE stresses that secrets and randomness sk, d, t, e, f are sampled from the same probability distribution Ψ. In addition, instead of directly picking a random $A \in S_A$, meta-PKE generates A using a random seed_A, which is widely adopted by most candidate algorithms.

Example 1 ***(NewHope-CPA-PKE).*** *NewHope-CPA-PKE defines* $S_A = S_{sk} = S_B = S_t = S_U = S_V = R_q$. *Bilinear mappings are simply multiplications of polynomials in* R_q. *Message* $\mathsf{pt} \in \{0,1\}^{256}$ *is encoded by multiplying it* *by* $\lfloor \frac{q}{2} \rfloor$ *and represented twice (four times).*[4] *Namely,* $Y = \mathsf{encode}(\mathsf{pt})$*, and the bit* pt_i *of the message appears at position* i *and* $i + 256$ *(and* $i + 512$, $i + 768$*) of* Y *by* $Y_i = Y_{i+256}$ $(= Y_{i+512} = Y_{i+768}) = \mathsf{pt}_i \lfloor \frac{q}{2} \rfloor, i = 1, ..., 256$*. The distribution* Ψ *is the centered binomial distribution* B_η *with* $\eta = 8$*. In order to compress the size of ciphertext, function* Compress *is introduced and it simply performs coefficient-wise modulus switching between modulus* q *and modulus 8 by multiplying it by 8 and then performing a rounding division by* q*.*

Example 2 ***(LAC.CPA).*** *LAC.CPA defines* $S_A = S_{sk} = S_B = S_t = S_U = R_q$ *and* $S_V = \mathbb{Z}_q^{l_v}$*. Bilinear mappings are simply multiplications of polynomials in* R_q*. Message* $\mathsf{pt} \in \{0,1\}^{l_s}$ *is first encoded as* $\mathsf{ECCEnc(pt)} \in \{0,1\}^{l_v}$*, then it is encoded as* Y *by multiplying it by* $\lfloor \frac{q}{2} \rceil$*, namely,* $Y = \lfloor \frac{q}{2} \rceil \cdot (\mathsf{ECCEnc(pt)})$*. The bit* $\mathsf{ECCEnc(pt)}_i$ *appears at position* i *of* Y *by* $Y_i = \mathsf{ECCEnc(pt)}_i \lfloor \frac{q}{2} \rceil$*. The secrets and randomness are sampled from the centered binomial distribution* $\Psi = B_\eta$ *with* $\eta = 1$ *or* $\frac{1}{2}$*. In particular, in calculating* $V \leftarrow t \times B + f + \mathsf{encode}(\mathsf{pt})$*, function* $(\cdot)_{l_v}$ *is introduced and used to take the first* l_v *coefficients of the polynomial* $t \times B$*. In addition, in order to minimize the size of the ciphertext, in implementation the lower 4 bits for each coefficient in* V *are discarded.*

4 A Feature of Meta-PKE

In meta-PKE construction, there is a key step

$$V \leftarrow t \times B + f + Y,$$

where B is part of the public key pk, V is part of the ciphertext ct, t, f are randomness, Y is the encoding of secret pt and $Y = \mathsf{encode}(\mathsf{pt})$. Usually, randomness t, f are sampled from a centered binomial distribution and codeword Y belongs to set $\{0, \frac{q}{2}\}$, the coefficients of t, f and Y are discrete integers. In particular, the number of possible values they can take are denoted as Ω_t, Ω_f and Ω_Y, respectively.

We observe that if B is chosen as an integer, each coefficient of V has at most $\Omega_t \times \Omega_f \times \Omega_Y$ possibilities. Further, if Alice chooses B so that each coefficient of V has exactly $\Omega_t \times \Omega_f \times \Omega_Y$ possibilities, V can reveal the values of t, f, Y (then pt) completely. In particular, NewHope-CPA-PKE and LAC.CPA also have this feature and we use the following theorem and corollaries to explain it.

Theorem 1. $t, f, Y \in R_q$*, and the coefficients* t_i, f_i *are in* $\{-D, ..., D\}$*,* $D \ll q$*,* $Y_i \in \{0, \frac{q}{2}\}, i = 1, ..., n$*.* $B \in \mathbb{Z}_q$ *and* $V = B \times t + f + Y \bmod^{\pm} q$*.*[5] *If* $2D + 1 \leq B < q/4D - 1$*, then* V *will reveal the values of* t, f, Y *completely.*

[4] NewHope recommends 2 parameter sets and they adopt different coding methods.

[5] For ease of understanding and explanation, we consider the modular reductions in $[-\lfloor \frac{q}{2} \rfloor, \lfloor \frac{q}{2} \rfloor]$, which corresponds to $[0, q-1]$ one by one. In particular, $r' = r \bmod^{\pm} q$ is the unique element in range $[-\lfloor \frac{q}{2} \rfloor, \lfloor \frac{q}{2} \rfloor]$ such that $r' = r \bmod q$.

Proof. Given that $t_i, f_i \in \{-D, ..., D\}$, $B \in \mathbb{Z}_q$ and $B < q/4D - 1$, we have

$$(t\times B+f)_i \in \{-DB-D, -DB-(D-1), ..., DB+(D-1), DB+D\} \subset (-\frac{q}{4}, \frac{q}{4}).$$

Considering that $Y_i \in \{0, \frac{q}{2}\}$, we have

$$V_i = (B\times t+f+Y)_i \in (\{-DB-D, -DB-(D-1), ..., DB+(D-1), DB+D\} \cup$$
$$\{-DB - D + \frac{q}{2}, -DB - (D-1) + \frac{q}{2}, ..., DB + D + \frac{q}{2}\}),$$

where

$$\{-DB - D + \frac{q}{2}, -DB - (D-1) + \frac{q}{2}, ..., DB + D + \frac{q}{2}\} \subset ((-\frac{q}{2}, -\frac{q}{4}) \cup (\frac{q}{4}, \frac{q}{2})).$$

Based on the above analysis, we have that $V_i \in (-\frac{q}{4}, \frac{q}{4})$ reveals $Y_i = 0$, and $V_i \in ((-\frac{q}{2}, -\frac{q}{4}) \cup (\frac{q}{4}, \frac{q}{2}))$ reveals $Y_i = \frac{q}{2}$. Further, when $B \geq 2D + 1$, the $2(2D + 1)^2$ elements in set

$$\{-DB - D, -DB - (D-1), ..., DB + (D-1), DB + D\} \cup$$
$$\{-DB - D + \frac{q}{2}, -DB - (D-1) + \frac{q}{2}, ..., DB + D + \frac{q}{2}\}$$

are different, thus V_i can determine values of t_i, f_i, Y_i uniquely and definitely. □

In NewHope-CPA-PKE, in order to compress the size of ciphertext, compression function Compress is introduced which simply performs coefficient-wise modulus switching between q and p by multiplying by p and then performing a rounding division by q. In this case, it is difficult to recover the value of f from Compress(V), because the compression function compresses adjacent integers into the same integer. In particular, we have the following corollary.

Corollary 1. *$t, f, Y \in R_q$, and the coefficients t_i, f_i are in $\{-D, ..., D\}$, $Y_i \in \{0, \lfloor\frac{q}{2}\rfloor\}$, $i = 1, ..., n$, $q = 12289$, $D = p = 8$. $B \in \mathbb{Z}_q$ and $V = B\times t+f+Y \bmod^{\pm} q$. If B satisfies certain conditions, then* Compress(V) *will reveal the complete Y and part of the information about t.*

Proof. See Appendix A.1 for the proof. □

Example 3 ***(NewHope-CPA-PKE continued).*** *In NewHope-CPA-PKE, $t, f, Y \in R_q, q = 12289, p = 8$, $t_i, f_i \in \{-8, ..., 8\}$, $Y_i \in \{0, \lfloor\frac{q}{2}\rfloor\}, i = 1, ..., n$. According to Corollary 1, if B satisfies $B < q/4D - 1$, $p(8B - D)/q > 1$ and $p(7B + D)/q < 1$, then* Compress$(V)_i$ *will reveal Y_i, and* Compress$(V)_i$ *$= 1$ and -1 will reveal $t_i = 8$ and -8, respectively; if B satisfies $B < q/4D - 1$, $p(7B - D)/q > 1$ and $p(6B + D)/q < 1$, then* Compress$(V)_i$ *will reveal Y_i, and* Compress$(V)_i$ *$= 1$ and -1 will reveal t_i is in $\{8, 7\}$ and $\{-8, -7\}$, respectively; ...; if B satisfies $B < q/4D - 1$, $p(B - D)/q > 1$, then* Compress$(V)_i$ *will reveal Y_i, and* Compress$(V)_i$ *$= 1$ and -1 will reveal t_i is in $\{8, 7, ..., 1\}$ and $\{-8, -7, ..., -1\}$, respectively.*

In LAC.CPA, in order to minimize the size of the ciphertext, in implementation the lower 4 bits for each coefficient in V are discarded. In this case, it is difficult to recover the value of f from $\overline{V}$, where $\overline{V}$ is the value after discarding the lower 4 bits of each coefficient in V, because the operation converts adjacent integers into the same integer. In particular, we have the following corollary.

Corollary 2. *$t, f, Y \in R_q$, and the coefficients t_i, f_i are in $\{-D, ..., D\}$, $Y_i \in \{0, \lfloor \frac{q}{2} \rceil\}$, $i = 1, ..., n$, $q = 251, D = 1$. $B \in \mathbb{Z}_q$ and $V = B \times t + f + Y \bmod q$. If B satisfies certain conditions, then $\overline{V}$ will reveal t, Y completely.*[6]

Proof. See Appendix A.2 for the proof. □

Example 4 ***(LAC.CPA continued).*** *In LAC.CPA, $t \in R_q$, $f, Y \in \mathbb{Z}_q^{l_v}$, $q = 251$, $t_i, f_j \in \{-1, 0, 1\}$, $Y_j \in \{0, \lfloor \frac{q}{2} \rceil\}, i = 1, ..., n, j = 1, ..., l_v$. In calculating $V \leftarrow t \times B + f + \mathsf{encode}(\mathsf{pt})$, function $(\cdot)_{l_v}$ is introduced and used to take the first l_v coefficients of the polynomial $t \times B$. According to Corollary 2, if $B = 175$, then $\overline{V}_i$ will reveal the values of $t_i, Y_i, i = 1, .., l_v$; if $B = 175x^{l_v}$, then $\overline{V}_i$ will reveal the values of $t_{l_v+i}, Y_i, i = 1, .., l_v$; if $B = 175x^{2l_v}$, then $\overline{V}_i$ will reveal the values of $t_{2l_v+i}, Y_i, i = 1, .., l_v$.*

5 The Recovery of Reused Randomness in NewHope-CPA-KEM and LAC.KE

NewHope-CPA-KEM is an IND-CPA KEM and it is constructed from NewHope-CPA-PKE. LAC.KE is a passively secure unauthenticated key exchange protocol and it is directly based on LAC.CPA. If randomness $\mathbf{t}$ is reused in NewHope-CPA-KEM and LAC.KE, then it can be recovered according to the results of the previous section.

5.1 The Reused Randomness Recovery Game

First, we define reused randomness recovery game in key exchange which is constructed from meta-PKE by using it to convey a secret pt. Since a KEM can be used as a key exchange, our game can cover both NewHope-CPA-KEM and LAC.KE.

Definition 1. *As shown in Fig. 2, Rand-Rec is the reused randomness recovery game, where oracle $\mathcal{O}$ simulates Bob's actions and reuses randomness t. Adversary $\mathcal{A}$ has access to this oracle to make multiple queries. When adversary $\mathcal{A}$ queries oracle $\mathcal{O}$ with pk', the oracle $\mathcal{O}$ generates secret pt, runs the encryption where randomness t is fixed, returns the ciphertext ct.*

The Rand-Rec game comes from Ding's signal leakage attack model [11], where the client Bob is static and reuses secret, a malicious server Alice can initiate key establishment with Bob which responds honestly.

[6] If the lower 4 bits for each coefficient in V aren't discarded, V will reveal t, f, Y completely.

Game Rand-Rec$_{\mathcal{A}}^{\mathcal{O}}$():	**Oracle** $\mathcal{O}$(pk')
1: KeyGen()→ (sk, pk)	1: generate secret pt
2: $\mathcal{A}^{\mathcal{O}(\cdot)}$(pk) → t	2: Enc(pt, pk', coinB) → ct, where randomness t is fixed
3: return t	3: return ct
	4: generate shared secret K

Fig. 2. The reused randomness recovery game

5.2 Recovering Randomness in NewHope-CPA-KEM

In NewHope-CPA-KEM (Fig. 3), if Bob reuses randomness **t** and malicious Alice can initiate key establishment with Bob which responds honestly. Based on the previous results, as long as Alice queries oracle $\mathcal{O}$ (initiates key establishment with Bob) 8 times[7] with different **b**, Alice can recover **t** completely. Then, **e** can be recovered by computing $\mathbf{e} = \mathbf{u} - \mathbf{a}\mathbf{t}$.

Alice		Bob
(pk, sk) ← NewHope.KeyGen()	pk = $(\mathbf{b}, \mathsf{seed}_{\mathbf{a}})$ →	
		coin $\xleftarrow{\$} \{0,1\}^{256}$
		pt‖coinB ← SHAKE256(64, coin)
	← ct = (**u**, Compress(**v**))	ct ← NewHope.Enc(pt, pk, coinB)
pt ← NewHope.Dec(ct, sk)		K ← SHAKE256(32, pt)
K ← SHAKE256(32, pt)		

Fig. 3. NewHope-CPA-KEM.

In fact, in NewHope-CPA-KEM, reusing randomness is disastrous. In order to protect against attacks involving disclosure of system randomness, NewHope-CPA-KEM computes pt and coinB by hashing random coin, rather than picking them directly. Further, coinB is used to sample randomness **t**. Therefore, the reuse of **t** actually stems from a reused coin. Since the final shared secret K is derived from pt by hashing, a reused coin will cause pt to be all the same in multiple conversations. Thus, the final shared secret K is all the same too. Therefore, it is very easy for Alice to detect that Bob is reusing randomness. Further, when Bob communicates with others as a responder using the same randomness, the shared secret is known to Alice.

[7] See Corollary 1 and Example 3 for more details.

5.3 Recovering Randomness in LAC.KE

In LAC.KE (Fig. 4), in order to keep the context consistent, random coinB is passed as an explicit input, which is different from the original specification of the algorithms [24].

$H: \{0,1\}^* \rightarrow \{0,1\}^{l_k}$		
Alice		Bob
$(\mathsf{pk}, \mathsf{sk}) \leftarrow$ LAC.CPA.KeyGen()	$\mathsf{pk} = (\mathbf{b}, \mathsf{seed}_{\mathbf{a}})$ $\longrightarrow$	
		$\mathsf{pt} \xleftarrow{\$} \{0,1\}^{l_m}$
		$\mathsf{coinB} \xleftarrow{\$} \{0,1\}^{l_s}$
	$\mathsf{ct} = (\mathbf{u}, \overline{\mathbf{v}})$ $\longleftarrow$	$\mathsf{ct} \leftarrow$ LAC.CPA.Enc(pt, pk, coinB)
$\mathsf{pt} \leftarrow$ LAC.CPA.Dec(ct, sk)		$K \leftarrow H(\mathsf{pk}, \mathsf{pt}) \in \{0,1\}^{l_k}$
$K \leftarrow H(\mathsf{pk}, \mathsf{pt}) \in \{0,1\}^{l_k}$		

Fig. 4. LAC.KE ($\overline{\mathbf{v}}$ is the value of $\mathbf{v}$ after discarding the lower 4 bits of each coefficient.)

If Bob reuses randomness $\mathbf{t}$ and malicious Alice can initiate key establishment with Bob which responds honestly. According to the previous results, as long as Alice queries oracle $\mathcal{O}$ (initiates key establishment with Bob) $\lceil \frac{n}{l_v} \rceil$ times with different $\mathbf{b}$, Alice can recover $\mathbf{t}$ completely. Then, $\mathbf{e}$ can be recovered by computing $\mathbf{e} = \mathbf{u} - \mathbf{at}$.

5.4 Recovering the Shared Secret in Another Session

In LAC.KE, the recovered randomness $\mathbf{t}$ can be used to recover the shared secret in another session, where the same randomness is used. In particular, we consider a scenario where Bob communicates with Alice and Carol as a responder using the same randomness $\mathbf{t}$, $\mathbf{e}$, $\mathbf{f}$.[8] If Alice gets Bob's reused randomness $\mathbf{t}$, then Alice can recover the shared secret between Carol and Bob.

When Bob communicates with Carol as a responder, Carol first sends $\mathsf{pk}' = (\mathbf{b}', \mathsf{seed}_{\mathbf{a}'})$ to Bob. Next, Bob chooses secret pt', reuses randomness $\mathbf{t}, \mathbf{e}, \mathbf{f}$, computes

$$\mathbf{u}' \leftarrow \mathbf{a}'\mathbf{t} + \mathbf{e},$$

$$\mathbf{v}' \leftarrow (\mathbf{b}'\mathbf{t})_{l_v} + \mathbf{f} + \lfloor \frac{q}{2} \rceil \cdot (\mathsf{ECCEnc}(\mathsf{pt}')),$$

discards the lower 4 bits of each coefficient in $\mathbf{v}'$ and gets $\overline{\mathbf{v}'}$ (Discarding the lower 4 bits of each coefficient is equivalent to shifting 4 bits to the right.), Then, Bob sends message $\mathsf{ct}' = (\mathbf{u}', \overline{\mathbf{v}'})$ to Carol, and computes the shared secret $K' \leftarrow H(\mathsf{pk}', \mathsf{pt}')$.

[8] We consider that $\mathbf{e}, \mathbf{f}$ are also reused. In fact, whether they are reused or not does not affect our analysis.

In the process, Alice intercepts $\mathsf{pk}' = (\mathbf{b}', \mathsf{seed}_{\mathbf{a}'})$ and $\mathsf{ct}' = (\mathbf{u}', \overline{\mathbf{v}'})$, shifts each coefficient of $\overline{\mathbf{v}'}$ 4 bits to the left and gets $\widetilde{\mathbf{v}'}$. Having got randomness $\mathbf{t}$, Alice computes

$$\lfloor \frac{q}{2} \rceil \cdot (\mathsf{ECCEnc}(\mathsf{pt}')) \leftarrow \widetilde{\mathbf{v}'} - (\mathbf{b}'\mathbf{t})_{l_v}, \tag{1}$$

$$\mathsf{pt}' \leftarrow \mathsf{ECCDec}(\mathsf{ECCEnc}(\mathsf{pt}')),$$

$$K' \leftarrow H(\mathsf{pk}', \mathsf{pt}').$$

Thus, Alice gets the shared secret K' between Carol and Bob.

In (1), $\widetilde{\mathbf{v}'} - (\mathbf{b}'\mathbf{t})_{l_v}$ actually produces an approximation of $(\lfloor \frac{q}{2} \rceil \cdot (\mathsf{ECCEnc}(\mathsf{pt}')))$ due to the noise caused by shift operations and unknown $\mathbf{f}$. However, these noises are relatively small and don't affect getting the accurate value. In particular, $\mathsf{ECCEnc}(\mathsf{pt}') \in \{0,1\}^{l_v}$ and $(\lfloor \frac{q}{2} \rceil \cdot (\mathsf{ECCEnc}(\mathsf{pt}'))) \in \{0, \lfloor \frac{q}{2} \rceil\}^{l_v}$, that is to say, each component of $(\lfloor \frac{q}{2} \rceil \cdot (\mathsf{ECCEnc}(\mathsf{pt}')))$ is either 0 or $\lfloor \frac{q}{2} \rceil$. By doing experiments, we found each component of $\widetilde{\mathbf{v}'} - (\mathbf{b}'\mathbf{t})_{l_v}$ is in $[110, 127]$ or $([235, 250] \cup \{0, 1\})$, namely, each component is near 0 or $\lfloor \frac{q}{2} \rceil$. Therefore, Alice can get the accurate value of $(\lfloor \frac{q}{2} \rceil \cdot (\mathsf{ECCEnc}(\mathsf{pt}')))$ according to $\widetilde{\mathbf{v}'} - (\mathbf{b}'\mathbf{t})_{l_v}$.

6 Conclusion

In this paper, we provide better insight into the resilience of NewHope-CPA-KEM and LAC.KE against randomness reuse. Since they are based on NewHope-CPA-PKE and LAC.CPA respectively, we start with these underlying PKEs. In particular, we first show that they share a common feature. Based on the feature, we recover the reused randomness in NewHope-CPA-KEM and LAC.KE. Since our method does't require Alice to change the public global parameter $\mathbf{a}$, it can apply to the situation where $\mathbf{a}$ is cached. Using the parameter sets recommended, the randomness can be recovered after several communications, which confirm that randomness reuse should be strictly avoided. After recovering the reused randomness in LAC.KE, we also demonstrate that these randomness can be used to recover the shared secret in another session where the same randomness is used.

Although underlying PKE can be used to construct IND-CCA KEM by applying the Fujisaki-Okamoto transformation [16,20], the re-encryption process in transformation allows Alice access to all the randomness. Our future work is to investigate if our attack is possible in other NIST candidates.

Acknowledgements. This work is supported by the National Key Research and Development Program of China (No. 2017YFB0802000), the National Natural Science Foundation of China (No. U1536205, 61802376).

Appendix A

A.1 The Proof of Corollary 1

Proof. According to Theorem 1, when $B < q/4D - 1$, we have that $V_i \in (-\frac{q}{4}, \frac{q}{4})$ reveals $Y_i = 0$, and $V_i \in ((-\frac{q}{2}, -\frac{q}{4}) \cup (\frac{q}{4}, \frac{q}{2}))$ reveals $Y_i = \lfloor \frac{q}{2} \rfloor$. Considering the function Compress performs coefficient-wise modulus switching between modulus q and modulus p, we have that $\mathsf{Compress}(V)_i \in (-\frac{p}{4}, \frac{p}{4})$ reveals $Y_i = 0$, and $\mathsf{Compress}(V)_i \in ((-\frac{p}{2}, -\frac{p}{4}) \cup (\frac{p}{4}, \frac{p}{2}))$ reveals $Y_i = \lfloor \frac{q}{2} \rfloor$.

Further, if B satisfies $p(8B - D)/q > 1$ and $p(7B + D)/q < 1$, then $\mathsf{Compress}(V)_i = 1$ and -1 will reveal $t_i = 8$ and -8, respectively; if $p(7B - D)/q > 1$ and $p(6B + D)/q < 1$, then $\mathsf{Compress}(V)_i = 1$ and -1 will reveal t_i is in $\{8, 7\}$ and $\{-8, -7\}$, respectively; if $p(6B - D)/q > 1$ and $p(5B + D)/q < 1$, then $\mathsf{Compress}(V)_i = 1$ and -1 will reveal t_i is in $\{8, 7, 6\}$ and $\{-8, -7, -6\}$, respectively; ...; if $p(B - D)/q > 1$, then $\mathsf{Compress}(V)_i = 1$ and -1 will reveal t_i is in $\{8, 7, ..., 1\}$ and $\{-8, -7, ..., -1\}$, respectively. □

A.2 The Proof of Corollary 2

Proof. Given that $t_i, f_i \in \{-1, 0, 1\}, Y_i \in \{0, 126\}$, V_i has at most 18 possible values when B is an integer in $\mathbb{Z}_q$. In particular, each possible value corresponds to a set of values t_i, f_i and Y_i. After discarding the lower 4 bits of V_i, adjacent integers in V are converted to the same integer in $\overline{V}$, which makes it difficult to recover the value of f_i from $\overline{V}_i$. However, if the public key $B \in \mathbb{Z}_q$ is chosen so that the coefficient $\overline{V}_i$ has at least 6 possibilities, $\overline{V}_i$ can reveal the values of t_i and Y_i. For example, if $B = 175$, then $\overline{V}_i = 4$ will reveal $t_i = -1$ and $Y_i = 0$; $\overline{V}_i = 12$ will reveal $t_i = -1$ and $Y_i = 126$;..., as shown in Table 2. □

Table 2. The values of t_i and Y_i revealed by $\overline{V}_i$ when $B = 175$

$\overline{V}_i$	4	12	0/15	7	10/11	3
t_i	-1	-1	0	0	1	1
Y_i	0	126	0	126	0	126

References

1. Alkim, E., et al.: Newhope: algorithm specifications and supporting documentation (2019). https://csrc.nist.gov/Projects/post-quantum-cryptography/round-2-submissions
2. Alkim, E., Ducas, L., Pöppelmann, T., Schwabe, P.: Newhope without reconciliation. IACR Cryptol. ePrint Arch. 2016:1157 (2016)

3. Alkim, E., Ducas, L., Pöppelmann, T., Schwabe, P.: Post-quantum key exchange–a new hope. In: 25th {USENIX} Security Symposium ({USENIX} Security 16), pp. 327–343 (2016)
4. Băetu, C., Durak, F.B., Huguenin-Dumittan, L., Talayhan, A., Vaudenay, S.: Misuse attacks on post-quantum cryptosystems. In: Ishai, Y., Rijmen, V. (eds.) EUROCRYPT 2019. LNCS, vol. 11477, pp. 747–776. Springer, Cham (2019). https://doi.org/10.1007/978-3-030-17656-3_26
5. Banerjee, A., Peikert, C., Rosen, A.: Pseudorandom functions and lattices. In: Pointcheval, D., Johansson, T. (eds.) EUROCRYPT 2012. LNCS, vol. 7237, pp. 719–737. Springer, Heidelberg (2012). https://doi.org/10.1007/978-3-642-29011-4_42
6. Bauer, A., Gilbert, H., Renault, G., Rossi, M.: Assessment of the key-reuse resilience of newhope. In: Matsui, M. (ed.) CT-RSA 2019. LNCS, vol. 11405, pp. 272–292. Springer, Cham (2019). https://doi.org/10.1007/978-3-030-12612-4_14
7. Bernstein, D.J., Groot Bruinderink, L., Lange, T., Panny, L.: HILA5 pindakaas: on the CCA security of lattice-based encryption with error correction. In: Joux, A., Nitaj, A., Rachidi, T. (eds.) AFRICACRYPT 2018. LNCS, vol. 10831, pp. 203–216. Springer, Cham (2018). https://doi.org/10.1007/978-3-319-89339-6_12
8. D'Anvers, J.-P., Guo, Q., Johansson, T., Nilsson, A., Vercauteren, F., Verbauwhede, I.: Decryption failure attacks on IND-CCA secure lattice-based schemes. In: Lin, D., Sako, K. (eds.) PKC 2019. LNCS, vol. 11443, pp. 565–598. Springer, Cham (2019). https://doi.org/10.1007/978-3-030-17259-6_19
9. D'Anvers, J.-P., Rossi, M., Virdia, F.: *(One) failure is not an option*: bootstrapping the search for failures in lattice-based encryption schemes. In: Canteaut, A., Ishai, Y. (eds.) EUROCRYPT 2020. LNCS, vol. 12107, pp. 3–33. Springer, Cham (2020). https://doi.org/10.1007/978-3-030-45727-3_1
10. D'Anvers, J.-P., Vercauteren, F., Verbauwhede, I.: The impact of error dependencies on ring/Mod-LWE/LWR based schemes. In: Ding, J., Steinwandt, R. (eds.) PQCrypto 2019. LNCS, vol. 11505, pp. 103–115. Springer, Cham (2019). https://doi.org/10.1007/978-3-030-25510-7_6
11. Ding, J., Alsayigh, S., Saraswathy, R.V., Fluhrer, S., Lin, X.: Leakage of signal function with reused keys in RLWE key exchange. In: 2017 IEEE International Conference on Communications (ICC), pp. 1–6. IEEE (2017)
12. Ding, J., Cheng, C., Qin, Y.: A simple key reuse attack on LWE and ring LWE encryption schemes as key encapsulation mechanisms (KEMs). IACR Cryptol. ePrint Arch. 2019:271 (2019)
13. Ding, J., Fluhrer, S., Rv, S.: Complete attack on RLWE key exchange with reused keys, without signal leakage. In: Susilo, W., Yang, G. (eds.) ACISP 2018. LNCS, vol. 10946, pp. 467–486. Springer, Cham (2018). https://doi.org/10.1007/978-3-319-93638-3_27
14. Ding, J., Xie, X., Lin, X.: A simple provably secure key exchange scheme based on the learning with errors problem. IACR Cryptol. ePrint Arch. 2012:688 (2012)
15. Fluhrer, S.R.: Cryptanalysis of ring-LWE based key exchange with key share reuse. IACR Cryptol. ePrint Arch. 2016:85 (2016)
16. Fujisaki, E., Okamoto, T.: How to enhance the security of public-key encryption at minimum cost. In: Imai, H., Zheng, Y. (eds.) PKC 1999. LNCS, vol. 1560, pp. 53–68. Springer, Heidelberg (1999). https://doi.org/10.1007/3-540-49162-7_5
17. Gao, X., Ding, J., Li, L., Liu, J.: Practical randomized RLWE-based key exchange against signal leakage attack. IEEE Trans. Comput. **67**(11), 1584–1593 (2018)
18. Greuet, A., Montoya, S., Renault, G.: Attack on lac key exchange in misuse situation. IACR Cryptol. ePrint Arch. 2020:63 (2020)

19. Guo, Q., Johansson, T., Yang, J.: A novel CCA attack using decryption errors against LAC. In: Galbraith, S.D., Moriai, S. (eds.) ASIACRYPT 2019. LNCS, vol. 11921, pp. 82–111. Springer, Cham (2019). https://doi.org/10.1007/978-3-030-34578-5_4
20. Hofheinz, D., Hövelmanns, K., Kiltz, E.: A modular analysis of the Fujisaki-Okamoto transformation. In: Kalai, Y., Reyzin, L. (eds.) TCC 2017. LNCS, vol. 10677, pp. 341–371. Springer, Cham (2017). https://doi.org/10.1007/978-3-319-70500-2_12
21. Huguenin-Dumittan, L., Vaudenay, S.: Classical misuse attacks on NIST round 2 PQC. In: Conti, M., Zhou, J., Casalicchio, E., Spognardi, A. (eds.) ACNS 2020. LNCS, vol. 12146, pp. 208–227. Springer, Cham (2020). https://doi.org/10.1007/978-3-030-57808-4_11
22. Kirkwood, D., Lackey, B.C., McVey, J., Motley, M., Solinas Jerome A., Tuller, D.: Failure is not an option: standardization issues for post-quantum key agreement (2015). https://csrc.nist.gov/csrc/media/events/workshop-on-cybersecurity-in-a-post-quantum-world/documents/presentations/session7-motley-mark.pdf
23. Liu, C., Zheng, Z., Zou, G.: Key reuse attack on newhope key exchange protocol. In: Lee, K. (ed.) ICISC 2018. LNCS, vol. 11396, pp. 163–176. Springer, Cham (2019). https://doi.org/10.1007/978-3-030-12146-4_11
24. Lu, X., et al.: LAC: algorithm specifications and supporting documentation (2019). https://csrc.nist.gov/Projects/post-quantum-cryptography/round-2-submissions
25. Lyubashevsky, V., Peikert, C., Regev, O.: On ideal lattices and learning with errors over rings. In: Gilbert, H. (ed.) EUROCRYPT 2010. LNCS, vol. 6110, pp. 1–23. Springer, Heidelberg (2010). https://doi.org/10.1007/978-3-642-13190-5_1
26. National Institute of Standards and Technology. Post-quantum cryptography standardization (2016). https://csrc.nist.gov/Projects/post-quantum-cryptography/post-quantum-cryptography-standardization
27. Okada, S., Wang, Y., Takagi, T.: Improving key mismatch attack on newhope with fewer queries. IACR Cryptol. ePrint Arch. 2020:585 (2020)
28. Peikert, C.: Public-key cryptosystems from the worst-case shortest vector problem. In: Proceedings of the Forty-first Annual ACM Symposium on Theory of Computing, pp. 333–342 (2009)
29. Pöppelmann, T., Güneysu, T.: Towards practical lattice-based public-key encryption on reconfigurable hardware. In: Lange, T., Lauter, K., Lisoněk, P. (eds.) SAC 2013. LNCS, vol. 8282, pp. 68–85. Springer, Heidelberg (2014). https://doi.org/10.1007/978-3-662-43414-7_4
30. Qin, Y., Cheng, C., Ding, J.: A complete and optimized key mismatch attack on NIST candidate newhope. In: Sako, K., Schneider, S., Ryan, P.Y.A. (eds.) ESORICS 2019. LNCS, vol. 11736, pp. 504–520. Springer, Cham (2019). https://doi.org/10.1007/978-3-030-29962-0_24
31. Qin, Y., Cheng, C., Ding, J.: An efficient key mismatch attack on the NIST second round candidate kyber. IACR Cryptol. ePrint Arch. 2019:1343 (2019)
32. Regev, O.: On lattices, learning with errors, random linear codes, and cryptography. J. ACM (JACM) **56**(6), 1–40 (2009)
33. Ristenpart, T., Yilek, S.: When good randomness goes bad: virtual machine reset vulnerabilities and hedging deployed cryptography. In: NDSS (2010)
34. Shor, P.W.: Algorithms for quantum computation: discrete logarithms and factoring. In: Proceedings 35th Annual Symposium on Foundations of Computer Science, pp. 124–134. IEEE (1994)

35. Wang, K., Jiang, H.: Analysis of two countermeasures against the signal leakage attack. In: Buchmann, J., Nitaj, A., Rachidi, T. (eds.) AFRICACRYPT 2019. LNCS, vol. 11627, pp. 370–388. Springer, Cham (2019). https://doi.org/10.1007/978-3-030-23696-0_19
36. Yilek, S., Rescorla, E., Shacham, H., Enright, B., Savage, S.: When private keys are public: results from the 2008 Debian OpenSSL vulnerability. In: Proceedings of the 9th ACM SIGCOMM Conference on Internet Measurement, pp. 15–27 (2009)

Author Index